THE LIFE & TIMES OF WALTER REUTHER

An Unfinished Liberal Legacy

JAMES TEN EYCK

228 Hamilton Ave.,
Palo Alto, CA 94301

ISBN 978-1-960946-16-4 (softcover)
ISBN 978-1-960946-18-8 (hardcover)
ISBN 978-1-960946-17-1 (ebook)

Printed in the United States of America.

CONTENTS

Part 4: Epilogue

CONTENTS

Part 4: Epilogue

A PERSONAL INTRODUCTION

This book is the culmination of a progress along divergent career paths and through evolving political sensibilities. It is colored by my life experiences and reflects my concerns for the future. It began with the thought of writing a biography about a man I admired from afar, but emerged instead as a drama in which the lead actor is off stage for several scenes and which continues to evolve after his death. Rather than tracing the progress of the man through the events of his life, the book focuses on the significant events and issues that shaped present-day America and views the involvement of the man in many of these episodes.

There is no shortage of biographies of Walter Reuther. They have been written by labor historians, journalists, family members, and friends of Eleanor Roosevelt. Many of these are listed in the bibliography and have provided insight and guidance to this effort. I am neither an historian, nor a journalist, nor an intimate with any of the labor, civil rights, or national leaders past or present. My perspective is that of someone coming of age during the Cold War, the Civil Rights struggle, and a period of a rising economic tide that lifted the opportunities for both working class families and white-collar professionals like my parents. I was drawn to write this book not to fill a void in the biographical accounts of Walter Reuther, but to affirm a political philosophy that has been relentlessly attacked and insufficiently advanced for the last quarter century.

The subject matter and its treatment reflect the environmental influences that have shaped my intellectual perspective. I grew up in a family of school teachers living in Central New Jersey. My parents were both Republicans by birth and nurture whose political interest was more a biennial obligation than a daily concern. Politics was rarely discussed over dinner or at any other time. We were very private people who generally spoke only in superficialities. The voids in meal-time conversation were filled by the radio—*Rambling with Gambling* and *Breakfast with Dorothy and Dick*[1] in the morning and Gabriel Heater with the news, Stan Lomax with the sports, and Fulton Lewis Junior with a right-wing commentary at dinner time. Lewis did not rant with the ferocity of Rush Limbaugh today, and his world view was quietly accepted at the dinner table.

My political bent was first on display in 1952 when I paraded around town with an oversized *I Like Ike* button pinned to my shirt. I happily subscribed to the family political tradition and developed an admiration for the hero of a war I was too young to experience at the time and a faith in his promise to end one that I was vividly experiencing in my nightmares. As part of the population drafted into the Cold War during the fifties, I was willing to believe in the righteousness of the cause and in the venality of the enemy. My own circumstances during the decade were comfortable and provided me little motivation for critical reflection on the prevailing attitudes of the community. Only the previous 21-year old voting age saved me from casting a vote for Nixon in 1960.

Like most teenagers, my personal philosophy developed during my college and young adult years when one's horizons expand and career paths narrow. My undergraduate years spanned a time when Elvis was in the Army and the blue suede shoes and white bucks were stashed away in a closet back home beside the memories tucked into the high school yearbooks. Folk music struck a responsive chord for a generation coming of age in the span between Elvis and the Beatles. We were awakened from the somnolent fifties by the growl of a Birmingham Alabama police dog and spent the fall of '62 like Schrodinger's cat in a state both alive and dead while the powers played nuclear chicken with our future. Mississippi began to burn. Joan Baez stopped singing about Henry Martin and Mary Hamilton, moved in with Bob Dylan, and covered his songs of angst, rebellion, and disillusionment. There was a lot more happening in the country than Gabriel Heater reported in the news, and a different opinion from the one Fulton Lewis expressed in his commentary.

My social and political sensibilities matured during the Civil Rights and anti-war movements of the sixties. Television had superseded radio as the media for conveying the culture, painting the contrasts between the promise and reality of America in black and white. It added a dimension to the news that voice and print alone could not convey. The March on

Washington was a particularly vivid moment when the country gathered around its television set and examined the depth of its soul. The mass exercise of participatory democracy delivered an affirmation of my faith in America. I felt Walter Reuther was there for me—a white man in stride with a drumbeat pounding in my veins, voicing the words that were running through my thoughts. The March planted a seed that slowly germinated into the writing of this book. Later in the long, extended decade I added my own footsteps to the marches demanding an end to an ill-conceived, divisive war. My core liberal beliefs solidified as the Republican Party of Goldwater and Reagan was distancing itself from me and my family's values.

The distinction between the political parties in the fifties and early sixties was not as much between liberal and conservative—there were people who were identified by those labels in both parties—as it was between pro-business and pro-labor affinities. My sympathies were with labor even before I worked summers at John's Manville during my last two years of college.

The company that produced asbestos pipes and siding for the construction industry was a major employer of college students during its busy summer months. After a brief interview during which the personnel manager asked me if I had any problems working with people he referred to using the N word, I was assigned to H-building where corrugated boards and shingles were produced. John's Manville was an open shop represented by what seemed to be a rather weak union. Summer help was neither required nor asked to join it.

African Americans were obviously concentrated in this one building, but still constituted a minority of its work force and included none of the summer help. The working environment in the building was congenial and the foreman was a decent boss. Workers of both races got along well enough with one another and with the summer help that was making the same hourly rate they were. The wage included a small piecework bonus that varied with the product run. I rotated through the various jobs on a long section of machinery that alternated between production runs of two different types of siding. There was a mixer man loading the raw materials at one end and a small crew removing the end product at the other. My primary job for much of the time was serving as the mixer man.

The mixer man's job was to dump two fifty pound bags of asbestos located to his right and three fifty pound bags of a binder located to his left into the machine, pull a lever to add an amount of pulverized scrap to the mix, then wait for the needle on a gauge to work its way down to a red line and repeat the process again. Only deliveries by the fork lift driver provided a diversion from the silent interplay between machine and man.

The job was dirty and far more dangerous than I was told at the time. Dust and asbestos particles were always floating in the air and clinging to my clothing. I was provided with a rudimentary face mask, but given no safety instructions mandating its use or information about the period of its effectiveness. The plant was hot and the mask uncomfortable to wear for long periods of time. There were many times when it was draped around my neck instead of covering my nose. There was no public notice at the time that the strange white fibers that could be peeled from the little rocks that kids brought to school for show-and-tell posed a significant health risk.

The production methodology used in H-Building was straight from the textbook of Taylor and Ford. Every job was reduced to a single repetitive task. Workers switched stations at regular intervals to provide some relief from the monotony, but each task required little skill and imparted little in the way of experiential benefit. The atmosphere in the workplace did not permeate with the intimidation practiced in the Ford plants of the thirties or the racial animosity in the Packard plants of the forties; the speed of the conveyor belt moving the product from its raw ingredients to a dried and hardened finished piece of siding was geared to the required curing and drying time of the material and not subject to the arbitrary speedup that plagued auto workers governed by the same Fordist principles. Union representation protected workers from the worst forms of abuse and arbitrary company actions, but at John's Manville production workers acquired few on-the-job skills and were ill-prepared to start afresh a decade later when the dangers of asbestos were widely touted and lawsuits and low demand for its products forced the company to shut down its Manville operation.

Between college and graduate school I worked for three years at IBM in Endicott, New York. The company had just introduced its

Series 360 family of computers and was experiencing a boom that was shared by its employees in the form of generous benefits including a partially subsidized stock purchasing plan. The company was famous for the way it treated its workers, and was rewarded in-turn by their loyalty. My time at IBM informs some of the material presented in Chapter 8, which is juxtaposed with the preceding chapter on the Treaty of Detroit. The Treaty was a designation applied specifically to the historic 1950 agreement between Reuther's UAW and General Motors, but is used here to include the set of agreements achieved by the union and the automobile industry between 1948 and 1956 which set the parameters for contract negotiations between labor and management throughout much of the industrial heartland. IBM, in contrast, was a non-union company whose generosity to its employees was based on the management philosophy of its "first family" and conditioned on its ability to maintain the phenomenal growth it experienced over its first seventy-five years. When the growth could no longer be sustained and a new breed of manager succeeded the old guard, the benefits were reduced and the promise of secure employment was rescinded. Contracts modeled after the Treaty of Detroit and business practices inspired by the success of IBM contributed substantially to the growth and stability of the middle class in the forty years following World War 2. Absent these protections, middle and working class families have been buffeted by a series of economic storms and seen the flow into their bank books from the growth of the national output reduced to a trickle.

IBM is important in this narrative for more than its labor policies. It was the primary engine driving the automation and globalization characterizing the current phase of capitalism. Its global aspiration was announced in its name—*International* Business Machines. It was one of the first American companies with a truly global reach, and its products made today's globalization of business possible. The company's original chief executive, Thomas Watson, Sr., envisioned a transnational layer of businessmen stitching the various conflicting national interests and political ideologies into a coherent commercial quilt that he marketed with the slogan "World Peace through World Trade." His exuberance for this mission nearly ruined himself and the reputation of his company, but IBM was too big and too important to bear public scrutiny for what may have been a deeper flaw in the free market system that nobody wanted to expose.[2] IBM provided the electronic brains that put the nation's astronauts into orbit and landed Neil Armstrong on the moon; it provided synapse for the eyes with which the American military scanned the horizon for enemy bombers and missiles; and it provided much of the equipment, funding, and job support for the education and development of the students filling the nascent high-tech sector. It has been described as a national treasure.

I enjoyed my time at IBM and took advantage of the recreational and educational opportunities it provided for its employees. But after three years my job satisfaction waned and the social opportunities available in Endicott dwindled. I traded the cubicle and blue suit and tie for the campus atmosphere and casual dress of academia. I took a leave of absence to complete the master's degree I was sampling piecemeal at IBM and never returned, much to the dismay of my more practically-minded mother.

My graduate school years encompassed the assassinations of Martin Luther King and Robert Kennedy, the invasion of Cambodia, the killings at Kent State, and the saga of Watergate. Events of the day crowded into the monkish pursuit of higher learning. Students of the period left the university with their ideological antennae tuned to a particular frequency. Those that stayed behind in academia were more inclined to maintain that setting as more powerful transmitters seeped into its band.

After forty years teaching physics and computer science, I was ready to retire and take up the pen. An age for reflection, an urge to write, and a concern about the narrative that was being written and prominently promoted in the country provided the incentive for undertaking this particular task. The book combines a history of the period and a biography of the man with personal recollections and observations in presenting an argument for a renewed effort to complete the unfinished liberal agenda.

In the succeeding chapters the career of Walter Reuther interweaves with the story of mid-twentieth century America. The central character becomes the lens for viewing the period through a particular focus. The period was expansive and contentious. It was marked by social movements for racial justice and economic reform. Suffragettes and temperance crusaders of an earlier era were followed into the streets by hunger marchers, unionists, civil rights activists, and anti-war protesters. Conflicts within the society played against a backdrop of war, ideological struggle for supremacy, the emergence of peoples of color from the periphery of world events, and the rapid evolution of technology that ushered in the post-industrial society of twenty-first century America.

After a brief overview of the life and times of Walter Reuther in the first chapter, the narrative looks back at the dawn of the twentieth century—a period over which the United States was poised to exert its influence. The new century began with a leap into modernity that was accompanied by a growing appetite for imperialism fueled by the country's recent success in the Spanish American War. It was a time in which the country was struggling to accommodate its new ambition with its founding creed, and a time in which the descendants of the framers of those documents feared the dilution of their Anglo-Saxon stock, that they regarded as uniquely suited for the obligations of self government, by a wave of immigrants from eastern and southern Europe.

The America that was set to exert its dominance over the twentieth century was troubled by the fissures that existed between descendants of the original colonists and recent immigrants, between industrialists and laborers, and by the legacy of its original sin of racism. Chapter three looks at the formative years of the labor movement in which the conflicting strands of the American identity were forged into a brittle alloy inside the melting pot. The chapter ends with the formative years of Walter Reuther and the two and a half year odyssey of the brothers Walter and Victor through the emerging German Reich and the Molotov autoworks of Soviet Russia.

The brothers returned to the United States to witness the birth of the CIO and became leaders in the sit-down strikes of the late thirties that changed the dynamic between capital and labor. Chapter four highlights the General Motors strike at Flint that put an exclamation mark on the emergence of the industrial union movement in America. Chapter five moves the struggle to Ford where the battle is not only between labor and management but within the office suites and the union halls as well. The Ford lifted from the pages of American mythology was a complex individual who allowed his inner demons to subvert a generous spirit and placed his good name, his industrial empire, and the son he loved but never truly respected at the disposition of a street fighter with associations in the Detroit underworld.

Chapter six covers the war years and the fragile peace within the United Autoworkers Union that papered over the factional differences within the leadership, and the discontent in the plants over the no-strike pledge their leaders had made. When the war years ended they were quickly followed by a long strike against General Motors that helped propel Reuther to the presidency of the UAW (Chapter 7). The post-war bargaining agreements initiated a pattern of labor contracts that provided the framework for the relationship between labor and management over the next quarter century.

The end of one war brought a chill from another. The Cold War underscored every facet of public concern. It narrowed the politics; it inhibited speech; and it drew a curtain of secrecy around the conduct of public affairs. Chapter ten details the McCarthy and HUAC hearings, the activities of the CIA in Iran and Central America, and the advocacy of "preventive war" by Navy Undersecretary Mathews and others. The chapter follows Reuther to Berlin and India, describes his encounters with Mikoyan and Khrushchev, his confrontation with Goldwater and his Republican colleagues during the McClellan Committee hearings on labor racketeering, and his bitter feud with George Meany.

The Cold War turned hot when a liberation struggle in Vietnam was viewed in the context of Cold War orthodoxy. Chapter eleven traces the origins and growth of this conflict into one in which the consequences for the former French colonies in Indochina was tangential to the perceived consequences for America in deviating from a strict adherence to the beliefs of Cold War fundamentalism. In the end, the war did little to alter the trajectory of the course of history globally, but it left casualties on and off the battlefield domestically of irretrievable loss and thwarted promise.

During the time in which the war in Southeast Asia was acquiring an American accent, the Civil Rights struggle was emerging from the churches and court houses and taking to the lunch counters, the buses, and the streets. The movement that appeared in the late fifties and early sixties had earlier roots in many communities. Chapter nine begins by tracing the development of the movement in Detroit and its somewhat uneasy relationship with the UAW. The union and the community leaders represented two very different, often antagonistic, constituencies, with different primary goals, but each came to recognize the essential need for the other in achieving their own success. The chapter continues by tracing the important events in the national struggle and the role that Reuther and the UAW played in the affairs of the movement.

Chapter twelve is titled *The Aftermath* and deals with the breakdown of the Cold War consensus over Vietnam, the aspirations, accomplishments, and disappointments of the Great Society, and the frustrations of Northern Blacks over the limited effect the civil rights legislation had upon their reality. Society splintered into contentious factions. Trust in familiar institutions and leaders wavered, and angry voices found a receptive audience. The first two years of the Johnson administration provided Reuther with more influence within the government than he previously enjoyed, but constrained his independence and marginalized his influence within the movements he had helped to spawn.

The End of an Era (Chapter 13) refers to the era spanned by the New Deal and the Great Society. The era ended in the last years of the Johnson presidency, but it was the election of Ronald Reagan in 1980 that delivered a repudiation of the policies of an expansive state. The Conservative narrative extols the accomplishments of the Reagan presidency, but a closer examination of that record reveals a much less flattering picture. Chapter thirteen examines economic performance during the last three Republican administrations and finds a lack of compelling evidence that a policy of lower taxes, particularly for the wealthy, and deregulation stimulated growth.

The last chapter is *The Post American Century*. The title given the new century does not necessarily imply that America's place will be superseded by some other nation in the coming decades, but that the circumstances that propelled its rise have changed. The new century is post colonial, post Euro-centric, and post industrial. The world has become much larger with more people and more nations expressing their identity, and it has become much smaller with the speed of travel and communication shrinking time and space. America's success in the coming years will depend upon how well it adapts to its new circumstances—particularly how well it adjusts its twentieth century mindset to twenty-first century reality.

America in the new century is driving into the future with its eyes constantly peering in the rear view mirror. The focus is no longer on the moon and beyond, but on retrenchment behind secure borders and fewer state services. The ideological offspring of Barry Goldwater and Ronald Reagan vow to dismantle the programs and institutions of an expansive state; while a battle-scarred opposition fights to preserve and extend the protections that it offers. The battlegrounds are familiar from the past—health care, social security, the work place, civil rights, housing, education, and the environment. The battle lines have shifted on many of these fronts, but the terrain is familiar from the sixties. The remainder of the narrative follows parallel threads through the social movements, conflicts, and political disputes of mid twentieth century America whose loose ends reach into the present. It is not structured around a man and a period in one chapter of the nation's history, but about the man and the moment within the sweep of a story still being told.

PART 1

Setting the Scene

CHAPTER I

The Liberal Warrior

More than anyone else in America, you stand out as the shining example of democratic trade unionism. Through your trials, efforts, and your unswerving devotion to humanitarian causes, you have made life more meaningful for millions of working people. Through moments of difficulty and strong obstacles, you have stood firm for what you believe, knowing in the long run "Truth crushed to earth will rise again." As I have heard you say, the true measure of a man is where he stands in moments of challenge and controversy, when the only consolation he gains is the quiet whisper of an inner voice saying there are things so eternally true and significant that they are worth dying for, if necessary. You have demonstrated over the years that you can stand up in moments of challenge and controversy. One day, all America will be proud of your achievements, and will record your work as one of the glowing epics of our heritage.

Martin Luther King, Jr.
May 17, 1961

On Saturday, May 9, 1970, a private Lear Jet carrying May and Walter Reuther, architect Oskar Stonorov, Reuther's bodyguard, Billy Wolfman, and two pilots took off from Detroit Metro Airport into patchy clouds and intermittent rain. The Reuthers and Stonorov were heading to the United Auto Workers (UAW) new family education center at Black Lake, Michigan for a final inspection tour before the facility was to formally open. As the plane neared the small airport in Pellston, Michigan the rain became steadier. Within three miles of the airport, the pilots noticed that the lights on runway 23, the one with a Visual Approach Path Indicator, were not all working and chose to land on runway 5 instead,[1] As the plane began its descent it ran into a bank of fog and relied on instruments to con-tinue its approach. Before reaching the landing area, the plane skimmed the top of a large elm tree. Both engines clogged with debris and shut down. The plane hurtled forward, plowing through a stand of trees, and burst into flames. All six passengers on board were killed.

The death of Walter Reuther occurred as an illustrious chapter of American history was drawing to a close. The era bracketed by the New Deal and the Great Society was marked by significant advances in economic, social, and racial justice. America reached for the moon and opened new doors at home. Blue collar families achieved a path into the middle class. New educational opportunities opened for returning veterans and the burgeoning population of their offspring. Racial segregation was outlawed and cultural and economic restraints on opportunities for African Americans and women were aggressively challenged. The post-war prosperity was shared across a broad spectrum of society. Areas of poverty remained, but there was a commitment to ameliorating the causes producing them. Despite depression, hot, and cold war, and civil disharmony, the country retained a sense of optimism and faith in its institutions.

Mid-twentieth century America was a time and place of no less glory and grandeur than Periclean Athens and Augustan Rome with similar hubris and troubled by similar tensions that newly acquired responsibility placed on traditional forms and values. The epic age produced a number of transcendent figures—Franklin and Eleanor Roosevelt, Henry Ford, John L. Lewis, Dwight Eisenhower, the Kennedys, Lyndon Johnson, Martin Luther King—and antagonists such as Hitler, Stalin, Mao, and Ho Chi Minh. The telling of history often magnifies the role of such figures at the expense of the chorus that develops the theme and sustains the drama. In twentieth century America it was the chorus—the suffragettes, the men who sat down in the factories and stormed the beaches of Normandy, the Blacks who faced a long, hot, Southern night after the cameras were turned off, and the youth who marched against an ill-conceived war—that prompted the lines of the other actors on the stage. Walter Reuther was a voice from the chorus whose role was enhanced as the scene progressed. In this narrative he is singled out as the most appropriate lens through which to examine the various progressive movements of the time.

Like Odysseus in the classical epic, the central figure of this account was a chieftain of a lesser domain whose influence was magnified by his insight, opportunism, and ability to devise a plan for every exigency. And, as with the classical hero whose adventures encompassed the full extent of the Mediterranean world, Reuther's footprints are found at or around all of the events and progressive movements of the time. The history of the period was written in the automobile factories of the Midwest, on the battlefields of Europe, in the rice paddies of Vietnam, on the buses of Montgomery, in the streets of Birmingham and Selma, Alabama, and at the Wall between the East and West divide in Berlin. Reuther's odyssey began at the Ford plant in Detroit, wound through the autoworks in Gorky, and circled back to the overpass entrance to the Ford River Rouge complex. He visited Hitler's Berlin in his youth, and returned later to a divided city as one of its champions. He marched with Martin Luther King in Selma and Memphis and stood with him on the steps of the Lincoln Memorial when he recounted his dream. In the union power game he grabbed the high card from the "Chance" deck for a stroll on the Boardwalk in Atlantic City with an opportunity to win high office and take a turn rolling the dice with the monopoly players in the board rooms of Detroit. He had a conversion plan for preparing an entry into one war and belatedly joined the chorus for disengaging from another. His influence was felt by the social democrats of Europe, the Labor government in Israel, and the independent nationalist Nehru in India. He was a confidant of Democratic presidents, a rival of George Meany, an anathema to Barry Goldwater, J. Edgar Hoover and Nikita Khrushchev, and a target of assassins on several occasions.

Walter Reuther was the most enduring of the progressive leaders that shaped the era, and the only one who was still on the national stage as the decade of the seventies began. John and Robert Kennedy and Martin Luther King were dead. Lyndon Johnson had retired to his Texas ranch and was in declining health. Hubert Humphrey was sidelined by his close association with an unpopular Vietnam War policy. Between the peaks of the first two Roosevelt administrations and the first years of the Johnson presidency, there was a long, sometimes deep valley of recrimination and intimidation from which few new liberal leaders emerged. The Civil Rights struggle produced many outstanding African-American leaders, but neither they, nor the country was of an age to gain them a wider platform. The death of Reuther and the others marked the end of the liberal era, but did not precipitate it. The nation was unable to digest the social changes that were occurring before a period of turbulence shifted the political landscape and unraveled the coalition that Roosevelt had stitched together.

Reuther exemplified the mid-twentieth century liberal. His passage from the Debsian Socialism he inherited from his family, through the filter of New Deal pragmatism, to the reformist and anti-communist agenda of the Americans for Democratic Action (ADA) was not atypical from the experience of many of his generation. The chronic illness of the economic order, with frequent cycles of remission and relapse, grew acute during the Depression years. The old remedies brought no relief. New prescriptions were advanced and tried. The period provided an opportunity for people outside of the usual politics, like Walter Reuther, to emerge and engage in an effort to reorient the social lattice along a different set of axes. Reuther was an idealist, but above all he was a pragmatist and an opportunist. This combination sustained his influence in the national life for over three decades.

Reuther's involvement in public life ranged far beyond the union hall. There were Reuther plans to deal with war preparedness and the return to a peace-time economy. He was prominently associated with all of the issues that persist to the present—civil rights, health care, education, automation, housing, and the environment. He appeared frequently in the halls of Congress to testify for his various initiatives.—to structure economic policy around a goal of full employment, to extend health care coverage, to convert idled defense plants to the production of housing units, and to create a Fair Employment Practices Commission with rigorous enforcement powers. He was in the forefront of the organizing drive in the factories during the thirties and was at the bargaining table during the landmark agreements of the fifties and sixties.

Reuther began his association with the automobile industry as a master tool and die maker in the sprawling Ford River Rouge complex in Dearborn, Michigan. He excelled at his work and was soon one of the highest paid hourly workers at Ford, and the youngest die leader in the factory.[2] He resisted the temptation to drift into a comfortable middle class life style, guided by a family sense of obligation to serve the cause of social justice.[3] When the Depression whittled away the work force in the auto plants in 1932, Reuther was fired from Ford for his union activity.[4] With little prospect of finding new work in the Detroit area, Walter withdrew his savings and together with his brother Victor began a two and a half year adventure during which the brothers experienced first-hand the rise of Hitler in their ancestral homeland and the industrialization of a largely peasant society in the Soviet Union.

When the brothers returned to the United States in the fall of 1935, the impetus for industrial unionization was building. The government, eager to put more wealth into the hands of struggling workers to boost the economy, was sympathetic to the goals of labor and passed legislation establishing the rights of workers to choose their bargaining agent. The Reuthers returned home just in time for Walter to attend the tumultuous AFL convention in Atlantic City where John L Lewis broke with the conservative leadership and formed the Committee (later Congress) of Industrial Organizations (CIO). Over the next five years Walter, Victor and Roy Reuther were in the forefront of the organizing efforts and confrontations that secured UAW-CIO bargaining rights throughout the automobile industry.

Two decades later, Walter Reuther was the only one of the leaders of these battles who was still in a position of authority in the labor movement. He had formed a coalition that unified the fractious UAW under his leadership, and had negotiated a set of labor agreements that established the pattern for wage and benefit settlements throughout much of American industry. Reuther rose and remained at the top with the same opportunism and tenacity of the nineteen year old boy who had talked his way past a security guard and personnel manager at Ford to test for a die leader's position requiring twenty years of experience.

Reuther the die leader retained a strong influence on Reuther the labor leader. A die leader had to lift the engineer's design off the page and render it in steel. The position required precision, attention to detail, an appreciation of the larger purpose, and an ability to improvise. A die leader had to work with the engineers and the skilled craftsmen on his team. These were the attributes that served Reuther the labor leader in devising the many "Reuther Plans" that caught the public's attention and elevated his role in the national drama well beyond the part of labor leader.

Reuther had his own blueprint for a new model of society that he labored to turn into artifact. He was at once the engineer, craftsman, production hand, and salesman of a liberal program for which the market alternately warmed and cooled and then withered away under an advertising blitz by its competition. The liberal brand has now been demeaned and the word liberal turned into a pejorative by a well-financed conservative campaign. That effort has been aided in no small part by the timidity of nominally liberal politicians and commentators.

The term "liberal" has had different connotations since first being used to denote a set of political beliefs. Classical liberalism had its origins in the writings of British philosopher John Locke. Locke conceived a system of government which recognized certain natural rights—life, liberty and property—that belonged to the governed and could not be abridged by an absolute monarch, hereditary lord, or an established religion.[5] He argued against the divine right of kings, and held that a ruler must be subject to the consent of his people. Locke greatly influenced Thomas Jefferson and his writings prompted insertion of the clause proclaiming the unalienable rights of life, liberty, and the pursuit of happiness into the Declaration of Independence.

These natural rights were not taken to be universal by the early liberal thinkers. Locke profited from the slave trade and was a principal author of the *Fundamental Constitution of the Carolinas* in 1671 which established a slave-holding aristocracy in the colonies. A century later Jefferson and Madison were unable to resolve the contradiction between their proclamation of unalienable human rights and their ownership of slaves. Classical liberals differentiated between men of property, which included them, and the people of little means who toiled in the fields and factories. The protection of property rights from an indebted underclass was just as central to their thinking as was protection from an autocratic ruler or an established church. Madison argued in the *Federalist Papers* for a constitutional republic to protect the sovereignty of individual property rights against the will of a majority that might infringe on those rights at some future occasion.[6]

Belief in individual freedom was tempered by the eighteenth and nineteenth century belief in the perverse nature of the common man. Men of property and rank were seen to be motivated by ambition, but the poor were thought to be condemned to their state by a lack of industriousness. Classical liberals embraced the free market as the optimal engine for allocating resources. They were convinced by Malthus that population growth would outpace production, and regarded the plight of the poor a necessary consequence of the economic reality, even a desirable brake on further population growth. Liberals were behind the Poor Law Amendment Act of 1834 in Britain that limited the provision of assistance to the needy. Protection of property demanded the enforcement of contractual obligations, unfettered access to markets, and the suppression of trade unions.

The corrective hand of the market proved incapable of moderating the frequency and amplitude of the business cycle. Panics of increasing severity occurred in America at roughly twenty year intervals culminating in the Great Depression The free market was never really free, but distorted by the favoritism bought by large financial interests. Wealth was not proportionally shared, and hardship was disproportionately born by the working man.

The indifference of capital to the plight of labor fomented a backlash against laissez-faire liberalism. At the outset of the twentieth century calls for a redistribution of ownership of the means of production gained a sympathetic ear with a large number of people in Europe and America. The appeal of Socialism in America was blunted by progressive legislation that appeared to mitigate the worst abuses of the capitalist system and by a repressive Espionage Act that limited free speech during the country's involvement in the First World War. A massive propaganda effort, undertaken in conjunction with the punitive measures of the Act, marshaled an unenthusiastic public into a patriotic fervor in support of the war and against the Socialist and Marxist critics of the war and the economic system that fed upon it.[7]

The Great Depression brought about a crisis of faith in the free market economy. While classical economic theory held that government could not allocate resources more efficiently than the market, John Maynard Keynes proposed that government's intervention was needed at critical junctures to regulate the level of economic activity. The Keynesian stimulus that ultimately ended the depression was defense spending for World War II, but Keynesian economic theory remains a key ingredient of modern liberal thinking. Social liberals envisioned a more expansive role for government in providing opportunity and security for is citizens. Arthur Schlesinger Jr., one of the intellectual pillars of mid twentieth century liberalism, gave the following rationale for the new social interpretation:

> "when the growing complexity of industrial conditions required increasing government intervention in order to assure more equal opportunities, the liberal tradition, faithful to the goal rather than to the dogma, altered its view of the state," and "there emerged the conception of a social welfare state, in which the national government

had the express obligation to maintain high levels of employment in the economy, to supervise standards of life and labor, to regulate the methods of business competition, and to establish comprehensive patterns of social security."[8]

The political sympathies of a classical and a social liberal are largely shaped by whether he or she believes the natural order is exemplified by an austere Jehovah or a compassionate Christ. The one belief does not entirely preclude the other and is only symbolic of its religious connotation. The classical liberal is today's libertarian or neoliberal conservative who values personal responsibility in an unfolding drama for which the script has been previously set. The social liberal assumes some responsibility for the community in a script that admits reinterpretation and amendment.

Schlesinger, along with others who included Walter Reuther, Eleanor Roosevelt, and Ronald Reagan formed the Americans for Democratic Action (ADA) shortly after the end of the Second World War to promote the social liberal agenda. The social liberal accepted private ownership of the means of production as a necessary economic efficiency, but saw a need for greater government involvement in ensuring the system worked for the greater common good. The ADA fashioned itself as the non-Communist voice of the left and proclaimed its anti-Communism as loudly as its liberal beliefs, but that did not stop the right from trying to isolate it on the fringe of American political thought during the McCarthy era.

The ADA became a vestigial limb of the Democratic Party. It wavered between the choices of remaining unaligned or trying to assume the intellectual core of the party. It achieved neither. The Democrats held the ADA at arm's length and denied them any major influence on party policy.[9] The ADA in turn chose expediency over principle in embracing Democratic candidates like Adlai Stevenson who did not support much of the liberal agenda and temporized on civil rights. The Democratic Party of the fifties, whose "luminary clock [...] proclaimed the time was neither wrong nor right"[10] for a concerted effort to end racial discrimination, appeased its Southern segregationist block and sacrificed principle for the chimera of party unity.

ADA liberals put party over principle in finessing their position on civil rights with the realities of electoral politics. The theologian Reinhold Niebuhr cited Stevenson's call for moderation as "statesman-like," and claimed "the South had made steady progress in racial justice."[11] Niebuhr argued for time "to give these organic processes of persuasion a chance to close the hiatus between the standard of equal justice and the mores of the community." Hubert Humphrey, who championed a progressive civil rights plank at the 1948 convention, retreated behind party lines in 1956 and cautioned that "patience" was important in overcoming discrimination. Humphrey said he was thinking more of "observance" than "enforcement" of the Supreme Court's Brown vs. Board of Education decision outlawing segregation in public schools.[12] Eleanor Roosevelt told the 1956 convention that the word "moderate" does not mean "stand-still." It means going ahead one step at a time in accordance with the realities, and the priority of importance."[13]

Electoral politics was not the vehicle for promoting social change, it only served to endorse and formalize change when the movement demanding it became impossible to deny or appease. The movement produced many notable black leaders and some prominent white allies, but, like the union organizing drive of the thirties, it was sustained by the many anonymous people who faced the fire hoses, police dogs, and Klan violence when the marches ended and the organizers went home.

Walter Reuther became the most visible white face in the drive for black equal rights. He drove that effort at a measured pace with his foot sometimes too heavy on the brake and at other times firmly on the accelerator. He was described as the "white Martin Luther King" by a group of participants during the March on Washington, but was dismissed as too compromising by black contemporaries within the union. However deliberate the pace, he was well out in front of other white liberal politicians of the fifties and sixties, despite the overtly racist cast of the workforce in the expanding Southern auto plants and the lingering racial hostility in many of the union strongholds of the North.

The other issue that dominated American life during the post-war period was Communism. The hoped-for peace at the end of the war quickly deteriorated into a struggle between the United States and the Soviet Union for dominance. The nation was swept by a wave of anti-Communist hysteria during the McCarthy era. Liberals who defended the rights of people expressing unpopular beliefs got branded as commie-symps or fellow travelers. The urge to disassociate themselves from the radical left rendered many liberals mute to and others complicit in the war on civil liberties waged by McCarthy and the House Committee on Un-American Activities (HUAC). When the red purges ended, the political spectrum had shifted toward the ultra violet.

Thousands of Americans were attracted to Communism during the Great Depression as an alternative to the system that had produced an economic crisis it seemed incapable of ending. In the years leading up to the Second World War, Communists worked with other left-leaning groups within the framework of the Popular Front. They were in the forefront of the industrial labor movement and the nascent civil rights movement of the thirties and forties. Their prominence in the social movements of the day far exceeded their appeal to liberal-minded voters. Enthusiasm for Marxist doctrine in America was tempered by the rigidity with which the Party leadership adhered to a script that was being written in Moscow. Many who flirted with Communism during the thirties became disenchanted with the Stalinist reality in Russia and drifted away from the Party in later years.

Walter Reuther worked closely with Communists in organizing the automobile plants during the late nineteen thirties, but split with them over ideological and internal political differences. Communists were a key component of the anti-Reuther caucus, and he made unwarranted Communist influence in union affairs a major rallying point for his supporters. After the Reuther group gained full control of the UAW Executive Board, Communists were removed from positions of authority in the union. Ousting Communists from positions of influence spared the union more intense scrutiny from HUAC, but robbed it of much of its previous dynamism and some of its most able organizers. Reuther concluded with other ADA liberals that a complete disassociation from domestic Communists was essential if they were to appeal to a broader constituency.

When Walter Reuther boarded the small plane for a brief Mother's Day get away with May, he might have been contemplating the next stage of his life. He was sixty-two, three years away from retirement. Black Lake was to be his legacy. It was an idyllic place away from the pace of the factory where union families could come to expand their horizons in a setting of natural and architectural beauty. Reuther hoped to recreate an atmosphere like he experienced at Brookwood Labor College, where many of the young idealists who spearheaded the organizational drives in the factories of the Midwest in the thirties first met and honed their skills. He hoped Black Lake would produce a new generation of leaders to carry on his fight for a just social and economic order.[14]

The opening of the Center was to be marked by a UN sponsored symposium on the environment that would bring together ecologists from seventeen countries to lay the foundations for the first world conference on the environment scheduled for Stockholm the following year.[15] Reuther had an abiding love of nature, and he embraced the environmental movement with his characteristic vigor. He was among the first supporters of Senator Gaylord Nelson's call for an observance of Earth Day, and relished the opportunity to address the first Earth Day celebration at his daughter's college.[16] He spent the morning before the fatal flight at his Paint Creek home planting trees he had purchased as a Mother's Day gift for May.[17] In retirement, Reuther would never be content to limit his voice to one issue, but environmentalism was a cause that neatly filled the breech between reduced responsibility and a continuing sense of social obligation.

When the plane disappeared into the overcast on its approach to Pellston, Reuther was beset by stormy weather behind him and on his horizon. The rumblings of thunder within the UAW that occasioned the first roll-call vote for president during Reuther's twenty-four year tenure in office broke into a torrential downpour shortly after with the invasion of Cambodia and the killing of four students at Kent State. Reuther easily turned aside the simmering challenge to his leadership, but realized a potentially long, difficult strike against General Motors loomed in the fall.[18] In the meantime, the Vietnam War and its extension into Cambodia were fraying blue collar support for his social and economic agenda. When images from Kent State swept across the TV screen in his living room, Reuther was horrified. He flew into a rage, and in his last public act before boarding the ill-fated flight, he penned an angry telegram to President Nixon warning of the enormity of the tragedy his actions were fostering.[19]

Reuther came late to the realization of the enormity of the tragedy that was Vietnam himself. The "author of the Peace Corps" had been an outspoken critic of the Dulles era reliance on dubious military alliances with dictators to contain Communism, but he was an ardent anti-Communist who believed in the necessity of containment. He initially supported the Kennedy-Johnson Vietnam policy and later muted his growing disenchantment with the war effort in deference to his association with Lyndon Johnson and his domestic agenda. When his old adversary, Richard Nixon, became president, Reuther felt free to express his opposition to the war, but by then it was too late. The country was too polarized. In Reuther's absence other figures defined the peace movement. His belated involvement in the anti-war effort was largely met with indifference by a new generation of activists.

Reuther's labor constituency was drifting to the right, swept along by a white undertow running counter to the economic tide that had lifted them into the lower reaches of the middle class. With John and Robert Kennedy, Martin Luther King, and Walter Reuther gone, and Edward Kennedy incapacitated by Chappaquiddick, there was nobody able to apply the brakes to the rightward drift of the electorate. As Reuther had warned, with no national planning to address the effects of automation and globalization, the vagaries of the market alone dictated how these forces diffused through society. Wealth slowed to a trickle into the lower economic strata and gushed into Wall Street. Factories closed in Flint and Cleveland and opened in Shanghai and Mumbai. Some people became fabulously wealthy but many more felt the strain of ebbing income, security, and expectations. Individuals, and the nation as a whole, tried to maintain their previous life-style by plunging into debt.

People who were becoming less secure, seeing their income stagnate while prices continued to rise, looked for someone or something to blame. The right pointed them to its favorite scapegoat—the government and the liberals who had inflated its role in society. From the thirties into the seventies the federal government had been a leveler of economic advantage, helping lower and middle income families to reap a larger share of the national product. The government provided opportunity and relief during the depression, a legal framework for organizing the industrial workforce, leadership during a period of hot and cold war, and a small helping hand when confronting hardship and old age. Government spending built public structures during the depression, provided cheap electrical power to the Southeast, created an interstate highway system for commercial and recreational transport, funded research and development that found expression in commercial enterprises, and "invented" the Internet. Government spending helped fuel the economic expansion, and there was general public support for its role in a mixed economy.

Attitude toward the government began to sour during the sixties and seventies. Disenchantment with the Vietnam War and riots in the cities fueled anxiety about the course in which the country was heading. Long gas lines, high inflation, and concern over forced busing, abortion, and public prayer brought the progressive era to a halt. The rise of the right was accompanied by a tsunami of corporate money flooding into the political process, by a concentration of media outlets in a few corporate hands, and by a decline in numbers and influence of organized labor. Campaign money and rigid ideology rendered the government increasingly dysfunctional, adding to public disrespect for the institution.

During the last fifteen years of his life, Walter Reuther fought George Meany for the soul of the labor movement. Reuther stole the public spotlight, but Meany prevailed within the council chambers. Meany presided over a gerontocracy that had little enthusiasm for an aggressive drive to organize the largely unorganized textile, petrochemical, and agricultural workers, and to increase labor's footprint in the South.[20] Meany retained his leadership position well into his eighties, retiring only months before he died, and many of the Executive Council members similarly served well beyond the customary retirement age. They were more interested in maintaining a status-quo than welcoming an influx of new members who might threaten their privileged position. Meany made clear within the organization and within the governing elite that he spoke for organized labor and that all decisions affecting labor were to be approved by him. Under his leadership the labor movement atrophied. There was no major effort to increase membership which peaked at about the time of the merger of the AFL and CIO. There was no planning to anticipate the effects of automation—to ameliorate the dislocation it caused and extend the opportunity it offered. Automation and globalization were left to run through the economy like an epidemic, devastating some sectors and some regions of the country while leaving others healthy and more prosperous. Among the early casualties was organized labor.

The traditional bastions of industrial unionism—auto and steel— were among the least prepared industries to weather the impact of globalization. America's steel industry was already ill at the end of World War II.[21] It had not modernized its plants and relied on government price supports and import barriers to remain profitable while European and Japanese producers reemerged from the war years with new, more efficient factories. The auto industry was blind to the impact of rising fuel costs and the level of internal demand for smaller, cheaper, more fuel-efficient cars. General Motors wrote the script for the industry's marketing strategy in a 1948 edition of its magazine *Folks*.[22] "Folks in the U. S. are inclined to like class and dash. Because of that, the popular American cars are big, fast, high-powered, advanced in styling, and a-sparkle with chrome." These big American cars were also relatively expensive. Almost half of the new cars produced in a year were bought by people in the top fifth income group. People in the bottom two-fifths of the population bought only eleven percent of the new cars produced annually and relied on used cars for their transportation.[23] The UAW pushed the industry to produce a small car for a broader segment of the public as early as 1949, but small cars did not have the same profit margin as the larger models, and Detroit adhered to its original script until it was blind-sided by the oil embargo in the early seventies.

The wounds suffered by American heavy industry during the onset of globalization were largely self-inflicted, but American workers suffered most of the consequences. As auto industry layoffs mounted, UAW membership declined. What had been the most dynamic agent for progressive change was now defensively fighting for its survival and the survival of its industry. During the heyday of the American automobile industry, UAW membership reached 1.5 million workers, and UAW funding invigorated the Civil Rights Movement, the farm workers struggle, and political action committees. With the decimation of its membership, its coffers were depleted, and its voice muted.

As a consequence of the diminished stature of the UAW, the Black Lake Family Education Center became a heavy drain on the union's treasury. From 2005 to 2010, the Center lost 23 million dollars.[24] In January, 2010, the UAW Executive Board decided to put the property on the market. That decision was rescinded later in the same year when a new leadership took office, but the new economic realities still threaten the legacy project of Walter Reuther. Black Lake is not just another asset the financially challenged union can no longer afford. The ashes of Walter and May Reuther were scattered over the Center grounds and their spirit lingers on the woodland trails and in the rustic venues. Reuther viewed the UAW as a vehicle for the intellectual and social development of the membership as well as for its economic advancement. He envisioned Black Lake as a place of inspiration for a new generation of unionists. It was a place of natural beauty where couples experiencing difficulties in their marriage might find a brief respite from the pressures of the job and home to try to restore their relationship.[25] Black Lake was conceived in an expansive era when we reached for the moon, and it now fights for survival in an era of lowered horizons—a time of retreat from the community back into the self.

Martin Luther King's personal tribute to Walter Reuther captures the character of the man and the role he played in enabling the realization of the American Dream. Unfortunately King's prediction that one day all America will take pride in those achievements rings hollow. In a small questionnaire given to fourteen students enrolled in a computer science class at a prestigious private university, none had heard of Walter Reuther nor could cite any of his accomplishments. When reported to several of the junior faculty, they too did not know of Reuther.

Part of the reason that Reuther has faded in the collective memory is that he is lost in the superficial telling of history—the recitation of dates, wars, and national leaders that typifies the scholastic curriculum. There is also an effort by people on the right to edit the historical record into a narrative celebrating their ideological conceptions. Text books in Texas and libraries in Arizona have been cleansed of material that is inconsistent or contradictory with this telling of the story.[26] The networks and media outlets also find it more profitable not to deviate very far from a revised standard version of the American liturgical text. With labor relegated to the margins of American society, there is little interest in the media to shoe-horn its agenda into the news cycle or to recall its past role in securing a better life for a broader swath of the population.

America is still a work in progress—a country trying to live up to the ideals expressed in the Declaration of Independence. When it looks in the mirror it often sees the photo-shopped image of itself staring back. To some, the image passes for reality—change represents distortion of a pleasing visage. Others can see the reality lurking behind the image, and work for change to bring it closer to the idealized depiction. Change needs vision. A proper gaze into the future requires a reflection from the past and inspiration from its role models.

The twentieth century had its leaders, its warriors, and its visionaries. Leaders and warriors leave their mark on the past, and visionaries shine a light into the future. Walter Reuther was a leader and labor warrior who was also a visionary. He has left a mark in the struggles for economic, social, and racial justice that defined mid-century America. But as a visionary, he remains relevant in the new century. The Reuther plans that have gathered dust in the archives for a half century provide a primer for a liberal alternative to the stagnation of middle class growth that has typified much of the post-liberal era in America.

CHAPTER II

The American Century

Take up the White Man's burden, Send forth the best ye breed—
Go, bind your sons to exile, to serve your captives' need;
To wait, in heavy harness, On fluttered folk and wild—
Your new-caught sullen peoples, Half devil and half child.

....

Take up the White Man's burden! Have done with childish days—
The lightly proffered laurel, The easy ungrudged praise;
Comes now, to search your manhood, Through all the thankless years
Cold, edged with dear-bought wisdom, The judgement of your peers.

Rudyard Kipling, 1899

At the end of the nineteenth century, the United States was emerging from a long period of internal expansion and reconstruction. The young nation was now a feisty adolescent eager to assert its place in society with its more mature European brethren. In the late nineteenth century,

European powers were busy establishing colonial dependencies in Africa and Asia to supply the raw materials needed to feed their industries and the markets to absorb the production needed to sustain their growth. The United States too craved a presence in Asia to foster its own economic growth, especially to fuel the development of its Western states. With western expansion completed and the frontier settled, the voices of Manifest Destiny were looking for new challenges to extend the imperial mission that they viewed as the obligation of their race, and for some, as a mandate from God. The opportunity arose when Cuba, the last of the Spanish colonies in the Caribbean, revolted against its colonial master. After a newspaper propaganda barrage and an explosion aboard the USS Maine in Havana harbor, the US was at war with Spain.

Its Inca gold long depleted, Spain was little match for the robust young opponent. Spanish soldiers, hardened by years of experience fighting a guerrilla war against the local revolutionaries, put up a stiff resistance against the largely inexperienced American forces, but could not withstand the resources that their opponent could marshal against them. As the nineteenth century drew to a close, the United States acquired the previously Spanish colonies of the Philippines and Puerto Rico, established a naval presence on Cuba, and found a national hero to lead it into the next century.

The twentieth century was to become the American Century. The United States was particularly well adapted by geography, geology, and institutional structure to assert its prominence over the course of the twentieth century. It was separated from potential rivals by two great oceans that made it all but invulnerable to sustained assault. It was able to emerge unscathed from the two great conflicts of the century that left the cities and industries of Europe and Japan in ruin. It was blessed with a huge deposit of iron ore on the edge of Lake Superior and abundant veins of coal in the mountains of Appalachia with a lake and river system that provided for cheap transport to the factories of Pittsburgh, Detroit, and Gary Indiana. It was self-sufficient in oil for the first half of the century and a major exporter of agricultural products. It placed few constraints upon the creativity and enterprise of its people and supported its population and industries with a comprehensive public educational system.

The dawn of the new century not only marked the ascendancy of a new power, but it uniquely represented a demarcation between distinct eras in the human experience. Unlike most transitions, where decades and centuries continuously flow from one into the next, the start of the twentieth century represented a quantum jump between a pre-modern and modern age. The automobile, the airplane, and the radio all came into being at the start of the twentieth century. The upheaval in science, the arts, and the common culture that occurred at the turn of the century was equally abrupt. When the ball dropped onto 1900, the automobile was still largely a curiosity owned by a handful of the wealthy; heavier than air flight was still a centuries old dream; the first trans-Atlantic radio broadcast had yet to be made; kinetescope movies offered a peep into a new entertainment industry; and the science, whose achievements produced the advances in communication and transportation that were to transform life in the twentieth century, was in crisis.

American society too was in a state of flux. The start of the twentieth century saw it struggling to adjust to new realities created by industrialization, increased immigration, and its expanded role on the world stage. Racial attitudes had hardened since Emancipation, and the African-American struggle for civil rights was foremost a struggle to survive the legal barriers and extralegal threats that denied them life, liberty, and the pursuit of happiness. Women were agitating for the vote and combating traditional occupational and intellectual constraints that limited the realization of their full human potential. The political system, always slow to adjust to new circumstances, was beginning the process of a century-long realignment of power.

Cars, Planes, and New Horizons

No product or industry influenced the development of twentieth century America more than the automobile, but the story of the automobile began in nineteenth century Germany. Work on an internal combustion engine started in the 1860's, but it wasn't until the end of the century that commercial production of automobiles began. The beginning of the automobile age may be dated to August 5, 1888, when Bertha Benz gathered her two teen-aged sons into the family car and drove off to visit her mother in Pforzheim. The distance between the Benz's home in Mannheim, Germany and Pforzheim was only about one hundred and twenty kilometers, but the trip lasted from dawn until dusk. The only fuel available in 1888 was benzene, sold in small containers at pharmacies as a cleaning agent, so Bertha had to make a number of fuel stops along the way. Other technical problems arose during the trip. The brake linings needed to be replaced; a chain had to be repaired; Bertha had to use a long straight pin to unblock a clogged fuel line, and she had to use a garter to patch frayed insulation on a wire.[1] When she arrived in Pforzheim, she wired her husband, Karl, to let him know her whereabouts. She returned to Mannheim by a different route the next day, and suggested a number of improvements to the prototype automobile Karl had designed, including the addition of another gear to enable the car to negotiate the uneven terrain encountered on a journey of any real distance. Bertha's jaunt was not altogether a pleasure trip. She wanted to convince her husband that there was a commercial market for his invention.[2] Her trip attracted a lot of attention along the route and generated a great deal of publicity. It succeeded in whetting the public appetite for a motorized personal conveyance.

Three years earlier, Karl Benz attached a four-stroke engine of his own design to a three-wheeled carriage that was driven by a pair of roller chains attached to the rear axle. Benz was awarded a patent in 1886 for inventing the first true gasoline-powered automobile.[3] The car that Bertha drove to Pforzheim and back was the third version of the original design. Sixty miles away, in Stuttgart, another automotive pioneer, Gottlieb Daimler and his long-standing associate Wilhelm Maybach were perfecting their own 4-cycle engine and adapting it for use on bicycles, carriages, and boats. Neither party knew of the other or had knowledge of the other's work. Daimler licensed his engine to two French companies, Panhard et Levassor and Peugot that began building automobiles commercially in 1891.[4] The Benz Velo was the first standardized automobile model, and 135 Velos were built in 1895.[5] The first American car company, founded by the Duryea brothers in 1893, produced 13 cars in 1896.[6]

Ransome Olds started the Detroit area auto industry. Olds invented an early version of the assembly line, and produced 425 cars in 1901.[7]

Three years later the Olds assembly line was producing 4000 cars a year, and for the first half of the decade he was the leading automobile manufacturer in America. Americans rode into the new century singing, "Come away with me Lucille in my merry Oldsmobile. Down the road of life we'll fly, Automobubbling you and I"

In 1903 Henry Ford started a company, named for himself, that brought the automobile to the general public. Ford improved upon the assembly line by installing a conveyor-based line in his Dearborn plant and introduced rationalization of the production process. Ford did two other things to bring the cost of an automobile within the price range of a wider public: he successfully challenged the Selden patent, and he raised the pay for his workers to the then unprecedented level of five dollars a day. With these moves he lowered the price of a car and created a wider market for his product.

George B. Selden had obtained a patent on his design for an internal combustion engine automobile, but he never actually produced a working model. For a number of years, Selden was able to extract a percentage on every car produced in America. Rather than contest Selden's claim, most of the prominent automobile manufacturers of the day paid a royalty to Selden and his Wall Street backers and passed the additional cost on to their customers. Ford refused to pay the fee and went to court to contest the claim. The Selden interests won the initial court case, but during the appeal, Ford's lawyer directed attention of the room out the window at some cars assembling for an automobile race and remarked to the Judge, "I see a Winton, a Duryea and many Fords out there, but I don't see a single Selden."[8] The appeals judge limited the applicability of the Selden patent to the two-stroke external combustion engine of the Brayton-type that was stipulated in the document and which was not used by any car maker of the day. Ford won his court case and established his reputation as a champion of the common man. In 1908, Ford introduced the Model T and soon after became the leading automobile manufacturer in the world.

In the same decades that the automobile was capturing the imagination of the public, the dream of heavier than air flight was being pursued on two continents. In 1891, Alberto Santos-Dumont and his family arrived in Paris from Brazil. Alberto's father was a French-born mechanical engineer who had employed the steam-driven technology of the day to extend his plantation and become the leading coffee producer in Brazil. After a fall from his horse left the "Coffee King" a paraplegic, he was no longer able to manage his vast estate, and he decided to retire back to his native France.

The young Alberto had always been intrigued by machinery and the future that was unfolding around him. He loved to indulge his imagination in the science fiction of Jules Verne, and by age ten had read the complete works.[9] When the family arrived in Paris, Alberto pursued his interest in flight. His earliest experimentation was with balloons. He also experimented with heavier than air flight, and in October of 1906, flew his plane, the 14-bis, a distance of sixty meters and at a height of three meters before a large crowd of witnesses. The feat won him the Archdeacon Prize awarded to the first aviator to fly more than twenty-five meters.[10] The 14-bis resembled an elaborate box kite with a motor, over which the pilot had little or no directional control. It contributed little to the evolution of airplane design.

During the same period, the brothers Orville and Wilbur Wright operated a bicycle shop in Dayton, Ohio. They had developed an early interest in flight from a toy helicopter with a rubber-band rotor propeller they had played with as children. Unlike Santos-Dumont, they were not independently wealthy, and their experimentation with flight compromised their income from the bike shop. Wilbur Wright realized that the central problem confronting fixed-wing flight was controlling the craft during turns and variable wind conditions. The brothers experimented with glider flights and wind tunnel tests to perfect a warped wing design and a 3-axis control mechanism that they submitted for a patent after a successful 1902 glider flight.[11] After a series of glider trials culminating with the 1902 flight, the brothers were convinced that they had solved the fundamental problem of control and began readying for a mechanically propelled flight. Their assistant in the bike shop, Charles Taylor, built a light-weight engine, while the brothers experimented with the propeller design.[12] Kitty Hawk, North Carolina, the site of many of their glider experiments, was selected for the first mechanized attempt because of the favorable wind conditions and seclusion it provided. On

December 17, 1903 Orville Wright flew for a distance of 120 feet at a height of 6 feet above the sands at Kitty Hawk while one of five witnesses, John Daniels, photographed the event.[13]

The Wright Brothers continued to improve the design they initially tested at Kitty Hawk, and ten months earlier than the Santos-Dumont flight near Paris, Wilbur flew the longest of several test flights near Dayton for a distance of 24.5 miles in front of a few invited guests.[14] The Wrights were secretive about their experiments with flight, and on the one previous occasion, in which they had invited the local press to witness a demonstration, the weather was bad and the flight was unsuccessful.[15] Reports by people from the Huffman Prairie area outside of Dayton of an airship circling in their skies were not taken seriously by reporters from the *Dayton Daily News*, and none ever took the trouble of going out to investigate for themselves.[16] With little unimpeachable testimony in support, the American and International press was dubious about their claims, with the *International Herald Tribune* headlining a story about the Wrights "Liars or Flyers."[17]

In 1906, the patent for their design was finally granted, and the brothers negotiated contracts with the United States Defense Department and a French company for the sale of their aircraft pending a successful demonstration of its capabilities and with the proviso that it be able to carry a passenger.[18] By 1908, Wilbur was ready to demonstrate a model of the Wright Flyer at an airfield outside of Le Mans. Before a large crowd of onlookers he exhibited his skill as an aviator and the capabilities of his plane with a series of loops and figure eights that far exceeded the accomplishments of his European rivals. Instantly the doubt about the brother's previous claims vanished and Wilbur became the toast of Paris. Ernest Archdeacon, sponsor of the Aero Club de France Prize awarded to Santos-Dumont, admitted that the Wrights were indeed the first to achieve controlled mechanized flight, and he had done them an injustice.[19]

Orville put on a similar demonstration for an American audience, but not without mishap. On a September 17th flight outside of Fort Myer, Virginia, he took off with his passenger, Lt. Thomas Selfridge. A few minutes into the flight, at a height of about 100 feet, the propeller snapped and the plane crashed. Lt. Selfridge suffered a fractured skull and died later that evening. Orville suffered numerous broken bones and ribs and was hospitalized for seven weeks.[20] The contract was extended for one more year to allow Orville to recover and complete the demonstration. On November 22, 1909 the Wright Company was incorporated and the brothers began producing planes for their customers.

The Wright's celebrity was short-lived. Their need to profit from their invention contrasted unfavorably with the motivation of the wealthy Santos-Dumont, who freely published many of his designs to promote flight for the well-being of mankind. The brothers had a public falling-out with Octave Chanute, an engineer, who collaborated with the Wrights on their glider designs, but who now claimed that they gave him insufficient credit for his contributions.[21] The picture of the brothers as greedy and less admirable was reinforced when they became embroiled in a bitter court fight with another American flight pioneer, Glenn Curtiss, over their claim of patent infringement. The fight between the Wrights and Curtiss sapped the energy of Wilbur and stunted the growth of the American aviation industry. Wilbur succumbed to a bout of typhoid fever in 1912 that his family believed was brought on by his depleted health from the strain of the patent fight. Aircraft innovation in the United States stagnated during the years of the patent fight, and it received little support from the government; so that when the United States entered World War 1 in 1917, it had to buy its fighter planes from European suppliers.[22] The dispute between the Wrights and Curtiss was ultimately resolved with Orville's 1915 departure from the company that the brothers had founded and the 1929 merger of the two companies into Curtiss-Wright.

Santos-Dumont went into business with Adolphe Clement's Clement-Bayard Company to build the world's first series production aircraft, the Demoiselle No. 20, in 1908. Each plane could be built in only 15 days and sold for 7500 francs. Three hundred of the planes were built and sold.[23] Santos-Dumont did not need to capitalize on his design. He released drawings of the plane for free to promote aviation as a vehicle for the prosperity of mankind.[24] Unfortunately, his own career as an aviation pioneer came to an abrupt end in 1910 when he was diagnosed with multiple sclerosis. Unable to fly his own planes, he retired to his native Brazil where he was welcomed as a hero. He built a grand home overlooking the sea in the hills above Rio, but became despondent over his illness and from seeing the invention he did so much to promote used to sow death and destruction in war. Alberto Santos-Dumont committed suicide in 1932.

While coal powered the steam and electrical-based Industrial Revolution of the nineteenth century, the twentieth century is frequently described as the oil age. Oil produces the fuel that powers the internal combustion engine, and oil is a primary raw material in fertilizers, synthetic materials, and even medicines. While the largest deposits of accessible oil are now located in the Middle East, it was the United States that became the first industrialized country to realize large oil deposits within its territory. Three states, California, Texas, and Oklahoma became the loci of the American petroleum industry. In 1900, California produced 4 million barrels of oil a year.[25] By 1910, California was producing 73 million barrels a year,[26] but the center of the industry was already moving elsewhere. On January 10, 1901, oil was discovered in the Beaumont region of Texas, near Spindeltop, and this field alone was soon producing 17 million barrels a year.[27] Additional fields were discovered throughout eastern Texas during the decade. At about the same time another huge oil field was discovered at Red Fork, Oklahoma near the city of Tulsa.[28] Tulsa became an oil capital, home to millionaires like J. Paul Getty and Waite Phillips.

The discovery of so much locally produced oil during this decade gave the United States an important advantage over other industrialized economies. The growth of its automotive industry and the expansion of its driving public were not inhibited by the high cost of fuel. Oil produced new wealth for the country that had already overtaken England as the world's leading economy.

The Current War and the Spread of American Culture

Developments in transportation technology accelerated America's economic growth relative to the rest of the world, but parallel developments in communication technology were more influential in establishing American cultural hegemony over the course of the century.

Two men, Thomas Edison and Nikola Tesla, one born within the United States and the other a recent immigrant, were largely responsible for the electrification of the North American continent and the development of many basic products and concepts that laid the foundation of the broadcast and entertainment industries of today.

When Edison began working on his incandescent bulb in 1877, electric arc lights were illuminating about a half mile of the Avenue de l'Opera, turning Paris into "the City of Light," and were transforming Broadway into "the Great White Way." The carbon arc lamp produced an intense shower of light that invigorated the night life of cities and proved suitable for illuminating high-ceiling factory buildings and auditoriums, but its blinding glare and short filament life made it impractical for general use in the home. The race was on to tame this new form of illumination for everyday use. Edison was among a handful of inventors working on an incandescent bulb, some of whom had limited success before he developed a bulb suitable for commercial production.[29] What separated Edison from his rivals was that he conceived the light bulb as part of a complete generating and delivery system and he had the financial backing of Drexel, Morgan bank and investors linked to the Vanderbilts to help bring his work to fruition. Edison spent $130,000 on the development of his system and by 1879 employed over 30 people with a variety of specialties. By contrast William Sawyer, his main American competitor, spent $4000 on his effort and never had more than 2 or 3 assistants aiding him.[30] Edison is pictured in the textbooks as a 19th century individual inventor, but he functioned more like the modern corporate director of research by the time he was ready to begin the electrification of lower Manhattan.

One young man coming to work for Edison in his laboratory was Nikola Tesla. Tesla came to the United States with a recommendation from Charles Batchellor, Edison's chief lieutenant in Paris[31] and the blueprint for a polyphase AC motor sketched in his brain. When he tried to interest Edison in his project he was rebuffed by the great inventor who was adamantly opposed to the AC alternative to his DC delivery system. Instead, when Tesla informed him that several improvements could increase the efficiency of his dynamos and lower their operating cost, Edison told him that there was fifty thousand dollars in it for him if he could do it. After Tesla made the suggested improvements and demonstrated the increased efficiency of the redesigned dynamos, he approached Edison for the promised bonus, but was told instead that he failed to understand American humor. The offer was made in jest. Not only did he not receive the expected reward, but when he tried to get his weekly salary raised from $18 to $25 he was denied. Tesla quit on the spot.[32]

Edison, through his Edison General Electric Company, had set up a power distribution network in New York City during the decade of the 1880s, but his direct-current distribution network had several severe limitations. Home and industrial users required different amperage, and had to be served by different power lines. More importantly, with DC generation the voltage could not be stepped up and down between the generating plant and the customer. Since electrical power is a product of voltage times amperage and is dissipated as heat by the square of the amperage times the resistance of the wire, the direct current generating plants had to be close to the customer. With alternating current, transformers could step up the voltage at the generating plant so that the current carried over the wires would be small and the loss to heat between the plant and customer greatly reduced. Step-down transformers allowed residential and industrial customers to be serviced from the same transmission grid.

Alternating current had many advantages, but Edison continued to argue against it on the grounds of safety. During the blizzard of 1888 the wind and heavy snow brought down numerous power lines that were left dangling from their poles long after the snow had melted. Edison buried his cables underground, but a hodge-podge of telephone, telegraph, and high voltage AC arc lamp wires sprouted like creeper vines over the streets and rooftops of lower Manhattan. One fine spring afternoon a 15-year-old street peddler went skipping down the road and grabbed onto a dangling wire as if to swing into an imaginary pond. The boy was electrocuted in view of appalled passers-by.[33] Several other deaths by electrocution provided Edison with the ammunition for attacking AC and his principal competitor George Westinghouse.

The "Current Wars" took a peculiarly cruel turn when a small-time electrician named Harold Brown added his voice in support of DC and issued a public petition to the New York State Legislature demanding that AC above 300 volts be banned as unsafe.[34] Edison offered Brown space in his laboratory and the assistance of two of his senior associates to substantiate his claims about the safety hazards of AC. Brown offered neighborhood kids a quarter for each stray dog they brought to the lab and then conducted tests on the unfortunate creatures to determine how much voltage they could withstand before they succumbed. Brown next took his gruesome act before a meeting of the New York City Electrical Control Board. A large black Newfoundland mix was brought into the meeting in a cage and wired to receive jolts of electricity. The dog evidenced increasing levels of pain as DC voltage was raised in steps from 300 to 1000 volts after which he was dispatched with 300 volts of AC.[35] The horrified spectators yelled their outrage at Brown, but, undeterred, he repeated the same demonstration with three other dogs four days later, and a short time later again in Edison's laboratory with two calves and a 1250 pound horse.[36]

The notoriety served to get Brown appointed as a consultant to the New York prison authority, which was looking for a more humane method of executing its condemned prisoners. Brown designed an electric chair powered by a Westinghouse AC dynamo and referred to his method of execution as "Westinghousing." The first man to be 'Westinghoused" required a second jolt of current that ignited his shirt and sent puffs of smoke escaping from the cap covering his head. Distraught witnesses to this more humane method of death were sent scurrying from the room amid the smell of feces and burning flesh.[37]

The scare campaign was not persuasive enough to offset the economic advantages of alternating current. By 1888 new AC plant construction was outpacing the growth of DC, and the incidence of electrocution by downed power lines was less than other hazards tolerated by city dwellers, even traffic accidents in the horse and buggy era.[38] The area serviced by an Edison power station was limited to a radius of a half mile around the plant. An AC generating station could be located outside of a city and service a much broader area. The lower amperage carried on the AC high tension lines allowed Westinghouse and other AC providers to save on the amount of expensive copper used in their transmission system. The lack of a suitable AC motor for industrial customers was the one main technical advantage that DC proponents could still claim.

After leaving Edison, the frail, ascetic Tesla worked at manual labor for a year until he found a pair of investors willing to subsidize his efforts to construct the polyphase induction motor that had lingered in his thoughts for the previous four years.[39] In short order Tesla produced a working prototype of a complete AC system that he introduced to the world at an American Institute of Electrical Engineers meeting on May 16, 1888.[40] The induction motor eliminated the commutator that sparked and wore down rapidly in more rudimentary AC motors. Tesla and his benefactors held forty patents for versions of the motor and other components of a complete system. George Westinghouse realized the importance of securing the rights to the Tesla patents and offered the Tesla Electric Company one million dollars plus a royalty of $1 per horsepower on all the articles in use that were covered by these patents.[41]

Armed with the Tesla patents, Westinghouse borrowed heavily to finance the rapid expansion of AC power. When he became overextended during the economic downturn leading to the Panic of 1893, Westinghouse had to approach Tesla about relinquishing his patent royalties. Tesla asked, what would happen if he didn't relinquish his claims, and he was told that he would then have to deal with the bankers because Westinghouse would lose control of his business. Tesla responded by tearing up the contract and telling Westinghouse he would save his company; that he would rather have the benefits to humanity that would come from his AC system than the money.[42] Tesla later said

"George Westinghouse was, in my opinion, the only man on this globe who could take my alternating current system under the circumstances then existing and win the battle against prejudice and money power. He was a pioneer of imposing stature, one of the world's true noblemen of whom America may well be proud and to whom humanity owes an immense debt of gratitude."[43]

Westinghouse saved his company and prevailed in the "Current Wars," but Thomas Edison lost his. The Morgan interests that provided Edison with the financial muscle to win the race to produce a commercially viable incandescent bulb and to electrify lower Manhattan became dissatisfied with his management and engineered a merger with a rival firm, removing the Edison name from Edison General Electric and the inventor from his role in the company.[44] In the final verdict on the War of the Currents, Westinghouse, with the Tesla patents as its trump cards, won the contract to build the generating plant at Niagara Falls and established 60 cycle AC as the standard in the industry.[45]

Delivery of electrical power to an increasing number of urban residential and industrial customers during the first decade of the new century did much to enhance worker productivity and increase leisure opportunities. Productivity gain, as much as unionization of the workforce, was instrumental in reducing the average work-day, and electric lighting extended the waking hours. Electric power in the home brought with it the technology of the time – the phonograph and later the radio, TV and various appliances.

At the 1893 Colombian Exposition in Chicago, Nikola Tesla demonstrated the transmission of high frequency electromagnetic waves to light fluorescent and incandescent bulbs that he had placed around the hall and held in his hand.[46] Five years later in Madison Square Garden he entertained his audience by piloting a toy boat around a tank of water using a hand-held remote similar to the devices controlling kids' toys today.[47] He subsequently built a similar oscillator and tuned receiver to transmit a signal between his residence at the Gerlach Hotel and his laboratory on Houston Street, thirty blocks away. Tesla found with a more powerful transmitter he could receive a signal on a ship twenty-five miles up the Hudson River, but he never attempted to transmit Morse code or voice.[48] Instead of developing a practical wireless communication system he began a Quixotic effort to eliminate the need for copper wires by transmitting energy through the earth.

The principle of radio wave transmission was first demonstrated by the German physicist Heinrich Hertz, but he made no attempt to develop the practical consequences of his experiment. Others, including Tesla and Marconi, developed the commercial implications of the technology.

In 1902, Marconi sent a wireless telegraph message from Cape Cod to a receiving station in Cornwall and has since been credited in the textbooks with the invention of radio. The actual credit for wireless telegraphy was a point of contention for decades with Edison lobbying for Marconi, and against his old rival, Tesla. It wasn't until 1943 that the litigation over the claim of priority was resolved when the Supreme Court upheld a lower court ruling that invalidated the main Marconi patent because it was anticipated by the work of Tesla and others.[49] Despite the ruling Marconi is still considered the inventor of radio in the popular discourse. Marconi won the 1909 Nobel Prize in Physics for his invention. Neither Tesla nor Edison was ever similarly honored. In 1915, *The New York Times* printed information from what it considered reliable sources that the two men were to be jointly honored, but the award went to two others instead. Animosity between the pair may have dissuaded the committee from making a joint award for fear that one or the other might refuse the honor.[50]

The wireless telegraph found an almost immediate application in ship-to-shore radio, but practical commercial broadcasting was still two decades away. Broadcast radio advanced step-by-step with essential contributions from Lee deForest, Edwin Armstrong, and others. Later innovators drew inspiration from Tesla and utilized his earlier work on high frequency resonance in their development of the field, but the pioneer failed to recognize the appropriate direction in which his research should continue and added little to the maturation of the science after 1900.[51] It wasn't until 1920 that the Westinghouse broadcasting station, KDKA in Pittsburgh, became the first commercial radio station in America.

Another new technology that first appeared at the turn of the century was motion pictures. In 1889 the flexible celluloid film strip was invented for Kodak by Henry Reichenbach, and two years later Edison and William Kennedy Laurie Dickson built the kinetoscope, a single-viewer peep show device in which a film strip was moved past a light and viewed through a lens mounted on the top of a cabinet that resembled a lectern.[52] Edison first exhibited the lab's invention at the Brooklyn Institute of Arts and Sciences in May of 1893, and one year later the first kinetoscope parlor opened in a converted shoe store in New York

City.[53] The first movie house had two rows of five kinetoscope cabinets arrayed against opposite walls with different film strips in each of the ten machines. Customers were charged a nickel to view any one of the films that ran for less than a minute and fifty cents to see all ten.

The next step was to project kinetoscope films onto a screen. A number of inventors in the United States and France developed movie projectors and vied for audience appeal with exhibits in saloons, vaudeville theaters, and amusement parks. The first full-time movie house in America opened in Pittsburgh in 1905.[54] The price of admission was five cents, and these early movie houses became known as nickelodeons. A show typically lasted about a half an hour after which a new audience was seated as the show repeated throughout the day. The picture was complemented with music performed by a pianist (and sometimes also a drummer) or from a Wurlitzer. The musicians had little advance indication of the content of the film and the music frequently did not reflect the mood of the action on the screen. Sometimes during a long repetitive day the musicians would entertain themselves and the audience by turning a romantic moment or a moment of melodrama into farce with a deliberately inappropriate musical background.[55] The American public flocked to these early theaters. Between 1906 and 1908 about 5000 nickelodeons opened in the United States.[56] In 1907, the Saturday Evening Post reported that the attendance at nickelodeons exceeded two million for the year. One year later, the daily attendance was over 200,000 people.[57]

The thing that drew the initial customers to the movie houses was the novelty, but to sustain interest in the medium, entertaining pictures were needed. An industry producing and distributing motion pictures arose to satisfy the public appetite for this new form of entertainment. The first feature length film, lasting 70 minutes, was titled *The Story of the Kelly Gang* and premiered in Melbourne, Australia in 1906. Edison's studio in Fort Lee, New Jersey was one of the early producers of motion picture entertainment in America.

Edison protected his prominence in the industry with a horde of patent claims and aggressive litigation efforts to enforce them. In 1907 Edison, George Eastman, the major French film producer Pathé Frères, Biograph, and several other industry leaders formed the Patents

Company which much like the holders of the Selden Patent extracted a royalty from every theater operator and producer in the United States. The independents, which included many of the names familiar to later generations of movie goers, resisted and got the majority of the patent claims nullified in court. Removal of the restrictions imposed by the Patents Company allowed the American film industry to flourish. By the time World War I started, the nickelodeon era had ended—giving way to a more mature industry with longer, better quality films playing in larger, more comfortable theaters served by national distribution networks that satisfied the public craving for fresh entertainment and the theater owners need for local diversity. With longer pictures and more elegant surroundings, the ticket price in the new movie houses was no longer a nickel.

During the second decade of the century the locus of the film industry moved from the East Coast to Los Angeles to take advantage of the light and the local scenery. Typical of the trend were the Warner Brothers who started a film exchange business in Pittsburgh in 1905 and expanded into the movie distribution business in 1912 before moving their operation to Hollywood and becoming producers of their own movies.[58] Studios required an available pool of actors to produce the quantity and quality of movies the public demanded, and after restrictions imposed by the Patents Company were lifted their names began to appear in the credits. Initially, stage actors were reluctant to perform in the movies, as it was considered unworthy of their talent, but as the industry matured, that view changed. Film actors started to become recognized from their performances, and a star system was born.

The movies, recorded music, radio, and later television have spread American culture throughout the world and made English a de facto Esperanto. The music of the American black underclass that had developed inside its own cocoon was now able to emerge with a new pair of amplified wings. Ragtime, jazz, and the blues transcended the night clubs of the Mississippi River towns and found an appreciative audience in the major cities of America and Europe. Rock 'n roll was a step-child of country and blues that voiced the concerns of American youth in the 1950s. It rapidly attracted a global audience of youthful devotees who appropriated many of the American cultural values that it celebrated.

Joshua's trumpets may or may not have brought down the walls of Jericho, but rock'n roll blasted some big cracks in the iron curtain.

The science that paved the way to these innovations was itself in crisis at the start of the new century. Maxwell's equations unified the forces of electricity and magnetism and led to the realization that visible light occupied one band of frequencies in the spectrum of electromagnetic radiation that also included Roentgen's x-rays and Tesla and Marconi's radio waves. But classical waves required a medium like water or air to support their propagation. If light were a wave, how did it travel from distant stars through the vacuum of space to reach the earth? Nineteenth century science postulated that a luminiferous aether permeated space and provided the stuff that carried the electromagnetic disturbances we perceive as light and detect in other forms on film and radio.

In 1887 Albert Michelson and Edward Morley conducted a series of experiments to detect the earth's movement through the aether. They built an interferometer that split a beam of light into two components traversing equal but perpendicular paths before rejoining and producing an interference pattern on the eyepiece. They expected to detect the presence of the aether by measuring the difference in velocity between the split beams when one component traveled parallel to the direction of the earth through the aether and the other perpendicular to it. The "head wind" experienced by the transverse beam was expected to cause a slight decrease in its velocity that would be detected by a shift in the detected fringe pattern ranging to 0.4 wavelengths as the orientation of the apparatus was rotated through the various positions it could assume. Despite the attention to detail of the experimenters and sensitivity of the equipment, no change in the fringe pattern was detected for any orientation of the device. The negative result led to explanations that included suggestions that measuring rods and clocks in the transverse and longitudinal reference frames did not maintain the same length and tick with the same frequency. Einstein explained the phenomena of time dilation and contraction of the measuring rods needed to accommodate the result of Michelson-Morley by rejecting the idea of an absolute reference frame such as aether provided and making the speed of light the one point of common reference between different inertial observers.

During the same period, developments in the field of thermodynamics produced a troubling result. The formula derived from classical theory for describing the radiation from a black body——a thermally isolated chamber with a small peep hole allowing radiation emitted by the walls of the chamber to be observed—not only failed to conform with the experimental results, but predicted that the amount of energy radiated as a function of frequency would increase indefinitely. The result became known as the ultraviolet catastrophe and would lead to the development of a radically new description of the natural world.

In 1901, German physicist Max Planck postulated that the heated atoms on the walls of the chamber were not free to radiate at all frequencies, but only those that were a multiple of a constant later named for him. The new theory produced results that agreed with experiments, but did not provide a satisfactory rationale for why such an assumption was valid in the first place. Even the reality of the oscillating atom was challenged by people like Ernst Mach who considered atoms useful theoretical concepts to explain certain phenomena, but, with no direct evidence of their existence, were unwilling to accept that the physical world had a fundamental underlying granularity.[59]

Five papers by Einstein published in 1905 were crucial in birthing two cornerstones of twentieth century science, Relativity and Quantum Mechanics, though only Max Planck and a handful of scientists at the time appreciated their importance. One paper, explaining Brownian Motion, the erratic movement of dust particles suspended in a gas or fluid, provided evidence supporting the existence of atoms. The photoelectric effect paper, for which he was later awarded the Nobel Prize, demonstrated that not only was radiation produced by discrete oscillations, but that light itself was composed of discrete bundles called photons. One of the other papers produced the famous formula $e = mc^2$, and the paper on special relativity combined time and space into a four dimensional universe with a speed limit – the speed of light. Einstein followed these triumphs ten years later with a new theory of gravity.

For over two hundred years, classical physics enunciated a world view that conformed to common experience. Whether one spends five hours on a jet plane or the same five hours waiting in an airport, one expects each watch to record the same elapsed time. Classical physics makes intuitive sense because it fits well with experiences of everyday life. Many of its precepts can be tested in a high school laboratory. It is only in the realm of the very small, or the very big, or the very fast – near the speed of light—that classical physics breaks down and is replaced by a world view more reminiscent of writings by Lewis Carroll or drawings of M. C. Escher. The modern world has produced many technical marvels that have made life more comfortable, but modern science, as well as modern art and literature, has introduced many difficult, and sometimes disquieting, concepts into the discourse.

While American inventors and entrepreneurs were prominent in generating the technological products that appeared at the start of the new century, American science lagged behind the basic science being done in Europe. The schools, networks, and tradition that produced generations of scientists in Europe, were not yet as developed in the United States at the start of the twentieth century. In the year 1900 the language of science was most often spoken in German.

Three factors led to the rise to predominance of American Science: money, government support, and the rise of Hitler. Studying the structure of the atomic nucleus required powerful particle accelerators that the economy of the United States was able build and deliver to research groups established at several well funded public and private universities. The opportunity to do research with the best available tools brought scientists from Europe to work with their American colleagues. The migration of scientists from Europe swelled as the Nazi Party became entrenched in Germany and beyond. This group of mostly Jewish scientists entered America to stay. The exodus of scientists from the Old World to the New was highlighted in 1933 when Albert Einstein accepted a position at the Institute for Advanced Studies in Princeton and later became an American citizen. By the sixth decade of the twentieth century the language of science was clearly English.

Race, Ethnicity, and Manifest Destiny

In January of 1901, Queen Victoria, "By the Grace of God, of the United Kingdom of Great Britain and Ireland Queen, Defender of the Faith, Empress of India" and longest reigning British monarch, died.

Her death marked a symbolic transition from an age dominated from sunrise to sunrise by one English-speaking people to the hegemony of another. Though she was long on title and short on real authority, the Queen's passing signaled a transition from the structure and mores of one century to the deconstruction of the next. The Queen's immediate heir was an overweight, self-indulgent, post middle-aged man, but the real inheritance passed over the entire extended family of crowned heads she left behind in Europe to the presumptuous commoner an ocean removed.

Within twenty years of her passing, the families that had long regarded Europe as their personal Monopoly game, where deeds were collected and swapped through marriage and war, were gone – reduced in rank and influence or removed entirely. The Great War that preceded their demise decimated an entire generation of young men. What started with traditional infantry and cavalry ended in the trenches with tanks, aircraft, and disease. In the wake of the slaughter and the vacuum created by the fall of monarchies, hyperinflation, and depression, repressive fascist and communist regimes arose. The "War to End All Wars" only produced a flawed peace that led to a second, even more destructive, conflict that left Europe and much of Asia devastated and divided. The Second World War ended with only one modern country having its land and industry unscathed by the conflict and its military presence displayed around the globe.

Queen Victoria was not the only prominent world figure to pass away in 1901. In September of that year, President William McKinley went to Buffalo, New York to open the Pan American Exhibition. On September 6 while greeting the public at the site's Temple of Music, McKinley was shot in the stomach by an anarchist. McKinley was rushed to a nearby hospital and operated upon by the top surgeon locally available, but the bullet could not be found. After the operation McKinley seemed to be recovering and was released from the hospital to convalesce at the home of the Exposition's director, but infection set in and McKinley died on September 14. After the operation an aide to McKinley had made an urgent request of Edison for use of an x-ray machine developed in his lab. The machine was dispatched on the first available train to Buffalo, but was never used to try to locate the bullet.[60] Eighty years later, Ronald Reagan received an equally serious wound in an assassination attempt, but aided by technological descendants of that x-ray machine and advances in medical science, surgeons were able to save the President's life, and he returned to duty a few weeks later.

McKinley's death promoted Theodore Roosevelt to the Presidency. The Rough Rider is known today as a progressive who championed the preservation of the wilderness and confronted the monopolists, but he was also a strong proponent of American exceptionalism. As Assistant Secretary of the Navy he advocated building a strong navy that, as President, he dispatched to points of call around the globe to advertise the presence of a new superpower. To facilitate the movement of the fleet between the Atlantic and the Pacific, Roosevelt needed to build a canal across the neck of Central America. When he could not get a favorable deal from Colombia, an uprising was fomented; the country of Panama was created; and a strip of land right through the new country's middle was leased to its benefactor.

Roosevelt's ascendancy to the Presidency in 1901 marked the culmination of a remarkable six-year period which saw him rise through a sequence of positions marked by distinguished accomplishment despite a brief tenure in each office. In 1895, he became president of the Board of New York City Police Commissioners. In this post he transformed one of the most corrupt police forces in the country into a professional organization by establishing standards and requiring new appointments be based on merit, not political patronage.[61] When McKinley became President in 1897, Roosevelt was appointed Assistant Secretary of the Navy. The title Assistant did not stop him from effectively running the Navy Department in the absence of any leadership from Secretary John D. Long.[62] When war was declared in 1898, the Navy was the one branch of service that was prepared for the conflict. Upon the outbreak of war, Roosevelt resigned his office and received a commission as Lieutenant Colonel of the First Volunteer Cavalry Regiment, a group recruited from cowboys from the western territories and friends of Roosevelt from the Ivy League schools of the East.[63] The unit's charge up San Juan Hill has become the lasting memory of this brief war. Roosevelt was nominated for a Medal of Honor for his heroics in leading the attack, but the citation was originally turned down. (In 1997, Congressman Rick Lazio of New York's Second District sent a recommendation to the US Army

Awards Branch nominating Roosevelt for the medal, which he received posthumously in 2001.) When the war ended later that year, Roosevelt resigned from the service to run for Governor of New York, and in 1900 was placed on the national ticket to run as McKinley's Vice President.

The election of 1900 was fought over the issue of the Philippines. Dewey's victory at Manila Bay had handed the United States an unanticipated prize that it did not quite know how to accept. The rationale for war with Spain was argued over events in the Caribbean. Imperialistic ambitions in the Pacific were strong, but complementary to the specific war aims. When the war ended, the disposition of the Philippines was left for future negotiation in the protocol signed by Spain and the United States on August 12, 1898.[64] As final negotiations proceeded, McKinley was persuaded by commercial interests, and the specter of Germany moving in to claim the Islands should the US relinquish them, to demand that the entire island group be ceded to the victorious country. On December 21, before the treaty was ratified by the Senate, McKinley issued a proclamation to the Filipino people stating that the authority of the United States was exerted over their land to protect their security and property, and resistance to this authority would be met with "firmness."[65]

During the War with Spain, the US military aided the return of the Filipino nationalist leader, Aguinaldo, to the Islands to lead resistance against the Spanish occupiers, but when that war ended and President McKinley proclaimed American sovereignty over the entire island group, Aguinaldo turned his revolt against the American presence. The revolt lasted over three years and cost an estimated 600,000 Filipino lives.[66] The occupation triggered a spirited debate within the US over what constituted the national interest and how the policy being pursued was rationalized with the ideals enunciated in our founding documents.

The argument for retention of the Philippines and the previous annexation of Hawaii was not only based upon commercial interest and development of the Pacific Coast, but also cited American exceptionalism and the obligations of a superior Teutonic race. One of the most fervent advocates for an imperialistic point of view was Senator Albert J. Beveridge of Indiana. In an address to the Senate he proclaimed that stewardship of the conquered lands was nothing less than a divine mission.

"God has not been preparing the English-speaking and Teutonic peoples for a thousand years for nothing but vain and idle self-contemplation and self-admiration. No! He has made us the master organizers of the world to establish system where chaos reigns. He has given us the spirit of progress to overwhelm the forces of reaction throughout the earth. He has made us adepts in government that we may administer government among savage and senile peoples. Were it not for such a force this world would relapse into barbarism and night. And of all our race He has marked the American people as His chosen nation to finally lead in the regeneration of the world. This is the divine mission of America, and it holds for us all the profit, all the glory, all the happiness possible to man. We are trustees of the world's progress, guardians of its righteous peace."[67]

It is not clear what burning bush or angelic visitation relayed the word from on high that Israel was out and Americans were now the chosen people of God, but Beveridge's view of manifest destiny and American exceptionalism had a willing audience of adherents within the country, and this view did nothing to hinder the mercantile ambitions of other voices for retention within the Republican Party. The imperialist cause was also aided by Kipling's poem, "Take Up the White Man's Burden," that was widely distributed throughout the country. It was primarily the catchy title and not the ironic verse that was used as a rallying cry for retention. Kipling saw the United States as heir to the British colonial mission and viewed Theodore Roosevelt as custodian of this mission. He sent Roosevelt an original copy of his poem in an 1898 letter in which he urged Roosevelt to be a good colonial administrator, and "put all the weight of your influence into hanging on permanently to the whole of the Philippines [...] since America is morally bound to build over again from the foundation."[68]

The Democratic candidate for President in 1900 was again William Jennings Bryan. Bryan was defeated by McKinley in the previous election when he campaigned against the monopolistic practices of the railroad barons that squeezed the livelihood of Midwestern farmers. Bryan was a pacifist that spoke out against a war with Spain, and in his acceptance speech at the 1900 Democratic Convention, he cautioned against American imperialism.

> "Those who would have this nation enter a career of empire must consider not only the effect of imperialism on the Filipinos but they must also calculate its effect upon our own nation. We cannot repudiate the principle of self government in the Philippines without weakening the principle here."[69]

In the giddy flush of victory and national pride, the appeal to the older virtues of our founding documents did not gain traction, and Bryan went down to a resounding defeat.

"'I told William McKinley it was a mistake to nominate that wild man at Philadelphia. Now look, that damned cowboy is President of the United States!'—Mark Hanna, on the funeral train carrying McKinley from Buffalo to Washington.[70] Roosevelt was added to the Republican ticket in 1900 as much as a means to sideline him from New York politics, as it was for his voter appeal as a charismatic national hero. He could be relied upon to advance the expansionist goals of the backers of his party, but his domestic agenda could not be reliably identified with the views of any segment of the party. His closest political friends and advisers included Henry Adams, Senator Henry Cabot Lodge, Secretary of State John Hay, and the conservationist Madison Grant. This group shared a connection with Harvard and an ancestry that stretched back to the early Puritan and Dutch colonists.

The biggest concern of this "Harvard elite" was the diminution of the influence of their class because of immigration from Southern and Eastern Europe and because of the rise of the nouveau riche capitalist class. The old elite did not think that the new capitalists shared their virtues of honest labor and civic obligation, and were sympathetic to efforts to limit the power of the trusts that they controlled.[71] They were more concerned about the huge influx of immigrants from the non-Teutonic, non-Anglo-Saxon regions of Europe, and the effect that these "inferior races" might have on the capacity of the body politic for self-governance.[72] The recent immigrants were concentrated in the big eastern cities like Boston where machine politics was run largely by and to the benefit of the immigrants who had wrested control from the previous ruling elite.

Albert Beveridge was not unique in believing that American exceptionalism rested on the particular fitness of the Northern European peoples that previously settled this continent. These great grandchildren of the founding fathers were feeling particularly isolated within a community that they long viewed with a sense of proprietorship.[73] Jewish immigrants from the ghettos of Poland and Russia were particularly foreign in their language, dress, and religion, and therefore subject to particular nativist animosity. Henry Adams, grandson and great-grandson of Presidents, sensed his relegation to the dust bin of history as inevitable and vented his outrage against the Jew. "The Jew has got into the soul. I see him – or her – now wherever he – or – she goes, and there must remain a taint in the blood forever."[74]

Others of the Anglo-ascendancy misappropriated scientific methodology to justify their belief in racial superiority. Henry Cabot Lodge painstakingly traversed page-by-page through Appleton's 6-volume *Encyclopedia of American Biography* to identify the racial extraction of all the eminent men and women that it listed. He discovered that of the 14,243 subjects, only 19 had roots in Southern or Eastern Europe.[75] He wrote that, "immigration from Great Britain has contributed ¾ of the ability from outside sources…if one adds settlers from Germany, France, the Netherlands, and Scandinavia, virtually all of the eminent Americans since the country's founding are accounted for."[76] Lodge presented this evidence without any consideration of the percentage of the total population each of these ethnicities represented or the length of time that sizable numbers of each of the various national groups had lived in America.

Lodge's selective use of data to confirm a strongly-held belief may be dismissed as normal operating procedure for a politician. More telling was that every major university in the United States and Great Britain at the time had scholars producing research on racial theory. A contortion of Darwin's theory of Natural Selection called Social Darwinism was used to examine the differences between the races and produce explanations for the superiority of the white race, particularly its Northern European branches.[77] Without the proper tools to study the evolutionary development of the human species, heads were measured, facial features were given unwarranted significance, and statistical studies of comparative racial achievements were used to promote racial doctrines. Louis Agassiz, the eminent zoologist and popular Harvard professor, held the belief that whites and Negroes belonged to different species, much as Neanderthals had once coexisted with our own ancestors. He stressed that it was "the scientist's obligation to settle the relative rank among these races [since] it will not do to assume their equality and identity."[78]

If racial superiority could be legitimized by providing scientific cover, then social engineering would not be an improper means to preserve and protect the superior race against threats to its distinctiveness that the melting pot might pose. Madison Grant, Chairman of the New York Zoological Society, Trustee of the American Museum of Natural History, and Councilor of the American Geographical Society, used the credibility of the titles his social standing accorded him to lend credence to his prescriptions for attacking what he believed to be racial suicide. In his 1916 book, *The Passing of the Great Race*, Grant states that the problem of racial suicide cannot be solved by encouraging indiscriminate breeding. He lamented the "Mistaken regard for what are believed to be divine laws and a sentimental belief in the sanctity of human life," and proposed "the elimination of defective infants and the sterilization of such adults as are themselves of no value to the community."[79] He numbers in this group "the ever increasing number of moral perverts, mental defectives, and hereditary cripples." Grant continues to state that "This is a practical, merciful, and inevitable solution of the whole problem, and can be applied to an ever widening circle of social discards, beginning always with the criminal, the diseased, and the insane, and extending gradually to types which may be called weaklings rather than defectives, and perhaps ultimately to worthless race types."[80] The book went through multiple printings in the United States and was translated into a number of other languages, including German in 1925. Grant received a fan letter from Adolf Hitler, who wrote "The book is my Bible. *Mein Kampf* was influenced by the book."[81] The book went through three revisions in seven years after its initial publication and generally received acclaim from reviewers, including an oblique affirmation from the fictional Tom Buchanan in the *Great Gatsby* who told Nick and Daisy that "it was a fine book, and everybody ought to read it."[82] Another enthusiastic reader was Theodore Roosevelt who wrote Grant that

> "It's a capital book; in purpose, in vision, in grasp of the facts our people most need to realize. It shows an extraordinary range of reading and a wide scholarship [...] It shows a fine fearlessness in assailing the popular and mischievous sentimentalities and attractive and corroding falsehoods which few men dare assail. [..] all America should be grateful to you for writing it."[83]

The efforts of Lodge and Grant culminated in the Immigration Act of 1924. The Act limited immigration to two percent of the foreign born of each nation living in the United States at the time of the 1890 census – the time that predates the mass migration to the United States from Eastern and Southern Europe. Immigration dropped to 20,000 per year from its previous figures of well over one-half million.[84] The Act was not repealed until the mid-1960s, and it prevented the immigration to the United States of many Jews seeking to flee Nazi persecution during the 1930s. Despite the placement of a plaque containing Emma Lazarus's poem, *The New Colossus,* in the interior of the pedestal of the Statue of Liberty in 1906 to express the Statue's symbolic greeting to new immigrants sailing into New York harbor, the "huddled masses yearning to breathe free" were not particularly welcome, and after 1924, were expressly excluded.

If European immigrants were viewed contemptuously by the earlier generations of European immigrants, the native-born African-Americans were regarded with particular disdain. In the South, they were segregated from the rest of society, given limited access to commerce, and too many times lynched for offenses against the prevailing culture as small as showing too little deference to a white neighbor or too little tolerance for their allotted place. In the North, real discrimination against black advancement existed in the schools, the workplace, and the neighborhood, but more insidious was the deep-rooted belief in the inferiority of the Negro race that manifested itself in a paternalistic attitude by the progressives and a toleration of the injustices by the politicians.

In 1900, the average life expectancy in the United States was forty-nine years, but for black American men it was only thirty-two and one half years.[85] In the last two decades of the nineteenth century, over 2,500 blacks were lynched in the South while the nation looked the other way.[86] The South was not reintegrated into the country, but allowed by Northern politicians, who dominated the national administration, a free hand in all matters outside of interstate commerce and defense.

When war with Spain broke out in 1898, African-American leaders were divided in their response. Some felt that concern for the rights of our "brown brothers" in Cuba rang hollow given the treatment of the black man at home, and that this was just another occasion to exert white control over another non-white race. They urged that blacks should not get involved in this enterprise.[87] Others, including Booker T. Washington, saw an opportunity for the black man to prove himself in combat and win respect from the larger population.[88] Black regiments had served with distinction in the Civil War and on the frontier, and, with a standing army of only 26,000 men when the war started,[89] the army offered blacks one of the few unfettered avenues to employment.

Four black regiments were ordered to report to staging areas in Tampa and Key West, Florida in March and April of 1898. The units consisted of the 24th and 25th Infantry and the 9th and 10th Cavalry that had been previously stationed on the Western frontier. When the 24th Infantry departed from Fort Douglas, near Salt Lake City, Utah, the townspeople lined the streets to give the regiment and its band a farewell tribute for their service.[90] When the 24th arrived in Tampa they were greeted with the same scorn and prejudice experienced by black civilians throughout Florida. The black regiments left Tampa in mid-June and arrived on the Southeastern tip of Cuba on June 22nd. Two days later they were engaged in some of the heaviest fighting of the war. First at Las Guasimas and a week later at El Caney and San Juan Hill, the black regiments fought side-by-side with the white 1st Regular Cavalry and the 1st Volunteer Cavalry – Theodore Roosevelt's celebrated Rough Riders.[91]

In the charge up San Juan Hill, the Rough Riders found themselves under attack from all sides and in danger of being cut to pieces. The

9th and 10th Cavalry were in reserve, and, when receiving word of the predicament of the Rough Riders, raced to their defense. In the words of a New York reporter viewing the battle "their aim was splendid. Their coolness was superb and their courage aroused the admiration of their comrades."[92] In the words of one Rough Rider corporal, "If it hadn't been for the black cavalry, the Rough Riders would have been exterminated."[93] Five black soldiers of the 10th Cavalry were awarded the Medal of Honor and 25 more were awarded the Certificate of Merit.[94]

The four black regiments participated in the heaviest fighting of the war, but the most dangerous duty that they faced may have been in the Yellow Fever hospitals during the occupation. Black soldiers came largely from the South and were less susceptible to the disease than their white counterparts. They were dubbed the "Immunes," though this was hardly the case.[95] Yellow Fever took a greater toll than combat on both white and black soldiers during the Spanish American War.

Theodore Roosevelt did not share the angst felt by those of his circle. He did not grow up in tradition-bound Boston, but in a more dynamically mobile New York. He believed in the power of the melting pot to fashion a uniquely American culture, but he railed against the hyphenated American. "A hyphenated American is not an American at all."[96] He nominated the first Jew, Louis Brandeis, to the Supreme Court, and appointed the first Jew, Oscar Solomon Strauss, to his Cabinet. He consistently supported the rights of the recent immigrants, and was sympathetic to the views of the muckrakers. Under his administration the Pure Food and Drug and the Meat Inspection Acts of 1906 were passed by Congress and a Department of Labor and Commerce was established. His Bull Moose Party platform in 1912 included a plank for women's suffrage.

The progressive Roosevelt, however, shared the belief in the superiority of the Northern white race that was common to his circle and to the native white population in general. He was receptive to the paternalistic obligations of the superior race as described by Kipling. Roosevelt outlined his attitudes on race during a February 13, 1905 speech to the New York City Republican Club. He cautioned against imposing radical changes in government policy to foster racial equality, but favored instead a gradual, largely passive, approach to achieving these ends. He referred to the white race as the "'forward race' who had the responsibility to elevate the status of the non-white citizens through training 'the backward race' in industrial efficiency, political capacity, and domestic morality." It was imperative that the "forward race" embrace this duty because, "if morality and thrift among the colored men can be raised, then those same virtues among whites would rise to an even higher degree." At the same time "debasement of the blacks will in the end carry with it debasement of the whites."[97]

In 1905 America, Roosevelt was considered a racial moderate. His views of white racial superiority did not prevent him from awarding some patronage jobs to blacks during his years in New York politics. Early in his presidency, he invited the black educator Booker T. Washington to the White House to seek his advice and asked him to dine with him at the close of the day. The event had symbolic importance for both the black and white communities. The gesture ingratiated Roosevelt with the black community, but social interaction between the races was an anathema in the South, and Roosevelt's relations with the Southern Congressional delegation remained strained for the rest of his presidency. Roosevelt continued to consult with Booker T. Washington for the duration of his time in office, but never again in the White House.[98]

Roosevelt was a firm believer in the law, but also an adherent to the social order. In a message to Congress he argued that "The greatest existing cause of lynching...is the perpetuation, especially by black men, of the hideous crime of rape." He went on in the same address to state "Let justice be both sure and swift, but let it be justice under the law, and not the wild and crooked savagery of the mob."[99] His racial views led him to the conclusion that the mob was acting in justified outrage against an actual act of Negro criminality, but that this anger needed to be ameliorated by the rule of law.[100] Roosevelt strongly disapproved of lynching, but he never proposed legislation to outlaw it.

The event that tarnished Roosevelt's legacy on race relations occurred in Brownsville, Texas on a hot August night in 1906. The first battalion of the black 25th Infantry had been transferred from Nebraska to Fort Brown, Texas earlier in the summer. The townspeople in segregated Brownsville did not want the black soldiers in their midst and petitioned the War Department for their removal. Secretary of War,

William Howard Taft, believed that racial prejudice was more than just a regional phenomenon, and refused to alter postings of black units to the South.[101] The citizens of Brownsville were not mollified by Taft's decision, and racial tensions between the townspeople and the troops became very strained by an alleged assault by a soldier upon a white woman on the night of August 12th. Two nights later a group of men in army uniforms began firing randomly on the street and into buildings in an attack that lasted several minutes and resulted in the death of a bartender and injury to a policeman. Witnesses from the town reported seeing black soldiers firing into the buildings, and military cartridge shells and discarded rifles were retrieved at the scene. Twelve members of the 25th were later arrested but not indicted for the crime.[102]

Two investigations were ordered by President Roosevelt: the first headed by Major August Blockston, and the second by Army Inspector General Ernest Garlington, a South Carolinian with deep-seated racial prejudice. From the beginning the presumption of the collective guilt of the black soldiers outweighed any testimony or evidence brought forward in the investigation. White witnesses were believed, black soldiers were assumed to be lying, testimony by the unit's white commander and chaplain was dismissed, and exculpatory evidence was ignored.[103] It took Blockston less than 48 hours to assert that the black soldiers were lying, and Garlington was predisposed to this opinion from the start. General Garlington stated during the proceedings that "The secretive nature of the race, where crimes charged to members of their color are made, is well known."[104] When asked directly if he thought colored people, generally, are truthful, he replied frankly "No, Sir, I do not." During the investigation the unit was assembled and those participating in the riot were ordered to step forward. None did. The order was next given for anyone having knowledge of the incident and of those responsible to step forward and volunteer that information. Again, none did. As a result, the entire unit of 167 men was charged with insubordination. Roosevelt waited until the day after the Congressional elections of 1906, so as not to jeopardize the black vote, to sign the dishonorable discharge papers of all 167 men, including six Medal of Honor winners and thirteen cited for bravery in the Spanish American War.[105]

Among the evidence discounted by the investigators was the testimony of the white battalion commander, Major Penrose that all of the soldiers were present at the 10:00 curfew and all of the battalion's rifles were similarly accounted for and none had been recently fired. The cartridges found at the scene of the raid bore double indentations, indicating that they had been loaded into the chamber twice. They were likely retrieved from the rifle range at the fort and used again in shooting up the town.[106] Major Penrose also testified to the easy availability of army uniforms to the citizens of Brownsville. None of this evidence or the exemplary record of many of the troops trumped pre-conceived racial stereotypes. In the wake of the Spanish American War and the Philippine Insurrection, valor in combat had done little to advance the status of blacks.

As the United States strode into the twentieth century, it had one foot firmly planted in the past and the other tentatively stretching toward the future. The country had already supplanted Great Britain as world's wealthiest economy, but the average citizen had an income similar to what the average Mexican has today.[107] In 1900, only about one third of American homes had running water and fewer than 15% had flush toilets. Only about 3% of homes had access to electricity. The typical worker spent sixty hours, spread over six days on the job. Ten percent of the population was illiterate, and the average adult had an eighth grade education. Only seven percent of the population finished high school.[108]

Jefferson's nation of small farmers was moving rapidly into cities like Pittsburgh and Detroit to work in the factories of Carnegie and Ford. In 1900, less than forty percent of the population was rural, and that percentage would decline dramatically over the next couple of decades.[109] The changing demographics necessitated changes in the institution of government. Theodore Roosevelt was the first twentieth century President to confront the need for government to legislate in the conflicting interests of business and labor, producer and consumer, farmer and banker. As industrialization proceeded along with rapid advances in communication and transportation, the nation was being stitched into a more cohesive fabric. The role of the federal government grew at the expense of the states. Roosevelt, like many of his successors, accrued more power in the office he occupied. The tensions between a rural past and an industrial present that surfaced at the beginning of the twentieth century persist into the twenty-first.

In the decade before the turn of the century, the nation developed an appetite for imperialism. Roosevelt championed this development, and later became the first American President to have a leading voice in the council of nations. From its founding, the republic was influential for the ideals it proclaimed, however inadequately it lived them, but now its influence stemmed more from its emergence as a self-confident economic and military power. The national appetite for imperialism, however, was counterbalanced by the gene for isolationism that George Washington fathered into the national DNA. In 1900, the nation was both eager and hesitant to step out onto the world stage.

The party platforms for the 1900 presidential election reflected this division. The Republican platform extolled the leadership of McKinley and trumpeted the unselfish purposes for which the nation had gone to war.[110] The Democratic platform reflected Bryan's concern that imperialism was inconsistent with the nation's founding principles. It cautioned against militarism and asserted that a small standing army together with state and volunteer militia was sufficient to provide an adequate national defense.[111]

In 1900 the Democrats were the party that advocated a smaller government and lower taxes. The Democrats relied upon a base of solid Southern support, and Bryan had appeal to more conservative rural voters. The Republicans of that era were the more progressive party. The Republican platform condemned laws and practices that denied blacks the right to vote as provided for in the 15th Amendment, but committed to no concrete steps to stop the discrimination. It stated that "the government must protect the person of every citizen when they are wrongfully violated or placed in peril," but gave no intention of proposing anti-lynching legislation. The document saluted women for their service in volunteer organizations and as nurses during the war and their "operation in education and industry," but made no mention of giving them the vote.[112] The Republicans vowed to protect labor by restricting immigration of cheap labor from foreign lands, while the

Democrats pledged strict adherence to the Chinese Exclusion Act, and its extension to all Asians.[113]

By the end of the "Roosevelt decade", a million cars were on the American road and electric power was being delivered to residential and commercial customers in most American cities. The nation was prosperous and self-confident. The government had taken an active role in the regulation of monopolistic practices of industry, consumer protection, and wilderness preservation. A chorus of progressive voices advocating a varied social agenda was growing louder and more confident of eventual success. In America's second full century the nation had become more industrialized, more urban, more heterogeneous, and, with internal expansion completed, more outward-looking.

CHAPTER III

The Formative Years

It is true that wealth has been greatly increased, and that the average of comfort, leisure and refinement has been raised, but these gains are not general. In them the lowest class do not share....The association of poverty with progress is the great enigma of our times....There is a vague but general feeling of disappointment; an increased bitterness among the working classes; a widespread feeling of unrest and brooding revolution....The civilized world is trembling on the verge of a great movement. Either it must be a leap upward, which will open the way to advances yet undreamed of, or it must plunge downward which will carry us back to barbarism

From *Progress and Poverty* by Henry George, 1879

Growing pains of an adolescent nation

The prosperity promised by the new technologies did not filter through all regions of the country and all classes of people. The boom-bust cycle of unregulated capitalism whip-lashed the hourly workers in the factories with irregular work and fluctuating wages. The mechanization of farming meant that farmers were driven to the banks to borrow money to increase their land holdings and purchase the equipment needed to remain competitive. They became squeezed between tight money, high transportation costs, and falling grain prices. Many became tenants on the land they once owned. The government and the courts provided little relief.

Between the end of the Civil War and 1900, the population of the United States tripled. Immigrants from Eastern and Southern Europe flooded into the industrial cities of the Northeast and Midwest. The country strained to accommodate its rapid growth. The railroads and the cavalry opened the plains for new settlements, and cheap land, embellished with deceptive tales of its abundance, drew people from the overpopulated cities and towns east of the Mississippi to the arid grasslands of the Southwest.

These population shifts occurred during a time when machines were dramatically increasing the productivity of the worker on the farm and in the factory. Before the Civil War, 61 hours of labor was needed to produce an acre of wheat. By 1900 the same acre of wheat could be produced with 3 hours and 19 minutes of labor.[1] The Bessemer Process produced the same amount of steel in 15 minutes that was formerly turned out in a day.[2] The factories and the farms grew bigger, and as the workforce expanded, the price of labor shrank. With more and more capital concentrated in fewer large enterprises, the model of the small business owner dependent upon the skill and devotion of his workers gave way to the reality of a small coterie of industrialists presiding over a large anonymous workforce of limited skill and individual value.

The exploitation of cheap, plentiful labor provoked a violent reaction during the Panic of 1873 and the years of depression that followed. When railroad companies moved to cut the already low hourly wages of brakemen by ten percent in 1877, workers at the Baltimore & Ohio railroad yard in Martinsburg, West Virginia went on strike and announced that no trains would leave the station.[3] The governor called out the militia to get the trains moving again. But after a brief confrontation between the strikers, supported by many unemployed townsmen, and the soldiers, the protesters stood their ground and the militiamen refused to fire upon the crowd containing many of their friends and relatives.[4] The militia stood down and the strike quickly spread from the station in Martinsburg to its terminus in Baltimore, and then around the Monopoly Board from the B & O to the Pennsylvania and Reading Railroads and off to the Midwest along the Burlington line. It spread to Pittsburgh and the stockyards and lumber mills of Chicago. It reached St. Louis where a general strike left the whole city under the effective administration of the local leaders of the Workingman's Party.

As the strike grew it awakened sympathy from the working class and spread to other industries. At its peak, the strike involved 100,000 workers and was supported by many times more of the unemployed. More than half the freight transported over the nation's rail network stopped running.[5] Local militia proved ineffective and unreliable in restoring the old order. Only federal troops were able to impose the will of the state. In Pittsburgh, the Philadelphia militia was summoned to break the strike because the sympathies of the local guardsmen were with the strikers.[6] The two Pennsylvania cities shared little in the way of common history, common tradition, or common affection. When the rival militia arrived in Pittsburgh, it received a barrage of insults peppered with a few stones and responded with gunfire. The city erupted in a riot that left scores of strikers, their supporters, and guardsmen dead, and millions of dollars in damage to the Pennsylvania Railroad's rolling stock and property. The militia was forced into a hasty retreat.[7] When the militia left, regular army units replaced them.

The strike was largely spontaneous. Only in Chicago and St. Louis was there active leadership from the Workingman's Party.[8] Over time the troops remained and the crowds dwindled. The fervor that erupted over the wage cuts and working conditions could not be sustained. When the strike ended over 100 people were dead; thousands arrested; hundreds of strike leaders fired; and the wage cuts remained in force.[9] Capital reinforced its intransigence against any future challenge to its prerogatives.

The strike highlighted the incomplete sentences and dangling participles in the American narrative. The words of the founders of the republic nestled alongside verses from the Bible in the minds of the faithful and were subject to as many interpretations. Americans from every social strata believed in "American exceptionalism," which was then taken to mean that the republican character of the state allowed it to escape the economic and societal upheaval, caused by rapid industrialization, that was troubling Europe. Republicanism admitted no aristocracy of birth or privilege but was otherwise sufficiently plastic to accommodate the situation and the audience attending to the message.[10] The laborer who was a committed republican did not regard his interest as separate from his employer, but in harmony in a community of equals. The Railroad Brotherhoods of the period functioned much like social clubs, complete with rituals and initiation ceremonies, that promoted sobriety, fellowship, and apprenticeship. The brotherhoods served as feeders of qualified candidates to the employers[11] in much the same way that the Negro churches supplied Henry Ford with African-American workers fifty years later.

The (white) American male defined his manhood as his obligation to be proficient in his craft, provide for his family, and participate in the affairs of his community.[12] A disconnect between American mythology and American reality widened as mechanization and monopoly diminished the skill required for the job and shifted personal responsibility from the local community to the seats of corporate authority. The ability of the laborer to advance his career narrowed and his influence in the community was diminished by the extra burden that low wages drained from his time and energy. The emergence of an aristocracy of wealth with privileges usually associated with the feudal lords and monarchs of Europe was seen as contradictory to the precepts on which the republic was founded.[13] The strikers of 1877 were reacting to the cuts that thwarted their ability to provide food and shelter for their families, restricted their role on the job and in the community, and thus stunted their manhood.

The commercial class found their expression of Americanism in the classical-liberal assertion of property rights and in the republican form of government that Madison proposed for their protection. The business interests celebrated the abundance of resources and enterprise that was elevating the young nation into world prominence and regarded labor unrest as an infringement on the rights of property and a subversion of the nation's "Manifest Destiny." Rather than a serious examination of the issues underlying the strike and the compatibility of democratic institutions with an encroaching corporate state, the establishment press dismissed the strikers as ruffians, malcontents, and the basest element, and relied on nineteenth century racial theories to shed the unrest of its American context and dress it in the guise of an unwelcome foreign influence. Immigration that diluted the original Anglo-Saxon and Teutonic stock was seen as incompatible with the republican tradition of self-government.[14] *The Nation* expressed the prejudice of the native elite toward the "huddled masses" in an editorial placing blame for the riots on factors extraneous to the root cause:[15]

> The kindliest thing that can be done for the great multitudes of untaught men who have been received on these shores, and are daily arriving, and are torn perhaps even more here than in Europe by wild desires and wilder dreams, is to show them promptly that society as here organized, on individual freedom of thought and action, is impregnable, and can be no more shaken than the order of nature...In what better provision, in the shape of the public force, should be made for its defense we have no space left to discuss, but that it will not do to be caught again as the rising at Martinsburg caught us; that it would be fatal to private and public credit and security to allow a state of things to subsist in which 8,000 or 9,000 day-laborers of the lowest class can suspend, even for a whole day, the traffic and industry of a great nation, merely as a means of extorting ten or twenty cents a day more from their employer, we presume everybody now sees.

Corporate muscle and government suppression did not quiet the labor unrest. Throughout the latter decades of the nineteenth century there were frequent strikes and new outbursts of violence. Attempts began to give the spontaneous eruptions more organization and political coherence. Radical thinkers rejected the capitalist economic system that they saw imposing a form of virtual serfdom upon the working class, and developed a growing mass of adherents in the factories and on the family farms. Labor unions emerged in parallel with the labor rebellions but developed a sense of disconnect with the culture and aims of the men in the factories, on the railroads, and in the mines.

The first national labor organization to appear in the United States was the Knights of Labor. The Knights were not originally a labor union, but an organization devoted to the improvement of the domestic and cultural life of the worker. It was a conservative organization that did not seek a reorganization of society. It opposed strikes and boycotts and sought an elevation in the status of the working class through self improvement and working through the political system.[16] As the strikes continued and multiplied, however, the Knights of Labor came to assume a more militant advocacy role.

In the mid 1880s the Federation of Organized Trades and Labor Unions made the 40-hour work week the centerpiece of their program.[17] They urged their members to strike companies that denied the 40-hour week. This precursor of the AFL had few members and little prestige, but the campaign for a forty hour week resonated within the rank and file of labor. Both Grand Master Worker Terrence Powderly of the Knights of Labor and Samuel Gompers, who would lead the American Federation of Labor for its first 40 years, opposed calls for a May 1, 1886 strike, and neither the new AFL nor the Knights had a strong presence in the plants.[18] It was only more radical local leaders that could call and organize a strike, but, despite Powderly's objections, many chapters of the loosely organized Knights rallied to the call for action.

The most confrontational of the 40-hour workweek strikes occurred in May, 1886 at the McCormick Harvester Works in Chicago. Thousands of strikers and their sympathizers blockaded the plant to prevent the police from escorting strikebreakers into it. On May 3, the standoff between the police and picketers flared into violence. The police fired into the crowd. Four people were killed; many more were injured.[19]

Albert Parsons and August Spies expressed the outrage felt by many in the community in *Arbeiter-Zeitung*, the organ of the International Working Peoples Association, and called for "Revenge! [...] To arms we call you, to arms!"[20]. Parsons was a Southerner who had fought for the Confederacy in the Civil War, but Spies and many others in the Socialist organization were German immigrants whose political ideology was rooted in the upheaval in their homeland after Bismarck's consolidation of the separate Germanic states beneath a heavy Prussian boot. The Socialists called for a rally in Haymarket Square the next night to protest the killings.

The rally began peacefully with about 3000 people listening to speakers denounce the police and the events of the previous day. Chicago mayor Carter Harrison attended the rally and was satisfied that the event would conclude without incident. When he left he ordered the police reserves to return home.[21] As soon as the mayor was gone, police Captain John Bonfield, the man who had initiated the action at the McCormick factory the previous day, ordered his men to charge with nightsticks into the crowd and break up the rally.[22] In the midst of the melee a bomb was thrown by some unidentified person in the crowd wounding sixty-six cops, seven fatally. The police retaliated by firing into the crowd, killing several and wounding up to 200 others.[23]

Parsons and Spies and six others were arrested and charged with murder. None of those arrested was charged with throwing the bomb and some of the men charged were not present in the crowd at the time of the riot. All were charged with publishing inflammatory stories and radical ideas that incited the labor unrest and precipitated the riot. *Arbeiter-Zeitung* urged its readers to arm themselves and meet force with force,[24] but this was the language of labor confrontation during the period. The *Chicago Tribune* and *Chicago Daily News* were equally vocal in providing their readers with instructions for building bombs and urging force against labor agitation.[25] The editors of the *Tribune* and *News* and the police who fired on the strikers were not indicted. The eight defendants were found guilty and seven were sentenced to hang. Despite international protest, Parsons, Spies and two of the other men were put to death. Another defendant committed suicide before his scheduled execution. The remaining defendants were later pardoned when a liberal governor, John Peter Altgeld, entered the state house. In pardoning the three surviving men, Governor Altgeld documented that the jury was selected by a bailiff determined to see a guilty verdict from a restricted pool favorable to the prosecution, the trial judge acted in a manner extremely prejudicial to the defense, and that key witnesses were coerced and bribed for their testimony. Governor Altgeld noted that Chicago Police Chief Ebersold in a later interview with the *Chicago Daily News* told of men in his force that worked to foment an anarchist threat to promote their own reputation.[26]

The Haymarket Square riot effectively ended the 40-hour workweek campaign and the Knights of Labor as an effective voice for the workingman. Membership in the organization declined dramatically after 1886. The American Federation of Labor (AFL) was formed in 1881 under the leadership of Samuel Gompers, but from the start its emphasis was on the skilled trades and its base was Protestant, native-born, and conservative. The United Mine Workers and Railroad Brotherhoods would later affiliate with the AFL, but it made no real effort to organize the unskilled workers in the mills and factories.

Hard times and the intransigence of the system to accommodate the needs of the underclass drove many people to explore alternatives to the unregulated capitalism that was producing such uneven dividends. Edward Bellamy's vision of a Socialist utopia in his novel *Looking Back* became a huge best seller in the mid 1880s. Bellamy's protagonist, Julian West, was transported 113 years into the future to wake from a hypnotic trance in the year 2000. Just as Rip Van Winkle woke from twenty years of sleep to find the American Revolution had settled him in a new country, West awoke to a new social order of greater abundance in which everyone shared equally according to their effort. People of greater talent that expended less effort than a person of lesser talent working to his full capabilities might still produce greater value, but would be accorded a smaller share of the national wealth. The book contained no polemics about current injustices, but provided a dream-like escape to a new possibility that avoided the unpaved roads and tortuous trails for actually getting there.

One of Bellamy's avid readers was Eugene Debs. Debs was born in Terre Haute, Indiana to an immigrant family from the Alsace region of France who had established a meat market and textile mill in their new community. Debs left school at age 14 to work in the rail yards first as a paint scraper, then as a boiler man. In 1875, he helped found a new lodge of the Brotherhood of Locomotive Firemen, and rose quickly to prominence within the union. By 1880 he was editor of the union magazine and Grand Secretary of the Brotherhood. The railroad brotherhoods of the period were much like the Knights of Labor, more a fraternal order than a collective bargaining agent. Debs did not support the railway strikes of 1877, and had not yet begun his philosophical journey to Socialism. Debs was elected to the Indiana General Assembly in 1884 as a Democrat.

By 1893, Debs views were beginning to crystallize around a more radical agenda. He left his position with the Brotherhood of Locomotive Firemen to found the American Railway Union (ARU)—the first American union uniting all workers from a single industry into a single organization. It had an immediate success when it struck the Great Northern Railway in April of 1894 and won many of its demands.[27]

In June of 1894 workers of the Pullman Palace Car Company went on strike and appealed to the ARU for help. Many of the strikers not only worked for Pullman, but lived in a town wholly owned and operated by the industrialist that he modestly named Pullman, Illinois. When a severe depression hit the economy in 1893, Pullman lowered wages five times over a period of months without lowering the rents he was charging his tenants or the price he was charging them for water and gas.[28] In their plea for help the Pullman workers offered the following indictment of their boss and landlord:

> "He owns the houses, the schoolhouses, and the churches of God in the town he gave his once humble name...the wages he pays out with one hand—the Pullman Palace Car Company—he takes back with the other—the Pullman Land Association. He is able by this to bid under any contract car shop in the country. His competitors in business, to meet this, must reduce the wages of their men. This gives him the excuse to reduce ours to conform to the market. His business rivals must in turn scale down; so must he. And thus the merry war—the dance of skeletons bathed in human tears—goes on..."[29]

The ARU was moved by the testimony it heard from the Pullman workers, but Debs urged restraint while the union assessed the situation.[30] Despite the advice, the Pullman workers had endured enough and walked off the job when three members of their grievance committee were summarily fired. Presented with the situation, the ARU voted over Debs's objection to support the strike. It vowed not to handle any Pullman cars.[31] Given the monopoly Pullman enjoyed on the supply of railroad cars, the ARU action effectively shut down the nation's railroads.

The railroads were knitted into a cohesive national network by the bankers, and chief among the banks was the House of Morgan. J. P. Morgan orchestrated the consolidation of the nation's railroads into six systems, four of which were completely or partially controlled by Morgan.[32] The House of Morgan was the lattice on which the American enterprise system grew. Its insurance companies collected the premium payments from millions of Americans and grew into a billion dollar reservoir of cash. The insurance companies fed the banks and the Morgan investment portfolio. The banks controlled the railroads.

In 1900 Morgan bought Carnegie's steel company for one half billion dollars.[33] He bundled it together with several smaller companies and formed U. S. Steel. The House of Morgan handled a $1.1 billion dollar stock offering and pocketed $150 million in commissions. The share price was much overvalued, but Morgan lobbied the Congress for tariff protection that allowed the company to keep the price of steel at $28 per ton, while management kept the price of labor low.[34] Banks, railroads, steel, and mines were all part of the Morgan empire. Morgan sat on the board of directors of 48 corporations. His fellow "robber baron" John D. Rockefeller sat on 37.[35]

Congress and the administrations of both political parties were responsive to the wishes of business, but to mollify an outraged public, Congress passed the Sherman Act in 1890 to prevent "combination or conspiracy" to restrain trade in interstate or foreign commerce. Three years earlier it created an Interstate Commerce Commission to regulate the railroads. Business interests lobbied to repeal the acts, but more astute businessmen counseled that the law worked more to the advantage of business than its detriment. Richard Olney, a lawyer for the railroads who was about to be named Grover Cleveland's Attorney General, told his clients:

> "The Commission, as its functions have now been limited by the courts, is, or can be made, of great use to the railroads. It satisfies the popular clamor for a government supervision of railroads, at the same time that that supervision is almost entirely nominal...It thus becomes a sort of barrier between the railroad corporations and

the people and a sort of protection against hasty and crude legislation hostile to railroad interests."[36]

Debs and the American Railroad Union were the people hostile to the railroad interests during the Pullman strike. Now the Attorney General, Richard Olney had a chance to make great use of the Sherman Act for the benefit of the railroads. He got an injunction against the strike on the grounds it was restraining interstate commerce by preventing the mail from being delivered. The injunction was ignored, and the strike followed the usual pattern of confrontation between strikers and militia, shots being fired, strikers killed and arrested, and finally defeat for the union.

The demise of the ARU was not an unwelcome outcome of the Pullman strike for the AFL. Before heading to an emergency meeting of the AFL Executive Council in Chicago to discuss a general boycott in support of the flagging strike, Samuel Gompers was quoted by a trade unionist within earshot as saying "I am going to the funeral of the American Railway Union."[37] He subsequently claimed he was misquoted by the anti-labor press, but he appeared more than eager to serve as a pall bearer. The AFL saw the power that big business and its allies in government brought down upon the industrial union, and had no appetite for challenging the hegemony of the entrenched interests. It was content to work at the margins of the system and ingratiate itself with more forward-thinking businessmen and sympathetic politicians. Adherence to a craft structure was seen as a necessary tenet for survival.[38]

Once the railroads were running again, Debs and other officials of the ARU were indicted for refusing to comply with the injunction. Debs was represented by Clarence Darrow, who had been a lawyer for the railroads, but followed his heart and defended Debs at financial loss. Debs was convicted, and sentenced to three months in jail. At his trial Debs denied that he was a Socialist, but during his time in prison he read the Socialist literature that was sent to him and met with the Socialist newspaper editor Victor Berger. Debs left prison crediting Berger and particularly the writings of Karl Kautsky for opening his mind to Socialism. "The writings of Kautsky were so clear and conclusive that I readily grasped, not merely his argument, but also caught the spirit of his socialist utterance—and I thank him and all that helped me out of darkness into light."[39]

Debs was not alone among the sons and daughters of the rural merchants and farmers who followed a path of disillusionment with an economic system that had confined them to its margins to espouse Socialism or other radical realignments of wealth and political power. Squeezed by high freight and storage costs, falling commodity prices, and the cost of land and equipment needed to be competitive, many farmers were being driven deeper into debt and tenancy on land they once owned. Particularly in the South, a crop-lien system fostered an increasing cycle of debt. The "furnishing man" would lend the farmer access to equipment and services at interest rates as high as 25%. Often the debt would accumulate until the farmer was forced to give up his land and work for "the Man"[40]

Faulkner described such a furnishing merchant in his novel *The Hamlet:*

> He was the largest landowner and head supervisor in one county and Justice of the Peace in the next, and election commissioner in both, and hence the fountainhead if not of law at least of advice and suggestion to a countryside which would have repudiated the term constituency if they had ever heard of it...He was a farmer, a usurer, a veterinarian...He owned most of the good land in the country and held mortgages on most of the rest. He owned the store and the cotton gin and combined grist mill and blacksmith shop in the village proper and it was considered, to put it mildly, bad luck for a man of the neighborhood to do his trading or gin his cotton or grind his meal or shoe his stock anywhere else.[41]

Throughout the farm belt, small farmers were at the mercy of the banks and a money supply tied to the government's gold reserves. With the population tripling over a period of four decades and the gold reserve increasing much more slowly, every dollar in circulation became more valuable. Money borrowed earlier had to be repaid with interest in dollars that were worth more than the ones originally obtained. By 1880 one quarter of the nation's farmers were tenants on land they once owned. Those who could not afford the rents became farm laborers.[42] The situation continued to get worse in the ensuing years.

A Farmers Alliance movement took root in Texas and quickly spread throughout the various crop belts that were so prominently delineated in our school geography lessons. By 1892 the Alliance counted two million farm families in its movement.[43] The Alliance combined political action with cooperative efforts to counter the influence of the banks. The cooperatives "bundled" the crops of many farmers into a single unit to obtain the best price and similarly purchased supplies in bulk to receive a discount for its members. In order for this cooperative effort to work effectively on a large scale the cooperatives needed seed money. When the banks refused to provide the cooperatives with the loans they needed, the Alliance tried to raise it from its members, but the farmers were too poor to create an effective bargaining agent. Less than half the money pledged to the cooperatives was received, and it was utterly insufficient to establish the Alliance as an agent for negotiating the price of farm produce in America.[44] The farmers lost another round in their struggle, and the banks won.

Henry Clay Frick best described the political situation in late nineteenth century America, and for much of the twentieth century as well, in a letter to the vacationing Andrew Carnegie. Frick expressed sorrow for the defeated Republican president, Benjamin Harrison, but attested that "I cannot see that our interests are going to be affected one way or the other by this administration."[45] Hayes or Cleveland, Cleveland or Harrison, Harrison or Cleveland—the interests of Frick and Carnegie, Rockefeller and Morgan were little affected by change of administration. The only shadow falling on the industrialists' political landscape was the threat of popular third party revolts. Senator Sherman expressed this concern in justifying his Anti-Trust Act. "You must heed their appeal or be ready for the socialist, the communist, the nihilist. Society is now disturbed by forces never felt before."[46]

Popular discontent never coalesced in one third party movement. There were regional alternatives to the two party system that had some success in local elections. Henry George, the author of *Progress and*

Poverty, received 31% of the vote as the Independent Labor candidate for Mayor of New York City and finished second, ahead of the Republican candidate Theodore Roosevelt who was making an early run for elective office.[47] Labor candidates fared well in Chicago and won the mayoral contest in Milwaukee and local elections in Fort Worth, Texas and Eaton, Ohio.[48]

The Farmers Alliance formed an independent People's Party (also called the Populist Party). The party sought to unify the exploited and dispossessed behind a common program, but its intended constituency was too diverse and too fragmented. The divisions between black and white, Protestant and Catholic, North and South, native stock and recent immigrant, farmer and laborer proved stronger than the need to unite against a common oppressor. The Populists ran as an independent movement for two election cycles before backing the Democratic candidate, William Jennings Bryan, in the 1896 election. Bryan was defeated by McKinley, and the Populist movement gradually drowned in the ocean of Democratic politics.

The election of 1896 offered something more than a Harrison-Cleveland choice for the voters. The dissident voice was not crying in the wilderness of third party irrelevance. Most Populists and many laborites and socialists had gathered within the Democratic tent, and, under the leadership of Governor Altgeld, pushed through a platform that not only called for free silver, but also demanded strict control of monopolies, proposed a graduated income tax and reduced tariffs, and repudiated President Cleveland's handling of the Pullman strike and his use of "government by injunction." Republican leader Mark Hanna was warned by one of his campaign workers that "the labor organizations are against us to a man…Impossible to teach them. They are more interested in the question of Federal jurisdiction over strikes than the money question."[49] Theodore Roosevelt had one solution to the class struggle threatening the established order. "The sentiments now animating a large proportion of our people can only be suppressed, as the Commune in Paris was suppressed, by taking ten or a dozen of their leaders out, standing…them against a wall and shooting them dead."[50]

Hanna and the industrial elite settled on a more subtle means of coercion. They threatened not the lives of the leaders, but the livelihood of the masses. Workers were forced to wear McKinley buttons and join McKinley Clubs. Mills were shut down prior to the election and the workers told they would not reopen if Bryan were elected. One employer told his workers they would be paid $10 a month if Bryan won the election and $26 a month if McKinley won.[51] Letters threatening the cancellation of orders if Bryan were elected were sent to manufacturers from their dealers and posted prominently inside the plants. The Goodyear Tire and Rubber Company conveyed the Republican campaign of coercion in a letter to their employees.

> "The stockholders and officers of the Goodyear Rubber Company wish to have it distinctly understood that a vote for Bryan and Sewall on the part of any of its employees will be regarded as an act committed directly against the welfare of the company and its employees, any employee working for or voting for the above mentioned ticket in the coming election may expect to be regarded by the officers as antagonistic to the company."[52]

The ballot box proved as ineffectual an instrument for fundamental change as the picket line.

The Socialists, Communists, and anarchists that so troubled Senator Sherman had a relatively small but significant following. The Socialist party had a membership of 100,000 people at its height, and its main newspaper, *Appeal to Reason*, had a circulation of a half million readers.[53] Other Socialist literature reached an audience as large again. Muckrakers exposing unsavory practices in the meat packing industry and the Rockefeller industrial empire made the public more favorably inclined to the socialist message. Socialists had their greatest success in Oklahoma where they boasted over 12,000 dues paying members and elected more than 100 of their candidates to local office and 6 to the state legislature.[54] A Socialist, Victor Berger, was elected to Congress in 1910, and one year later 73 socialist mayors and 1,200 lesser city officials were elected in 340 communities across the country. Socialist candidate Eugene Debs received over 900,000 votes representing over 6% of the total cast in the presidential election of 1912.[55] The Socialists and other radical parties never gained more than single digit support nationwide in the general elections, but the possibility that a restive electorate could rally around an alternative economic philosophy disquieted the political and business elite. A growing socialist presence frightened the establishment into enactment of the consumer oriented legislation of the Progressive era.

Progressive era legislation was meant to deflect popular outrage and save the capitalist system, not substantially change it. Theodore Roosevelt confided to his brother-in-law "I intend to be most conservative, but in the interests of the corporations themselves and above all in the interests of the country."[56] The Milwaukee Journal printed that "the conservatives fight socialism blindly [...] while the Progressives fight it intelligently and seek to remedy the abuses and conditions upon which it thrives."[57]

The Progressive era changed perception much more than reality. Enforcement of the anti-monopoly statutes by the government and courts was lax. Change in the system of interlocking corporate dependencies was largely cosmetic. Working conditions in the factories changed very little. Women were largely peripheral to the labor movement around the turn of the century, but they formed 20% of the workforce and were heavily concentrated in the garment industry.[58] One woman recalled the conditions in the sweat shops where they labored.

> dangerously broken stairways [...] windows few and so dirty [...] The wooden floor was swept once a year [...] Hardly any light but the gas jets burning by day and by night...the filthy malodorous lavatory in the dark hall. No drinking water [...] mice and roaches [...] how we suffered from the cold in the winter. In the summer we suffered from the heat. In these disease-breeding holes we, the youngsters with the men and women, toiled from seventy to eighty hours a week! Saturdays and Sundays included! A sign would go up on Saturday afternoon: 'If you don't come in on Sunday, you need not come in on Monday.' Children's dreams of a day off shattered. We wept for after all, we were only children"[59]

Women working at the Triangle Shirtwaist Company in New York City went out on strike in 1909. They called for support from other sweatshop workers throughout the garment district and twenty thousand workers walked off their jobs. Black and white women walked the picket lines together through the cold winter months. The women endured the cold, the police harassment, arrests, and prison. Police harassment of the women on the picket lines eased only after the predominantly Jewish women from the garment industry were joined by suffragettes and sympathetic ladies from the fashionable sections of the city.[60] After months of struggle, the companies settled and agreed to most of the strikers' demands.

Women won some concessions, and gained leadership roles in the International Ladies Garment Workers Union (ILGWU), but conditions improved very little in the sweat shops. On May 25, 1911, a fire, perhaps from a spark from one of the gas jets used to light the building, started in a rag bin on the eighth floor of the Triangle Shirtwaist Factory building and quickly spread to the two floors above. More than half a million people worked above the seventh floor in New York City buildings in 1911, but the city fire department had no ladders that reached above a seventh floor.[61] Fire laws required factory doors to open outward and be unlocked, but at the Triangle Shirtwaist Factory the doors opened inwards and were locked.[62] Workers found themselves trapped inside an inferno. In a scene repeated ninety years later during another New York tragedy, workers jumped from the ledges of the burning building, some singly, some embracing one another in a last desperate moment of companionship before splattering on the concrete below. Many others, men, women, and children made their way down the "dangerously broken stairways" to find the doors to their escape locked. One hundred and forty six people, mostly women, died in the Triangle Shirtwaist fire on that day.[63]

The Triangle Shirtwaist Factory fire was particularly horrific, but far from unique. Other workplace fires that took only a few lives went almost unnoticed. The United States Commission on Industrial Relations reported in 1914 that 35,000 workers were killed in industrial accidents during the year and 700,000 were injured. Nineteen fourteen was not unique. Similar statistics were recorded during every year of the period. Many injured workers were disabled and unable to perform their previous job any longer. During hearings by the Commission on Industrial Relations, Harris Weinstock, a member of the Commission questioned John Osgood, the President of a Rockefeller controlled coal company in Colorado, about company responsibility toward workers who were killed or injured on the job. He was told that dependents of workers killed on the job were compensated in some cases, but in others, they were not. If a worker for Osgood's company were crippled for life in an industrial accident, Weinstock was told he received no compensation from the company. The burden was thrown entirely upon the family of the injured worker.[64]

The situation in the factories and mines and on the farms and railways appalled many Americans. A great many more were either kept unaware of the conditions faced by those beyond their own neighborhoods by the establishment press or were willing to accept the situation as part of the natural order of things. The late nineteenth and early twentieth centuries were awash with attempts to provide a scientific basis for claims of racial and ethnic superiority. When Darwin sent the wrong message or was considered to be the wrong messenger, justification for the social order was found somewhere in the Bible.

Russell Conwell, a law school graduate and a minister and one of the founders of Temple University, lectured extensively on the "Acres of Diamonds" that awaited anyone willing to put in the effort to get rich. Getting rich was taken to be a Christian duty, and being poor, a sign of moral failure.

> "I sympathize with the poor, but the number of poor who are to be sympathized with is very small. To sympathize with a man whom God has punished for his sins...is to do wrong...Let us remember there is not a poor person in the United States who was not made poor by his own shortcomings."[65]

Throughout the American experience there has been no shortage of Russell Conwells who preen like Pharisees in the temples of power and grant the poor and unfortunate no more comfort than the promise of an "undiscovered" tomorrow. A Puritanical thread is woven through the fabric of America that binds the church and state in common cause, like elusive dark matter that draws the Constitutional separation back to an original focus. It knits a political and religious consensus in support of commerce. Its religious establishment interprets the ancient texts and scholarly manuscripts, highlighting the passages it holds most sacred while scribbling notes and comments in the margins. It has functioned like the Grand Inquisitor in Ivan Karamazov's dream, but here, an inquisitor intent to purify the teachings of Jesus from any of the Socialist tendencies he may have expressed. It has produced a homespun Jesus, worn like a designer label of personal virtue—a plastic Jesus, safely affixed to the dashboard altar, or a slimmed down Jesus, pasted to the rear bumper where he doesn't diminish the jealous, vengeful Jehovah of the Old Testament.

Many of the newer immigrants came from different religious traditions. In 1892, the eleven year old Valentine Reuther arrived in America with his father Jacob, mother Christina, and two siblings. The Reuther family settled in the small Illinois hamlet of Effingham where a relative had settled some years previously.[66] Jacob Reuther was a Christian Socialist whose pacifism and advocacy of what is now identified as "liberation theology" put him at odds with Bismarck's militarism and with the Lutheran establishment on both continents. Jacob Reuther was a devout believer, but not of the message being delivered by the Lutheran church in Effingham, Illinois. When the long treatises on Christian theology that he wrote to the local pastor had no effect on the teachings preached at the Sunday service, Jacob Reuther withdrew from the church and held his own services at home for his family and any like-minded neighbors. In Jacob Reuther's sermons man's duty to his fellow man had as much emphasis as his obligation to God. The Reuther patriarch never counseled his family to seek "Acres of Diamonds." The family legend holds that when the steamer bringing them to America entered New York harbor and passed the newly erected Statue of Liberty, Jacob Reuther put his arm around Valentine and told his son, "a man should always fight for freedom and brotherhood."[67]

The Rise and Fall of the Wobblies

The Knights of Labor declined rapidly in number and influence after the Haymarket riot linked its 40-hour week campaign with the radical voices that rallied around it. By the turn of the century it had virtually ceased to exist. By then more than 80% of the organized workforce was affiliated with the AFL.[68] The AFL was the voice of the skilled craftsmen whose middle class aspirations were limited by few impediments. Craft unions were concerned with apprenticeships, credentials, and exclusivity. Their focus was local. Their members wanted to become part of the establishment, not overturn it. The AFL also accommodated railway and mine workers within their ranks, but the association between these unions and the parent organization was always more tenuous. The path to the middle class rarely ran through the mines or along the tracks. The AFL had little presence among the unskilled workers in the factories and made little attempt to establish one.

Samuel Gompers made speeches about equal opportunity, but his organization made scant effort to include blacks. Gompers voiced the indifference of Northern "liberals" to the plight of Southern blacks when he told a Southern audience "I regard the race problem as one with which you people of the Southland will have to deal; without the interference, too, of meddlers from the outside."[69] Gompers and his AFL were part of the Progressive bulwark against the advance of alien Socialism.

The AFL abandonment of the unskilled and working poor opened the way for an avowedly Socialist union to form and proselytize among these workers. In Chicago in 1905 a group of Socialists and radical labor leaders including "Big" Bill Haywood, Eugene Debs, and Mother Jones met and formed the Industrial Workers of the World (IWW). The IWW became known for no transparent reason as the Wobblies. The Wobblies called for one big union accommodating all the working people of the country.[70] They disparaged the AFL fragmentation into crafts and regional jurisdictions. The IWW founding document cited the meat packing industry in Chicago as a prime example of AFL inadequacy

"The directory of unions of Chicago shows in 1903 a total of 56 different unions in the packing houses, divided up still more in 14 different national trades unions of the American Federation of Labor. What a horrible example of an army divided against itself in the face of a strong combination of employers."[71]

The IWW proclaimed that the working class and the employing class had nothing in common and were locked in struggle. They had no interest in establishing a business relationship with the employers. They advocated direct action. By "direct action" they meant industrial democracy. One IWW pamphlet described what it meant by direct action: "Shall I tell you what direct action means? The worker on the job shall tell the boss when and where he shall work, how long, and for what wages and under what conditions."[72]

The Wobblies did not advocate violence, but vowed to respond to any violence directed against the workers in kind. Joseph Ettor, an IWW organizer described the ultimate power that the worker possessed was not one with a gun in his hand, but with his hands in his pockets refusing to participate in the old system. The aim of the organization was to educate and train the worker for a final general strike—a capitalist catastrophe— that would complete the expropriation of prerogatives now exercised only by the capitalist.[73]

The message was both naive and intoxicating. The IWW never had more than ten thousand members at any one time, but its willingness to go anywhere and support any group of workers earned them respect beyond their numbers. They were everything the AFL was not. They were militant; they were inclusive; they welcomed blacks and women into their ranks; and they spoke to the unskilled and semi-skilled workers ignored by the AFL.

The IWW prominently supported the 1912 American Woolen Company strike in Lawrence, Massachusetts. The workforce in the woolen mills was predominantly women whose families were from diverse immigrant backgrounds. The strike began spontaneously when several women found their paychecks had been reduced without any prior notice.[74] The women, who were working for an already inadequate $8.76 a week,[75] stopped their looms and walked out of the factory. The next day they were joined by 5,000 others at one of the other mills in the city. Within days 10,000 workers were in the streets picketing the mills.[76] They called for help from the IWW, who sent Joseph Ettor to Lawrence to organize the strike activities. Ettor directed the establishment of soup kitchens and helped organize the procurement of enough food supplies to feed 50,000 people and enough fuel to get the strikers through the Massachusetts winter.[77] Money arrived from IWW locals and Socialist organizations throughout the country.

The authorities reacted to the strike by calling in the police and local militia. The police presence at a parade of strikers led to confrontations and rioting. One of the strikers was shot and killed. The city blamed the violence on the strikers. Ettor and his deputy Arturo Giovanitti were charged with inciting some unidentified person to commit the murder.[78] Martial Law was instituted in the city. Citizens of Lawrence were forbidden to gather and talk on the streets. Twenty-two companies of militia and two troops of cavalry were assembled in Lawrence to enforce the Martial Law decree, but still the strike continued.[79]

In February the food began to run out. The IWW arranged through the Socialist community in other cities to have children of the strikers leave Lawrence and stay with volunteer families while their mothers continued the strike. An initial group of 119 children was welcomed by a cheering crowd of 5,000 people when they arrived at Grand Central Station to meet their New York host families. City officials reacted to this exodus by forbidding any future departures of children and dusting off an old law that allowed them to charge the parents of these children with child neglect. The IWW disregarded the warning and continued to send groups of children to host families in New York and other smaller New England towns. A group of 40 children was headed for Philadelphia on February 24, when they and their supporters were attacked by police as the children were about to board the train in Lawrence.[80] The attack on the group of children and their minders and the brutal police tactics used during the assault sparked widespread outrage. Public sentiment for the strikers and against the police tactics swelled, and the American Woolen Company decided to give in and offer raises of 5 to 11% and reinstate all the workers without discrimination.[81]

As soon as the strike ended the I. W. W established a Defense Committee to raise funds and support for Ettor and Giovanitti. Their murder trial began on September 30, 1913, six months after the successful outcome of the strike. The day the trial began a crowd of 15,000 people participated in a 24-hour demonstration strike, rallying outside the courthouse in support of the accused.[82] Unlike the Haymarket trial, a fair jury was selected from over 600 panelists questioned, and the weakness of the government's case was not buttressed by rulings from a hostile bench. The defendants were acquitted of all the charges against them. A crowd of 10,000 people took a day off from work in Lawrence to celebrate the verdict and the successful outcome of the strike.[83]

The year 1912 marked the high point of Socialism in America. The party achieved success in numerous local elections, and Debs received over 6% of the popular vote in the Presidential election.[84] Socialist politicians, looking to broaden their political base, began to distance themselves from the anarchistic rhetoric and sometimes violent tactics of the Wobblies. In 1913 Big Bill Haywood was ousted from his seat on the Executive Council of the party.[85] The move put Debs in the uncomfortable position of defending the rationale behind the move, yet remaining close to the IWW and its leader. Helen Keller deplored the move in a letter she wrote to the *New York Call.* "It is with deepest regret that I have read the attack upon Comrade Haywood [...] such an ignoble strife between two factions which should be one, and that too, at a most critical time in the struggle of the proletariat [...] Shame on us!"[86]

Bloody Ludlow

Despite the Socialists' disavowal of the IWW and Progressive legislation, both real and cosmetic, to smooth the rough edges of the capitalist system, the American workplace in 1913 remained a tinderbox. A strike that began in the coal fields around Trinidad, Colorado erupted into fourteen months of open warfare between the miners, agents of the companies, and elements of the state militia. The strike began at the Rockefeller owned Colorado Fuel & Iron Company in September of 1913 when, after the murder of a labor organizer, eleven thousand miners lay down their picks and walked out in protest over the low pay, dangerous working conditions, and feudal environment of the company controlled towns.[87] Management responded to the challenge by evicting the strikers from their company-owned hovels. The miners took to the hills. Tent cities sprang up on the mountain sides surrounding the mines, and pickets continued to block entrance at the company gates.

The striking miners and their families faced intimidation by hired thugs from the Baldwin-Felts Detective Agency and the bitter Rocky Mountain winter that dumped four feet of snow on the region in mid December, but they showed no indication of bowing to the pressure the company applied. Both sides showed no reluctance to settle old scores with violence, and both stockpiled weapons and ammunition in preparation for an anticipated attempt to end the strike by force. Faced with a potentially explosive confrontation, Governor Ammons activated the state militia with orders to act as a buffer between the two sides, provide protection for non-striking miners to enter the mines, but not to permit the importation of strikebreakers from outside the affected areas.[88]

The militia was not a very professional force. It was led by General John Chase and included a company of hastily recruited mine guards and sheriff's deputies that Lieutenant Karl Linderfelt had assembled when still working for the interests of the coal companies.[89] Chase, in full regalia, and 931 guardsmen arrived outside the Ludlow colony and were greeted by a brass band playing martial music that was assembled for the occasion.[90] After the pageantry of his entrance, Chase settled in assuming powers he did not possess and was not granted. He declared martial law and with a judicial apparatus heavily weighted with company representatives and supporters began arresting strikers he deemed responsible for the violence.[91] One of those arrested was Mother Jones.

Mother Jones, a self-described hell raiser, emerged in the labor wars of the 1890's from a hazy past shrouded in innuendo. When the strike was called in the Colorado coal fields she arrived to encourage the polyglot audience of "her boys" with emotional appeals they could feel, if not always words they could understand. After Chase arrived he sought to silence her and had the eighty-two year old lady confined under guard at the San Rafael Hospital on the outskirts of Trinidad. The arrest of Mother Jones sparked a protest rally by the wives and supporters of the strikers. A group of over a thousand women marched up Commercial Street in Trinidad and turned on to Main where their path was blocked by General Chase in front of a line of mounted militia men. Chase ordered the marchers to disperse and, when they continued their advance, rode his horse into the throng causing some minor injuries to several of the marchers. In the confusion, the horse reared throwing Chase to the ground and drawing laughter and ridicule from the women. An embarrassed and infuriated Chase remounted his steed and ordered his troopers to charge the phalanx of women with cutlasses drawn and disperse the marchers. There were several reporters witnessing the scene and recollecting recent similar incidents in St. Petersburg, Russia. The *Denver Express* ran a headline "The Great Czar fell! And in Fury Told Troops to Trample Women." The article went on to mix references to Humpty Dumpty with allusions to the depravities of the French Revolution.[92]

Scenes like the cavalry charge on defenseless women brought the long-simmering conflict in the coal fields under scrutiny of the United States Congress. An inquiry was launched that dispatched investigators to Colorado and dragged John D. Rockefeller Jr. into a Senate hearing room. By 1914 the labor vote had become sizable and more focused and needed to be courted by career-minded politicians. Corporations, whose monopolistic practices had been scrutinized by muckrakers and revealed in anti-trust cases, could not rely on the government to enforce their policies as they did during the railway strikes of the previous century. The hearings generated some heat and noise and made Rockefeller squirm under some uncomfortable questioning, but then they ended. The investigators went home. Rockefeller retreated back into his Pocantico Hills estate, and the situation in the coal fields became more desperate.

The Rockefeller backed management refused to consider recognition of the United Mine Workers Union as a bargaining agent for their miners and refused to even be in the same room with UMW officials.[93] Attempts by the governor and President Wilson to submit the dispute to arbitration were rejected out of hand. As the dispute dragged on past February, the resources of both the state and the union were nearly depleted. The state of Colorado was in debt for nearly $700,000 in maintaining a force of 695 men overseen by as many as 397 officers in the field for six months.[94] Money to pay the men had never been appropriated and they received only promissory notes in lieu of cash.[95] The UMW was also nearly out of funds needed to compensate the strikers and their families and was desperately looking for any escape from what they recognized as a lost cause. By mid March the man the Rockefeller manager referred to as "our little cowboy governor"[96] reduced the size of the guard deployment to a company of 200 men under the immediate command of Lieutenant Linderfelt. A second company consisting mostly of mine guards, sheriff's deputies, and local vigilantes was hastily assembled, sworn in to the National Guard, and put on the payroll of the Colorado Fuel and Iron Company.[97]

On April 20th, one day after the many Greek inhabitants celebrated the Orthodox Easter, Linderfelt sent to Major Hamrock a note passed to him by a woman claiming her husband was being held against his will in the Ludlow colony. Hamrock summoned the leader of the Greek contingent at Ludlow, Lou Tikas, to a meeting where Tikas assured him that no such person was present in the colony. In Tikas's absence the strikers noticed the repositioning of Linderfelt's company and they deployed in defensive positions.[98] Tikas raced back to the camp and yelled at the men to return to their tents, but it was too late. The guardsmen opened up with machine gun fire on the tents below.[99] The embattled miners had dug protective trenches inside their tents and fired back. The attack on the tent colony increased in ferocity. The Guardsmen moved down the hills firing into the colony forcing its inhabitants to flee. Thirteen people were killed by the gunfire.[100] The leader of the strikers, Lou Tikas, and two others remained in the camp and were captured by the Guard. While two men held Tikas by the arms, Guard commander, Lt. Linderfelt hit him over the head with his rifle butt. Tikas was later found shot in the back. His body was left beside the railroad tracks for three days in sight of passing trains.[101] After the murder of Tikas and the two others, the Guard set fire to the tents.

The following morning one of the workers going through the wreckage of the tent colony lifted a metal cot covering a trench dug inside one of the burned tents and found the remains of two women and eleven children.[102] The events of April 20th became known as the Ludlow massacre. The *New York Times* deplored the tactics, but not the necessity of breaking the strike in the first place.[103] Elsewhere, outrage was vented in rallies in front of the state house in Denver and in front of the Rockefeller's headquarters in New York.[104]

Hundreds of miners and their sympathizers took up arms and headed to the hills surrounding Ludlow. Telegraph and telephone lines were, cut, mine entrances dynamited, and company guards were killed. Two days after its editorial deploring the tactics employed at Ludlow, the *Times* warned "With the deadliest weapons of civilization in the hands of savage-minded men, there can be no telling to what lengths the war in Colorado will go unless it is quelled by force [...] The President should turn his attention from Mexico long enough to take stern measures in Colorado."[105] Ludlow escalated class warfare into open hostility.

Woodrow Wilson had intervened in the Mexican civil war to protect the business interests of American industrialists who controlled upwards of 47% of the Mexican economy.[106] An incident in which a half dozen American seamen were briefly held captive occurred near the port of Veracruz, and when the Mexican government refused to fly the American flag and offer a 21 gun salute in apology, the port was shelled and 200 Mexicans killed on the same day the bodies of the thirteen women and children were discovered in Ludlow.[107] Wilson did turn his attention to Colorado long enough to send in federal troops to quell the upheaval. The strike petered out. Sixty-six men, women, and children were dead. The union did not win recognition, and the strikers never got their old jobs back. No member of the Guard or private militia was ever charged with a crime.[108] Union officials and strikers charged with crimes were either acquitted or had convictions overturned.[109] The coal field war ended like most military conflicts with the guns stilled, the soldiers gone home, prisoners released, and the survivors left to rebuild their lives.

America Enters the 'Great War'

American involvement in the multi-party civil war raging in Mexico was not sufficient to deflect the class struggle raging in the United States with an appeal to patriotism. The terrible conflict in Europe provided another opportunity.

W. E. B. Du Bois wrote in the *Atlantic Monthly* that the carnage endured to move the battle lines forward a few kilometers in the countryside of France was to move the borders a few hundred kilometers forward in divvying up Africa. The "neutrals" of Asia and Africa and the

Middle East were the spoils for which the war was being fought. The capitalist system needed the new wealth of these unexploited regions to give its working class a "share of the loot" and sustain its preeminent position in Western Society.[110] A lecture that Woodrow Wilson had delivered at Columbia University supported Du Bois's thesis. Wilson told his audience that "Concessions obtained by financiers must be safeguarded by ministers of state, even if the sovereignty of unwilling nations be outraged in the process [...] the doors of the nations which are closed must be battered down.[111] In 1914, Wilson's Secretary of State, William Jennings Bryan, the Populist who once decried the Midwestern farmers being crucified on a cross of gold, now applauded his President who had "opened the doors of all the weaker countries to an invasion of American capital and American enterprise."[112]

Wilson ran for re-election in 1916 on the slogan of "a nation being too proud to fight." By the spring of 1917, he found the affront to American shipping posed by German U boats too great a provocation to ignore. American commerce benefited from the war. The Morgan steel companies made $348 million in profit in 1916.[113] Their banks owned millions more in British debt. By the time the United States went to war with Germany, in April of 1917, its corporations had made over 2 billion dollars in war profits from the Allies.[114] The United States economy was very dependent upon its war profits to avert slipping into recession and reprising the class conflict seen at Ludlow. The House of Morgan and other bankers were in need of an allied victory to secure their loans. By 1917 an allied victory was very much in doubt. The Russian front had collapsed, and half the French units were experiencing mutinies. Arrival of the fresh American troops changed the dynamics of the battle.

Wilson characterized the American effort as a "War to End all Wars" and to "make the world safe for democracy." These lofty goals did not translate into popular support. The public had little appetite for war, and the German and Irish immigrants had no sympathy for the British. Only 73,000 answered the call to volunteer for military service in the first month of the American involvement in the war.[115] Debs announced at a March 7th rally at Cooper Union that he would rather be shot as a traitor than go to war for Wall Street.[116] To make his declaration of war credible, Wilson had to elicit popular support and institute a draft.

Wilson recruited the talents of George Creel, a veteran Kansas City journalist, to sell the war to the American people. Creel was named as head of the Committee for Public Information (CPI). Creel was from a Southern family that had been loyal to the Confederacy. He admitted that "an open mind is not part of my inheritance. I took in prejudices with mother's milk and was weaned on partisanship."[117] Part of the job of selling the war was to stigmatize its critics.

Creel enlisted the establishment press and Hollywood to popularize the war. Newspapers were given guidelines on what was acceptable to print and fed stories the government wanted published. German atrocities were magnified or fabricated from incidents that warranted a different interpretation. Hollywood produced a stream of films with titles like: *The Kaiser: The Beast of Berlin, To Hell with the Kaiser,* and *Pershing's Crusaders.*[118] Seventy-five thousand "4 minute men" were recruited to stand up at public events and give a prepared 4-minute speech boosting the war.[119] Even novelists and cartoonists were enlisted to provide images and short stories that would feed the war frenzy. The CPI issued numerous "Red, White, and Blue books" by noted public figures including liberals and socialists such as Walter Lippmann and John Dewey.[120]

The other aspect of Creel's effort was to defuse the anti-war message that was widely expressed at the time of Wilson's war declaration. This effort was buttressed in June, 1917 by passage of the Espionage Act. Wilson first proposed such legislation in his 1915 State of the Union address, declaring "There are citizens of the United States [...] who have poured the poison of disloyalty into the very arteries of our national life; who have sought to bring the authority and good name of our Government into contempt...to destroy our industries...and to debase our politics to the uses of foreign intrigue [...] Such creatures of passion, disloyalty, and anarchy must be crushed out."[121] Actual espionage was never the real concern. The provisions of the act were structured to stifle dissent. The act made it a crime "to convey false reports or false statements with intent to interfere with the operation or success of the [military] [...] to cause or attempt to cause insubordination, disloyalty, mutiny, refusal of duty in the military [...] or to willfully obstruct the recruiting or enlistment service of the United States."[122] The act prescribed a maximum fine of $10,000 and up to 20 years in jail for people found guilty of such "insubordination." One year later the Sedition Act amended the original law to include, "any disloyal, profane, scurrilous, or abusive language about the form of government of the United States..."[123] The government now had the statutes it sought to fight its foes in Europe and its critics at home.

To aid this effort the Justice Department sponsored an American Protective League. The League claimed to have three million members dedicated to sniffing out cases of disloyalty. The *New York Times* editorialized that "It is the duty of every good citizen to communicate to proper authorities any evidence of sedition that comes to his notice."[124] Other newspapers echoed the same message.

Newspapers and magazines printing a different message were denied mailing privileges by the Post Office. *Appeal to Reason* muted its criticism of the war to remain in circulation. *The Masses*, a monthly literary and arts magazine out of Greenwich Village that welcomed opinion pieces from Socialist writers like John Reed and Max Eastman, refused to moderate its anti-war stance, and was forced out of print when its second-class postage rate was rescinded.[125] The most bizarre episode of censorship concerned the film *Spirit of 76*. The federal government moved against the film and its producer on the grounds that its depiction of atrocities committed by the British during the Revolutionary War questioned the good faith of our ally, Great Britain. The case of *U. S. v. Spirit of 76* resulted in a ten year sentence for the producer.[126]

The government used the Espionage Act to go after the IWW. In September of 1917, agents from the Department of Justice conducted 48 simultaneous raids on IWW offices. Seized documents were used in evidence against 165 leaders of the labor organization, charged with conspiring to hinder the draft, encourage desertion, and impairing the war effort with labor disputes.[127] One hundred and one of the defendants went on trial in April, 1918, and, after a trial lasting five months, all were convicted. Bill Haywood and fourteen others were sentenced to 20 years.[128] Big Bill Haywood jumped bail and fled to Russia where he remained until his death ten years later. The IWW was effectively broken. It would be another 15 years before the drive for industrial unionism reemerged.

In June, 1918, Debs emerged from visiting three socialists incarcerated for opposing the draft in Canton, Ohio and spoke for two hours to a crowd that had assembled across the street from the prison. During his speech he refuted the claim that Socialists were pro-German. "I hate, I loathe, I despise Junkers and Junkerdom, I have no earthly use for the Junkers of Germany and not one particle more for the Junkers in the United States." He continued to say "Wars throughout history have been waged for conquest and plunder [...] The master class has always declared the wars; the subject class has always fought the battles."[129] Two weeks later Debs was arrested for encouraging resistance to the draft because there had been draft age men in his audience. Debs called no witnesses to refute the charges during the trial, but instead requested he be allowed to speak in his defense. He admitted to obstructing the war in his address. "I have sympathy with the suffering, struggling people everywhere. It does not make any difference under what flag they were born or where they live."[130] Debs was found guilty and sentenced to ten years in prison.

Debs would receive over 900,000 votes for President again in 1920 when he ran from his prison cell in the Atlanta penitentiary,[131] but the Socialist percentage was down from its 1912 levels, and Socialist candidates received less support in local contests. Socialists were divided over the war and again over the emergence of the Marxist regime in Russia. A number of prominent Socialists like Jack London, Upton Sinclair, and Clarence Darrow supported the war effort.[132]

Wilson governed mostly from the right in his attitudes toward business, labor, and minorities, but through his university background he had established a rapport with liberal academics who shared his foreign policy goals. Wilson was the first U.S. President who acted to proactively spread democracy. He most likely believed that an allied victory would make the world safe for democracy and even that such an outcome could put an end to great power conflict.

By 1917, it became obvious to the combatants that the huge loss of life could not be sustained. Continuation of the war was leading to mutinies and demonstrations that augured revolution like the one taking place in Russia. Both sides needed a quick, decisive victory. The Germans gambled that if they announced they were abandoning the marine warfare protocols that had been established after the sinking of the Lusitania and adopted a policy of unrestricted submarine warfare, they could deprive England of the food and materials needed to sustain its war effort before American troops could reach the front in any substantial numbers.

In the spring of 1918, Germany launched the offensive it hoped would win the war. In the first major advance in the long stalemated struggle, the Germans got within 75 miles of Paris and began lobbing artillery shells at the city from railway mounted cannons. Four divisions of Australian troops, rushed down from the Somme, managed to halt the German advance. By summer the allies were ready to counterattack. Again it was the Australian and Canadian troops at the center of the line that spearheaded the allied advance. By August the Germans were pushed back to where they were when their offensive began, and American forces were arriving at the rate of 10,000 per day. New tactics and new technology had reduced the impact of the submarine campaign against allied shipping to more of a nuisance than a critical threat. The German generals realized the war was lost and began lobbying for peace before their position became more tenuous. By November the German army had retreated back to the Siegfried Line and the Kaiser abdicated. A truce was called and both armies stopped fighting on November 11th. It was now time for the leaders to "make the world safe for democracy."

The United States entry into World War 1 gave Wilson a seat at the table when the leaders met in Paris to negotiate the terms of the German surrender and redraw the map of the World. Wilson stipulated in his Fourteen Points that the final peace should include free trade, open seas, militaries sufficient only for domestic safety, and establishment of a League of Nations. He also allowed that the interests of the native population be given equal weight with the colonial power in the questions of sovereignty,[133] but missed a chance in Paris to meet with Ho Chi Minh and discuss the interests of the Vietnamese people in the question of their sovereignty.

The French suffered most from the War and insisted on making Germany pay heavy reparations. They got back Alsace and the parts of the Lorraine they lost in the Franco Prussian War. Other slivers of Germany were awarded to Denmark, Poland, and Belgium. Strict limits were placed on German arms, and German colonies in Africa and the

Orient were taken from them and divvied up among their European neighbors. The German foothold in China was not given back to the Chinese, but to Japan.

The stiff penalties imposed upon the Germans created the conditions for hyperinflation and depression. The front lines never reached the German homeland during the war, making it difficult for the German public to reconcile their defeat and the harsh conditions inflicted upon them by the Treaty of Versailles. Chief of Staff Hindenburg did not admit the dire conditions facing the German Army at the end of the war and encouraged the right to claim that Germany was stabbed in the back by the Socialists, Marxists, and Jews.

Countries pieced together out of the ruins of the Hapsburg and Ottoman Empires proved equally unstable. Far from creating a peace to end all wars, Versailles and surrounding treaties created conditions for a Second World War and subsequent wars over the breakup of Yugoslavia, the disposition of the British Mandate for Palestine, the failure to carve out a Kurdish state, and the clumsy arrangement of Ottoman provinces into Lebanon, Syria, Iraq, and Kuwait. The United States Congress that eagerly rallied to Wilson's call for war was reluctant to endorse his plan for peace. The United States never ratified the Treaty of Versailles.

The war did not make the world safe for democracy, but it did make the capitalist system in the United States more secure from the Socialist challenge. The government wielded the heavy axe of patriotism to dismantle the Wobblies and impugn prominent leaders of the Socialist movement. The left fractured into ideologically incompatible camps of liberal reformers, social democrats, Marxist ideologues, and Leninist radicals. With pressure from the Socialist alternative diminished, the Progressive Era in American History came to an end.

When the war ended, war profits flowed through the American economy, and electricity flowed into middle class homes in most of the cities and towns. A new, liberating music played on the phonographs, and soon the radios, across the land. Women occupied more university seats and felt liberated from political, sexual, and cultural constraints. Automobiles toured the roadways. The economy boomed and promised an upward mobility to any one clever enough or enterprising enough to seize the opportunity. In 1927, the twenty-year old Walter Philip Reuther left home in Wheeling, West Virginia to seek a better opportunity in the automobile factories of Detroit.

The Making of a Labor Leader

After the fall harvest of 1899, Valentine Reuther left the family farm in Effingham, Illinois and joined his older brother Jacob in Wheeling, West Virginia. With Jacob's help, Val Reuther found a job as a laborer in the Riverside Ironworks. A laborer worked twelve hours a day, six days a week for $1.50 a day.[134] Val Reuther looked for a better opportunity to earn more to pay off debts to his brother and help his family back in Illinois. He saw that the men who maintained the furnaces in the rolling mill earned about five times the pay for the same 12-hour shift, so he became friendly with the foreman in the rolling mill and expressed an interest in learning a "heater's" job. He would show up an hour before his laborer shift began and watch and learn the work of the men tending the ovens. When one of the heaters called in sick one day, Val was there to fill in. A relief job soon opened for him and he was promoted to a skilled position covered by one of the craft unions operating in the plant.[135]

Valentine Reuther attended the union meetings and joined the discussions on the social issues faced by the men in the plant. He was dismayed by the attitude the skilled tradesmen had toward the common laborers. There was a prejudice against the new immigrants who formed the bulk of the unskilled labor force, and no interest in accommodating the unskilled into their membership. Valentine Reuther argued that the skilled and unskilled workers had common interests and that their small group of elite tradesmen had little clout standing alone against the well-organized corporate bosses.[136]

When the craft union struck over the long hours and poor working conditions, Val was at odds with his union over its exclusiveness, and was marked by the company as a troublemaker for trying to unite the categories of workers whose mutual antagonism they played to their advantage. As Val predicted, the strike ended in failure. The plant closed, and the old management never resumed operation in the facility. Valentine Reuther was out of a job.

Steel was now the backbone of the Ohio River industrial base, but in the pre-Civil War days, Mefflin Marsh started a company in Wheeling that hand rolled Virginia tobacco into the long stogie cigars that became popular with riverboat men who navigated up and down the Ohio-Mississippi system. The cigar makers built one of the strongest early unions and were most noted for the cultural and educational activities they initiated on behalf of the largely immigrant workforce. The union employed "readers," reading both the news of the day and literary classics to the men as they cut and rolled tobacco in factories. Samuel Gompers began his career in labor as a reader for the cigar makers union.[137] Valentine Reuther became a lifelong aficionado of both the stogie and the educational emphasis of the union for the men producing it.

Wheeling was also home to factories producing glass and calico, and, by the late nineteenth century, breweries bottling 800,000 gallons of beer annually.[138] There was a sizable population of German immigrants in Wheeling, and two things for which the German culture was famous were music and beer. Those two German traditions helped Valentine Reuther find his next job. Val was a member of the Beethoven singing society, and it was at one of its meetings that he learned that the Schmulbach Brewing Company was looking for drivers to haul kegs of beer to outlying areas around Wheeling. The pay was much less than a skilled worker in the steel mills made, but the work was outdoors and driving the horse-drawn wagons brought back fond memories from his rural past.

The elder Reuther brought his union sympathies to the new job. He organized workers in the brewery and was granted a charter from the International Brewery Workers' Federation. He insisted that all classification of workers be represented by a single union, and resisted efforts by the Teamsters to split the drivers away from the men and women in the factory.[139] Valentine Reuther proved himself a skilled negotiator who maintained a cordial relationship with management. He avoided strikes by understanding the other party's needs and how they could be accommodated while meeting the demands of the workers. The respect the Schmulbach Brewing Company had for Valentine Reuther's talents as a speaker and his persuasiveness was evidenced when they gave him three months of paid leave during the debate over Prohibition to travel the state and present the brewer's argument.

The job at Schmulbach's frequently brought Val to the Hofreuter saloon across from the brewery for lunch. Hofreuter served a complimentary meal with the purchase of a mug of beer, and Val had an eye for the pretty redheaded cook that had recently started working at the saloon.

Anna Stocker was the eleventh of twelve surviving children born to Jacob and Agatha Stocker in the Swabian region of Germany. Swabia was considered in Germany at the time to be a conservative province whose people were known for their frugality. Anna's father Jacob, owned a farm near the village of Scharnhausen, but his main occupation was wagon making. Agatha and the children were left to do most of the farm work. Jacob died when Anna was only fifteen, and the army took each of the Stocker males when they reached the age of military service. One-by-one the children left home, leaving Agatha more dependent upon Anna to maintain the farm. When Anna's brothers finished their military obligation, they often left the claustrophobic environment of the Stoker farm. Some were enticed by the call of the New World. Her oldest brother Jacob sailed for Buenos Aires and later settled in Brazil. Karl and later Theodore relocated to Wheeling. Two older sisters also preceded her to America.

With each departure, Agatha became more possessive of Anna. Anna fell in love with Fritz Glohr, the son of a store keeper, whose espousal of social democracy marked him in the village as a radical. Agatha disapproved of the lad, and vowed she would never allow her daughter to marry beneath the Stocker social standing in the village. Anna and her mother often quarreled, and one day Anna shouted at her mother in frustration, "If you don't let me marry Fritz, I will go to America!" To her surprise, Agatha responded, "Go ahead, I'd rather have you go to America than marry him!" Anna was taken aback, but too proud not to follow through with her threat. Fritz promised that he would follow her to America, but months turned into years and the first love of her life never followed Anna to her new country.[140]

Valentine Reuther was infatuated with Anna Stocker. She enjoyed his company, but remained committed to the belief that Fritz would soon join her in the New World. Valentine escorted Anna to practice sessions of the Beethoven singing society and became a regular guest at brother Karl's farm where Anna lived. After two years of waiting for Fritz, her friendship with Val blossomed into love and the two were married on June 9, 1904.

The couple began life together in a nineteenth century cocoon while the twentieth century emerged around them. Val and Anna rented an upstairs flat with no running water, kerosene lamps, and an outside privy. After the children arrived and the family needed larger quarters, Val had a new house built in South Wheeling, but could not accept the idea that the privy be accessible from the living quarters of the house. He compromised and allowed access from the back porch at Anna's insistence.[141] Val's job with Schmulbach's affirmed their connection with the horse-drawn world of the late century.

One year after their marriage, Ted, the first of the Reuther children arrived. Walter was born two years later in 1907, then Roy in 1909 and Victor in 1912. Eleven years after Victor's birth the couple's last child, daughter Christine, was born.

Valentine Reuther took to his role as a labor leader. He was selected by the Brewers International to be their representative in the Ohio Valley Trades and Labor Assembly. He soon became a prominent voice in the regional organization. West Virginia was a coal mining state, and the young brewers rep became a spokesman for coal and steel as well as beer. In his last years, Valentine Reuther recounted to his sons his earlier struggles against the child labor law that permitted twelve year old boys to work and sometimes die in the depths beneath the Appalachian hills of his adopted state.

> It had been the practice of the coal mine employers in West Virginia to work the children of the miners who worked for them. If a man had a son of eleven or twelve years, they would frequently lay off the father so that the family would be compelled to make the child work in the mines or else do without bread, because they never had any cash money. They were required to buy at the company store, where prices were from twenty-five to thirty percent higher than in other stores. And these children, naturally, if they met with an accident, they perished.[142]

He continued to describe his six year effort in Charleston to prohibit the practice.

> At the fourth session I appeared before the committee that had the bill under consideration and I told them… that if this bill is not passed and you read an account in the daily papers where children of that tender age had again been killed in the mine, then ask your conscience who the guilty party is.

After a sixth effort finally produced a law prohibiting the employment of children under the age of eighteen, he affirmed his belief that when the ballot was used effectively by the working people of the state, it was the strongest weapon they possessed.[143]

The German circle in Wheeling brought Val Reuther in contact with a second cousin, Philip. The two hit it off and Philip introduced Val to the Socialist literature coming out of the Debs organization. Val was attracted to the words of Debs, and saw that Socialism complimented the Christian humanism taught by his father. He became a supporter of Debs, and as his involvement in Socialist politics grew, a close friend of the Socialist leader.

With a growing role in the West Virginia labor movement, Valentine Reuther realized he needed to become better educated. Like many children in the farming communities, he left school after seven years to help the family in the fields. Now as an adult, he enrolled in correspondence courses to improve his English writing and grammar, and read avidly everything from the Socialists Jack London and Upton Sinclair, to the German classics of Goethe and Schiller, to the ancients. Only Victor was able to finish high school in the traditional fashion, but all the Reuther children were exposed to books and discussions at home, and taught the value of an education.

In 1914 West Virginia became a dry state. The Schmulbach brewery was forced to shut its doors and Valentine Reuther was out of work. The family was forced to skimp and look for ways to cut expenses. The house on Wetzel Street in South Wheeling had a mortgage that strained the depleted family budget, forcing the Reuthers to squeeze into the downstairs of the house and rent out the top floor. Potatoes became the staple of the family diet, and Ted's clothes were refitted for all his younger siblings.[144]

Anna opened a small restaurant, but disaster soon followed. One day when Valentine was moving soda bottles into the ice box, one exploded in his hand and sprayed glass fragments into his eye. He was rushed to the doctor's office, worried about his future. He feared that if he were sedated, the doctor might remove the eye, so, fortified with medicinal whiskey, and held down by two husky volunteers, Valentine Reuther endured the pain while the doctor removed the fragments with a pair of tweezers.[145] The ordeal was for naught. Valentine lost sight in the eye, and years later when prosthetic eye replacements became a more attractive option, the eye was removed.

The next few years were very difficult for the family. Valentine worked sporadically in low paying jobs. When each of the older boys reached an age when they could find work, they left school and earned money to supplement the family income. Valentine recognized his educational shortcomings, and insisted that each of his sons learn a useful trade. At age 11, Ted and later Walter, worked after school as apprentices in the Northwood Glass factory for forty cents a day.[146] Walter was an indifferent student in the traditional subjects when he was young, but excelled in the shop classes.[147] He spent long hours working with his teacher learning the art of tool making.

The Reuthers' economic struggles were exacerbated during the war years by the hostility toward German-Americans that the Creel campaign to support the war effort abetted. The teaching of German was discontinued in many schools, and at a war bond rally in downtown Wheeling, recordings of the German classical composers—Beethoven, Mozart, Schubert, and Brahms—were thrown on the sidewalk and trampled by the patriotic throng. Val's Socialist politics and friendship with Debs made him and his family particular targets for abuse. The family could wake up in the morning to find paint splattered on the door of their house, or threatening letters stuffed into their mailbox.[148] The German background, Socialist father, and homespun clothes made the boys recipients of the cruel taunts that all too frequently plague the adolescent years.

Debs was incarcerated in the Moundsville, West Virginia federal penitentiary in 1919, awaiting transfer to Atlanta, and Valentine Reuther was a regular visitor. On the last visit before Debs was transferred, Val brought Walter and Victor with him. The two boys of twelve and eight remember a gaunt old man in prison garb, but with a twinkle in his eye, who patted them on the head and greeted them affectionately. The ride home was indelibly burnt into their memory. Their father was visibly shaken when he left the jail with tears running down the side of his face. No one spoke for most of the journey home. Finally, Val began shaking his head and repeating "How can they imprison so kind and gentle a man!"[149]

Even after the Armistice, President Wilson was deaf to all calls for clemency for Debs. Debs was finally pardoned in 1921 by Wilson's successor, Warren Harding, who invited him to the White House so he could meet the man over whom so much passion had been aroused. After meeting Harding, Debs returned home to Terre Haute where 50,000 supporters gathered to celebrate his release.[150] By the time of his pardon, Debs was an old man who receded from public life in the years before his death.

After Val recovered from the accident, his cousin Philip found him work at a brewery across the river in Ohio.[151] When that state turned dry, he found a job on a county road gang, but could not escape his ill fortune when a chip from a stone flew up and struck him in the good eye. The eye swelled up, and Val was temporarily blinded. The experience caused him to hasten the completion of his correspondence course, and that enabled him to find a job selling insurance for Metropolitan Life.[152] Valentine Reuther had made numerous friends in South Wheeling from his union work, and his own experience underscored the need for a measure of security that insurance could provide to the working man. Val proved an adept salesman, and the family finally felt relief from the years of financial hardship following the passage of Prohibition in the state of West Virginia.

The easing financial picture allowed Ted to leave the glass Factory and finish eighth grade. He followed his elementary education with an intensive course in bookkeeping at the Elliot Business School.[153] Ted found a job as a timekeeper at the Wheeling Corrugating Company and soon moved into the company's accounting office. His position kept him abreast of company hiring plans, and when an apprentice tool making position became available, he alerted Walter of the opening. Walter received an excellent recommendation from his shop teacher, Mr. Schneider, and cited some additional experience as an apprentice at the Glass Works. He got the job, and the sixteen year old Walter Reuther quit high school and went to work making eleven cents an hour as an apprentice tool maker.[154]

Factory work was a dangerous occupation in the 1920s with over 100,000 disabling injuries occurring each year.[155] Walter Reuther was nearly one of those. He and three other men were lifting a 400 pound die with oil on the underside. The die slipped from their control and came crashing down on Walter's big toe. As he was being carried to an ambulance on a stretcher, he yelled to a fellow worker, "Bring me my toe! I'm not leaving without my toe!"[156] The bloody toe was dutifully retrieved and placed on the stretcher, but when he reached the hospital, the doctor told him that the damage was too extensive and the toe could not be saved. Reuther insisted that he try, and, like his father before, refused anesthesia to be sure that his wishes were obeyed. The doctor was right. A few days after the operation, he had to be rushed back to the hospital and have the toe amputated. He resolved the injury would not cripple him or prevent him from playing his favorite sport—basketball. He recounted in later life how during his Ford years he organized the Highland Park team that won the plant championship.[157]

With Valentine's improving financial situation and contributions to the family coffers from Ted and Walter, the two younger boys were not under pressure to curtail their education. Roy, developed a keen interest in electronics. He was the "first kid on the block" to acquire a radio kit and build his own receiver that got the pioneering Westinghouse station KDKA loud and clear.[158] Electronics proved a greater attraction than high school, and Roy quit school to work long hours at little pay as an apprentice in a Wheeling electrical firm.

After Valentine's employment stabilized, daughter Christine was born. The birth was difficult and Anna was hospitalized for an extended time. To provide a safer environment for his daughter and a healthier one for his wife, Valentine found a farm on Bethlehem Hill outside of the city. The farm needed a lot of work, but could be purchased within the family resources. The whole family went to work doing plumbing, carpentry, and masonry. Roy wired the house for electricity. The outdoor privy was remodeled for Val's comfort, but the rest of the family had an indoor facility for their use as well. With KDKA, electrical wiring, and indoor plumbing, the family moved into the not so new century.

Anna Reuther was a devout Lutheran who believed that the teachings of Christ should be practiced in daily life. Val was educated by the Lutherans in his childhood, and briefly considered a career in the ministry, but his focus was fixed on man's obligation to his fellow man. His formal attachment to a Lutheran church ended when a newly arrived pastor chose Labor Day as an occasion to attack the labor movement in his sermon. Victor reports seeing his father flush and squirm and finally, unable to contain himself, rise, and in a loud voice confront the young cleric.[159] He then led his family out of the church. Victor kept casting his eyes heavenward expecting some divine judgment to descend upon his father. Anna insisted that the boys continue to attend Sunday School and church services on Sunday, but Val never set foot in the door of the church again.

He supplemented the boys' church attendance on Sunday with a weekly debating lesson. They were assigned a topic—an issue of the day like child labor, women's suffrage, Prohibition—and told which side of the debate they were to argue. Occasionally Val would change their sides at the last minute and impress upon them that to effectively argue for one point of view they had to know the rationale for the other. Val would critique their performances and evaluate both the logic they used and the rhetorical skill with which they debated. The boys would prepare at the library during the week and sometimes stand on a tree stump on the farm and practice their delivery in front of a bemused cow. [160]

Years later when Walter was the head of the GM section of the UAW, the *Detroit Free Press* wrote that, "Debating is in the Reuther family blood."[161]

> The Reuthers' father was a union official who set out early to prepare his sons to carry in his footsteps [...] Contrasting personality traits resulted. Walter, now

union GM chief, and Roy, a union international representative, found a little bombast would sink Victor, now a leader in the union war work conversion effort. Victor compensated by becoming precise. No Supreme Court jurist can read a nationally important decision with more finality than Victor can summon to back up a routine report on union finances [...] Working together, the three are deadly.

After three years working in the Wheeling Corrugating Company tool room, Walter Reuther was ready to leave home and head to the manufacturing center of Detroit. As his father wished, he possessed a skill that could be expected to provide security. He left home with the blessings of his family; with forensic tools to supplement the ones he carried in his toolbox; and with the family credo "a man should always fight for freedom and brotherhood" nurtured into his core.

Walter Reuther Arrives in Detroit

Walter Reuther arrived in Detroit on the last Saturday of February, 1927.[162] On Sunday he made the rounds of the auto plants looking for work. He found a job as a drill press operator at Briggs Body Works at three in the afternoon and started a twelve hour shift at 5:30. He worked thirteen hour shifts twenty-one nights in a row, making sixty cents an hour.[163] The pay was low, the working conditions were bad, and the work was not challenging. When he learned that Ford was looking for Die Leaders, he lined up to apply.

A Die Leader is usually a man in his late thirties or forties with years of experience behind him. When the nineteen-year-old kid arrived at the gate saying he was there to apply for one of these jobs, he was dismissed by the guard and told to leave. Reuther had to use the negotiating skills that would mark his later career just to get past the gate keeper. He insisted that "I'm not just a kid, I'm a Die Leader and I'd like to be interviewed." When the guard still refused him entry, he asked him "Are you a Die Maker or are you a Die Leader? How can you look at me and tell what qualifications I have?" He told the guard that if he had such skills he ought to be inside making a lot more money. Reuther would not go away and demanded to see the man who was competent to make the judgments on whether he had the necessary skills. The back and forth went on for three hours, before the guard relented and said he'd "probably catch hell for this, but I can't get rid of you," and let him inside.[164]

Once inside, Reuther next confronted a skeptical employment manager. He told the man that he had just spent the last three hours going through the same fight and did not want to go through another three hours of the same discussion. Again his persistence paid off, and the employment manager reluctantly called the chief master mechanic. Mr. Gardham, the chief mechanic, arrived and asked where the die leader to be interviewed was. When the employment manager gestured toward Reuther, Gardham became furious and asked why was he called down here.

Reuther spoke up and said, "Maybe you wouldn't have come if you had known I was waiting. But you're here. You've got the blueprints under your arm. It will only take a few minutes to find out how competent or incompetent I am. You've got nothing to lose."[165]

Gardham acquiesced and unrolled the blueprints of some very complicated dies and asked some highly technical questions. He was impressed by the answers and admitted "You know much more about this than one would believe looking at you."[166]

Reuther insisted that he knew more than his appearance indicated and told the older man that if he were given a chance and couldn't do the job, he would leave voluntarily. Gardham agreed to the deal. He told Reuther that he had never done this with anyone he'd ever employed before, but if he were willing to work for two days without knowing what he'd be paid, he'd be watched carefully and the company would decide whether it would keep him and how much they would be willing to pay. Reuther agreed, and hurried off to put in his last twelve hour shift at Briggs and give them his notice.[167]

Before Reuther could start working at Ford, he had to get his tools from Briggs. The tools belonged to the worker, but he would have to get written clearance from the superintendent to remove them from the plant. That became a problem. The superintendent did not want him to leave, offered a raise, and threatened to withhold his signature. The standoff lasted all night until the superintendent realized that Reuther was determined to leave, and signed the release. He got no sleep before starting his first shift at Ford. After the second day, Gardham and two foremen came over and told him that he had surprised them. They didn't think he had the skills that he had, and they would be happy to employ him at $1.05 per hour.[168]

In landing a job that led to his promotion to die leader, Walter Reuther joined the working elite. A dollar five an hour was very good pay in 1927. Walter sent half of his pay check home to help his family, but when he turned 21 in September, 1928, his father wrote him that he was to stop sending money home to them. He was a man now and needed to provide for his own future. Reuther inherited the Swabian frugality from his mother, and spent very little of the money he was making. He used his savings to buy a lot in Dearborn, and two smaller lots in another subdivision.[169]

Within a year of joining Ford, Reuther was working the three thirty to midnight shift at the River Rouge plant. He had ambitions of becoming an engineer and enrolled at Fordson High to complete his high school education. The schedule of classes during the day, a factory shift from 3:30 until midnight with occasional overtime, and then homework before a late bed and an early repetition of the same routine the next morning required the stamina for which he was noted during many long negotiations later in his life.

For the first time in his life, Walter Reuther was relatively well-off. He quickly rose to the rank of Die Leader and had forty men working under his direction.[170] His activities reflected a desire to be part of the emerging society as much as an ambition to reform it. Despite the grueling schedule of work and school, he found time and energy to organize a club with a group of other young men, who, like Walter, were completing high school while working full-time jobs. The club was called the 4C Club: the four C's standing for cooperation, confidence, comradeship, and citizenship.[171] Walter was the president, and a new friend, Merlin Bishop, was secretary. The club provided mutual support for a group of people determined to pull themselves up by their bootstraps. It engaged in fairly mundane fund raising activities to help disadvantaged students complete their education. It numbered a bank president and the principal of Fordson as honorary members. The club was recognized by various civic groups in the city, and Walter and Merlin Bishop were paraded before the Rotary and Kiwanis Clubs as the officers of this worthy organization.[172]

After Reuther completed his high school education, he enrolled at the City College of Detroit (CCD, now Wayne State University). It was now 1929, and in the fall of that year, the stock market crashed. The Roaring Twenties came to a screeching halt. The economy sputtered and stalled while Treasury Secretary Andrew Mellon stripped its gears, shifting into reverse.

Back home in West Virginia, Victor was enrolled in his first year of study at the University of West Virginia. His letters to Walter became more frequent and reflected more disillusionment with the academic environment at WVU. He hated being forced to participate in compulsory ROTC training, and he found the juvenile rituals associated with the fraternity system personally repugnant. Victor made frequent visits to the Scotts Run mining camps on the outskirts of Morgantown, and became despondent over the deplorable conditions that he witnessed there. He found the student body of WVU to be willfully oblivious to the plight of their less fortunate neighbors, and he wrote to Walter that they had to do something in their lifetime to right these grievous wrongs.[173] Walter suggested that they could have the greatest impact as lawyers advocating for the poor, and suggested that Victor join him at CCD to prepare for a career in law.

Merlin Bishop credits Victor's arrival in Detroit with Walter's rediscovery of his Socialist heritage. Bishop remembers his friend as a "very frugal fellow [who] invested his money, so I think at that point he was more interested in making money. His mind hadn't got onto social problems until Vic came and got him stimulated."[174] Walter, Victor, and Merlin Bishop were part of a housing cooperative formed to help defray costs and support one another's educational aspirations.

The trio were not satisfied with an intellectual understanding of the social issues discussed in the classroom. They extended their inquiry into the laboratory. To understand the charity available to the destitute, the three posed as indigents and went through a humiliating delousing process to spend a night in a Salvation Army flophouse. When the class discussion veered into criminology and prostitution, they went on a "whoreology" tour of the red light district to hear the personal stories of girls forced into prostitution. To understand the human cost of the depression, they toured the Hoovervilles to bring back pictures and testimony of families that had lost their homes and livelihoods.[175]

Reuther and his friends also started a Social Issues Club on campus and obtained its affiliation with the League of Industrial Democracy, a Socialist group originally founded in 1905 with Walter Lippmann, Clarence Darrow, Upton Sinclair, and Ralph Bunche as charter members.[176] Affiliation with the League provided an opportunity to attract well-known Socialist speakers like Norman Thomas and Scott Nearing to campus. The first issue confronting the club was the college's intent to start a ROTC chapter on campus.

Pacifist sentiment was strong after the carnage of World War I was examined with more dispassion in the post-war years. The many students of CCD, who, like Walter Reuther, were working their way through college, had little interest in playing soldier during the precious time they spent on campus. The Social Issues Club led the fight to keep ROTC off the campus. They were joined by Professor Walter Bergman, a World War I vet who, with like-minded vets, had formed a pacifist chapter of the VFW in the city. Bergman spoke at one of the club's student meetings and was promptly fired by the Board of Education.

The ROTC battle evolved into a battle over Bergman's right to freedom of speech and the retention of his job. Lillian Hernstein, the leader of the American Federation of Teachers in Chicago came to Detroit to defend Bergman before the Board of Education. Walter and Victor Reuther also appeared before the Board. Walter introduced himself as a Ford worker and a Dearborn landowner before defending the professor's exercise of free speech.[177] The appeals worked. Bergman was reinstated by the Board, and the Social Issues Club gained membership and clout on campus.

When Walter Reuther filled in his membership application form for the 4C Club, he wrote that, "I seek knowledge that I may serve mankind."[178] Before the market crash, he did not seem to regard service to mankind and pursuit of his own ascendancy into the moneyed class as incompatible. The depression confirmed for him his identity with the working class. The 4C Club was a group of upwardly mobile young men working with the establishment to help promote other working class youths with the same ambitions. The Social Issues Club was an avowedly Socialist organization, committed to class struggle to free working people from the chains of wage slavery.

The 4C and Social Issues clubs reflected two aspects of Reuther's approach to achieving social justice. The first expressed an attempt to crash the middle class party through education and technical competence. The other method was to raid the party and confiscate the bootleg casks of excess wealth hoarded by the in-crowd.

If Reuther were motivated by money during his 4C days, then money was a means to no discernible end. Reuther never outgrew the frugal habits of his Spartan childhood in Wheeling. It is more plausible that he relished the technical challenge of a die leader's job, the leadership role the job entailed, and the affirmation it accorded him. Reuther's heroes included Thomas Edison and Luther Burbank: men of craft and science who had "elevated civilization from the rut of superstition, fear, and religion."[179] Despite a record of perfect attendance at Sunday School back in Wheeling,[180] Reuther discarded much of the ritual and dogma of the religious practice observed by his mother while retaining his father's humanism. He had an almost naive faith in the basic goodness of humanity and in the power of technology and education to unlock this vast potential.

As the Depression deepened, layoffs in the auto industry soared. Over half the 1929 workforce was idled three years later.[181] The 4C Reuther took the advice of a sympathetic foreman and joined the Masons. Membership in the Masons at Ford was a trump card for getting a promotion or retaining one's job during periods of layoffs. During the same period, Reuther was actively campaigning for the Socialist Presidential candidate, Norman Thomas. Walter and Merlin Bishop traveled throughout Michigan in an old Buick with a speaker's platform attached to the back bumper and a sign reading 'Vote for Norman Thomas—Repeal Unemployment' fastened to the roof.[182] In Dearborn, where political rallies not approved by Ford were not sanctioned by city officials, Reuther used the lot he had purchased to stage his rally. When the cops arrived to disperse the crowd, they informed him that he was on private property and must vacate at once. Reuther triumphantly whipped out his deed and told them "I know. I own it!"[183]

The Masonic ring he flashed in the tool shop and his ability as a die leader kept Reuther employed at the Rouge despite his joining the Automobile Workers Union and marching in the funeral procession for the workers killed during the Communist organized 1932 Ford Hunger March. His political activity finally brought him into the scrutiny of the Ford Service Department. On September 30, 1932 Walter Reuther was terminated despite an employment record that listed him as a "first class worker." When he left Ford, he was making $1.45 an hour—one of the highest paid workers on the factory floor.[184]

When Walter returned home that day, he was smiling and greeted his brothers (Roy had recently joined them in Detroit) with the news, "Guess what happened to me today? I feel like a liberated man!"[185] He and Victor were now free to undertake the European adventure they had been contemplating.

A European Adventure

Walter Reuther had become friendly at work with John Rushton, an older toolmaker who had visited the Soviet Union in 1930. After Rushton, a devout Communist, was fired for his participation in the Hunger March, he returned to the Soviet Union with his wife and two teenage daughters to work at the Gorky Autoworks plant.[186] The Gorky facility was modeled after the Rouge and was preparing to produce a version of the Model A that was being discontinued in the United States. Soviet technicians had been assigned to the Rouge since 1931 to study Ford production methods and prepare to transfer machines and technology to Gorky. Rushton pictured the Soviet Union through the lens of an enthusiastic believer to his young colleague. Once in Gorky he wrote Reuther of the need for skilled die makers at the plant, and, with his recommendation, Walter Reuther was offered one of the positions allotted to the skilled Detroit workforce. The Soviet agency in the United States was so interested in securing the talents of Walter Reuther they consented to offer a position to his unskilled brother Victor as well.[187]

The brothers finished out the semester at CCD, but left college short of the credits needed for their degrees. Walter withdrew his savings from the bank barely a week before a bank holiday was declared and the bank collapsed. They left Detroit in December of 1932 for a brief visit to Wheeling to say goodbye to their parents. While in Wheeling, Walter gave Victor a crash course in tool and die making in his old high school machine shop. At their farewell party, Walter was quoted in the local paper with saying "We are going to study the economic and social conditions of the world, not the bright lights."[188] The two spent their last night in the New York home of Norman Thomas before boarding the German-bound steam ship that carried them to the adventure that awaited.

When the SS *Deutchland* steamed into Hamburg harbor on February 24, 1933, the city was in turmoil. Uniformed troopers paraded in the streets. Nazi swastikas and competing Communist and Social Democratic banners flew from buildings all over town.[189] The contact they had been given by a CCD German professor turned out to be an avid Nazi supporter.[190] After a disagreeable brief encounter, they located some distant relatives who put them in contact with Social Democratic dock workers who gave the pair a sense of the anti-Nazi feeling in the port city.

News of the Reichstag fire reached the Reuthers on March 1st, and they boarded a train for Berlin to see for themselves the events unfolding in the capital. When they arrived, the ruins of the building were still smoldering. The scene around the building was reminiscent of the atmosphere surrounding a major sporting event, with hawkers selling Nazi propaganda sheets and other paraphernalia. The pair joined a tour of the gutted building whose Brownshirt guides pulled books from the shelves in offices of Communist deputies to reveal pages hollowed out to hide a revolver.[191] This was the Nazi evidence of a planned, armed uprising.

Norman Thomas had supplied them with credentials and the names of some Socialist university students who might provide them a place to stay during their time in the city.[192] The students lived in a housing cooperative on the top floor above a large warehouse. The visitors enjoyed a couple of evenings of spirited discussion and companionship before the March 5th elections. They attended one of the last meetings of a group of Social Democratic activists in the rear of a wine seller's establishment. The participants spoke in whispers to lament the inability of the progressive forces to put aside their differences and unite against the imminent Nazi takeover. Group members were now planning to go into exile in Switzerland or the Netherlands. When the meeting adjourned, the participants left in small groups at irregular intervals to avoid a beating from the Brownshirt thugs patrolling the streets.[193]

The night before the vote, the two Americans ventured into a crowd of twenty-five thousand Nazi partisans in Franz Joseph Platz listening to the martial music and peeling church bells that set the tone for the piped-in voice of Hitler punctuated at the close by the banned anthem, Deutchland Uber Alles, blaring defiantly from loudspeakers. When the pair returned to their coop, they found their friends barricading the doors and windows against what they knew would be an impending raid.[194]

Three days after Franklin Roosevelt told the American people that the only thing "they had to fear was fear itself," the German people went to the polls and gave Adolph Hitler 44% of the vote. Later that evening a large contingent of war veterans paraded through the Brandenburg Gate, down Unter den Linden, and past the reviewing stand where General Ludendorff purged the memory of the country's defeat in a nostalgic reawakening of the right.[195] With support from other nationalist and conservative parties, Hitler became Chancellor of Germany.

The anticipated raid came one day later. The lights above the warehouse went out at 2:00 in the morning. At 3:00 there was a crash of the door downstairs being battered down. Brownshirts could be seen milling outside. The leaders who were the targets of the raid escaped through the back window on a rope ladder that had been positioned in anticipation of this eventuality. The first down was Emil Gross, a leader of the young Socialist resistance to the Nazi movement. By the time the Storm Troopers reached the top floor, the people they were after had vanished. Walter and Victor Reuther showed the intruders their American passports and were warned they should find other lodging. The next day they headed South toward their mother's family home in Swabia.[196]

The politics that divided Germany, also divided the Stocker clan. The boys stayed with their Uncle Ernst and Aunt Karolina in the village of Ruit. Ernst was a typographical worker in the city of Esslingen, who had been active in the Typographer's Union. Another uncle lived down the road in the small village of Scharnhausen. Uncle Adolph was a conservative farmer, who served as the Deputy Mayor of his village. As Deputy Mayor he would preside at parades and other local festivals. Unable to afford the full Nazi uniform, he contented himself with the swastika armband and Nazi hat. The two uncles were separated by temperament and lifestyle. They had little but family connections in common, and politics strained those tenuous bonds. In a heated exchange after Ernst expressed his reservations about Hitler, Adolph reddened with rage, and thundered "When we march on Moscow, I hope I shall have the privilege of shooting you down if you oppose me!" Adolph presented his two American cousins with a photograph of himself astride his plow horse giving the Nazi salute. That particular memento found a deserving place on the privy wall back in Ruit.[197]

The boys used Ernst and Karolina's home as a base while they waited for their work visas from the Soviet Union to arrive. When they did not arrive as anticipated, the boys purchased a couple of bicycles and set out to tour the immediate European neighborhood. They pedaled through the Black Forest into France, then down the Rhone Valley to Cannes and across to Italy. The beauty of the Mediterranean coast was a brief diversion from the ugliness they had witnessed in Germany. When the pair reached Pisa, they were exhausted from a particularly arduous day of cycling in terrible weather. They decided to check their bicycles and take the train to Rome. As it turned out, they had picked the very day Hitler was visiting Italy to help Mussolini celebrate the tenth anniversary of the Fascist state. The train carrying the Reuther boys was shunted off to a siding while the train bearing Der Fuhrer sped past.[198]

In Rome they found the same uniformed partisans marching in the streets, the same propaganda pouring out of the official organs, the same mindless crowds chanting "Duce, Duce, Duce." In Rome however the history seemed to swallow up this little ripple in time. It was the architecture, the ceiling of the Sistine Chapel, and the monuments of antiquity that dwarfed the demonstrations rumbling through the Eternal City in the recollections of the two brothers.[199]

From Rome, their tour passed through Florence and Venice and on to Austria. In Vienna the Socialists still garnered up to 70% of the vote, but in the rural countryside swastikas could be seen sprouting like dandelions after an April shower. The annual May Day celebration was officially banned, but the citizens of Vienna turned out anyway, and like in the scene from *The Sound of Music*, joined arms, and paraded around the city in defiance of the ban.[200]

A respite in Switzerland from the turmoil infecting its neighbors almost turned into tragedy for Walter Reuther. Inspired by the Swiss countryside, the boys decided to have a go at mountain climbing. Before attempting a more challenging slope, they made a practice assault on the relatively easy Mount Pilatus. Once above the timberline the rocks became wet from melting snow and the path narrowed. Walter Reuther stepped too close to the soft edge and lost his balance. As he started to slip down the side of the mountain, he grabbed hold of a shrub conveniently growing near the edge of the path. Reuther held on for dear life while his alpenstock plummeted over a thousand feet to the rocks below. Victor crept over to the edge of the path and held his walking stick down to where Walter could grab it. Slowly he managed to pull his brother back up to the path and safety. In shock, the two leaned back against the side of the mountain until their hearts stopped pounding in their chests and some strength returned to their limbs.[201] All thoughts of further mountain climbing adventures were abandoned. The brothers returned to Uncle Ernst and Aunt Karolina in Swabia.

There was still no word from Gorky on their entry visas. The wait they expected to take weeks was now over three months. With time on their hands, and little to do in the village, the boys and their two older cousins, Erna and Julia, and Julia's boyfriend, headed to the nearest big city, Stuttgart, to take in a movie. Their curiosity about the "New Germany" led them to choose a Goebbels produced propaganda film about a virtuous Hitler youth who falls into the evil clutches of depraved, criminal Communists. At the close of the film a huge swastika appeared on the screen and the sound track played the Horst Wessel song. This was the signal for the whole audience to stand, give the Nazi salute, and join in the singing. When the Reuther party remained seated, the crowd became ugly and started yelling "Communist pigs! Swine! Throw them out!" Walter Reuther reacted quickly to try to defuse the situation and buy time for their escape, by speaking loudly in English to his brother. When the audience realized they were foreigners, they were able to get out of the theater with only a stream of verbal abuse trailing their departure.[202]

Since the entry visas to the Soviet Union had not arrived, the Reuthers decided to go "on the road again," and attend the Second International Socialist Conference in Paris before continuing on to England. On the way into France they decided to pass through the Rhineland and look up Peter Reuther, a relative on their father's side. They had no address for "Uncle" Peter, so they stopped at the police station in Edigheim and asked the constable, a man named Massar, if he knew where Peter lived. Massar warned the brothers that Uncle Peter was a dirty Communist with whom they should have no truck.

At that moment Massar spotted Uncle Peter walking past the police station and. hailed him in a brusque voice. Once inside the two men traded insults about their political leanings. Uncle Peter, described by Victor as looking like a German Rip Van Winkle, challenged Massar to go ahead and arrest him, then at least he would have to feed him.

It was not a very pleasant way to be introduced to one's American relatives who dropped in unexpectedly after forty years of distance between the two branches of the family. The boys admired "Uncle" Peter's spirit, and were upset to learn that Massar did arrest him after their departure for embarrassing the German state in front of foreign visitors.[203]

Their experience at the Second Socialists International was also a downer. The attendees were only able to lament the state of their movement in the face of Fascism. There was little agreement between the factions and the generations. The image Victor retained from the conference was that of Otto Wels, leader of the Social Democrats in the Weimar Republic, near tears in trying to explain the collapse that brought the Nazis to power in Germany.[204] The conference had more the air of a funeral than a christening or marriage.

Their travels next took the pair to England. There the boys met Fenner Brockway, a parliamentarian from the Independent Labor Party. Brockway supplied them with names and addresses of contacts throughout the country. He advised them that they should attend the British Trade Union Conference that was soon to be held in Brighton. It was also Brockway who put them in touch with the Soviet Consul General in London, who informed them there was additional paperwork to be done before their visa applications could be processed.[205]

In Brighton, Brockway introduced the pair to Jennie Lee, a vivacious, young Scottish coal miner's daughter, who championed women's suffrage and Socialist causes, and was active in trying to organize an anti-Fascist front in the years before World War II. She was particularly interested in hearing what the two young men had observed in Germany. Lee, and her future husband, Aneuran Bevan, became life-long friends of the Reuthers. As Health Minister in the Labor Government of Clement Attlee, Bevan was largely responsible for creating the British National Health Service. As Arts Minister in Harold Wilson's Government, Jennie Lee authored the Open University System.

The Reuthers stopped in Amsterdam on their return to Germany to reunite with Emil Gross. After Gross had escaped down the rope ladder from their coop during the Storm Troopers' raid, he made his way to Amsterdam, where he became a link in the anti-Nazi German underground. While they were in the Dutch city, Gross recruited the Reuthers to deliver several messages to contacts in Germany. The boys realized this was more than a get acquainted tour of the social conditions away from the bright lights. Before heading into Germany they mailed their diaries back to Wheeling, and committed to memory the names and addresses of their contacts and the messages they carried before destroying any slips of paper that contained information that should not fall into the hands of the Nazis. Their principal contact was someone using the name Fritz living in Gelsenkirchen in the Ruhr. Like in the script of a Hollywood spy movie, they were to locate Fritz by visiting a bookstore and asking the proprietor if he had a copy of a rare book. The brothers were told in the first couple of stores they visited that they did not have a copy of the book requested, but were given the name and location of a store that might have it. After several referrals, the boys encountered a man who came out of the back room when he heard the name of the book they were seeking, and told them that he did not have it, but could lead them to someone who might if they came back after closing hours. When they returned, they were led to a house where Fritz and two friends were living. The Reuthers imparted their news of Gross and the instructions he had for them.[206]

The brothers later learned that Emil Gross had crossed back into Germany using false identifications several times and had been caught during one such attempt and sent to a concentration camp. They had presumed he had fallen victim to the Nazi terror and had not survived the war until one day in 1957 Victor Reuther received a call that there was a German newsman waiting outside who would like to see him. When he asked the name of the reporter, he was surprised and delighted to learn it was Emil Gross. The two flew out to Detroit that evening to reunite with Walter, now President of the UAW.[207]

Back in Germany, the brothers traveled to Berlin to see if there was any news about their visas. The Consulate had no word, but promised to send an air mail letter to the tourist agency in London to inquire about the delay. It was now November 11th, Armistice Day, and it had been ten months since they had left New York. On November 12th, the Germans were holding an election that would make the aged von Hindenburg President, and confirm Hitler as Chancellor. There was no chance that Hitler would get only 44% of the vote and need to form a coalition in this election. All parties except the Nazis were banned. The German "election" also coincided with the time that President Roosevelt recognized the Soviet Union. Whatever the cause, the entry visas appeared the next day.[208]

Into the "Workers' Paradise"

The brothers spent nearly two years in the Soviet Union. During their time in the country, Walter contributed a number of letters to the English language *Moscow Daily News*—some extolling the progress of the Russian worker, some critical of administrative inefficiency and lack of safety precautions. The letters written to friends back home were generally positive, often enthusiastic, about the progress the country was making and the relationship between the workers and the bosses that existed in the Gorky plant. The Soviet years and the youthful exuberance about their Russian experience would haunt them for much of the rest of their lives.

The two young men arrived in Moscow on the seventeenth of November, 1933. The Russian winter had arrived before them. Temperatures already dipped to thirty-five degrees below zero.[209] The trip to Gorky involved a night spent sleeping in an unheated rail station filled with peasants newly liberated from the land, but not from the garments and smells that lingered with them. The local train from Moscow to Gorky was slow and had few amenities. The trip ended with a six-mile tram ride from the station to the auto plant. The brothers were crammed into the carriage with little space to shift position. When they arrived at the plant, they found their jackets had been slit with razor blades and the contents of their pockets looted.[210]

Despite the rude introduction, the boys were predisposed to see the makeup on the Soviet face and overlook the blemishes. They had witnessed the rise of the Nazis in Germany and Austria and the incapacity of the progressives in England and France to respond to the challenge. Perhaps they had looked to the Soviets for hope. The Spartan conditions of the Gorky complex added to the sense of creating something new in a location far removed from the bright lights—a made-to-order laboratory for "studying the economic and social conditions of the world."

As a tool and die leader, Walter Reuther derived satisfaction from teaching recent peasant farmers the technical skills of a tool and die maker. He noted the pride that his charges derived from being part of the effort to lift the standard of living of their countrymen. In a letter to the *Moscow Daily News* he effused "The untrained workers of yesterday are taking rapid strides that soon will overtake auto workers anywhere in the world."[211]

Reuther particularly enjoyed the camaraderie he experienced at Gorky. There was a cafeteria set aside for the foreign workers, but the brothers chose to eat with the native workers. Lunches rarely consisted of more than cabbage soup and black bread, but after the meager meal the workers would congregate in the Red Corner where "A foreman produces a guitar, strums a few chords. A greasy mechanic and a red-kerchefed *Komsomolka* forgetting work, swing into gay dancing. Everybody keeps rhythms, shouts and laughs. I enjoy every minute here."[212] Such a scene would be unthinkable at Ford, where even smiling was taken as a sign of laziness

Reuther also seemed to enjoy the *subotnik*, or volunteer community service that the workers were occasionally called upon to perform doing such jobs as assisting the ice harvest from the Oka River in the early Spring or digging up the potato crop in the fall. These occasions had the flavor of a Midwestern barn raising with music, dancing, and a more substantial meal usually following the work. It was only later that the Reuthers realized that the work was less voluntary than they originally thought.[213]

In Gorky, Walter Reuther had his first love affair. Parties at the American compound proved a magnet for Russian girls. They flocked to the American compound—as much for the better food and better selection of merchandise provided the foreign workers as for meeting the exotic foreigners. Walter was attracted to a beautiful local girl named Lucy. When he spotted her at one of the compound parties, he used his limited Russian vocabulary to invite her back to their next social event. Lucy, the daughter of a railroad official, was poised and well-educated.[214] Unlike many of the girls that came to the compound, she fell in love with the man, and not the amenities the place provided. After several dates, the relationship blossomed, and Walter asked Victor if he could find another apartment. Lucy moved in with Walter.

A few weeks later Lucy told the brothers about a friend of hers, Victoria, who had had a falling out with her Austrian boyfriend. Victor began seeing her, and soon the two were sharing a room. That liaison lasted about two weeks when Victor learned she had been buying clothes at the foreign workers' store and selling them for a profit on the black market. The black market "went violently against [Victor Reuther's] grain."[215] Victoria was asked to leave.

Before they left for Europe, the boys had made a pact with each other that they would not marry. They planned to be active in the labor movement when they returned and expected to face hardship and possible jail. It would not be a lifestyle for a family man. They vowed to remain unencumbered, if not celibate. Lucy and Walter agreed that they would relish their time together, but the affair would not go beyond the time in Gorky.[216]

From his correspondence it is fair to say that Walter Reuther enjoyed his time in the Soviet Union. He had his first real romance. He could feel he was living his 4C commitment to "serve mankind" by helping to raise a peasant population into an industrial workforce. He was recognized as an *udarnik* or superior worker, and that provided him with additional vacation time and travel privileges. As *udarniks* the Reuthers were part of the Gorky contingent that stood on the reviewing stand at the 1934 May Day parade, a short distance from Stalin and members of the Politburo, to celebrate the first entirely Russian made car produced at Gorky.[217] Walter Reuther wanted to think that a state where workers shared in its management and reward was being created, and he characteristically flung himself into that effort.

In January, 1934, shortly after arriving in Gorky, Victor Reuther wrote a letter to Melvin and Gladys Bishop that, in several different versions, was used at every opportunity by the Reuthers' enemies to try to defame their character and stigmatize the causes with which they were identified. Melvin Bishop was the brother of their former housemate Merlin Bishop, and he and his wife were friends of the Reuthers through their work during the Thomas campaign. Over the years that friendship turned sour, and Melvin Bishop was implicated in an assassination attempt that almost cost Walter Reuther his life.

In the letter, Victor described the brothers' enthusiasm for their chosen endeavor, "…the daily inspiration that is ours as we work side by side with our Russian workers in our factory, the thought that what we are building will be for the benefit and enjoyment of the working class, not only of Russia, but for the entire world, is the compensation we receive." [218] He went on to give an idealized description of the factory floor democracy they witnessed at Gorky. "Mel, if you could be with us for just one day in our shop meeting and watch the workers as they offer suggestions and constructive criticism of production in the shop. Here are no bosses to drive fear into the workers. No one to drive them in mad speedups. Here the workers are in control. Even the shop superintendent has no more right in these meetings than any other worker."[219]

Victor continued to describe the hour-long lunch break where workers eat "wholesome plain food" while being entertained with music from a band playing in an adjoining room, after which they adjourn to the Red Corner to read papers and technical magazines, play, or just sit and chat. He described a party held in the clubhouse in the city built to house and service the factory workers. "Imagine, Mel, Henry Ford throwing a big party for his slaves. Here the party was no gift of charity from someone above for we own the factory, we held the meeting, and decided to have the party, and it was paid for from the surplus earnings of our department."[220]

The brothers' embrace of the Soviet model was in part quickened by their disillusionment with the Second Socialist International they had attended in Paris. Victor warns in his letter "Keep your eye on the S.P. It is being affiliated to the Second International. I am not certain it is 'drifting' in the right direction, certainly not in the light of recent events." The letter proclaims that. "[Soviet] leadership, the proletarian dictatorship, have not sold out to the owning class like the S. P. in Germany and the Labor Party in England."[221]

The letter to Melvin Bishop was written shortly after the Reuthers' arrival in Gorky from the night that was descending over Germany. By the time they were ready to leave the Soviet Union, distortions in their idealized image of the proletarian dictatorship would be all too apparent. After the assassination of Leningrad boss Sergei Kirov in December, 1934, Stalin began a ruthless purge of any real or perceived enemies. The show trial of the alleged assassin was broadcast into the Gorky plant during lunch hours.[222] Even earlier, an Italian worker with a Russian wife and family who the Reuthers knew as a "gentle, sensitive person who rarely talked politics"[223] was awakened by a knock on the door and whisked off to Siberia. Periodically arrests were made at Gorky, and nobody would dare speak with or acknowledge the remaining family members for fear of being identified with the arrested party. In his memoirs many years later, Victor wrote that, "it was only on those rare occasions when we were alone with friends on a walk through the woods or perhaps in a rowboat in the middle of the Oka that we could talk to any Russian worker about his opinion of the Stalin regime and the political oppression that was hanging like a sword over his head."[224]

Many foreign workers returned disillusioned from their Soviet experience, but not the Reuthers. Walter Reuther continued to defend the Soviet system for two years after his return to the United States.

Despite the evident primary role of the Communist Party in the tripartite plant governance system, he retained an idealized picture of workplace democracy colored by the hues in the range of the spectrum his vision was prefigured to detect. Perhaps the many months observing the Nazi takeover of Germany dimmed the critical eye directed toward the Soviet dictatorship. The brothers regarded the Soviet Union as a bulwark against the rise of Fascism sweeping across Europe.[225] It was also true in the early years of the CIO that a working relationship with the Communists was as big a calling card in the union hall as displaying a Masonic ring on one's finger was in the tool room at Ford.

The Melvin Bishop letter accumulated greater amplification with the continued positive correspondence coming from the Reuthers. Several versions appeared in Socialist publications and FBI files. Different versions were read into the Congressional Record and the NLRB report on the "Battle on the Overpass."[226] The version promulgated by Reuther's Conservative critics ended with the closing "Carry on the fight for a Soviet America, Vic and Wal."[227] Victor always maintained that he ended the letter with "Carry on the fight." The phrase "for a Soviet America" was added later by someone wishing to discredit the Reuthers. Whatever the youthful sentiments of the pair, from the time Walter Reuther became head of the GM Department of the UAW he was an outspoken critic of Soviet style Communism, and a leader in the effort to purge the CIO of Communist influence.

Conservative critics ignored the role and motivation of Henry Ford and other industrialists in their participation in the Soviet economy during the same period. Ford entered into an agreement to sell 400 cars to the Soviets in March 1919, short months after the Bolshevik Revolution.[228] Edsel Ford told his foreign department manager at the time to "keep in as close touch with Russia, through various channels in New York, as possible"—but keep it confidential.[229] The Gorky project was the result of negotiations that involved Ford Production Manager Charles Sorenson and high Soviet officials including at times Anastas Mikoyan and even Stalin himself. Ford's architect, Albert Kahn, expressed the company policy succinctly "Our own attitude has been this—that we are not interested in their politics. We feel, as Mr. Ford has so well expressed it, that that which makes for the upbuilding of Russia is bound to prove a benefit to all nations, America included."[230] It almost had the ring of a quote attributed to another automobile executive twenty years later. To paraphrase—"What's good for Ford is good for America."

Early in the summer of 1935, Walter and Victor Reuther decided to return home. They had saved most of the rubles they had earned at Gorky, and the Soviet currency could not be taken out of the country. They decided to spend their Soviet earnings seeing more of the country. As *udarniks*, they were entitled to papers giving them travel privileges that included seating priority on trains and permission to visit regions of Asian Russia that few Westerners were permitted to see.[231]

After a tearful parting between Lucy and Walter at the Gorky station, the Reuthers boarded the west-bound train for Moscow, and then headed south through the Ukraine where they viewed the Dnieper Dam project, collective farms, and Black Sea villas that had been turned into resorts for workers.[232] In the Georgian town of Batumi, the boys returned to their hotel from a mountain climbing excursion to find Lucy perched on her suitcase waiting for them.[233] Despite the pre-non-nuptial agreement that the two had reached, her strong feelings for Walter were evident, and the long, lonely trip to Georgia may have sprung from hope for more than just a chance to extend the long goodbye. The Reuthers planned to hike the military highway through the Caucasus to the village of Ordzhonikidze, and Walter persuaded his brother to let Lucy accompany them on this leg of their tour. The terrain was rough, the nights were cold, and Lucy was not dressed for the rugged conditions. By the time they reached their destination, she realized she was not able to keep up with their activity and only another sad goodbye waited at the end. The couple parted for the last time, and Lucy returned by train to Gorky.[234]

Walter and Lucy corresponded for some time afterward through intermediaries like John Rushton whose translations compensated for Walter's limited facility with Russian. He learned shortly after returning to America that Lucy married another American engineer in Gorky.[235]

The next leg of their tour took the pair on a steamer across the Caspian Sea to the fabled city of Samarkand. On the boat they met a schoolteacher and social worker who invited them to her school and told them of her work to free the Muslim women of the area from having to wear the horsehair veil. They noticed many of the older women in the city retained the veil but most of the younger ones did not wear it. The teacher explained to them how months of clandestine meetings led to a rally where hundreds of women removed their veils and threw them into a fire, lit for the occasion. Unfortunately, that night some of the women were murdered by Muslim fundamentalists.[236]

When they reached Tashkent on the Uzbek-Kazakh border they were told that they could go no further. The Eastern Muslim provinces were not securely under Soviet control, and travelers would have to return to Moscow and take the Trans-Siberian railroad to make their way to China.

The trip from Moscow to the Manchurian city of Harbin took eleven days. The Reuthers shared a cabin with a pair of English brothers and an aloof, middle-aged Englishman looking every bit the retired British colonel as the Hollywood version portrayed by Alec Guinness. When their cabin mate learned they had worked for twenty months in the automobile factory in Gorky and traveled extensively through the remote Asian regions of the Soviet Union, he suddenly became attentive and started asking detailed questions about their work and their experiences. When he identified himself as Hayley Bell, an ex-Colonel and aluminum manufacturer with offices in Shanghai, Walter kidded him about being an exploiter of the workers. Bell enjoyed the repartee and asked him what he thought they would do to a chap like him in a country like this. Walter answered "they would probably shoot you."[237] Bell burst out laughing, and a rapport was established between the two young Socialists and the older colonial capitalist.

When the train reached the border, the passengers learned that this part of Manchuria had been seized by Japan and was now called Manchukuo. The five cabin mates did not have visas for Manchukuo, which had not been recognized by either Britain or the United States. Bell refused to write on his passport and issue his own visa to Manchukuo and his cabin mates followed suit. The Japanese border guard told them "no sign, no visa, no train." The train went on to Harbin without them. There was a three day wait at the remote border crossing before another train was scheduled to arrive. This time Bell swallowed his pride and wrote

Manchukuo and his name onto his passport and his younger companions followed suit. Bell telegraphed the British Consulate in Harbin "Lt. Colonel Hayley Bell has just recognized the state of Manchukuo. Now sixty million British subjects may feel free to follow suit."[238]

One local custom in Harbin particularly disturbed the Reuther brothers. They would not allow themselves to be pulled along the streets of Harbin in a rickshaw, much to the amusement of Hayley Bell. At one point in the day, a rickshaw carrying Bell dressed in a white linen suit with a white pith helmet whizzed past, and he called out to them "Observe the British imperialist."[239] When they reached Peking (now Beijing), a speaking engagement at Yenching University on the outskirts of the city had been arranged for the Reuthers by the University President. The two resolved to hike the distance, but found themselves followed by an ever increasing number of coolies pleading for their business. The Reuthers realized the coolies needed their patronage much more than their working class solidarity. They convinced their bearers at one point in the journey to exchange places and let them pull. This gesture of class consciousness ended in exhaustion far short of their destination and the appointed order of things was sheepishly restored.[240]

China was in flux when the Reuthers arrived. Chiang Kai-shek's Kuomintang controlled the major cities, but little else. The Japanese had appropriated much of Manchuria, and Mao's Communists operated in the countryside. Severed heads of Communists that had been executed by Chiang's soldiers stared down from posts as warnings to others inclined to challenge his authority.[241] The value placed on human life in pre-War China was driven home to the pair when they boarded the steamer in Nanking that would carry them down the Yangtze to Shanghai. Starving peasants struggled to jump aboard, but were clubbed into the river and left to drown by hired Sikh guards. When the boys appealed for someone to try to save the drowning peasants, they were met with shrugs and told, "they would have died of starvation anyway."[242]

In Shanghai the Reuthers had a final meeting with Hayley Bell who invited them to the International Club where he introduced them as a couple of Bolsheviks. They last saw him on the dock waving goodbye to his quirky young companions as their boat pulled out for Japan. It was only after the war that they learned their friend had died and been eulogized by Winston Churchill for his contributions to the war effort as Britain's primary secret agent in the Far East.[243] Hayley Bell was also the grandfather of the actress Hayley Mills.

Their connection with Bell at the Manchukuo border alerted Japanese authorities to be suspicious of the Reuthers' presence in their country. During their bike tour from Osaka to Tokyo, they were aware of a shadow that accompanied them along the way.[244] When they finally reached Tokyo they were broke. The American embassy helped find them a job on the *SS Hoover* bound for Honolulu and Los Angeles. After two and a half years, Walter and Victor Reuther were headed home, steeped in experiences from a world on the verge of madness and uniquely prepared for service in the world that awaited.

PART 2

Chasing the American Dream

CHAPTER IV

Sit Down and Fight

There once was a union maid, she never was afraid
Of goons and ginks and company finks and the deputy
sheriffs who made the raid.
She went to the union hall when a meeting it was called,
And when the Legion boys come 'round
She always stood her ground.

Woody Guthrie

Walter and Victor Reuther arrived home in the fall of 1935. Like few other Americans, the two young men had experienced first-hand the forces that would shape the design of the next half century. Walter was now twenty-eight. Victor, five years younger. Their experience abroad fortified the sense of social obligation inculcated in them by Valentine Reuther. The pair resolved to dedicate their energy to the struggle for social justice, and vowed to remain single for the foreseeable future in priestly devotion to their cause. By the end of the next year, those vows would be nullified, and the two young men would be leaders in the mass movement reshaping American society.

With his savings depleted and black-listed from employment in the automobile factories, Walter Reuther embarked on a lecture tour of Midwest campuses. The Sunday debating sessions orchestrated by his father had made Reuther a persuasive speaker with a compelling experience to relate. His lectures drew an audience beyond the Socialist youth groups arranging the events. Reuther was generally positive about his experience in the Soviet Union, emphasizing the shop floor democracy in setting production quotas over the political repression manifest in the consolidation of Stalin's power. By Christmas, the speaking tour brought him to Brookwood Labor College in Katonah, New York where his brother Roy was teaching.

Brookwood was founded in the aftermath of World War I when there was an enthusiasm for providing an education to workers without the money or credentials to attend college which were generally a privilege reserved for the more well-to-do. Under the directorship of Tucker Smith, a Quaker pacifist with strong ties to the Socialist Party, the labor college now catered more to campus youth, radicalized by the depression and drawn to the peace movement. Brookwood became a Mecca for idealistic young radicals to deepen their understanding of the labor movement, form bonds, and establish their credentials as labor organizers. Len De Caux, a Brookwood student during this period and later a CIO publicist, described his experience at the school as one of "ease, security, the fresh-air pleasures of the well-to-do...Spiritually, Brookwood was a labor movement in microcosm—without bureaucrats or racketeers—with emphasis on youth, aspirations, ideals."[1] Brookwood was a well-spring for a generation of labor activists.

Roy Reuther was a student at Brookwood in 1933 and later became an instructor in a worker's education program sponsored by the Federal Emergency Relief Administration (FERA). Roy was selected to head the FERA program in Flint where he set up a curriculum similar to the one at Brookwood with courses in labor history, public speaking, and "labor dramatics," offering a radical approach to labor relations. Roy was the most personable of the Reuther boys, and his energy and competence made him popular with workers harboring union sympathy that signed up for his courses. Within weeks of his arrival, Roy orchestrated worker testimony before an NRA committee investigating labor relations in heavy industry.[2] General Motors got him fired from the FERA program, but not before he had established a working relationship with unionists in Flint and earned their respect. After his time in FERA, Roy returned to Brookwood as an instructor and circuit lecturer.

From his association with Tucker Smith at Brookwood, Walter Reuther was introduced to several like-minded young people who would become instrumental in building his West Side Local. George Edwards, the National Student Association leader, conducted a League for Industrial Democracy (LID) workshop at Brookwood during the summer of 1935, and a young Dallas newsman, Frank Winn, spent much of that year at the labor college. Both were key participants in the Kelsey-Hayes strike one year later.[3] Brookwood lectures by people like Norman Thomas and Robert Lynd found future UAW stalwarts Brendan Sexton and Nat Weinberg in the audience.[4] Time and factional politics would erode some of the friendships formed during this preparatory interlude, but Brookwood provided an atmosphere where visionary youth found reinforcement of their beliefs and made common cause in their aspirations.

Tucker Smith provided Victor Reuther with a job in 1936 doing labor outreach for a Quaker-funded Emergency Peace Campaign. Brookwood became the base from which he visited satellite programs and established a network of contacts in the industrial cities.[5] Smith offered Walter Reuther a comparable position at Brookwood that would eventually send him to Pittsburgh or Detroit to head a Brookwood branch campus in one of those cities. Walter was intrigued by the idea, but developments in Detroit led him to decline Smith's offer.

Soon after Walter and Victor returned home in the fall of 1935, Walter drove to Atlantic City with a group of friends to witness the AFL convention. At the 1935 convention on the boardwalk, a high tide of industrial fervor sent its breakers crashing against the slowly shifting sands of the labor establishment. The Wagner Act protecting the worker's right to organize had just been signed into law by President Roosevelt, and there was a good deal of ferment in the manufacturing centers to organize on an industrial basis. The leadership of the AFL, however, was politically conservative and committed to organizing only along craft lines. The old guard of the AFL were uncomfortable with the younger Socialist and Communist organizers active in the industrial movement.

The AFL had stalled organizing efforts in the plants by their rigidity. It created federal unions in the industrial sector under direct control of the Federation leadership, who appointed their officers and determined their agenda. These federal unions served as little more than catchments for gathering together workers in an industry until sufficient numbers were accumulated to be parceled into the various crafts that could be identified in the manufacturing process. Unlike the building trades where crafts such as plumber, carpenter, and electrician were easily differentiated, changes in the manufacturing process frequently redefined the roles of workers in the plants and blurred the distinctions between categories of workers. Activists in the plants resented the fact that they were not allowed to choose their own officers and chafed under the fragmentation and caution imposed by the AFL.

The AFL leader most committed to the idea of industrial unions was John L. Lewis of the United Mine Workers (UMW). Many of the mines were directly owned by the steel companies they supplied, and Lewis reasoned that his union would have more leverage over these operations if steel workers were organized, particularly if that union were under the influence of John L. Lewis.

A UMW lieutenant Heber Blankenhorn remembers a chance encounter he had with Lewis on the boardwalk during one of the nights of the convention. Blankenhorn greeted Lewis and asked him if he was still thinking of organizing the workers in basic industries on an industrial basis. Lewis clasped Blankenhorn's forearm in a firm grip and replied in a mystical tone.

> "I have been thinking of nothing else for a year. Day and night. Last night I could not sleep. I sat in my bathrobe, at the window, facing east looking over the sea. Mrs. Lewis called, asking why I did not go to bed, what was I waiting for? I said I was waiting for the sun to rise…I shall go back to my hotel now and tonight I shall sleep for the day is here and I am ready."[6]

When the sun rose the next morning Lewis took his fight to the convention floor. The votes were not there to adopt a minority resolution favoring the organization of basic industries on an industrial basis, but the convention setting provided a theater to address his message to a different constituency—the young radicals in the gallery like Walter Reuther and the rank-and-file beyond the boardwalk in the union halls of Pittsburgh and Detroit.

Lewis began the morning sparring with his rivals. He struck first at two of the spokesmen for the old guard, Matthew Woll and John Frey, by proposing that any AFL official holding office in the National Civic Foundation (NCF) could not simultaneously serve on the board of the AFL. The NCF was founded in 1900 with the intent of establishing better relations between management and those segments of labor deemed to be responsible and willing to work within the framework of the capitalist system. Mark Hanna, a prominent Republican businessman, expressed the intent of the NCF, declaring in print, "Now, my plan is to have organized union labor Americanized in the best sense and thoroughly educated to an understanding of its responsibilities, and in this way to make it an ally of the capitalist, rather than a foe with which to grapple."[7] The NCF was dominated by businessmen and prominent politicians, but for many years Samuel Gompers of the AFL served as first vice-president of the organization. The NCF was regarded as reformist in its day. Its effort to include elements of labor in the capitalist panoply contrasted with the outright hostility to any accommodation with labor expressed by the National Association of Manufacturers (NAM). The NCF was created to stem the growing appeal of Socialism during the years prior to the First World War, and its founder, Ralph Easley, saw the adamant stance of the NAM as furthering this trend. He described enemies of the NCF as "the Socialists among the labor people and the anarchists among the capitalists."[8]

By 1935 the NCF had become increasingly anti-labor, and the Lewis resolution gave Woll and Frey little choice but to resign from the NCF board. He struck another blow against them with a resolution barring publishing advertisements from companies with a record of union busting in the AFL monthly journal. Again the pair offered no resistance. After the initial jabs were thrown and parried, the resolution to issue industrial union charters to workers in mass-production industries was brought to the floor by a craft unionist sympathetic to the Lewis challenge. Matthew Woll offered a "long desultory Philippic"[9] in rebuttal. Next Lewis took the floor and proclaimed he had been seduced in San Francisco (1934) by fair words. "Now I am enraged," he thundered, "and I am ready to rend my seducers limb from limb."[10] When an exchange with William Hutcheson of the Carpenters Union became heated and ended with Hutcheson calling Lewis a bastard, Lewis made good on his warning. Lewis vaulted a row of chairs, sprang at Hutcheson, and knocked him back against a table with a well-placed right hand to the jaw. As a bloodied Hutcheson was being escorted from the hall, Lewis calmly readjusted his tie, lit a cigar, and strolled to the rostrum.[11] With one dramatic gesture the CIO was born.

The CIO started as an insurgency within the AFL called the Committee of Industrial Organizations. Besides Lewis' UMW, only Sidney Hillman's Amalgamated Clothing Workers (ACWA), David Dubinsky's International Ladies Garment Workers (ILGWU), Thomas McMahon's textile workers, and Max Zaritsky's cap makers aligned with Lewis' Committee. None of these unions represented part of the industrial core that the CIO sought to attract, and most of the leaders were unwilling to risk a divorce from the AFL and the respectability it represented. John Brophy, an off-again-on-again Lewis associate from the UMW was named the director of the new organization with Lewis as its chairman. The UMW, ACWA, and ILGWU each ponied up $5000 to give the Committee an initial operating budget.[12]

Whatever the CIO lacked in money and organization, it made up for in the star power of its Chairman. As the AFL was preparing to hold a convention in Miami, John L. Lewis traveled to Akron and Cleveland on January 19, 1936 to deliver an afternoon and evening address to rubber and auto workers. Despite freezing temperatures and a raging blizzard, both halls were filled to capacity and loudspeakers broadcast the message to thousands more braving the cold and snow outside. Lewis did not disappoint. He derided the migratory flight of the AFL leadership from the beaches in New Jersey in the summer to the beaches of Florida in winter. He touted industrial democracy and promised to liberate industrial workers from the antiquarian practices of the AFL. He castigated the enemies of labor and quoted the Bible to reinforce his cause.[13] He toured the Midwest industrial belt like a rock star with overflow crowds awaiting his every appearance.

The Akron rubber workers who braved the blizzard to hear John L. Lewis speak in January struck the Goodyear Tire and Rubber

Company in February. When the company tried to revert to a three shift schedule, in place prior to the Depression, without notifying the union, a spontaneous walkout of 500 workers in Plant 2 resulted.[14] The company plan meant a longer workday for the same pay for the workers on the first three shifts and layoffs for many of those on the fourth shift. The walkout quickly spread throughout the Goodyear complex. Inside the plants workers staged a sit-down to prevent the company from operating the plants with scabs, while outside a huge picket line surrounding the eleven mile perimeter of the complex was formed.[15] Among those rushing to Akron to reinforce the picketing rubber workers was Walter Reuther.[16]

The CIO did not initiate the strike, nor did it have any real organizational structure within the rubber plants when the walkout began. The strike provided the opportunity the CIO sought to demonstrate its relevance to industrial workers disillusioned by years of AFL neglect. It supported the fledgling United Rubber Workers (URW) with money and organizational support. When the strike ended, the CIO won few concessions from Goodyear, but the fact that the company signed any contract was regarded by the press as a victory. The company refused to dismantle the Industrial Alliance, the company union, but the strike had galvanized the latent militancy of the workers, who now flocked to the URW.

While Walter Reuther was walking the picket line in Akron, he was still contemplating Tucker Smith's offer to teach at Brookwood. The job in Katonah offered him contact with the progressives in the labor movement and a regular paycheck, but his heart was leading him to Detroit. Reuther sensed that the Atlantic City AFL Convention and the enactment of the Wagner Act, protecting workers' rights to organize, had created an opportune moment for organizing in the basic industries that he and other social activists were eager to seize. Encouraged by his brothers and his friend Merlin Bishop to remain in Detroit and be part of the auto workers organizing drive, Walter wrote to Tucker Smith and explained the "necessity" of his remaining in Detroit.[17]

Reuther committed to the role of union organizer, but having been blackballed from working anywhere in the industry, he first had to become affiliated with one of the UAW locals. Many of the early locals consisted of no more than a handful of militants sympathetic to the agenda of the Communist Party. Reuther needed Communist backing to gain membership in one of the fledgling Detroit area locals, and worked closely with the party during this period. Nineteen thirty six was the time of the Popular Front when Communists, Socialists, and other voices on the left worked cooperatively to advance shared objectives. Whether the young Reuther harbored a brief affinity with Communist ideology or opportunistically cooperated with influential party members to advance his own career, Communist backing secured his membership in Local 86 at the GM Ternstedt plant.[18]

Reuther had worked six years at Briggs and Ford before his European adventure, but never at Ternstedt. He was accepted by his new colleagues for his previous work in the industry and his energy and commitment as a union organizer. Reuther later revealed that the Ternstedt local had only 13 members in a plant employing about 12,000 workers. "The constitution of our union said you had to have fifteen members to have a charter. We had only thirteen. We paid for two people by taking up a collection every month for two guys who hadn't joined yet."[19]

Reuther's mission was not to organize the workers in the big GM plant. That job would come later. The first priority for Reuther and other labor activists was to wrest the young UAW from the control of its complacent AFL leadership. The test of that effort would occur at the April 1936 convention in South Bend, Indiana. Walter Reuther was elected as a delegate to the South Bend convention by the Ternstedt local. "I was elected by acclamation. I stood before this great mass meeting of organized workers—there were five others there besides myself—and thanked them for the great honor."[20] When the assembled agreed that the unemployed Reuther be given the money in the local treasury to finance his trip, the financial secretary reached into her purse to produce a five dollar bill. Reuther was handed the local's wealth with an admonition to bring back any change.[21]

The biggest impediment to organizing workers in the auto industry was the AFL. The AFL yielded to pressure in 1934 to convene a national conference of the fragmented unions representing different segments of the auto industry, but placed this consolidated group under the direction of an eleven member executive committee appointed by the AFL national leadership. At the 1935 convention of the newly organized United Autoworkers of America (UAW), the delegates voted overwhelmingly to elect their own leadership, but AFL president William Green stepped to the podium and intoned "By the power vested in me and upon orders of the Executive Council, I will now appoint the officers of this international union."[22] Green named Francis J. Dillon president; Homer Martin vice-president, and Ed Hall secretary-treasurer.

Delegates arrived at the 1936 convention in South Bend eager to oust Dillon and select their own leaders. Dillon and the AFL leadership to whom he reported incurred the fury of the rank-and-file for aborting a massive strike that spread from an Auto Lite parts plant to the Chevrolet transmission plant in Toledo and then giving way on many of the worker demands in reaching an unfavorable settlement. Homer Martin declared "Dillon has pursued a positively impossible policy. If he is allowed to remain in his present position he will only further destroy the automobile workers' unions."[23]

The convention brought Communists and Socialists to South Bend, eager to participate in a great social upheaval. It brought representatives from the CIO, primed to steer the convention in a direction it was anxious to go. It brought the voices of the new immigrants from Eastern and Southern Europe together with xenophobic old settlers from Appalachia. It brought socially conservative delegates from Kansas City and Atlanta. Scattered among the delegates were Dillon supporters and company spies. The only voices not heard in South Bend were those of the African Americans concentrated in a few Chrysler plants and in the River Rouge complex of Ford.

When the meeting convened, the name of the relatively unknown 28 year old redhead was prominently introduced to the gathered in the opening skirmish of the proceedings. Voices of the old order, some perhaps company agents that wormed their way deep into the union structure, challenged the credentials of Walter Reuther over the fact that he never worked at the Ternstedt plant. The charge was true, but such a technical violation was hardly unique to Reuther at this convention. Reuther claimed that he had worked briefly at Ternstedt under an assumed name and was vouched for by Wyndham Mortimer and Leo Krzycki, the national Chairman of the Socialist Party.[24] In a test of strength between the progressive and conservative factions at South Bend, Reuther was seated, but elements of the old guard raised the issue on a daily basis and kept the name Reuther in front of the delegates throughout the proceedings.

Reuther reveled in the attention accorded him by his opponents. At one point during the proceedings he rushed to the podium with a copy of the Hearst *Chicago Herald-Examiner* newspaper that blared a provocative false headline claiming that the UAW had quit the AFL. Reuther roused the delegates with a spirited attack on Hearst and the power which his newspaper chain wielded against the legitimate rights of the working man. He reported to his brothers later "I had the entire convention on its feet fighting mad."[25] When he finished his attack on Hearst, he turned to the body of the article, which gave an accurate, balanced account of the convention proceedings, and differentiated the working journalists from the editorial board at the paper. He called upon the journalists at Hearst to join the ranks of the CIO and affiliate with the Newspaper Guild.[26] Reuther's resolution denouncing Hearst won unanimous endorsement from the gathering and brought congratulatory telegrams to the convention from John L. Lewis and Heywood Broun, head of the Newspaper Guild.[27]

When the convention ended, a Rubicon had been reached, but not crossed. William Green bowed to the sentiment in the hall and freed the union from direct Federation control. Francis Dillon declined to seek the presidency of the quasi-independent union, and the convention elevated Homer Martin to the post. Martin, an ex-pastor and collegiate hop-skip-and-jump champion, had become a spokesman for Kansas City auto workers after his pro-labor sermons had run afoul of the views of the more conservative parishioners in his Baptist congregation who compelled him to seek other employment. He was hardly a radical, but he retained the evangelical flair of his previous calling and had a strong rapport with the transplanted white Southerners who formed a significant segment of the auto industry's workforce. The convention had adopted a Reuther-endorsed resolution to expand the number of vice-presidents, and the able Communist Wyndham Mortimer was elected to one of the three posts. George Addes, a leader of the Toledo strikes, was named secretary-treasurer. The UAW did not leave the AFL as Hearst erroneously trumpeted, but viewed its jurisdictional restraints in the words of Walter Reuther as "just black on white."[28]

Reuther's prominence in South Bend made him a floor leader of the Michigan delegation[29] and led the Michigan caucus to elect the 28 year old to one of four seats apportioned to the state on the UAW Executive Board. His elevation to the board again prompted his opponents to challenge his credentials and the Michigan election process that placed three Detroiters and nobody from Flint on the board. Homer Martin backed Reuther's position that the purpose of the election was to place the four best men on the board regardless of the city from which they came, but he left Walter Reuther as the only member of the executive board without a geographical region, a salary, or a paid staff.[30]

Walter Reuther had another reason for turning down Tucker Smith's offer to teach at Brookwood and remain in Detroit He had become acquainted with an attractive red head named May Wolf, a teacher active in Socialist Party gatherings attended by Reuther. The couple met, not quite by chance, one cold December evening on a Detroit streetcar and got to talking. That was the beginning of a brief two-month courtship that consisted mostly of "dates" at union or Workman's Circle branch meetings.[31] Without superstition, on Friday, March 13, 1936 "[Walter] grabbed her hand on an uncharacteristic impulse, and they hurried to the justice of the peace to be married. On the way, they asked two surprised strangers if they could spare a few moments to be witnesses."[32] After the brief civil ceremony the newly married couple rode off to Mount Clemens, Michigan where Walter addressed an evening labor rally.[33]

Walter Reuther broke his vow of priestly devotion to a single call. It helped that May was as passionately devoted to the same cause as Walter, but passion for a cause and one another begins to wear when buffeted by frequent separations, constant sacrifice, and conflicting priorities. The letters exchanged during Walter's many travels reveal the strains the couple endured and the longing they retained for each other.

May Wolf was Jewish, Walter Reuther, Lutheran, but in the family history of both partners progressive politics trumped religious orthodoxy. May was active in Socialist Party conclaves and in the attempt to organize Detroit area teachers before she ever met Walter. After they were married, she supported the family with her sixty dollar a week teacher's salary and devoted many of her spare hours to helping manage the office of her husband's West Side Local. When the local grew and the office work mushroomed, she quit her teacher's job and worked full-time at the local headquarters for the meager sum of twenty dollars a week.[34] As Walter Reuther's role grew and his station increased, May saw her role diminish. Eventually, after the birth of their first daughter, Linda, in 1941, May Reuther settled into the role of mother and housewife common to most educated, ambitious women of the day.[35]

When Walter Reuther notified his brother Victor that he was married, there was a moment of disbelief that his brother would break their pact without so much as a prior discussion, then a feeling of liberation that he was now free to follow his own heart. Victor had fallen in love with Sophia Goodlavich, a young student at Brookwood whose parents had immigrated to America from what was then part of Poland when they were teenagers. Sophia and Victor were married in Peekskill, NY in July of 1936.

The Road Ahead

April Fool's Day in 1936 found Walter Reuther married and sitting on the Executive Board of the newly liberated UAW. It also found him with no job, his savings depleted, and no assigned responsibility within the union. Reuther's foes could not disqualify him at the South Bend convention, but they contrived to place him in a situation where he seemed doomed to fail or stagnate into irrelevancy. Instead, one year later he had built one of the largest, most dynamic locals in the UAW. Reuther captured a brief window when the "tide [was] taken at the flood" and with hard work, astute planning, and guts saw his effort "lead on to fortune."

Reuther left South Bend with little more than a title. He had to recruit a staff, raise money to cover basic expenses, and carve out a base from which to confront the most powerful corporations in the country. From his unsuccessful attempts to skirt around the blacklist and find a job in the industry he realized the extent to which a monolithic labor policy dictated by the big three companies permeated the whole industry. Company based unions in a parts supplier or a single plant were impotent against the pressure exerted by an auto giant that could change suppliers or redirect production to another facility. Only an industrial based union covering a wide swath of the industry could mount an effective challenge. Reuther began organizing his base in the UAW by convincing six separate locals operating in six Detroit area plants "to agree that none...in isolation could get anywhere on its own. Therefore we ought to create an amalgamated local union and pool our membership, our resources, and our efforts to do something meaningful in terms of organizing the unorganized."[36] The amalgamated union located on the West Side of Detroit was chartered as Local 174 with Walter Reuther as its first president. The six unions combined had a total membership of 78 people.[37]

Now that Reuther had a local, he had to rent an office. He found space in a building on the corner of Michigan Avenue and Thirty-fifth Street once belonging to a bank that closed during the depression. The corner was a streetcar transfer location for workers traveling to the huge Ford River Rouge plant. Dave Miller, a union loyalist working at the Cadillac plant, remembered Walter showing May and himself the old bank that Walter said could be rented for $10 a month. The three did not have $10 between them at the time.[38] Reuther borrowed $350 from Miller and got a secondhand desk, a mimeograph machine, and a typewriter for his new headquarters. Most of the money was used to rent a sound truck to alert the workers toiling in the West Side factories of the new union presence in their midst.[39]

Upon returning from South Bend, Reuther finally succeeded in landing a job at the Coleman Tool and Die shop on the West Side. His skill as a craftsman had not diminished during his enforced absence from the trade, and despite having a second full-time occupation as a union leader, the quality of his work drew notice from his superiors. After little over a month on the job, he completed a perforating die with over 200 perforating punches with tightly specified tolerances. When the inspector tested the die on a copy of the morning paper it cleanly pressed all of the punches without a single burr. The inspector complimented Reuther by telling him "that is one of the best jobs we have put out in this shop in some time." Reuther told him to save his compliments for the boss because he was going to ask for a wage increase. The floor boss at the shop was called "Highball John" for the way he rode the people under him. When "Highball John" came over to check the work, Reuther told him "If this job is as good as the inspector claims, I ought to get a ten-cents-an-hour raise." "Highball John" told him he would check with the old man—plant owner Frederick Coleman—and get back to him. The next morning at seven o'clock "Highball John" came over to Reuther and informed him that he was getting his raise. At nine o'clock the same morning "Highball John" fired him for incompetence. Reuther's wage demand drew attention to his organizing activities inside the shop. Reuther replied to "Highball John" that "[he] was going to finish the job of organizing this shop before you physically throw me out of this plant."[40] That was the last job Walter Reuther held in the automobile industry.

The loss of a steady income increased the financial burden on the pair of newlyweds, starting a new life together while at the same time pouring their resources into the fledgling local, but it gave Reuther time to devote his full energy to building the union. Reuther worked closely with Communists Dave Miller and Bill McKie to establish contacts with workers inside the plants. From September into December Reuther and McKie would meet for morning coffee and review the list of names that McKie had prepared for Reuther to contact. With workers afraid to be seen talking to anyone from the union in the presence of company spies, many of these contacts took place in the workers' homes or while taking a stroll through a city park.[41] These contacts proved essential in establishing a core of unionists and union sympathizers within the plants the local planned to organize.

The union movement nationwide got its biggest boost from Franklin Roosevelt's landslide election victory in November of 1936. Roosevelt's election victory was an affirmation of his New Deal policies, and it dragged into office on his coattails progressive governors in the industrial states of Pennsylvania, Ohio, and Michigan. The election of Frank Murphy as Governor of Michigan proved to be as instrumental in the events that followed as the re-election of the President himself.

A poll of autoworkers taken in the spring of 1935 revealed a substantial 88 percent expressing a preference for "no union."[42] At the time, the poll results were seen to reflect the workers' sentiments about the AFL as much as their disinclination to organize for better pay and working conditions. The years prior to 1935 were marked by labor unrest, but the organizing effort of the AFL was tepid, the company unions were weak and fragmented, and most strikes ended in defeat. Subsequent to the publication of those poll results, the picture for labor changed dramatically. The country was emerging from the depths of the Depression. The auto companies were again expanding their workforce, and New Deal legislation had imbued workers with a new-found sense of militancy. The formation of the CIO and the Roosevelt landslide prompted a sense of optimism that job actions could improve the lives of workers.

After years of the depression, most workers no longer held out hope that their current station was just a stepping stone on the path to a middle class life. They felt as welded to the assembly line as the machines that dictated the pace of their existence. They were more inclined to view themselves as part of a class struggle and accept the union as the instrument with which they would wage battle to gain more control over the dehumanizing aspects of their existence. Franklin Roosevelt added impetus to the union movement when he declared during the campaign that "If I were a factory worker, I would join a union." This quote would be pasted on every factory gate in Detroit in the fall of 1936.[43]

Wages were an issue in the labor disputes, but the more overriding concerns were the working conditions and lack of security faced daily by an autoworker. Hourly rates for the same type of work varied considerably within the industry and even within an individual plant between the sexes and the races. At the top end, these rates appeared rather generous, at the bottom, appallingly low. But even workers making the top rate found their annual earnings diminished by the irregularity of auto industry employment. The introduction of yearly model changes meant production workers faced extended periods of layoffs during the model changeover period, and skilled tool and die workers could be transferred to lower wage production tasks when the tools for the new model year were readied. On the production floor there was little redress from the ever quickening pace of the line. When workers grew too old or too infirm to maintain the daily rhythm of the shop floor, they faced loss of the only profession for which they were prepared to enter with no security to see them through their remaining years. Ford was a singular example, but throughout the industry shop floor discipline was frequently harsh, and arbitrary, with few mechanisms for pursuing a grievance. Walter Reuther summed up the situation workers faced in the plants: "When men walked into their jobs, they left their dignity, their citizenship, and their humanity outside."[44]

Reuther Builds His West Side Local

The trolley leaving the Thirty-fifth Street transfer stop rolled straight to the Rouge, but to get there Reuther had to first win over the workers in the lesser plants that formed much of the industrial base on his West Side turf. The sound truck and covert meetings brought awareness of the new local inside the plants, but to organize on a mass scale dramatic action was needed to draw reluctant workers to embrace the new union. The Roosevelt landslide had already emboldened workers at Bendix in South Bend and Midland Steel in Detroit to strike and win concessions from a management that was startled by the solidarity and union sentiment expressed by the workers.[45] Reuther knew it was time to assert the viability of his union and his leadership. He selected the Kelsey-Hayes Wheel Company as his target.

Kelsey-Hayes was selected for a number of reasons. Unlike the Rouge or the GM Fleetwood and Ternstedt plants, it was not too big to tackle, but with about 4000 workers in 2 units, it was not an insignificant employer. It was a major supplier of wheels and brake drums for Ford that could cripple Ford production if a long strike ensued. The Bendix strike prompted Ford to transfer brake dies from Bendix to Kelsey, whose labor situation was considered more stable.[46] The paternalistic management of Kelsey-Hayes had accommodated an AFL federal union presence in the company for the previous three years. The AFL union waxed and waned in membership as its impotence was made apparent, but it had established some union sentiment in the Kelsey workforce and a sense of complacency in Kelsey management. Clandestine meetings between Reuther and workers from the West Side plants were often penetrated by spies, resulting in discharge of men or women harboring union sentiments. At Kelsey-Hayes, there were few people discharged for meeting with Reuther, and union activists were able to be hired using their real names.[47]

The main impetus for the union movement in Kelsey-Hayes came from the skilled workforce—the inspectors and foremen whose white collar aspirations were frustrated by the Great Depression. The old AFL federal union was led by Michael Manning, a man in his forties who had hired on at Kelsey in 1930 as an inspector and been promoted to foreman in 1935. Manning was an ally of Francis Dillon and had strongly opposed the revolt against the old leadership at the South Bend convention. Manning served as chairman of the AFL's Detroit Autoworkers Council, but, typifying the attitude of the AFL leadership, he did not believe the autoworkers had the ability to organize an industrial union. "They are not experienced enough to conduct it and they have no money to run it," he reported to the AFL bosses after the Atlantic City convention brought the issue of industrial unions to the fore.[48]

The Secretary-Treasurer of the moribund federal union was Frank Manfried, an electrician from a German-Jewish family from New York who came to Detroit to find work in the auto industry. He was hired at Kelsey after being excluded from employment at Ford because of the company's anti-Semitic hiring bias.[49] At Kelsey he saw his wages cut by 30% during the Depression after he was demoted to the production line.[47] Manfried belonged to the same generation as Reuther and was a strong backer of CIO affiliation in Atlantic City.

Kelsey-Hayes President George Kennedy was judged "a fair guy" by Manfried and "[the fairest man] in the city to work for"[50] by Michael Manning. Kennedy recognized the pressures coming from Washington and from an increasingly militant workforce and sought to accommodate them by taking a paternalistic approach to the union sentiment in his plant. He paid some of his production workers ten cents an hour more than other parts suppliers in the city[51] but there was a wide disparity in wages within the workforce, particularly between men and women doing the same job. The average wage in the auto industry had shrunk by almost half of what it was before the Depression, and the average at Kelsey was less than half the average pay at Ford.[52] Kennedy sought to dampen worker discontent by establishing a system of elected "watchmen" that functioned as shop stewards in settling minor grievances. He accepted the AFL presence in his plant, but refused to recognize it as the sole bargaining agent for his workers. He refused to hold an NRA labor board election in 1935, claiming "[it was the steadfast policy of the company] to deal with any individual employee, or with any group of our employees... in relation to hours, wages, or other working conditions."[53]

With failure by the federal union to win recognition as sole bargaining agent for Kelsey workers, its membership drifted away. The AFL union had a membership of 2500 at its peak, but with its ineffectiveness that number dwindled to a stalwart few. Frank Manfried summarized the weakness of the AFL union when he later recalled "We did not have anybody that actually knew [what to do] and we...were just beginning, with the result that we were maneuvered."[54]

Walter Reuther provided the aggressive leadership the old union lacked. Working with Manfried, he established key contacts within the company and was tipped when job openings occurred at the plant. Reuther issued a call to his old college roommate Merlin Bishop and his brother Victor to come to Detroit and take jobs at Kelsey-Hayes. Brookwood acquaintances George Edwards and Frank Winn arrived from Dallas to participate in the effort. Edwards joined Bishop and Victor Reuther on the shop floor in Department 49. Department 49, where brake shoes were assembled for Ford, was singled out as the target for a work stoppage because it had the greatest concentration of devoted unionists and because it was central to the production process in the plant.

Walter Reuther began the battle at Kelsey Hayes with about a dozen dedicated lieutenants stationed in Department 49 and perhaps 35 committed unionists in the whole plant whose workforce now approached 5000 people.[55] Tuesday, December 11 was set as the date the job action would occur, but only about ten people in the plant knew the plan in advance.[56] With no income of his own, no financial support from the international, much of the family earnings plowed into the organizational effort, and no certainty how the workers at Kelsey would embrace his efforts, Reuther embarked on a gambit that had a high risk of failure and severe consequences in the event that it did.

On the 11th more of the core unionists were alerted that something might happen that afternoon. About twenty minutes before the scheduled shift change, a husky Polish woman, who had fainted on the job once before, fell to the floor in an apparent faint. Immediately Victor Reuther pulled a switch to stop the line and shouted, "Strike! We've had enough of this speedup!"[57] Bishop and Edwards and a few of the plant militants ran through the plant yelling strike and pulling switches to stop production. Soon a crowd of bewildered workers from both shifts gathered around Victor Reuther, who had mounted a shipping crate and began regaling the workers about the brutal speedup that they had been forced to endure and the need for a union to win better pay and working conditions. As the crowd continued to grow, the plant personnel manager Charles Danzig approached Victor and demanded to know what he was doing. Victor replied that he was explaining to the workers why the plant needed a union. Danzig demanded that he get back to work. Victor replied that the only way these men would get back to work was if Danzig and Kennedy sat down with Walter Reuther.[58] Danzig said "Who the hell is Walter Reuther?" When informed who he was and how to reach him, Danzig put in a call to Reuther who was waiting by the phone at the Thirty-fifth Street headquarters.

Danzig barked to Reuther, "I want you to tell these men to get back to work."

Reuther replied, "Where are you?"

Danzig informed him that he was in the plant, to which Reuther replied, "I'm outside the plant and can't tell anybody to get back to work as long as I'm here. Send a car over to pick me up and take me into to the plant, and I'll talk to the guys."

When Walter Reuther arrived at the plant, Victor was still perched on his crate extolling the virtues of a union. Walter took over his brother's platform and continued to exhort the workers about the union. Danzig grabbed his trousers and demanded to know, "What the hell is this? You're supposed to tell them to go back to work."

Walter replied, "I can't tell them to do anything until I first get them organized."[59]

Five hundred workers from all over the McGraw Avenue plant were packed into Department 49 for hours listening to the strike leaders rally them to the union cause.[60] Finally, management agreed to hold talks with Reuther and an elected strike committee the next day and the workers returned to their jobs.

Negotiations over the next two weeks went nowhere. The company was willing to give on the salary demand, but adamantly refused to offer recognition to Local 174 as the bargaining agent for its employees. George Kennedy was under pressure from the Employer's Association of Detroit (EAD) and it hard line President Chester Culver not to give any concessions to the union.[61] The company stalled for time, expecting to wait out the workers until the job action lost momentum and the insurgency dissolved. Personnel Manager Danzig circulated through the plant offering individual workers raises in an attempt to get them to abandon the union.

The company also tried to revive the moribund company union, sending telegrams to all its employees inviting them to a union meeting on the afternoon of the second Sunday of the strike. This provided Reuther with another theater to surprise the company and renew the optimism and spirit of solidarity in the workers. Reuther scheduled his own meeting earlier on Sunday then led 500 fired-up workers over to the company meeting with their invitations in hand. The company spokesmen were escorted off the stage by a handful of tough union hands, and Reuther and area organizer Richard Frankensteen took over the meeting and orchestrated a vote to disband the rival company union and join the UAW. Hundreds of new membership cards were signed that Sunday afternoon.[62]

Kennedy and the EAD now realized they were dealing with a much more capable and determined opponent than the timid federal union, and they toughened their position. The following Monday the company rejected outright union demands to disband the company union and recognize Reuther's local as the sole bargaining agent for its workers. It also reneged on an agreement to allow the elected strike committee to report on negotiations in both of the company's facilities.[63] Reuther felt he had little choice but to call a sit-down strike for both plants. About 500 men were called upon to occupy the plants with the remainder of the membership assigned picketing and support duties.

The sit-down strike was the union weapon of choice during the rise of the CIO, but once the shop doors closed and the men were alone in the expanse of the near empty plant, the uncertainties and fears played on their minds. The company exploited the workers' vulnerability by threatening dismissal if they didn't vacate and later sending telegrams purportedly from family members experiencing an emergency. George Edwards proved especially valuable inside the plant during the sit-in. The former National Student Association President commanded respect from the workers, and was instrumental in holding them together in the face of company pressure.

On the second day of the sit-down, Merlin Bishop sent an urgent appeal to Reuther: "Walter, *please* send some food in for us. We had only bread and coffee so far, and it is now 2:00 PM."[64] The men in the plant were becoming restless. Reuther had planned for a series of short work disruptions that would compel the company to bargain on wages, the speed up of production, and recognition of Local 174 as the sole bargaining agent for Kelsey-Hayes workers. The sit-down forced the local to provide logistical support to a much bigger union offensive.

The small staff at the Thirty-fifth Street headquarters had to secure provisions from sympathetic local merchants, set up soup kitchens, and bolster the resolve of the men inside the plants with a substantial, spirited picket line outside. In addition to food, musical instruments and Christmas decorations were sent in to the plant, and country music ensembles, barbershop quartets, and holiday choirs formed to bolster spirits and relieve boredom. As the days passed a camaraderie developed between the men and their commitment to the union strengthened.

The supporting staff at headquarters consisted mostly of the Reuther family. Walter barely slept during the two weeks the plants were occupied. May called in sick from her job and prepared handbills that were distributed to the workers. Sophie helped with chores in the office and translated the union literature into Polish. Victor remained outside the plant to assist his brother and spent a considerable time manning the sound truck, blaring instructions to the pickets and encouragement to the men inside. Frank Winn became the press secretary for the local, briefing reporters and issuing press releases to counter the flow of propaganda issuing from the company spokesmen. An agreement between the railroad workers and the young leader of the Detroit teamsters, Jimmy Hoffa, to honor the UAW picket lines ensured that no goods would leave the Kelsey facilities.[65]

Unable to win a quick surrender inside the plants, the company sent in a dozen strikebreakers on the first Friday to get some production started and encourage the less committed workers to trickle back to work. Bishop led a contingent of strikers who trapped the scabs in a first-aid station, while Walter Reuther summoned a force of thousands of workers from around the city to surround the plants. The scabs were given fifteen minutes to leave the plant by Bishop, and his ultimatum was echoed by a chorus of "fifteen minutes" and "throw the scabs out" from the large crowd assembled outside.[66] Kelsey management demanded that the police, but Mayor Couzens, conscious of the union support that secured his election and the mood of the country in the wake of the Roosevelt landslide, refused to give the order.[67] An agreement between Reuther and city officials to allow the strikebreakers to leave the plant peacefully averted a riot, and checked another company gambit.

As the strike entered its second week pressures to find a settlement increased on both the company and the union. The lack of brake shoes and wheels had forced Ford to curtail production and lay off workers. When a rumor surfaced that Ford was going to send in a contingent of its infamous plant security men to remove the dies and ship them over to the Rouge, Reuther and Frankensteen reinforced the picket lines with workers from around the city while the men inside barricaded the doors and prepared to resist any attempt to remove their most important asset. The attack never came and the union rolls were swelled by thousands of new members, inspired by yet another union victory.[68]

Harry Bennett, the Ford satrap for all personnel policy, informed Kennedy that he either settle the strike or Ford would look for other suppliers.[69] Ford looked upon its suppliers and their association, the EAB, in much the same manner George III had looked upon his colonists and their meddlesome legislatures. Bennett's ultimatum served notice on Kennedy that he could not simply let the strike drag on and wait out the union.

Reuther too, was under pressure to get a settlement done quickly. The meager union treasury could not sustain a long work stoppage, and the fast approaching Christmas holiday loomed as a date at which the men's desire to spend time with their families might seriously erode their support for the job action. When John Gillespie, Bennett's tough lieutenant in charge of the Ford supply network called Frankensteen and asked him to specify the union's minimum demands, an unsatisfactory settlement for both sides was hammered out. The union got its minimum wage increased to 75 cents an hour for both sexes. Victor Reuther saw his hourly rate double and some women saw theirs triple, but there was no immediate raise for the skilled workers who formed the backbone of the strike effort.[70] There was only a statement by Kennedy that overtime pay and wages for people in the higher brackets would be adjusted. Significantly there was no recognition of the UAW as sole bargaining agent for the Kelsey workers, and no commitment to disband the company union. There was a promise not to discriminate against union workers.

When Reuther and Frankensteen took the agreement to the men in the plant, they faced a tough fight. George Edwards was dismayed by the accord and told Reuther that the failure to win higher wages for the skilled workers would breed resentment once they returned to work. Reuther replied "Yes, and they will fight to raise their pay once they are back to work."[71] Chester "Moon" Mullins, the "hillbilly anarchist" led the stiffest resistance to the pact and based his final resistance on the fact that he just "did not trust the bastards."[72] Reuther finally prevailed in getting the men to come out by telling them that the resources of the UAW were needed for the upcoming campaign with General Motors. If the union were to win that, then all of the demands made upon Kelsey would be met, but if they lost, the entire union struggle would be in jeopardy.

The men left the plant on December 23—two days before Christmas. Some of their misgivings were assuaged by the heroes' welcome they received from the men and women waiting outside. To many of the production workers and much of the general public, the union had won a victory at Kelsey-Hayes. The local survived and began to prosper. The 78 members it claimed before the strike at Kelsey had now grown to over 3,000 and before the end of 1937 would grow to more than 35,000.[73] True to Reuther's prediction, soon after UAW victories at GM and Chrysler, Kelsey-Hayes, as other supplier plants on the West Side, recognized the UAW as the sole bargaining agent for their workers, and agreed to a 20% reduction in the speed of their assembly line.[74]

The management of the Kelsey-Hayes strike was a personal triumph for the young Reuther. He showed his mettle in the face of a much more entrenched adversary. He displayed resourcefulness in parrying every initiative of the company, and organizational skills in managing the logistics of supplying the needs of the men in the plants. He was a leader to whom thousands of workers entrusted their livelihood during the strike and deferred to his judgment in accepting the settlement.

When the union finally won recognition at Kelsey-Hayes, Reuther was subjected to the corrupting influences that came to stigmatize the labor movement. The insurance agent that handled the Kelsey account showed up in his office one afternoon and informed him of the deal he had negotiated with the company personnel director in which the two would split the commission. He was now offering Reuther one-third of the next contract.[75] Reuther was irate and threw the man out of his office, but the incident apprised him of the extremes needed to forestall corruption in the organization when he became president of the union.

The Battle of Bulls' Run

On the UAW fight card, Kelsey-Hayes was one of the preliminary matches. General Motors was the main event. Many on the Executive Board felt that GM was too big and too diversified for the nascent UAW to challenge and that Chrysler, with much of its production centralized in Dodge Main in Hamtramck, was the more inviting target. Instead, without authorization from the board, Fred Pieper, an ally of Homer Martin, called a strike in the Fisher Body plant in Atlanta. Two days later, the Kansas City GM plant went out on strike. Kansas City was the home base of President Martin, and his role in instigating these actions in the periphery of the GM empire was evident.

With two plants on strike, Homer Martin wired the imperious GM President William Knudsen on December 20th to request a meeting.[76] Martin and UAW Secretary-Treasurer George Addes met with Knudsen the next day. Knudsen, commenting on the Kelsey-Hayes strike three days earlier, said that "General Motors believes that collective bargaining is here to stay."[77] During the meeting with Martin and Addes he qualified that statement by refusing to bargain nationally with the UAW and instead suggesting that the Atlanta and Kansas City strikes be negotiated separately. Martin, to the dismay of the leadership of both the UAW and the CIO, did not object to Knudsen's proposal and stated afterward that his meeting with Knudsen was "completely amicable."[78]

Martin's subsequent meeting with John L. Lewis was anything but amicable. In the GM corporate structure, the individual plant managers were given much leeway in meeting the production standards anticipated by the GM top management, but the corporate culture and personnel decisions affecting that culture were strictly enforced at the top. In any negotiation within an individual plant, the union would be dealing with the full weight of the General Motors Corporation and all the redundancy built into that organization. It would be a recipe for disaster. A chastened Martin drafted a letter to Knudsen demanding a national conference between labor and management. Knudsen never replied.

The premature job actions in Atlanta and Kansas City alerted GM to imminent labor problems and it moved to transfer essential dies from the Fisher Body plants in Flint to other GM facilities less likely to be struck. Flint was a company town. GM controlled the city governance, the police, the local press, and even much of the local clergy.[779] Even so, there was a fledgling union presence in the plants that was manifested a month earlier when a sit-down in the Body-in-White Department of Fisher Body One forced the company to reinstate three welders who had been fired after winning some concessions during a brief job action the previous day.[80]

Wyndham Mortimer had been assigned to Flint shortly after the South Bend convention. Mortimer assumed the task of merging the separate unions in the city into one amalgamated Local 156. Mortimer met with small groups of workers in their homes, but soon discovered that the local ranks were infested with company spies, and workers meeting with him were summarily fired shortly afterward. Mortimer worked tirelessly against a backdrop of hostility from company agents and from a significant Klan presence in the city, but he had difficulty relating to the workers in Flint and leaders of Local 156 asked the CIO to replace him with Bob Travis.[81] Travis delivered much the same message as Mortimer, but with a cadence more attuned to the autoworker's ear.

Travis became aware of the organizational work done by Roy Reuther during his time in Flint as a FERA instructor and requested he be dispatched to Flint as his assistant. Travis and Roy Reuther trod much the same ground as Mortimer, but in a more favorable climate. The LaFollette Committee on Civil Liberties focused a public spotlight on the extent of General Motors' network of spies and tipped Travis and Roy Reuther to the identity of spies on the local executive board. At the next union meeting, after receiving a tip, Roy Reuther stood before the assembled and announced that they had uncovered a stool pigeon sitting in their midst. The crowd yelled "name him, name him," but Roy continued with a denunciation of any Judas that would sell out his brothers for thirty pieces of silver. As the crowd grew more impatient and more resentful of the traitor in their midst, Roy finally acceded to the demands and said, "Perhaps this lonely creature would prefer to rise and confess before I am compelled to identify him publicly. I will count to ten and if he has not risen to his feet, I will point him out. One..." Only the voice of Roy Reuther slowly intoning each number like a boxing referee standing over a helpless pugilist disturbed the silence draping the hall. When he finally reached ten and the man had not risen to his feet, he pointed to the local board member John Stott. A visibly shaken Stott rose from his seat and was escorted from the hall by a pair of burly union men who were previously assigned the task. Stott was warned that for his own safety he should leave Flint immediately.[82] The drama made good theater for the people in the hall and signaled that the union now had an ability to aggressively ferret out a corporate spy lurking in its midst.

When the company tried to remove strategic dies from the Flint Fisher Body plants, the union had little choice but to occupy the plants and prevent the transfers. A sit-down strike was called at both Fisher Body One and Two on December 30, 1936. John L. Lewis originally tried to discourage the sit-down fever sweeping the auto plants, but once the plants were occupied, he committed the full resources of the CIO to the strike. Lewis emphasized that "attempts to settle this widespread confusion through local plant conferences and with plant managers devoid of authority would be a futile waste of time."[83] It was Lewis, not Homer Martin, who would dictate the course of this strike.

After the occupation of the Fisher Body plants in Flint and Cleveland, both sides sparred cautiously, feeling each other out during the opening rounds of the conflict. Both sides went to the court of public opinion to solicit support that might serve their course of action later. General

Motors also went to the court of Judge Edward D. Black to secure a court order for the union to evacuate the occupied plants immediately. When the sheriff went to the plants with 100 policemen and 60 plant guards to enforce the edict, he was greeted with jeers and catcalls, and retreated without securing compliance of the order.

Once again Homer Martin frustrated Lewis and the UAW hierarchy by rushing to assure the country that the strikers would obey the court order and vacate the plants.[84] An angry Lewis dispatched Homer on an organizing odyssey to the unreached plants in the hinterland. With Martin out of the picture, the CIO looked for other ways to react to the court order. CIO counsel Lee Pressman learned that Judge Black owned 3365 shares of GM stock worth almost a quarter million dollars.[85] The judge was completely discredited and forced to disqualify himself from the case.

With the legal route temporarily thwarted, the company next decided to confront the union head on with a rival organization more beholding to General Motors. GM encouraged the formation of a group called the Flint Alliance that claimed to represent men and women who were satisfied with their jobs at GM and just wanted to get back to work. The Alliance was founded by a former Buick paymaster and Flint mayor, George Boysen, who disingenuously claimed "we merely wish an enrollment for its moral effect toward soothing the strike movements and restoring peace in Flint and men and women to their jobs."[86] With GM support, Boysen was able to employ a New York public relations man to publicize his movement. He claimed 15,000 workers joined his Alliance on the first day it was formed.[87] Joining the Flint Alliance only required filling out a membership card with no dues or fee to join. It was a safe way for an auto worker to register affinity with the company regardless of his true feelings. The union labeled the Boysen movement a company union and trumpeted that message through the sound system mounted on a car usually manned by Victor Reuther.

The Flint Alliance was able to enlist a large majority of the hesitant Flint workforce, but was not able to dislodge the unionists from the plants or shrink the picket lines around them by either "moral effect" or vigilante tactics. After nearly two weeks of stalemate during which production of GM cars was severely curtailed, the company moved to reopen the plants. On January 11th they shut off the heat in Fisher Body Two, and posted about twenty company guards at the gate to prevent food being delivered to the strikers inside. The commitment of the men inside Fisher Body Two was considered more problematic by both the union and GM than that of those in the other plant where union sentiment had a longer, more expressive history. The police were getting ready to move, and Fisher Body Two was their first target.

Victor Reuther was at strike headquarters when word of the company and police moves was received. He drove the sound car on side streets and back alleys to reach the plant. Once situated, he instructed Red Mundale, the strike leader in building # 2, to send a detachment of about thirty people down to persuade the guards to open the gates and let food be delivered.[88] When the detachment confronted the guards, they just stepped aside and let the squad of strikers open the gates and bring in food from a union supply truck. The company guards had no heart for their assignment. They entered the plant and phoned that they were being held captive to cover their ignominious retreat. The GM security guards spent the night of the confrontation locked inside the women's restroom.

The police attack was planned long before the guards reported their alleged captivity. The police arrived wearing gas masks and lobbing tear gas canisters at the second floor windows of the plant and at the pickets outside the building. The men inside the plant were prepared for the occasion. They had stocked piles of pound and a half hinges on the roof and strung tire inner tubes between steel bars in the roof structure to serve as giant slingshots. Every canister of gas was answered with a barrage from the roof. When the police moved close to the plant, the strikers hit them with blasts of cold water from the plant fire hoses. In the sixteen degree Fahrenheit cold, the drenched cops were quickly incapacitated. After the first assault, the police retreated, regrouped, and attacked again. The second assault was also repulsed, but not before some of the frustrated cops fired rounds of buckshot at the pickets. Thirteen pickets were wounded.[89]

Throughout the battle Victor Reuther poured forth a steady stream of instructions and encouragement from the sound car. At one point he saw a second floor window open in the building across from Fisher # 2 and a rifle pointed directly at his post. He quickly alerted the slingshot operators to the direction of his assailant, and a well-placed volley of hinges drove the gunman from his perch. Victor was later proclaimed the "General" of the Battle of Bulls Run by Bob Travis for his work in directing the union forces from his seat in the sound car.[90] General Motors also singled him out later as an instigator of the violence and secured a warrant for his arrest. He was hustled out of Flint by the UAW.

After the second assault was repulsed, the strikers had a brief respite to prepare for the next attack. The strikers used every spare car available to them to blockade both ends of Chevrolet Avenue leading to the plant. When the third assault came, the police brought longer range tear gas missiles that were fired from beyond the barricades into the pickets and building. Men were choking and vomiting from the fumes, but then a fortunate shift in the wind began blowing the gas back at the police.

At the height of the battle, Genora Johnson approached Victor Reuther's sound car and asked if she could use the loud speaker. The batteries were running low, but Reuther said there was nothing to lose in giving her a chance to speak. She rebuked the police with "Cowards! Cowards! Shooting into the bellies of unarmed men and firing at mothers of children." The crowd of onlookers who were cordoned off behind the police barrier grew silent at the sound of a woman's voice coming from the sound car. Then Johnson addressed the women in the crowd: "Break through those police lines and come down here and stand beside your husbands and your brothers and your uncles and your sweethearts."[91] After a few moments one woman began to move forward. A policeman grabbed her by the back of her coat, but she slipped out of the coat and came forward.[92] Soon other women followed her lead, and men and women in the crowd surged forward. The "bulls" retreated a final time, and the Battle of Bulls' Run was a celebrated union victory.

The violence on January 11th brought Governor Frank Murphy to Flint. Murphy arrived in Flint shortly after midnight when the violence was winding down. The Governor called out the National Guard to secure the peace, and got a commitment from GM not to provoke the situation by turning off heat in the buildings or preventing the men from receiving food. Murphy worked tirelessly for the next three days to negotiate a deal between the company and union to have the strikers leave the occupied plants in return for the company agreeing not to resume production or transfer dies from these plants while negotiations continued. On January 15, the Governor received a letter from Knudsen and two other GM executives stating that the UAW agreed to leave the occupied plants in Flint, Detroit, and Anderson, Indiana as "soon as practicable" and that GM would meet with UAW representatives to bargain on the basis of its proposal. The letter further stipulated that GM would take no reprisals against the strikers and would not try to reopen those plants or remove equipment from them for the duration of a negotiation period that should not exceed fifteen days.[93] The Flint strikers were skeptical of the company's intentions, but Mortimer, Travis, George Addes, and Ed Hall labored to convince them that it represented a big concession by GM and it represented a victory for the union.

Walter Reuther had pulled workers out of the West Side Fleetwood and Cadillac plants earlier in the week, and these plants along with the Guide Lamp plant were the first to be evacuated. The Flint plants were about to be evacuated when Bill Lawrence, a reporter for the United Press, happened by chance to see a press release in the office of Flint Alliance publicist Larry Williamson stating that Knudsen and Boysen had agreed to meet the next day to negotiate a contract. Lawrence stopped by the union headquarters on his way to cover the story of the men leaving the Fisher Body plants, and told Travis of the planned meeting between GM and the Flint Alliance leader.[94] Travis informed John Brophy of the CIO who notified John L. Lewis. Lewis was furious, and immediately called Mortimer and Travis to call off the evacuation of the plants. When Lawrence arrived at Fisher Body Two, he saw Wyndham Mortimer racing up the stairs, shouting "The evacuation is off! We've been double-crossed."[95] Pressed by Lawrence to explain what had happened, Mortimer replied "You should know. You told us."

The insincerity of the GM pledge to Murphy became more apparent when Cadillac workers on the West Side received telegrams soon after leaving their factories ordering them to report for work two days later. In Anderson, Indiana, General Motors did little to discourage a strong Klan presence in the town from intimidating strikers and burning the union headquarters.[96] The agreement negotiated by Murphy became a dead letter when GM notified the press that it did indeed intend to negotiate with Boysen.

As the stalemate dragged on, the union situation was becoming desperate. The company again went to court and got another injunction ordering the strikers to leave the plants by February 3. The union did not have the resources to maintain a long strike, public opinion was turning against the wave of sit-downs washing through the basic industries, and pressure was mounting on Governor Murphy to end the illegal occupation of the plants. Kermit Johnson, the union leader in Chevrolet Four realized that his plant produced the engines for virtually every Chevrolet sold in the world. If that heavily guarded plant could be shut down, GM would be forced to negotiate. One night Johnson showed his wife Genora the sketch of a plan to capture the plant.[97] Chevy plants number 8 and 6 were located near plant number 4, and in Johnson's plan workers from those two plants would help secure number 4. A diversion was needed to draw the Pinkertons and local vigilantes that GM had assigned to Chevrolet Four away from the building long enough for the union men to occupy and secure the plant. The plan called for an attack on Chevrolet Nine to be approved in a larger council of strike leaders that included several suspected GM spies. Only a handful of the most trusted people were to know the true target. When the attempt to shut down Chevrolet Nine occurred, GM would shift some of its security from nearby plants, including number 4, to thwart the takeover of the apparent target. Only then would Travis and Roy Reuther lead a second group of strikers into number 4.

When the plan was presented at a Socialist Party meeting, Walter Reuther was firmly opposed.[98] He thought the workers at Flint did not have the necessary experience to carry out such a plan and that a futile attempt would only further demoralize the men in the Fisher Body plants and weaken the union effort. Reuther's opposition caused the plan to be rejected, but Genora Johnson did not give up. She wrote to Norman Thomas, the oft times presidential candidate of the Socialists, seeking his support for Kermit's plan. Thomas referred the letter to the Socialist Party Labor Secretary, Frank Trager. Trager thought the plan had merit and came to Flint to assess the situation for himself. He found a committed core of workers at the Socialist's headquarters in Pengelly

Hall, and at the next meeting of party leaders spoke in favor of the plan. Walter Reuther still opposed the idea, but Roy Reuther voted with the majority to approve the plan.[99]

Genora Johnson received world-wide recognition for her role in the Battle of Bulls' Run, but the contribution of this 23-year-old woman was far more pervasive than that singular event. On the first night of the strike Genora witnessed a number of wives yelling at their striking husbands that if they did not come out of that plant immediately, they would divorce them.[100] A number of chastened husbands climbed down the ladder from their second floor redoubt and followed their wives home. Genora Johnson resolved to create a supportive female cadre that would feel a much greater part of their loved ones' struggles at work. She formed a Women's Auxiliary that grew to over 1000 members.[101] Women from the Auxiliary attended classes in public speaking so that they could present the woman's perspective more effectively, and learned lessons in labor history and the role women played in the turn of the century garment workers strike. The men resisted the idea of women involved in union affairs at first, but most came to appreciate the positive affect it had upon their marriage.

After January 11th, Genora Johnson formed a Women's Emergency Brigade to stand shoulder-to-shoulder with the men on the picket line and to respond to situations like the planned takeover of Chevrolet # 9. Genora addressed a large gathering of the Women's Auxiliary and proposed the new brigade. She stressed the dangers that could be faced and the sacrifices that would be required. When she was finished, a woman in her seventies was the first to stand up. Johnson told her no, that this would be too hard for her, to which the woman replied "You can't keep me out. My sons work in that factory. My husband worked in that factory before he died and I have grandsons in there."[102] She then stepped forward and signed her card in front of the rest of the women. Four hundred women joined the Emergency Brigade. They wore red berets and a white arm band with E B stitched on it. Genora Johnson organized the brigade in military fashion. She selected five lieutenants and named herself the captain.

When the feint against Chevrolet # 9 occurred, the Emergency Brigade was in the center of the action. The plan to allow the corporate spies to alert GM and draw much of their security force into building 9 worked to perfection. The men attempting to take over that plant were taking a terrible beating. One of the bloodied strikers inside broke a window and called out, "They're gassing us in here."[103] The women rushed into action, breaking windows to let air into the building. The men assigned to take over plant # 9 did not know they were a diversion for the main attack. They put up a spirited fight and were severely beaten.

When the battle in number 9 was fully engaged, Ed Kronk and Walter Reuther who had come up from Detroit with members of their "flying squadrons" converged upon Chevrolet # 4 from two directions. The roughly 100 Detroiters from the two groups entered the plant and signaled the union members inside to pull the switches and shut down the plant. With security absent, the plant was readily seized, but the men inside needed time to secure the entrances before the police arrived.

When the battle at Chevrolet # 9 ended, Genora Johnson sent the Emergency Brigade back to Pengelly Hall to await further instructions, then proceeded with her five lieutenants as inconspicuously as they could toward Building # 4. The small troop arrived just before the police and distributed themselves across the main gate. When the police arrived and ordered them to move aside, they refused and engaged the cops in a discussion of how they would act if roles were reversed and they were in the plant and their wives out front. While the banter was distracting the police from their assigned duty the rest of the Emergency Brigade arrived wearing their red berets singing Solidarity Forever.[104] The gates were not breached, the plant secured, and the day ended with the UAW holding the jewel in the crown of the GM empire.

On February 1, the UAW took possession of Chevrolet plant number 4. On February 2, Judge Paul Gadola issued an injunction ordering the strikers to vacate Fisher Body One and Two and threatened the union with a $15 million fine if the injunction was disobeyed.[105] Both the union and the company had played their high cards. Whether the forecast on February 2 was for an early settlement or 6 more weeks of labor strife lay in the hand of Governor Murphy.

Judge Gadola's injunction could only be enforced by the National Guard, and only Murphy could order the Guard into action. As Governor, it was also Murphy's obligation to enforce the law, but Murphy temporized, seeking to avoid a bloody confrontation that enforcement of the Judge's order would produce. Murphy responded to his critics on the right by saying "I'm not going down in history as 'Bloody Murphy!' If I sent those soldiers right in on the men there'd be no telling how many would be killed. It would be inconsistent with everything I have stood for in my whole political life."[106]

Murphy's political life before and after the events in Flint exemplified his underlying humanity and his commitment to those things he stood for. As a judge in the 1920's he presided over the emotionally-charged Ossian Sweet murder trial and ensured that a black defendant received a fair hearing from a not often color blind judicial process. As Mayor of Detroit at the start of the Great Depression, Murphy established an unemployment committee of civic leaders to identify all the residents of Detroit who were unemployed and not receiving welfare and charged the committee with the task of delivering aid to these people. Murphy also founded the United States Conference of Mayors and served as its first President. After leaving the governorship, Murphy became the Attorney General of the United States and founded the Civil Liberties Section inside the Justice Department. Murphy was appointed to the Supreme Court in 1940 and served on the High Court until his death in 1949. While on the Court, he was accused of ruling more from the heart than head and a strict adherence to the law. His opinions usually favored women, minorities, and the disenfranchised. His most memorable dissent was his fierce opposition to the internment of Japanese Americans during World War II which he termed "legalized racism."[107] Murphy offered a synopsis of his judicial philosophy in writing an opinion in the 1944 case of Falbo v. United States which included, "The law knows no finer hour than when it cuts through formal concepts and transitory emotions to protect unpopular citizens against discrimination and persecution."[108]

On the morning of February 3, John L. Lewis boarded a train for Detroit from Washington's Union Station with a melodramatic departure quote from Tennyson to the assembled reporters: "Let there be no moaning at the bar when I put out to sea."[109] Lewis realized that Murphy held the trump cards and made sure he held them back until after the CIO had made its game. Upon arriving in Flint, Lewis made sure that the Governor's moral compass was aligned with its historic pole.

He responded to Murphy's threat to enforce the law by reminding him of his family history.

> "Your grandfather was executed for resisting real law, law passed by the Lords Spiritual and Temporal and assented to by the Commons and sealed with the King's imprimatur. My compliments to your ancestors and I hope they will be able to look down and be proud of their Governor Frank P. Murphy, who was willing to resist not the law but a General Motors' suborned injunction."[110]

For nine days Lewis parried and finessed and played his hand with swagger. When the General Motors team of Knudsen, Donaldson Brown, and John T. Smith were in the midst of presenting a strong, coherent argument to the CIO chief, he used reports of a Pinkerton spy snooping around his Washington home to interject "What's the basis for your statement? Some lousy Pinkerton? I want to know who of you sent a Pinkerton bastard to spy on me and my home in Alexandria. I look on my home as my castle and I guard my privacy jealously. Who sent that Pinkerton, was it you Brown?" Donaldson Brown was visibly taken aback and claimed he had no idea what Lewis was talking about. "Was it you, Smith?" Smith insisted upon his ignorance of the matter. "Well how is General Motors run anyway? What about the third one, you Knudsen?"[111] When Lewis finished his diatribe the GM negotiators were flustered and lost the thread of their previous argument.

The corporation could not get the federal or state government to intervene on its behalf, but it had one ally using its influence to end the strike—the AFL. The parent organization disassociated itself from its rebellious offspring and endorsed the company's bargaining position. When Knudsen produced a telegram from AFL President William Green declaring that his organization opposed granting exclusive recognition to the wayward UAW, Lewis calmly stood up, reached for his overcoat, coldly stared at William Knudsen, and offered a bit of sarcastic advice. "Now that Mr. Green and the AFL have entered this picture, I suggest that you gentlemen also invite Haille Selassie, because he certainly has as much of a following among your workers."[112] Even Knudsen appreciated the humor and the truth behind Lewis's bit of theater.

As the days passed and the company could move neither the men in the plants nor the government officials, its bargaining posture softened. Nineteen thirty seven was a good year for automobile sales, but the production of Chevrolets had dropped from 50,000 a month in December to just 125 in the first week of February.[113] John L. Lewis held firm against Judge Gadola, Governor Murphy, Labor Secretary Frances Perkins, and President Roosevelt that he would not order the men from the plants until the company recognized the UAW as exclusive bargaining agent for its workers.

Finally on February 11, an agreement satisfactory to Lewis was worked out between Murphy and GM. Murphy, Knudsen, Brown and Smith came to Lewis' hotel room where they found the CIO chief in bed. Murphy informed Lewis that a satisfactory agreement had been reached and that he should sign the document at the top, to which Lewis replied that he would sign it at the bottom because there would be no agreement unless he approved.[114]

The agreement recognized the UAW as the bargaining agent for its members, promised no discrimination against union members and no interference with the union's right to organize. It promised to begin negotiations with the UAW on the union's January 4th list of demands, and it promised not to engage with any other bargaining group in the 20 GM plants that were struck for a period of 6 months. It was not a complete victory for the union, but a significant departure from General Motors' history of intransigence against any attempt by its employees to organize independently.

Many of the workers in the Flint auto plants were transplanted Southerners who retained the prejudices of their former home. General Motors, also, was particularly discriminatory in its hiring policies. There were few black workers in Flint, and all were either in the Buick foundry plant or doing janitorial work. Only one of the sit-downers was black. Roscoe Van Zandt remained in Plant 4 when it was occupied by the strikers. On the first night he took his meal apart from his fellow workers, but that was a cause of embarrassment to many in the plant. The Fisher Body plant had seat cushions that the union men used for sleeping, but the engine plant had only one table and blanket. When deciding who among them who should get the table, the workers voted to give it to Van Zandt because he was the oldest and least able to endure the cold, hard floor. The nine days during which the plant was occupied provided the first opportunity any of them had to get to know this black man on a personal basis. When the workers marched out of Plant 4 in triumphant procession, it was Van Zandt who was chosen to lead them out bearing the American flag.[115]

Once GM fell with a thud, the lesser companies scurried to make their deal with the union. As Reuther predicted, Kelsey-Hayes now recognized the UAW as the bargaining agent for its workers and acceded to many of the union's earlier demands. Other suppliers recognized the inevitability of a union presence, negotiated their own contracts. The last of the West Side supplier firms to bow to UAW pressure was Federal Screw in 1938. One year after the wave of sit-ins that washed through the industry broke against a wall of public reaction, the parts supplier, its biggest customer, Ford, and the Detroit police resolved to challenge the union head on. The brief spurt of confidence that the recovery of 1936 and 37 had provided was dissipated. Unemployment was back up to 19 percent.[116] Federal Screw had cut its workforce by more than half and many of those still working were on reduced hours. People were reminded that the Great Depression had been ameliorated, but it was not yet over.

Federal Screw wanted to negotiate a 20% wage cut with the union. Local 174 representative Stanley Novak was told by his management counterpart "Things have changed in the City of Detroit. Labor is going to be put in its place, any strikes, sit-downs or otherwise, will no longer be tolerated."[117] Reuther did not want to give in on the wage reduction for fear it would precipitate similar demands from other companies in the industry and critically weaken the union. Novak told Reuther that the shop was still 75% organized, morale among the workers was good, and that the company was still making a profit.[118] Reuther prepared for a strike.

Federal Screw initiated the strike by unilaterally declaring a 10 cent hourly reduction in wages. For the first two days of the walkout,

Detroit police shepherded about thirty workers through the union picket lines to keep the plant operating. To counter the large police presence acting on behalf of the company, Reuther called on thousands of out-of-work autoworkers from all over the city to help man the picket line. He also called in the flying squadrons from Kelsey-Hayes and other heavily unionized plants on the West Side. These squadrons were made up of tough young militants, willing to answer the call to stiffen a picket line or protect a union rally anywhere in Southeastern Michigan. Like the Women's Emergency Brigade in Flint, they wore distinctive outfits and sported armbands that marked their elite status in the ranks of the labor army.

Between three and five thousand pickets marched behind a large American flag around the Federal Screw plant. Opposing them were about 600 police, including a mounted unit.[119] At about the time of the shift change the police charged and the battle was waged. The labor battles of the late thirties were like barroom brawls in cowboy movies. No arrests were made. The antagonists battled it out with fists, clubs, bottles, and bricks until one side backed off. The area around the Federal plant was Stanley Novak's turf. Neighborhood residents supported the strikers, and offered shelter and aid while the fight lasted. The Detroit police were littered with members of the Ku Klux Klan and its Black Legion offshoot. They were held in low esteem by much of the community. It was the union that claimed to speak for law and order, and it was they that they were exercising their legal rights to picket. When the police attacked community residents dumped refuse and contents from their toilet pots down on them from their upper story windows. The police were withdrawn, and the company was forced to capitulate. Pay was restored to the pre-strike level, overtime and seniority rules were improved, and Local 174 won sole bargaining rights for Federal Screw workers.[120]

Federal Screw was an impressive victory for the union and for its leader, Walter Reuther. It was also a much resented setback for Ford in its effort to defeat the union before the battle reached the gates of the River Rouge. Reuther drew the attention of Ford Security chief Harry Bennett and his thuggish assistant John Gillespie. Ford agents rented a house in Reuther's neighborhood during the Federal strike and kept track of the movements of Walter and May Reuther.[121] On the evening that the local signed the new contract with Federal Screw, two of these operatives knocked on Reuther's door with guns drawn.

One of the men, Willard Holt, had direct ties with John Gillespie and the Ford Service Department. The other, Eddie Percelli, was a small-time Detroit hoodlum. When inside, they were surprised to find the Reuthers were not alone. It was Sophie Reuther's birthday, and a small party of family and friends had gathered to celebrate. The thugs were there to take Reuther "for a ride," but the unexpected appearance of so many people flustered them, and when one of the friends jumped from a second story window to alert the neighborhood of the trouble, the pair ran off without their quarry.[122`] Reuther survived the first of several attempts on his life.

After signing the agreement with General Motors, John L. Lewis turned his attention back to steel. Steel had always been the first target in his sights, but the shop floor militancy of the autoworkers forced him to postpone those efforts and deal with autos first. With autos, the drama was carried by the young militants, who defended the occupied plants and planned the maneuver to capture Chevrolet Plant # 4. Lewis only played a major role in the final act, where with kingly presence he resolved the conflict and restored a balance to the troubled realm. Steel would be a completely Lewis production.

Lewis began his organizing campaign in steel shortly after the Atlantic City convention that gave rise to the Committee of Industrial Organizations. Lewis realized that the sentiment for an industrial union was strong in the Amalgamated Association (AA) that represented steel workers in the AFL, and gave the AA leaders an ultimatum to either be part of a Steelworkers Organizing Committee (SWOC) he was forming, join the CIO, and receive substantial financial help from the United Mine Workers, or defy the wishes of its membership and be swept aside by the organizational drive he was preparing to launch. When William Green refused to budge on the issue of organizing on an industrial basis, the AA had little choice but to accept Lewis's dictum. Lewis named one of his top lieutenants, Phillip Murray, to head the SWOC, and the old AA leadership was subordinated to Lewis and his team.

On January 9th, 1937, two days before the Battle of Bulls Run, Lewis was having lunch with his friend Senator Joseph Guffey at the Mayflower Hotel in Washington, when Myron Taylor, Chairman of the Board of United States Steel, and his wife entered the hotel dining room and nodded a greeting to Lewis.[123] After seating his wife, Taylor returned to Lewis's table and, in a moment reminiscent of the old Dean Witter television commercial, the pair had a brief conversation while the dining room fell quiet and the other patrons strained to hear what the two men discussed. When Lewis finished his meal, he went over to the Taylors' table and continued the conversation for another half hour. The two men agreed to continue the dialog in Taylor's Mayflower suite the next day. Events in Flint interrupted these meetings, but when he returned from Detroit, Lewis and Taylor resumed their discussions in Taylor's Upper East Side townhouse.

On Sunday, March 1, Lewis collected together in his New York hotel suite Sidney Hillman of the CIO, and Phil Murray and Len Pressman of the SWOC leadership and informed them that he had just reached an agreement with Myron Taylor on a contract with US Steel.[124] After summarizing the details of the agreement, he instructed Murray and Pressman to go to Pittsburgh the next morning and meet with US Steel President Benjamin Fairless, and Fairless would sign a contract with the SWOC. Murray and Pressman were stunned. The leaders of the SWOC had no idea that secret negotiations were taking place and had no input into the terms of the agreement.

The agreement called for a basic forty hour week with time and a half for overtime. It granted an across the board wage hike, and established a rudimentary grievance and seniority procedure. It recognized the SWOC for those workers it represented, but did not recognize it as the sole bargaining agent for all of its employees.

The agreement met the minimum requirements for both parties, but the popular press reported it as a great victory for labor. US Steel under the leadership of Judge Gary had been among the most intransigent companies in accepting a union role in their plants, and news of any recognition of the SWOC was regarded as a major concession from the company.

United States Steel needed labor peace. It was negotiating a big contract to supply armaments to the British government that could not be fulfilled if the company were to experience any prolonged labor stoppage.[125] Taylor realized that the SWOC was having success in organizing among steelworkers, and many of the erstwhile company unions were declaring independence and aligning with the CIO. US Steel watched the President and Governor of Michigan take a hands-off approach to the GM strike and realized it could not rely upon government support in any confrontation with the union.

John L. Lewis also had reason to avoid a costly strike. Unlike the autoworkers that were organized by young militants like the Reuther brothers, the steelworkers were organized from the top down by merging more sedentary AFL affiliated or independent unions into the SWOC. The majority of steelworkers were not yet members of the union, and Lewis could not be sure of the commitment of the rank and file. The deal gave the CIO a presence in the plants that they would be able to exploit in future negotiations.

The steel and auto unions had different beginnings and different histories throughout the CIO years. Steel was molded by its autocratic founder, John L. Lewis. Lewis, at heart, was a traditionalist Republican, whose vision of social change had no clarity beyond the factory gate. Auto unions were pieced together from the outside in by a cadre of young idealists with a broader social vision. Auto plants were arranged around a moving conveyor belt that could be shut down at several critical points by pulling a switch. The whole plant was vulnerable to a small band of committed unionists. Steel plants had few critical junctures and furnaces that had to be cooled and damped down over a period of days. There was less opportunity for a spontaneous job action and more control at the top to prevent it in the first place. For the next fifteen years, steel and autos would find themselves pulling apart more often than pulling together.

The Battle Within

In the fall of 1937, the CIO returned to its birthplace, Atlantic City, to celebrate its past success and bright future. It now boasted nearly 3.5 million members,[126] and had won great victories against the biggest giants in American industry—General Motors, United States Steel, and Goodyear Tire and Rubber. The convention brought together all shades of the political spectrum and all geographical regions of a loosely stitched together nation. They came to toast the one man in the center holding this improbable coalition together—John L. Lewis.

Off the Boardwalk, away from the salt water taffy and arcade fantasies, America was retreating into its nativistic shell. The recovery that ushered in the Roosevelt landslide and the victories being celebrated in Convention Hall had sputtered and stalled. The economy was heading into another deep recession. Factories that were hiring at the beginning of the year were now trimming their workforces. Roosevelt's popularity had ebbed; his court packing bill was bitterly resented. Continued unrest in the factories had soured public opinion on labor. The CIO was increasingly painted as red, lawless, and foreign. The industrialists who were in retreat in the winter and spring had now regrouped and were prepared to regain the initiative.

The UAW had fomented a revolution in the plants that had enhanced the power of individuals on the shop floor and thrust responsibility of shop floor governance upon the leadership. Now it faced the more difficult task of uniting the diverse forces that had carried out the revolution and governing the actions of its membership in the quasi coalition it had established with management. Management was eager for it to fail and ready to exploit any opportunity to rid itself of this troublesome entanglement.

The union did not disappoint corporate management that looked for it to fail and crumble. Homer Martin proved as incapable of leading the union as he was in negotiating with General Motors. He was a transitional figure from the old AFL federal union who was never comfortable with the radicals who built the UAW-CIO from the ground up. He saw the continuing unrest in the plants as an opportunity to purge them from their leadership positions.

Shortly after the successful conclusion of the strike at Flint, the UAW split into two competing factions. The faction backing Martin called itself the Progressive Caucus, and included Richard Frankensteen and R. J. Thomas as its most prominent members. The Unity Caucus opposing them included Socialist, Communist, and liberal activists such as the Reuther brothers, Wyndham Mortimer, Bob Travis, and George Addes. The names chosen for the two caucuses were complete misnomers. The Progressive Caucus consisted of the more conservative and reactionary elements within the union. The Unity Caucus vowed to maintain the unity that brought success to the union, but was united by very little else internally.

The Unity Caucus represented most of the core unionists that put their bodies on the line in Flint and Dodge Main and elsewhere, but after the success of those efforts, union membership swelled with a different sort of worker, and many of these newly minted members gravitated toward Martin and his "Progressives." The makeup of the two caucuses reflected the divisions in the rank-and-file between Protestant and Catholic, native and foreign born, rural and urban.

Martin was intent on purging the Communists and anyone else he considered red from the UAW. He began by removing Roy Reuther, Henry Kraus, and Bob Travis, the leaders of the Flint strike, from the UAW payroll. He moved Victor Reuther out of Detroit and dismissed Merlin Bishop and Frank Winn from the union. He prepared to go after the elected officers in the Unity Caucus at the Milwaukee convention in August of 1937. Martin probably had the votes in Milwaukee to complete his purge but for the appearance of John L. Lewis who urged re-election of the entire current leadership. "[The formation of the UAW was one of labor's] most outstanding achievements, and I think that the officers who led you throughout that enterprise and to the objective of success are deserving of your commendation."[127] Lewis wanted stability and a strong executive role, but he feared the purge being contemplated by Martin would fracture the evenly divided union.

Martin bowed to Lewis's authority, but he never gave up his intent to establish his own absolute dominance of the UAW and purge his rivals. As long as his popularity within the rank-and-file remained high, he had reasonable expectation of ultimate success, but his appeasement of General Motors and erratic leadership steadily eroded that popularity.

The visibility of the union in the daily lives of its members lay with the shop stewards who handled the day-to-day grievances workers had with their immediate bosses, the plant foremen. It was the shop steward who ensured that working conditions stipulated in the national contract were adhered to in the individual fiefdoms inside each plant. GM recognized the authority wielded by shop stewards and used all its corporate muscle to prevent an effective shop steward system from being established in its plants. The original contract substituted a bureaucratic committeeman system to handle grievances that left workers provoked by company violations with little recourse but initiation of a wildcat strike.

Before beginning negotiations on a second contract with the UAW, GM demanded assurances that it had the right to unilaterally discipline any workers engaged in an unauthorized strike. Martin readily capitulated to this demand, writing Knudsen on September 16th, 1937, "the corporation will be allowed to discharge, or otherwise discipline, union members known to be or found guilty of instigating unauthorized strikes."[128] Going further, Martin committed the UAW to taking "effective disciplinary action" against those identified by GM as wildcat strike instigators.

Martin's surrender to GM's demands was met with outrage in the shops. Walter Reuther led the attack against the terms of the contract Martin seemed on the verge of signing with GM. His publicist, Carl Haessler issued a detailed response to Martin's initiative that was mailed to every local in the country. Reuther hastily arranged a meeting of delegates from more than 40 GM plants from around the country at the Tuller Hotel in Detroit. Reuther demanded repudiation of the Martin letter, and suggested that now was the time for the union to reassert its power and demand a shop steward system in GM plants.[129] The majority of those attending agreed. Martin was roundly denounced at the conference and Reuther emerged as the champion for worker rights.

Martin and his Progressive colleagues quickly reacted to rank-and-file outrage and repudiated the contract they had been negotiating, but their change of heart was cosmetic and too late. A brief work stoppage at a Fisher Body plant in Pontiac over layoffs, speedup of production, and the transfer of work to a non-union plant in Linden, New Jersey ended when the company agreed to listen to the workers' grievances. Instead, the next day GM refused to listen to any grievances and fired four people it considered instigators of the previous job action. The company cited Martin's letter as justification for its action. On November 17th about 500 workers again occupied the Fisher Body Plant and began another sit-in. The strike action drew support from thousands of other workers in Pontiac who gathered in the union halls and enthusiastically applauded speakers who denounced Homer Martin and the agreement he had made with GM.[130]

Pontiac had been a Martin stronghold in the ongoing factional dispute. Its demographics—Protestant, conservative, small town—mirrored that of the Martin constituency. Now that constituency was in open revolt against the policies of their leader. Martin's appeal to the workers to return to work was ignored. Reuther and Mortimer urged the Executive Board to authorize the strike and support the militancy of the workers. The Board deliberated for five days while the situation in Pontiac became increasingly tense. Finally it was John L. Lewis and Earl Browder of the Communist Party that sent the men back to work.

Lewis saw how much the terrain had changed over the past six months and was not prepared to challenge Knudsen's threat that authorization of an illegal strike would put into question the value of a contract with such an unreliable partner. Lewis believed in the sanctity of contracts and had not been averse to the sentiments expressed in Martin's September letter. The Communist Party in New York did not want to jeopardize the legitimacy they had achieved during the era of the Popular Front, and ordered their members in Pontiac to end the sit-down immediately.[131] Reuther had little choice but to go along with the Executive Board order to return to work, but benefited from his earlier support of the Pontiac workers.

The Pontiac strike outcome and the unfavorable settlement negotiated with GM were disastrous. Shop steward activity in the GM plants was further diminished. The number of committeemen was reduced and the time allotted for them to handle grievances cut in half. Shop stewards were forbidden from collecting dues on company property, and Martin was given the right to exclude any other union official from meeting with GM management. The contract was termed a "wretched surrender" by Reuther,[132] but with depression conditions returning and the plants empty, there was little he could do but hold his nose and sign the accord.

The shifting allegiances and intrigues that occurred during this first round of factional warfare were reminiscent of the Byzantine court. The Unity faction, was unified only in its opposition to Martin. The Reuther group was uncomfortable in its alliance of convenience with the Communists, and others in the Unity faction had little love for the headstrong, young Reuther. Martin, the ardent anti-Communist, came under the influence of Jay Lovestone, the former head of the American Communist Party. Lovestone wormed his way into the union leadership councils after a succession of opportunistic transformations. In 1929, Lovestone was denounced from the podium as a right deviator during a Moscow meeting of the presidium of the Communist International. When he refused to recant positions that sparked the denunciation, he was removed from his post, and he left the party. He formed an opposition party that originally had the name Communist in its title, but after a succession of name changes and policy shifts, mention of Communism was dropped entirely from his revolutionary movement. By 1937 Lovestone's anti-Stalinist message supported Martin's feelings toward his opponents. Whether practicing Communists like Mortimer, Socialists like the Reuthers, non-ideological foes like George Addes, or opportunists like Frankensteen, all opposition was viewed by Martin and his Lovestonite advisers as part of a Stalinist conspiracy.

Martin responded to challenges to his leadership with purges and strong-arm tactics. The factional dispute was papered over during the 1937 Milwaukee Convention through the intervention of John L. Lewis, but the compromise left Martin with greater authority and a two-to-one control of the executive board. Martin used his new authority to consolidate his leadership of the union. Two heroes of the Flint campaign, Victor Reuther and Robert Travis were transferred to the UAW hinterlands. When Victor refused the new assignment, he was fired for economy reasons. Victor took a new position as education director within his brother's West Side local.[133] Another popular Socialist, Emil Mazey, was ousted by Martin from his position as chief organizer of the Briggs local.

Martin raised Frankensteen to the position of Assistant President, even though no such position was provided for in the constitution, but as Martin's incompetence became more evident and his position weakened, Frankensteen was wooed into the Unity Caucus by the Communists' proposal that he could become the unifying figure in the factional struggle. Frankensteen was no Communist, but he thought his own ambitions might be better served by distancing himself from the erratic Homer Martin.

Frankensteen's switch to the Unity Caucus was part of a deal that gave another former Progressive partisan, Richard Leonard, a seat on the Michigan CIO Council that had been promised to Victor Reuther. Walter Reuther flew into a rage when he learned that the Communists in the Unity Caucus had gone behind his back and made a deal with his rival. The double-cross delivered a particularly painful sting because Reuther had resisted enormous pressure from his colleagues in the Socialist Party, including his wife and brothers, to sever his connections with the Communists and "build the [Socialist] party" inside the UAW.[134] Reuther remained faithful to the Unity Caucus because his pragmatism governed his actions. He knew that New Deal reforms had sapped the appeal that Socialism once held for compassionate, progressive-minded youth, and he knew the power that the Communists wielded among hard-core unionists in the plants. He had regarded his alliance with them as essential for checking Martin and preserving a vibrant union.

When Reuther found Frankensteen huddling with two prominent UAW Communists at the April, 1938 Michigan CIO conference in Lansing, he burst into the room and demanded to know "What are you bastards doing? Don't you realize you are going to destroy the Unity Caucus, which is the only thing that can save this union?" After he was coldly rebuffed, he blurted out "If you carry out this double-cross, then count me on the other side, not only in this fight, but from here on out!"[135]

In April 1938, there was no other side for Reuther to join. The Martin presidency was leading the union to inevitable disaster. The "Reuther Group" became a third faction within the UAW power struggle. As Martin's support continued to wane, Reuther became the primary beneficiary. Reuther emerged as the most recognized anti-Communist voice within the union.

Frankensteen's defection spurred Martin into more desperate actions. On June 13, 1938 he announced to the Executive Board that he was suspending Frankensteen, Wyndham Mortimer, Ed Hall, Walter

Wells, and George Addes from the Board, and ordered the five men to stand trial before an emergency meeting of the full Board two weeks later.

The trial degenerated into a farce with an awkward beginning and a predetermined end. Before the meeting began, partisans from both caucuses engaged in a free for all. The *New York Times* reported that "blood flowed freely."[136] The trial opened with the five defendants greeting Martin with a Nazi salute and a chorus of Heil Hitler. During the trial, the defendants turned the tables on Martin by revealing letters published in the *Daily Worker* that had been stolen from the Manhattan apartment of one of Jay Lovestone's friends. The correspondence revealed Lovestone's influence over Martin and exposed a purported Martin and Lovestone plan to negotiate a sweetheart deal with Ford. The trial closed at a subsequent meeting with four of the defendants expelled from the Board and Wells suspended for three months.

Lewis was forced to intervene again in the messy affairs of the troubled union. He put the UAW under the direct control of the CIO and dispatched Phil Murray and Sidney Hillman to Detroit to negotiate another compromise. The expelled officers were reinstated, but Martin resisted tutelage from Murray and Hillman. He reacted by calling Lewis a dictator and a threat to the CIO[137] When Martin tried to reestablish his authority by opening unsanctioned negotiations with Harry Bennett and Henry Ford he began a process that would lead to his eventual ouster.

The Board finally had enough of Martin's high-handed behavior and in his absence scheduled a special meeting to elect new officers in Cleveland on March 20, 1939. Martin responded by suspending fifteen board members, including Walter Reuther, and calling his own convention to be held two weeks earlier in Detroit. The anti-Martin convention named R. J. Thomas as the compromise candidate for president, retained George Addes as Secretary-Treasurer, named Reuther the national director of the General Motors department, and placed both Reuther and Frankensteen on the Board. Two prominent Communists: Ed Hall and Wyndham Mortimer left Cleveland without a position in the UAW hierarchy.

The Martin convention attracted delegates representing 60,000 union members, less than half the total represented in Cleveland. After he was replaced by Thomas in Cleveland, there was no place left for Martin in the CIO. On April 17, he met with William Green and accepted an AFL charter for his breakaway union.

Power Under Control

The thirty-two year old Walter Reuther now had the most important labor position in the country. The union presence in General Motors was tenuous, and the emergence of Martin's AFL rival provided GM with a more compliant alternative it would try to exploit. In May, 1939, when Reuther assumed his new responsibilities, only 6 percent of GM workers were paying dues to the UAW. In Flint, the symbolic birthplace of the UAW, only 500 of the 42,000 GM workers were members in good standing of the union.[138] Reuther assessed the state of the membership as "demoralized and disillusioned."[139] Organizational activity by the union had all but ceased to exist.

Reuther confronted the situation he faced with characteristic vigor and confidence. His first act was to visit with the union councils that had been established to provide the leadership with access to the wishes and grievances of the rank-and-file in the individual plants. These meetings cheered Reuther by revealing a more militant spirit among the council activists than the lagging commitment of the larger body that was reflected by the drop in the collection of dues. The meetings also served to legitimize Reuther's appointment by establishing recognition of his leadership from the elected representatives of the membership.

The other strategic move made by Reuther was to bypass his ideological brethren from the West Side Local and fill his GM staff with men from the Progressive Caucus who had refused to follow Homer Martin out of the CIO. The GM workforce profiled as being the most sympathetic to Martin's message, and he retained his largest influence among GM workers. As Reuther accrued greater responsibility, he represented a more diverse group of workers, and realized he had to broaden his base to accommodate a wider range of views. The addition of men like John Livingston, George Merelli, and Art Johnstone reinforced the CIO flanks along Martin's ideological and geographical base.

The meetings with the local councils affirmed support for sole representation of the UAW, a more vigorous shop steward system, and a guaranteed annual wage. Reuther promised national negotiations at the earliest possible opportunity, but he admonished his listeners that "We must demonstrate that we are a disciplined, responsible organization, that we not only have power, but that we have power under control."[140] He emphasized that unauthorized strikes would not be tolerated. "We who claim the right to strike must assume the responsibility of striking when it is right to strike."[141]

General Motors sought to exploit the union weakness by requesting an NLRB ruling on the union's jurisdiction, followed by an election to determine if its workers still expressed a preference for the UAW. Reuther had determined that Martin's support in the plants was not very substantial but there was also a diminished appeal for CIO style activism. He could not be sure of the outcome of an NLRB vote. A dramatic action was needed to counteract the company strategy and reinvigorate the disillusioned workers.

Reuther, in collaboration with Bill Stevenson, a veteran of the old MESA union strike of tool and die workers in 1933, devised a brilliant, but risky, strategy for getting GM to the bargaining table. The Roosevelt recession was receding and GM was preparing for a banner year. The plants were hiring again, and there was a greater sense of security among the workers. Reuther realized that the tool and die makers, whose wages and professional standards were being undercut by the outsourcing of work to non-union shops, formed the most reliable cadre of union stalwarts, and a strike of these skilled workers during the summer when GM was retooling for the next model year would attack GM where it was most vulnerable. The gambit was risky. If the strategy failed, both the union and Reuther's leadership position within it would be dealt a crippling blow.

Reuther's plan won approval from Hillman and Murray of the CIO and from the UAW Executive Board, and was endorsed overwhelmingly in strike votes taken at the affected GM tool rooms. On July 5th the skilled workers at Fisher # 21 walked out on strike. The next day four more Detroit plants were struck. Reuther staggered the closing of the GM plants to build a daily momentum behind the effort to bring GM to the negotiating table. By the weekend, the walkouts spread to Cleveland and Saginaw. Without the dies, production of the new model cars could not begin. Thousands of production workers were laid off, and GM faced the prospect of beginning the new model year with no product to sell. When the Michigan Compensation Commission ruled that laid off workers who were not themselves on strike were entitled to unemployment insurance, GM realized that it faced the possibility of a long strike and reached a settlement with the union.

The autocratic William Knudsen harbored an instinctive dislike for the brash young Reuther, and insisted upon direct negotiations with Phil Murray of the parent CIO. Reuther served as a technical adviser to Murray during the proceedings, and at one point during a particularly grueling session, Knudsen peered over at Reuther and said, "Young man, I wish you were selling used cars for us." When Reuther objected "Used cars?" Knudsen retorted, "Yes, used cars! Anybody can sell new cars."[142]

The concessions GM granted to the union were relatively minor. But the fact that the automotive giant signed its first company-wide wage agreement since 1937, was viewed by most of the GM workforce and by the public-at-large as a union victory carried huge symbolic importance. Support for the UAW-CIO in the GM plants was rejuvenated. When the NLRB representational elections were held in the spring of 1940, the UAW-CIO received 68 percent of the vote cast.[135] Martin's AFL union prevailed in only five plants outside of the Michigan nexus of the GM empire, and as these plants realized the futility in dealing with the corporate giant from such an isolated base, they returned to the CIO fold.

Once again, as in the building of the West Side Local, Walter Reuther, working with few resources other than his own energy and ingenuity, achieved a remarkable personal triumph. The union that had been severely weakened by two years of ineffectual leadership and factional warfare was restored to a new level of legitimacy within the industry giant. With power under control, the UAW and General Motors approached the next contract with expectations of the benefits that each might receive from the other.

In the 1940 negotiations, GM presented a new face across the table from the UAW team. William Knudsen had departed to Washington to serve as the head of the National Defense Advisory Commission. He was replaced as president of GM by "Engine" Charlie Wilson. Wilson was given the nickname "Engine" to distinguish him from "Electric" Charlie Wilson who was heading GE during the same period. GM's Wilson came from a much different background than his predecessor and held a more enlightened view on the role of labor unions.

"Engine" Charlie had belonged to a union in his youth and claimed to have voted for the Socialist Debs in the 1912 election.[143] He graduated with an engineering degree from Carnegie Mellon and worked as an Engineer at Westinghouse before coming to GM and climbing its corporate ladder. Unlike Knudsen who had little time for labor relations and detested the negotiating process as well as many of the people sitting across the table from him, Wilson immersed himself in labor issues and recognized that the company had more to gain from working with the union in trying to reduce the level of labor unrest in its plants than it did in trying to defeat it. Wilson and Reuther would sit across the table from one another for twelve more years and each developed a respect for the other. Wilson once called Reuther "the ablest man in American industry."[144]

Against the ominous background of the Nazi blitzkrieg through Western Europe, the two men struggled to reach an accommodation that would normalize the relationship between the two adversaries. Nobody in the room or in the country wanted a strike. In the end both sides got the thing they wanted most.

The union got recognition as the "sole exclusive bargaining agent" for almost all of GM's hourly workers. It also won the right for its shop stewards to collect union dues and solicit membership on the shop floor. The contract awarded GM workers a "CIO bonus" of a week of paid vacation, and established a five million dollar fund for equalizing the wages for workers performing the same tasks in different parts of the country. The wage standardization clause had broad implications because over time it created a national standard for wages within a company and between companies in similar industries. It had a side effect of reducing the pay differentials between different categories of work. This eventually led to a revolt of the skilled workers that provided Reuther with his great victory in 1939.[145]

The company also got what it wanted—control of the production process. It remained adamant against granting any authority to union shop stewards or its own foremen in settling individual grievances. Company foremen were instructed to be firm, but respectful, and not to deviate from the 72-page little gray book that codified the 1940 agreement.[146] Accommodations with individual workers or small groups of workers were not to be made at the local level. Grievances were monitored closely at corporate headquarters to ensure that deviation from company guidelines was not occurring in any of the individual plants. The contract stipulated that "the right to hire; promote; discharge or discipline for cause; and to maintain discipline and efficiency of employees, is the sole responsibility of the corporation."[147] Paragraph 78 in the agreement reinforced the language governing managerial responsibility for shop floor work rules with the declaration that, "production standards were subject to the full authority of local management."[148] Charlie Wilson summarized the negotiations to management guru Peter Drucker: "A union is a political organization and needs adversary relations and victorious battles. And a company is an economic organization and needs productivity and discipline. At GM we get both."[149]

With "power under control" Reuther was put in the position of enforcing the terms of the contract while having virtually no control over the resolution of day-to-day flashpoints that spark work stoppages and wildcat strikes. This was the same dilemma that Homer Martin handled so maladroitly. Two years after arguing in union council for authorization of the wildcat strike in Pontiac, Reuther now was part of the GM-UAW apparatus that demanded forbearance from its workers. He was never able to break through the Maginot Line of defense that the company erected around paragraph 78, and he spent the next thirty years probing for ways around it.

By 1940 the young Walter Reuther stood with the aging John L. Lewis as the most accomplished labor leader in the country. The young radical who had worked in the Molotov Auto Works in Gorky and fought in the front lines of the labor battles of the late nineteen thirties, had matured into the pragmatic leader of the UAW General Motors Division. He had broadened his base beyond his Socialist colleagues who helped spark the growth of the West Side Local. He became the inheritor of much of the Progressive legacy after the passing of Homer Martin from the CIO scene. The man who short years earlier attacked red baiting as "playing the bosses game"[150] was now the voice of anti-Communism within the CIO.

Reuther never abandoned the idealism that drew him to Socialism, but he grew less-and-less involved with the party before formally resigning his membership in 1938 to support Frank Murphy in his reelection bid for Governor. Victor Reuther described the slow withdrawal of the two brothers from Socialist politics. "…the trade union movement offered far greater possibilities for social gains, for legislative improvement, than did the vehicle of a political party….Why should one waste his life with a third party in a country where traditionally third parties have only been little splinter groups?"[151] The pragmatic Reuther would spend the next quarter century driving this "vehicle" in the direction of social gain and legislative improvement.

CHAPTER V

The Battle of the Overpass

I was 12 years old when Pat Brooks heard about the money Ford was paying. He went up first, and then brought us up to Detroit. We moved in with some of our kin in MacComb Street. It was kind of crowded there, but the house had toilets indoors and electric light. Down in Alabama we had outhouses and kerosene lamps. My stepfather got a job with Ford, and we got a place of our own in a frame tenement in Catherine Street.

Joe Louis

After winning and securing UAW recognition at General Motors and Chrysler, the union was ready to ride the thirty-fifth street trolley down to the River Rouge complex and confront the last recalcitrant member of Detroit's Big Three. Ford no longer enjoyed the preeminent position in the industry that it once held, but it was a family-owned business still ruled over by its legendary founder. Henry Ford was adamantly opposed to any union encroachment into his domain and he retained a mythical stature with much of the public. To confirm its legitimacy in the broader culture, the CIO-UAW had to win recognition from Ford.

At the beginning of the twentieth century, Henry Ford was better known for racing cars than building them. Racing and endurance competitions offered auto builders like Ford an opportunity to demonstrate their creations before investors looking for an opportunity to establish themselves in this new business and seeking the right person to back. Ford had success racing an earlier model at Grosse Point, Michigan against auto pioneer Alexander Winton, but when Ford, with the help of his assistant C. Harold Willis, built his most powerful new model, the 999 racer, a more daring hand was needed at the wheel. Ford hired a bicycle racer who "lived on speed"[1] named Barney Oldfield to drive the car. In a well-publicized race at Grosse Point in 1902, Oldfield guided the 999 around the three-mile course leaving his nearest rival ½ mile behind at the finish.[2]

Ford's racing successes attracted the attention of Alex Malcomson, a modestly wealthy timber baron who was looking to enter the auto business. Malcomson and Ford attempted to attract additional investors and raise an initial capital of $100,000, but came up far short of this goal. John Gray, a Detroit banker, was persuaded to invest $10,000 in the enterprise and was named president of the new company. Ford was given the post of vice president of the company and along with Malcomson awarded 25 ½ % of the stock. Gray was awarded a 10% share in the company and Albert Strelow was given a small block of stock in exchange for use of his woodworking shop which became the first Ford factory. The brothers John and Horace Dodge, who supplied motors for Olds, were retained to supply motors and other components for Ford and were awarded 5% of the stock each. John Dodge was also named a director of the company. Malcomson's personal lawyers, John Anderson and Horace Rackham were each given a 5% stake in the company, but contributed nothing but free legal advice to the enterprise. The initial capital investment amounted to only about ⅓ of the original goal.[3]

Malcomson installed one of his own employees, James Couzens, as secretary and business manager of the company. Malcomson wanted to retain some control over the day-to-day operation of the enterprise, and he selected the bright, young Couzens to manage the business operations of the firm. Couzens was awarded a 2 ½ % stake in the company. In the distribution of ownership of the new firm, Wills was given nothing. He was retained only with a verbal promise by Henry Ford that Ford would share a fixed percentage of his earnings with Wills.[4]

Ford's earlier forays into producing automobiles for the marketplace ended in failure because Ford remained the part-time hobbyist more interested in improving his prototypes than dealing with the issues of building to scale and marketing a standard 'frozen' design.[5] This time Ford found success with a modestly priced car that Couzens touted as "the most reliable machine in the world. A two cylinder car of ample power for the steepest hills and the muddiest roads, built to stand the severest strains. The same genius which conceived the world's record maker—the 999—has made possible the production of a thoroughly practical car at a moderate price."[6] Couzens kept Ford focused on building that 'two cylinder car with ample power' and not drifting back to the 999 and the challenge of building for the track.[7]

Three years after the incorporation of the Ford Motor Company in 1903, ownership of the company devolved to Ford and Couzens. Gray died. His heirs retained their 10% share in the company, but the title of president went to Ford. Strelow cashed in his earnings and bought into a British Colombian gold mine. Malcomson and Ford had a falling out over the market the company should target. Ford wanted to build a sturdy inexpensive car for the mass market and Malcomson thought the only profitable course was to build higher performance cars for a wealthier clientele. Ford garnered the support of the majority of the board and was able to maneuver his partner into selling his stake in the business.[8] The company now was successful enough for Ford and Couzens to get a bank loan of $175,000 for the pair to acquire Malcomson's shares. The company reorganized with Ford as the head, John Dodge as its vice president, and Couzens as its secretary-treasurer.[9]

Couzens was instrumental in the success of Ford. It was Couzens that developed the company's sales force, and Couzens that presided over a purchasing department that was able to negotiate favorable deals from Ford's suppliers. When the volume of buying at Ford became such a large share of the market, Couzens was able to negotiate deals with suppliers that left them so little margin of profit that the only way they could survive was to extract higher margins from Ford's competitors. He also pioneered the practice of delivering stripped down cars to distribution centers where parts were delivered in bulk for final assembly and delivery. John Anderson wrote in 1916 that "it was due to [Couzens'] efforts that the company became a success. Neither Ford nor Couzens could have done it alone."[10]

Whenever Ford deviated from the formula of offering a practical car for a moderate price, his sales suffered.[11] With the introduction of the Model T in 1908, he fully committed to producing a durable car at a popular price. It was practical to drive and maintain. It had 5,000 standardized parts that could be purchased at any Ford service center.[12] It was especially popular in rural America, where, unlike many of its rivals, it could travel on any road, no matter how rocky or muddy that road might be. By 1914 Ford was selling 200,000 Model Ts a year.[13] To keep up with demand, Ford improved the assembly line by introducing the automated lifted belt.

The man most responsible for expediting the Ford manufacturing process was Charles Sorensen. Sorensen devised the conveyor system that moved the work piece down the shop floor where each worker performed his simple set of operations in the time each piece was at his station.[14] The challenge of matching the speed of assembly with the speed with which the components were delivered was addressed by Carl Emde, a German-born master mechanic, who designed specialized machine tools and directed where they would be best located to avoid bottlenecks and assure the efficient operation of the whole manufacturing process.[15] Two of Sorensen's assistants, P. E. Miller, and William Knudsen were also instrumental in development of the Ford manufacturing process.

With the success of the Model T, Ford became increasingly autocratic. Like most autocrats, he became intoxicated with notions of his own genius. He required that his star shine brightest in its own firmament, and when any other star began to rival his, it was quickly extinguished. Couzens was forced out of the company in 1915. Wills had a falling out with Ford and left the company soon afterward. Knudsen left Ford to eventually become the president of General Motors, Dodge terminated his association with Ford to later join forces with Walter Chrysler, and even Sorensen was ultimately forced out toward the end of the old man's reign.

The automated manufacturing process turned mechanics that enjoyed building substantial pieces of the whole car into automatons, responsible only for performing routine repetitive tasks. The one constant in the life of the auto worker was the line. It dictated the rhythms of his day and streamed the visions of his night. He was the servant of the machine—the interchangeable part, lacking a skill, lacking pride, and lacking control of his own circumstances. If he were to complain about conditions in the plant, he would be taken over to a window, shown the crowd gathered below, and told if he didn't like his job there were plenty of others willing to take it. The line replaced the need for heavy labor or specialized skill with tedium. Henry Ford called it "a boon for factory workers who have no brains,"[16] at least none that he and his Security Department were willing to concede them.

Ford no longer appeared on the shop floor to fraternize with the workers.[17] Instead he introduced a rigid system of supervision that not only monitored their performance in the plant, but controlled their afterhours behavior as well. The work was tedious, the plants were cramped, and the regimentation was oppressive. The turnover of the workforce was as high as 40 to 60% each month.[18] To meet the manpower challenge that threatened to derail his production quotas, Ford proclaimed an offer of five dollars for an eight hour day.

The promise of a five dollar a day wage embellished the legend of Henry Ford and stabilized his work force. In his autobiography, Ford wrote of the five dollar a day wage that "it was to our way of thinking an act of social justice, and in the last analysis we did it for our own satisfaction of mind. There is a pleasure in feeling that you have made others happy."[19] Later in the same book he admitted that, "The payment of five dollars for an eight-hour day was one of the finest cost-cutting moves we have ever made."[20] Ford may have acted with the best interest of his workers at heart, but in serving up some nuggets from his philosophy he later claimed, "I do nothing because it gives me pleasure. I give nothing for which I do not receive compensation. I do not believe in charity."[21] Ford made sure his workers earned their wage by regularly speeding up the line and subjecting them to the tyranny of his Service Department.

Ford was not unique in recruiting agents to spy on his employees and combat any sentiment that might be considered pro union. Other companies employed firms like Pinkerton to supply their eyes and muscle. Ford created his own private police force. The man he put in charge of this small army was Harry Bennett. Bennett was hired by

Ford in 1916 as a watchman. He had been a boxer in the navy and was working as a clerk at the time Ford hired him. The five foot six Bennett had a toughness that Ford admired and an unwavering devotion to his boss. He rose to head the internal security group that Ford called his Service Department. Bennett had full control over hiring and firing Service Department employees, and this control later extended to the entire company including executives. He filled his legion with ex prize fighters like himself, cops that had been fired from the force, and former gangsters. Bennett served on a Michigan parole board, which gave him a good opportunity to authorize the release of some of the applicants to the custody of the Ford Motor Company. The "gentlemen" that Bennett recruited into the ranks of the Service Department included the likes of "Legs" Laman, a small-time rum runner and kidnapper who had served the law as a snitch during his time in custody, Sam Cuva, who had served time for shooting his mother-in-law, and the Detroit gang leader, Chester Le Mare, who, in 1929, was granted the very lucrative fruit and vegetable concession at the River Rouge plant.[22] The only criteria that mattered was having a suitable demeanor for the job and unquestioned obedience to Harry Bennett.

His close association with Henry Ford provided Bennett with connections to prominent people like J. Edgar Hoover. Hoover and Bennett shared similar attitudes toward organized labor and other progressive movements, and Bennett ran an intelligence operation that was hardly less formidable than Hoover's FBI. The two men became good friends and regular golfing partners.[23] Both Hoover and Bennett shared a particular antipathy for Walter Reuther.

Ford was a very austere man bent upon fostering his own values upon the larger society. As a virtual dictator in his plants he was able to impose those values upon his workers. Small talk was not allowed. Even smiling, whistling, or humming was taken to be a sign of laziness. The "right atmosphere" was enforced by the Service Department. The intimidation of Bennett's goons was described by Keith Sward.

> "For years after Bennett came to power, it was the proud, undisguised aim of the Service Department to blot out every manifestation of personality or manliness inside a

Ford plant...Bennett's mercenaries finally mastered every tactic from the swagger of the Prussian drill sergeant to outright sadism and physical assault. On the night shift they would jolt an incoming worker out of his wits and take the starch out of his system by flashing a light in his face and shouting at him. 'where did you get that badge?' or 'who's your boss?' Another intimidating practice that came into being under Bennett's rule was the act of shaking 'em up in the aisles. In this case a workman summoned to the employment office for any reason at all, even one that was totally unrelated to his work, would be shoved and pushed along the aisle by a pair of officious Servicemen like a felon in the custody of the police."[24]

The success of the Model T provided Ford a platform to address a national audience. He considered himself to be a practical sociologist with a prescription for "right living" in a healthy society. In his plants, the "practical sociologist" supplemented his Service Department with a Sociology Department headed by the Reverend Samuel Marquis, Dean of the Episcopal Cathedral of Detroit. Sociology Department representatives would visit Ford employees at home and keep charts on their moral steadfastness. Drinking and smoking were frowned upon as was divorce, and the practice of a male employee taking on a male border to defray the cost of housing was considered an "evil custom"[25] by Ford and the good Reverend. Only those deemed fit to be "profit sharers" received the full five dollar a day wage. Those deemed sociologically deficient had to be reevaluated regularly before they could qualify for the full wage.[26] Workers found living unworthily would see their pay checks cut or their jobs in jeopardy.

With Sorensen and Bennett assuming a larger role in managing the day-to-day operations of the company, Ford devoted more of his energy to other projects. Not content to foster his morality upon his workforce, he sought to influence a wider audience through a publishing enterprise: *The Dearborn Independent*. In the *Independent* he crusaded for the Midwestern virtues he practiced: church attendance and early rising. He advocated staying on the farm to his rural readers. Ford was never comfortable with the century he did as much as anyone to create. He railed against the capitalists whom he considered unproductive and dishonest. Ford never considered himself a capitalist. He was beholden to them in the formation of the company, but after the success of the Model T, he was able to extract himself from all outside control.

In Ford's mind many capitalists were also Jewish. He never surmounted the anti-Semitism that was all too common in nineteenth century America. The only Jew that Ford and countless other kids growing up in the rural heartland knew was Shylock as introduced to them in *McGuffey's Reader*. McGuffey's Shylock was not berated and spat upon by Antonio on the Rialto, and did not bleed when he was pricked, McGuffey's Shylock was only the vengeful usurer, excerpted from the full text, devoid of Christian charity, insisting on his pound of flesh. In *McGuffey's Reader* Shylock was an exemplar of a race whose "...authors were incapable of the diction and strangers to the morality contained in the gospel."[27] Ford and generations of American school kids learned reading and writing and 'rithmetic taught to the tune of a heavy-handed Calvinistic hickory stick.

Ford used his publication to print numerous anti-Semitic diatribes. In one article he claimed "Jews were the conscious enemies of all that Anglo-Saxons mean by civilization."[28] In 1921 Ford reprinted the infamous *Protocols of the Elders of Zion* in a book titled *The International Jew*. The original document was a fabrication coming out of Tsarist Russia in 1903 that purported to contain the details of a Jewish plot to achieve global hegemony through the degradation of morals and control of economics and the press. The *Times* of London exposed the Protocols as a fraud in the same year that Ford's book appeared, but Ford's endorsement of the fraudulent document was seized upon by the Nazis as a justification for their anti-Jewish campaign. Hitler was a great admirer of Ford and hung a full-length portrait of the industrialist in his Munich office.[29] In 1938 Ford accepted the Award of the Grand Cross of the German Eagle from the Hitler government that had already begun its reign of violence against its Jewish citizens.

Ford's diatribes against *the Jew* were not necessarily reflective of his attitudes toward particular Jews. The two real-life Jews who figured most prominently in Ford's life were the architect Albert Kahn and the

Dearborn rabbi Leo Franklin. Ford relied on Kahn to design his factories and developed a friendship with Franklin that was sufficiently close for Ford to make presents of new cars to the rabbi on his birthday. The ambiguous feelings Ford harbored for *the Jew* and the Jews in his circle were reflective of the contradictions he exposed in many facets of his character. In much of the personality he revealed to the public, Henry Ford showed an inability to connect the general with the particular He disdained charity, but could be generous. He could distance the tyrannical regime he imposed in his plants from the image of himself as the champion of the worker. After the attacks on Jews appeared in the *Dearborn Independent,* Kahn continued to design Ford's factories right up to his death in 1942, but refused to meet personally with the industrialist in the Rouge again, and Franklin refused the delivery of his new car. When Ford learned of the rabbi's refusal to accept his gift, he showed the disconnect between his philosophy and practice by naively asking Franklin "have I done something to offend you?"[30]

Ford's bigotry against Jews was not duplicated in his public attitude toward blacks. At the beginning of the depression, a delegation of prominent black citizens approached Ford and expressed their concerns about discrimination in the pattern of layoffs. Ford promised the group that he would maintain the same percentage of blacks at the River Rouge plant as blacks were represented in the population of the greater Detroit metropolitan region. Thereafter, blacks accounted for 10% of the plant's workforce, and, under Ford's dictatorial regime, some blacks were promoted to positions of greater responsibility, including a small number of foremen.[31]

Ford hired two African-Americans, Donald Marshall and Willis Ward, a former University of Michigan football star, to oversee the hiring of black workers at the Rouge and ensure compliance with his pledge to the community delegation. Marshall and Ward used an alliance of black ministers to find suitable recruits for the labor force. Ministers that were part of the Ford labor supply chain were those that shared his Republican politics and attitudes toward labor relations. Since most African-Americans at the time voted Republican and were not supportive of unions that failed to support equal opportunity for them, Ford's attitudes were echoed by many in the black community. Keeping on the good side of Ford brought with it rewards. Ford became a benefactor of compliant black churches in the Detroit metropolitan area that were suffering loss of revenue during the depression. He donated a parish house to the Saint Matthew's Episcopal Church where Marshall attended and taught Sunday school. He also made generous contributions to the Second Baptist Church and the black Inkster Village project.[32] Ford provided a venue for African-American artists like Marian Anderson and Dorothy Maynor on the Ford Sunday Hour radio show at a time when black musicians were largely absent from the white stage.

By 1938, the black populace had switched its allegiance to the Democratic party of Franklin Delano Roosevelt and softened somewhat its opposition to the unions. Black voices inside the churches were dissenting from Ford's policies. When one church invited the Back labor leader A. Phillip Randolph to address the congregation, members from that church were threatened with firing at Ford. Black ministers were warned by Marshall that if pro-labor speakers were to appear in their church, Ford would never hire another member of that congregation.[33] The association between Ford and the Black churches was exposed in a 1938 magazine article by Dr. Horace White entitled *Who Owns the Negro Churches?* White's revelations caused a furor and prompted Marshall and Willis to create a number of Republican clubs in the black communities of Wayne County to replace the churches as the conduits for work at Ford.[34]

Whether Ford's motives were altruistic or self-serving, his actions benefited his motor company and his image, as well as the black community of greater Detroit. The Ford that championed black employment and black entertainers provided a counterpoint to the Ford that tyrannized his workers and railed against the Jews. The biographers of this complicated man, including Ford himself, had another chapter to either embellish the legend or soften the tone of the man they were painting. Blacks were given an opportunity for work that others denied them, and Ford was provided with a group of workers who were grateful to the company and antagonistic to the union. If Ford were true to his claim of doing nothing for which he did not receive compensation, then the reward for his patronage of the African-American community was a Praetorian guard for the defense of his industrial empire.

The River Rouge Complex represented the culmination of the industrial age and foreshadowed its later evolution. The complex was located on the Rouge River in Dearborn, just upstream from its confluence with the Detroit River. It was over a mile and a half wide and a mile long. It had its own docks and was served by over 100 miles of dedicated railroad track. A power station on the site produced the electricity that ran the entire complex. At the completion of the extended complex in 1928 it was the largest vertically integrated manufacturing center in the world. Iron ore, coal, and tires would enter at one end of the complex and thirty-four hours later the new Model A cars would roll off the assembly line at the other.[35] During the 1930s, as many as 90,000 workers were employed at the Rouge complex.[36] On the silver screen and on the artist's canvas the power and regimentation of the Rouge provided a metaphor for the industrial age. Charley Chaplin succumbed to the drudgery and speed-up of the assembly line and got caught in the gears of the machinery that dictated his existence in *Modern Times*. Jail became a preferred alternative to the kind of freedom experienced outside. After his visits to the Rouge, Diego Rivera depicted anonymous laborers toiling inside a maze of belts and wheels, pipes and furnaces, cloistered behind a neo-classical facade of white marble and polished halls on murals painted in the Detroit Institute of Arts Museum.

Even as the extended facility was being completed, it was already obsolete. Vertical-integration lacked the flexibility of having independent suppliers offer competitively priced components that were purchased on the basis of need. In time of slow economic activity, the vertically-integrated plant would have idle capacity that would not encumber its more nimble competitors. But the Rouge plants did give Ford some protection in the labor wars from being overly vulnerable to a strike at a key supplier. With 90,000 workers concentrated in one complex, the Rouge became the main battlefield in the struggle for union recognition within the industry.

A year after the final stage of the River Rouge facility was completed the stock market crashed. The depression years followed. The Detroit auto factories employed just over 470,000 workers in 1929. By 1931 that figured had declined to under 257,000, and few of those employed worked full weeks.[37] Thousands still trudged to the employment lines in front of the plant gates each morning with scant hope of finding work, but with no other place to turn. The relief roles in the city swelled to over 200,000 people and another 150,000 discouraged workers left Detroit and returned to their former home towns.[38] Henry Ford showed little sympathy for the plight of his workers. He minimized the severity of the depression, and refused to pay into a fund for the unemployed. In March of 1931 he wrote an article in which he blamed the poor for the circumstances they faced. "These are really good times, but only if you know it…The average man won't really do a day's work unless he is caught and cannot get out of it."[39]

As the depression dragged on with little being done by either the government or the employer, the situation of the unemployed became increasingly desperate. Prolonged periods of inadequate nutrition produced real hunger. Foreclosures and evictions fueled the anger of men with empty stomachs and diminished pride. On May 7, 1932, Communist organizers led a hunger march of thousands of unemployed workers from Detroit to the Rouge plant in nearby Dearborn. When the marchers reached the town border they were met by a wall of Dearborn police and told to disperse. An uneasy standoff ended with fire hoses and rounds of tear gas being turned on the demonstrators. The crowd was not deterred, and maintained its resolve to deliver their message at the gates of the Ford factory complex. Finally an order to fire was given. Four marchers lay dead on the ground. A fifth marcher, a black man named Curtis Williams, died shortly afterward. The four white men: Joe DeBlasio, Coleman Leny, Joe York, and Joe Bussell were buried in the Woodmere Cemetery, within view of the giant smokestacks looming over the Rouge complex. Curtis Williams was denied burial in the white cemetery. His ashes were scattered over the Rouge from an airplane hired by the union. Many years later a headstone for the fifth victim was placed beside those of his four comrades in struggle.

A New Awakening

Almost one year to the day another march down another street in another city ferried Franklin Delano Roosevelt to the White House for his inauguration. In his address to the nation, he pledged himself "to a new deal for the American people," one in which they would have "a more equitable opportunity to share in the distribution of national wealth."

As promised in his address, Roosevelt aggressively pushed the powers of his office to the limits of the Constitution, and sometimes beyond. He was able to shepherd legislation through Congress with great urgency but conservative opponents resisted New Deal initiatives in court with some success. After the National Industrial Recovery Act was struck down by the Supreme Court, the protection of collective bargaining it offered labor was strengthened and re-codified in a new National Labor Relations Act sponsored by Senator Wagner. In January of 1937 the Court upheld the constitutionality of the new labor law.

With an improving economy and an administration with a friendly attitude toward labor, the CIO unions flexed their muscles and won concessions from Big Auto and Big Steel. The secondary companies in these industries, however, were not prepared to follow the leader and submit to union representation in their shops. Ford and the Little Steel companies of Republic, Youngstown, and Bethlehem drew up their defenses to fight the unions on the shop floor and fight the New Deal in the courts and at the ballot box. The momentum that the union gained at Flint was on the line when the battle shifted to Ford.

As May approached, it was time to take the fight to Ford. With the Rouge heavily guarded by land and water, the Reuther brothers took to the air in their initial foray against the auto maker. Walter and Victor rented a small plane, and had it fly low over the plant complex at a shift change. As the plane circled above, Walter exhorted the workers below over a loudspeaker to choose the benefits of union membership. The plane flew as low and slowly over the plant as safely possible, but the usually eloquent words of Walter Reuther just dissipated into the hum of the plane engine and traffic on the ground and the expanse of the spring afternoon sky.[40] The verbal message was lost, but the visual message of the bold intrusion into Ford airspace made an impression about the resourcefulness of the union and of the young Walter Reuther.

In order to win, the union needed to secure the sympathy of the public and the confidence of the workers in the plants. It had to wage a public relations war for these two constituencies. Sensitive to the charges leveled by the Ford publicity machine that it was red and alien to the ideals of the country, the UAW had to convince the public that it sprang from the best traditions of America in the fight against injustice and oppression. It began this campaign by plastering billboards throughout the region with messages like "Unionism is Americanism" and "Fordism is Fascism."

The UAW also needed to recruit leaders inside the plants who were willing to risk their jobs and their safety to spread the union message. To convince workers, intimidated by Harry Bennett's spies and goons, that the union was powerful and ready to challenge the Ford regime, Reuther believed that a demonstration of union strength on Ford turf was needed. The UAW commenced its effort to organize Ford by planning a highly visible leafleting campaign at the gates of the Rouge. It obtained a permit from the Dearborn City Council to distribute its leaflets at the Rouge complex on May 26. In preparation for what he knew would be a potentially dangerous situation, Reuther opened two union halls on the outskirts of the plant, and made two reconnaissance trips to the Miller Road Overpass near Gate 4, where the leaflets were to be distributed.[41] The overpass had been built by Ford, but leased to the Detroit Street Railway Commission. It provided workers arriving by streetcars that stopped on the other side of the highway a safe passage to the factory. It was not designated as private property, and was frequented by street vendors with no connection to Ford. To lessen the risk of a dangerous confrontation with the Service Department, journalists, clergymen, and staffers from the Senate Committee on Civil Liberties were invited to observe the event.[42]

At about noon on the 26th, journalists and photographers began arriving at the Miller Road overpass. When they arrived there were about 25 cars filled with burly men wearing sunglasses already parked along the street. These men in dark glasses threatened the photographers and warned the newsmen to get out of the area. Reuther spent the morning addressing a rally of about 100 members of the women's auxiliary of his Detroit West Side local 174. The women were to leaflet the plant at the shift change later in the afternoon. At about 2:00 he arrived at Miller Road along with Richard Frankensteen, the man in charge of the Ford campaign, Robert Kanter, and J. J. Kennedy, the UAW East Side Regional

Director.[43] When the leaders arrived, *Detroit News* photographer, James "Scotty" Kilpatrick asked them to pose on the overpass in front of a large Ford sign. Desiring publicity for the Ford campaign, the group obliged Kilpatrick and mounted the two flights of stairs to the overpass. As they were smiling for the camera, a group of Servicemen marched up behind them and began attacking. Frankensteen had his coat pulled up over his head to incapacitate him while four Servicemen punched and kicked him and knocked him to the concrete. There, two men pulled his legs apart and another man repeatedly kicked him in the groin. One of his assailants ground his heel into the union leader's abdomen before putting his full weight down on it. Kanter was pushed off the overpass and fell thirty feet to the ground.[44]

Reuther was kicked and beaten and pushed down the two flights of stairs, only to be beaten some more when he reached the street. In describing his treatment to the NLRB inquiry later, he said,

> "Seven times they raised me from the concrete and slammed me down on it. They pinned my arms…and I was punched and kicked and dragged by my feet to the stairway, thrown down the first flight of steps, picked up, slammed down, and kicked down the second flight. On the ground they beat and kicked me some more."[45]

As the attack against the leaders raged, the ladies of the auxiliary were arriving on the trolley cars. They became the next target of the Service Department members. Some women were pushed back on the trolleys and others dragged off and beaten. The Dearborn police stood back and watched while the rampage continued. One cop was appalled by the scene and urged the servicemen beating a woman to stop before they killed her.[46]

After the union leafleters were beaten or dispersed, the servicemen went after the reporters and photographers. They confiscated notebooks, smashed cameras, and demanded photographic plates. Kilpatrick managed to get back to his car, hide the plates of the photos he had snapped during the confrontation, and dupe the thugs into accepting some unimportant plates sitting on his front seat. Before Kilpatrick and other reporters arrived back at their office, Henry Ford was on the phone to Managing Editor Fred Gaertner claiming that it was loyal Ford workers, not Bennett's Service Department men, who beat the union organizers.[47] The photos showed otherwise, and Gaertner ordered the City Editor to print the story, and "tell the boys to write it as they saw it."[48] Kilpatrick's pictures appeared in the *Detroit News* the next day, and the national media picked up the story via the wire service. Pictures of Frankensteen, with his arms incapacitated by the coat pulled over his head, being beaten by several of Bennett's thugs and the bloodied and swollen faces of Reuther and Frankensteen after their ordeal appeared in publications across the country and around the world.

The visual impact of the photos was damaging to the image of Ford, who retaliated by pulling advertisement from the *Detroit News* and the publications of Henry Luce, who was feuding with Ford at the time and whose magazine, *Time,* wrote a particularly unfavorable account of the company's actions during the episode.[49] Ford redoubled his efforts to place the blame on Communist agitators seeking to discredit the American free enterprise system. The impact of the photos also started a sentiment for creating a Pulitzer Prize for Photojournalism that would be established several years later.

Ford got a reprieve from the bad publicity his Service Department garnered on the Miller Road overpass four days later, when another labor confrontation turned violent and captured the headlines. A Memorial Day march of striking workers on a Republic Steel plant in Chicago was halted with gunfire by the Chicago police. The gunfire was reported to have erupted after a branch was thrown at the police by one of the demonstrators. Ten people were killed and thirty wounded.[50] Communists, including the future General Secretary of the American Communist Party, Gus Hall, were prominent in the Steelworkers Organizing Committee (SWOC) that called for the demonstration, and the press was quick to emphasize this aspect of the massacre. A coroner's jury exonerated the police response as justified homicide to what was called in the press a 'Red riot'. When Roosevelt responded to a union plea for help with an assertion that what the American people were saying was "a plague on both your houses," the strike was effectively broken and the union was forced to go back to work without a contract.[51]

With the setback at Little Steel and efforts to enroll the workers at Ford stymied by the Service Department, the gains won in the winter months of 1936–37 by the CIO became more tenuous by the fall of that year. Management, caught off guard by the strength and tactics of the union earlier, had regrouped and prepared to counterattack. Ford and the other auto executives used their advertising and editorial muscle to shape opinion. Media ownership was generally sympathetic to the management position and worked to paint a picture in the public mind of labor unrest as a radical assault on the institutions of the American free enterprise system. In a 1940 survey by Fortune Magazine of which individual had done the most for the working man, Henry Ford beat out Senator Wagner, Labor Secretary Perkins, and John L. Lewis by a wide margin.[52]

The Ford publicity blitz doomed an electoral challenge to the pro-business power structure in the city of Detroit by the UAW. The union assembled a slate of five candidates headed by Walter Reuther, Richard Frankensteen, R. J. Thomas, and labor attorney Maurice Sugar to contest for seats on the City Council. The optimistic outlook with which the campaign began in the spring of 1937 crashed into the reality of the enormous power the business elite wielded. The Detroit newspapers were almost as reliable an outlet for Ford generated opinion as the *Dearborn Independent*, and they emphasized the Communist connections of the union organizers. The controversial radio priest, Father Coughlin, added his voice to the anti-union, anti-red crescendo, and asked his listeners if they "wanted Detroit run by labor tyranny?"[53]

The five labor candidates survived the preliminary round of voting in September, but in the November election, the media campaign and get-out-the-vote drive waged by Ford and the other auto executives resulted in a voter turnout that was nearly double the usual figure for a City Council election. The union ticket was soundly beaten. In his first and only try for political office, Walter Reuther finished fourteenth in a field of eighteen candidates.[54]

The Detroit city election provided management with a rehearsal of its strategy for defeating labor. They intended to hold out against the unions in the factories and battle pro-union legislation in the courts until the next presidential election in 1940 when they would use their media power and organizational skill to regain the White House and Congress and reverse the policies of the New Deal. The second round of the struggle for recognition was as crucial for the union as was the wave of sit-downs that culminated in the initial successes of 1937.

While the labor push in the factories was meeting resistance, the internal power struggle within the UAW was diverting energy from the battle at hand. It quickly became apparent that Homer Martin was not the man to lead the union in the struggle it faced. The early victories were won by the spontaneous action of the men in the plants and the guidance of some of the lower level leaders like the three Reuther brothers and Richard Frankensteen. Walter Reuther and Richard Frankensteen, the brothers in battle at the Overpass, were the two most dynamic young leaders of the movement and the two most ambitious. Pictures of the two bloodied but unbending victims of the Rouge assault made them instant heroes of the rank and file. Both men knew that the person responsible for getting a contract with Ford would likely become the man to lead the union in the not too distant future. The rivalry between the factions in the leadership mirrored a growing rivalry between the two men.

The husky Frankensteen, a former tackle on the University of Dayton football team, was the UAW organizing director for the Detroit area and in charge of the Ford campaign. He had planned on a teaching and coaching career when he graduated from Dayton in 1932, but during the height of the depression a promised position fell through for lack of funding. Frankensteen had worked summers in the Chrysler Dodge plant since the age of fifteen, and with few prospects to use his college education more productively he went to work at Dodge. At Dodge he became active in the company union that he helped to reorganize as an independent in 1935. He merged his Industrial Workers Association with the UAW later that year and during the sit-downs in the winter of 1937 won recognition from the Chrysler company when efforts to roust the strikers from the plants were repulsed. Frankensteen studied law at night while working at Dodge, but ultimately decided that "There are lots of lawyers and lots of school teachers, but there is a need for leaders among the laboring men. I feel I should do all I can."[55]

After Frankensteen merged his independent union with the UAW, Reuther pushed his candidacy for the executive board, even though he was not on the executive committee himself. At the start of the Ford campaign Frankensteen was a Martin loyalist, and was rewarded with the position of first Vice President of the union. Reuther was on the Ford organizing committee because the Rouge was located within the geographical bounds of his West Side local. The stunt with the plane and the canvassing effort were both Reuther initiatives. Reuther was convinced that the presence of newsmen and community representatives would deter Bennett from unleashing his goons on the union leaders and prevailed upon Frankensteen to sanction the event. Three months after the Battle of the Overpass, during the period of the NLRB hearings in Detroit, Reuther pushed for another leafleting action at the Rouge, this time with the company of a thousand sturdy union men. Frankensteen was not convinced of the wisdom of the action, and became increasingly irritated at Reuther's efforts to dictate the direction of the committee he headed. He refused to sanction the action, and when Reuther skipped an executive board meeting to lead the leafleting event, the two men exchanged angry words.[56] Frankensteen got Homer Martin to order Reuther back to the meeting or face expulsion from the board.

On August 11, the leafleting event transpired without Reuther and the two other union organizers. A thousand union men arrived at the Miller Road gate during the shift change armed with their leaflets. The possibility of another violent confrontation brought local and national reporters, along with representatives of the State Police, investigators from the NLRB and Senate Civil Liberties Committee to the Rouge to observe the proceedings. Mrs. Cornelia Pinchot, wife of the former governor of Pennsylvania joined the observers to see if "Dearborn was still in America."[57] Ford Servicemen, outnumbered by the union leafleters, did not interfere with their activity. They stood back and glared at workers who tried to surreptitiously take the handbill on their way out of the complex. The second shift workers entering the plant were much more reluctant to accept the offering, and some made a show of wrinkling it up and tossing it away in view of the watchful Ford security men.

The union considered their effort to be a success and planned to return regularly to demonstrate their resolve and to make a show of union presence in the heart of the Ford empire. That plan was thwarted when Ford prevailed upon the Dearborn City Council to pass a handbill ordinance against the distribution of printed literature in congested areas of the city during certain hours of the day. The congested areas included all of the entry points of the Rouge complex, and the certain hours coincided with the times of shift changes at the Ford plant. When union organizers appeared at the plant in defiance of the ordinance, they were hauled off to the police station, held for a few hours, and then released with no charges being filed. This approach prevented the union from making its case to the workers changing shifts, and also prevented it from having a test case to challenge the questionable constitutionality of the law in a court of appeals.[58.]

Dearborn was the epitome of a company town. The city was reliably Republican. Its elected officials were filtered through Harry Bennett's Republican machine, and they retained that support only if they adhered to the Ford position. The police chief and many of his officers were former Ford Servicemen, and they often served as adjuncts to their former colleagues.[59] The Ford strategy effectively limited union influence in Dearborn for the next two years.

Other cities with Ford plants did not have such a compliant political structure. There the Service Department was more aggressive in ensuring that the union message did not get a foothold within their facility. The most extreme example of Ford's forcible suppression of any pro-union sentiment, whether it related directly to the auto industry or not, occurred in Dallas, Texas. Dallas was far away from the UAW base in the Midwest, and the conservative South was barely within the peripheral vision of the most ardent labor activist. That did not stop Bennett from recruiting a group of toughs from one of the Dallas area plants and augmenting this body with a small core of his Servicemen from Detroit. The unit was supplied with pistols, blackjacks, and rubber hose, and directed to instill the "fear of God" into any suspected agent of the union. On June 23, 1937, they ambushed a visiting UAW organizer and left him badly beaten with fractured ribs. Afterward, with few real UAW members to dissuade, they went after prominent members of the community that harbored pro labor sympathies. Their next victim was George Baer, an organizer for the Dallas area millinery workers. Baer was beaten into unconsciousness and lost several teeth in the encounter. W. J. Houston, a liberal Dallas attorney, was attacked leaving his neighborhood drugstore, and given a beating that required hospitalization. Their next target was A. C. Lewis, a Dallas businessman who confided in a neighbor that he was sympathetic to the idea of labor unions. The thugs mistook Lewis's twin brother for their intended victim, and gave him a severe thrashing. Four months after the beating, Archie B. Lewis died of pneumonia. The NLRB investigators compiled twenty-five volumes of testimony about the company activities in Dallas, including that of Ford Service agents who were willing to come forward and testify against their employer. The NLRB documents do not charge that the beating was a contributory factor in Archie Lewis's death, but the dying Lewis implored his brother to see that those who killed him were tracked down and received justice.[60]

In 1938, the Ford campaign settled into a period of sporadic skirmishes, and the factional conflict within the union boiled into full-scale war. When it was revealed Martin was negotiating an unauthorized sweetheart deal with Ford and dickering with the AFL to take his union out of the CIO, his position in the UAW became untenable.

Martin proclaimed the naive belief that Henry Ford did not know the conditions in his plants and would be amenable to UAW representation once he realized the true state of affairs.[61] Harry Bennett confirmed that meetings took place, but reaffirmed Ford's contention that the company had been "fair and just" toward its employees and had no intention of recognizing a union. The UAW briefly split into two rival unions, but the body under control of Martin's opponents steadily garnered the support of the rank-and-file, and Martin's rump union slipped into irrelevance.

The Last Bastion of Resistance Falls

With the factional dispute, at least for the moment, resolved, the UAW was ready to resume the campaign against Ford. During the intervening two years, the Supreme Court had ruled sit down strikes to be an "illegal seizure of buildings in order to prevent their use by the employer in a lawful manner."[62] The union got better news when a Dearborn municipal judge, Lila Neuenfeld, ruled that the city handbill ordinance was unconstitutional. The City of Dearborn and the Ford Motor Company both appealed to the Wayne County circuit court to issue an injunction to restrain the union from leafleting at the Rouge while Judge Neuenfeld's decision was appealed. On December 7, 1940, circuit court judge James E. Chenot issued an injunction, but not the one Ford was seeking. Judge Chenot lambasted the ordinance as a mockery of constitutional guarantees and issued an injunction that forbade any future enforcement of the city ordinance. Two days later the UAW was out in force with 35,000 handbills at every entrance to the Rouge.[63] The union vowed to reappear every two weeks with 50,000 copies of its handbill, *Ford Facts*.[22]

The UAW received additional good news on February, 10, 1941 when the Supreme Court refused to review the Cincinnati Circuit Court of Appeals decision upholding the NLRB finding of Ford's flagrant violation of the National Labor Relations Act. The company was forced to reinstate with back pay certain union men who were fired four years earlier, halt its violations of the act, and signify its compliance with the ruling by posting notices of the terms of the judgment throughout its plants. The compliance notices stated in print that workers were entitled to exercise their right to organize without interference from management.[64] The formidable industrial fortress had been breached. Workers now felt free to flock to the union halls, and organizers who had been forced to keep their affiliation secret showed up at work proudly displaying their union buttons.

Management never developed a coherent strategy for dealing with the new turn of events. The election of 1940 provided a conservative Republican Congress, but returned Roosevelt to the White House with a strong endorsement of his leadership by the electorate. With war raging in Europe and the Orient, the public was ill-disposed toward labor unrest, but neither was it sympathetic to the union-busting activities detailed in the NLRB indictment of Ford. Years of dictatorial, myopic management had reduced Ford to third place in market share and threatened the continued viability of the company. It was no longer in a position to announce some dramatic wage increase like the five dollar a day pay to forestall the organizing efforts of the union.[65] Instead it vacillated between conciliation and harassment.

Within weeks of the Supreme Court ruling, the union had gained enough membership that it was able to establish its presence inside the Rouge. Departments with sufficient union representation elected shop stewards who initiated grievance proceedings over issues that had festered for years. Stung by the courts and faced with the infectious militancy of his workers, Ford granted small concessions on one issue after another. On one occasion a delegation of shop stewards ventured to Harry Bennett's office to protest the firing of two dozen union partisans from their departments without notice or explanation of cause. To their surprise they were ushered into Bennett's office, offered chairs and cigars from his humidor, and received a cordial hearing of the grievance. After listening to the steward's complaints, Bennett offered an apology for the actions of one of his subordinates, summoned the unfortunate scapegoat to his office, and dressed him down in front of the union delegation.[66]

The "new" Harry Bennett did not usurp the body of the old prize fighter, but was only a costume worn on occasion to maintain the appearance of compliance with the Labor Relations Act. Underneath his costume Bennett explored every device available to forestall union recognition. The first option that presented itself came in the person of Homer Martin, now the head of his small AFL affiliate. Martin sought to reestablish his credentials as a spokesman for the autoworkers by organizing Ford, and Henry Ford viewed Martin as a pliant adversary who would not demand from the company more than it was willing to offer. Donald Marshall spread the word in the black community that Ford was amenable to the AFL, and Bennett's Servicemen made up for a dearth of AFL organizers within the plants, by assuming that role themselves.[67]

Ford's belated attempt to circumvent the UAW by recognizing its AFL rival had little chance of success, but great potential for calamity. Ford's white workers had embraced the UAW and were not about to switch to the timid AFL alternative, particularly if it was seen as a wedge for blacks to drive between the workers and their preferred agent. Homer Martin's courtship of the black community threatened to ignite the racial tinderbox that was Detroit.

Bennett's goons did not completely forgo their customary approach to labor relations. Union activists were intimidated and dismissed faster than the grievance mechanisms could get them reinstated. The company's most successful ploy for thwarting the union advance was moving shop stewards from their current department to one in another section of the vast complex. The union stalwart retained his status and salary within the company, so the transfer did not result in a violation that could be grieved, but it deprived his old unit of their recognized leader and located the activist in with a group of strangers. Harry Bennett phrased the company attitude toward the union for a *Time Magazine* article when he boasted "We will bargain with it because the law says so. We will bargain till Hell freezes over, but they won't get anything."[68]

Ford harassment and dismissal of union floor leaders instigated work stoppages that usually redressed the immediate demand, but threatened to draw the union into a premature general strike. The union had petitioned the NLRB in December, 1940 for an election to determine who, if anyone, the workers wanted to represent their interests in the plant. Despite legal challenges employed by the company to delay the vote and buy time to try to splinter the union, the UAW was confident of the eventual outcome. It expected to gain recognition as the bargaining agent for the Ford workers through the mechanisms stipulated in the National Labor Relations Act, and was eager to avoid any action that might jeopardize their position. They wired the President urging an NLRB election at the earliest possible time, and indicated the union was willing to accept any form of conciliation the state or federal government was willing to invoke, but would be forced to strike if Ford Service was not restrained from violating the law and dismantling the grievance mechanisms recently established within the company.

By the first of April, Ford and Bennett decided their best gambit was to precipitate a crisis that would either force the union to back down and lose face or into a strike that Ford was determined to win. Ford retreated to his Georgia estate where he was removed from any direct involvement with the happenings in Dearborn, and Bennett instigated the provocation by firing the eight Rouge employees who had composed the overall grievance committee in the plant. In announcing his action, Bennett provided no reason for the dismissals, but proclaimed the decision was final, and that the union could "bargain till Christmas, but we won't put the eight men back to work.[69] Faced with this sudden provocation, the men in the rolling mill plant quit working. About one hundred Dearborn police were summoned to the plant to restore order, but, when confronted with over a thousand workers rushing to the scene from around the complex, they abruptly departed. The stoppage at the rolling mill building quickly spread to the whole Rouge complex.

The union was confronted with the situation it sought to avoid. Its only recourse was to endorse the strike. Occupation of the Rouge was ruled out, not only because sit-downs were now illegal and could be broken by state or federal troops, but also because the Rouge was so formidably walled and guarded, that workers occupying the plant could not be supplied with food and water from the outside. The UAW pulled its workers from the plant and ringed the complex with thousands of pickets. When street barricades were ordered removed, a moving belt of cars that slowly circulated up and down Miller Road for days prevented normal access to the facility.[70] Both sides gambled that the other would be forced to yield.

The union proclaimed it would end the strike when three conditions were met. The eight men had to be reinstated, bargaining arrangements in the plants had to be restored to pre-strike conditions, and an immediate NLRB election was demanded.[71] Bennett responded to the strike by appealing for federal and state intervention. He couched his appeal in patriotism and raised the specter of "communist terrorists." He alleged in a wire to the President that sit-down strikers in the thousands had occupied the plant and were destroying tools and dies destined for the manufacture of airplane parts.[72]

Unfortunately for Bennett, none of his allegations were true. Two reliable observers, James Dewey, the federal conciliator, and James Sweinhart, a representative of the firm that was handling publicity for Ford, were on the scene reporting the situation they observed at the plant. Both attested that it was Bennett's Servicemen and a few thousand recently recruited blacks from the South that were occupying the plant, not the union men. Dewey made arrangements with the union to allow for safe passage out of the plant, but when he tried to address those inside, he was drowned out by a crescendo of noise orchestrated by the Servicemen. Sweinhart reported that Servicemen were physically preventing anyone from trying to leave the plant.[73]

The charges of sabotage were also baseless. Five days after the strike started, Bennett arranged an inspection tour for reporters to verify the damage he claimed was being done to Ford equipment. The company was claiming that $100,000 worth of "wanton destruction" had been done to material vital to the defense needs of the nation.[74] Bennett's gambit of inviting an inspection tour with his own men occupying the plant was ill conceived. A *Detroit News* reporter familiar with the automobile manufacturing process carefully inspected hundreds of tools and only found one that may have been damaged in some unknown manner.[75] The tour did not produce the favorable coverage Bennett intended. Union president R. J. Thomas challenged Bennett to call in the FBI to investigate his claims of sabotage, but the offer was never accepted.

Company pleas for outside intervention were intended to tap public anxiety over the wars in Europe and Asia that were threatening to spill across the oceans and break against these shores. In this case, however, even patriotism did not prove to be a last refuge for a scoundrel. The President knew the true situation at Ford, and dismissed the impact of the strike on the nation's defense effort as inconsequential.[76] The automobile industry's outright rejection of Reuther's plan to use excess capacity in the auto plants to build planes short months earlier, and their claim then that excess capacity in the auto factories could not readily be converted to other military production made company warnings now ring particularly hollow. The only defense work occurring in the Rouge at the time was the construction of a new plant to produce engines for the B-24 bombers that were to be built in a new Ford plant being constructed at Willow Run. The UAW-CIO picketers agreed to allow the AFL construction workers into the facility to continue their work in the national interest. Bennett was to submit a list of names of the construction workers who were to be allowed to pass through the picket lines to the State Police. In a blatant display of hypocrisy, the large majority of names on the list were not those of construction workers, but strong-armed reinforcements for the men occupying the plant.[77]

Bennett always counted on violence and intimidation to compel the authorities to force an end to the strike. Picket lines appeared at the plant by 6 AM on the day after the spontaneous walkout. One hour later several hundred blacks charged out of the plant armed with clubs and knives and attacked the picketers. The line broke and thirty-six of the unionists were sent to the hospital. By 9 AM the picket lines reformed and a second assault from the plant began. This time the union pickets were armed with clubs and baseball bats and the attack was repulsed.[78]

As the strike took root, Ford tried to organize a back to work movement. On the second night of the strike, Homer Martin appeared at a rally of over 3000 blacks in his new role as an AFL organizer urging a back-to-work march on the Dearborn facility.[79] The prospect of such a march raised fears of a race riot. Ford may have encouraged this fear to prod the authorities to intervene against the strikers. Local and national black leaders rushed into the neighborhoods to forestall plans for the march. NAACP leader Walter White extracted a promise from the UAW that union seniority rules would not be used against blacks in times of high unemployment then set about diffusing the tension in the neighborhoods. White convinced local black leaders that African-Americans had more to gain cooperating with the union to ensure a successful outcome from the strike than being seen as bastions of the Ford regime. White and several prominent local pastors were able to dampen sentiment for the march to Dearborn, and the AFL helped diffuse the situation by labeling Martin a strike breaker.[80]

With the threat of the march averted, White headed to the Rouge to try to talk the black workers out of the plant. The union provided the NAACP leader with a sound truck and assurances of safe passage through the picket lines for any worker leaving the plant. His stature did not make his task any easier. White described the hostility toward the union that he encountered as he walked the picket lines and pleaded with workers occupying the buildings.

> "I walked the picket line and attempted to talk to a Negro inside who brandished a frightening weapon several feet in length made of tool steel which he had sharpened to razor keenness. In answer to my plea that he come out of the plant he told me in exceedingly profane and biological language what he thought of unions in general and of me in particular. He said that Ford's was the only place in Detroit where he had been able to find a job

to support himself and his family, and that the union had not done a blankety-blank thing to break down employment discrimination in other Detroit plants."[81]

Eventually about one third of those inside were talked out of the factories by White, and the rest left at the urging of federal conciliator Dewey several days later.

Michigan Governor, Murray Van Wagoner, came to Detroit at the outset of the strike, but with no inclination to accede to the Ford request for troops. Van Wagoner was a moderate Democrat who had defeated the Ford-backed Republican candidate in the recent election. He was resolute in stipulating that only mediation would resolve the crisis. The union promptly agreed to mediation, and as Bennett's other options dwindled, he too agreed to meet the Governor and explore mechanisms for a settlement. Ford's reluctant acceptance of mediation was reflected in its choice of negotiators that it sent to the meetings. The Ford team consisted of a Ford Company lawyer and low level employees from the Service Department including a former boxer known in local ring circles as One Round Hogan.[82]

Ten days after the strike began, it was over. The union won on all its basic demands. The agreement stipulated that five of the eight dismissed shop stewards be immediately reinstated, and the previous grievance process restored. Unresolved differences were to be submitted to a mediation board, and, most importantly, an NLRB sponsored employee election was to be expeditiously scheduled.[83] That election took place on May 21, 1941. Eighty-three thousand votes were cast by workers from the Rouge and two other Ford plants. The ballot offered three choices: the UAW-CIO, Homer Martin's former AFL union, or no union at all. The UAW received 72% of the vote. No union was the choice on only 4% of the ballots, and the AFL affiliate received the remainder of the votes.[84] Much of the AFL support came from black workers who thought Ford favored the Martin-led group. With the election defeat of the AFL affiliate, Homer Martin's career as a labor leader came to an end.

The UAW had won the right to be the bargaining agent for the Ford workers, but still faced Bennett's stated threat that he was not obligated to accede to any of their demands. The historic antagonism of the company toward the union created the prospect of a drawn-out bargaining process, but pressures from without and within the Rouge fortress led to a surprisingly swift, groundbreaking agreement.

Ford, the 'practical sociologist', was approaching his eightieth birthday. After he was gone, his fortune would pass to his survivors, his company would be managed by other leaders, only his reputation would remain a lasting presence in the world of the quick. The NLRB hearings threatened to destroy that. A particularly able NLRB investigator aided by a large staff had assembled a damning array of witnesses whose testimony would change the narrative of Ford's treatment of his workforce from the five dollar day to the intimidation and criminal behavior of his Service Department.[85] Ford had exhausted every effort at his disposal to delay or halt the hearings, and as contract talks took place, only an agreement with the union could circumvent the proceedings.

In June of 1941, the sounds of war were growing louder and closer to home. American industry was being mobilized to supply the beleaguered British armed forces and to defend the homeland. Lucrative contracts were at stake and Ford's posture toward labor and past support of the German Bund and the America First movement put him at a disadvantage in getting his share of the rewards. He needed a labor settlement, but had difficulty abandoning his years of hostility toward the union.

The final push to sign a contract with the UAW came from his family. Ford's son, Edsel, was the nominal president of the company, but was given little real authority by his domineering father. Henry Ford delegated more authority to Harry Bennett than to his son. Edsel was aware of how stagnant business practices had become at Ford, but suggestions to adopt some of the changes occurring throughout the rest of the industry were viewed by his father as a repudiation of his leadership. The company was hemorrhaging talent and losing its competitiveness. Edsel had been urging for several years to begin normalizing conditions at Ford by recognizing the inevitability of the union, but the elder Ford resisted losing any control over his empire.[86]

The large pro union vote by his workers in the NLRB election seemed to dishearten the old man. His closest associates confided that he was never the same afterward.[87] Just as negotiations reached a critical stage, Ford vowed to close the company rather than sign a contract with the union. This last defiant impulse was damped by his wife, Clara, who was distressed at the prospect of racial violence that his actions might unleash and threatened to walk out of their home if he were to do such a thing. Ford later admitted "I'm sure she was right. The whole thing was not worth the trouble it would make. I'm glad that I did see it her way. Don't ever discredit the power of a woman."[88]

With the NLRB hearings underway, the declining fortunes of his company, and his wife's threat to leave him ringing in his ears, the aged industrialist had little choice left. On June 20, Ford abruptly did an about face and committed to the most generous contract the UAW had yet been awarded. Besides the standard grievance framework and pay raises bringing Ford workers up to the prevailing industry rate, the company granted the union a closed shop and a dues check-off arrangement. The agreement also required all workers engaged in plant protection to wear badges or distinctive uniforms to indicate their function. The dreaded Ford Service Department was renamed the Division of Plant Protection, and their ability to intimidate the workforce was greatly curtailed.[89]

The union negotiators walked away from the signing ceremony with broad smiles on their faces. Surprisingly, Harry Bennett, signing the agreement for the company, also had a Cheshire grin on his face when he met the press. With the agreement the NLRB hearings in Detroit and nine other pending cases were automatically closed. Instead of the incriminating testimony from the government witnesses, the public got to hear Bennett extol the generosity of his boss. The company issued a press release proclaiming that with this agreement "once more, as ever in the past, the Ford Motor Company was setting an example for other industrialists" and had committed itself "to address every problem from the viewpoint of its workingmen."[90]

The little ex-pugilist had other reasons to feel smug. Bennett and Ford believed that if they could not keep the union out of their shops, they could take it over once it was allowed inside. By agreeing to a closed shop, the union could not keep the former Servicemen that were now switched into jobs on the line from becoming members. Assigned to their new tasks, these former enforcers elbowed their way into nominations for the shop steward positions that would determine the effectiveness of the union inside the plant. This tactic failed at the Rouge and other plants with a union presence before the settlement when the "Bennett candidates" won few votes from the rank-and-file in local elections.[91]

Experiencing little success with infiltration, Bennett next tried enticement. He embarked upon a campaign of charm and flattery toward the union officials, from the lowest shop steward to the most senior leaders. Bennett and Ford entertained the likes of R. J. Thomas and CIO president, Phil Murray, and played on the vanity of union leaders by suggesting that the union was too small a stage for men of their talent and intimating that they could have a more fulfilling career in business or politics.[92] Whether it was their devotion to the cause for which they had been fighting, the realization that any sign of selling out to the company would be punished by the rank-and-file, or the salutary example of Homer Martin sitting in the Ford Administration Building like a relic in the museum of labor antiquity, the attempts to turn the leaders to the dark side of the force proved futile.

By the time the Ford charm offensive ended, America was at war. The union pledged not to strike during the period of national sacrifice, and the company reverted to its old habit of delay and intimidation in an attempt to goad the workers into an action that would discredit the union in the eyes of the public. In the face of company provocations and disregard for the established grievance procedures, the UAW requested that all unsettled grievances be adjudicated by an outside umpire as established with the other automobile companies. After some delay, Ford agreed, but continued to delay by rejecting all of the names proposed by the union. After five months elapsed, the company agreed on the choice of Dr. Harry Shulman, a former professor of law at Yale. America had been at war for almost a year and a half before Dr. Shulman made his first ruling.[93]

At about the same time, Edsel Ford died. Edsel was the voice for moderation and reform within the company—the patron of the Arts who brought the Communist painter, Diego Rivera, to the Rouge and resisted calls to erase the artist's conception of *Detroit Industry* from the walls of the Institute of Arts. The old man, who had marginalized his son during his lifetime, was devastated by his death. He became more detached from the affairs of the company. Edsel's wife, Eleanor, his twenty-six year old son, Henry Ford II, and Harry Bennett were added to the Ford Board of Directors. The elder Ford returned in name as the President of the company, the young Ford was named Executive Vice President, and Harry Bennett assumed greater responsibility in the day-to-day management of the corporation.[94]

In 1945, Henry Ford suffered a stroke. Control of the company passed to the twenty-eight year old vice president who had spent his apprenticeship preparing for the moment. His first action as chief executive was to fire Harry Bennett. Edsel's son sacked the man who had tormented his father and thwarted his efforts to restore the company to its former prominence. When Henry the second reported his action to Henry the first, the old man is reported to have merely shrugged and said "I guess Harry is back on the street again."[95]

The younger Henry continued the palace revolution at Ford by airing the stale atmosphere that had permeated the institution for the previous quarter century. Over 1,000 of Bennett's minions were shown the door, and top talent was recruited from outside the company.[96] Ernest R. Breech left the presidency of the Bendix Division of GM to assume the position of Executive Vice President at Ford. Breech served the inexperienced Ford grandson as a mentor. Executives from GM and Montgomery Ward were brought in to direct planning and purchasing, and capable mid-level executives who had languished under the Bennett regime were afforded a greater measure of responsibility. Ford's old propagandist, W. J. Cameron was replaced by the public relations firms of Elmo Roper and Earl Newsom.

For years Ford had been navigating the commercial seas without a compass. Planning was centralized. Important decisions were made by dictatorial fiat. The pace of the model changeover lagged behind its rivals. Accounting practices confined the flexibility of management in a straight jacket. When Ford's grandson assumed control of the company, accounting methods at Ford were little different from the work Bob Cratchit might have done for Scrooge and Marley in Victorian England. Management had no way of measuring how each of its various units was performing and how its resources would be best allocated.[97] The young man with little experience in the industry was faced with a Herculean task of cleaning the old man's Aegean stable.

In addition to Breech and other high executives that were lured from his competitors, Ford recruited ten bright young graduates of Harvard who had served during the war as systems analysts with the Air Force. These new recruits, dubbed the "whiz kids", included Robert McNamara, the future Secretary of Defense, and Arjay Miller, like McNamara a future president of the company, and J. Edward Lundy who helped establish Ford Finance's reputation as a model for corporate America. The whiz kids formed the core of the design team which took the 1949 Ford sedan from concept to production in a mere nineteen months.[98] The 1949 sedan was the first new design by Ford since 1942, and it became an instant success, vaulting the company back up to the number two position in sales. The company that Franklin Roosevelt briefly considered nationalizing during World War II had regained its health and direction.

The grandson of the 'practical sociologist' majored in Sociology himself at Yale. His ascendancy marked a new chapter in labor relations at Ford. Shortly after his elevation to the presidency, he articulated his views on labor in an address before the Society of Automotive Engineers titled "The Challenge of Human Engineering." He reiterated his intention to work with the union and excoriated the industrialist who neglected the human factor in managing his business.[99] Through the years, Ford developed a close working relationship with Walter Reuther. The first company pension plan was negotiated with Ford in 1949, and in 1955 the union won a Supplementary Unemployment Benefits plan from the company, marking the first step in achieving Reuther's goal of a guaranteed annual wage. Away from the bargaining table the two men found common cause in issues affecting their community and nation. Reuther and Ford partnered in efforts to revitalize Detroit after the 1967 riots, and jointly founded the United Way campaign. Reuther remarked on a number of occasions that when the primary goal of a negotiation was a wage increase the union would target General Motors, but when the goal was an innovation in social welfare, it would target Ford.[100]

On April 7, 1947, Henry Ford died. Eulogies poured in from around the country extolling his achievements. One hundred thousand mourners filed past his body as he lay on view at his historical recreation of Greenfield Village.[101] At an appointed hour on the day of Ford's funeral, workers in all industrial establishments in the state of Michigan were requested to stand at their station and pause for one minute of silent tribute for the man who symbolized the American automobile industry.

In Ford's case, Shakespeare's Antony got it backwards. It was mostly the good that remained and the evil that was interred with his bones. The anti-Semitism, intimidation of his workers, and small-mindedness were separated from the rags-to-riches story, the five dollar day, and his acts of generosity by the word BUT. Henry Ford had these foibles..., BUT he was the protagonist of an American success story who rewarded his workers with the five dollar day. Harry Bennett and Ford's publicist, W. J. Cameron, were easy villains to blame for the excesses in deed and word of the Ford regime. Harry Bennett and the word BUT protected Ford's legacy as staunchly as the Service Department had defended his industrial empire during his lifetime. To the public looking for a hero, the territory on the other side of the BUT was not a place many were interested in exploring.

In many respects Henry Ford symbolizes an America that still yearns for an idealized past and is discomfited by the erosion of its Anglo Saxon bloodline. He was a pioneer of the twentieth century whose two feet were firmly planted in the religious and pioneering traditions of the colonial past. His writings tout a Calvinist pursuit of divine redemption through the avoidance of sin rather than by a resume of charitable service. His definition of sin was broadened to include any of the socially undesirable practices with which he disapproved, and he strove with a missionary zeal to instill his values in the culture. Ford, as the self-taught mechanic who disdained intellectual achievement, is an exemplar of the America that elevates ingrained belief over scholarship.

CHAPTER VI

The War Years

England's battles, it used to be said, were won on the playing fields of Eton. This plan is put forward in the belief that America's can be won on the assembly lines of Detroit.

Walter Reuther
Introducing 500 Planes a Day plan, 1940

On July 4th, 1940, as Americans were celebrating the anniversary of their Declaration of Independence, the army of the mother country was completing its evacuation from the beaches of Dunkirk. The Battle of France was over. Ten days earlier, a jubilant Adolph Hitler danced a jig at the French surrender ceremony staged on the recreated site of German humiliation twenty-two years earlier. With the battle of France over, the Battle of Britain was about to begin, as was the battle for the future course of the United States.

Franklin Roosevelt had presided over eight of the most turbulent years the country had experienced, and claimed he was eager to return to his home in Hyde Park. He may have yearned for the tranquility of his Hudson River estate, but the captain who had steered the American state through the troubled waters of the Great Depression was not ready to leave the bridge in inexperienced hands while the storm raging across both oceans threatened the homeland. Roosevelt had accrued vast new power in the office of the presidency, and the office had become synonymous with the man. More than an oversized ego convinced him that there was no other person of comparable stature and ability to lead the nation through the perilous times ahead.

Only tradition stood between Roosevelt and the third term he craved. All previous sitting presidents adhered to the precedent set by George Washington in limiting their period in office to two consecutive terms. For Roosevelt to break with this tradition would require a disavowal of such an intent, a weak Democratic aspirant to the position who could be swept aside with little loss of political capital, and an irresistible call from the party and the country for him to seek a third term. The operation had to be contrived without the appearance of it being contrived.

The Democrat who stepped forward to presume the post-Roosevelt leadership of his party was James Farley, the man who managed Roosevelt's first two campaigns. Farley was a political operative who could be rewarded with a patronage job, but he had no qualification for higher office. His delusional aspirations were akin to a James Carville or Karl Rove stepping out from behind the curtain to audition for the lead. Roosevelt did nothing to dampen Farley's expectations or suggest he planned anything other than his own retirement. In a conversation with Farley a week before the convention, Roosevelt reiterated his desire not to seek reelection and his intention to so inform the convention. But when pressed by Farley to make a Shermanesque declaration that he would not run if nominated nor serve if elected, Roosevelt replied that he would have no right to decline a genuine draft in these perilous times.[1]

Every delegate and party leader at the Chicago convention center knew that neither Farley nor any candidate other than Roosevelt had a realistic chance of defeating the Republican nominee, Wendell Willkie. Influential Democrats were urging Roosevelt to break with convention and run again. The UAW Executive Board added its voice to the crescendo of pre-convention imprecations urging the President to run for a third term, but to finesse the break from tradition, the semblance of a genuine draft had to be maintained. The President's advisers determined that the convention chairman, Alben Barkley, would deliver a message to the assembly from Roosevelt expressing his desire to retire from public life, but not shutting the door to accepting a draft from the floor. The message delivered to Barkley read, "You…have known and understood that I have not today and have never had any wish to remain in the office of President…after next January. You know, and all my friends know, this is a simple and sincere fact. I want you to repeat this simple and sincere fact to the convention."[2]

Barkley summarized the message at the end of a rousing speech extolling the progress made over the past eight years, then ended by stating, "He wishes in all earnestness and sincerity to make it clear that all delegates to this convention are free to vote for any candidate. That is the message I bear to you from the President of the United States, our great leader, Franklin Delano Roosevelt."[3] After a brief hush permeated the assembled, the Chicago machine of Mayor Kelly went to work. A voice emanating from somewhere in the basement of the convention center rumbled through the loud speakers in the hall. "We Want Roosevelt!" The crowd took up the chant—"We Want Roosevelt!" The galleries packed with Kelly loyalists erupted in 'spontaneous' demonstrations for the President. "Chicago Wants Roosevelt!" "New York Wants Roosevelt!" "The World Wants Roosevelt!" The demonstration went on for over an hour.[4] There was nothing left for Farley to do the next evening than to move that the renomination of Franklin Delano Roosevelt be made unanimous. When it was learned that the voice coming over the loudspeakers belonged to Chicago Superintendent of Sanitation, Thomas McGarry, Republican opponents noted that Roosevelt was summoned to another run by the voice from the sewers.[5]

Roosevelt had stepped on toes and alienated some of his earlier supporters by aggregating unprecedented power within his office. In particular, the attempt to thwart Constitutional restraints by packing the Supreme Court with additional justices alienated people sympathetic to his overall agenda and enraged his conservative opponents. There was also a strong isolationist block determined to resist any gesture toward Britain that might draw the country into war.

Roosevelt tried to remain aloof from the fray and project an image of confident leadership, but by mid-October Willkie began cutting into his lead. It was then announced that he would make five campaign addresses in five large Northeastern cities that would be broadcast live to a national audience. Roosevelt's opponents also took to the air.

John L. Lewis was a life-long Republican who had supported Roosevelt in 1936, but soured on the President because of personal differences and because his pacifist sensibilities were offended by his perception that Roosevelt was maneuvering the country into war. (Lewis' aversion to violence did not always pertain to his personal conduct as evidenced during the AFL convention in Atlantic City four years earlier.) Lewis' ego had recently added considerable girth from indulging on the desserts of his previous achievements. His October 25th radio address was mean-spirited and delusional. He accused FDR of "overweening, abnormal [...] dictatorial ambitions," and claimed "the reelection of President Roosevelt would be an evil of the first magnitude." He charged the President with scheming to involve the country in the foreign war, and couched his appeal in a grim calculus of a Roosevelt reelection: "You, who may be about to die in a foreign war, should you salute your Caesar?" And to the 'mothers of the nation' he queried "May I hope that on Election Day you [...] with the sacred ballot [will] lead the revolt against the candidate who plays a game that may make cannon fodder of your sons?"[6] Lewis ended his address by incredibly casting the presidential election as a referendum on himself. Lewis reasoned that Roosevelt could be reelected only with the support of labor, and asked America's workers to "sustain" or "repudiate" himself with their votes as if *he* were running in the election. He promised to resign as head of the CIO if Roosevelt were reelected.

Lewis's tirade frightened Roosevelt, saddened many rank-and-file workers who worshiped him, and infuriated many other labor leaders. Walter Reuther took to the air in a thirteen city hookup to reiterate labor support for the President. "The personal spite and hatred of one man will not switch labor's votes from Roosevelt," Reuther vowed. "The issue is wholly and simply Roosevelt or reaction. American labor will take Roosevelt."[7]

After Roosevelt was reelected, Lewis made good on his promise. He resigned as head of the CIO and retreated with his mine workers back into the AFL. His behavior became more erratic. He called several ill-timed, ill-advised coal strikes during periods of national emergency that roused public ire and abetted a conservative Congress in passing restrictive labor legislation. Like Ford, Lewis played a defining role in creating the modern industrial society of post-war America, but he was every bit of an autocrat as the industrialist. Neither man was able to check his ego nor adapt his institution to the norms of the democratic society in which it resided, and both allowed the excesses of their latter years to tarnish the image they forged through their accomplishments.

Lewis was succeeded at the CIO by Phil Murray, an avuncular, soft-spoken Scotsman who was a Lewis protégé and head of the Steelworkers union. The affable Murray proved an ideal choice for containing the factionalism and rivalries that continually threatened to implode the young organization whose early physical development outpaced its coordination and maturity.

Another loose cannon who threatened to derail Roosevelt's bid for a third term was Joseph Kennedy, the patriarch of the political family that dominated Democratic Party politics for much of the latter half of the twentieth century. Kennedy was skeptical of the British ability to withstand the German blitz and fearful of the consequences of a wider war. He was not averse to a fascist state in Germany, and favored Chamberlain's appeasement of Hitler to Churchill's uncompromising rejection of any negotiations with the Nazi dictator. Kennedy made several attempts to meet personally with Hitler without State Department approval to "bring about a better understanding between the United States and Germany."[8] Kennedy had a long association with Roosevelt and his son James, but his fears that Roosevelt was steering the country into the European conflict prompted him to plan an endorsement of the President's GOP opponent.

Kennedy flew back to Washington from his post in Britain on a transatlantic sea plane common in the era when the range of a passenger plane was roughly the distance between Labrador and the west of Ireland. Kennedy had contemplated a much earlier, more visible arrival back home, where he planned to play an active, probably disruptive, role in the political drama, but his departure from Britain was delayed by the blitz and his not wanting to be accused of a cowardly retreat from his post in the face of danger. When he arrived at La Guardia Field on October 27th, two days after the Lewis broadcast, Roosevelt went to lengths to ensure that his homecoming would be neither visible nor disruptive. The minute his plane touched down he was met at the bottom of the steps by Secret Service agents who gave him a handwritten invitation to dinner from Roosevelt and escorted him to a special phone connection with the President. FDR was having lunch with the Speaker of the House Sam Rayburn and his young Texas colleague Lyndon Johnson when the Kennedy call was put through. Accounts of the conversation indicated Roosevelt greeted Kennedy like a long-absent friend. "Ah Joe, it's good to hear your voice…Come to the White House tonight for a little family dinner. I'm dying to talk to you." While uttering the last sentence he was said to have smiled broadly to his lunch guests and made a gesture of slitting his throat.[9]

Since Kennedy was still the Ambassador to Great Britain, he could not graciously decline the President's invitation. To ensure that he had no opportunity for mischief before meeting with Roosevelt, the President had him escorted across the tarmac to a waiting plane, flown to Washington, and escorted by motorcade to the White House. During the plane ride to Washington, his wife, Rose, was said to have cautioned him about how ungrateful a repudiation of the man who had appointed the first Catholic to the Court of St. James might appear to the public.[10]

Kennedy was accorded little time alone with the President during the course of the evening. Finally, before agreeing to endorse the reelection of his party's nominee, he told Roosevelt that he had some things he needed to get off his chest. He complained about being bypassed by State Department officials carrying messages between Roosevelt and Churchill and being left completely in the dark about the agreement to lend five hundred vintage destroyers to Britain in exchange for the lease of British naval bases in the Caribbean and Canadian Maritimes.

Roosevelt distanced himself from the actions of his subordinates, and told Kennedy that these "officious men" would be dealt with after the wartime emergency no longer necessitated their continuance in the administration. Such "insolent" men would not be allowed to treat old, trusted friends like Kennedy in such an off-handed manner. Whatever inducements were used privately to extract an agreement from Kennedy to issue a statement of support for Roosevelt were only secondhand rumors attributed to close family members. John Kennedy was told that

Roosevelt dangled a presidential run in 1944 before his all too receptive father. James Roosevelt reported that his father offered his support for the political careers of Joe Kennedy's sons, but if the elder Kennedy betrayed him their political future would never occur.[11] Both versions seem plausible interpretations of the parts of the conversation the two participants were most eager to hear and convey.

Kennedy's message of support for the President, when it was widely anticipated he would endorse Willkie, forestalled any last-minute momentum the challenger was hoping to gain. Roosevelt's return to active campaigning swung the momentum in the race back to the incumbent. On October 28th, Roosevelt went to Madison Square Garden to address an audience that overflowed out into the streets and expanded to forty or fifty million via radio. He never mentioned Willkie by name, but listed the accomplishments of the New Deal and named Republican legislators who tried to block his reforms and who now attempted to rebuff his efforts to aid the forces of democracy in the ongoing war. The list of Republican obstructionists ended each time after a brief pause with the names Martin, Barton, and Fish. The crowd inside the arena quickly caught the spirit and after each pause, echoed back the refrain of Martin, Barton, and Fish. Willkie was no isolationist, and was not an opponent of many of the New Deal programs, but Roosevelt adroitly photo shopped Willkie into the obstructionist, isolationist class photo along with Martin, Barton, and Fish.

The name Fish escaped from the mouth of the President like a venomous hiss from the confluence of two of the Anglo Saxon tongue's more turbid phoneme streams. Hamilton Fish was FDR's mid-Hudson neighbor and the Representative from Roosevelt's own home district. The two political rivals from Dutchess County today are commemorated by a pair of bridges, appropriately twenty miles apart that provide two different routes across the expansive Hudson River. Hamilton Fish Sr. was succeeded in office by his son, Hamilton Fish, Jr., a moderate Republican, who, as a member of the House Judiciary Committee, cast a vote for the impeachment of Richard Nixon. The grandson of Fish Sr. attempted to hold the seat for the family while running as a Democrat, but was defeated.

The short campaign established the claim that Franklin Roosevelt was the person best able to lead the United States through the difficult period ahead. Wendell Willkie was a capable, intelligent man whose views on the world situation were very similar to Roosevelt's. But Willkie had one conspicuous handicap. He had been a Republican for less than a year before becoming the party's nominee. Willkie had backed FDR in his first campaign, and the Wall Street lawyer did not have an allergic reaction to the New Deal. Roosevelt demonstrated his complete dominance of the party he headed from the "spontaneous" chants of "We want Roosevelt" at the convention to his handling of the ambitious Kennedy before he could cast his own shadow across the race, whereas Willkie had to march in the same parade as Martin, Barton, and Fish and shuffle his feet to keep in step with his adopted party. Willkie was asked to lobby the Republican Congressional leadership on behalf of the Lend-Lease deal to send old destroyers to Britain in exchange for the use of naval bases in the Canadian Maritimes, but demurred because as a newly minted Republican he was not ready to get in a struggle with the party old guard at a time he was trying to unify them behind his candidacy.

The election campaign of 1940 did not paralyze the governing process in the manner of today's over-produced, over-budgeted, tightly-scripted Hollywood blockbuster campaigns. Events in Europe would not allow an escape from the responsibilities of elected office. In September, Congress passed the Selective Service Act despite the prolonged efforts of Fish to dilute the scale and involuntary nature of the bill. Willkie supported the measure, but, as with the destroyers for bases exchange with Britain, was unable to convince the majority of his party to follow his lead.

As the campaign progressed, American attitudes toward the war began to change. On June 25th a Gallup Poll found that 64% of the public said that it was more important to stay out of the conflict than to back Britain. By October 20th, the public was evenly divided between the two choices, and on November 19, the balance had shifted to 60-40 in favor of backing Britain even if it meant being drawn into the war.[12] The numbers reflected confidence in Roosevelt's leadership and support for his actions in authorizing the destroyers for bases exchange and extending the neutrality zone far out into the Atlantic, but it also reflected the admiration felt for the British in withstanding the German blitz and the resolution to endure expressed by their leader, Winston Churchill.

On Election Day Wendell Willkie received more votes than any other Republican presidential candidate had ever won, but Franklin Roosevelt received five million more. Roosevelt won in all of the nation's two hundred largest cities except Cincinnati, and all of the industrial states of the Northeast and Midwest except the UAW stronghold of Michigan, where a significant vote for the Socialist Norman Thomas allowed Willkie to squeak out a seven thousand vote margin of victory.

The third Roosevelt term presented a different challenge from the first two. War production provided the economic stimulus that brought unemployment, which had stubbornly settled into the low double digit range for much of the second term, down to pre-depression levels. The fact that such a massive infusion of government spending was the prescription for the sick economy written by Keynes has been discounted by conservative opinion, unwilling to credit the medicine for the cure. With the Depression effectively over, there was no further effort to expand the New Deal.

By mid-summer of 1940, before the election campaign began in earnest, Roosevelt had already shifted his focus from the New Deal social-economic agenda to war preparedness. He privately told his chief political operative Thomas Corcoran "Tommy, cut out this New Deal stuff. It's tough to win a war."[13] In May he created a National Defense Advisory Commission that included the former General Motors President William Knudsen as head of production planning. The Commission included other prominent businessmen, and Sidney Hillman of the CIO as the union hall bloke invited to a country club soiree. The wealthy businessmen served on the Commission for a salary of one dollar a year and became referred to as the "dollar a year men." In July, the President reorganized his cabinet and brought a number of prominent Republicans from the internationalist wing of the party into his inner circle. He made Henry Stimson, Secretary of State under Hoover, his Secretary of War and Henry Knox, Alf Landon's running mate in 1936, Secretary of the Navy. These appointees brought into government with them a coterie of business associates who came to occupy the front row seats previously filled by the New Deal liberals.

In response to the German advance into France and the Low Countries, Roosevelt pushed the peacetime draft through Congress, tripled the defense budget, and coupled the destroyers for bases agreement with an extension of the 'neutrality zone' far out into the Atlantic. He called for the construction of fifty thousand aircraft per year—a number far in excess of the total number of planes in service across the globe in 1940.[14]

Nineteen forty was a good year for Franklin Roosevelt; it was also a very good year for Walter Reuther. Before 1940, Reuther was best known to the public as the other guy in the photo with a battered Richard Frankensteen after the Battle of the Overpass. By the end of the year he emerged as a successor to Lewis as the public face of organized labor. Barely a week before German forces goose-stepped down the Champs-Elysées, Reuther was able to solidify the UAW relationship with General Motors. In August he emerged at the UAW convention in St. Louis as the leader of the pro-Roosevelt internationalist wing of the union. It was Reuther who gave the radio response to Lewis in the last days of the campaign; and it was Reuther who grabbed public attention in December with a plan for realizing Roosevelt's desire to build fifty thousand planes a year.

Reuther's deferred his defection from the Unity Caucus in 1938 because Martin represented the more immediate concern and there was nothing he could do but bide his time and strengthen his own position. By 1940 he was ready to make a clean break with his former Communist allies and with vestiges of the ideology he may have worn more comfortably upon his return from Gorky. The Molotov-Ribbentrop Pact of August, 1939 and subsequent Soviet usurpation of territories in Poland, Finland, and the Baltic States delegitimatized the Communist Party in the eyes of most Americans. Before the pact, Communism had an appeal among Finnish and Polish Americans. After Soviet troops rolled into those two countries, people from these immigrant groups became staunchly anti-Communist.

Communists became much more isolated within the union. The Reuther forces in St. Louis seized the opportunity to push through a resolution condemning "the brutal dictatorships, and wars of aggression of the totalitarian governments of Germany, Italy, Russia, and Japan."[15] They backed this up with a resolution, passed over the objection of George Addes, barring members of an organization declared illegal by the U. S. government from holding union office. Reuther then took the floor to overwhelm Communist efforts to forestall a UAW endorsement of a third term for President Roosevelt. The Communists cited the opposition to a third term by John L. Lewis and echoed his fear that a war would unleash the same reactionary forces that destroyed the progressive movement during the last Great War. Reuther countered the arguments that Roosevelt was insufficiently liberal. Waving a copy of the Proceedings of the 1939 Convention above his head, Reuther recalled "the beautiful resolution that [Communist floor leader] Nat Ganley introduced praising Roosevelt, because those were the days of the People's Front. That is no more; there has been a deal between Stalin and Hitler, and therefore People's Front and collective security have been put in the ash can once and for all." He concluded by resolving the choice between following the lead of John L. Lewis or backing the President by declaring "Let Lewis lead the CIO and let Roosevelt lead the nation."[16] The auditorium erupted in cheers and subsequent attempts to prevent an endorsement of Roosevelt were greeted with whistles and jeers. Only thirty Communist delegates voted against the resolution.[17]

The Popular Front was relegated to the ash can not only by the German-Soviet alliance, but also because the young Socialists who were mentored by Norman Thomas and Tucker Smith at Brookwood Labor College were migrating out of the party into collaboration with socially progressive internationalists who joined together to form the Union for Democratic Action (UDA). Walter and Victor Reuther had seen the rise of Hitler during their time in Germany and knew this was not a war fought primarily for imperialistic design on markets and resources. Churchill had included labor in the manufacturing, procurement, and manpower allocation planning for the war effort, and the workers living in the East End of London were bearing the brunt of the German bombing campaign. Word of German atrocities was slipping through the Nazi facade. The radical anti-militarism at the core of Socialist teaching had no answer to the threat posed in this conflict. Thomas widened the breach between his party and his young protégées when he shared the platform at a May 1941 anti war rally with Charles Lindbergh, the aviator and America First spokesman who had been vocal in expressing his sympathy for the German regime.[18]

500 Plumes a Day

In the summer of 1940, as German forces were poised on the French coast and Luftwaffe planes were bombing London and the industrial Midlands, Reuther observed the progress on construction of a new Packard aircraft engine factory each morning on his way to work. He knew it would be two years before the plant would be finished, staffed with a trained workforce, and equipped, ready to begin delivering engines for badly needed planes. He feared two years might be too late to supply the planes Roosevelt envisioned for the defense of Britain. He also feared that labor was being marginalized by the dollar a year men using the national emergency to erode the gains recently won by workers. Reuther thought the same mass production methods used to produce automobiles could be employed to build airplanes—"a car with wings."[19] With characteristic vision, vigor, and self-assurance, Reuther formulated a plan addressing both national and parochial interests.

Reuther authorized a detailed survey of idle capacity in the Detroit area plants. He knew much of the machinery that would be needed for the new plants would duplicate machines already available and underutilized in existing plants. He noted that:

> At present the auto industry never operates at more than 80 – 90% capacity, and then only for a few months a year. The rest of the year it operates on reduced schedules, and many plants shut down completely. If automobile production were spread evenly over a 19-month period, it would be possible, without reducing the total output of autos, to convert a large portion of this machinery to the manufacture of planes.[20]

Skilled labor was also subjected to the same model-year cycle volatility:

The automobile industry has the largest reservoir of skilled labor in the world. More than twenty-five thousand tool and die workers, jig and fixture men, pattern makers, draftsmen, and designers are employed in the auto industry. Each year thousands of the industry's most skilled craftsmen work at top-speed for a few months to adapt old machinery to new models. When completed, only a skeleton crew of these skilled workmen are retained. Three to four thousand are shifted to ordinary production jobs, while more than ten thousand are laid off until needed again. More than one half of the tool and die makers averaged less than 6 months of work a year.[21]

Reuther proposed delaying the new model year for six months and pooling the unused labor and machinery to build the various components for a single model pursuit plane that could be mass produced and supplement the production of bombers and planes of special design being constructed in the aviation plants. To coordinate the scheduling and assignment of labor and responsibilities between the various plants and companies, Reuther proposed a tripartite aviation production board consisting of three representatives each from government, management, and labor, and vested with full authority "to organize and supervise mass production of airplanes in the automobile industry."

Finally Reuther recognized the opposition that his plan would engender within the aircraft and automobile industry establishment and sought to deflate it by elevating the discussion to a question of patriotism.

Though we propose payment of a fair profit to each manufacturer in accordance with his share of the work, we foresee the fears this plan may arouse on the part of some managements. They may prefer the government to finance entire new engines and aircraft plants. Aviation companies may look with misgiving on a production program that would inevitably cut the cost of planes by putting their production on a mass production basis.

But we believe the average management executive would not put forward these selfish considerations at a time of crisis.[22]

The plan recognized the only feasible way of reducing start up delay and dislocations associated with a shift from civilian to defense production. It had obvious patriotic appeal. It also contained a few caveats for labor, for the UAW, and for the Reuther faction within the union. The tripartite board represented an element of national industrial planning that management always strenuously resisted. If it could be introduced as a temporary war-time measure and demonstrate achievements, there would be a case for continuing it after the war. The plan also embodied a goal it would take Reuther another twenty-five years to realize—a guaranteed annual wage. By leveling the crests and valleys in employment caused by the model-year changeover with regular defense work, an autoworker would enjoy the security of a regular paycheck.

Much of the defense work was being directed by the war planners to areas outside of the traditional union strongholds in the Northeast and Midwest. Using existing auto plants for defense related production would keep government money flowing into unionized plants. In particular, the aircraft industry was mainly located in Southern California "the white spot of the open shop."[23] Reuther's rival within the UAW, Richard Frankensteen, was in charge of the union membership drive within the aviation industry, but in the shops, the locals were dominated by Communists. Diverting aircraft production from California to Detroit would enhance Reuther's strength within the union and diminish that of his rivals.

The plan went through a dress rehearsal of sorts in November, 1940, when a group of skilled tradesmen from over a dozen Detroit area factories assembled at Cass Technical High School and endorsed the technical feasibility of the plan. By December it was ready to be unveiled. Reuther worked with UAW publicist Edward Levinson and journalist I. F. Stone in drafting the report. He gave his proposal the catchy slogan "500 Planes a Day" to draw public attention to it. As he had hoped, the plan immediately became a focus of public scrutiny and drew praise from many quarters of the internationalist press.

The plan was presented to the President shortly before Christmas by UAW President R. J. Thomas and CIO President Phillip Murray. Thomas showed the limitation of his vision, when he initially responded to Reuther "Screw you. You are not going to make a horse's ass out of me. Union men should stick to their knitting."[24] Murray saw that the plan contained elements of his own industry councils idea for protecting labor's interests in the defense plants, and Thomas consented to join him in presenting the plan to Roosevelt, who was favorably impressed. After the meeting, the President fired off a copy of the proposal with a memo to his production chief, Knudsen "I don't know whether you have seen all this. It is well worth our while, I think, to give a good deal of attention to his program."[25]

Knudsen was willing to hire Reuther to sell his company's used cars, but he was not about to let the thirty-four year old redhead sell the country a plan that infringed on the auto industry's control over its production schedule. He may also have been jealous that the young upstart who recently sat across the bargaining table from him was now usurping his prerogatives in his role as war production manager. In any case, Knudsen was not about to give a good deal of attention to Reuther's program. Treasury Secretary Henry Morgenthau expressed the situation succinctly when he quipped "There is only one thing wrong with the program. It comes from the 'wrong' source."[26]

Reuther and his plan received a whirlwind of publicity in the days between Christmas 1940 and mid-January 1941. He met with the President, presented his plan to a nationwide radio audience, was embraced by the embattled New Dealers surviving Roosevelt's swerve to the right, and impressed the Washington press corps with his passion and mastery of his presentation. Joseph Rauh, the organizing force behind the UDA and future Reuther friend and confidant, gushed with enthusiasm after witnessing the press conference. "This young man took Washington and all of its cynical reporters by storm that day [...Reuther's plan] was the greatest thing he ever did [...] because it combined his gigantic knowledge of the social forces in America, his mastery of the technical forces, and his idealism."[27] Blair Moody, the Washington correspondent of the usually industry friendly *Detroit News* probably gave Knudsen some indigestion when he reported "[Reuther's plan was] being seriously regarded as perhaps the most constructive production proposal ever to come from the ranks of organized labor."[28]

Whatever favorable breezes the Reuther plan may have had at its back when it was first launched, it soon ran into serious headwinds from the vested interests. Government defense spending spurred a recovery that led to the sale of four million cars in 1941. The industry was in no hurry to sacrifice the profits from civilian production and preferred that the government build new plants instead of adapting existing plants for military purpose. Industry heavyweights attacked the feasibility of the plan. Iconic GM Chairman Alfred P. Sloan publicly stated on November 20th, 1940 that auto plants could not be adapted for defense production. "Only about ten or fifteen percent of the machinery and equipment in an automobile factory can be utilized for the production of special defense material."[29] The company president, Charles Wilson, asserted management's prerogatives, claiming that "this is none of his business [...] If Reuther wants to become part of management, we will be happy to hire him."[30] But a union Vice President had no right to speak like a corporate executive.

There was also a strong current of isolationism in the industrial heartland. Some industrialists feared that Britain would be forced to accept Hitler's peace terms, and a heavy commitment to defense production would leave them with an over capacity, and the buildup would be paid for with increased taxes and more government involvement in the economy. Others, like Henry Ford, were adherents of the America First movement represented by Lindbergh. Ford turned down a lucrative contract to build Rolls Royce plane engines for export to Britain.

The aviation industry disputed Reuther's contention that planes could be built with the same mass production techniques as automobiles. They too were looking for the government to award them with new plant capacity. The President of the Aeronautical Chamber of Commerce, Colonel John H. Jouett, rebutted Reuther's contention that mass-production could greatly increase the volume of planes produced monthly. "These aircraft manufacturers have made lifetime studies of aircraft production. They would be the first to adopt mass-production methods wherever possible."[31] He argued the impracticality of Reuther's plan by multiplying the 500 planes a day figure with costs of building a single plane using the hand-crafting technology of the industry. Reuther countered by contrasting the cost and manufacturing space it would require to build six thousand Chevrolet's a day using production methods of the aircraft industry.

In the early months of 1941, advocates of the Reuther plan sent a memo to the President stating that War Department figures showed that only two Flying Fortress bombers had been delivered to the Air Corps during the previous month. Presidential Aide, Harry Hopkins, intercepted the memo and doubted the accuracy of the claim. The author of the memo, Wayne Coy, was told to go back and recheck his facts and not feed the President such misinformation again. The reprimanded Coy dutifully double checked his sources and found that indeed the original number was inaccurate. The Air Corps had received only one bomber during the month. The second one had been delivered a little later but was added to pad the previous monthly total.[32]

Since the specifics of the plan proved difficult to refute on their merit, the opposition shifted its attack to the plan's author. When Reuther's name appeared in the holiday season headlines, J. Edgar Hoover—the self-appointed crossing guard at the line between acceptable and unacceptable free speech—dug into his scrapbook of juicy gossip and dirty secrets to send a belated Christmas message to Knudsen, Senator Cox of Georgia, and other friends on his holiday mailing list who would most appreciate hearing from him. Featured in the Hoover correspondence was the FBI version of the letter from Gorky. The original letter was reprinted in the Young People's Socialist League paper *Challenge* in 1934 with the closing, "Keep up the fight, Vic and Wal." Liberty League propagandist, Joseph Kamp reprinted a doctored version that closed with the phrase, "Keep up the fight for a Soviet America, Vic and Wal." in a 1937 pamphlet attacking the CIO. It was the Kamp version that made its way into the FBI files, and it was this version that Senator Cox read into the Congressional Record when he denounced Walter Reuther, calling him "as violent a red as ever turned on the American public by Russian Communism."[33] The accusations came at a time when Reuther was trying to eliminate Communist influence within the union. The exuberance the young Reuther brothers may have felt at the beginning of their Gorky adventure had been tempered by events, age, and responsibility, but the stain of that "original sin" remained in the FBI files for the rest of Walter's life, and was trotted out by Hoover like the family photo album and shown to special friends whenever an occasion warranted.

By the summer of 1941, Hoover's antipathy toward the Reuther brothers spurred him into preparation to consign all three to "custodial detention" should the United States enter the war. In August he sent copies of the Reuthers' "detention cards" to the Detroit Bureau office. The Detroit bureau chief, John Bugas, realized the consequences such an action could spark and wrote back to Hoover:

> In view of recent developments in this country in labor circles, and in view of the stand that WALTER REUTHER has taken against Communistic elements, and further in view of the fact that it is apparent from newspaper articles that WALTER REUTHER is cooperating with the Office of Production Management in certain matters, it is believed that the Bureau would want to reconsider the information submitted, and probably not consider REUTHER for custodial detention at this time.[34]

Thwarted in a chance to pounce on his prey when war-time emergency might draw them into his web, Hoover retreated back into the shadows to wait for the next opportunity to entangle his victims. Reuther's enemies were not only lurking on the right. On the left, his opponents within the labor movement were eager to find any crumb of scandal that might fall on their plate. The letter from Gorky was used internally to show the brothers' hypocrisy as it was externally to paint them red. As war drums grew louder, mocking Reuther's draft status became a steady refrain from the anti-Reuther chorus at UAW events. Reuther registered for the draft early in 1941, and R. J. Thomas requested he be given a deferment because of his responsibilities as GM Division head. Reuther's draft board was unpersuaded and classified him 1-A with a reporting date of May 21st. CIO President Phil Murray joined Thomas in appealing the board's decision on the grounds that union leaders should be accorded the same consideration as their management counterparts. The draft board again was not persuaded to defer him on occupational grounds, but did lower his classification when it learned that Reuther's wife May would lose her secretarial position in the union if her husband were to be drafted. The arrival of the Reuther's daughter, Linda, in February, 1942 cemented his deferred status for the duration of the war.

The thirty-four year old Reuther, who had lost part of his big toe in a shop floor accident in his youth, would probably not have been cleared for combat in any case, but since he was given a deferment because of his wife's dependency instead of an occupational deferment, his critics accused the "plan man" of cowardice. At the UAW's August, 1941 convention, John Anderson, one of the leading Communist voices in the union, reminded delegates that the man who had introduced a resolution denouncing the Party for its attempts to undermine defense efforts was himself "a man that would sooner face cameras than bullets...He hid behind the skirts of his wife, and every man in the hall knows that."[35]

When the Japanese navy brought the war to American shores on December 7th, industry had to abruptly switch from a civilian to a war economy. As Reuther had predicted, there were serious dislocations in the initial months of the war. The automobile companies had not delayed the introduction of the 1942 models by six months as the Reuther plan suggested, and when production of passenger cars was ordered terminated by January 31, 1942, over 350,000 auto workers in Michigan alone were unemployed while industry made the conversion to war production. Industry sources blamed the situation on the government for lack of planning, but Reuther ridiculed these claims. "They had Mr. Knudsen down there, surrounded by hundreds of dollar-a-year men, who spent all of their time looking around to see how they could protect their own individual interests [...] And so when they say the government was responsible, they are merely saying that the dollar-a-year men from industry, who were running the government, were representing industry instead of the needs of the nation."[36]

By the time of Pearl Harbor, the original Reuther plan to use surplus capacity in the auto plants to build pursuit planes was dead, buried in the recesses of the Office of Production Management. Shortly after the Japanese attack, he made a renewed effort to revive critical aspects of the original plan. In a January OPM meeting, Reuther proposed pooling all the Detroit area tool and die facilities under the supervision of a "central agency to route the tooling jobs to see that the right job gets to the right shop in terms of machinery and tools and manpower."[37] He cited as an example of the need for coordinated industry-wide pooling the 800 skilled tool and die men at GM Ternstedt who were idled while Ford was desperately seeking workers to build the twelve hundred dies needed to start production at its Willow Run bomber plant.[38] He also called for the big three automakers to build a single model tank from a common pool of dies.

The corporate expatriates in OPM were no more inclined to allow labor a role in war-time planning with bombs falling on United States territory than they were when the bombs were falling on London. GM's Charlie Wilson, the man who claimed to have supported Debs in his younger days, now called the idea of government sponsored pooling of industrial resources in time of emergency tantamount to the "complete socialization of industry."[39]

Much as the industrial managers in OPM tried to dismiss Reuther and bury his plan, neither the man nor his program would go away. With the initial chaos in moving the county to a full military footing, voices beyond labor and its usual allies were chastising industry for its intransigent stance against an idea with much compelling rationale. General Motors decided to try to put discussion of the Reuther plan to an end by holding a debate at which it hoped the corporate view, given full exposure, would raise enough issues with the labor proposal to quiet many of the plan's advocates. General Motors rented a hall, hired George Denny, host of radio's popular *Town Hall of the Air* show, to be the moderator, and invited over 200 journalists to witness the debate and pose questions to the participants. The debate took place on March 31st, 1942. The two participants, Wilson and Reuther, each were accompanied by three technical advisers. Ben Blackwood, a senior GM tool and die man who assisted Reuther in compiling shop floor data for the plan, Victor Reuther, and an organizer for the Designing Engineer's Union of the CIO sat at the table with Reuther. Wilson was flanked by members of his Engineering and Executive boards. The event went on for six straight hours. Wilson spoke with deliberation, often reading from notes or messages passed by his associates. Reuther spoke rapidly, rarely referring to notes. Reuther addressed his counterpart as Mr. Wilson; Wilson referred to him as Walter. Reuther claimed that introduction of the 1942 models "represented the greatest waste of skilled man production and man hours that has ever taken place in America at a time when we needed every single skilled man hour we could get."[40] Wilson countered that "In October, 1940 [the industry agreed] it would subordinate any tooling program on new models to the necessities of the defense program. The trouble was that the orders for defense material did not come out fast enough for us to get at the job." Wilson claimed that "lacking large defense orders [...] the industry would have had to lay off huge numbers of workers" if it delayed or canceled production of the 1942 models.[41]

This line of reasoning seemed more an indictment of Knudsen and the industry captains on the OPM than a deficiency in the Reuther plan, but six hours of sometimes contentious exchange and oftentimes tedious recital of technical detail created enough fog to obscure any clear winner in the debate. At the end of the long session the two rose from the table, shook hands, and marched arm-in-arm to a large war poster reading. PLEASE, KEEP THE BOMBS AWAY. The pair pointed to the message and jointly vowed "That's our job and we'll do it!"[42] The Detroit News judged the debate to be a draw, but the outcome a victory for America.

The debate may have had little effect in damping enthusiasm for the Reuther plan, but spurred by five billion dollars of defense orders, American industry was able to hold labor at arm's length and relieve changeover bottlenecks more rapidly than anticipated by effectively implementing resource pooling through industry cooperation and subcontracting. Reuther's initiative did garner public approval for labor's readiness to commit itself fully to the war effort. In his 1943 testimony before a Senate committee, Chrysler president K. T. Keller proudly stated that eighty-nine percent of his company's machine tools had been converted to war production, and, at war's end, could be converted back to civilian production again. This testimony prompted *Washington Post* publisher, Philip Graham, to conclude that Reuther was eighty-nine percent right all along.[43] After defeat of the axis powers, additional tribute was accorded Reuther by the business magazine *Fortune*. "Reuther was on the right track. Compared with many industrialists who sat back and hugged profits and [...] the aimless agencies of Washington, the redheaded labor leader exhibited atomic spirit of action. He never let up."[44]

War planning had brought Reuther to Washington and to the attention of people in and around government. He became a darling of the post New Deal left that had gathered into the UDA. He formed close friendships with a number of people who would be part of the Washington scene for years to come. He encouraged the UAW to establish a Washington office and spent a good deal of his own time in the city. Washington invigorated Reuther, who listed his hobbies in his *Who's Who in Labor* entry as "wood & metal craft work, development of economic & production plans."[45] In the war-time capital he had an opportunity to use his technical skills to work on problems of critical import, and he had a sympathetic audience of government officials and journalists to give weight and voice to his grand vision. He was able to transcend the role of labor leader, but astutely realized that his influence would fade like the cherry blossoms of springtime if he were to step too far away from his labor base.

Reuther was officially a member of the Labor-Management Policy Committee of the War Manpower Commission, but unofficially he acted as a close associate of Sidney Hillman and Undersecretary of War Robert Patterson. Upon assuming their government responsibilities in the summer of 1940, Patterson and his deputy Robert Lovett quickly became frustrated by the pace of industry conversion to military production. They were intrigued by Reuther's 500 Planes a Day proposal and developed a respect for his ability and energy. After war was declared and the Reuther plan shelved, the pair continued to consult with him about ways of relieving production bottlenecks in the supply chain. Reuther believed that Fordist mass-production technology, properly channeled, would provide the abundance necessary to achieve his social vision. In essence, he was a product of the Ford shop and its apostle in Gorky. Fordism was his hammer and he devoted much of his energy during the war looking for 'nails' where the best practices of the auto shops could be substituted for hand crafted methodology common in many other industries.

A lack of tools for producing the ground gears used in making aircraft engines created a backlog of up to two years in the machine tool shops.[46]

Reuther argued that shaved gears used in the auto industry would work just as well as ground gears for all but the relatively few gears in a plane engine requiring the tightest precision. After the idea was savaged by the generals and experts from the aircraft industry, he prevailed upon Patterson to have Pratt & Whitney ship two finished engines to the Ford factory in Dearborn that were to produce duplicates of the Pratt & Whitney design. At Ford, he arranged to have the gears in one of the engines replaced with shaved gears and then have both delivered to the Air Corps for block and flight testing without mentioning the alteration. Testing confirmed that shaved gears would be more than adequate for most engine parts resulting in a dramatic increase in the rate engines were produced.

Patterson, who was recruited into the War Department from the New York bench, and Lovett, a Wall Street Lawyer, came to rely upon Reuther for technical advice. When it was discovered that M-4 tanks were being produced faster than they could be equipped with a 75 millimeter cannon, Patterson reported the problem to Reuther, who went to the arsenal near Philadelphia with Ben Blackwood to get a better understanding of the problem. They discovered that after the gun barrels were bored to within a few millimeters of their final size, they were then honed to perfection in a process requiring eight hours. The pair recommended that the auto industry practice of broaching be tried instead. The final barrel diameter was reached after the initial boring process by pulling through a broach containing successively larger diameter teethed rings to achieve a smooth barrel machined to its final tolerance. Broaching reduced the processing time for producing the guns from eight hours to one minute.[47]

Production problems were not limited to tools and manufacturing methodology. Accommodating the workers who would fill the new defense jobs posed another challenge to military planners. Most of the new factories being readied for defense production were located away from the industrial heartland in places like Ypsilanti, Michigan; Wichita, Kansas; Long Beach, California; and Tacoma, Washington. Workers chased after the federal dollars flowing into the factories. There was a parade of skilled workers lured into better paid jobs with other companies and a migration from the rural South into defense jobs in Michigan and California. Housing, in chronic short supply, was inadequate to accommodate the new arrivals.

In the fall of 1941, Reuther pushed the UAW to support a federally funded "Defense City" project outside the Ford Willow Run bomber plant being built near Ypsilanti. Reuther flung himself into the effort with his customary energy. He engaged his friend, the architect Oskar Stonorov to design a city for over fifty thousand people. Stonorov, who was born in Germany and educated in France, Switzerland, and Italy, was well-schooled in the modern aesthetic represented by movements such as the Bauhaus school. Stonorov's concept of a planned community with well integrated shops, schools, parks, and pedestrian walkways tempered Reuther's faith in the practicality of factory-built modular homes. Reuther's enthusiasm for the project proved contagious, and Sidney Hillman and other New Deal liberals in the administration set about allocating resources and securing funding for it. When Hillman reported the plan to Roosevelt, the President said the Defense City would be a "city of homes, well planned and designed, and owned by defense workers, as a symbol of the America we are defending and the America we are rebuilding for the future."[48]

The project was never built. It faced one insurmountable obstacle. Henry Ford was adamantly against it. Ford had located the plant in Washtenaw County near the small city of Ypsilanti to escape the influence of the union and increasingly unsympathetic city politicians and judges. He owned Washentaw County, and he intended to keep it solidly Republican and overwhelmingly white. He built the federally funded plant as an L-shaped building, with two turntables installed in the assembly line at the join, so that the complex would reside entirely within the one county.[49] Ford refused to sell land he owned near the plant for development and encouraged neighboring farmers to do the same. In the face of Ford's opposition, the idea for a "Defense City" was scrapped. Ford only relented to a scaled down community of bungalows and trailers near Willow Run when the shanty towns and trailer camps springing up around the plant threatened a health emergency, and the intolerable living environment led to an unacceptably high turnover rate in his workforce.[50]

Reuther had friends in the highest places. FDR greeted him warmly as "my young red-headed engineer,"[51] and Eleanor Roosevelt became a close confidant and life-long friend. She greased his entry into the liberal establishment and served as a conduit for channeling his ideas directly to the President. He was similarly valued for his initiative and energy by people in the War Production Board (WPB). Knudsen's successor, Donald Nelson, called Reuther "quite a fellow [...] Three fourths of the dollar-a-year men around this place are scared to death of that little fellow. And, you know they ought to be scared of him—because he's smarter than they are."[52]

While he himself was welcome in the corridors of power, his union was not. In October, 1942, the Wall Street banker Ferdinand Eberstadt offered to make him his "partner" in relieving the most persistent commodity and labor bottlenecks hindering the war effort. Reuther asked if the offer represented a real or token recognition of the labor movement. Eberstadt replied "No, I want you. I don't want the labor movement."[53] Reuther told Eberstadt that he felt he was already making a contribution in production management, an area he thought he knew best, and turned the offer down. Shortly afterward he was made a similar offer by "Electric" Charlie Wilson, the former General Electric boss, which he also turned down.

In the spring of 1943 he was nominated to fill one of two newly created posts of labor vice chairman in the WPB. Reuther seriously considered the offer. He wanted a chance to involve labor in a meaningful role in war-time production planning, and he wanted to protect the interests of workers in the infighting within the agency. He was dissuaded from accepting the offer by his brother Roy who wrote that accepting the post would be "suicide." The bureaucracy had been functioning for over a year with little or no labor input. He warned his brother that he would be blamed for all the unpopular measures affecting labor with no effective apparatus in place to give the position any real authority. Roy cautioned "if you come to D. C. and are here for six months or a year— you will have to start out at the bottom of the UAW again."[54]

The War Within the Union

In the spring of 1941, labor unrest in the United States was distracting the nation from its war preparations. The long struggle at Ford was nearing its end game, and the final act began in April with the spontaneous revolt precipitated by the firing of the eight union members of the grievance committee at the Rouge. The Ford strike was seen publicly as a predictable product of the intransigence of the company with little bearing on national defense mobilization. Ford was well known for his isolationist and pro-German views and for his rejection of a contract to build plane engines for Britain. His labor difficulties generated little sympathy in Washington.

Other strikes by the UAW against companies engaged in government contract work raised official concern. The Allis-Chalmers Company in Milwaukee made turbines, generators, and construction equipment needed for the defense effort. In the spring of 1941, the Allis-Chalmers workforce was divided between a minority faction favoring an AFL craft union and a militant UAW local led by Harold Christoffel. Christoffel worked closely with the Communists and had formed one of the most combative flying squadrons in the UAW. Company president Max Babb used the division between the workers to undermine the UAW local at every opportunity. In March, Christoffel's local struck. Sidney Hillman rushed to Milwaukee to try to work out a compromise on union security, but his efforts were unsuccessful. Stimson and Knox demanded the plant be reopened immediately. Three days of bloody riots in which Christoffel's flying squadron battled both police and company loyalists left the union with a black eye and a bloody nose on the pages of the nation's newspapers. To forestall use of the military to halt the strike, Hillman urged Roosevelt to set up a tripartite National Defense Mediation Board (NDMB), and he won reluctant acceptance of the board from the CIO executive council. The CIO forced mediation on the local, but Christoffel was regarded as a hero by much of the rank-and-file for defending a worker's right to strike. A unanimous UAW Executive Board, though privately happy to see the Allis-Chalmers situation out of the headlines at a time when the confrontation with Ford was reaching a crucial climax, assured its members in an editorial in the union paper, the *United Auto Worker*, that the right to strike was the "Keystone of Liberty."[55]

Union leaders in 1941 were engaged in a delicate balancing act between the militancy of their rank-and-file and the impatience of the war bureaucracy and the general public with labor disruption of defense preparations. Walter Reuther read the tea leaves as well as any politician and knew that a strike at General Motors in April of 1941 would imperil the upcoming NLRB certification vote at Ford and undermine his own influence in Washington. He knew that ninety-five percent of the production in GM plants was still devoted to the civilian marketplace, but conceded the point to Wilson that GM workers engaged in the defense effort would not strike. Reuther was looking for the same ten cent an hour increase won by the steelworkers and acquiescence to a union shop by the automaker. Priorities on the shop floor included a shop steward system like the one in place at Chrysler and a stronger stance against the speedup.[56] The large GM local in Flint was never in Reuther's camp and was overwhelmingly opposed to Hillman's reliance on the NDMB to sheath the union's most effective weapon—the strike. Other large GM locals were as adamantly opposed to Hillmanism and to Reuther's seeming timidity to press their case. A large Buick local and the Fisher Body No. 1 local demanded his dismissal as GM Division director.[57]

Reuther had no choice but to call a strike, but two days before the date set, Labor Secretary Frances Perkins intervened to certify the dispute to the NDMB. A relieved Reuther immediately called off the scheduled strike. George Addes took the opportunity to criticize his rival for his hasty capitulation, declaring "We must follow an aggressive policy, not one of appeasement."[58] He was expressing the sentiments of much of the Executive Board and the majority of the rank-and-file. The NDMB ultimately granted the ten cent an hour raise, but left the shop floor structure intact.

Next, the scene of labor unrest shifted to California and the rapidly growing aircraft industry that was concentrated on the West Coast. The UAW expanded its full title to include Aeronautical and Agricultural workers within its jurisdiction, and made a concerted drive to organize the new workers pouring into the Southern California plants. The skilled older workers familiar with the pre-war cottage industry days wanted either no union or were inclined toward an AFL craft representation, but the new employees proved fertile ground for UAW recruitment. The Aeronautical Chamber of Commerce enforced a fifty cent an hour wage on semi-skilled workers.[59] This figure was far below the prevalent rate in the auto factories and comparable to the rates paid in the Southern textile mills. The Communist Party was strong in Southern California, and the

UAW organization effort was lead by party members Lew Michner and Wyndham Mortimer.

Negotiations broke down in May, and Richard Frankensteen flew to Los Angeles to authorize a strike. Frankensteen was hoping the dispute would be referred to the NDMB where he could expect a favorable ruling on the main issue of wages, but the NDMB was swamped with cases and slow to schedule a hearing. When Michener and Mortimer were confronted with a wildcat walkout on June 4th, they decided to expand it into an authorized strike. The strike drew an immediate condemnation from Secretary of War Stimson who was "morally certain" that defense strikes were "instigated by Communist and other subversive elements."[60] He wanted an immediate Army takeover of the plant, but Hillman and NDMB Chairman William Davis prevailed upon the military to give the UAW a chance to end the strike before any action was taken. Frankensteen again flew to California and demanded Mortimer end the strike. Mortimer refused and Frankensteen took over the local, suspended its negotiating team, and fired the organizers. Wyndham Mortimer, who had served as a mentor to Reuther and was the senior UAW official who signed the original contract with GM, was now without a position in the union.

Frankensteen went on national radio to declare the strike a wildcat and denounce the "infamous agitation and vicious underhanded maneuvering of the Communist Party." Frankensteen's message may have played well with his radio audience and the military planners back in Washington, but it had no effect on the men on the picket line. Frankensteen had a frightening confrontation with militant strikers in a bean field outside the Inglewood plant at which he made no progress in ending the walkout, but did manage to escape the encounter unharmed. The Army was dispatched to reopen the plant and the strike ringleaders were fired. The Army did help the UAW reconstitute the local under new leadership, and the NDMB awarded most of what the union requested including a substantial pay raise. The *United Auto Worker* trumpeted the union victory under the headline "Responsible Unionism Wins at Inglewood."[61]

On June 22, 1941 Hitler's armies invaded the Soviet Union. Communist opposition to the defense build up instantly ceased. The changing party line was reflected in a pair of resolutions Communist leaders of Plymouth Local 51 submitted to the Wayne County CIO council. A resolution to "take America out of the war and keep it out of the war"[62] was quickly followed by one urging all-out aid to the Soviets. To the chagrin of the Plymouth local, both resolutions came up for a vote at the same meeting.

Reuther sought to repeat his triumph in St. Louis at the 1941 convention in Buffalo. After the North American Aviation strike he found common cause with his old rival Richard Frankensteen in an attempt to remove Communists from positions of influence in the union. The lynchpin of Communist strength was Secretary-Treasurer George Addes. Addes was not himself a Communist, but party loyalists were able to find cover under his protective wing and formed the largest power base in his caucus. As controller of the union finances, Addes maintained many loyalists in the union bureaucracy through his patronage. Removing Addes from his post would not only leave the Communists weakened and exposed, but also remove the biggest obstacle in Reuther's ascent to the top. The pair went to Buffalo united in purpose to replace Addes as Secretary-Treasurer with Richard Leonard. The Reuther and Frankensteen families cemented their new relationship by vacationing together in the Shenandoah en route to the convention.

When Reuther arrived in Buffalo the scene appeared set for a repeat of the previous year's triumph. Victor chaired the constitutional committee and Reuther loyalist Tom Doherty, the important Credentials Committee. Edward Levinson had prepared a detailed agenda for the meeting and an extensive brief rationalizing the decision to oust Addes.[63] But UAW conventions of the period were like political conventions in the days before they became scripted, made-for-TV infomercials. Delegates came together from all parts of the country. Most came with purpose, but all came for a good time. There were rallies and demonstrations. Bands played. Delegates wore distinctive hats identifying their locals and paraded around the hall, carrying banners touting their candidates for high office. There were long, boring speeches and short, spirited ones; and in the evening there was always plenty of alcohol and late night poker games.

The delegates were not necessarily representative of the rank-and-file, but were those, typically more skilled and better educated workers for whom service to the union provided some small financial benefit and a measure of prestige. A UAW convention was a democratic forum where each of these delegates was determined to be heard, on or off the floor. Such a gathering could not be reliably scripted.

The convention began with a credentials fight over the seating of the delegates from Allis-Chalmers Local 248. Tom Doherty's committee refused to seat Christoffel and his loyalists on the technical grounds that the nomination and election occurred on the same day contrary to constitutional procedure. The real reason this technicality was cited was purely political. Christoffel and his men could be expected to be strong Addes supporters. The rationale for not seating the Local 248 delegates was more about their actions during the abortive strike than the technicality. Christoffel's flying squadron was accused of strong-arming his opponents within the local to continue the disastrous strike. Richard Leonard summed up the case against the local:. "The issue before this convention is a simple question of whether or not [..].the highest tribunal of our organization is going to put the stamp of approval on the worst kind of strong-arm political racketeering in this union."[64] Sixty percent of the delegates sided with Leonard, voting to uphold the Credentials Committee's ruling against seating the Christoffel delegation.[65]

While the Reuther forces were winning that fight on the floor, the campaign to replace Addes was unraveling behind the scenes. Phil Murray did not want to see the largest union in the CIO in the hands of an ambitious young leader building his own independent power base inside and outside of the CIO framework. Murray's representative at the convention, Alan Haywood, took Frankensteen aside and told him that the CIO wanted George Addes as Secretary-Treasurer. He assured Frankensteen that the Addes camp would back him for a vice presidency if he gave up his opposition to Addes's reelection.[66] Frankensteen realized that he would never play any part but second fiddle in an orchestra conducted by Reuther, and was ever ready to switch allegiances as opportunity dictated.

The next floor fight involved the disposition of the leaders involved in the North American Aviation strike. Mortimer, an avowed Communist, was sacrificed, but Addes and Frankensteen concluded a deal that merely suspended Regional Director Lew Michner from the Executive Board. Reuther pushed for a stronger penalty but was defeated. Murray put Michner on the CIO payroll and within a year he was reelected to the Executive Board.[67]

Reuther's defeat in the fight over Michner signaled the direction in which the convention was heading. Twice representatives from the Credentials Committee traveled to Milwaukee to conduct new elections for Local 248, and twice the Christoffel loyalists prevailed. On the sixth day of the gathering, Christoffel took to the podium and gave a ringing endorsement of the struggle his local waged to protect the right of workingmen to strike. When the Christoffel loyalists arrived in the hall on the ninth day of the convention, they were given a thunderous welcome from the assembled.[68] It was now obvious that Addes would retain his position on the Executive Board.

Debate over the amendment to bar Nazis, Fascists, and Communists from holding union office was spirited and personal. The Addes forces focused their attack on Reuther. Copies of the Gorky letter were distributed to anyone willing to accept, and a recitation of Reuther's earlier associations and his denunciations of red-baiting as the "boss's ploy" for sowing discord in the union ranks were emphasized by his opponents. There were demands that Socialists should be included with the unholy trio and not enjoy a privileged status within the union. After all the political points were made, the convention voted overwhelmingly to support the Reuther amendment. Most of the Communists in the union were "closet Communists," unwilling to come out and reveal their affiliation with the party. In the summer of 1941 it was politically correct to be against Communism, but not against individual Communists who had championed the workers' cause for years.

When the convention ended, Addes was handily reelected, and Reuther barely held on to his Michigan board seat. He had overplayed his hand leading into Buffalo and his close association with Hillman and the warfare state alienated him from the militant sentiment being expressed on the shop floor. He would need to recapture the support of the rank-and-file if he were to challenge the forces aligned with Addes again.

Immediately after Pearl Harbor, the labor movement made a no strike pledge for the duration of the war. Labor disputes were to be arbitrated by a National War Labor Board that had authority to set wage rates and impose upon unionized plants the obligation to enroll all new workers in a certified union within fifteen days of employment unless they choose not to join. Labor initially endorsed the bargain, but soon realized that it was wedged between corporate pressure for additional concessions and the militancy of its rank-and-file.

With the nation now at war, President Roosevelt demanded a seven day week in all defense plants.[69] The imperative of the moment notwithstanding, the reality in the plants spoke of steel shortages, conversion delays, and layoffs. The auto industry had resisted calls by Reuther and others to adapt to war production sooner and more quickly. It now promptly reacted to the President's demand for a seven day week by calling for the elimination of premium pay on weekends even though it was in no position to implement a full round-the-clock production schedule for many months to come. General Motors demanded that the UAW forgo premium weekend pay in the 1942 contract negotiations. Walter Reuther invited GM president Charlie Wilson to present the company's rationale for asking its workers to give up this benefit at a February meeting of union leaders from ninety GM plants. The appearance of a GM president at a union event was unprecedented and appreciated by those in attendance, but his presentation was unpersuasive. Time and a half for Saturdays and double time for Sundays was negotiated during a time of high unemployment to discourage the practice of maintaining a smaller workforce by having those employed work more overtime. Wilson now argued that union insistence on maintaining this benefit in time of full employment and a national emergency represented "business as usual for the union."[70] Reuther countered by citing figures that showed company profits per employee were thirty-nine percent higher over the first nine months of 1941 compared to the same period the previous year.[71] Then he challenged Wilson's claim of business as usual. "Mr. Wilson and three other top executives of General Motors are drawing [combined] salaries and bonuses of $6,644,437 a year. Maybe these things ought to be brought up when Mr. Wilson talks of sacrifices and business as usual."[72]

Reuther may have effectively countered Wilson's argument in February, but by March conservatives in Congress threatened to pass a law requiring unions to give up premium pay for the duration of the war along with other concessions. Roosevelt pressed Murray to forestall hostile Congressional action by voluntarily accepting a war time discontinuance of premium pay. WPB chief Donald Nelson gave labor thirty days to act or the government would press for a law to require it.[73] Murray bowed to the pressure and the UAW leadership had little choice but to follow his lead.

The capitulation on premium pay was unpopular in the union shops, and the union needed to portray the concession as part of a shared patriotic sacrifice. George Addes and Walter Reuther collaborated to develop a plan they called "Victory through Equality of Sacrifice." The plan called for rationing and price controls, and a rigid ceiling on executive pay and corporate profits. Salaries would be capped at $25,000 per year (about eight times the average annual wage in 1942).[74] Eleanor Roosevelt praised the plan as a constructive suggestion in her *My Day* newspaper column,[75] and three weeks later the President sent a message to Congress calling for a program of Equality of Sacrifice that included the $25,000 yearly salary cap. Congress was only willing to spread the sacrifice so far. It weakened the President's price control program and gouged loopholes into his rationing schedules. As for the cap on salaries, R. J. Thomas observed that "Congress paid no more attention to that part of the President's program than to an individual that would go to church and burp."[76]

Labor was on the defensive and industry looked to take full advantage of the strength that the war emergency and their new influence in Washington provided them. In the 1942 contract negotiations, GM pushed to reduce union influence on the shop floor where its presence was most directly felt by workers. It called for a reduction by one half of the number of grievance committeemen and requested the ability to make unilateral changes in work rules. It demanded the union stop making accusations of speed up over its efforts to increase defense production.[77] Reuther went into the negotiations wanting twelve and a half cents an hour average increase in wages and a union shop. He ended up getting from the National War Labor Board (NWLB) imposed settlement a four cent pay hike and maintenance of membership clause which bound current members, and those new employees volunteering to join, to the union for the duration of the contract.[78]

Wages during the war years were controlled by the formula used by the NWLB to settle the 'Little Steel Strike' against Bethlehem, Republic, Youngstown and other smaller steel producers. By late spring of 1942, labor and commodity shortages had caused inflation to jump fifteen percent over an eighteen month period. Many felt the official figure was grossly understated, but the formula of limiting wage increases to fifteen percent of the rate on January 1, 1941, with possible small adjustments in specific cases, used in settling the Little Steel strike became the basis for all cases referred to the NWLB.[79] The little steel formula did not have the intended effect of controlling inflation, but remained a guide for NWLB settlements for the duration of the war.

The maintenance of membership clause was also a fixture of NWLB rulings, thanks largely to the influence of board member Wayne Morse, the future Oregon Senator and Vietnam War critic. Maintenance of membership prevented management from flooding the ranks of its workforce with non-union employees and drowning the influence of the union in its plants. Maintenance of membership helped the union ranks to grow to thirty-five percent of the non-agricultural workers in the country by the end of the war.[80.]

The GM settlement in 1942 produced one significant milestone. It established a policy of equal pay for equal work between the sexes. The decision was more nuanced than a flat declaration of principle. It continued to categorize jobs into men's and women's occupations and left room for disputes over which job descriptions belonged in which of these classifications. A question of whether women aircraft inspectors should be paid at the men's rate was resolved by the NWLB by substituting the terms "light" and "heavy" for "men" and "women" in the contract language and paying inspectors ten cents an hour less than the hourly rate for "heavy" jobs.[81]

The UAW initially regarded the influx of women streaming into traditionally male jobs as a threat to the wage scale. By 1942 women represented twelve percent of the GM workforce and this percentage doubled again in a year. The war emergency had turned the depression era labor surplus into a period of scarcity and women were becoming a more significant segment of the UAW membership. Confronted with the new reality, the union moved to protect the male wage scale by extending its applicability to women rather than by trying to exclude them from the higher paying jobs. Victor Reuther, serving as chairman of the union's policy committee, authored a clause in the negotiating brief that stated "wage rates for women shall be the same as for men where they do work of comparable quantity and quality in comparable operations."[82] The NWLB ruling upheld the union position and Rosy the Riveter got the full pay that she deserved.

At the 1942 convention there was rare accord in the leadership and dissension in the ranks. Reuther seconded the nomination of Addes for Secretary-Treasurer with a call to rally 'round the flag. "There is one fight that we have got and that job is against Hitler, so I say, lets vote Brother Addes in unanimously. Let's support the officers of this union, back Phillip Murray and President Roosevelt, and knock hell out of Hitler."[83] In seconding Reuther for one of the vice presidencies, Addes, a bit less enthusiastically, called Reuther able and energetic, and noted his recent desire to work together with others of us to establish unity in the organization.

Thomas, Addes, Reuther, and Frankensteen were marching in step at the front of the column, but the men in the ranks were grumbling and unsure whether they were advancing or in retreat. They had seen their wages nearly frozen by the little steel formula while inflation soared ahead. They had given up premium pay for weekend work and surrendered their right to strike. They did not appreciate the strategic imperatives faced by their leaders. Down in the trenches the tactics carried a strong smell of defeat. The convention delegates showed their displeasure with the leadership by refusing to increase dues fifty cents a month and paring back pay raises for the top officers. "Pay them like bosses and they begin to think like bosses" muttered one of the disgruntled back benchers.[84]

War time controls and calls for equality of sacrifice had limited result in leveling the effects of the abrupt industrial conversion from consumer products to military and from labor abundance to scarcity. The Little Steel formula only limited wage rate increases in cases adjudicated by the NWLB. Wages paid by small tool and die shops not party to a NWLB settlement rose much faster than those in comparable jobs at GM and other big unionized employers as manufacturers scrambled to attract skilled workers and grab a share of the defense dollar. GM maintenance workers fumed at seeing AFL craftsmen who were installing the new tools in their plants earning better wages than they were. Much of the labor discontent at the outset of America's participation in the war was not caused by a lack of "pie on the table" but by the relative size of the piece everyone was given.

Conversion to defense production not only opened new theaters in the war between labor and management, but also sparked new battles in the rivalry between the AFL and CIO. The AFL, like the CIO, agreed to forgo premium pay for the duration of the war, but the AFL exercised less central control over their semi-autonomous craft lodges than their rival, and individual lodges in the AFL felt free to ignore the commitment made by William Green and the parent organization. The UAW lost an NLRB representational election to the International Association of Machinists of the AFL at the Curtiss-Wright Aircraft plant in Buffalo because the IAM did not relinquish the right to premium pay. IAM organizers played up the claim that they were not party to such an agreement. "The CIO sacrifices workers' pay, workers' overtime as the CIO's contribution to the war effort. Big of them, huh?" "While the AFL has been loyal to the country, it has also been loyal to its members. It has not felt called upon to make sacrifices of workers' pay or of labor's gains."[85]

The UAW was stunned by this defeat and sent an emergency appeal to Roosevelt for an executive order mandating all of labor relinquish premium pay for the duration of the war. When the President hesitated, Victor Reuther's War Policy Committee drafted a resolution proclaiming that the UAW would withdraw its sacrifice of premium pay within thirty days unless the government made the policy obligatory for all defense workers.[86] Thomas, Reuther, and Frankensteen rushed to Washington to meet with the President and obtained an agreement for the desired executive order.

In January of 1943, Reuther compiled statistics showing GM and other large firms hoarding labor by working some of its employees less than forty hours a week while hiring others to relieve labor shortages. Reuther urged the President to order an immediate forty hour week to be extended to forty eight hours within sixty days. Three weeks later Roosevelt mandated a forty-eight hour work week.[87] The immediate effect of this order, with time and a half for overtime, was a thirty percent increase in the weekly paycheck for all defense workers who had been working a forty hour week.

The most divisive issue facing labor in 1943 was incentive pay for piece work. The War Production Board campaigned to increase war production with incentive pay. The WPB was heavily influenced by the auto executives in its midst who argued for a reorganization of much of the work into piecework projects with the workers partially compensated by an incentive-based formula. Roosevelt took a firm stance against revision of the Little Steel formula, and many in the CIO were inclined toward incentive pay as the only way to circumvent the constraints that the formula placed on pay increases. Richard Frankensteen viewed incentive pay as an opportunity for the Aircraft Division to organize workers whose wages were fixed at a lower rate than California dock workers by the NWLB formula. He complained that, "We no longer have the approach we once had of telling these workers that if they join up with us, we have a very tangible something to put into their hands…that we will get them five, ten or fifteen cents an hour and their retroactive pay."[88] Piece work was common practice in that industry, so incentive pay represented a tangible benefit to most workers.

Most autoworkers associated incentive based schemes that existed in the plants before recognition of the union with speedup, arbitrary and incomprehensible rate calculations, and attempts by management to discourage worker solidarity. Walter Reuther seized upon rank-and-file antipathy to piece work to highlight his differences with his rivals Addes and Frankensteen. He denounced piece work as a violation of the union's commitment to labor solidarity and argued that it would wreck efforts to win industry wide wage standards. He countered calls for "local autonomy" by insisting "if this union does not [...] begin to think in terms of wages with the whole industry, we are going to go into a postwar situation where the shop having the lowest wages is going to have the job and the shop having the highest standards is going to be on the street. We have got to take labor out of competition!"[89] Reuther coupled his opposition to piece work with a call for a more aggressive push for revision of the Little Steel formula. He warned "if labor even indicates that it is considering piece work, such an attitude will be used to make the labor and wage freeze stick."[90]

The loudest call for piece work came from the Communist Party. The greatest battles of the war were being waged on the Russian front in the winter and summer of 1943, and the party was demanding an all out effort to support our Russian ally. It called on workers to adhere to the no strike pledge and agree to concessions demanded by the government, not as a retreat, but as a progressive step toward victory. In a pamphlet *Production for Victory* that was distributed widely in the factories and union halls, Communist leader Earl Browder forecast that all war time wages would be tied to an incentive plan, and that workers should shed their prejudice and look upon the time and motion study firm of Bedaux as an ally of the labor movement that would "help smash Nazism everywhere in the world."[91]

Communist advocacy of incentive pay provided them another opportunity to attack the plan's staunchest critic, Walter Reuther. Labor frustration with wage controls and the government's resistance to any significant modification of the Little Steel formula provoked job actions in the mines and in a number of industrial settings including the Chrysler plants of Detroit. Reuther urged labor to make a stand against wage controls and not retreat into acceptance of incentive pay, but his preferred battleground was the war-time agencies in Washington, not the picket lines of Detroit. He continued to support the no strike pledge and condemned the "wildcat" action at Chrysler.[92]

Reuther's reaction to the Chrysler strike did nothing to dissuade Earl Browder from linking him to some Socialist/Trotskyite conspiracy to deflect the war effort. Browder denounced him as "less bold and more hypocritical" than Lewis.[93] Browder conveniently forgot that he had called the President a warmonger during the days of the Hitler-Stalin nonaggression pact. Now he was inventing a narrative where "Unlike his brother, Victor, who has been openly against the war throughout, Walter has shown an ability to support the war with great energy when that also serves the purpose of his ambition."[94] Reuther was not immune from marrying policy initiatives with ambition, but the war effort was a cause both brothers championed from the beginning. Browder's attacks did little to change Reuther's message of opposition to Communist influence, incentive pay, and wage controls that was widely applauded at delegate conferences leading up to the 1943 convention.

The harmony in the leadership that existed in Chicago the previous year had grown dissonant during a year of factional competition to appeal to the disquiet fomenting in the plants. The Reuther caucus arrived in Buffalo for the convention prepared to secure a strong statement against incentive pay and make another attempt to unseat Secretary-Treasurer George Addes. The anti-Reuther forces were similarly resolved to accomplish their agenda. The convention was polarized into two camps, and the rival factions serenaded each other with little campaign ditties sung to the tune of Reuben and Rachel. The Reutherite version began:[95]

> Who are the boys who take their orders
> Straight from the office of Joe Stal-een?
> No one else but the gruesome twosome,
> George F. Addes and Frankensteen.

The Addes camp retaliated with its version, beginning:[96]

> You have given the workers nothing
> Except hot air and steam,
> And when the votes have all been counted
> We'll still have Addes and Frankensteen!

The national emergency no longer papered over the divisions in the union leadership nor curbed the ambitions of the rivals. Buffalo marked a resumption of a struggle for control of the union that would not be resolved until either Reuther, Addes, or Frankensteen managed to oust from power both of the other two.

Nineteen forty three would not be the year such a decisive victory would be achieved. The Reuther caucus won a resolution opposing incentive pay by a two to one vote, but when the votes for the officers "had all been counted," the Executive Board "still had Addes and Frankensteen." George Addes survived the attempt to unseat him by seventy one votes. Reuther and Frankensteen were elected first and second vice presidents respectively.[97]

The votes that returned Addes to his post came from the increasingly influential Negro caucus. The union victory at Ford and federal fair employment initiatives markedly increased the number of African Americans in the union. By 1943 these numbers translated into a significant increase in the number of black delegates attending union conventions. With the Addes and Reuther factions so closely divided, the Negro caucus attained an influence well beyond its actual strength in numbers. At the Buffalo convention the Negro caucus pushed for a reserved minority seat on the Executive Board. The proposal was supported by Addes and Frankensteen and opposed as a case of reverse Jim Crow by Reuther and Thomas. The motion was defeated, but Addes's support for the proposal secured him the votes that provided his margin of victory.

Victory in Sight

Nineteen forty three was the decisive year of World War II. Many hard, deadly battles lay ahead, but the course of the war was set. The Germans were in retreat on all fronts, never able to mount another major offensive except a last desperate gambit in the Ardennes. The Japanese perimeter in the Pacific continued to shrink after the Battle of Midway in June, 1942 and their defeat at Guadalcanal in January, 1943. The Germans lost almost one million men during the winter of 1942–1943 at Stalingrad, and in their last major offensive of the war, were defeated in the great battle of Kursk.

The Germans committed about three quarters of a million troops to the battle and the Russians positioned nearly two million men and women about a well-prepared sequence of defensive lines stretching back a depth of over two hundred kilometers.[98] The German offensive stalled within two weeks of its launch in July of 1943, and for the rest of the summer the Germans slowly retreated before a withering Soviet counter offensive. Kursk featured the largest concentration of tanks, artillery, and aircraft in the history of warfare. The Soviets suffered a staggering eight hundred and fifty thousand dead and wounded at Kursk and during the ensuing counter offensives.[99] German losses were about one fourth the Soviet total,[100] but in the wake of Stalingrad, these were unsustainable for maintaining the ambitions with which Germany began its campaigns of conquest years earlier. Nineteen forty three ended with the Eastern front steadily creeping back toward the German homeland and American, British, and free Polish forces climbing the boot of Italy. The Battle of Britain had been won by the RAF, and now British and American bombers were pummeling Germany's industrial base.

With the threat from Hitler and Tojo receding, Roosevelt was suddenly confronted with a new crisis coming from a familiar adversary. The coal miners were suffering under the constraint that the Little Steel formula placed on their wages while inflation was devouring their purchasing power. The miners were hungry, tired, and ready to rebel. When the mine operators refused to negotiate a new contract, John L. Lewis defied the no strike pledge and pulled the miners out of the coal fields.

During the second and third Roosevelt administrations, John L. Lewis was the only public figure in the nation with a persona that rivaled Roosevelt's. Both men filled whatever room they occupied. Both men evoked either love or hatred from their countrymen, and each came to roundly detest the other. Lewis believed Roosevelt to be indecisive, procrastinating, and lacking a deep sympathy for labor.[101] After the sit-in at Flint, he came to consider the president dishonest. Lewis felt he was deceived by Roosevelt before heading to Flint and was not receiving a reward for the large contribution he made to the president's re-election campaign.[102] Roosevelt felt he was being used by Lewis in his organizing message that "The President wants you to join a union."[103] Both men had huge egos and neither was about to defer to the other.

Lewis was caught between an unsympathetic War Labor Relations Board, a group of mine operators who knew the cards out against him and refused to bargain, and a president who was out to destroy him. He held only one high card in his hand and that was the strike card. Lewis knew there was over a month's supply of coal above ground and he was not about to imperil the war effort in his game of brinksmanship, but when he struck he was denounced in the halls of Congress and in the bars and barbershops on main street. He was vilified as a traitor in the reliably anti-union press and depicted shoveling a heap of coal on the grave of a fallen soldier by one political cartoonist.[104] The full weight of the government came down upon him and his union. Roosevelt nationalized the mines and ordered the miners to get back to work; courts issued injunctions; Congress passed punitive legislation; but the miners only took direction from John L. Lewis, and he held firm. In the end, Lewis won the battle. The miners got more than they originally requested. But the cost of that settlement to both Lewis and the labor movement was very steep. Lewis retained the support and respect of his miners, but he was marginalized in the broader labor movement and loathed by many of his countrymen. Labor received a black eye that ultimately contributed to a hostile Congress and passage of the Taft-Hartley Act.

By the fall of 1943 U. S. war production peaked.[105] The Normandy invasion was more than six months away, but the war planners already envisioned an approaching end to the European campaign. Some old contracts were not renewed and new orders were less forthcoming. The small producers were particularly hard hit as most new orders went to the major suppliers and those firms pulled more of their subcontracted work back in-house.[106] Donald Nelson, the man who succeeded Knudsen as head of the War Planning Board (WPB), wanted to avoid the delays and lack of planning that plagued the effort leading up to war and address the problem of reconversion promptly. He sought to allow firms with no military contracts to ease back into civilian production. Nelson saw the futility of trying to manage the allocation of resources and manpower between the thousands of companies supplying tens of thousands of consumer products ranging from automobiles and appliances to soaps and bobby pins. He devised instead a four-point plan which would lift restrictions on the use of aluminum and magnesium, permit manufacturers to place orders for machinery that would be filled when there was no military or priority need for those machines, allow the company to demonstrate that it was capable of producing the product it wanted to market, and be cleared to begin production when a WPB field officer certified that the producer was no longer needed for war work, the resources and manpower were available, and the war effort would not be adversely affected.[107]

The Nelson plan encountered immediate opposition from two powerful lobbies. The dollar-a-year men in the WPB and scattered throughout the war-time bureaucracies envisioned a reconversion timed to begin with the end of military production and orchestrated to allow each major producer to recapture the percentage of the civilian market that it had prior to the start of the war.[108] They balked at a plan that might give small manufacturers a head start toward establishing a presence in markets they had previously monopolized. These industrialists had an ally in the military which wanted no relaxation of scarcity and no deviation of public psychology from an obligation of national sacrifice. The brass conducted an extensive media campaign to keep the public focused on the obligation of rationing and in the continuing need for selfless dedication to the task of accelerated military production as orders were being cut back and material surpluses were starting to occur.[109] In the end the Armed Services prevailed at home and abroad. Nelson was eased out of his job and the power structure that dominated American life before the war emerged from the conflict with its privilege unchallenged and its power reinforced by an expanded military presence in the post-war framework. Small businesses were shunted to the periphery of war planning, asked to assume much of the sacrifice, and left to compete for market and influence after the war in an economy rigged to favor the entrenched interests.

With the pace of war-time production slowing and the eventual outcome of the war no longer in doubt, labor grew more restive about adhering to its no strike pledge. The debate at the 1944 Convention in Grand Rapids was heated on and off the convention floor. The union now had divided into four factions: the Addes-Frankensteen caucus, The Reuther group, a group of Thomas loyalists who usually sided with Addes but were in no sense his partisans, and a rank-and-file caucus committed to overturning the no strike pledge.[110] The 1944 convention goers were not content to regale one another with campaign songs. Fist fights broke out in the hotel lobby, causing damage to the furniture and prompting Addes to warn that no city would welcome this union again if the delegates didn't exercise more self-control.

The debate on the floor was just as contentious. None of the four principal leaders was ready to abandon the no strike pledge, but each needed to convince the rank-and-file of his militancy. Thomas vowed to the unruly assembly that he would resign as president if the no strike commitment were defeated. He was jeered, and, despite his office, allowed only five minutes to present his case for continuance. Following a plea from Phil Murray, immediate repeal of the pledge was rejected by a two to one margin.[111]

Next the competing factions tried to placate the militants by proposing resolutions stipulating the conditions, short of complete Allied victory, under which the no strike restriction would be lifted. The Reuther proposal of removing plants no longer doing defense work from a no-strike commitment was judged too easily circumvented by industry and defeated. A Thomas-Addes-Frankensteen proposal to let the CIO and UAW Executive Board decide after the defeat of Germany when to lift the pledge was also defeated. Faced with having no policy at all, Reuther and Thomas proposed that the no strike pledge be reaffirmed subject to ratification by the entire membership in a referendum conducted through the mail.[112] That proposal passed and the convention settled in to choosing its leaders.

Addes faced no real competition for his spot on the Executive Board at this convention. The contests in doubt were those for the two vice presidencies. Reuther and Frankensteen again vied for the first vice presidency spot with Richard Leonard also competing. Leonard had twice been the Reuther choice to run against Addes and now set out on his own to win higher office. Leonard wanted the vice presidency and refused to commit to withdraw in favor of Reuther should Frankensteen win the first election. As feared, Frankensteen won the first vice presidency with 5,444 votes to 4,528 for Reuther and 385 for Leonard.[113] Despite Leonard's poor initial showing, he posed a threat to Reuther in the second race as a potential recipient of the anti-Reuther vote.

The CIO feared that a Reuther defeat might split the union and intervened to try and prevent it. Pressure from Alan Haywood, working the convention floor for Phil Murray and the CIO, did not dissuade Leonard from continuing his candidacy. Leonard would not budge, but Reuther learned that vote trading in a number of the divided locals had exaggerated the size of Frankensteen's victory and ensured him of more support in the second election.[114] The final tally gave Reuther a comfortable victory over Leonard and a third candidate from the rank-and-file caucus.

The UAW left Grand Rapids with the leadership that had presided over the union during the war intact, but the attention now was focused on the post-war period. German super weapons like the V-2 rocket and jet aircraft arrived too late to alter the inevitable outcome. After one last desperate punch glanced off the chin of the American defenders of Bastogne, Hitler was left with no place left to retreat, save to his bunker and his final fate.

One of the last casualties of the war in Europe was the Commander-in-Chief. Franklin Delano Roosevelt died at his Hot Springs retreat on April 12, 1945—barely more than two weeks before Hitler committed suicide and three weeks before Germany's formal surrender. The man who had guided the country through its Great Depression and its great war could rest in the knowledge that he had, like Lincoln, brought it through a most troubled period of history. Now, as with Lincoln, the post-war problems would fall squarely on the shoulders of a man outside the inner circle of his predecessor.

Roosevelt began his fourth term with his third vice president. Harry Truman rose to national prominence during the war as chairman of a Senate committee combating waste and mismanagement in the war effort. He was added to the ticket in 1944 after prominent party insiders, realizing Roosevelt's health had deteriorated to an extent that he was unlikely to serve a full fourth term, persuaded the President to dump the liberal Henry Wallace in favor of a reluctant Harry Truman. Despite his ill health, Roosevelt rarely conferred with his Vice President and left him unaware of major policy decisions. On the day of Roosevelt's death Truman first learned of the Manhattan project—a secret Joseph Stalin had known for some time.

Truman had to make the awful decision to use the bomb on Hiroshima and Nagasaki to end the war. He also faced the daunting task of abruptly down shifting from a war economy to peacetime with millions of veterans returning to the civilian workforce. Removal of war-time measures like rationing and wage and price controls required as deft a government hand as was needed in instituting them in the first place. Workers were poised to shed the no strike commitment and make up for wages lost to inflation during the war years. Consumers feared a new round of inflation would eviscerate their savings. Roosevelt had won the war. Truman was faced with securing the peace.

The United States came out of the war in good shape. Pearl Harbor was the only piece of U. S. territory that suffered a major attack. Its civilian population was spared the ravages inflicted upon the people of London, Coventry, Hamburg, Dresden, Warsaw, Leningrad, Hiroshima, Nagasaki, and countless other places large and small. The country's factories and railways were unscathed. Its farmlands were not rutted with tank tracks and bomb craters. Its farmers did not have to worry about mines lurking beneath their fields. American companies were sitting on large reserves of cash, ready to fuel reconversion to a peacetime economy. Reuther reported that GM had set aside 48 million dollars already by May of 1943 for reconverting its machines after the war. With Europe in ruins, Asia and Africa yet to awake, and Germany and Japan battered and occupied, there was no foreign competition for the domestic market and only one economy prepared to meet the needs of a war-torn world.

American workers also fared well during the war. Constraints on wage rates imposed by the Little Steel formula were more than offset by the amount of overtime worked and the number of promotions, job reclassifications, and improved employment opportunities that occurred. Fifteen million workers, nearly one third the work force, acquired new jobs during the war years. Manufacturing wages rose sixty-five percent after Pearl Harbor—twenty-seven percent when inflation and new taxes were taken into account. The bottom two-fifths of the population saw their income rise sixty percent by 1945—more than double the gain in the other quintiles. The gains made by the lowest income groups were reflected in a decline by one third in the infant mortality rate and an increase of three years for whites and five for blacks in average life expectancy.[115]

Labor navigated through the war-time bureaucracies that regulated its activities and emerged larger, stronger, and determined to regain the initiative it sacrificed during the period of national emergency. Labor realized that the conditions that propelled working class gains during the war emergency—labor scarcity, massive government spending, and a mandated forty-eight hour week with overtime—would not persist after reconversion. The task it faced was to bring the real wage rate back to the pre-inflationary levels of 1941 and find a new purpose for keeping the factories built solely for defense production running at full capacity during peacetime.

Richard Frankensteen, echoing the dream of Alberto Santos-Dumont, proposed the spare capacity in the aircraft industry be used to build low-cost, small airplanes that would open the benefits and joys of flying to a larger segment of the population, particularly to those people living away from the major metropolitan areas and not adequately serviced by existing forms of transportation.[116] Walter Reuther saw a different need. He recognized the inadequacy with which the government addressed the housing shortage problem during the war. Now with millions of servicemen returning, the need for affordable housing was more acute. He proposed that idled aircraft factories be converted to produce prefabricated house components for returning veterans.

Housing was always a high priority on Reuther's social agenda. It was a tenet of his faith in Fordism that the capability of the mass-production engine could make the American Dream affordable for all of its citizens. The Cold War eventually ensured that aircraft factories would continue to be devoted to their original purpose, but the low interest, no down payment VA loans available to returning service men and women created a market that led developers to apply some Fordist methods to their industry. William Levitt brought his experience building mass-produced military housing units using uniform, interchangeable components home from the war, and he mass produced low cost homes at the rate of about thirty a day.[117] By standardizing his parts and rationalizing his labor, Levitt created the modern American suburb.

By 1963, a white middle class was firmly established, but the conformity that the engine driving its growth imprinted upon it was also sedating its spirit. The dream of Reuther and the realization of Levitt's mass-produced affordable housing had metastasized into a formless sprawl, devoid of boundaries between adjacent towns and neighborhoods, with little delineation between the lives of the neighbors themselves. The folk singer Pete Seeger voiced the individual's complaint against the excesses of Fordism with his rendition of Malvina Reynolds song, *Little Boxes*. The song began describing houses built of ticky-tack that all look just the same."[118] The next verses lamented the identical lives of the people living in the little boxes and the little boxes into which the lives of successive generations were being groomed to fit.

Levittowns were contractually restricted to whites-only until Supreme Court rulings in the fifties struck down the legal basis for such restrictive covenants.[119] Well into the nineties they remained predominantly white. Blacks did not participate in the post-war home ownership boom, and were excluded from the new suburbs by discriminatory practices. Housing in the cities and poor rural communities remained substandard and in short supply. Government programs initiated by Truman to replace slums and shanty towns with affordable public housing suffered from poor planning, inadequate funding, and the piggybacking of local civic and cultural projects onto federally funded urban renewal projects.

Reuther retained an interest in making affordable housing available to all people throughout his life. He never let go of the idea of devoting unused industrial capacity to build housing components. In testimony before Congress in December, 1969, just months before his fatal plane crash, he outlined a plan for creating incentives for plants engaged in defense work to convert to civilian production without undue disruption to the workforce and the community. Housing was cited as a primary need converted defense plants could begin to address.[120]

Walter Reuther saw in Fordism a potential to liberate people from the drudgery of just trying to get by, not its capacity to stuff them into neat little boxes. Reuther envisioned the working man having the means and opportunity to participate in the cultural and intellectual life of the community. His answer for accommodating the size of the workforce with the capacity of the economy to absorb its production was the shorter work week. He argued in 1945 that gains in productivity achieved by technological advances spurred by war research and improved production methods could produce as much wealth in a thirty hour week as had been produced in the forty hour week. Reuther argued his ideas in a *New York Times* forum with Chamber of Commerce President Eric Johnston and industrialist Henry J. Kaiser. The workaholic Reuther proclaimed that "Work in itself is not an end. It is a means to an end. The end is a more abundant life, to be able to conquer the job of feeding and clothing ourselves in as little time as possible, so that as civilized men we can enjoy the finer things—culture and education. That is the struggle."[121] Johnston retorted with a dismissive bit of sophistry "if you carry Mr. Reuther's proposal to its absurd conclusion, no one should work at all and then everyone would be rich."[122] Kaiser argued that more material goods, not more leisure was what the public wanted. Anyway "most of us will want to work more than thirty hours a week."[123] Of course Henry J. Kaiser did not work on an assembly line.

Reuther was already sensitive to the challenges posed by automation. He welcomed the increased productivity it promised, but wanted to ensure that its benefits would be distributed fairly. For the next twenty-five years he argued for a national commission to study the effects of automation and how dislocations caused by it might be anticipated and minimized.

National planning was a central theme in every "Reuther plan." He followed up his calls for a role for labor in the war-time production planning process with a proposal for a Peace Production Board where representatives from labor, management, agriculture, consumers, and government would oversee the reconversion effort. In Britain, where labor was given an integral role in the war effort, the establishment of peacetime planning boards, like that proposed by Reuther, became a natural outgrowth of war-time collaboration. In the United States, labor was kept at arm's length in the war production planning, and now was accorded no more space in the reconversion effort.

Labor was restricted to an adversarial role with management, with the playing field limited to wages, benefits, shop floor discipline, and grievance. Labor, management, and consumers were not invited into a collaborative effort of national purpose. They were left to compete in the democratic forum as separate interest groups petitioning government for favorable treatment, usually at the expense of one or both of the other two. In this dynamic the post-war climate favored the selection of a new hybrid species—a military-industrialist—whose voice was louder, whose stature was taller, and, most importantly, whose wallet was thicker.

Unlike after previous wars, the military did not simply stand at ease and fade back into a traditional role and profile. When the Second World War ended Washington was left with a new permanent fixture sitting astride the southern bank of the Potomac. The huge, five-sided building made no pretext of capturing the classical grandeur of the Capitol, but the statement it made and the size of the bureaucracy it housed identified it as the lodestone of what President Eisenhower would call the "Military-Industrial Complex" America was to become a permanent war-time state—not to collect empire as Britain had done, but to exert its influence and reinforce its commerce and diplomacy.

The dollar-a-year men did not just go home after the war either. They maintained their ties with the military. Retired colonels and generals found their way into corporate executive suites and onto corporate boards. Military and corporate lobbyists doubled down on efforts to keep the federal pipeline flowing through the Pentagon out into deep corporate pockets. The Cold War gave the process added impetus, but by the time of Eisenhower's farewell warning in 1960, it was already self-sustaining. The end of the Cold War found new enemies to fear and costly new projects to fund.

CHAPTER VII

Labor Battles and The Treaty of Detroit

They put horses to pasture, they feed them on hay,
Even machines get retired some day.
The bosses get pensions when their days are through,
Fat pensions for them, brother, nothing for you.
...Who will take care of you,
How'll you get by
When you're too old to work and too young to die?

Joe Glazer

On August 14th, 1945 Japan surrendered. World War 2 was over. Crowds celebrated in the public squares. The troops were feted with parades and honors; the generals driven through the canyons of New York in a deluge of confetti. And then it was over. The crowds went home. The twenty thousand workers at Willow Run were saluted and given Army-Navy E's, then told to go home too. The country didn't need them anymore. Henry Ford didn't need the plant that produced nearly 9,000 Liberator bombers in the last two years of the war.[1] Around the country defense plants were shutting down and work hours being trimmed. The overtime and employment fluidity that kept wages abreast of inflation during the war was gone. The corporations were awash in war profits, and the workers were determined to break the shackles of Little Steel and hike the basic rate to at least the pre-inflationary level.

Two days after the Japanese surrender, President Truman issued an executive order permitting wage increases that would not result in increased prices. Walter Reuther had been preparing for this moment since June. His team had compiled a seventy-six page brief containing a sophisticated analysis of General Motors sources of income and costs and even a comparison of the company's share price in relation to wages and inflation over the previous four years.[2] The union document indicated that GM could increase labor costs thirty cents an hour and realize its pre-war profit margins without raising car prices. Two days after the President's announcement, Reuther submitted his brief to GM and demanded a thirty cent an hour increase with no subsequent rise in prices.

Reuther next sold the UAW on his one at a time strategy. The union could not afford to confront all three of the largest manufacturers at the same time. He argued that a better course would be to single out one company for job action while keeping the others working. Workers in the unaffected plants would continue to pay into the union coffers to support their striking colleagues, and the targeted company would feel the loss of market to its competitors in a year of anticipated high demand.

On October 3rd Reuther received his response from GM. The company president, Charlie Wilson, rejected the union demand outright, claiming a thirty percent increase in wages would require a thirty percent price rise. General Motors appeared no more willing to return to its pre-war profit margins than its workers were prepared to allow war-time inflation to devour their incomes. Wilson proposed instead that Reuther join him in asking Congress to increase the standard work week to forty-five hours.[3] Such a suggestion was hardly serious. Any industrialist with an ear to the word in his plants would realize the unrest such an attempt would unleash, and Wilson would have known Reuther was publicly advocating a shorter work week as a means of avoiding a post-war recession.

The parties were at an impasse. Reuther petitioned the NLRB for a strike vote as required by law. He then began a media offensive to convince the public of the reasonableness of the union perspective and to position his union as an advocate for the consumer in the post-war readjustment of the economy. In the *New York Times Magazine* he tied the union's negotiating strategy to a call for strengthened buying power needed to fuel a healthy economy.[4] He continued the offensive by arranging a debate with George Romney, general manager of the Automobile Manufacturers Association, on the popular *Town Meeting of the Air* program. When negotiations with General Motors opened on October 19th, Reuther invited the national press to be in attendance, and then apologized for the company's 'shyness' when GM demanded they be barred[5] Transcripts of the proceedings were provided reporters by a stenographer attached to the union delegation.

Company negotiations were conducted by personnel boss Harry Coen, a man with strong racist and anti-Semitic sentiments[6] and Harry Anderson. Their tone was belligerent and condescending. Reuther wasn't following the script that a labor leader was supposed to mouth, and the two corporate functionaries seemed at a loss to recognize the cues to recite their appointed lines. The transcripts reveal the tone of the meeting and the complete disconnect between the parties.[7]

Coen:	There is nothing sincere in your approach. It's just another chance for you to get up on a soapbox before more people. [...] Is the UAW fighting the fight of the whole world?
Reuther:	We have been fighting to hold prices and increase purchasing power. We are making our little contribution in that respect.
Coen:	Why don't you get down to size and do the job you're supposed to do as a trade-union leader and talk about money you'd like to have for your people and let the labor statesmanship go to hell for a while? [...] You say we can't raise prices, and if we say we have to raise prices you don't want thirty percent but you are going to have the thirty percent or else [...]
Corbin:	[Elwin Corbin, UAW official interjecting] Do you mean if we came in here with a thirty percent wage

	demand and offered to join with you before the OPA (Office of Price Administration) for a thirty percent increase in the price of cars, you would talk business?
Coen:	We don't ask you to join with us on the price of cars. It is none of your damned business what OPA does about prices.
Corbin:	The hell it isn't! I intend to *buy* a car.
Reuther:	But don't you think it is constructive for us to relate our wage question to prices?
Coen:	Nobody else is doing that but you. You're the fellow who wants to get the publicity out of this whole thing. You want to enhance your political position. That's what this whole show is about….
Reuther:	[…] when Reuther comes and there is what you say is an attempt to be a statesman, you think that is bad. I think if I didn't do it that way it would be bad. I think if we came in here on a selfish basis and said, "We want ours and the world be damned," then you should take our pants off.
Coen:	I don't think the people out on the picket line care anything about wage theories. What does the man carrying a sign say about GM books?
Reuther:	He doesn't care anything about GM books, provided you give him a satisfactory wage increase.
Coen:	That is right.
Reuther:	But if you say, "No dice, we can't give you a wage increase," he says, "Let's look at your books to see why you can't."

The proposal was intended to give Reuther a political boost within the UAW. But it was much more than a political ploy by an ambitious leader. Reuther's ambition was married to a vision of a more equitable society. His genius lay in recognizing an opportunity, engineering an attractive product, and moving decisively while the opportunity existed. Harry Coen recognized ambition, but to him, ambition had always been wedded to power, status, and wealth.

The question of General Motors' ability to raise wages and still realize a fair profit on the sale of its cars was not something the company wanted discussed in public. Any evidentiary analysis of the Reuther brief might have evolved into a broader discussion of how GM profits compared to companies in more competitive industries and where the line between fair and excessive profits should be drawn. GM wanted these questions left unasked. It never presented a detailed refutation of Reuther's claim or made a counter offer based on its own calculations. Instead it resorted to labeling Reuther's concept of building a more stable economic foundation by empowering more consumers as socialism.

Coen never paused to examine Reuther's logic and consider whether a larger market might add more revenue to the company's coffers than a higher profit margin. Instead he leveled the charge of Socialism:[8]

Reuther:	Unless we get a more realistic distribution of America's wealth, we don't get enough to keep the machinery going.
Coen:	There it is again. You can't talk about this thing without exposing your socialistic desires.
Reuther:	If fighting for equal and equitable distribution of the wealth of this country is socialistic. I stand guilty of being a Socialist.
Coen:	I think you are convicted.
Reuther:	I plead guilty.

The preliminary meeting illustrated the gap between the two parties. It was almost a month later before the company made its first concrete offer—a ten cent an hour increase.[9] The union dismissed the offer as a 'bribe' aimed at undermining union militancy without providing adequate protection against inflation. Reuther made an immediate counter proposal. The union would accept the verdict of an impartial arbitration board if the company would open its books for a realistic appraisal of what constituted a fair settlement and agree not to raise prices on its automobiles. He gave the company twenty four hours to respond.[10]

Reuther kept the pressure on the company. The union was being fair and civic minded. The company, arbitrary and uncompromising. President Truman delivered a radio address in which he gave a sympathetic recitation to the workers' plight and voiced the same concern as Reuther about the need to stimulate demand to avoid a recession.

> "I wonder how many of you know that many war workers have already had to take, or will soon have to take, a cut in their wartime pay by one-quarter or more. Think of what such a decrease in your own income would mean to you and your families [...] Unless checked, the annual wage and salary bill in private industry will shrink by over $20 billion [...] The corner grocer is going to feel it, as well as the department store, the railroads, the theaters and gas stations, and all the farmers of the nation. It is a sure road to wide unemployment."[11]

Reuther wired his congratulations to the President and contended again that GM would not have to raise prices to satisfy the union's demands. Truman, however, opened the door ajar to permitting price increases where justified to cover the cost of labor agreements.

In a vote conducted by the NLRB, 70,853 workers favored a strike to enforce UAW demands on GM with only 12,438 opposing.[12] When GM did not respond to the offer for arbitration by Reuther's deadline, GM workers in 95 plants across the country walked off the job. Three days later, Harry Anderson, GM vice president for labor relations, rejected arbitration, calling the union proposal "not an offer of arbitration, but a demand for abdication,'" and vowing management would not turn over its responsibilities to arbitrators.[13]

The GM strike of 1946 took on a different character entirely from the violent confrontations that marked the union battle for recognition in the thirties. Now there was no violence; no attempt to keep the plants running with scabs; no confrontations on the picket lines. This strike was fought in the court of public opinion—a venue in which Reuther proved very adept and the corporation surprisingly maladroit.

Since the company wouldn't agree to an independent arbitration board, Reuther recruited his own citizens panel to review the contentions of the parties and offer an assessment of the competing positions. The citizen's panel included a St. Louis banker, the national president of the PTA, prominent Protestant and Catholic clergymen, and Walter White, executive secretary of the NAACP.[14] The Reuther panel was distinguished but overwhelmingly sympathetic to the labor movement. GM refused to meet with the group, ensuring a one-sided presentation of the argument. Reuther seized the high ground when he said he would reduce his demands from thirty percent to as low as one percent if an accurate reading of the books demonstrated that was all GM could afford to offer without raising prices.[15] This 'magnanimous' gesture was rejected out of hand by the company, prompting Walter White to write later that he was surprised at how inept the company was in handling its public relations.[16] Not surprisingly, the citizens committee supported Reuther's contention that GM could afford to raise wages without increasing prices. It went on to praise Reuther's proposal as "[lifting] the whole matter of collective bargaining to a new high level by insisting that the advancement of labor's interest shall not be made at the expense of the public."[17]

Reuther had conducted numerous strikes before. He knew that public support, or at worst public neutrality, was critical in maintaining the pressure essential for labor success. Public support was like swelling the picket line with thousands of invisible, but decidedly present, extra bodies. He was a conductor cuing in each section of his ensemble where the score required. There were the returned veterans, walking the picket line wearing their recent uniforms and carrying placards reading "I did not fight over there to protect GM profits over here." Union organizers were dispatched to the Kiwanis and Rotary clubs across the country explaining the importance of the strike in terms of community buying power. Letters were sent to shopkeepers asking "How many du Ponts shop at your store?" Buttons were sold bearing another Reuther slogan—"We fight today for a better tomorrow. I gave to win higher wages—no price increase." Finally, the chorus of prominent voices—Eleanor Roosevelt, Wayne Morse, Henry Luce, Harold Stassen, and others—were melded together to form a Citizen's Committee to Aid the GM Strikers.[18] Luce's magazine empire put Reuther on the cover of its December 3rd issue of *Time* and gave him favorable publicity in *Life* and *Fortune*. The business magazine noted that:

> "He believes that labor's political and economic power must be brought to bear for one great purpose: to gain for labor—and thus, he believes, for the consumer—a true partnership in the U. S. productive machine. To this mission, thirty-eight year old Reuther brings an energy and native intelligence unmatched by any other union leader."[19]

The orchestrated labor campaign was in tune, and resonating with a receptive audience.

General Motors reacted to the union pressure two weeks before Christmas by canceling its old contract containing the NWLB maintenance of membership clause and declaring its hostility toward any union security clause in the future.[20] Negotiations broke down and both sides "settled their heads for a long winter's nap." President Truman was coming under increasing pressure to take action against a mounting nationwide wave of strikes. On December 3rd he appointed a fact-finding committee chaired by Lloyd Garrison, a member of the old NWLB, and containing Milton Eisenhower, then president of Kansas State College, and Walter Stacy of the North Carolina State Supreme Court. The committee was charged with investigating the issues in the strike and making its recommendations to the President.[21]

On December 19th, one day before the fact-finding committee was to hold its first hearing, Alfred P. Sloan, Donaldson Brown, and Wilson of GM convened a parlay in New York's Waldorf Astoria Hotel with their counterparts from the steel industry, General Electric, Westinghouse, and other companies under attack from the CIO to ensure their resolve to adhere to a hard line in their negotiations.[22] The corporate counteroffensive was not being led by Wilson and the auto men back in Detroit, but by the financial interests and the du Ponts in the East.

The hard line adopted by the corporation was emphasized in the choice of their chief counsel at the hearings: Walter Merritt, a person Reuther called "the cave man of American labor relations."[23] Merritt's involvement in management attempts to thwart union organizing efforts dated as far back as a 1906 Danbury hatters strike that he crippled by securing a broad injunction against the striking workers. Merritt announced at the outset of the hearings that his delegation would not be part of further proceedings if ability to pay was considered relevant to issues in the case. Garrison and his committee waited for confirmation by phone from Truman before stating that ability to pay would be relevant to the committee's consideration of the case. Garrison urged both parties to return to Detroit and try to work on a resolution over the Christmas break. When the fact-finding committee deliberations resumed on December 28th, Merritt and his delegation stood behind their chairs and asked if ability to pay was still under consideration. When informed by Garrison that it was, the GM delegation walked out.[24]

The company walk out was a public relations triumph for Reuther, but the widening strike into steel, electrical workers, the rubber industry, and beyond was not a welcome show of labor militancy, but an indication that the union fight was being taken over by the more traditional unionists content to limit negotiations to wages, benefits, and job security and not be concerned about the larger economic impact of their bargain. The Truman panel was able to get a look at GM financial records, and recommended to the President on January 10th that the company could grant an increase of nineteen and one half cents an hour without necessitating an increase in prices.[25] The panel's verdict stipulated a pay rise less than two thirds of what was requested by Reuther, but it noted that when production from new plants came on line it would greatly increase the company's profitability, allowing it to pass on those profits to its stock holders and its consumers in the form of lower prices and better quality.

Reuther was eager to establish a principle, now seconded by the fact-finding board, and indicated his willingness to settle on terms outlined by the board. The company rejected the conclusions claiming they were based on "an unsound principle" that a rich company be forced to pay more for labor than a less well-to-do one.[26] Ironically, years later when George Romney made a counter argument that a small company should not be asked to pay as much for labor as a big one during a Congressional hearing, Victor Reuther took him aside during a break and asked if U. S. Steel gave him a favorable price because his was a small company? Victor told him the answer was no, that GM would actually get a better deal because of the size of its purchase. He then asked "Why do you ask an American [Motors] worker to sell his labor in the marketplace under circumstances less favorable to him than those that govern the sale of a cold ton of steel?"[27]

In fact the committee figure of nineteen and one half cents had more to do with the situation in the steel industry than what GM could afford without raising prices. The American steel industry was already sick, showing the early symptoms of the illness that would incapacitate it once the newly reconstructed factories of Germany and Japan were producing high quality steel more cheaply. For years the steel barons stood behind a wall of protective tariffs and low commodity and transportation costs, resisting modernization of their plants and fearing over capacity. By the time of the great wave of post-war strikes, the industry had low productivity and diminished prospects for growth. It was more than content to establish a pattern of letting Washington set its wage and price standards, and relying on it for protection against foreign competition—a bargain that passed the costs of its inefficiencies on to the consumer.

On January 15th, 1946, U. S. Steel President, Benjamin Fairless indicated to President Truman that he would seek an agreement for an eighteen cent an hour increase of wages in the steel industry.[28] Negotiations between Fairless, the more militant anti-union leaders of Little Steel, and Phil Murray produced no agreement, so Truman proposed an eighteen and one half cent wage increase. Steel would not agree without a price hike, and Murray took his 750,000 members out of the mills and mines. Truman was caught in the middle with his "good angel" Chester Bowles sitting on one shoulder telling him to hold the line on prices, and his "naughty angel" Treasury Secretary John Snyder sitting on the other shoulder urging him to be more elastic in stretching the price guidelines.[29] Finally the "naughty angel" won out and the CIO and the steel industry agreed to an eighteen and one half cent increase in wages. Three days later the OPA authorized a price hike for steel of slightly more than five dollars a ton.[30] Truman called the deviation from price control a "little bulge."[31] It was the first little bulge, but far from the last until the whole OPA framework became so contorted and elastic that it served little purpose, and its critics had no trouble abolishing it altogether.

The steel agreement set the industry pattern. One-by-one the other unions signed on to the eighteen and one half cent standard set by steel. The Ford and Chrysler Divisions of the UAW were among the first in line. When the Communist dominated United Electrical Workers went behind Reuther's back and negotiated a separate eighteen and one half cent deal for their GM workers, the strike was lost. Old line unionism had won out. The penny difference between the Truman panel's recommendation and the industrial standard set by steel became a symbolic exclamation point between a complete company triumph and a face-saving crumb for Reuther.

With management pricing prerogatives secured, GM Chairman Sloan, who wanted to repeal the New Deal like Prohibition before it,[32] left the remaining bargaining to Wilson, who just wanted to start building cars again. The final union security deals and rules governing seniority and transfers were hammered out. On March 13th, 113 days after it began, the great GM strike came to an end. Walter Reuther was not present at the signing ceremony where Phil Murray, representing the CIO inked the agreement for the union.

Reuther lost on both main issues. He was not able to force the company to raise wages and hold the line on prices, and the negotiated wage increase was substantially less than the thirty cents an hour sought. R. J. Thomas complained that the GM strike was "called six weeks too early and ended a month too late."[33] Still Reuther emerged as the leader most attuned to the mood of the rank-and-file. Despite the hardship of foregoing almost four months of pay, the GM workers remained committed to the effort. When it was over, it was Phil Murray and the Communists of the United Electrical Workers who were blamed for "selling out" and backstabbing the union. The workers may not have "cared anything about wage theories" at the beginning of the strike as

Harry Coen sneered, but by the time it was over they recognized that the "hollow nickels of inflation" they won made them no better off than before.

Reuther Heads From the BargainingTable to the Boardwalk

Post-war labor relations had entered a new era. The government, that helped foster the growth of the labor movement in the thirties and mediated the relationship between labor and management during the war years was now stepping aside, permitting an increasingly hostile Congress to blunt labor's most effective weapons. Industrial leadership was passing from the generation of men like Alfred Sloan and Henry Ford, who wanted to see the New Deal "repealed" like Prohibition, to men like Charles Wilson and Henry Ford the Second, who saw labor as a useful ally in placating their workforce and making it better able to consume their product. The new industrialists had a sophisticated appreciation of the post-New Deal terrain and knew how capitalism could flourish in that environment. Wilson proved more than willing to help his workers buy a car, but stood adamantly opposed to letting them help drive his vehicle.

Labor was desperately searching for a new direction. The old style militancy of John L. Lewis alienated a growing white-collar middle class and put only inflationary "wooden nickels" in the pockets of workers. In the UAW, the heavy-set, tobacco-chewing, poker-playing Thomas was becoming an anachronism. He was always considered a transitional figure—a non-divisive choice of Phil Murray and Sidney Hillman to lead the union out of the Homer Martin wilderness, but not the person who would lead it into a promised land. Reuther's supporters feared that Communists would become more entrenched in the Addes machine through patronage and soon propel their man to the top post. They urged Reuther to challenge for the presidency.[34] Reuther was at a peak of popularity for his militant leadership of the GM strike. He realized this was his opportunity. As the GM strike was winding down, he announced his candidacy for UAW president.

The ink was barely dry on the GM contract when the UAW delegates marched straight from the picket line to the Boardwalk for their 1946 convention. Atlantic City was cold and windy in late March. The beaches were empty; the Million Dollar Pier was deserted; the casinos were years in the future. The hotels on Park Place and Boardwalk this time of year rented for rates that would only get you a room on Mediterranean and Baltic in season. Atlantic City was cheap and the UAW was broke. The number of dues paying members was less than half the war-time peak of 1.2 million.[35] The aircraft plants were particularly hard hit with the cessation of war-time orders.

The Reuther group arrived in Atlantic City expecting to win. A preliminary headcount indicated they had well over the number of votes needed to elect their candidate, but UAW conventions were never predictable. They were boisterous and rowdy; water balloons were dropped from upper-story windows, and fights broke out between supporters of the rival factions. More than salt water taffy was available on the Boardwalk to induce wavering delegates to vote for Thomas, and there wasn't a shortage of Reuther partisans willing to pretend to be an uncommitted, if only to keep the girls away from their intended targets.

The real threat to Reuther's election did not come from call girls or water balloons. The danger lay in the role Phil Murray would play in swinging sentiment in the hall to Thomas. There was always a coolness between Murray and Reuther, and the GM strike exacerbated their differences. Murray was wary of an independent rival gaining control of the UAW, and reading in *Fortune* that "Reuther brings an energy and native intelligence unmatched by any other union leader"[36] did little to endear the brash young redhead to his nominal boss. It was no secret that the CIO preferred Thomas. The only question remained how determinedly Murray would campaign for the incumbent?

There was little Reuther could do to curtail Murray's effect on the convention, but he would not react passively to the script dictated by his rivals. Reuther was not included in the delegation assigned to escort Murray from his hotel to the convention floor, but the official snub did not keep Reuther from appearing on stage with Murray. Reminiscent of the persistence with which he had once talked his way past the security guard and into a job at Ford, Reuther joined up with the escorts on route to the hall and wedged his way toward Murray. Richard Leonard remembered:

"Walking down the boardwalk, I was alongside Phil and I was getting my heels kicked by Walter trying to get up alongside Phil. As we hit in back of the convention hall, Walter had Phil by the left arm and he walked right up the steps with Phil, you know, onto the platform. And I overheard the conversation. I guess Phil wasn't sure if Walter was a candidate at that point. I think Phil probably was trying to prevail upon him not to be a candidate. I remember Walter saying, 'Well, damn it, Phil I'm going to run.' And so he did."[37]

In his address to the delegates, Murray denounced as "a diabolic, detestable lie" the rumor that he was party to the GM fact-finding board's low estimate of the figure GM could afford in wages without the need to raise its prices.[38] He praised Thomas for "very extraordinary and unusual services" in helping establish the World Federation of Trade Unions, then referred to Thomas as "this great big guy for whom I have such a distinct fondness."[39]

The Thomas delegates played up the "fondness" that Murray had for their man. The CIO floor representatives, Hillman and Haywood, lobbied delegates for Thomas on the convention floor, and the girls hired for the occasion lobbied for Thomas in the hotel rooms at night. By the time of the vote, Reuther's substantial lead had dwindled. The issue was in doubt.

Polling of the delegation lasted four hours. The name of each local was read out by the clerk and the votes for each candidate recorded. The number of votes allotted to a local was based on the size of its membership. Each convention delegate represented about one hundred members and votes were broken down as fine as three places to the right of the decimal. It was a long, tedious process. Only a few people in the hall were keeping an accurate tally. As the roll call was nearing the end, a great shout rang out after the votes of a pro-Reuther local were called out. Delegates from Brendan Sexton's Willow Run local hoisted Reuther onto their shoulders and began celebrating. The demonstration seemed to indicate that Reuther had just reached the magic number needed for victory. In fact he hadn't. The demonstration was a ploy by Sexton to stampede the remaining votes to the presumed winner.

When the voting ended, Reuther had his victory. His share was just 50.7 percent of the vote.[40] Questions lingered long afterward whether Sexton's demonstration gave Reuther the votes he needed for the win. His opponents were certain the ploy swung the election to Reuther, but Leonard Woodcock, who was keeping the vote tally for the Reuther forces that day, was satisfied no votes were changed, only the enthusiasm with which they were announced.[41]

The Reutherites hit the night spots of the shore community to celebrate. The abstemious Reuther fulfilled a campaign pledge and had a beer and a cigar with the boys. For the night, memories of the struggles and triumphs of the early days and visions of the opportunities ahead mingled with the overpowering aroma of tobacco and the heady effervescence of beer.

The remainder of the convention gave them little else to celebrate. Thomas did not perform the ritual surrender expected from defeated union leaders, and Addes chose to maintain his alliance with the Communists rather than accept a compromise offered by Reuther.[42] The Communists retained significant influence inside the union and were not prepared to see it diminished without a continued fight.

The transfer of power formalities began right after the final vote was certified when Alan Haywood approached the dejected "big guy" with the offer of a mid-level post in the CIO bureaucracy. Thomas was expected to retire from the UAW and slip gracefully into the obscurity of his new office. But before he had time to come to terms with his defeat and accept his new position, he was seduced by a Communist-led draft movement to contend for the office of First Vice President.[43]

The Reuther forces had selected Melvin Bishop, the recipient of the letter from Gorky years earlier, to be first vice president. They had not anticipated Thomas would be a candidate, and that sympathy for his defeat and gratitude for his years of service would siphon off enough support from the previous day's majority to handily defeat Bishop.

Addes was reelected without opposition, and the second vice presidency went to Richard Leonard, the erstwhile Reuther loyalist who wouldn't allow Reuther a free path to the vice presidency in 1944 and whose heels he ran up on rushing to get close to Phil Murray earlier in the week. Addes loyalists prevailed in the majority of the Executive Board races as well. The only moment of cheer for the Reuther group came in the election of the progressive Socialist Emil Mazey to the seat vacated by Bishop. Mazey would have to wait to occupy the chair he had won until his return from service in the Philippines.

The 1946 convention was the last for long-time Reuther rival, Richard Frankensteen. The burly ex football star fulfilled a campaign pledge he made during an unsuccessful 1945 run for Mayor of Detroit and resigned from the UAW. He faded from public view into a private life removed from the turbulence of the formative days of the union. In a 1975 interview, Frankensteen reminisced about the factional struggles that marked that period of his life. He told the interviewer "In my judgment the factionalism never could have ended until Walter Reuther became president of the UAW. He wouldn't let the fight die. I don't say that as a criticism of Walter. He was a very capable man who had a seething ambition which would not have ended until he got what he wanted."[44] He expressed no bitterness over the 1943 election battle that produced the doggerel linking "the gruesome twosome, George F. Addes and Frankensteen" with the Communists in the union. "That was politics. I never had any political ideology."[45] Frankensteen died two years later with little public notice of his passing.

The Communists survived the Reuther election with their power largely intact. Six months after the Japanese surrender the country was not ready to listen to the drumbeat for another war. The Communists still had a voice in the national conversation—tolerated but not popular on the left and excoriated but not excommunicated by the right. Churchill's Iron Curtain speech at Westminster College three weeks before the UAW convention was considered by many to be unduly provocative. Victor Reuther and Nat Ganley found common ground in a resolution at the convention condemning the speech and attacking the United States, Great Britain, and the Soviet Union for their "old imperialist, war-inciting methods of power politics,"[46] though Ganley objected to the Soviet inclusion in Reuther's wording.

The UAW left the Boardwalk more divided than when they arrived. Reuther faced an Executive Board controlled by his rivals. No executive and legislative branches controlled by rival parties could be more dysfunctional than the 1946 UAW leadership. The majority on the board met privately to draft policy statements that Reuther never saw before they were formally presented at a meeting of the full board. At the board's first meeting after the convention, the Addes faction presented a completely worked out economic plan that repudiated much of the theory behind Reuther's GM strike strategy, including using ability to pay as a metric for fashioning non-inflationary wage demands.[47]

The antagonism went beyond matters of policy and colored the daily interplay in the office. Even the secretaries took sides. Reuther loyalists in departments dominated by the Addes camp would seek out a secretary favoring their man to type their reports.[48] There was no cooperation at the top either. Addes would not let Reuther see the books until Reuther discovered a clause in the by-laws that said all checks drawn on the union account needed the president's signature. Reuther contacted the UAW bank and notified them that no check was valid until he verified the check number by phone. He then threatened to stop approving paychecks until he was given access to the books. His opponents complied because, as he later said "Those fellows hated my guts, but they loved their paychecks."[49]

In jockeying for advantage in the factional deadlock, Reuther and Thomas made a deal in which Thomas would be named the director of the Competitive Shops Department, which was in charge of organizing non-unionized plants. The post provided Thomas with an ability to appoint a large staff dependent on his patronage. In return, Thomas supported naming Victor Reuther to head the Education Department and Frank Winn to head Publicity.[50] The deal gave Thomas a portfolio from which he could establish a power base aligned with, but independent from, the Addes camp. Reuther got control of the union newspaper and the department which became the most strategically important piece of real estate in the factional war.

The Education Department was where the "battle for the hearts and minds" of the rank-and-file was waged. Victor Reuther fired Addes loyalists from staff positions in the department and filled its ranks with Reuther loyalists. He recruited Brendan Sexton, Lewis Carliner, and Mrs. Mildred Jeffrey to fill the top positions on his team.[51] They established a leadership training school at a CIO resort area in Port Huron, Michigan. Courses in public speaking, parliamentary law, and labor history were offered to students carefully selected for their potential usefulness in the upcoming local delegate selection battles. The courses provided the locals with trained spokespeople, able to contend with management in grievance and work rule disputes and to promote the union on the shop floor. Graduates of leadership training classes were expected to assume active roles inside the locals and provide a counterbalance to activists versed in Communist ideology.

The Education Department sponsored a huge seminar in Cleveland in the late fall of 1946. Over a thousand attendees listened to speakers from the non-Communist left like Eleanor Roosevelt, OPA administrator Chester Bowles, and Walter White of the NAACP provide a liberal agenda for union militancy and argue against factional quarrels that "to satisfy personal ambitions or grudges could mean destruction of the union."[52] Between the formal sessions White reported "There was an undercurrent of tension and caucusing [...] No quadrennial convention to select a Presidential candidate by any of the political parties was ever more steeped in political maneuvers than the Cleveland meeting."[53] The Communists had always exerted influence beyond their actual numbers because of the intellectual foundation they provided for programs championed by non-ideological leaders like Addes and Thomas. At events like the educational conference in Cleveland, the Reuthers got to set the agenda, provide a social-democratic alternative to the Communist narrative, and empower a cadre of shop floor activists with the tools and arguments to counteract Communist influence.

In the two years since the end of the war, Communism had become a much bigger issue with the public at large and within the union movement. The Republicans gained control of both houses of Congress in 1946 for the first time since 1930 by riding a wave of public discontent over paralyzing strikes and out-of-control inflation. The Republicans needed a bogeyman to scare voters over to their agenda. They found it in Communism.

The 80th Congress introduced Joseph McCarthy to the Senate and Richard Nixon to the House. It came into power resolving to curtail the power of the unions, and used the issue of Communist influence within the labor movement to forge public sentiment for restrictive labor legislation. The Communist dominated Local 248 of Harold Christoffel and Robert Buse provided the headlines bolstering their argument.

The militant union and intransigent management of Allis-Chalmers were in a state of perpetual conflict, frequently peppered with work stoppages and strikes. A 1946 strike was six months old when the Communist card was played. Management leaked personnel files of union leaders to the *Milwaukee Sentinel* showing their connections to the Communist Party.[54] A month later negotiations broke down, and the company issued a back to work order. The workforce was divided in its loyalty to the union and many workers were eager to return to the job. Violent clashes erupted. Local officers and shop floor leaders underscored their allegiance to the class struggle by signing Communist nomination petitions, and nomination petitions were openly distributed on the picket line. The mainstream media widely publicized the Communist character of the strike.

Walter Reuther feared the actions of Christoffel and Buse could result in the desertification of the UAW local at Allis-Chalmers. It was also adding impetus to the Taft-Hartley legislation making its way through Congress. Reuther fumed "Why did they place this gigantic club in the hands of their management with which to beat our union to the ground?"[55] He and Addes both felt that the only way the strike could be saved would be for the local leaders to be replaced, but the strike committee retained the support of Thomas and CIO Regional Director Joseph Mattson.[56]

Management refused any resumption of negotiations with the local leadership. A Wisconsin Labor Relations Board certification election was scheduled for January 26, 1947, and the outcome was far from certain. Reuther received a call that management was willing to reopen negotiations, but only with top leaders from the CIO. He advised Phil Murray of the offer and notified Thomas that he and John Brophy of the CIO would meet with the company officials. As the date for the election drew near, Thomas became convinced that the local would win re-certification by a four to one margin. He denounced Reuther for "swallowing a corporate divide-and-conquer scheme" and announced that negotiations were terminated until after the vote.[57]

The union barely survived in a close vote that the company immediately challenged. But its problems were hardly over. The House Un-American Activities Committee swept into town for hearings on the Communist involvement in the UAW local. Thomas, Buse, and Christoffel were dragged before the House Education and Labor Committee where all three were grilled and denounced. The UAW witnesses received particularly hostile questioning from freshmen legislators Richard Nixon and John F. Kennedy.[58] The Senate was no more willing to buy Reuther's argument that the post-war strikes were a product of employer intransigence and flawed government policy. The Congress was readying the legislation that became the Taft-Hartley Labor Relations Act of 1947 that placed restrictions on a union's ability to strike and required union officers to sign loyalty oaths.

The Allis-Chalmers strike collapsed in March, prompting Reuther to report to the Executive Board "Our failure at Allis-Chalmers was the result of the open interference on the part of the Communist Party in the affairs of the local union involved...There were people in leadership positions in that local who put loyalties outside of their union, outside the rank-and -file, and outside of this country [...] That is why we lost."[59]

Defeat in the Allis-Chalmers strike did little to quiet the factional battle within the UAW. Despite the temper of Congress and the mood of the country, the anti-Reuther majority on the board were not willing to give up support for their Communist allies nor find common cause with Reuther in defending the union against an assault from the right. The struggle for control colored every aspect of union endeavor as the next convention approached.

Reuther's opponents on the Executive Board had what they thought was a trump card that they played late in a July, 1947 Executive Board session as Reuther was hustling to catch a flight to Washington for a White House meeting. The Addes group had been secretly negotiating a merger with the Farm Equipment Workers (FE) under which the FE would join the much larger UAW, but retain an autonomous identity within the union and be awarded a block of 430 convention votes.[60] The Reuther forces were caught by surprise. They did not have the votes to block board approval of the merger, and the addition of 430 votes from a Communist-dominated union would likely doom Reuther's reelection chances at the upcoming convention. Unable to delay a vote on the merger, Jack Livingston, a Reuther lieutenant on the board, was able to attach a proviso to the resolution that the merger would be conditional subject to the approval of the membership in a referendum.[61] The Addes forces did not see a danger in this proviso. The merger made sense on practical grounds. The FE had been in jurisdictional disputes with the UAW in the past, and an alliance could be justified on grounds of labor solidarity. Ratification by the membership would remove any doubts about the legitimacy of the merger.

The referendum provided Reuther and his allies with a challenge and an opportunity. Reuther had attracted a talented staff around him. Men like Don Montgomery, Jack Conway, Leonard Woodcock, and Nat Weinberg helped their boss turn the Addes putsch to their advantage. Reuther and his team out-maneuvered and out-hustled the opposition throughout the short campaign. Squads of loyalists were dispatched to every UAW center coast-to-coast and from Canada to the Gulf to deliver Reuther's message to the membership. George Addes had saved R. J. Thomas from the potential embarrassment of a debate with Reuther at the convention on the Boardwalk, but foolishly allowed himself to be drawn into an encounter with his forensically skilled opponent in Detroit. Reuther demolished George Addes in their debate. The Reuther forces opposed the merger on the technical grounds that it created an autonomous unit, not based on geographical parameters, in violation of the union by-laws. But the real focus of opposition was the Communist orientation of the Farm Equipment Workers union.

Livingston's proviso of requiring membership approval for the merger to take effect over-trumped the Addes play and secured the needed trick for game. Reuther's message resonated with the men and women on the shop floor. The merger was rejected in the referendum by a margin of more than two to one.[62] The rank and file was tired of the factional divide at the top of their union. The Allis-Chalmers debacle accentuated Reuther's warnings that Communist loyalties were with the agenda of the party, even if it came at the expense of the interests of the workers.

The heat coming from the 80th Congress had helped defrost the relationship between Phil Murray and Walter Reuther. By the time the

UAW returned to the Boardwalk for its 1947 convention in November, Murray had come to accept Reuther, if not yet to have "such a distinct fondness" for him. He briefly interceded for the retention of George Addes as Secretary-Treasurer, but was told it was too late for "peace in our time."[63] In his remarks to the convention, Murray recalled the pledge he and Reuther had made to each other the last time they were together on the Jersey Shore:

> "I took his good little right hand in mine and I patted his red locks. 'Walter,' I said, 'I am going to support you.' He said, 'Phil, I am going to support you.' And he did, and I did."[64]

Murray and Reuther would grow closer to each other over time, but in 1947 they had a working relationship and a growing mutual respect.

The Reuther forces came to the Shore promising to end factionalism and protect the workers from outside influences. They rallied under the slogan of "UAW Americanism for Us." Unlike the previous convention, there was no drama; the opposition forces were resigned to their fate and did not offer a prominent candidate to challenge Reuther. In turn Addes, Thomas, and Leonard were trounced by Reuther-backed candidates: Emil Mazey, Richard Gosser, and John Livingston.[65] Only four seats on the twenty-two member Executive Board were retained by Addes supporters, and two of those immediately jumped over to the Reuther side.[66] When the UAW left the Boardwalk, it had a new slogan "Teamwork in the Leadership and Solidarity in the Ranks."

R. J. Thomas now accepted a low-profile job in the CIO bureaucracy. George Addes left the union and opened a nightclub. Dick Leonard drifted into a CIO post in the desert Southwest. Of the three men whose ambitions jostled the union from side to side as they struggled to reach the front of the line—Addes, Frankensteen, and Reuther—only one remained to escort it into a period of relative peace and tranquility.

The Assassination Attempts

The peace for Reuther was short-lived. On the afternoon of April 20th, 1948, Walter telephoned May that the Executive Board meeting was running late and that she should put his dinner on the back burner and expect him to get home well after dark. The meeting lasted until 8:30 that evening and Walter and his chief associate Jack Conway stopped off at the UAW headquarters to take care of a few chores before he headed home. When he arrived at his home on the corner of Appoline and Chippewa, it was after 9:30. He parked his car in front of the house on Appoline and entered through the front door. He sat down at the kitchen breakfast bar and ate a dish of warmed over stew, then went to the refrigerator to get a bowl of sliced peaches. Just as he turned to respond to a remark by May, a blast from a 12-gauge shotgun shattered the kitchen window and ripped into its target. Four pellets tore into his arm and a fifth passed through his chest. The brunt of the blast was absorbed by a kitchen cabinet behind the spot Reuther was standing the instant before he turned to address his wife.[67]

If Reuther had parked as usual on the side street and entered through the kitchen door, he would have run straight into an ambush. If he had not turned the moment the shot was fired, the buckshot would have gone straight through his chest. Reuther was lucky to be alive. The fast reaction of his neighborhood helped to keep him alive. A neighbor, alerted by the gunshot, rushed over to the Reuther house and saw Walter lying on the floor in a pool of blood. The man then ran down the street to summon the neighborhood doctor. Dr. Lenzi hurried over, administered morphine for the pain, and worked to staunch the bleeding.[68]

Once Reuther believed he was going to survive, his greatest fear was losing the use of his arm. Seeing the arm dangling at a crazy angle by his side brought back memories of the accident at the Wheeling Corrugating Company where he lost part of his big toe. Reuther pleaded with the doctor not to let anyone amputate his arm. To calm his patient and increase the chances of saving the arm, Dr Lenzi immobilized it in a sling while waiting for the ambulance to arrive.[69] Doctors at the hospital held out little hope that he would regain use of his arm. Surgery to repair the damaged radial nerve offered slim hope for success, but the skill of the surgeon and the indomitable will of the patient beat the gloomy odds.

After months of physical therapy, and years of forcibly making the hand grasp tools and squeeze rubber balls, Reuther gradually regained use of the arm.

Just over a year after Walter Reuther was shot, his brother Victor was targeted in a similar manner. Victor had not considered himself to be sufficiently important to be marked for assassination, and had taken few precautions to reduce his vulnerability to attack. He had purchased a small cocker spaniel that doubled as a watchdog and family pet, but had no security fence, floodlights, or bodyguards.[70] On several occasions when he arrived home from work, he would see a car parked across from his house start up and speed away, but he attributed this to his sudden intrusion into the guilt-ridden passion of teenage lovers. In May, 1949, he began receiving phone calls from the local police precinct informing him of complaints from an unnamed neighbor about the late night barking of his dog, telling him to do something about it. The dog did wake up the family on occasion, and when Victor came down to check on him he sometimes noticed a car moving away from in front of the house.[71] The police would not say which neighbor issued the complaint so that the problem might be straightened out between them. Instead a policeman came to the door and told Victor that this was a final warning. He had to do something about the dog. Reluctantly, the family gave the dog to friends.

On the night of May 22nd, one day after the dog was given away, the Reuthers entertained family friends—Dr. William Lowrie and his wife. After the Loweries left, Sophie Reuther wanted to read an article in the *New York Times* and Victor replaced a dull bulb with a brighter one to give her more light. He then settled down to read himself. Suddenly there was an explosion. Sophie thought at first that the new bulb had blown out in spectacular fashion, but soon realized something much more horrible had occurred. Victor had been hit in the side of the face. His glasses were shattered; his partial was driven back into his throat, making it difficult to breathe; his collarbone was broken and pellets had ripped open his chest. He staggered to his feet and managed to pull the denture out of his mouth before collapsing to the floor. He remembered thinking of all the things for which he needed to live, and praying, not yet Lord.[72]

Dr. Lowrie was notified and he had the ambulance diverted to the Henry Ford Hospital where he was resident. By the time it arrived, Dr. Lowrie had assembled a top flight surgical team and Victor was rushed into emergency surgery. Sophie had to sign papers permitting the doctors to remove her husband's right eye, but it was just a formality. The shot had already done that. Victor's life was in the balance for a couple of days before it became evident that a second Reuther had survived a second assassination attempt.[73]

Anna Reuther had rushed to her son's bedside after Walter was shot, and expressed a mother's misgivings about the danger her son faced in the career he had chosen. She urged him to give up his union work and perhaps try writing as a safer alternative.[74] After Victor's shooting, the Reuther clan gathered at Walter's new Longfellow Street home (the corner house on Appoline and Chippewa was considered too exposed to adequately secure) and held a family council. This time Anna had a different message to relay:

> "I've been thinking about this and, you know, mothers in the whole history of the world have to wrestle with this problem of losing their sons. Too many mothers have lost their sons in wars. I haven't lost any of my sons in wars. But you boys have made a decision—made a decision to give your time and your energy to the labor movement. That's what you believe in, and if you believe in it, as I know you do, you must be prepared to give your life to it."[75]

Walter later claimed, "I came out of that meeting feeling I could lift a mountain with one hand."[76]

His mother gave her blessing for his union work, but his wife and daughters felt that mountain descending upon them. Linda was six at the time of Walter Reuther's shooting. She had been asleep when the shot sounded, and was told her father had cut himself on the broken window. The police activity in their home and her father's long absence gave ready lie to that explanation. The shot inflicted more lasting damage on her than on her father. May had already retreated into the role of mother and homemaker expected of women at that time, so the security fence, guard dogs, and bodyguards that became part of their everyday life represented just a further isolation from the world of routine banter and grand design she once inhabited. Lisa was less than a year old at the time, so the new arrangements were the life she always knew. For six year old Linda, the world that was just opening up to her suddenly closed like a prison door. The ever-present bodyguard, the dogs, and the fence isolated her from her schoolmates and marked her as different at an age when it was most important to be like everyone else. Linda found her father remote and Teutonic—a gigantic national figure that dwarfed her own identity rather than nurturing it.[77] In time she came to admire her father, but love and respect her mother.

Being Walter Reuther's daughter meant always living in the shadow of fear. The bodyguards and security were a constant reminder of the dark forces that still harbored an intense hatred of their father, but there were also the dangerous situations his activism led him to seek out. When Walter and May went to Selma to stand with Martin Luther King after an earlier march was brutally assaulted by a white mob, Lisa awoke screaming from a nightmare in which men in white sheets lit into the marchers with clubs, separating her parents and searing the contorted face of her mother into her inner reality.[78] When Lisa picked up the phone on another occasion, she was thrilled to be greeted by the voice of Dr. King, but before she could hand the phone over to her father she also heard the distinctive click of the third party on the line.[79] J. Edgar Hoover hung over the family like a dark cloud. He did not content himself with persecuting only the father. Reuther's daughters, parents, siblings, and even May's family all had their pages in the "scrapbook" of this avid collector of tasty tidbits and dirty secrets.[80]

After the attempt on Walter Reuther's life, several congressmen and cabinet officers urged the FBI to enter the investigation. UAW lawyers Joseph Rauh and Irving Levy received a commitment from Attorney General Tom Clark that he would speak to Hoover about getting the FBI involved, but Clark reported back the next day "Fellows, Edgar says no. He says he's not going to send the FBI in every time some nigger woman gets raped."[81]

The investigation of both shootings remained in the bungling hands of the Detroit police. The investigatory work was mostly done by police detective Albert DeLamielleure. Reuther did not lack for enemies who might want to see him dead. There were the Communists, the hard line industrialists, and his rivals in the union. George Addes appeared at police headquarters immediately after word of the shooting to remove all doubts of his involvement. As the investigation progressed the name of Santo Perrone, a Detroit mobster with ties to the Mafia, became more entangled with events surrounding the case. DeLamielleure never seriously pursued this connection. He was always directing the investigation and other investigators toward this Communist in Europe or that Communist fled to Mexico. When Victor first returned home from the hospital, DeLamielleure insisted on speaking with him alone in his bedroom and asked whether he had been having any recent trouble with his wife.[82] Only his condition prevented Victor from slugging the cop for implying that his wife had anything to do with the shooting.

As 1948 stretched into 1949 and Christmas was only days away, the investigation was going nowhere. Then, three nights before Christmas Eve, Jack Pickering, a reporter for the *Detroit Times* received an anonymous phone call giving him a lead on a story that dynamite had been planted in the union headquarters building when "the big guy" was in the office.[83] An initial police search failed to turn up the bomb, but around midnight, a watchman found a rain-soaked box, wrapped like a Christmas present, lying just outside a seldom-used basement entrance. When the present was unwrapped, investigators found thirty-nine sticks of dynamite—enough explosives to bring down the building and cause severe damage and possibly deaths in a GM building twenty-five feet away.[84] The rain caused the fuses to sputter out and prevent the gift finding its intended recipient.

This latest attempt on Reuther's life finally brought the FBI into the investigation. In a rare move, the Senate voted a resolution requesting the President to direct the FBI to become involved in investigating the shootings after the attempt on Victor's life.[85] Six months later they finally entered the case. There was enough evidence to enable Efrem Zimbalist, Jr., the actor portraying an agent on the TV drama *The FBI*, to crack the case. Zimbalist always "got his man" by the end of the show. The real agent-in-charge was more inclined to follow the leads DeLamielleure fed him that nourished the bureau's obsession with Communism. Unlike the image the FBI painted for itself on TV, the government agency had no particular interest in pursuing this case, and through either indifference or collusion never "got its man."

Since neither the local nor federal police displayed any interest or ability in solving the case, the UAW hired a pair of its own investigators. The UAW team of Heber Blankenhorn, an investigator for the NLRB into corporate spying on labor back in 1936, and Ralph Winstead, a former federal investigator, focused their investigation on leads developed during grand jury testimony in 1946 into a string of beatings surrounding the battle between Emil Mazey and Melvin Bishop for the position of East Side Regional Director.[86] Mazey was expected home from military service at war's end, and had a strong base of support in the large Briggs local. Several key Mazey supporters were beaten severely soon after Carl Renda was awarded a contract for hauling scrap iron from the Briggs plant. Renda had no trucks, no yard for sorting and processing the materials, and no prior experience in the business. The actual hauling was subcontracted out, but grand jury testimony revealed he cleared $53,000 in 1946 and $101,000 in '47.[87] When the grand jury, and later the Kefauver Senate Crime Investigating Committee, asked Briggs controller George Lilygren why Renda was awarded such a lucrative contract, he testified that purchasing director W. J. Cleary told him the directive came directly from company president Dean Robinson, and there was nothing he could do about it. Asked to speculate about the reasons for awarding such a lucrative contract to such an unqualified person, Lilygren said he thought it bought the company relief from labor troubles.[88] Cleary was not able to confirm Lilygren's account. He had died under suspicious circumstances earlier.

Mazey defeated Bishop in the 1946 election, and shortly after occupying Bishop's old office happened to absent-mindedly hit the P key on Bishop's telephone number finder pad. The name Santo Perrone with his private number flashed back at him.[89] Perrone became the key figure in the grand jury investigation. Santo and his brother Gaspar had a long association with the Michigan Stove Works Company run by John Fry. The Perrone brothers were working as core makers in the plant in 1934 when the Mechanics' Education Society struck the firm. The Perrone brothers were enlisted by Fry to recruit strikebreakers and put an end to this early organizing effort. The Perrones performed their task with brutal effectiveness and were rewarded by Fry. Santo got the scrap hauling contract, and Gaspar, by verbal agreement, took over operation of the foundry. The Stove Works plant was ideally situated on the Detroit River for smuggling contraband and illegal aliens into the country. During the time when there was supposedly an active investigation into the Reuther shootings occurring, twenty illegal Sicilian immigrants were rounded up in a raid on the Stove Works plant.[90]

Success in efforts by the UAW to organize workers in the Stove Works plant fluctuated with the jail time of the Perrones. The brothers were sentenced to six years in Leavenworth for liquor law violation in 1936, and the CIO organized the plant. Fry was named Detroit Deputy Police Commissioner while retaining his leadership of the Stove Works. Fry arranged to have the brothers paroled after serving 29 months of their sentence, and they returned to their positions in the plant. The Stove Works local evaporated soon after the heat of the Perrones' return was felt by the local's organizers.

Winstead reported to the grand jury that a series of meetings took place in 1943 and 1944 between Fry, Harry Bennett, Dean Robinson of Briggs, and others with Santo Perrone and Tony Dana in attendance.[91] Bennett was unable to swing some scrap metal business from Ford to Perrone, but Robinson was introduced to Perrone's son-in-law, Carl Renda, and when he assumed leadership of the Briggs company from his father-in-law in 1945, Renda got the scrap metal contract. The beatings of Mazey supporters began soon afterward.[92]

The grand jury also heard testimony that Carl Renda would drive to Briggs with his car loaded with cartons of cigarettes, which were scarce in the immediate post-war environment, and hand them out for free to certain shop stewards and committeemen from the plant.[93] Nathan Silverstine, who had been production manager of all Briggs plants before leaving the company, told the grand jury that it had been expressed to him that the beatings were related to a battle within the union and that somebody higher up in the union, a vice president of some department, involved in that battle had to be on the take.[94]

The grand jury returned no indictments. A compelling narrative had been woven, but there was not enough evidence obtained to proceed further. Most of the investigatory work was done by detective DeLamielleure, and several witnesses were frightened out of testifying by threatening phone calls that could have been made only if word of their appearance had been leaked in advance.[95] Melvin Bishop was exonerated of involvement in the beatings before a UAW inquiry, but was dismissed from the union staff soon after Reuther gained full control of the union late in 1947.[96] The friendship between the Reuthers and Bishop, evident in the 1934 letter from Gorky, had soured. Youthful idealism had wilted in the steamy atmosphere of shop floor politics, and now the former friend was involved with people suspected of trying to kill the Reuther brothers.

When Reuther gained control of the union and Reuther partisans like Mazey took over operation of union activities on the East Side, a concerted attempt was made to clean up gambling operations and numbers running in those plants. It was at Reuther's instigation that a grand jury was seated to investigate the beatings at Briggs[97] and it was Reuther who was disturbing the familiar relationship people like the Perrones enjoyed with elements of the Addes caucus. This may have given the criminals reason to want him dead.

In the fall of 1949, the *Detroit News*, which had offered a "Secret Witness" plan to provide anonymity for potential informants, received a brief message, "Would you please Make Quiet Investigation of Clarence Jacobs Regarding the Walter Reuther Shooting." Two days later another note suggested they make this inquiry at an Esso station across from the Stove Works factory. It said that the owner of this gas station was "closely allied" with Jacobs.[98] The *News* passed these leads on to chief Detective DeLamielleur who knew precisely who owned that gas station. He had just secretly purchased the Canton Bar, under his brother's name, two doors away from Santo Perrone's gas station.[99] Jacobs was more difficult to locate. He had jumped bail and fled to Canada in 1948 after his arrest for illegally reentering the United States following an earlier deportation. No attempt was made to find him and question him about the accusation.

In 1953 the statute of limitations was about to run out on Walter Reuther's shooting when an investigator from the union located Joseph Ritchie, the nephew of Clarence Jacobs, in a Canadian jail. Ritchie agreed to talk to the investigator after he was released from custody and an elaborate arrangement was made to pay Ritchie $25,000 for his testimony without alerting the Perrones of the transaction.[100] Ritchie received an initial payment of $5000 and returned to Detroit to be questioned by the Wayne County prosecutor. In January, 1954, six years after the attempt on Walter Reuther's life, Prosecutor O'Brien announced a solution to the Walter Reuther shooting, and that arrest warrants had been issued for Santo Perrone, Clarence Jacobs, Carl Renda, and Peter Lombardo. O'Brien later made public the statement signed by Ritchie:[101]

I was in the car the night Walter Reuther was shot. For about four or five years I had been working for Santo Perrone. I made about $400 or $500 a week. In the occupation, I was—well, it just wasn't what people would call work. Clarence Jacobs approached me for this particular job. He told me I would get five grand. I was approached about five days before it happened and asked if I wanted to go. This conversation took place in Perrone's gas station. Perrone asked me several days before the shooting if I was going on the job. I said I was. I didn't ask a lot of questions. These people don't talk things over very much. All I knew was that Perrone had once said: "We'll have to get that guy out of the way." Did he mean Reuther? Yeah.

The night of the shooting I was picked up in the gas station. The car was a red Mercury. I don't know who it belonged to. I sat on the back seat. Jacobs drove. And Peter Lombardo was in the front seat with Jacobs. I was there in case there was trouble. If anything happened, I was to drive the car away. Jacobs did the shooting. He was the only one who got out of the car. I don't know how long he was gone. It's hard to remember time. I heard the report of the gun. Then Jacobs got back in the car and said: "Well, I knocked the bastard down." We took off in a hurry.

After the job they dropped me back at the Helen Bar (renamed the Canton Bar by DeLamielleur), about 200 feet from the gas station. I don't know what they did with the car. I heard later it was demolished and junked. I haven't any idea what happened to the gun. I had some drinks at the bar and then went and saw Carl Renda. He said, "I have something for you." He got a bundle of cash and handed it to me. I went downtown and met a girl. I stayed with her until four in the morning. Then I took a taxi to Windsor. I didn't count the money until I got to Canada. It was exactly five grand.

Ritchie was housed in a three room suite in the Detroit Statler as a material witness in the Reuther shooting case. He was kept under guard by Detectives Wayne Glisman and William Krupka[102]. On the afternoon of January 8th, he told the detectives that he wanted to take a shower, stepped into the bathroom, and turned on the water. An hour later, the water was still running and the detectives began to get suspicious. They entered the bathroom to find the shower empty and Ritchie gone. Soon afterward a reporter from the *Detroit Free Press* received a call from someone in Windsor identifying himself as Ritchie saying everything he told the police was a lie.[103]

That ended the investigation into the Reuther brothers attempted murder cases. The FBI quietly closed its investigation in 1952, two years after it entered the case.[104] No credible attempt was made to extradite Ritchie from Canada. He later gloated how he conned the UAW out of $25,000.[105]

The unwillingness of the authorities to vigorously investigate the shooting emboldened Carl Renda to claim he was a victim of malicious prosecution and sue the UAW, five of its officers, and a state police lieutenant for 5.2 million dollars.[106] The main witness for the defense in this civil lawsuit was Ralph Winstead, but days before he was to testify his frozen body clad in fisherman's gear was pulled from Lake St. Clair. The coroner ruled the death accidental. The Michigan Circuit Court found for Renda and awarded him $400,000 in damages. The

UAW immediately appealed and in an out-of-court settlement in 1963 reluctantly handed Renda a check for $12,500.[107]

No leads were developed in the bomb attempt. There was plenty of evidence to conduct a credible investigation into Victor Reuther's shooting, but none was made. The shotgun was left at the scene of the crime along with one of the shells. And one of the neighbors had noticed the car that was hanging around the Reuther home in the days before the shooting and was able to give a detailed description of its occupants.[108] Neither the FBI nor the Detroit police tried to develop these leads. When the neighbor came forward as someone who might be able to identify suspects in the case, his offer was ignored. After Victor intervened to try to force some progress in the investigation, DeLamielleur brought four or five boxes of photos of people who had been arrested in the past over to the neighbor's house and dumped them there. A few days later the neighbor began receiving phone calls threatening him and his family with death if he continued to cooperate with the investigation. The man suffered a heart attack and later moved to Florida to get away from the situation in Detroit. None of the neighbors said that they had called in complaints about the barking dog, and there was no record in the police precinct of such a complaint.[109]

Neither law enforcement agency wanted to solve these crimes. The Detroit police acted to cover them up and may have been involved in their commission. The Kefauver Committee shined a spotlight on the penetration of the mob into the economy of the nation, and this publicity forced Santo Perrone to relinquish his hauling contract. But once the committee left town and the TV lights were turned off, there was no further interest in pursuing the connections between elements of the business community, corrupt labor officials, rogue police, and organized crime.

The Treaty of Detroit

One of the visitors to Walter Reuther's hospital bedside after the shooting was Charlie Wilson. Wilson and Reuther were always paired in public on opposite sides of the bargaining table, but privately the two men shared a mutual respect and, as much as their different circumstances allowed, a friendship. Labor relations were always about more than nickels and dimes for both men, and this visit was more than a courtesy call on a stricken adversary. The next round of contract negotiations was nearing, and the unresolved issues from the bitter 1946 strike were on the minds of both people.

Reuther warned during the 1946 strike that "The grim fact is that if free enterprise in America is to survive, it must master the technique for providing full employment at a high standard of living, rising year-by-year to keep pace with the annual increase in technological efficiency."[110] He later elaborated on the issues at the heart of the strike. "The strike was about two questions. It was about the right of the worker to share—not as a matter of collective bargaining muscle but as a matter of right—to share in the fruits of advancing technology. The other issue was why should workers be victimized by inflationary forces, over which they have no control, which erode their real wage position?"[111]

Now Wilson confessed "You did not persuade us on those two basic principles during the strike. But when it was over, I began to realize that you were right, and that the two principles you had advanced were sound."[112] Wilson was signaling a new flexibility in the company bargaining position and a new accommodation with the union. The 1950 agreement would be called the "Treaty of Detroit" and hailed in the press as groundbreaking, but the full terms of that treaty were negotiated in a series of contracts that began with the deal between the UAW and GM in 1948 and culminated with Supplementary Unemployment Benefits being granted in 1955.

The years following the post-war wave of strikes and the gutting of war time price control regulations saw inflation spiraling out of control. Many voices in the business community argued for the traditional remedies of tight money, cuts in government spending, a tough stance in labor negotiations, and a "healthy" dose of unemployment to wring inflation from the economy.[113] General Motors had reason to resist this prescription. It was in the middle of a $3.5 billion expansion program to increase its production capacity by over 50%.[114] It needed a growing population of consumers able to buy its cars, and it needed stability on its production floors.

Wilson proposed a long-term contract that featured a cost of living adjustment for inflation and an annual increase of 2% above the negotiated base salary (AIF) to allow workers to share in the growth in productivity of their labor. The cost of living adjustment (COLA) would provide an increase of one cent for every 1.14 point quarterly rise in the Bureau of Labor Statistics (BLS) index of inflation, and would also decrease wages a penny for each 1.14 point decline in the index with a floor of five cents below the base wage of the contract.[115]

Reuther was initially cool to the idea. The concept of linking wages to changes in the cost of living fixed the real wage scale at the current level and precluded the option of seeking a bigger slice of the corporate pie for the workers. Labor also feared the escalator going down in the COLA formula would translate into a decline in wages during the anticipated post war depression.[116] But the GM offer came with a hefty eleven cent an hour boost in the base wage and an agreement that cost of living adjustments would be made on a corporation-wide basis. It was an offer the union "couldn't refuse." Reuther praised the agreement for breaking the "big business conspiracy" that had kept wages down during the inflationary period following the 1946 wave of strikes, but he termed it a "holding operation" to protect GM workers during the current reactionary climate. He vowed a continuing commitment to price controls and a larger base rate.[117] GM sought a five year contract, but the union would only agree to a two-year "trial offer."

Reuther was forced to come to the defense of the deal a year later when the BLS index declined and workers were confronted with a three cent an hour decrease in their wages. There was predictable grumbling in the union halls. Reuther confronted the rank and file discontent by mobilizing a public relations effort to defend the agreement as "a tremendous victory"—a progressive deal that preserved real wages of autoworkers.[118]

As the UAW warmed to the deal they had signed, General Motors became more convinced of its soundness. Annual productivity growth accelerated well beyond the 2% reserved for the workers, and production loss due to labor disruptions declined dramatically. Harry Anderson, who had replaced the irascible Harry Coen in the corporate chair at the bargaining table, expressed the company's satisfaction with their partner

"The UAW did a remarkable job of administering the contract…The experience through the period from 1948 to 1950 was very, very good."[119]

The two years of labor peace with GM provided the union space to pursue its social agenda. The federal government had abrogated its responsibilities to provide for the welfare of its citizens after the war, so the unions looked to the corporations to provide health and pension plans for their employees instead. By 1949, the monthly social security benefit paid to retirees had shrunk in real terms to about one eleventh the monthly take home pay of an autoworker.[120] Retirees were forced to make the equivalent of about three days of working class wages last for a whole month. Reuther contrasted the plight of retired wage earners with the rich pensions set aside for executives like Charlie Wilson. In every campaign he was ready with a slogan to marshal public sentiment behind a compelling call to arms. In the pension fight, the situation facing retirees was characterized as being "Too Old to Work and Too Young to Die."

John L. Lewis had breached the solid wall of corporate resistance to including pension plans in contracts for unionized workers during a series of coal strikes in 1946 and 1947.[121] Lewis negotiated deals in which the coal companies put the money earned by the retiree into a fund administered by the UMW. The companies were not required to set aside money for funding each employee's pension on an annual basis. Instead they were obligated to contribute the full amount due upon retirement[122] Reuther regarded such a scheme as actuarially unsound, and was proved right ten years later when the companies were no longer able to pay the obligation they made in better times.

Reuther selected Ford as the target for his pension campaign. Ford had shown a willingness to consider a weaker version of retirement protection in the 1947 round of negotiations, and Henry Ford II seemed more inclined toward working with the UAW to engineer a new social order than other corporate executives of the period. Ford was still a family owned company and was less subject to the dictates of the bankers and fund managers on Wall Street than other publicly owned corporations of the day.

Reuther made "Too Old to Work and Too Young to Die" the centerpiece of the 1949 Ford contract negotiations. He determined that $100 a month was the minimum needed for a retiree to subsist on in 1949 and demanded that the company pension plus social security should total at least that amount.[123] He also insisted that the plan be actuarially sound. Unlike the UMW and later the Teamsters, the UAW would not administer the pension fund itself. The company would have to establish a pension account and fund it on an annual basis so that when an employee reached retirement age, his or her pension money would already be fully committed.

Ford acquiesced to the union demand, and committed to a fully funded pension plan that allowed workers with thirty years of service a retirement income of $100 a month. This was not a princely sum, even in 1949, but it provided a subsistence income, and it was a foot in the door.

Chrysler balked at following Ford's lead on funding on a "pay-as-you-go" basis and endured a 104 day strike as a consequence. When finally settled, the UAW did not get the fully-funded pension plan they had received at Ford, but the damage to Chrysler was much more severe. It lost over a billion dollars in potential sales over the period of the work stoppage and lost forever its chance of overtaking Ford as the number two automaker in the country.[124] The UAW did not win the complete package it sought in that strike, but it flexed its muscle and demonstrated the unwanted consequences of resisting the industry pattern established in previous agreements.

The Chrysler strike confirmed the control Reuther now exercised in the union. The Chrysler workers endured a three and a half month strike over the question of whether the company's pension offer was actuarially sound. The term may have had little meaning to them at the outset, but they were willing to trust Reuther that the concept was worth a work stoppage. The assassination attempts had generated an outpouring of support for the leader and muted criticism from opponents who still maintained influence in powerful locals.[125] The UAW was unified as never before, and ready to ratify the grand bargain that it tepidly accepted two years previously.

When contract negotiations with General Motors began in 1950, the planks for an agreement had already been laid in previous accords—COLA/AIF, an "actuarially sound" pension scheme, and management control over production scheduling. Both sides were comfortable, if not happy, with the arrangement. There was little of the foreplay that usually accompanied labor negotiations before they reached the climactic last stage. The talks were held in secret with Reuther only becoming personally involved in the last days. An agreement was announced before the old expiration date with no threat of a strike looming on the horizon. The base rate was raised; the COLA/AIF computations were sweetened slightly; the pension total was raised to $125 a month for retirees with 25 or more years of service; there was a partially-paid health insurance plan; and the UAW was granted a modified union shop, which required new workers to join the union for one year, after which they could voluntarily leave it. The feature that made this agreement particularly groundbreaking was the five year length of the deal.[126]

The establishment press applauded the civility with which the two sides reached accord and the new era in labor relations that it signified. *Business Week* heralded the deal as "industrial statesmanship of a very high order." *Fortune* gave it the title "Treaty of Detroit."[127] And *The New York Times* speculated that Walter Reuther's next surprise might put him on the road to the White House.[128] Reuther himself touted the COLA/AIF as being one of his union's proudest achievements, and claimed, GM was forced "to abandon the practice of capturing in the market place through higher prices what it yields at the bargaining table in higher wages."[129]

Daniel Bell, writing for *Fortune*, took a less sanguine view of the arrangement Reuther had established with the auto giant.

> "GM may have paid a billion for peace, but it got a bargain. General Motors has regained control over one of the crucial management functions...long range scheduling of production, model changes, and tool and plant investment. [It was the first contract] that unmistakably accepts the existing distribution of income between wages and profits as 'normal' if not as 'fair' [...] It is the first major union contract that explicitly accepts objective economic facts—cost-of-living and productivity—as determining wages, thus throwing overboard all theories of wages as determined by political power and of profits as 'surplus value.'"[130]

Autoworkers' earnings would double in real terms over the decade, but the presence of the union on the shop floor, where the rank and file experienced the stresses and frustrations of their jobs, declined.[131] The "pattern bargaining" agreements extended salary and benefit gains won from GM to other manufacturers and industries, but allowed those firms to insist upon management shop floor prerogatives in return. The number and responsibility of shop stewards in a GM plant was restricted by contract. Grievance disputes and issues of seniority were "kicked upstairs" to an arbitration board established by the corporate and UAW leadership.[132] Local officials would hear grumbling about speedup and favoritism in promotions and reassignments, but not be able to do much about it. As the UAW relationship with management became more institutionalized, Solidarity House in Detroit became more removed from the union halls in Flint, Dearborn, and Hamtramck.

With company pensions complementing social security, the union renewed its efforts to increase retirement income for everyone. Now they had a new ally. The auto companies had a reason to see the government benefit rise and lower the share for which they were obligated. In the span of a few weeks Congress did what it hadn't done in over ten years: increase the social security benefit. Congress responded to power— Corporate power—not need. Once the industry added its voice to the lobbying effort, retirees saw their social security checks steadily rise and keep pace with increases in the cost of living. Attempts by unions to enlist the big corporations into a campaign to federalize other welfare benefits like health care met with far less success.[133]

Two months after the "Treaty of Detroit" was signed and ratified by the UAW membership, North Korea invaded its Southern counterpart and the United States was again at war. The conflict tested the durability of the relationship between the union and the automakers and the viability of the "treaty" cementing that association. War time wage and price policy threatened to freeze auto workers' wages, effectively blocking the automatic escalators in the contract from taking effect. Such a policy placed a disproportionate burden on the working class. Reuther and UAW vice president Richard Gosser bluntly warned the economic stabilization board that any tampering with the COLA/AIF formula would surely cause "unrest and instability" in the auto plants.[134] Reuther's implied threat gave policy chief Alan Valentine pause, and won a brief respite from attempts to include the escalator clauses in the board's wage freeze regulations. When these clauses came under pressure again from lobbying efforts by the National Association of Manufacturers, Harry Anderson of GM broke ranks with the NAM and offered a vigorous defense of his company's arrangement with the union.[135]

Together, the union and the industry forestalled attempts to alter the basic agreement of 1950, but despite the escalators in the contract, autoworkers saw their purchasing power decline over the first two years of the war. Inflation surged and consumer demand was strangled by tight money. The appetite for cars was starved, and the redirection of the economy from civilian to military production caused pockets of high unemployment in the auto industry. Labor had little voice in the war planning boards, and Reuther's appeals to direct more military spending into the auto communities hardest hit with layoffs were initially spurned. Dissatisfaction was bubbling in the ranks, particularly in Local 600 where Carl Stellato led an insurgency, demanding the autoworkers get more of the spoils from the defense spending. Reuther pushed back, working with the Michigan Congressional delegation to direct more government work into areas of highest unemployment. Late in 1951, the Truman Administration bowed to pressure and announced it would make every effort to place defense contracts in areas hardest hit by the new economic priorities.[136]

The five-year contract became an increasingly cumbersome burden to bear. The side effects of the war had invalidated the premises upon which it was structured, and voices of discontent grew louder inside the locals. After two years Reuther demanded it be reopened. He justified his action by claiming that contracts are "living documents" that need to be revised to reflect changing circumstances.[137] He accentuated his demands by not intervening in a wave of wildcat strikes that swept through GM and Ford factories in 1952 and '53 over local grievances that normally were settled quickly by intervention from the national officers. At its peak over 100,000 autoworkers were on strike and production was greatly curtailed.[138]

The Korean armistice in 1953 led to a renewed demand for cars. GM was willing to buy labor peace to return to full production. The original terms of the "treaty" were revised to increase the total pension to $137.50 per month, add an additional penny an hour to the annual productivity raise, increase skilled tradesmen's pay ten cents an hour, and put 19 cents of the 24 cents an hour COLA increase over the length of the contract into the base.[139] The revisions in the GM contract quickly diffused through the rest of the industry. GM bought labor peace, and Reuther quieted rumblings within his constituency. He did make himself vulnerable to criticism from corporate executives who denounced the renegotiation of a contract as a violation of trust, and from the new president of the steelworkers union, David McDonald, who later wrote "I knew this knife cuts both ways. I could still remember vividly the misery and chaos caused by the coal companies in the 1920's when they abrogated signed contracts. I believe these contracts should be binding on both parties for the length of the agreement."[140] Reuther realized that five years was too long and unpredictable a time for the length of a contract. Future contracts would be no longer than two years duration.

From the time the original GM deal was struck in 1950, Reuther began planning his next initiative—the guaranteed annual wage. Work in the auto factories was geared around the yearly model change. It was concentrated into an approximately six month period of intense preparation and heavy production followed by a slack period when surplus workers were furloughed. The relatively high hourly wage often did not translate into an adequate yearly income. The problem was originally highlighted by Franklin Roosevelt in a 1936 campaign speech in Detroit during which he recalled a meeting with autoworkers who brought their grievances to the White House two years earlier.

> "One of them, a former Marine who served through battle after battle in France, told me he was a machinist and that his pay was a $1.25 an hour or $10 a day. I told him 'I thought that was a pretty good wage scale,' and his reply was this: yes, Mr. President, it is a good hourly rate and a good daily rate, but last year I worked only 68 days. In other words, the total income of himself, his wife, and his children was $680 for the year. On this yearly

pay total he had lost the home, on which he had paid down hundreds of dollars." Roosevelt offered a solution: "I stressed the need of spreading the work more evenly through the year…It is my belief that the manufacturers of automobiles…must, by planning, do far more than they have done to date to increase the yearly earnings of those who work for them."[141]

Fifteen years later, little had changed. Reuther's *500 Planes a Day* plan offered a statist approach to providing steady employment during a period of national emergency that he hoped would permeate post-war industrial culture. Resistance to both the statist approach and change of common industrial practice proved much too strong to effectively challenge at the time. Reuther realized that an extensive campaign to educate the public about the issue would be needed to prepare a climate for successful negotiations.

The union used the four year period between signing the GM contract in 1950 and the round of negotiations scheduled for 1955 to prepare for the most difficult negotiation of Reuther's presidency. Nat Weinberg was given the task of preparing the union strategy. He established a research team to analyze North American and European literature on job security, chart the auto industry's historic pattern of hiring and layoffs, and scrutinize state and federal unemployment compensation laws.[142] While the union was preparing its negotiating position, it simultaneously began its public relations offensive. Writing in the *Annals of the American Academy of Political and Social Science* of March 1951, Walter Reuther announced that the next bargaining objective of the UAW would be the guaranteed annual wage. He described the issue as "more than a matter of economic justice to the wage earner. It is a matter of economic necessity to our nation, for freedom and unemployment cannot live together in democracy's house."[143]

The biggest hurdle faced by Weinberg's team was incorporating private unemployment compensation with the various state and local benefit plans. The initial reaction was that state laws would have to be amended to allow integration of public and private unemployment benefits and in the process would lead states to reduce the public commitment by like amount, leaving the workers no better off. Weinberg credits Leonard

Loesser, director of the autoworkers Social Security Department with convincing him that public and private unemployment benefits could be effectively combined under existing laws to provide a livable income during periodic intervals of unemployment.[144] Weinberg had a much more difficult time convincing a skeptical board.

A draft of the study committee's plan was presented at the 1953 convention where it was approved in principle. Reuther next appointed an advisory committee of eminent economists to review the draft proposal. The committee made a critical analysis of the draft, prompting a number of revisions. Formation of the committee also sent a signal to the auto companies that the union was serious about making supplementary unemployment benefits (SUB) the cornerstone of its 1955 bargaining position.

While the SUB plan was being developed, the union continued its public awareness campaign. Reuther stressed that the idea behind SUB was not to reward idleness, but to provide a financial incentive for the companies to distribute their work more evenly throughout the year. UAW officials and staffers presented the union position in a variety of public forums. More importantly, it took its plan to the membership in local union meetings, regional conferences, summer school classes, weekend forums, and night classes. The rank and file had a chance to examine and discuss the plan and offer a number of criticisms and suggestions that the academic panel had failed to consider.[145]

The UAW kept Ford and GM appraised of its thinking, and suggested joint study panels which the industry rejected. Ford took the union initiative seriously and empanelled its own experts to study the union proposal and develop its own thinking.[146] General Motors was now headed by Board Chairman Frederick Donner. Charlie Wilson had gone on to become Secretary of Defense in the Eisenhower Administration. Donner was more inclined to the intransigent position of the DuPonts and the Wall Street interests who felt that accommodation with the union on this issue would weaken and perhaps destroy the corporation. It dismissed the union effort out of hand and spent no effort studying union documents or developing its own thinking on the matter.[147]

The UAW brought four years of preparation into the negotiations. It would target Ford and establish the contract there as the pattern for the rest of the industry. Ford was chosen because of its apparent willingness to consider the union position, and because Henry Ford II had always shown a disposition to include social issues on the corporate agenda. It prepared for the eventuality of a strike, both as an expedient and as an advertisement of its commitment to securing supplementary unemployment benefits. It temporarily increased dues by $5 a month and was in the process of building a $25 million strike fund.[148] The union had done its homework, made its case with the public, and amassed the resources for a protracted battle.

The union's greatest asset in the negotiations was its lead spokesman. From the Sunday debating sessions organized by his father back in Wheeling to the time he talked his way into a toolmaker's job at Ford— from Kelsey-Hayes to the Treaty of Detroit, Walter Reuther was a force that dominated every discussion with his intellect, his persistence, and most of all his sheer energy.

On the other side of the table for Ford sat John Bugas. Bugas was the FBI field officer in Detroit back in 1940 who forestalled Hoover's attempt to send the three Reuther brothers to an internment camp during World War II. A few years later he was hired by Harry Bennett to work in the Personnel Department at Ford. He was one of the few Bennett recruits to survive the changing of the guard at Ford. The GM negotiations were handled by Louis Seaton: a man who had sat across the table from Reuther in 1950 and 1953, and whose continuing role in the corporation would be like the man on a basketball team assigned to guard Michael Jordan.

The GM contract was scheduled to expire on May 29th, the Ford contract two days later. Auto negotiations would always start with Reuther detailing the union offer. The UAW proposal called for an SUB that together with state unemployment benefits would provide about 70% of a worker's salary during periods of layoffs.[149] Reuther never missed an opportunity to educate his audience. Company representatives and reporters would often start a pool on how long he would speak.

When he finished, Seaton presented GM's counteroffer—a stock option plan in which the company would match dollar-for-dollar a worker's contribution to buy the number of shares he or she was able to purchase. A catch in the GM offer was that workers could not have access to their money until the stock matured, and if withdrawals were made because of some emergency like a layoff, the worker could only withdraw money they contributed. The company money would be retained and the stock withholding ended.[150] Reuther described the offer a "wheel-of-fortune deal" in rejecting it. "Hell, that's for the provident!" he said "I'm interested in the folks who can't take care of themselves."[151]

It was with Ford that the serious bargaining would occur. GM would be pressed to follow the pattern established there if a contract with supplementary unemployment benefits could be negotiated. Ford requested a four day delay in the talks to study the union offer. During the delay, Reuther obtained a one week extension of the GM contract so that the Ford contract would terminate first.[152] When Bugas returned to the table and began reading the company proposal, Reuther stopped him after the first page. He had heard it all before. It was the GM proposal with the names of the companies changed. Reuther called the offer of the same package just rejected at General Motors an insult to the intelligence of the union and the company. The exchanges at the table became heated. Reuther barked at Bugas "You have just bought yourself a strike!" He then reminded the Ford negotiators how previous strikes led to the decline of Willys-Overland and prevented Chrysler from overtaking Ford in 1949. In a parting shot at the company's appropriation of the GM negotiating position he asked Bugas "How will you produce Fords on the Chevrolet assembly line?"[153]

Bugas retorted that the company had taken a survey of workers in its plants, and that they preferred the company offer by a margin of 9 to 1.[154] Reuther promised that he would take the offer to the UAW National Council and the delegates would vote on the offer. To allay criticism that he would misrepresent the company proposal he invited Henry Ford II to come to the meeting and present the plan himself. Ford politely declined and suggested that the company workers should have a chance to express their opinions of the offer.[155]

The National Council unanimously rejected the offer. A majority of the Executive Board urged an immediate strike, but Reuther said "Not yet." He had another card to play at the negotiating table. When he returned to the talks, he greeted Bugas warmly and suggested that "Maybe we were a bit hasty, John."[156] He invited Bugas to join him in a separate room for a private meeting. When they were alone together Reuther encouraged Bugas to go through the company plan point-by-point. He asked detailed questions and made comments like "That's very interesting," that allowed Bugas to believe he was buying into the proposal. Bugas became more animated and confident of a breakthrough. When Bugas was nearing the end of his presentation, Reuther asked "You say a survey showed the workers are in favor of this plan?" "Overwhelmingly," was the reply. Reuther then sprung the trap. He offered to put it to a vote of the UAW membership at Ford. "If they vote for yours, we'll sign a contract containing your proposal. If they vote for ours we'll sign a contract with that. Since you say they want yours by nine to one, you're not taking any chances." After seeing his red-faced adversary squirm, Reuther later remarked "Poor John, I thought he'd die."[157]

When Ford returned to the table the next day, they came with the proposal developed by their own team that had analyzed the union's SUB proposal. Real negotiations began and a marathon 26-hour bargaining session led to an agreement. The SUB clause in the agreement provided workers with twenty-six weeks of unemployment benefits giving them 65% of their wages for the first two weeks and 60% for the remaining twenty-two.[158] It was less than the UAW wanted, but in Reuther's words, it was a foot in the door.

Reuther emerged from the session looking like he had had eight hours sleep and a morning shower. Bugas looked like he had just spent twenty-six straight hours in tough negotiations. Reuther hardly paused for breath. He took the Ford agreement over to Seaton and began round two of the benefit fight. Five days later he got a "Chinese copy, even to the patch on the pants" from General Motors. When Reuther asked what was meant by that, he was told the story of a sea captain who asked a Chinese tailor to make him a duplicate of the pants he was wearing. He got the duplicate including a patch like one on the old pair.[159] General Motors had not done its homework and had to rely on the hope that Ford had accurately done theirs. Harry Anderson admitted later "I would like to congratulate Mr. Reuther for having gone to Ford first, because we would have never agreed to this otherwise [...] This is the first time the president of General Motors Corporation has ever signed a contract that he didn't understand."[160] Chrysler meekly followed the leaders a little later. The agreements proved fortuitous for UAW members two years later when during the 1957–58 recession idled workers received about $13 million in benefits.[161]

The recession in the late fifties exposed rust that began to appear in the industrial belt of the Midwest. For the first time in the century steel imports exceeded exports. The new mills rising up from the war ruins in Europe and Japan were more efficient than their aging American counterparts. Volkswagens and soon Toyotas and Datsuns began to appear on the American road and Kaisers, Studebakers, Hudsons, Packards, and Ramblers in rapid succession disappeared. Ford could endure an Edsel, but Kaiser could not survive a Henry J or Hudson its tortoise-shaped Hornet. The smaller companies did not fit the "pattern" from which industry-wide deals were cut, and they could not assume the social burden relegated to them by the state. The corporate welfare state had inherent limitations.

After 1955, the bargaining became more ritualistic. Some new benefits were acquired in later contracts, but the settlements were mostly variations on established themes. In 1967 the guaranteed annual wage was effectively won. SUB benefits reached 95% of wages for up to a full year,[162] but this "penalty" did little to smooth out the production cycle of the big three companies. The companies still had the ability to set prices in a less than competitive market and pass the "penalty" on to consumers. The parameters of contract discussions were firmly established. The ability of the UAW to bargain for the consumer was greatly curtailed. The companies resisted all attempts to include prices in labor negotiations. They assumed the social cost of health care rather than join the union in lobbying for a national plan. The terms of employment established in Detroit trickled through the rest of the economy unevenly. The large corporations adopted similar packages. Smaller firms provided less generous benefit packages, and many small businesses could afford no benefits at all.

The Merger

The 1955 agreement was the last major achievement of the CIO. The young radicals of the thirties and forties had matured. They had staged a revolution that society first resisted and then absorbed. Some of the dreams from Brookwood had been realized, but that only made the remainder more elusive. Union members were now part of the new middle class. They were becoming comfortable and starting to migrate into the suburbs. The men who shook up the establishment were now part of it. The UAW moved into a modernistic new headquarters building on land that once belonged to Edsel Ford, while the CIO moved back home to live with its aging parent—the AFL. Walter Reuther had a room in both houses, but found the room in Solidarity House confining and was never made to feel welcome back "home" with the AFL-CIO.

Shortly after Dwight Eisenhower was elected president in November, 1952, Phil Murray unexpectedly died. Twelve days later, the 82-year old William Green succumbed to his infirmities. The nation had a popular new Republican president who brought to Washington with him a Republican controlled House and Senate. The deaths of the long-serving leaders of labor's two houses occurred just as the movement faced a hostile Congress, an indifferent administration, and an untethered Joe McCarthy fanning an anti-left hysteria that kept labor on the defensive. The circumstances were ripe for a rapprochement between the two branches of unionism, whose philosophical differences had narrowed over the past fifteen years.

George Meany, the AFL Secretary-Treasurer was chosen to succeed Green by vote of the organization's executive council. Meany had been assuming many responsibilities from the aging Green, and his ascension to the top spot was a matter of course. Since John L. Lewis had withdrawn his UMW from the AFL umbrella years earlier, the leadership of the biggest labor body was largely united and complacent.

The CIO was always a more chaotic organization. The men who lined up behind John L. Lewis in 1936 consisted of young idealists and committed ideologues. Communists, Socialists, Trotskyites, Liberals, and Catholic proponents of social doctrine enunciated by Popes Leo XIII and Pius XI nurtured the CIO into existence and fought with one another as fiercely as they fought with management. The ideological differences overlaid core differences between the two biggest unions within the organization—autos and steel. The steelworkers were first organized by the autocratic Lewis and run by his protégés, Murray and now David McDonald, ever since. It was the largest union within the organization, boasting one quarter of the total membership. It was the flagship union of Lewis and Murray. The steelworkers were designated to set the tone for the CIO in the bargaining rounds of 1937 and 1946, but it was the UAW that grabbed the initiative each time, first at Flint, then in the GM strike of 1946. Steel was now an ailing industry with aging plants and low productivity growth. The UAW resented the fact that Murray had undercut its bargaining position in 1946 and agreed to an eighteen and a half cent an hour package that provided for an increase in the price of a ton of steel. Steel negotiations would ultimately end up at the White House where wage and price increases would be settled and a degree of protectionism afforded.[163] From the Treaty of Detroit onward, autos set the tone for other industries to follow.

After Reuther gained full control of the UAW, he and Murray papered over their differences and established a cordial working relationship. There was no such cordiality between Reuther and Murray's successor. David McDonald had once been secretary to John L. Lewis in the 1930s and shared the antagonism of his old mentor toward the UAW leader. McDonald spoke for the business unionists within the federation who had no appetite for social crusading and wanted to depoliticize the CIO and concentrate solely on bargaining for wages and benefits. Reuther was by far the leading figure in the CIO and was being urged to seek the presidency by leaders of some of the larger unions within the body.

The man directly in line to succeed Murray was sixty-four year old Alan Haywood, an Englishman who emigrated to America after the First World War, but never lost the thick Yorkshire accent that made his speech difficult for the American ear to follow. Reuther viewed Haywood as a caretaker who would hold the seat for a couple of years until McDonald could establish his credentials and assume the job for himself.

Once again Reuther returned to the Boardwalk for an election battle. The CIO elections used a system where each union cast a number of votes equal to the size of its dues paying membership. Haywood was supported by the majority of convention delegates, but, except for the steelworkers, Reuther was the choice of the large unions and won a narrow victory. He did not improve his chances for a harmonious transition, when, prior to the vote, McDonald made light of his candidate's impending defeat by telling Reuther "At least we have come to like each other better." Reuther rebuffed his rival by responding "I would say we have come to *know* each other better, Dave."[164]

The CIO had been the incubator, nurturing the infant industrial unions through their formative period. Once the individual members had grown into strong, independent bodies, the only thing holding the organization together had been the leadership of Phil Murray. "Uncle" Phil was the tough Scottish coal miner, with the avuncular demeanor, who had nursed the fledgling unions through their growing pains and provided the advice and resources for their battles. He was held in deep respect and affection by the many unionists who worked with him. Thomas Harris, a lawyer working at CIO headquarters in Washington, expressed the feelings of the people in the building for their late leader. "Murray had an extremely sweet disposition. Murray knew everybody in the building, knew them by their first names, knew their families, spent a lot of time on their purely personal matters. He was a kindly father figure."[165]

Walter Reuther had the respect and admiration of those who worked closely with him, but he would not be described as "a kindly father figure" by any of them, not even his own daughters. He did not engage in small talk and rarely inquired about the families of his friends.[166] He was a man driven by big ideas and big purpose. He was a polarizing figure—admired by his supporters, hated by his adversaries. He divided his time between Solidarity House in Detroit and the CIO headquarters in Washington, but was rarely seen by most of the Washington staff.[167] He probably knew few by their first or last names.

Running the CIO was not like running the UAW. As one labor leader described the two jobs "Unions have to be run, really, with a pretty firm hand. The president of it has to be the unquestioned number one man [...] But this type of experience is not so ideal when you move in and try to run a federation [...] of autonomous unions."[168] Murray had the personality and disposition for leading a federation. Reuther did not. Feuding with the leader of the largest union within the federation was not a recipe for success.

The CIO headquarters had been the preserve of the United Steel Workers since its inception. Most of the staff were people affiliated with McDonald's union. Reuther brought in Paul Sifton and Robert Oliver to act as his representatives in Washington, and late in 1953 he brought Victor back from his assignment in Europe as CIO liaison with the International Conference of Free Trade Unions (ICFTU) to manage affairs in Washington.[169] During his tenure as CIO president, Walter Reuther was preoccupied with the effort to reopen the 1950 GM contract and preparation of the proposal for supplementary unemployment benefits in the 1955 contract talks. Administration of CIO affairs was left largely to others.

Reuther's stated interest in the CIO presidency was to deny it to McDonald in three years time.[170] He also planned to explore a merger with the AFL. The CIO was no longer the same instrument for social change that battled police and management goons for recognition in the factory towns of the 30s and 40s. It won those early battles and carved out its own niche in the establishment. Now, a generation later, there was less-and-less distinction between it and the older AFL. The older organization was bigger, richer, and spoke with a louder voice in Washington. A merger joining the two houses of labor made sense.

Reuther wanted to resurrect the organizational momentum that stalled in the post-war years. He envisioned an aggressive labor membership drive in the unorganized factories, textile mills and petrochemical installations of the South and in the rapidly expanding white collar workforce.[171] He saw the potential of a merged AFL-CIO, relieved of wasteful and divisive jurisdictional disputes, bringing wage and benefit improvements to millions of unorganized workers and increasing public support for social reforms dear to his heart. Within two days of his election to the top CIO post he met with Meany to explore a merger.

The merger of the two federations was a marriage of convenience, not of love. Reuther was urged by his brother Victor and his closest associates Donald Montgomery and Brendan Sexton not to do it.[172] They told him he was fooling himself to think that the AFL could be made into an agency for social change. Reuther, fresh from his acclaimed success at the negotiating table, may have underestimated Meany and thought he would be the dominant personality within the combined group. Threats by David McDonald to leave the CIO and forge a new alliance with Lewis's UMW and the Teamsters may have also contributed to his willingness to proceed with the merger.[173] On December 2, 1955, Walter Reuther closed the last CIO convention with the promise "This is not the end. This is part of that great historic struggle that goes on as long as hope beats within the human breast." Three days later he and Meany lowered the gavel to convene the first convention of the combined federation. Away from the hoopla on the convention floor, Brendan Sexton and other UAW staffers held a wake for the old CIO. "We sat around and wept," Sexton recalled. "I was just heartbroken."[174]

Meany became the president of the AFL-CIO. Reuther settled on the office of director of the Industrial Union Division (IUD). The Industrial Union Division consisted mostly of the old CIO unions, and Reuther planned this to be the power base from which, with added AFL support, he would launch the organizational drive he hoped would invigorate the labor movement. UAW vice president John Livingston was named director of a new Department of Organization that was formed to give impetus to the membership campaign. The "prenuptial agreement" and the constitution of the merged federations provided the structure for "an organizing campaign worthy in size and scope of [a] new trade union movement."[175]

Sexton's misgivings were quickly confirmed. Reuther pledged $4 million from the UAW and the old CIO to support the organizational drive and sought a matching amount from the far richer AFL. No such additional support materialized. The leaders of the old trade unions were more concerned with jurisdictional questions and whether an influx of new members might upset the existing leadership arrangements that maintained them in power than they were about increasing the voice of labor in the national dialog.[176] They were quite comfortable with the status quo.

George Meany and his colleagues frustrated every attempt at a serious organizational effort. In 1961 Reuther's Standing Committee on Organization presented a detailed plan for an organizational drive to the Executive Council that was approved in principle. The largely unorganized workforce in retail and distribution was a particular focus of the effort. There were twenty separate trade unions with jurisdictional claims to parts of this industry, and nineteen of the twenty were prepared to work out an arrangement supporting the membership drive. Meany allowed the one intransigent union to veto the whole effort. Meany admitted much later that he felt no need to increase his federation's membership size. He thought it was large enough as it was.[177]

Migrant workers on the farms and vineyards of California were among the poorest and most exploited laborers in the country. Initial attempts to organize them met with little success and were aborted by Meany. He expressed an unwillingness to commit additional resources to reinforce the organizational drive when the amount of dues expected to be collected from such a membership would not come close to covering the cost of the effort.[178]

Years later Cesar Chavez emerged as leader of an independent National Farm Workers Association and led the grape pickers out of the vineyards on strike. That strike became much more than a labor dispute. It was the embodiment of a Latino civil rights movement. The migrant's cause was supported by black civil rights leaders, white clergymen, and student groups. It was reinforced with a nationwide boycott of grapes.

The UAW and the Packinghouse Workers backed the strikers with financial aid, but the AFL-CIO moved more deliberately. Reuther introduced a resolution at the December 1965 AFL-CIO convention in San Francisco to support the striking farm workers. The resolution was adopted by the convention, but little practical support was forthcoming.[179] The old AFL trade unions contributed little financially or emotionally to the farm workers, and Meany declined to go with Reuther to Delano to support the strikers on the picket line. In August, 1966, after the National Farm Workers' Association affiliated with the AFL-CIO, Meany reluctantly agreed to a proposal by Reuther to set up a committee of Executive Council members to ensure the farm workers received sufficient financial support and assistance for their strike. Walter Reuther, the one Council member who had been to Delano in support of Chavez, was left off the four-man committee.[180]

Reuther helped arrange for Senator Robert Kennedy's Migratory Labor subcommittee to visit Delano. He expected that when Kennedy saw the conditions in the vineyards his passion would be stirred.[181] Kennedy arrived to see the peaceful picketers being arrested by the local sheriff's deputies. When pressed for an explanation, the sheriff told Kennedy that it was for their own protection. He had been told by the growers that if he did not get the pickets out of there, the growers would kill them.[182] Kennedy was incensed by the methods the growers and local officials used to intimidate the strikers and their attempts to disrupt his hearings. He felt a sense of moral outrage at seeing the conditions in which the migrants lived. He became publicly identified with La Causa and helped draw public attention to it. Increased public awareness strengthened the boycott of grapes and led to breaks in the grower's resistance to the union.

Once the farm workers union was admitted into the AFL-CIO, Meany made every effort to keep Chavez away from Reuther. Chavez was instructed not to go to Detroit to participate in a UAW fund raising effort for his union. He went anyway, and against the wishes of the leadership, invited Reuther to accompany him to Mexico to negotiate with labor officials there to stem the flow of strike breakers into the vineyards and lettuce fields of California.[183]

Under Meany's stewardship the American labor movement atrophied. The federation's interest in protecting the status quo was a reflection of the age and world view of its leadership. The AFL-CIO Executive Council may have only been exceeded in average age and tenure in office by the College of Cardinals and the sitting Justices of the Supreme Court. Executive Council Members were allowed to remain on the Council after they retired from an active role in their union and no longer directly represented any of its workers.[184] This patronage arrangement ensured a solid majority for George Meany in Council proceedings.

Previous presidents of the AFL died in office after a long tenure. Samuel Gompers had headed the AFL for thirty-eight years when he died at age seventy-four, and William Green led the federation from the time of Gompers' death until his own in 1952. Meany served into his eighties before relinquishing his post to his long-time associate Lane Kirkland two months before his death. Any notion that the relatively young Reuther may have had in 1955 about succeeding his older counterpart in seven years was not based on historical evidence. Meany had no intention of retiring at sixty-five or any time soon thereafter. In any case, the organization he headed had too much inertia to be turned in a different direction no matter how determined the captain.

The union between the two rival federations was never one of love or even deep mutual interest. When disillusionment set in, it quickly turned to animosity. Meany and Reuther fought like Michael Douglas and Kathleen Turner in *The War of the Roses*. They exchanged slights and insults. They fought over Nehru and neutrality; they fought over meeting with Mikoyan and Khrushchev; they were at odds over supporting the March on Washington; and ultimately they were divided over what was dividing the country—Vietnam.

Reuther was an irritant to Meany, but not a threat. Reuther was like an itch he could not scratch. Meany was a business unionist who had worked his way through the AFL bureaucracy to become Green's chief lieutenant. He had never conducted a strike or even participated in direct contract negotiations. He was an experienced bureaucratic power builder, and he was very good at it. Meany isolated Reuther within the AFL-CIO and outflanked him in the halls of Congress and at the White House. Meany was able to block Reuther's appointment to the United States UN delegation, and veto appointments of Reuther nominees to government positions. Power recognized power, and it was Meany who held the power in organized labor.

Reuther viewed organized labor as a vehicle for promoting a broader social agenda, and he missed few opportunities to expand upon his subject. He was confident in his ability to convince his listeners of the rectitude and cogency of his vision or at least negotiate a "foot in the door" compromise. He was prone to talk too much and for too long. He annoyed people like Meany and McDonald for whom labor had a more limited agenda, and he even distanced potential supporters by the insistence with which he pressed his arguments. Executive Council meetings became uncomfortable for the other participants when differences of opinion between Reuther and Meany were elevated into a test of wills.

Few of Reuther's ideological brethren subscribed to his ascetic life style. His complaints about holding the winter conferences of the Executive Council in luxurious settings like Miami Beach and San Juan during times of high unemployment won little sympathy from his colleagues. David Dubinsky vented his annoyance at Reuther one year for causing the conference to be moved to Washington. He complained to Reuther "You don't like to mix business and pleasure. All right. But I do!"[185]

After twelve years of living together and repeated efforts by friends of labor to patch up differences, the UAW left the AFL-CIO. For Reuther, it was twelve years wasted in an unhappy relationship. For labor and the general public it was a wasted opportunity. Both Meany and Reuther share blame for the failure of labor to exert a more influential voice in the direction America was heading. Reuther made a bad decision to initiate a merger with a federation that shared neither his vision nor his expectations for what the merger might achieve. He allowed himself to be drawn into a schoolyard brawl with Meany. Meany stood by and watched while the ranks of labor thinned and its influence declined.

By the time the UAW left the AFL-CIO foreign cars were commonplace on American streets, foreign steel was a common ingredient in American made products, and American companies were building many of their new plants on foreign shores. In the last years of his life, Walter Reuther spent most of his energy defending the gains his union had won in previous negotiations, not extending them.

After leaving the AFL-CIO, Reuther was like a man who escaped one bad marriage only to rush into another. He paved the way for his union's exit from Meany's federation by forming an improbable alliance with the Teamsters.[186] Reuther had been party to the decision by the AFL-CIO to evict the Teamsters when the extent of the corruption inside the union was made public by the McClellan Committee's hearings. Now, a decade later, he was willing to "kiss and makeup." In this new federation both parties had something to gain. The Teamsters had become bigger and richer than ever after they were booted from Meany's federation,[187] but they remained stigmatized by their criminal past. They needed to brighten their image by bathing in the reflection of their respectable new partner. The UAW needed to combine the size and resources of the Teamsters with its own to belatedly launch the organizing drive Reuther envisioned over a decade earlier.

The new Alliance for Labor Action actually worked during the brief years Reuther had left. Neither the UAW nor the Teamsters got in one another's way. Jimmy Hoffa was tucked away in federal prison, giving the Teamsters a respite from public scrutiny. Reuther and Frank

Fitzsimmons had known each other back in Detroit, and had a more common framework of experience than the son of a German Lutheran Socialist had with the son of an Irish Catholic plumber from New York. The two leaders both urged an end to the Vietnam War, and Reuther was given a free hand to pursue his social agenda.[188] The Alliance conducted several successful organizing efforts in the South, and ties with community unions in Watts and other poor urban areas were strengthened. Reuther enthused that "We have been accomplishing more reform in the AFL-CIO from outside than when we were in it."[189]

That was a brief mirage. The new alliance was short lived. The Teamsters had not exorcised their criminal ghosts. Hoffa reappeared to reclaim his old job only to disappear into folklore narratives of the mob. The nation had turned a page, and Reuther had turned sixty. He would not live to see the edifice he and his union had constructed slowly being dismantled. That fate befell Victor who never came to terms with the give backs the union made to keep the once great corporations afloat.[190]

The "Treaty of Detroit" brought twenty years of middle class growth and a leveling of income disparity. When those twenty years ended, the original terms were not renewed and wealth began flowing, slowly at first, then with increasing speed, into fewer-and-fewer hands

CHAPTER VIII

IBM, the Vanguard of Post-Industrial America

(to the tune of Glory, Glory Hallelujah)
Overseas we also make our marvelous machines.
Round the globe in every land, our service is supreme.
IBM's fine products are the joy of kings and queens.
We serve humanity.

Song of the IBM

The 1964 New York World's Fair provided a canvas for corporate America to paint a surrealistic picture of itself and the future within its gaze. General Motors took its visitors on a "fun house" ride through a cool dark tunnel into a scale model of *Futurama*. After a glimpse of land rovers crawling over the surface of the moon, the fantasy tour returned to earth and witnessed aquacopters scavenging the deep for its bounty and a submarine delivery network transporting the riches to shore. Leaving the ocean floor and the underwater resorts for the great-great grandchildren of the jet setters, the tour visited the rain forest where a giant factory on wheels could fell a swath of trees with a powerful laser set in the tip of a giant arm riding in front of a mechanical brute that would grind up the timber and stumps and leave a paved highway in its wake. The sound track enthused that resources of the jungle would be opened for exploitation, bringing "progress and prosperity to the tropics." The tour concluded at the city of tomorrow—a creation of steel and concrete where "plazas of urban living [rose] over freeways." Towering superskyscapers and covered moving sidewalks minimized any contact with daylight these future city dwellers were to experience. Centrally located airports, surrounded by ribbons of concrete, and "swift and efficient" electronically paced travel routes sped people in, out, and about the city of tomorrow, but the rivers of concrete had few islands of relaxation—parks, sidewalk cafes, open air markets—that make a city habitable. Nature was subject to the laws of economics in the corporate mindset of 1964, not the other way around.[1]

Across the highway on the other side of the fair from the GM building was Eero Saarinen's egg-shaped IBM pavilion. GM offered visitors a designer's mockup of the future, but it was the computer giant that the public most associated with the world of tomorrow. IBM did not have to project a hazy vision of some distant time. Its machines were already part of people's conception of the future. Visitors to the IBM pavilion witnessed the current state of the art in computer technology— language translation and handwriting recognition. People could feed a card with a handwritten date into the machine and it would almost instantly spit out another, imprinted with some important event that took place on that occasion.[2]

The two corporate giants also offered two different models of labor relations. General Motors was a unionized company that negotiated with the UAW a series of contracts during the fifties that collectively formed the pattern for labor contracts throughout much of heavy industry. IBM was the poster child for welfare capitalism—a non-unionized company with an enlightened management that provided security, generous benefits, and advancement opportunities for its workers. Its employment practices served as a cynosure for the growing number of companies in the technology sector with a predominantly professional and skilled workforce.

The 1964 World's Fair was an occasion to celebrate the future less than one year after the trauma of the Kennedy assassination and one year prior to the Gulf of Tonkin Resolution. Ford introduced its Mustang to the public, IBM was rushing its system 360 into production, and General

Motors still had the swagger to dream big dreams. The party in Flushing Meadow provided no Tesla Coil or AC generating system to astonish an audience, only a Disney World version of *Tomorrowland*.[3] As the decade played out, the fair placed a period at the end of a long paragraph rather than serving as the opening phrase of a new chapter.

At the end of July, 1964, the IBM manufacturing plants in Endicott, NY shut down for a customary two-week break, while the bulk of the workforce took their vacation. Work activity in much of mid-twentieth century America still had seasonal fluctuations, and vacation time was structured around manufacturing schedules. The newly hired college graduates who had not accrued any vacation time spent the two weeks in the classroom learning FORTRAN programming, circuit analysis using IBM nomenclature, and company history.

The IBM history class was taught by Mike Supa, a blind man who once had served in the corporate offices in Westchester County, but found the pace of the day and the traffic more suited to his needs in the less bustling Southern Tier town of Endicott. Supa had established a friendship with the company chairman, Thomas J. Watson, Jr., during his time at corporate, and still received the occasional phone call from the boss, which he signaled to any co-worker within earshot with a hearty "Hello Tom." Mike Supa had a special relationship with the company, with its leader, and with the company town of Endicott that made the history course much more than a bland recital of selected events and accomplishments.

Supa detailed the role the government played in the company's success. The company later to become the core component of IBM was the supplier of machines for tabulating the census data in the late nineteenth century. Later the government bought from IBM machines for managing social security information during the depression years, armaments during the Second World War, and specialized computers to fit aboard the limited interior in the space capsules of the 1960s. As with other leading companies, the government was neither peripheral nor an impediment to IBM's success, but instrumental to it.

IBM was a famously non-union company. It set up shop in places like Endicott and Poughkeepsie, New York where union penetration was minimal and wage competition favorable. Historical roots, neighborhood influences, and the philosophy of its first family laid the foundation for the relationship between the company and its employees, but, according to Supa, Watson Jr. made sure his employee benefits remained an industry gold standard by keeping abreast of the auto negotiations and awarding any new benefit that was likely to emerge before it percolated through the rest of the economy. Supa related that during his time at corporate Watson introduced him to two of his visitors—Henry Ford II and Walter Reuther[4].

IBM and the Southern Tier communities grew up together. In 1964 pieces of the interstate system sat around the Triple Cities of the Southern Tier like disconnected Matchbox play tracks awaiting the rekindled interest of their owner to complete the assembly and speed his traffic around the loops and interchanges of his imagination. Route 81 would point north to Syracuse and the Canadian border and south through the Poconos and Blue Ridge toward "Malfunction Junction" in Knoxville, Tennessee. The newly expanded 17 would rush its traffic past the Roscoe Diner, once a busy landmark on the old road, through the Catskills, and toward the sprawling malls of Paramus, New Jersey. In three years time the last pieces of track would be snapped into place and the Triple Cities of the Southern Tier would be joined into the network lacing together the bits and pieces of America.

In 1964, Endicott was still a place not very accessible to the rest of America. Endicott was IBM and IBM was Endicott. The gleaming white IBM buildings straddled McKinley Avenue at the intersection of North Street and trailed down North to the east. The row of white IBM buildings was broken on the west by the old red brick tannery mills of the Endicott-Johnson shoe company. The shoe factory still sported the look and smell of a nineteenth century sweatshop, despite the proximity of its upscale neighbor. The company brand no longer appealed to the taste of a more affluent middle class and the run-down buildings housed a small remnant of what had been a large immigrant workforce. The locals claimed it was not uncommon for a person to have labored his adult life behind the forbidding facade of those brick buildings and bequeath his kin millions from the shares of IBM stock he bought for a song in the twenties and thirties.

In contrast to the occasional blue collar millionaire slaving away amongst the tanning vats in the shoe factory, local legend told of the janitor at IBM heading to work in the morning dressed in a suit and tie that he would exchange for his work clothes once he reached his locker at the plant. Neither story was likely typical, or even true, but both had no shortage of believers in the community. IBM was all about image—the image it conveyed to the public was the best advertisement for its product.

In 1964 IBM was surging to the top of the Fortune 500 ranks and its workforce overflowed the space in the row of white buildings on North Street. Some departments were moved into a one-story building in Vestal across the Susquehanna River from the main plant complex. There was another facility on the west side of the town in the village of Endwell. Further to the west there was the Glendale Manufacturing Research Laboratory, and continuing west on route 17C for another twenty miles one reached the Federal Systems Division in Owego where the on-board computers for the space program were developed and produced.

A similar concentration of IBM facilities dotted the Mid-Hudson River Valley from Kingston in the north, to the main plant in Poughkeepsie and the cluster of satellite locations catching its overflow, to the chip plant in nearby Fishkill, and continuing south to the Thomas J. Watson Research Laboratory in Yorktown. Much of the corporate hierarchy was housed in Rockland and Westchester counties.

In addition to IBM, upstate New York was home to General Electric in the Mohawk River Valley around Schenectady, Carrier Corporation in Syracuse, Xerox and Eastman Kodak in Rochester, and the Corning Works where ceramic dishes and materials for the Mercury capsules were fabricated. Kodak and Xerox shared with IBM the reputation as model corporate citizens. New York was still an industrial heavyweight that could pretend to its claim as the Empire State.

If one worked for IBM in the Southern Tier, one rarely encountered anyone socially who did not. It seemed everyone in town was an IBMer through work, or through marriage, or by relation. There was little going on in the community outside the row of white buildings and their nearby satellites. Drink was a favorite after work pastime for the single crowd. There was clam night at Sharkey's on Tuesday and happy hour at the

Red Lion on Friday. A steady influx of service technicians brought to town for classes on the latest additions to the product line drowned the lonely night time hours in the little club on McKinley Avenue featuring exotic dancers. The proscriptions against alcohol consumption by the elder Watson were famously flaunted by the second son, Arthur, during his brief sojourn into the production end of the family business. The second Tom Watson relaxed the company leash on its workers' after-hours activities.

The Southern Tier provided little in the way of cultural activities for its residents. The Binghamton branch of the SUNY system was preparing to abandon the World War 2 Quonset huts that served as its temporary home and move onto its new campus along the Vestal Parkway, but it had little connection to the community. The campus leaned hard left, the community veered to the right. The pending move from pre-fabs to brick and mortar did not entice name entertainers or celebrity speakers to book a date on the make-shift campus.

The Dave Clark Five found its way to the Triple Cities during the British Invasion in 1964. American bands found more reason to simply avoid the roads less traveled. The region was served by a small airport north of Endicott and its carrier Mohawk connected cities in Upstate New York with the major metropolises on the East Coast. The Utica, NY based airline was low on the corporate food chain and was consumed by a slightly larger flying fish, Allegheny Airlines, shortly after the British rock group flew out of town.

The remoteness of the region had proved attractive to one group of "tourists." On November 14, 1957, Mafia bosses and their lieutenants from around the country arrived at the Apalachin home of Joseph Barbara to resolve tensions in the organization after the assassination of Albert Anastasia and the push for preeminence by the author and beneficiary of the hit, Vito Genovese. One vigilant state trooper, Edgar Croswell, who was aware of a traffic ticket given to mobster Carmine Galante after a visit to Barbara's home a year earlier and subsequently kept regular tabs on the comings and goings at the Barbara estate, learned that Barbara's son had been reserving a large number of rooms at local motels and had placed a large order for meat with a local butcher. Croswell increased his watch on the Barbara property, and when he found numerous luxury cars with out-of-state license plate numbers belonging to known criminals parked in the driveway, he called for reinforcements and set up roadblocks around the property. In a scene worthy of its depiction in the 1999 Robert DeNiro comedy *Analyze This*, many of the old, out of shape bosses took off trudging through the woods surrounding the Barbara house, ruining their expensive suits and losing some hundred dollar bills along with their dignity. Fifty-eight of the attendees were caught. Those apprehended got off with little or no punishment, but it was no longer "a glorious time before Apalachin"[5] for the mob. FBI Director, J. Edgar Hoover could no longer deny the existence of the American Mafia. After the meeting Hoover created the "Top Hoodlum Program" that stepped up the surveillance and pressure on the bosses and led to the eventual indictment of Genovese and others.

Sports appealed to the local taste more than the refined fare of art and theater. The PGA conducted an annual tournament on one of the area golf courses, and fans of formula one racing could make the short journey to Watkins Glen to see international racing stars compete in its grand prix. The area was home to the Binghamton Triplets of the NY-Penn League. The Double A Triplets were a Yankee affiliate in 1964 and played in Johnson Field. The field was built in 1913 and was slated to be torn down in 1968 to make way for another stretch of I-81. When it was demolished in 1968, a replacement was not built and the Yankee affiliate moved to West Haven, Connecticut.

IBMers moving into the area had little interest in minor league baseball, high school football, or the Broome Tech basketball team coached by Dick Baldwin, the winningest JUCO coach of all time. The company provided the outlet to continue their athletic endeavors. IBM provided country clubs for employees in Endicott, Poughkeepsie, and Owego. The one in Endicott had an 18-hole and a 9-hole golf course that employees could use for a nominal charge. The club house had a pro shop, a small bowling alley, a gym with several basketball courts, a coffee shop, and class rooms where Syracuse University professors offered graduate engineering and science courses to the IBMers it accepted into its degree programs. The company picked up a substantial share of the employee's tuition upon successful completion of the course.

The club had several softball diamonds and a lighted football field. It organized leagues in softball, football, and basketball. The competition was keen, and champions were determined in each sport. Trophies were handed out at an annual banquet the company threw for the winners.

IBM Endicott seemed to thrive in its backwater environment. With little diversion, the workers, many of second and third generation in the IBM family, pursued their calling with a monkish dedication to their labor and devotion to their employer. There was little in their world outside of what IBM provided for them.

IBM was central in the lives of the Southern Tier communities in which it grew and enjoyed its adolescence, but the Southern Tier was becoming less central to the company. By 1964 the hub of company manufacturing activity had shifted to Poughkeepsie and the Hudson Valley. Poughkeepsie was only 70 miles north of New York City and a two hour trip by rail from Grand Central Station. It was a more attractive location for many of the young engineers and programmers the company was eager to recruit.

The Hudson Valley was not the only location drawing the company's focus away from its Endicott operations. The International Business Machines Company was rapidly growing beyond its New York roots. It had a major presence in San Jose, California where a nascent Silicon Valley was growing around the Berkeley and Stanford campuses. It was setting up shop in the Raleigh-Durham Research Triangle in North Carolina and in Rochester, Minnesota and Burlington, Vermont; and its plants in Europe and Japan were an increasingly core part of its corporate structure.

The Cash

The story of IBM begins to the west of New York State in late nineteenth century Dayton, Ohio. IBM might be considered a step-child of John Patterson's National Cash Register (NCR) Company of Dayton. Patterson was a complex man whose idiosyncrasies and impact upon the course of industrial development parallel in many respects with those of Henry Ford. He was a tyrant, innovator, social critic, paternalistic boss, ruthless monopolist, philanthropist, hero, and convicted felon. His conviction was later reversed on appeal. NCR was both a pioneer in the office products industry and a pioneer in improving workplace relations.

After graduating from Dartmouth, Patterson and his brother started a business selling coal in Dayton. He realized that coal was a generic product. To distinguish his company he relied upon aggressive advertising and superior service that included guaranteed delivery schedules and accurate receipts.[6] The business prospered and he acquired interest in mines and a miner's supply store. To Patterson's dismay, the store was losing money even though it was well-positioned to be profitable. He determined that the clerks were regularly shortchanging the open drawer where the proceeds and receipts were kept.[7]

Elsewhere in Dayton, saloon keeper James Ritty was experiencing the same problem. In 1878 Ritty had just returned from a sea voyage to Europe, and during his return he noticed on a visit to the engine room a device that counted the number of revolutions of the ship's propeller. Back in Dayton he built a machine that applied a similar mechanism to the task of tabulating sales.[8] He called his invention "Ritty's Incorruptible Cashier" and waited for the customers to arrive. Few did. One who did purchase two of Ritty's primitive cash registers was John Patterson. Within six months of the purchase the miner's store turned a $5000 profit.[9]

Neither Ritty nor any of the successors to whom the patent was transferred made a go of the cash register business. Meanwhile, Patterson saw his business ventures taken over by a group of New England capitalists and began looking for a new enterprise to engage his passion. In 1883 the National Manufacturing Company that held the Ritty patents issued new stock. The Patterson brothers bought it all and, for $6500, John bought the shares owned by George Phillips, gained control of the company and changed its name to National Cash Register.[10] After the purchase, he realized he had bought a failing business that could not sell all of the limited number of machines the rundown factory could produce.

Patterson did not wait around like Ritty and his successors for the customers to find him. He assembled a list of 5,000 prospective clients and deluged them with mailings describing the virtues of his marvelous machine. Patterson's list eventually grew to over 1.5 million companies.[11] He supplemented the mass marketing campaign with a professional sales force headed at one time by Thomas J. Watson, Sr. Patterson assigned his salesmen set territories, paid them on commission, and ensured they were well-trained, well-dressed, knowledgeable, and respectful.[12] This sounds unremarkable today, but was innovative at the time. He rewarded the salesmen that met their quotas by inviting them to a year-end sales convention.

The Panic of 1893 plunged the country into a severe depression and initiated a wave of labor unrest highlighted by the Pullman strike. Shoddy work and sabotage by resentful workers plagued manufacturers including National Cash Register. When a $50,000 shipment of cash registers were returned from England as defective, Patterson moved his office down to the shop floor to understand the extent of the problem. He realized that he too would be resentful working in the dimly-lit, unsanitary, and dangerous environment that typified the late nineteenth century factory floor. He stated that "[when] I looked further into conditions, I had frankly to confess there was no particular reason why they should put heart into their work."[13]

Patterson set about changing the environment and the opportunities for advancement of his workers. He cleaned up the debris littering the factory floor, put safety shields around machines that presented a danger, and granted his workers a wage increase. He went beyond improvement in safety and sanitation in the existing factory and hired architect Frank Andrews to build a new NCR campus with steel-framed, glass-walled buildings that provided natural light and the ability to open windows for natural ventilation. Patterson complemented his vision of interior space by hiring John and Frederick Law Olmsted to landscape the grounds of his complex.[14]

The benefits bestowed on the workers at "the Cash" included subsidized lunches, a free clinic at an NCR dispensary, and a dressing room and shower facility on the company premises. Patterson left Dartmouth with an A. B. degree and a profound distaste for the liberally educated class of his day, but had a great respect for learning and self-improvement. He toyed with the idea of being a school teacher before entering the coal business, and considered teaching, at least lecturing, to be part of his greater mission. He initiated a paid suggestion program, later also implemented at IBM, to reward workers for ideas that would advance the success of the company. He opened a lending library for his employees, opened a night school, and began a program of free lectures and concerts for his workforce. Workers taking advantage of these opportunities had a path for advancement in the company.[15]

Like Ford and his initiation of the five dollar day, Patterson considered the benefits he bestowed on his employees to be the smartest business decision he made. The lower turnover and greater productivity of his workforce more than offset the cost of his benevolence. Seeing his mission in the world to advance human welfare beyond his factory doors, he opened his plant to visitors and offered them the opportunity to view the fruits of his methods for themselves. He was frequently available to lecture to his guests before the tour, and in case they missed the message, he plastered signs "It Pays" prominently throughout the factory.[16]

About 30,000 visitors per year might tour Patterson's model factory, but many of his fellow industrialists were not impressed by his bridging barriers of class distinction and were not inclined to follow his lead. Undeterred Patterson, like Ford the practical sociologist, published his message in *The NCR Weekly*, a company organ that proclaimed on its masthead that it was "Published in the interest of all concerned in all the NCR Companies, Owners, Makers, Office Forces, Sellers, Users, Nonusers, Clerks, Cashiers, Customers, Servants, Children, and others, if there are others."[17]

One cause close to Patterson's heart was reform of the municipal government in Dayton. He railed against the corruption, patronage, poor quality of education, and lack of recreational space for years to little avail. In 1907 when he couldn't get a rail spur that he wanted built without first paying a bribe, he convened a meeting of the local leaders and lectured them about all of the ills plaguing the city. He called out the names of all the people he felt responsible for the mess he considered the city to be experiencing, many of whom were in attendance, and cited their specific misdeeds. Finally he closed the meeting by threatening to pull his company, all of its employees, and the $4 million dollars it generated for the community annually out of Dayton. The *Dayton Evening Press*, edited by James M. Cox, ridiculed the event as a "Grand Meeting at the Glue Factory, [complete with] hot tea and hot air."[18] Five years later, home rule for Ohio municipalities was incorporated into the state constitution in the administration of Governor James Cox and Dayton adopted the city-manager form of government advocated by Patterson.

Patterson paid his executives handsomely but subjected them to his imperious dictates and arbitrary firings. Charles Kettering, the genius who electrified the cash register, was fired and rehired several times. Patterson thought that equestrian skill developed strong leadership traits in his executives and would order up a 6 am riding session. During one such event Kettering almost fell off his horse and was fired for his lack of riding skill.[19] Kettering, whose laboratory space was always cluttered with tools and parts, may have offended Patterson's sense of order. Patterson never particularly cared for the inventor and fired him on several other occasions, but engineering supervisor Edward Deeds kept rehiring him.[20]

Kettering and Deeds saw the potential for reward in the nascent automobile industry in the first decade of the twentieth century and worked nights in a barn behind the Deeds house to develop an improved ignition system that greatly extended the life of the battery. The pair sold the invention to Henry Leland of Cadillac who ordered 8000 units of the system for his 1912 model.[21] Kettering quit his day job at NCR and co-founded the Dayton Engineering Laboratories Company, better known as Delco. This was the beginning of a long association with General Motors and at the time of his death in 1958 the prolific inventor had acquired more patents than any other American except Edison. His inventions included the self-starting recharging ignition system, spray paint auto finish, anti-knock fuel additives, the diesel locomotive, and freon refrigeration systems.[22] He also co-founded the Sloan-Kettering Cancer Institute in 1945 after his wife Olive was stricken with the disease. Sloan's management skill and Kettering's inventiveness combined to vault General Motors ahead of Ford and into the leadership of the automotive industry. He retired from General Motors in 1947 and spent the last decade of his life as a popular lecturer.

At NCR Kettering fed his creative appetite by hanging out with people in the sales department to understand the problems customers were experiencing and what they were asking the company to help them do. One of his best friends in sales was Thomas Watson. Just as Kettering used the information about the marketplace that he picked up from conversations with those in sales, Watson gained an appreciation of the technical side of the business from Kettering.

Patterson routinely abused his managers and subjected them to his sometimes bizarre notions and obsessive adherence to passing food and health fads. On a European trip Patterson hired Charles Palmer, an ascetic little Englishman, as his personal trainer and placed him on the Board of Directors of NCR. Palmer claimed an ability to read people's faces. Patterson put him to work on his executive committee and fired some of those who failed this scrutiny. The boss believed the system was the engine of the firm's success, not any one individual (besides himself). He operated under the principle that "When a man gets indispensable, let's fire him."[23]

One of those fired for pushing back against the dictates on food and healthy living habits was the company's general manager, Hugh Chalmers. Chalmers later went on to lead a prominent auto parts business, but he took his firing by Patterson very personally. The two men filed suits and counter suits against each other and fought a very public battle that spilled out of the court room and into the newspapers.

Despite the erratic behavior of the boss, top talent flocked to NCR. The company paid extremely well, provided a practicum on management that served as a precursor to the training of an MBA today, and offered a distinguished network of alumni for finding the next job. A later chief executive wrote in his autobiography that in the years between 1910 and 1930 one sixth of the corporate leaders in America once worked for NCR[24].

To his workers Patterson was benevolent, to his executives he was an erratic tyrant, and to his competitors he was a ruthless thug. NCR achieved a dominant position in its market because of the quality of its product and the professionalism of its sales force, but that was not enough for Patterson. He was not content with the biggest piece of the pie; he wanted the whole thing and pushed as hard as John D. Rockefeller to make sure he got it. The first approach would be to bring the competitor to the NCR factory and overwhelm him by the sight of the efficiency of its operations. He would next be escorted to the "Gloom Room," where the products of defunct companies were displayed, and be given a buyout offer.[25] If this "soft" approach did not work he was bombarded with law suits that sapped his time and resources to defend. In one example Patterson wrote that "If a patent is granted to the Lamson Company we will bring suit. If we lose we will take it to the Court of Appeals. It will take five or six years of litigation and probably cost Lamson $100,000 before they would have the legal right to use their invention."[26] The last line of attack was to target customers considering a competitor's product with "knockout men." The knockout man would visit the customer and tell him that the machine he was considering violated NCR patents and he would be subject to a lawsuit if he were to buy it. If he were already under obligation to the competitor, the NCR man would offer to cover his legal expenses if he backed out of the deal. By 1907 NCR claimed a 96% share of the market.[27]

The strong-arm tactics used by Patterson and his firm brought an indictment under the Sherman Anti Trust Act for the boss and 29 of his key executives including Thomas J. Watson. Unlike in other anti-trust cases, the NCR defendants faced criminal, not civil, charges. The main witness for the prosecution was Hugh Chalmers, who escaped indictment for his own role in the escapades of his former colleagues and took his revenge on Patterson for his firing. Chalmers's description of the extent to which the executives at NCR had gone to stifle competition was devastating. In the spring of 1913 all but one of the defendants were convicted, fined $5000, and sentenced to one year in jail.[28] The sentences were appealed but short of a miracle the men seemed headed to prison.

Divine intervention occurred shortly after the sentences were handed down. On the Monday after Easter in 1913, the skies opened up over Dayton and dropped as many as 11 inches of rain on the city. At 6 AM the next morning Patterson inspected the levees and determined they would not hold. He convened a meeting of this executive committee and announced that there was going to be a flood. He ordered his factory to immediately start building row boats to evacuate the affected residents. His commissary was ordered to bake 2000 loaves of bread and his purchasing agents were dispatched to locate beds, clothing and medical supplies.[29] While the meeting was still in progress the levees broke and the city was flooded. The city government was completely incapacitated. NCR, on higher grounds and supplied with its own power, was the only functioning government in place. NCR rowboats ferried the stranded to the company campus where they were sheltered in the factory buildings and in a hastily erected tent city. His old antagonist, Governor Cox, formally delegated Patterson the authority he had already assumed, and state and federal officials came to him to coordinate their activities.

Three hundred people lost their lives and property damage totaled $100 million,[30] but prompt action by Patterson prevented a worse disaster for the city and made him a national hero. There was a campaign to get President Wilson to issue a pardon, but Patterson rejected this effort proclaiming his innocence and his intention to fight the original conviction in the appeals process.[31] In the heady atmosphere of the authority he possessed in the aftermath of the flood, he fired off an angry telegram to the *New York Times* vowing that if the presiding judge at his trial set foot in Dayton he would throw him in jail. Watson intercepted the telegraph before it reached the *Times* and saved his boss the stain that it might have left on the halo he was wearing had it been printed.[32]

Perhaps in reaction to public sentiment, the appeals court reversed two counts of the convictions and sent the third back to lower court for a retrial that never occurred. Vindicated, Patterson blamed his co-defendants for getting him into the mess and began firing them.

During the thirty years surrounding the turn of the century, Dayton was a magnet for creative thinkers and entrepreneurs, much like Silicon Valley today. It was home to the Wright brothers' bicycle shop, Charles Kettering and his DELCO laboratory, and the ambitious and talented people that flocked to NCR. It was a laboratory for technical, social, and municipal engineering. It gave the country James Cox, governor and presidential candidate, and Thomas Watson. John Patterson, the eccentric martinet, presided like a Medici over the life of his city during these florid years.

Thomas J. Watson Sr.

Thomas J. Watson, Sr. grew up near the Southern Tier community of Painted Post, a small town just west of Elmira. He attended elementary school in a little wooden one-room building, and later attended the Addison Academy, where, like many boys of his time, he ended his public education to enter the workforce after his sixteenth birthday. His first job as a public school teacher lasted one day before he quit and began exploring other possibilities. He was drawn to commerce and took a year-long course in accounting and business at the Miller School of Commerce in Elmira. He left the Miller School in 1891 and found a $6 a week bookkeeping position in Painted Post.[33] After a year he drifted into sales and spent the next few years trying to sell sewing machines, pianos, and organs in the rural communities outside of Elmira. When he realized that the ten dollars a week he was being paid by Bronson's Hardware Store would have been much more had he been on commission, he quit in indignation and moved to Buffalo where he found a job selling sewing machines for Wheeler and Wilcox.[34]

Watson's brief tenure at Wheeler and Wilcox came to an abrupt end when after stopping at a bar to celebrate a sale, he emerged hours later to find his horse and buggy gone – stolen along with his sample merchandise. Watson was fired and forced to compensate his employer for the lost property. Word of the mishap spread and shadowed Watson's attempts to find new employment."[35] The episode had a profound impact upon the senior Watson, and explained the strict temperance policy he later enforced upon his employees at IBM.

Watson's early career was plagued by missteps and failure. His next job, selling shares of the Buffalo Building and Loan Company for an unscrupulous broker named C. B. Barron also ended abruptly and badly. Barron absconded with the loan funds and Watson's commission. Watson next opened a butcher shop in Buffalo that soon failed, leaving him with no money, no job, and few prospects.[36]

The one thing the failed butcher shop did leave with Watson was an NCR cash register for which he had to arrange transfer payments to the new owner of his establishment. During his visit to the NCR office in Buffalo, he met the branch manager, John J. Range. Watson began bugging him for a job in sales, and after several weeks, was offered a position as sales apprentice to Range. Watson had spent much of his early business career in sales, but was not yet very good at it. He credited much of his later success to what he learned from Range.[37] Under the tutelage of his mentor, Watson became the most successful NCR salesman in the East, earning $100 a week.[38] His success drew notice at the Dayton headquarters, and he was assigned to head the struggling sales office in Rochester, NY. Watson complemented an aggressive sales campaign with knockout tactics (including sabotage) against Hallwood, the main competitor, and established an NCR monopoly in his territory.[39]

During his time in Rochester, Watson worked closely with Hugh Chalmers, who became general manager of NCR. After four years in Rochester, he was told by Chalmers to secretly board a train for Dayton and meet with Patterson and him at the corporate headquarters. Chalmers had noted the aggressive approach Watson had used in Rochester to establish NCR domination of the market there, and tabbed him for a special assignment. NCR had been losing customers to businesses that bought and resold used NCR cash registers from businesses that either failed or were upgrading to a newer model. Chalmers and Patterson devised a plan to drive out this form of competition by creating a phony used cash register company with Watson as its president.[40]

From 1903 until 1907 Watson ran the American Second-Hand Cash Register Company. The ostensibly legitimate business would set up in a store front in a section of town where other second-hand businesses were located, and, using NCR supplied funds, pay premium price for machines that it resold at prices below the competition. Watson's tactics drained the supply of used machines from an area and undercut the price his competitors could afford to offer. When a competitor could no longer squeeze a profit from the business, Watson offered generous terms to buy the failing enterprise with the condition that the seller sign an agreement not to operate a second-hand cash register business in the many territories in which Watson's company operated. When the competition was eliminated in an area, Watson lowered his offering price for used machines, raised his selling price, and turned the profits over to NCR. The phony enterprise was never intended to be profitable, but Watson managed to not only eliminate competition from reconditioned old NCR machines, but to turn a profit for his secret partner while doing so.[41]

In 1907 Watson was rewarded for his service. He was reinstated on the NCR payroll, brought to Dayton, and made an Assistant Sales Manager. Three years later he was elevated to the position of Corporate Sales Manager. Under Watson's leadership, sales of cash registers soared to over 100,000 in 1911, nearly double the volume sold two years earlier.[42] Patterson rewarded him with a townhouse in the exclusive neighborhood where he and other NCR executives lived and with a new Pierce Arrow automobile. Watson's success also put him in the cross hairs of the temperamental Patterson.

When 1912 arrived, the poor rural lad who once sold musical instruments to the farmers around Painted Post for $10 a week celebrated his success. He was part of the Dayton social elite, given to wearing fine clothes, driving expensive cars, and standing near the top of the NCR management pyramid. He was to meet and become engaged to Jeannette Kittredge, the daughter of a prominent Dayton businessman. Then, on February 22, the world of Thomas J. Watson came crashing down around him. He was one of thirty NCR executives indicted on three criminal charges that each carried a maximum one year prison sentence and $5000 fine. The star witness for the government was the man who set up the shadow second-hand cash register company and knew intimately the details of Watson's involvement with it, Hugh Chalmers.

One year later, almost to the day, Patterson, Watson, and twenty seven of the other defendants were convicted and faced a year in jail. When the Dayton flood occurred a few weeks after the verdict was handed down, Watson was in New York on company business, and he arranged for relief trains to deliver needed supplies to the stricken city.[43] Shortly after the flood waters receded and the city began to dry out, Watson and Jeannette Kittredge were married. Patterson attended the small gathering of family and friends assembled in the Kittredge townhouse for the ceremony and waved them off on their honeymoon to the West Coast. When the couple returned, Jeannette was pregnant with Tom Junior and Patterson was not in a welcoming mood. He wanted Watson out and went out of his way to publicly humiliate him and let him know his days at NCR were coming to an end. Whether on his own initiative or after a final push from Patterson, Thomas J. Watson and two of his closest associates walked out the door of NCR for the last time on an unusually warm and sunny November afternoon in 1913.

Watson's prospects were anything but sunny and warm. He was given $50,000 in severance pay by Patterson and allowed to keep the Pierce Arrow, but there was still a 1-year jail term hanging over his head and the record of the trial fresh in the minds of prospective employers. His wife was pregnant; his mother in declining health; and his ties with

Dayton severed. Still, when he looked back on the building complex he had just left for the last time, he is reported to have told his two friends that he would go out and build an even bigger business.[44] If true, or not, it became part of his legend.

The Next Chapter in the Life of T. J. Watson

Watson was profoundly shaken by the trial and by seeing his reputation shredded in the daily accounts of its proceedings, but he remained convinced throughout the rest of his life that he had done nothing wrong. The case brought against NCR was as much a case against the unfettered capitalism of the day as it was against a particular corporation. NCR was a particularly aggressive team in exploiting the tactics that the referees had ignored in the past. Now, suddenly, they were being flagged, and the individuals familiar with the game were left to question why they had drawn a penalty.

Watson was not bitter, like Hugh Chalmers, about his departure from NCR. He had received a first-class business education at one of the most progressive corporations of the day. He had proved to himself at the American Second-Hand Cash Register Company that he could run a business and against expectations make it profitable. He also left with scars from the earlier drinking episode in his Wheeler & Wilcox days and the NCR anti-trust trial that labeled him a criminal. He resolved that in his future business endeavors he would be squeaky clean. Now, with a possible jail term hanging over his head, he needed someone to give him a chance.

That chance came from Charles Flint, a diminutive sixty-four year old man with a mustache and mutton-chop whiskers, who began his business career at W. R. Grace retrofitting cargo ships with cannon and torpedoes for delivery to South American dictators.[45] In his later years he moved his activities to Wall Street and formed as many as 24 trusts, some more successful than others. His latest effort merged the International Time Recording Company of Endicott, NY, the Computing Scale Company of Dayton, Ohio, and the Tabulating Machine Company of Washington, D.C. These three businesses had very little in common, but Flint believed the product diversity would help insulate the parent company from downturns of the business cycle in any one of the industries. The conglomerate seemed headed for disaster with debt nearly double the combined assets.[46] Flint was looking as much for a miracle as for someone to manage the struggling business. He heard good things about Watson from a friend in Rochester, and was not put off by his legal problems. On May 1, 1914 Thomas J. Watson, Sr. was named General Manager of the Computing-Tabulating-Recording Company (C-T-R). One year later after his conviction was overturned by the Court of Appeals he was given the title of President.

The Tabulating Machine Company founded by Herman Hollerith was the centerpiece of the new company. Hollerith worked for the Census Bureau from 1879 to 1892 and secured patents for a punched card format and machines to tabulate and rapidly interpret census data. Hollerith formed a company to market his inventions and won the contract to supply the Census Bureau with his machines for the 1900 census. The job of producing the census report from the collected raw data, which usually took ten years to complete, was finished in two. The successful application of his inventions left Hollerith searching for other customers to sustain his business between the ten year census cycle. Foreign governments, who also conducted a census of their population, were potential customers as were large corporations like railroad companies that used passenger mileage data to efficiently schedule service on their lines. Hollerith, much like Patterson when he entered the cash register business, had to analyze the requirements of potential clients and sell them on the need for his product, before he could sell the product itself. In 1911, Hollerith, in failing health, sold his company to Flint, and with it the obligation to develop a market for its product line.

It was left to the sales force at C-T-R to convince skeptical clients of their need for the type of equipment the company was offering. Watson built upon the experience he had acquired at NCR to establish high standards for his salesmen. They became known for their well-groomed, dark-suited, highly professional bearing. Salesmen were put on a commission, given a territory, and provided with regular training. Emphasis was placed on knowing the customer and tailoring a solution to his special needs. The corporate image conveyed professionalism, expertise, and a sense of intimacy with its clients. It went a long way toward creating a niche for the company's products.

Watson initiated a set of practices at C-T-R that included songs and slogans as well as individual incentives to instill a sense of corporate pride and loyalty. THINK became the company byword, and THINK signs were plastered prominently on company walls and on the covers of company notepads. He adopted the suggestion box from NCR and created an open door policy that provided an opportunity for any employee having a complaint to bring the problem directly to any manager in the organizational hierarchy, including the boss. He sponsored company sports programs, a company band, and company outings to encourage a sense of community within the "C-T-R family." He brought in Roger Houston and Joe Rogers, the two men who were fired with him from NCR, but rejected recommendations from his directors to recruit new managers from the outside in favor of finding and promoting talent from within.[47] These men would have more loyalty to the company and help create a more cohesive unit.

The corporate culture of C-T-R developed around Watson. He became the image of the company both internally and to the public. Loyalty to the company was expressed by patterning one's dress after Watson's and conducting one's professional and private life according to his expectations. The omnipresent THINK signs were not only admonishments to think creatively, but to also think like Watson and anticipate the opportunities and potholes in the directions in which he was steering the company.

Watson's influence at C-T-R bore quick results. After four years, company revenue doubled to $2 million dollars and its geographical reach expanded into Europe, Asia, Australia, and South America.[48] By 1924 the company's global reach and it's president's grand vision prompted its name change to the International Business Machines Corporation, later abbreviated as IBM.

When Flint added Hollerith's company to the trust he constructed, he made two concessions to the inventor. Hollerith received a ten year consulting contract that stipulated he had to approve any changes or improvements to his machines and he was "not subject to the orders of any officer or other person connected with the company."[49] The Tabulating Machine Company had two senior engineers: Hollerith, who lived and worked in Washington, and Eugene Ford, who lived and worked in Uxbridge, Massachusetts. Hollerith became increasingly remote and temperamental. He refused to build new machines and often refused to approve improvements Ford made to the existing line.[50]

The Census Bureau balked at the charge Hollerith presented for the 1900 census and commissioned one of its engineers, James Powers, to design tabulating machines for the 1910 census. By the end of the decade Powers' tabulating equipment was technologically superior to Hollerith's and eating into the market share of C-T-R. Still the name Hollerith was as synonymous with tabulating machines as Hoover with vacuum cleaners. His association with the company was still more of an asset than a liability, but it presented Watson with the task of navigating through the obstacles he created without bruising his ego on the way by.

Watson valued the importance of a good research and engineering team from his association with Kettering at NCR. He convinced Ford to move to New York and start recruiting the best engineers he could find. Ford's first recruit was Clair Lake who designed a printer attachment for the C-T-R tabulating machines that enabled the company to regain the technological advantage over Powers. Watson added Fred Carroll and James Bryce to the team Ford assembled and provided the group with laboratory space and funding more generous than a company of its size was thought able to afford.

When Watson arrived at C-T-R, he had no grand strategy for building a company that would be bigger and richer than Patterson's. His approach was more motivational than strategic. Over time he came to appreciate that the tabulating machine was at the forefront of a vast data processing market that his company was positioned to capture and which he resolved to monopolize. Watson called a meeting of his executives on October 27, 1927 to discuss the future, and he told the assembled "There isn't any limit for the tabulating business for many years to come. We have just scratched the surface in this division [..] the potentialities are greater, and we have done so little in the way of developing our machines in this field."[51] Watson retained his 19th century appetite for monopoly and knew the recipe for building one required a generous supply of patents.

C-T-R and later IBM used its talented research group and key acquisitions to stuff its corporate briefcase full of patents. James Bryce alone was credited with more than four hundred. No one patent in those early years was more valuable than Clair Lake's redesign of the original Hollerith card into the 80-column IBM card that remained a standard storage device into the seventies. Lake replaced the round punch slots with rectangular boxes that could be squeezed closer together to enable each card to hold 960 bits of data. The design was patentable and worked only with IBM tabulating equipment. IBM offered a machine for transferring data stored on cards of the old design onto the new, but it would not license its patent on the cards to other competitors. The cards were the storage device of the era. Once a company had its vital data stored in boxes of IBM cards, it was reluctant to go to the expense of converting to another format. The cards locked customers into a long-term relationship with IBM. A card press invented by Fred Carroll could produce 1,000 cards per minute. IBM was the sole producer. It could produce them cheaply and sell them at a substantial mark up.[52]

Watson made an early decision to focus on large-scale, custom-designed solutions. This decision came to define the approach that C-T-R and later IBM would follow during much of its growth spurt. As much as General Motors became known for its big, high profit-margin cars, IBM became known for its "big iron," high profit-margin computing engines.

Watson built a first-class sales and customer service force and a first-class research and development team, but paid little attention to manufacturing. He took to heart what he learned from Range and Patterson about sales and Kettering about the importance of research and engineering, but the man who plastered THINK signs all over his walls did not pay close attention to the message IT PAYS that Patterson delivered to the skeptics questioning the benefits he showered upon his workers. Like Patterson when a shipment of defective cash registers was returned from England, Watson was awakened to problems in his factories when he received numerous complaints from the field like the one coming from a customer in Paris who balked at paying a full month's rent for a machine that was down for a good portion of it.[53] IBM needed to fix problems on the manufacturing floor if it were to achieve the success its leader envisioned. Watson needed one more tutor to complete his education.

The example of good corporate citizenship and good industrial relations was found in the company living next door. George F. Johnson was the son of a poor factory worker who at age 13 got a job as an apprentice at a bootmaker's factory in Ashland, Massachusetts. He followed his father into the job of treeing—attaching the accessories in the final step of the process of building a shoe. In 1881 he got a job as treeing foreman at the Lester Brothers shoe factory in Binghamton, NY. He was an effective manager and he gained more-and-more responsibility in the company. In 1890, Lester Bros. was bought by Henry B. Endicott. Endicott was an investor who knew nothing about the shoe business. He tapped Johnson to manage the factory. In two years, Johnson increased production form 1,000 pairs of shoes a day to 18,000 pairs a day.[54] In 1899 Endicott sold half the business to Johnson and allowed him to run it.

Johnson never forgot his humble origins. He described his philosophy to a biographer: "I don't believe that a man can own a company. It belongs to the community, to the public."[55] He was George Bailey in *It's A Wonderful Life* before Frank Capra created his character. George F., as he liked to be called by his workers, built houses and sold them to workers at cost. His own house was in the same neighborhood, and when he lowered the workday from 9 ½ to 8 hours, he was serenaded by his grateful workers.[56] He provided free legal advice and medical care. In 1919 he introduced a profit sharing plan. On a trip passing through Binghamton, President Wilson stopped and told a crowd of assembled Endicott-Johnson workers that "If the same spirit which exists between you and [management] existed everywhere, there would be no question, no trouble, no difficulty [...] between the employer and the employee."[57]

Johnson was the epitome of the welfare capitalist that Wilson regarded as an antidote to the labor unrest and Socialist ferment stirring within pre-World War 1 America. Johnson labeled his approach a Square Deal and spelled out tits terms in a pamphlet that was provided to every newly hired worker. Management promised fair treatment and additional benefits to the worker: "Certain claims of your family are recognized.

Medical and Hospital service is yours. Privileges of many kinds are yours." In return workers were expected to "give [management] a 'Square Deal'; which means fair return for what you receive—an honest effort to do the work well, and a fair and sufficient amount of it."[58] George F. Johnson was a humanitarian with a sincere interest in his employees' welfare, but he was also a shrewd industrialist who realized, like Patterson, that "It Pays" to buy his workers' loyalty with a Square Deal.

Before Endicott bought Lester Bros., the town that would be renamed for the financier was a sleepy little village of fewer than 10,000 nestled between the Susquehanna River on the south and North Street, the last east-west road before the railroad tracks. By 1920 the population of the town tripled.[59] Many of the newcomers were immigrants from Italy, Greece, and Eastern Europe drawn by reports from earlier arrivals about the generous benefits and relatively pleasant working environment at the factory. Many of the new arrivals located on the hill on the north side of town or in the neighboring town now called Johnson City.

When C-T-R arrived in the second decade of the twentieth century, it found itself an upstart in a place where the shoe company set the standards. The two towns just west of Binghamton, Johnson City and Endicott were named for the shoe company owners, and the George F. highway was the main road connecting them. Johnson spent lavishly on parks that he provided free of charge to the communities. He paid his workers better, treated them better, and was regarded as something of a saint by workers and the President of the United States alike. Watson set up shop in Endicott with the taint of his recent conviction hanging over him.

The relationship between Watson and Johnson progressed from cool at the beginning, to business-like, and after a while to one of mutual affection.[60] Johnson courted Watson to make his community the model for a progressive business culture. Watson warmed to Johnson and came to realize that he would have to match or exceed the pay and benefits Johnson provided if he were to attract and retain the best workers and make them feel part of the mission he established for his company. The other benefit of Johnson's generosity to his workers that Watson valued was that Endicott-Johnson was immune to the outbreak of unionism that was spreading through much of the rest of the textile industry at the time.

The Great Depression fell like night on the bright sky and sunny future the new technologies promised. For Watson it came at a time when he had just set his course on establishing and dominating the data processing market. He was not one to let the business cycle interfere with his plans and ambitions. During the 1921–22 recession he complained that every American company was sending out the message that business was bad. He told his colleagues, "What we want to do as a company and as individuals is get back to this message of better business and advertise it."[61] Throughout 1922 that is what he did in advertisements, speeches, and interviews. The period of sustained prosperity that he forecast, or willed, arrived in 1923 and carried through to the end of the decade.

Watson treated the start of the Great Depression in the same way. It was an inconvenience. He didn't expect it to last more than a couple of years, and he would just ignore it and will it away with the same optimistic message he used in 1922. He still remained committed to dominating the vast market he saw opening before him. He realized that the best asset the company had was its skilled and committed workforce. Endicott kept humming while the rest of the nation suffered.

IBM did not slow down for the hard times. It sped up. Watson believed that innovation would yield products that companies could not resist. He saw that automation had made only a 5% penetration of the market for accounting machines and believed that even in hard times new customers could be lured into buying the hot new products his lab would develop.[62] In 1932 IBM broke ground for a million dollar research laboratory across the street from its Endicott factory that would house all of its researchers and engineers. The size of the workforce increased during the depression.

Watson kept expecting the depression to end, but despite his pronouncements it wouldn't go away. IBM could sustain his program of producing for inventory for two, maybe three years after which the company would be in deep financial trouble. Time was running out. The board of directors considered replacing Watson, but delayed any action.[63] With dust blowing over the plains and brownshirts strutting through the streets of Germany, the end of the depression seemed nowhere in sight. Watson needed a miracle.

In 1913 Watson and his fellow defendants were saved by an act of God. In 1935 he was saved by an act of Congress. On August 14, President Franklin Roosevelt signed the Social Security Act. At the stroke of a pen a massive new market for tabulating equipment was created. Businesses had to report to the government the money collected for each employee, and the government had to process the data supplied by every employer. There was only one company that was prepared to supply the tabulating equipment and replacement parts that this task required. Watson bet the company on the belief that the depression would be over in two or three years. He was wrong, but luck was on his side. IBM emerged from the depression stronger than before and gained a huge technological lead over competitors such as Remington Rand, whose research and development efforts stalled during the period.

Across McKinley Avenue from the white stucco facade of IBM, Endicott's other industry faced the bleak days of the Depression without the prospect of an untapped new market waiting over the horizon. Shoes were a commodity that people patched up and wore longer when times were tough. In the face of falling revenues George F. Johnson struggled to maintain his Square Deal policy. Johnson had to cut wages by 20%, reduce hours, and institute a policy of work spreading to avoid layoffs. Employees were required to contribute 5% of their reduced pay to support the previously free Medical plan.[64] When Johnson lowered the stock dividend from 10 to 6 percent, he came under pressure from shareholders and some of his board members who objected to company funds being used to support employee medical care and relief efforts in the Broome County communities.[65] George F. expressed his determination that the pain be shared between labor and capital in a 1931 letter to his son, who had assumed the day-to-day management of the firm.[66]

> But as long as I am on earth to vote, I will never give the stockholders any more than I am willing to give the workers. When we took away from the common stockholders two dollars of their five dollars dividend, we took away at least two and a half from the workers, of their wages. By taking away from the workers we were

able to earn three dollars which we now propose to give to the common stockholders.

Tension between financial interests and the Johnsons' efforts to preserve as much of the paternalistic culture as they could persisted throughout the Depression years. Johnson went through the bad years warding off legal challenges to his policies.[67] His frustration with the selfishness of the shareholders and their assumption that the company existed only for their benefit mounted and his letters became more bitter.[68]

> Can a stockholder be considered—or even a collection of stockholders—as owners of the Industry, because they have invested their cash, hoping for a liberal return, and caring nothing about how these returns are earned, only that they receive them in the largest possible way? Are not stockholders willing and happy, and quite ready to sell out their interests? And do they not do it when it pleases them? How could a stockholder or group of stockholders claim to "own" the business, caring nothing for the earnings paid to the workers, or the values sold and delivered to the customers? Are they not in fact parasites—one and all, and every one with selfish interest, 'reaping where they have not sown'—demanding of Management, consideration of their interests which is not their due, and which they themselves have no respect for?

Watson and Johnson entered the Depression years vying to outdo each other in the benefits they offered their workers. The long period of hard times exposed the limitations of welfare capitalism. IBM was in the vanguard of the industry of the future and emerged stronger with its culture intact. Endicott Johnson was part of an industry headed down the road to distant shores with cheaper labor. It emerged with the Square Deal rounded at the corners and its ability to provide for the health and security of its workers substantially diminished.

Watson was one of the very few businessmen who supported Franklin Roosevelt and the New Deal. Most considered Roosevelt a traitor to his class and schemed to engineer his defeat in the next election. Watson may have seen something of himself in Roosevelt when they first met while FDR was governor of New York. Watson described how he became a supporter of Roosevelt after that first encounter: "People realized they were listening to a man who had a new idea. And a man who was not afraid to stand before them and say, 'This is the truth as I see it,' regardless of precedent—because precedent had proved itself to be wrong."[69] We can surmise if he would have been receptive to Roosevelt before he had met George F. Johnson, but by the time Roosevelt was elected president, much of the New Deal was already in place in Endicott, NY.

In a message Watson addressed to all IBM employees in 1933 he described the reasons why he supported Roosevelt's program:

> "There is no question in my mind but that the New Deal will mean certain restrictions in regard to some methods that have been employed by certain people, and corporations whereby they, perhaps, will not be able to profit as much for the benefit of the few. In our own business, I am looking forward to an era, under the New Deal, in which we shall be able to pay everybody more money—and I am looking for that in every industry. I believe it is coming."[70]

George F. Johnson must have smiled broadly when he read that speech.

Watson and Roosevelt became pen pals during his administration. Watson wrote the President regularly, with increasing frequency by 1935–36. Roosevelt was less diligent in his replies, but also warmed to Watson at the outset of his second term. The IBM Chairman served as a bridge to the business community and, in later years, an emissary to foreign leaders. Watson wrote to Roosevelt about his ideas for reducing the national debt, for managing TVA, and about countless other ideas he had for managing the economy.[71] In most of his letters the businessman was at the heart of the recommendation. The memo below captures the tone and substance of Watson's correspondence late in the President's first term.[72]

Memo from TJW to FDR, Mar. 6, 1936

"The best suggestion I can make for quick restoration of confidence is for you to make a good neighbor radio talk in which you will express confidence and appreciation in those business and financial institutions which are being conducted along sound and progressive lines. I feel that a close analysis of the whole picture will show that the majority of business and financial leaders are putting forth their best efforts to do a good job in the interests of everyone concerned. The proof that industry has been giving consideration to the working people is borne out by the fact that in 1860 the average annual wage of industrial workers was $288.00 and the working day was in many cases as high as 16 hours. The average annual wage for the entire country in 1929, including women, who did not figure in industry in the '60s, was $1,325.00, and the working day was down to 8 hours."

This memo initiated an exchange between Watson and the Acting Commissioner of the U. S. Bureau of Labor Statistics arguing the validity of Watson's numbers.[73.] Roosevelt did not reply himself and did not make such a talk.

Watson considered himself part of FDR's campaign team as the second term election approached. The memos became more frequent and often used the pronoun *we* when discussing the challenges and accomplishments of the administration. One memo extols the accomplishments of Roosevelt's first term.[74]

Sept. 24th, 1936 memorandum from TJW to FDR

> This record has brought to our country such remarkable recovery, under which all classes of people have benefited, that if properly presented there can be no question as to your re-election. Factory employment in July 1936, as compared with March 1933, shows an increase in the number of workers of 55%. [...] and from March 1933 to July 1936, there has been an increase of approximately 90% in man-hours and 11% in payrolls. Production of pig iron and steel ingots is back to normal and is approximately 5 times as great as it was at the same time in 1932. The output of our auto industry exceeds any year in our history, excepting 1929, and is more than 3 times what it was in 1932. the electrical industry in this country is making and selling more current in 1936 than it did in 1929 or any other period. Farm income is greater now, despite the drought, than at any time in six years.

Roosevelt may have found Watson to be useful, albeit a bit of a nuisance, in relaying the opinion of business, but he was not even a footnote in the later biographies of the thirty-second President. There is no indication that Watson's letters caused Roosevelt to do anything he wouldn't have otherwise. There is also no evidence that Watson's relationship with Roosevelt influenced the awarding of the Social Security contract to IBM. IBM was the only company positioned to meet the demand. Though Social Security was publicly debated before it was signed into law, Watson told business reporter Peter Drucker that he had not anticipated the act and did not realize the enormous requirement for tabulating equipment that it entailed.[75]

After the Social Security Act saved IBM, Watson's business legacy was secured. He had fulfilled the pledge he made to himself and his two companions when he walked out the door at NCR for the last time in 1913. He had built a struggling company on the verge of collapse into a thriving enterprise on the verge of dominating a new, seemingly limitless market. He had equaled and surpassed the accomplishments of Patterson. Now, in his sixties, he looked to play a bigger role on the world stage.

World Peace Through World Trade

Watson parlayed his celebrity, the connections he established with the political, business, and social elite of Europe on his frequent trips to establish and monitor IBM satellite companies, and his connections with the Roosevelt administration to rise to prominence in the Foreign Department of the American Chamber of Commerce, which also functioned as the American section of the International Chamber of Commerce (ICC). In 1935 he was elected president of the ICC to be installed at the next Congress in 1937. In his role as president-elect he got to choose the next convention site. He promised the attendees the largest, most grandiose Congress yet, then, with the flair of a modern chairman of the Olympic Committee announcing the winning bid to host the upcoming games, he told the delegates "We are going toooo… Berlin!"

The Nazi campaign of arrests, harassment, exclusion, and confiscations of property waged against Jews escalated during the two years that passed between the 1935 and 1937 Congresses. International pressure to isolate the rogue regime continued to mount. Yet in 1937, Watson, chanting his mantra of "World Peace Through World Trade," led his band of international businessmen into the German capital.

The setting was as grandiose as Watson promised. The businessmen were wined and dined at parties thrown by the Goebbels and the Goerings.[76] A night at the opera began with an unannounced arrival of Hitler dressed in his familiar brown uniform. The sight of der Führer making his way to the former royal box draped with a swastika flag brought the crowd of international businessmen, including Americans, to its feet. When the call *Sieg* crackled through the applause greeting his arrival, the response *Heil* echoed back from the gathered. Watson began to raise his arm in the Nazi salute with many of the others, but caught himself before it was fully extended.[77] The Nazis spared no expense in trying to impress their guests including a banquet for a crowd numbered in the thousands at a picturesque eighteenth century castle built by Friedrich Wilhelm III on Peacock Island just outside the city. The extravagant affair cost the hosts four million Reichsmarks.[78]

The incoming president of the ICC, along with his Dutch predecessor and another pro-Nazi delegate, was granted a private meeting with Hitler. Afterward he reported to the *New York Times* that Hitler told them "There will be no war. No country wants war, no country can afford it."[79] It is what Watson wanted to hear and what he wanted to believe. Not lacking in self esteem, he may have believed that he convinced Hitler that access to raw materials and markets would open for Germany if he were to forgo an effort to secure them by military action. In business and international affairs he was a man of consequence. His place on the world stage was confirmed for him during the banquet on Peacock Island when Goebbels and Economics Minister Hjalmar Schacht hushed the crowd and called Watson to come forward. Schacht then draped a red, black and white ribbon with the Cross of Merit of the Decoration of the German Eagle with the Star attached to it around the neck of his guest. It was the second highest honor Germany could bestow upon a foreigner.

In the late colonial period Britain and France had access to the resources of their possessions and client states in Africa, the Middle East, and South Asia. The United States possessed a vast territory spanning the breadth of a continent that was rich in resources and it dominated the commerce of its neighbors to the south. Germany, Italy, and Japan were relatively small nations, poor in resources, without the colonial empire of Britain and France to feed them materials and provide them with markets. Had Watson advanced the cause of *World Peace Through World Trade* ten years earlier, it would have been prescient, but he was still a pipsqueak in the world of international commerce back then, and the West was not ready to scrap the provisions in the Treaty of Versailles that dragged Germany into the clutches of its most extreme faction. In 1937, in the fairytale setting the Nazis wrapped around the Congress, the delegates ignored the dark human drama transpiring on the other side of their fantasy island. There was not even a mention of the huge refugee problem the Nazi pogrom was inflicting on its neighbors [80].

For three years the German Eagle hung like an albatross around Watson's neck. After the Congress of the ICC left Berlin in 1937, the brutality and aggressiveness of the Nazi regime unleashed greater horror on its Jews and dissidents and demanded more territorial concessions from its defenseless neighbors. On May 13, 1938 Germany absorbed Austria into the Third Reich and began rounding up Austrian Jews. On September 30th the European Allies appeased Hitler at Munich and ceded half of Czechoslovakia to Germany. It would only be a matter of months before Hitler seized the rest of the country. Finally two weeks after Kristallnacht, Watson felt compelled to write Hitler a mild rebuke and urge the Nazi dictator to observe the Golden Rule. In a letter dated November 25, 1938 he wrote:[81]

> ...upon my most recent return [from Germany] I find a change in public sentiment and loss of good will to your country [...that] I feel it is going to be difficult to accomplish mutually satisfactory results in connection with our trade relations. The change in sentiment referred to has been brought about through the decisions of your government in dealing with minorities, and I respectfully appeal to you to give consideration to applying the Golden Rule in dealing with these minorities. [...] If your Excellency would follow up this act of kindness with policies inspired by its humanitarian effort, it would, in my opinion, be the one way by which those interested in the exchange of goods and services and high ideals might find the opportunity to help Germany regain the valuable trade and good-will which she has lost.

The letter was mis-addressed and returned ostensibly unopened later. Hitler never officially read the advice to employ the Golden Rule. Still Watson kept the German medal and persisted in his efforts to appease Hitler and grant him access to the raw materials he craved through an international trade pact. Rather than simply make a graceful exit from the stage of international diplomacy as his term as ICC President came to an end, Watson urged his fellow delegates to the 1939 Congress in Copenhagen to adopt a resolution calling for a group of businessmen from the United States, Britain, France, and the three Axis powers to meet and negotiate a new international trade policy designed "to give all governments of the world a fair opportunity to share in the resources of the world" and then lobby their respective governments to approve the deal these business leaders would broker.[82] Watson was characteristically enthusiastic about the resolution he championed. He wrote Roosevelt about his role in presenting the resolution and stressed the non-governmental aspect of the proposal. He asked for a private meeting with the president upon his return and added that he had a private message from Danish King Christian X to relay.[83]

Watson's letter and his role in the ICC Congress hit the State Department like a left hook to the jaw. He received a note of "thanks for your letter regarding the activities of the Congress" from Secretary of State Cordell Hull who had received a similar letter as the one sent to Roosevelt from Watson.[84] The true feelings at the State Department were expressed in an internal memo from an assistant secretary during deliberations about how to respond to the industrialist.[85]

> It occurs to me that it is most unfortunate that Mr. Thomas J. Watson, as an American serving as the president of the International Chamber of Commerce, should have sponsored a resolution of this character. It may well be that this resolution will return to plague us at some future date.

Shortly after the Copenhagen Congress ended, Germany invaded Poland and World War 2 began. Stories of deportations and concentration camps appeared in papers such as the *New York Times*. The United States remained on the sidelines for two more years, but Watson increasingly felt the sting of bad publicity. Finally on June 6, 1940, after Belgium and the Netherlands had fallen before the German blitzkrieg, as German Panzers raced toward Paris, and as Luftwaffe bombers signaled the start of the Battle of Britain with raids upon coastal installations, Thomas J. Watson returned the Nazi medal to Hitler and sent a copy of the letter to the *New York Times*.[86]

Your Excellency:

At the time of the Congress of the International Chamber of Commerce in Berlin in June, 1937, at which I was elected President of that body, we discussed world peace and world trade. You made the statement that there must be no more wars, and that you were interested in developing trade with other nations. A few days later your representative, Dr. Hjalmar Schacht, in the name of the German Government, conferred upon me the decoration of Merit Cross of the German Eagle (With Star) in recognition of my efforts for world peace and world trade. I accepted this decoration on that basis and advised you that I would continue to cooperate in the interests of those causes. In view of the present policies of your Government, which are contrary to the causes for which I have been working and for which I received the decoration, I am returning it.

Yours truly,

Thomas J. Watson

The gesture of returning the medal drew widespread praise and quickly restored Watson's reputation in the United States. He was not the only prominent individual to espouse an admiration for Hitler's Germany in the 1930's or to receive a decoration from that state. The industrialists in the ICC were content to traipse after him to Berlin and to approve the resolution he proposed in Copenhagen. Henry Ford and Charles Lindbergh were two other American icons who accepted medals from Hitler. Unlike Ford, anti-Semitism did not enter into Watson's calculus for maintaining his ties with the Nazi regime.[87] His ego may have over-reached in thinking that he could achieve a reconciliation that would diminish the chance of war, but other than ego, his motivation was "just business." Fortunately for him, those business dealings did not receive public scrutiny until long after he was dead and his reputation secured.

The German Connection

IBM's German connection began in 1910 when Herman Hollerith licensed all off his patents to a German machine salesman named Willy Heidinger. Heidinger created the firm Deutsche Hollerith Maschinen Gesellschaft, called Dehomag for short, which leased Hollerith machines in Germany. Heidinger paid Hollerith a 10% markup on the machines he imported plus 25% of the royalties on the rentals.[88] When Flint purchased Hollerith's Tabulating Machines Company, the Dehomag arrangement was assumed by C-T-R. In 1922 hyperinflation in the Weimar Republic rendered Dehomag's revenues in marks virtually worthless. It could not pay the royalties it owed C-T-R. Heidinger faced bankruptcy and was forced to sell his company to Watson. The terms of the transfer gave C-T-R 90% of the shares in Dehomag. Heidinger retained the other 10% to maintain the appearance of joint German ownership, but he could only sell those shares back to C-T-R when he left the company.[89] Heidinger resented the deal he was forced to make and hated Watson, but the two men needed each other and endured a long contentious relationship.

By 1933 IBM had established subsidiary companies throughout Europe and other parts of the world. Dehomag was its most successful foreign venture and accounted for over half its overseas revenues.[90] German industry was in the forefront of utilizing Hollerith technology to expedite its accounting and inventory control operations and for improving its manufacturing processes. The German appetite for Hollerith machines only increased when the Nazis came to power in 1933.

Soon after establishing their Reich, the Nazis ordered a census in the largest German state, Prussia. Dehomag won the lucrative contract to supply the Reich with tabulating equipment for processing the census data. Business opportunity in Germany blossomed at the same time the risks and impediments became steeper. Watson was never averse to taking a risk when he sensed an opportunity. Despite calls for a boycott on German exports and attempts to topple the regime through sanctions, IBM made plans to build a one million dollar manufacturing plant in the Lichterfelde district of Berlin.[91]

Throughout much of this pre-war period IBM hid its involvement in Germany behind the name Dehomag. German Hollerith machines displayed the name Dehomag. Financial dealings with the German subsidiary followed a labyrinthine accounting trail of red and black ink designed to avoid taxes and German restrictions on money transfers. Dehomag profits found their way to New York early in the period through some accounting gimmickry that produced a paper loss for Dehomag and "royalty" payments to IBM.[92] By 1935 the royalty loophole disappeared and Dehomag profits were blocked from leaving the country. They had to be either reinvested in Dehomag, or German rental properties, or funneled to New York through subsidiaries in Switzerland, Holland, or Denmark where exemptions from the prohibition on transfer of profits existed.

During the thirties Watson was "on tour," visiting his widespread subsidiaries more often than a contemporary rock star playing the concert halls of the world. He would meet with business leaders, kings, and political leaders and never fail to write to Roosevelt about his conversations with the prominent among them. Almost always his trips took him to Germany where the three penny opera being performed between himself, Heidinger, and the economic machinery of the Reich required his greatest attention. Despite these difficulties, he made decisions that promoted his German interest at the expense of his subsidiaries in neighboring states. Watson met with Heidinger in October of 1933 and made a secret arrangement that granted Dehomag commercial authority to solicit business and deliver Hollerith technology outside of Germany in competition with IBM subsidiaries already operating in those territories.[93]

On January 8, 1934 Dehomag celebrated the opening of the Lichterfelde plant. Nazi dignitaries and Walter Jones, the manager of IBM European Operations gathered first in the Karstadhaus census complex where Hollerith machines were busily clanking out statistics on the Prussian census. Heidinger enthused in the setting and the company of dignitaries "I feel it almost a sacred action. I pray the blessing of heaven may rest upon this place." Then he proceeded to contrive a chilling metaphor to describe the "sacred action" that was click, clack, clanking away behind him.[94]

"The physician examines the human body and determines whether...all organs are working to the benefit of the entire organism. We [Dehomag] are very much like the physician in that we dissect, cell by cell, the German cultural body. We report every individual characteristic...on a little card. These are not dead cards, quite the contrary, they prove later on that they come to life when the cards are sorted at a rate of 25,000 per hour according to certain characteristics. These characteristics are grouped like the organs of our cultural body, and they will be calculated and determined each with the help of our calculating machine."

If Heidinger had stopped here, a visitor from New York may have been allowed to rationalize that this was just another business venture, but the committed Nazi went on to make clear that IBM was selling more than its machines. It was selling its soul.

"We are proud that we may assist in such task, a task that provides our nation's Physician with the material he needs for his examinations. Our Physician can then determine whether the calculated values are in harmony with the health of our people. It also means that if such is not the case, our Physician can take corrective procedures to correct the sick circumstances...Our characteristics are deeply rooted in our race. Therefore, we must cherish them like a holy shrine which we will—and must—keep pure. We have the deepest trust in our Physician and will follow his instructions in blind faith, because we know that he will lead our people to a great future. Hail to our German people and *der Führer!*"

From the census-complex the gathering motored to the Lichterfelde plant where two columns of Storm Troopers bracketed the walkway into the plant and military band added pomp to the ceremonies. Speeches by Jones, Heidinger, and German Labor Front representative Rudolph

Schmeer praised Watson, recounted the company history, reveled in the employment it would provide, and honored the man who was creating this new prosperity—Adolph Hitler. Jones wired a translation of all the speeches delivered at the ceremonies back to Watson, who wrote Heidinger a personal letter congratulating him on "the manner in which he conveyed his thoughts."[95]

IBM's commitment to Dehomag grew steadily with the rise of the Third Reich. In 1935 it expanded the Lichterfelde plant and opened other facilities around the country. As the demand for Dehomag's Hollerith machines grew, the appetite for punch cards became voracious. IBM held the patent on 80-column punch cards and was the only supplier. German census and industrial planning would have been crippled had IBM withheld their product. It had no such intention. An eight month supply of cards shipped from America was stored in the Lichterfelde plant and neighboring warehouses.[96] After 1935, card printing plants were built in Germany and Austria to accommodate the demand. As German troops pushed their way through the territories of Germany's neighbors, Dehomag followed along, sometimes pre-positioned, to tabulate the census, schedule the trains, and organize the logistics of the military and of the death camps.

IBM fought to retain ownership of its profitable subsidiary before, during, and after the war. During the war it lost operational control over Dehomag, but used its European headquarters in Geneva to safeguard IBM interests whenever ownership questions arose.[97] Heidinger died of illness in 1944. By then he had been removed from his position in the company by Hermann Fellinger, the custodian from the Reich Economics Ministry who had been given oversight of Dehomag and other IBM subsidiaries in the occupied countries. Fellinger guarded IBM interests as diligently as if he had been appointed by Watson. He performed his duties so well that he was allowed to continue in his role by the occupation authorities for some time after the fall of Hitler's Reich. The occupation forces needed the Holleriths to make their own inventory in a war ravished country filled with victims, collaborators, villains, and lost and stolen property. Questions of IBM's role in facilitating Hitler's program of mass murder and conquest never arose. By 1947 IBM regained control of its European affiliates and formed what would become IBM World Trade.

It wasn't until 2001 that IBM's activities in Nazi Germany were publicly aired in a book titled *IBM and the Holocaust* by Edwin Black. Black assembled evidence of IBM's involvement in a crime of premeditated mass murder as assiduously as a lawyer for the prosecution, but by the time of publication of the book, the main defendant had been dead for fifty years and the company had seen numerous leadership transitions since the Watsons were in charge. The company got little more than a kick in the shins from the bad publicity. The pain from a kick in the shins hurts for a while, but soon goes away, and the black and blue bruise it leaves fades over time.

IBM did not refute the charges made by Black, but questioned his methodology. In its first press release, concurrent with publication of the book, It summarized the history of the period in three short phrases: Dehomag supplied Hollerith equipment to Nazi Germany, not unlike the commercial activity of other foreign-owned companies; Dehomag came under control of the Nazis prior-to and during World War II, Watson returned his Hitler medal (presumably washing his hands of any company involvement with that government). It went on to cite the loss and destruction of records during the years of conflict. It asserted that all existing company documents relating to its involvement with Dehomag during the period in question were donated to research libraries at NYU and Hohenheim University in Stuttgart for scholarly inquiry.[98] In an addendum issued one year later it amplified its defense by quoting the review in the March 7, 2001 *New York Times Book Review* that Black "does not demonstrate that IBM bears some unique or decisive responsibility for the evil that was done." It backed up this testimony with an assertion that some unnamed, well-respected academic expert found the charges leveled by Black to be "implausible" and called the book "deplorable."[99]

The *Times* reviewer, Richard Bernstein, based his conclusion on two flimsy propositions: other businesses were doing the same thing, and the country that produced the V2 and the Messerschmitt would have developed the technology to identify and kill as many as six million people without IBM's help.[100] Neither absolve IBM of its responsibility; both are flawed. Bernstein creates a moral distinction between someone who sells rope and someone who uses the rope to hang people.[101] The metaphorical rope salesman here wasn't operating a hardware store. He was selling the rope to a particular customer. If the rope salesman were selling to a housewife, he would be safe to assume that the rope would end up as a clothesline. If he sold it to a hangman, he would likewise know the purpose for which it would be used. IBM was not like other companies in that its product was unique. It was not like a car that could be driven out of the showroom and never seen again. Hollerith machines had to be "programmed" for the specific job required. And they were not sold; they were leased and regularly maintained.

The second argument is equally facile. Before the Lichterfelde factory was built, Germany had to import machines from IBM in America. IBM had a near monopoly on the technology and was the only firm with a capacity in the depression years to produce machines in the volume Germany required. It also was the sole distributor of the 80-column punch card. If IBM had withheld its technology from the Reich, it would have had to start a whole new industry from scratch at a time when its financial position was weak and it needed infusions of trade and credit from abroad. It would have certainly pursued its plans of genocide by every means at its disposal, but it needed prompt censuses processed within months of completion to establish precise names and locations of its intended victims within Germany and the countries it annexed and conquered. Speculation that the Holocaust would have been so thorough and claimed as many victims without the technology acquired from IBM is merely that—speculation. Germany did produce the V2 and the fighter jet, but by the time it did its fate was already sealed. Thankfully it never did produce the atomic bomb.

If Bernstein's argument that "everybody was doing it" is used to absolve IBM, it then becomes a more general indictment of Capitalism, or at least the unregulated marketplace left to the guidance of the *Invisible Hand*. The *Invisible Hand* provides neither moral guidance nor special insight. It rewards the right choices and punishes the wrong ones, but provides no certainty what those right and wrong choices might be. In the context of the 1930s there was an expectation among many businessmen that Germany would dominate Europe, either through conquest or hegemony. To abandon Germany was to possibly forgo a future role in Europe. German mistreatment of the Jews in the period leading up to the invasion of Poland was extreme, but not unique. Other trading partners had terrible human rights records too. The United States itself practiced slavery and segregation for the first 200 years of its independence and engaged in campaigns of ethnic cleansing against its native population. Looking back from a distance of seventy-five years, Watson's behavior seems reprehensible. But with only an amoral *Invisible Hand* for guidance, he made at the time what he hoped was a smart business decision.

Watson described himself as an internationalist. "I am an American citizen. But in the IBM I am a world citizen, because we do business in 78 countries and they all look alike to me—every one of them."[102] Such a declaration reflects the credo of a salesman—a man traveling from one business client to the next, one business culture to another; ingratiating himself with his hosts, some of whom he would find personally compatible, others much less so; but always they were the face of a company with whom his sole focus was on making a sale. Watson was eclectic in his choice of heroes. He felt as close a bond with Mussolini as he did with Roosevelt. He saw in both men a strong leader with a plan and the conviction to see it carried out. He once said of Mussolini,

> "One thing which has greatly impressed me in connection with his leadership is the loyalty displayed by the people. To have the loyalty and cooperation of everyone means progress—and ultimate success for a nation or an individual business...we should pay tribute to Mussolini for establishing this spirit of loyal support and cooperation[103]"

He may have been speaking of himself and the culture he established at IBM—the songs, the signs, the ubiquitous pictures of the leader, and the autocratic rule of one man. Ultimately that culture failed him in his dealings with Dehomag and the Third Reich. There were no second thoughts, no independent voices raised, no brakes applied. IBM had a mission to dominate the world of data processing that it pursued with a single-minded purpose.

War and Growth

When Watson joined C-T-R he bargained for a deal that would pay him 5% of the corporate profits after dividends were paid. At the time it did not seem like much. The company had no profit and meager prospects. By 1935 that situation had changed. Newspapers reporting the ten highest paid executives in the country listed Watson at number one with a salary of $365, 358. It was over $150,000 more than the salary paid to either Walter Chrysler or Alfred Sloan of General Motors. The papers dubbed Watson the $1000 a day man at a time when many people never earned that much in a year.[104] Watson was by no measure the wealthiest man in the country. He did not own the company like Ford or have a substantial block of stock like Sloan and Chrysler. But the publicity the story generated brought letters asking for help from old school friends in Painted Post and former colleagues at NCR whom the Depression had battered and in some cases broken. Watson was generous to many of them, sometimes giving more charity than was warranted, but a letter appealing for a job from an unemployed Hugh Chalmers went unanswered.[105]

Watson relished publicity about himself when it promoted IBM. He cultivated publishers like Henry Luce and Frank Gannett who responded with often laudatory stories about the technology coming out of his lab, the gamble he was taking during the Depression, and the benefits he was providing for his employees. He made it a mission to be reported in the papers meeting with foreign leaders and hosting benefits for the opera and the Metropolitan Museum of Art. He promoted his company through himself. The news about his salary was not part of the message he wanted told. It set him up for negative stories from detractors. After he accepted the Nazi medal he learned how quickly his image could change. He began seeing his name appear in an unflattering context at the moment he was pouring a lot of money into establishing a pavilion at the New York World's Fair of 1939 and 40. Watson envisioned the Fair as an opportunity to identify IBM with its Disneyesque version of the future. For his contribution, IBM was given one special day at the Fair each year. As the 1940 IBM Day approached, The publicity was not about the company and its approaching date at the Fair, but about its Chairman and the Nazi medal he had accepted three years earlier.

Once again, as in Dayton years earlier, an event bringing misfortune to others brought Watson praise for his leadership in a time of crisis. IBM Day in 1940 was to be a huge celebration of the company's success and a demonstration that it was now ready to walk with the giants like Ford and General Motors. Watson invited every IBM employee and their spouse to attend the Fair on his dime. He would provide the transportation, lodging, meals, and Fair tickets at a cost to the company of one million dollars.[106] He took out full-page newspaper advertisements to publicize the event. IBM chartered twelve trains to bring employees into New York for the day at the Fair.[107] Two of the trains made it safely into the city. A third train made a brief stop at Port Jervis, a town on the state line with New Jersey. While the third train was stopped at Port Jervis, a fourth rounded a blind bend of track, not anticipating that it was blocked in front. It was unable to come to a full stop and plowed into the rear car of the stationary train. Fortunately nobody was killed, but many were injured—thirty-five seriously.[108] Watson jumped into a limousine, scooped up his daughter Jane and his right-hand man Fred Nichol and raced to Port Jervis. Watson and his daughter and Nichol visited the more seriously injured who were crowded into two small hospitals that were overwhelmed by the number of casualties. He called down to New York to arrange for doctors to be brought to Port Jervis and arranged for another train to bring those stranded in the small town into New York where medical attention was arranged for those needing it.[109] Just as he had when he organized relief trains to deliver supplies to the flood victims in Dayton, Watson reacted instinctively, efficiently, and generously in the face of a crisis. His handling of the situation also brought Watson the kind of media attention he relished.

While IBM was celebrating in New York, Hitler was overrunning Belgium and the Netherlands. Neville Chamberlain was out; Churchill was in; World War II was on in earnest. The United States remained on the sidelines for another year and a half, but preparations for war were starting. On July 8, 1940 Watson called in the press and announced that he was making available to the Federal Government the manufacturing facilities of IBM for the manufacture of essential war materials. He would freeze his salary at the 1940 level and would make only 1.5% profit on the sale of all war related goods. That profit would be placed in a fund to support the families of IBM servicemen killed or wounded in conflict.[110]

Watson made a commendable patriotic offer for which he was deservedly praised. In committing his company resources to the war effort, however, he was also hatching plans for IBM to win a bigger share of the peace to follow. Like other industrialists at the time, he didn't plan to convert his manufacturing facilities in Endicott to the making of purely military goods. He would find or build factory space someplace else, and aggressively seek war-related contracts to provide work for enough people to double his workforce. The difference between Watson and the others was that Watson didn't intend to shrink the company back to its previous size when the war ended.[111]

Watson was again taking a gamble that risked the viability of his company. The new hires would be put through a brief training period and ingrained in the IBM culture. To let them go when the military contracts expired would create a rift in the fabric of that culture. They were to become part of the IBM family. To maintain the company at double its size would require it to double its commercial market in an economy that everyone expected would enter a post-war recession. Watson had a strategy to accomplish it, but he would also need luck.

IBM only rented its machines. When a customer upgraded to a new machine, the old one was brought back to the plant, reconditioned, and leased to another customer. IBM profits depended upon keeping its machines in circulation. Watson planned to cut back production of commercial data processing machines and spare parts during the period of national sacrifice to meet just the minimum needs of its current customers. New orders would go to the military and customers with a war-related priority. Production of military hardware would fill the new factory space and the residual capacity of the Endicott plants. The research laboratory in Endicott would be put to work designing a new generation of machines that would meet the pent up demand for data processing machines from commercial customers at the end of the war. To attract new customers and avoid flooding its traditional market with leased machines returned by the government at war's end, IBM would go after the small businesses it had previously ignored. The returned machines would be geared down to a lower performance level and offered at a lower rental price to small businesses and to businesses in war-ravaged Europe that could not afford the standard models.[112]

In the fall of 1940 IBM got its first War Department order to produce 100 machine guns a month. The company purchased 215 acres overlooking the Hudson River just south of Poughkeepsie, NY to build factory space for filling its military orders.[113] By March of 1941 the two small converted food processing buildings on the site housed 250 workers turning out the first order of 100 guns a month.[114] By 1942 the United States was in the war and virtually all of company business was war-related. IBM built and expanded factory space in Poughkeepsie, mostly at government expense, as new war orders poured in. In addition to machine guns, IBM produced aircraft cannons, three-inch tank guns, bomb fuses, bomb sights, fire control instruments for Navy planes, and parts for other military contractors.[115] The military had a huge need for tabulating equipment and punch cards. It consumed virtually all of the punch card equipment IBM produced. The company grew rapidly during the first years of the war. Its workforce increased from 12,656 people in 1940 to 21,251 by 1943.[116]

The new workers were integrated into a company known for its generous benefits. In the late twenties Watson matched and even exceeded the benefits George F. Johnson provided his workers in the factories next door. IBM matched the salaries the larger shoe company paid. Johnson had a golf course for his workers, so IBM built one too. When company revenues took off after the Social Security Act was signed, Watson became an industry pioneer in providing a two week paid vacation for his people. His workers repaid his benevolence with their loyalty. When the United States entered the war, Watson announced that every serviceman from the company would continue to receive 25% of his salary while on duty and have a guaranteed job waiting when he returned.[117] The gesture cemented the bond his workers felt for their company, but it meant that postwar business had to provide revenues to absorb four thousand returning servicemen into an already expanded workforce.

The Prince

As the war dragged on Watson approached his 70th birthday. The old salesman was running a company that had become bigger and more geographically diverse, but had nothing to sell. It had one customer that offered contracts for which the company had to bid. In addition to the tabulating machines that were the heart and soul of his business, the company was producing armaments about which he knew little. For thirty years, Watson had been a virtual one man show in the management of IBM, but now the responsibility was becoming too much for one elderly man to handle alone.

Watson always planned for his son Tom to succeed him, but Tom was in the air force and not yet ready to take over so significant a role. Watson's right hand man, Fred Nichol, was in the words of the poet "not Prince Hamlet nor meant to be, but an attendant lord." For most of the thirty years that Watson ran IBM, Nichol was in an office close by to tidy up the cluttered affairs of his boss. After thirty years of following in the wake of his turbulent leader, Nichol was mentally exhausted and required a leave of absence that became extended. IBM had no leadership pyramid or usual chain of responsibility, only a cluster of people around Watson. The people closest to him in that circle can best be described as competent assistants, not dynamic leaders. To find the man to assume the job of managing the day-to-day operations of the company, Watson had to look deep into his organization and find the 38 year old Charley Kirk.

Kirk was gregarious, competent, and held in esteem by his workers. He would have been an ideal choice to lead the company if Tom Junior was not reading for the part. Young Tom was, in many respects, Prince Hamlet—haunted not by his father's ghost, but by his overbearing presence. He lashed out in angry shouting matches with his father only to lapse into periods of depression so deep he could not get out of bed and attend his classes. Tom was bright, but not in a way that is measured by the yardstick used in academia. He barely escaped from prep school with a passing grade. When his father tried to get him into Princeton, he was told by the Dean of Admissions that his son was a "predetermined failure."[118] The senior Watson called in a favor from the President of Brown University and got Tom admitted there. During his whole undergraduate experience, Tom felt the presence of the university president looking over his shoulder and reporting to his father the ups and downs of his academic progress.[119]

After graduation in 1937, Tom joined IBM as a salesman, and spent an unhappy three years trying to elude his father's shadow and prove himself worthy of the role he had been predestined to play. That proved impossible. Every recognition he received was due to his name, not his achievement. Every customer he visited received him as his father's son, not his company's salesman. When his father moved some of the company's biggest accounts into his sales district so that he qualified for the 100 Percent Club, he had had enough.[120] During his college days he took up flying. Soaring above the clouds in a machine under his own control was the only place where he could feel free of his father. When the United States prepared for war in 1940, he seized an opportunity to get out from under his father's shadow and joined the Air Force.

In the Air Force the brooding young prince found his own wings. He was assigned as an aide-de-camp to Major General Follett Bradley, Commander of the First Air Force. One of Bradley's missions was to arrange the delivery of American made planes to the Russians. Bradley and Tom Watson made several trips into Russia. On one of the missions Tom was put in charge of the flight crew. He badgered and blistered and micromanaged them in the same way his father often treated his managers and his family. The men resented him and told him they would rather be given a combat assignment than another mission with him. He was alert enough to realize he was treating his men the same way that his father controlled him. He backed off and allowed the men to take more responsibility for their work. Two weeks later the crew volunteered to fly another mission into Russia under him.[121] Bradley provided the kind of support his father was never able to give. He gave Tom the responsibility and encouragement to build his self-confidence and overcome the insecurity that plagued him from childhood. When the war ended, Tom contemplated a career as an airline pilot or owner of his own airline company. The pull toward IBM, however, was still there. His father realized his old approach would only drive his son away and used more subtle means to try to deromanticize Tom's notions about flying.[122] Faced with a difficult decision about his future Tom turned to the one person who could offer the fatherly advice he desperately wanted—General Bradley. When he told Bradley about his plans to pursue a career in the airline industry, Bradley looked at him and said "Really! But I thought you would go back and run IBM." Young Thomas J. Watson, Jr. then asked Bradley the question that had troubled him throughout his young life. "General Bradley, do you think I can?" "Of course," the General replied.[123]

When Tom returned to IBM, Charley Kirk was playing the role of the Prince. Tom was his understudy. He could not accept the role or the thought that Kirk, only eight years his senior, could block his ascent to his hereditary throne for as many as twenty two more years. If the elderly Watson were to suddenly die, Kirk might be the choice of the Board of Trustees to succeed him. The fact that Kirk had the love and respect of the workforce that Tom had yet to earn only made his resentment stronger. The two men were from different worlds. Kirk rose from a working class background in Ohio to become a factory manager in Endicott. Tom came from prep schools, the ivy league, and the country club set. Tom regarded his rival as too crude and uncultured to represent a great company like IBM.[124] For two years the pair feuded and tried to upstage one another, until one day in 1947 Tom stormed into his father's office and threatened to quit unless something was done to change the situation.[125] Watson decided to send the pair and their wives to an ICC meeting in Switzerland and an extended tour of IBM facilities in Europe where Tom would introduce Kirk to the people he knew there. While the pair was away, Watson would have time to think about a solution to the problem. He may have hoped that the extended time away from work together, joined by their wives, might reduce the friction between the two men, but the mutual animosity only grew deeper. Then tragedy once again intervened to relieve Watson from a difficult situation. After attending a banquet thrown for the visiting Americans in Lyon, France, Charley Kirk suffered a massive heart attack and died. The path was now clear for Tom to ascend to the company throne, but the old man was not yet ready to stand aside and let him have it.

The Watson's had three other children besides Tom—two daughters named Jane and Helen, and a younger son named Arthur, but who the family and close friends called Dick. Dick Watson experienced the same angry outbursts and scoldings from his father as Tom, but unlike his older brother who deflected the rage right back at his father, Dick absorbed it and said nothing.[126] Dick's sense of insecurity was only heightened by seeing the defiance of his older brother compared to his own resignation in the face of his father's fury. Dick compiled the same mediocre academic resume as Tom, but managed to get into Yale and showed proficiency for language acquisition that would serve him well in his future role with IBM.[127] Before the senior Watson died he established IBM World Trade as an independently operated arm of the company and gave his second son the job of running it.

Watson never considered a company role for his daughters. His eldest daughter Jane had the personality and brains to be an outstanding leader,[128] but her father and the society of the time steered her in another direction. Professional women at IBM up until the war years had to leave the company when they married. The policy had been in effect since the founding of the company, but was justified by one IBM executive during the Depression years who stated that once the woman married it should be the responsibility of her husband to provide for the family, and she should not be bringing home a second income at the expense of some unemployed man.[129] Watson did not envision his daughter taking the company vows and leading a cloistered existence within its embrace.

Watson began hiring women to assume positions of responsibility in 1935 after a friend of Jane's challenged him to explain why there were no career paths for women in American industry. Watson knew of no good reason why not and the first class of women recruits arrived at the IBM school in Endicott in the summer of 1935.[130] The career paths would only be in the fields of customer relations and personnel, but few other industries provided women a path for advancement or as much as a foot in the door. The IBM school graduated 67 men and 25 women that summer and dispatched them to field offices around the country.[131] Many of the managers in those offices did not share Watson's enthusiasm for employing women in positions of responsibility and refused to accept the women sent to them. Watson told them if they didn't accept the women, they didn't get anybody and fired all of the men in the class except for the few that their superiors were able to protect.[132] One woman hired later, Ruth Leach, was promoted to the position of Vice President in 1943. She became the first woman to reach that level in IBM and one of the first in corporate America.

When the war ended in 1945 the economy spluttered briefly and then soared ahead on the tail wind of the pent up demand for consumer products that were unavailable during the war. Watson's gamble once again paid off. The company was bigger and aggressively expanding its sales force into every corner of the land. But when the younger Watson joined the company he saw signs of deterioration and areas of vulnerability. The company was growing old around its aged leader. Nichol and other key executives had retired or left and their positions were either left unfilled or filled by people Tom Junior considered less able.[133] More seriously, the younger Watson viewed the research laboratory that was the pride of his father and the envy of the industry during the Depression years as stale, filled with older men whose wizardry in building the electromechanical machines of their era had little relevance for designing the electronic calculating machines that were emerging from the innovative spurt caused by the war.[134] Watson won his bet on the post-war economy, but misjudged the way the playing field shifted during the years of conflict. He anticipated that after the war no other company in his field could match the research funding that IBM would have to accelerate the introduction of new products into the marketplace, but with the advent of the Cold War, government money continued to pour into research and fund projects that fathered commercial products once the new technology matured.

World War 2 propelled the world into the Atomic Age, the start of the Space Age, and the birth of the Computer Age. IBM came to dominate the first four decades of the Computer Age, but took very tentative steps to get its feet wet before it was ready to dive into that pool. It got its first taste of things to come when it teamed with Harvard researcher Howard Aiken in 1939 on a project that was a precursor of the modern computer, but more properly an extension of IBM punch card technology. IBM became involved with Harvard when Watson dispatched one of his executives, George Phillips, to the campus to meet with deans and faculty to determine whether the company might establish a relationship with the Cambridge, Massachusetts university similar to the one that it enjoyed with Columbia.[135] While on campus, Phillips was approached by Aiken who told him he could build a super calculating machine out of accounting machine parts with additional work and wiring that would far exceed the speed of any existing calculating machine. On hearing Phillips' report Watson was unimpressed but decided to commit an initial $15,000 to the project and provided Aiken with laboratory space in Endicott.[136] Clair Lake was assigned to work with him on the project. The machine dubbed the Mark 1 was finished and ready for testing in 1943. It was described by Tom Junior as consisting of "2 tons of IBM tabulating machines synchronized on a single axle, like looms in a textile mill."[137] The rather ugly looking contraption was encased inside a cover designed by the art deco artist Norman Bel Geddes. It stood 8 feet tall; reached a length of 51 feet; and cost IBM $500,000 plus the use of its lab and engineers.[138] It was carted up to Harvard and readied for its August 6, 1944 introduction to the public.

Watson saw no practical value in the Mark 1 other than forging a relationship with Harvard and garnering publicity for IBM. On August 5th he and Jeannette took a train up to Boston expecting to be greeted by Harvard dignitaries who would have a limo waiting to escort them to their hotel. Instead only the IBM branch manager was waiting with his small Chevy and a copy of the *Boston Post* carrying a banner headline "Automatic Brain for Harvard."[139] IBM was not mentioned in the article as a co-inventor or the financial backer. Harvard had jumped the gun with its press release without consulting IBM. The Mark 1 got the publicity Watson craved, but his company did not get any of it. A furious Watson returned to New York and ordered his engineers to build a better machine than Aiken's and he gave them eight months in which to do it. IBM entered the computer age out of revenge.

While IBM was assisting Aiken to build the Mark 1, it became aware of a more ambitious project underway at the University of Pennsylvania. Two young engineers, J. Presper Eckert and John Mauchly, with support from the Army, were building the first all electronic computer. The machine was called the Electrical Numerical Integrator and Computer (ENIAC). Tom Junior and Kirk journeyed to Philadelphia to examine the ENIAC shortly after Tom rejoined the company in 1946 and came away unimpressed by it. In an unairconditioned room, unbearably hot from the 18,000 vacuum tubes at the heart of the processing unit, the pair of IBMers watched the ENIAC compute trajectories for artillery shells to hit a distant target. Both doubted there was a commercial market for a machine that was expensive, unwieldy, and unreliable.[140] Shortly afterward Mauchly and Eckert offered IBM an opportunity to own the rights to the ENIAC after they lost the backing of the university in a dispute over patents. Watson offered to hire the pair and provide them with a computing laboratory, but they wanted to form their own company and sell it to IBM along with their services. Watson told them no deal and then expressed relief when they left that he had not agreed to buy them out. He told his listeners that "This guy Mauchly wears those loud socks. I wouldn't want him in my business anyway."[141]

Mauchly and Eckert formed their own company and received backing from two of IBM's biggest customers, the U. S. Census Bureau and Prudential Insurance, among others for a commercial machine whose acronym was UNIVAC. That news jolted IBM into the age of electronic computing.

Bryce and his team of Endicott engineers met Watson's deadline and built a machine they called the Selective Sequence Electronic Calculator (SSEC) that combined 12,500 vacuum tubes and 21,400 mechanical relays into a gigantic hybrid that was more than twice the size and more than 250 times faster than the Mark 1,[142] but it was still just an expensive curiosity with no commercial market. It became the centerpiece in another IBM million-dollar advertising effort. Watson had it installed on the ground floor of the IBM corporate headquarters building on Madison Avenue in full view of curious passers-by, and provided researchers free access to its use.

Young Tom had not been impressed by his first inspection of the ENIAC but he was convinced that electronics was the future of data processing, and unless IBM fully embraced this future it would fade into obsolescence. Tom was much more impressed a few weeks after he returned from Philadelphia with a machine that one of the IBM engineers built in his spare time while the company was focusing on what Watson determined were the five most important products to emerge from the company at the end of the war. The machine was fed by a card reader but used vacuum tubes internally to perform additions and multiplications for calculating payroll information. Watson Junior urged his father to rush the machine to market, and when the IBM 603 Electronic Multiplier was introduced in 1946 it received a surprisingly receptive response.[143] Somewhat embarrassed by the limitations of the machine that went almost directly from the inventor's basement to the showroom floor, Watson pushed his engineers to build a more complete machine that could also divide and be programmed to solve some equations. Soon the 603 was superseded by the IBM 604 Electronic Calculating Punch. It proved to be a big success despite a glaring flaw embodied in the last word of its name—Punch.

The 604 used a card reader and card punch for its input and output. The electronics inside worked ten times faster than the punch card technology could feed it data.[144] It spent 90 % of its time sitting idle. The ENIAC used magnetic tape for its data delivery that worked much faster and stored its information more compactly. Watson stubbornly held on to the IBM card as the main repository for an institution's vital data. He believed that businesses and other customers would not trust this information to a medium as vulnerable as magnetic tape. Sagging beneath the weight of floors filled with card boxes, many of IBM's biggest customers were telling his son the opposite message.[145]

Watson Senior – The Last Act

Watson was over 70 when the war ended. His friend Franklin Roosevelt was dead, and he didn't warm to his successor, Harry Truman, for some of the same reasons Tom did not find common ground with Charley Kirk. Watson was less conspicuous on the world stage but still active behind it. After Roosevelt's passing, the one man that he saw capable of filling the void was General Dwight D. Eisenhower. Watson worked with Eleanor Roosevelt and her sons to try and convince Eisenhower to run for president as a Democrat, but Eisenhower was not interested and did not feel it was right for a career soldier to hold high political office.[146] He was not interested in becoming Army Chief of Staff or in running a business, but he was looking for a way to continue to serve his country.

Watson served as vice chairman of the Columbia University Board of Trustees and the university was seeking a replacement for its retiring president. Watson convinced the board that Eisenhower would add more prestige to the name of the university than someone from academia and worked to convince a skeptical General that Columbia was the right choice for him. Perhaps because Eisenhower's brother Milton was president of Kansas State University at the time, the idea of running a college began to intrigue him and he yielded to Watson's persuasion and accepted the position. During the two years the former general served as Columbia's president, Watson became his confidant. He introduced him to other businessmen and New York society.[147] In 1952 when Eisenhower decided to run for President as a Republican, Watson stepped into the background and did not betray his party loyalty, but remained a friend and confidant of Eisenhower over the last three years of his life.

On election night in 1952 the pundits were predicting a close race between Eisenhower and his Democratic opponent Adlai Stevenson. By this time televisions dominated the living rooms of middle class America. This would be the first election night television coverage to reach a wide audience. CBS decided to spice its district-by-district, state-by-state count of the numbers by adding an analyst that would interpret the numbers and see through the trends to give its anchor, Walter Cronkite, an early insight into who was going to win. This was no ordinary analyst, but what Cronkite referred to as the Electronic Brain—UNIVAC. The thing sitting in the studio with Cronkite was not even the real UNIVAC, but a wooden facade with blinking lights to look like the real thing. The UNIVAC relaying its wisdom back to Cronkite via a teletype machine hidden in its dummy was back in Mauchly and Eckert's lab in Philadelphia. CBS told its audience the truth and stationed veteran reporter Charles Collingswood in the Philadelphia lab. Eckert and the man who programmed the UNIVAC to interpret election data, Max Woodbury, were on hand to explain to Collingswood how the machine worked. At about 8:30 P.M. Eastern time UNIVAC typed out on its printer "It is awfully early, but I will go out on a limb. UNIVAC predicts: Eisenhower 438 electoral votes, Stevenson 93." Unable to print more than double digit numbers, it put the odds at 00 to 1 for an Eisenhower win.[148]

The prediction seemed unbelievable and was not reported by CBS. The public relations stunt for CBS and UNIVAC's parent company,

Remington Rand seemed like it was turning into a fiasco. Woodbury went back and redid his formulas and UNIVAC put the new odds at 8:7 for an Eisenhower victory. This tally was reported by Cronkite at 9:15. In the meantime TV sets were switching from NBC to CBS as more people became aware of and curious about the Electronic Brain that was predicting election results. One of those TV sets that was glued to CBS was located in a luxury apartment in Manhattan where Thomas Watson Sr., eagerly awaiting news of his friend's election, suffered the indignity of seeing that the men basking in that triumph were Eckert and his old business rival James Rand.

Woodbury double checked his new set of instructions and found an error. When that error was corrected UNIVAC again forecast the original Eisenhower landslide. Election results were now confirming the accuracy of the 8:30 prediction and CBS admitted to its audience that UNIVAC had correctly predicted the final result long before the network was willing to trust it. James Rand had pulled off a public relations coup worthy of the old master. The name UNIVAC became synonymous with computer in popular discourse. IBM found itself in the unfamiliar role of chasing a rival, trying to catch up.

The election night embarrassment rattled the walls of IBM with the force of a 7.0 magnitude earthquake, but IBM already had its challenger to UNIVAC waiting in the wings. Shortly after the outbreak of the Korean War in 1950, the United States was desperate to re-mobilize and increase its defense spending. IBM sent representatives to the Pentagon and defense laboratories to assess their needs and heard their pleas for more computing power. When they returned, the IBM team conveyed the desires of the people with whom they met to Tom Watson and proposed a bold solution. Instead of building computers configured for each specific task, as was the custom of the day, they recommended that IBM build a general purpose computer that would serve most of the needs of their individual clients. To preserve patent rights, they proposed that IBM build the machine they dubbed the Defense Calculator itself and not seek government funding. They estimated that building the prototype would cost three million dollars and the whole program would cost three or four times that.[149]

Changing of the Guard and the Birth of the Digital Age

Tom Watson was eager to push IBM headlong into electronics and was receptive to the proposal, but the company had amassed a debt of $85 million, the largest corporate debt in the country.[150] The debt was a symptom of the company's success, not its troubles. IBM rented its machines rather than selling them. When the post-war demand for IBM equipment soared, the company had to borrow at 2% interest to pay the cost of building new machines that would eventually return monthly rents that more than covered the debt repayments. Old Thomas Watson agonized over the size of this debt. Young Thomas better appreciated that the debt was necessary for making the company more profitable in the longer term. He was not afraid to go deeper into debt to fund a project he saw as being vital for the company's future, but before he proposed it to his father, he told his people to figure out what the rental fee for the new machine would be and go back to the people in the defense labs and see what the market for it would be. They determined a rental fee of $8000 per month and came back with the news that they found 11 takers for the Defense Calculator and the possibility of another ten.[151] With a market for the machine in hand, Tom went to his father and received permission to go ahead with the project.

As development continued, the initial rental estimate doubled, but the commitments from customers remained firm. Work proceeded at a brisk pace in the Poughkeepsie facilities. The first Defense Calculator rolled off the production line in December, 1952—one month after the election night triumph of UNIVAC. Watson renamed the new machine the IBM 701 and readied it for its introduction to the public in April, 1953. The SSEC was removed from the lobby of the IBM building on Madison Avenue, and the space was readied for the new arrival. John von Neumann, William Shockley, and J. Robert Oppenheimer were among the scientific elite on hand at the product introduction ceremony to underline the contribution the 701 would provide to American science. Oppenheimer called the 701 "a tribute to the mind's high splendor."[152] One of the most distinctive features of the 701 was that it was housed in separate compartments, each about the size of a large refrigerator, that could be wheeled through a door and rapidly assembled in a customer's intended space. This feature was prominently displayed to the people on the street stopping to gaze through the windows at the latest technological wonder. It proved a popular selling point for the 701. With the unveiling of the 701, IBM took a big stride in reestablishing its dominance of the data processing market.

Watson Senior still ruled as company Chairman, but young Tom was named President in 1951 and the 604 and 701 were the calling cards that announced his role at IBM now corresponded to his title. The transition from father to son also signified that the company's vital core had moved from Endicott to Poughkeepsie. Old Tom's men still held sway in Endicott, and punch card technology was still a large part of the firm's business there. The people young Tom hired were concentrated in Poughkeepsie building computers. Young Tom never enjoyed his time in Endicott and enthused about the atmosphere in the Poughkeepsie labs. Watson Junior recounted in his memoirs that:

> "You only had to visit Poughkeepsie to get a sense of the fundamental change taking place in engineering. Our laboratory back in Endicott had always felt to me like a stuffy museum—a place where ideas were scarce and had to be jealously guarded and preserved. But Poughkeepsie was wide open—the ideas seemed as abundant as air, and you had the impression of a limitless future. The old Endicott inventors worked in isolation from one another; in Poughkeepsie everybody believed that collaboration was the only way to move a complicated electronics project along. There was tremendous imagination and inventiveness everywhere you looked."[153]

The son's time in Endicott was colored by the unhappy experiences during his first stint working for dad. In the same autobiography he shows little personal attachment to the legacy established there. He wrote:

> Endicott is a little river town in the western part of New York State, not far from where Dad got his start selling sewing machines. In winter the weather is perpetually gray and damp, and whenever the wind blew over the

tannery of the giant Endicott-Johnson Shoe Company, all of Endicott stank. Yet I think to Dad it was the most beautiful place on earth. I spent two miserable winters there in 1937 and 1938."[154]

With the introduction of the 701 and the follow up arrival of the 702, designed for the business environment, IBM was back in the race to capture the bulk of the potentially huge data processing market. Two events propelled it into a lead that would continue to widen. The first leg of the competition between IBM and Remington Rand in 1952 to go IBM's way was winning the contract to develop computers for the SAGE project. After the Russians tested an atomic bomb in 1949, the Air Force awarded a contract to MIT to design an air defense system to detect the presence and position of potential Russian bombers. MIT scientists designed the parameters of the system, then sought candidates to supply the computers to meet the requirements they had established. The candidates included the defense contractor Raytheon and vacuum tube suppliers RCA and Sylvania, along with Remington Rand and IBM.[155] Remington hired retired General Leslie Groves, the director of the Manhattan Project, to deliver their pitch. IBM won the contract because it had the human and physical resources to deliver a product most promptly. When SAGE was conceived, computers were in their infancy. Programming was done by toggling switches or plugging wires into a panel like at a telephone exchange. Once the computer was programmed to run a particular job, data was entered, the processor performed its functions, and an answer was spit out. SAGE required computers to run continuously at a time when vacuum tubes burned out more frequently than cheap light bulbs and to handle interactively the data of planes entering and leaving the monitored air space.

IBM delivered 40 SAGE computers before the program was terminated. SAGE turned out to be a piece of Cold War folly that was obsolete by the time it was operational. Sputnik was the final blow it received. Intercontinental missiles and satellite delivery systems rendered a defense against aircraft useless. But for IBM, the program provided a valuable experience working on technology that was far in advance of the computer systems in use at the time.

The second piece of fortune that landed in IBM's lap came courtesy of a fumble by Remington Rand. *Time* planned to run a story on automation and sent a reporter over to the Remington Rand building in Manhattan. Remington was not very welcoming, so the discouraged reporter stopped in to the headquarters of the other computer company located in that part of town.[156] She was promptly directed to the office of Tom Watson and a protracted series of interviews between *Time* reporters and IBM executives resulted in a lengthy cover story about the company and its products. The face of Thomas Watson Junior appeared on coffee tables and newsstands across the country in March of 1955 with a robotic characterization of the devices that went Clink, Clank, Think posing impishly behind him.

IBM had regained its footing and reestablished its public image. In 1956 Eisenhower again defeated Stevenson in the Presidential Election, but this time IBM was in the television studio forecasting the margin of victory in the race.

Watson named his son President in 1951, effective January 1952, but he still sat in the big wood-paneled suite on the top floor. He was like a child with an electronic toy that he had assembled and positioned and set in motion—now able to sit back and watch its activity unfold, but still there to give a nudge when things got stuck or pieces moved in unintended directions. With Tom established in title, if not yet in full possession of the role, of president, Watson had one last major act to perform: establish a position for his other son, Dick.

In 1950, Watson, four years short of his 80th birthday, made two lengthy trips to Europe and South America to set up IBM World Trade as an autonomous subsidiary of the parent company. He set up a system where IBM factories in each of the larger countries would make certain parts for other IBM facilities as well as for themselves and earn foreign exchange credits to import the components they did not produce themselves from elsewhere in the company. Plants in each country assembled only the finished machines for their domestic market. Watson's version of an IBM common market, established ten years before the real thing, enabled the relatively small European plants to satisfy their internal demand and avoid the high tariff barriers in place after the war.[157]

He created a truly global company from national units stitched together by common needs and a transnational IBM culture. He recruited foreign nationals, mostly aristocrats who had lost property and privilege in the war but were still well connected to people of influence, to manage the operations in each country.[158] IBM in France and Germany would be as French or German as any other company operating in those lands. Frenchmen would sell to other Frenchmen; Germans to other Germans; Brits to other Brits. The old "internationalist" told people that the United States contained only 6% of the world's people. He wanted to sell to the other 94% as well.[159]

In 1948 he had dragged a reluctant Dick and his new wife Nancy with him on a two month tour of IBM facilities in Europe. Watson kept Dick at his side throughout this "honeymoon" and introduced him to old European colleagues as his assistant. Everyone knew that this ready-made, fully-furnished subsidiary was being fashioned as a coming of age present for the young "assistant." In 1953, the old emperor split his realm and made his second son the ruler of its Eastern half.

On May 8, 1956, Watson called his son Tom into his office and made him the Chief Executive Officer of the firm. The 82-year old man, for whom IBM was like a vital organ, was aware of life slipping away and was preparing for his departure. There was a last nostalgic trip to Endicott with Jeannette to preside at the sports trophy dinner on the 18th of May and a brief board meeting and honorary luncheon on the 22nd. He showed up briefly one last time six days later[160] then retreated to his home in New Canaan, Connecticut where he died on June 19, 1956.

System 360

The company Watson bequeathed his sons continued to grow rapidly. By 1960 seventy percent of the computers installed in America were produced by IBM.[161] The work force grew from just over 21,000 at the end of the war to 85,588 in 1957 when the company revenues passed the billion dollar mark for the first time.[162] The company financed this rapid growth by running a debt of $300 million.[163] To maintain its rate of growth without further increasing this debt, it issued new offerings of stock—the corporate version of printing money.

By the early sixties IBM had distanced itself from its old rival Remington Rand, but faced a new challenge from two companies larger than itself—RCA and General Electric. Tom Watson Junior went all in on a gamble to secure the market before any new challenger could gain a foothold. IBM would build a family of six computers ranging from the smallest that would rent for $2000 a month to the high end model renting for $115,000 a month.[164] All of the machines would be compatible with the software and peripherals produced alongside the new computers. Six different engineering teams were put to work designing and building the different models. Other engineers and technicians were fashioning the disk drives, tape drives, printers, and terminals that all had to be able to connect with each of the processors. The most challenging piece of the project proved to be writing the software which stretched to over a million lines of code. In addition, the company realized that much of the processing power wired into the circuit boards holding the tubes and transistors in their earlier models would soon shrink into the integrated circuits drawing interest from researchers in labs around the world. To insure its own hold on the essential functionality of its product, IBM decided to produce the components for the new system itself.

Plans for System 360 came out of a late December, 1961 strategy session. A group of managers and engineers from divisions geared to competing with each other were brought together and charged with developing a bold strategy for spurring growth at a time when the steep slope it had maintained for several decades was beginning to plateau. To speed their effort, the group was booked into a motel in Connecticut two weeks before Christmas and told not to return until they agreed on a proposal to present to the company's executive committee.[165] A more cautious management would have weighed the risks in backing such a plan and charted a safer course, but IBM and its long-time leader had never steered away from opportunity because the course was risky. Tom Junior inherited his father's gene for taking the tide at its crest and following it to fame and fortune.

The cost to IBM to produce System 360 ballooned to over five billion dollars.[166] At one point the heavily indebted company was forced to "print more money" and issue another $370 million stock offering just to meet operating expenses and payroll.[167] Driving expenses higher was the speed with which the project needed to be completed. The dynamic computer market would not let IBM wait and introduce the new machines over an eighteen month period beginning on April 7, 1964 as it originally planned. By mid 1963 IBM's machines were obsolete and competitors' models had two or three times their performance capabilities.[168] The whole line had to be introduced at once, even if some of the models in the display were still dummy shells with only the promise of their capabilities and delivery date attached to their cabinet. On April 7, IBM brought trainloads of reporters, business analysts, and prospective customers up the Hudson from Grand Central Station to Poughkeepsie to witness the biggest product unveiling in IBM's history.

The initial roll out was fraught with delays and under performance. The biggest problem was getting the software delivered on schedule. IBM attempted to speed up its arrival by assigning an extra 2000 programmers to the effort[169] but that only slowed things down further. The new people had to be shown what had been done and how their contribution would fit in with the work of others. The people who had climbed the learning curve to become more productive had to take time to train the new arrivals. Project manager Fred Brooks later described the problem by saying, "the bearing of a child takes nine months, no matter how many women are assigned."[170] The earliest machines had to run using scaled-down temporary software.

By 1966 the early problems were fixed and fully functional machines rolled off the assembly lines. IBM survived its anxious times and was now poised to prosper. By the end of the year it had over 7000 systems installed and over four billion dollars in revenues.[171] IBM was saved by its culture—not just the effort by the people in its labs and factories, but by its image in the marketplace. Customers knew IBM from its reputation and were willing to wait and suffer through early delays to stay with the company they trusted for their products and the service that came with them.

System 360 established IBM's dominance of the market for the next fifteen years. RCA and GE never became factors in the computer business. Six years after the 360, the company introduced its next generation of computers, incorporating the integrated circuits that were emerging from the labs and filtering into products. The technology changed in the System 370, but the basic architecture remained the same.

The only thing that did not turn out as hoped for by IBM was Tom Watson's attempt to groom his brother to succeed him when he reached his sixtieth birthday. The World Trade organization the senior Watson crafted for his youngest son to manage succeeded as the old man had envisioned. By 1960 World Trade was generating revenue of $350 million dollars a year and growing twice as fast as its domestic partner.[172] Dick Watson's natural charm, language fluency, and skills as a diplomat served him well to keep the mechanism running smoothly. When Al Williams, who Tom Watson named president in 1961, expressed his firm intention to retire in 1966 at age 55 and enjoy the leisure his hard work had earned, Dick was brought back from World Trade and groomed to replace him. Tom planned to step down as Chairman in 1973 and allow Dick to have a seven or eight year run leading the company.[173]

Dick was put in charge of the engineering and manufacturing aspects of the 360 project in 1964, but his years at World Trade did not prepare him for the responsibility of bringing a major product line to market. He did not hold up well under the pressure of meeting production schedules. When delays and production problems threatened to derail the whole project, Tom had little choice but to relieve his brother of his substantive role and give him an inflated title with no direct project responsibility. Dick was no longer in line to succeed his brother and left the company in 1970 to become Ambassador to France. By this stage of his life he had a problem with alcohol, and on one flight back from France it led to an ugly incident that forced him to resign his post. Two years later he fell down the marble stairs at his New Canaan home and died at age 55.

The New Frontier

As Franklin Roosevelt had served as his father's political north star, John Kennedy was the leader most admired by son Tom. His wife, Olive, had become friends with Jack and two of his sisters in school, and spent time during summers in the late thirties at their Hyannisport home.[174] After marrying Tom, the couple remained close to the Kennedys through shared interests in activities like sailing and skiing and through shared ideals. When Jack decided to run for president, Watson pledged him his personal support, but felt he could not give a public endorsement without drawing his company into the murky waters of partisan politics.[175] Kennedy was hardly more popular among Watson's business associates than Roosevelt had been among his father's. Tom Watson did not bombard the new president with advice or assume the role of roving diplomat like his father. He served on various commissions during the Kennedy years, but described his role with the administration as mostly that of a witness.[176]

The younger Watson did not use the media to link his company's name with his own like his father did before him, but the success of IBM under his leadership placed him in the national spotlight and elevated his role in the community. He came to serve on advisory committees and business forums. During the last years of his administration, President Eisenhower created a Commission on National Goals to chart an agenda for the next decade and beyond. Eisenhower persuaded prominent businessmen, labor leaders, academics, and civil rights leaders to come together and forge a set of national objectives with bipartisan support from a broad and influential constituency. Separate panels produced recommendations on issues such as civil rights, foreign policy, unemployment, and urban decay. Watson chaired a panel on technological change that included Walter Reuther, a young George Schultz, Bell & Howell president and future Illinois Senator Charles Percy, and IBM Chief Scientist Manny Piore. The Commission issued its report after the 1960 election, and the Eisenhower appointees produced a document that could have been a blueprint for the New Frontier. It recommended federal enforcement of voting rights, federal support for the arts, and efforts to deal with ingrained poverty.

During the deliberations of his panel, Watson was forced to re-examine his thinking about the effect automation had upon the people it displaced. His company was a pioneer in the field of office automation. IBM salesmen touted the cost effectiveness of their products by telling their clients how many clerks each new machine would be able to replace. Watson always felt comfortable in the belief that greater productivity leads to an economic expansion that would absorb the people his machines were replacing,[177] but now he had to step out of the

Economics 101 classroom and into the laboratory where those theories were tested. His first exposure to the plight of real individuals came when he appeared as a guest on an Edward R. Murrow documentary. The first segment of the show featured a man of advancing middle age who had been made redundant at his job in the meat packing industry. He was a man of limited education with no marketable skills who wanted to work, but could not find a job and had visibly succumbed to the despair of his situation. Watson did not dismiss the man's plight as a case of individual weakness or imprudence as other businessmen might, but saw it as a human tragedy.[178] He came to appreciate that the ability of the economy to reabsorb someone displaced by automation is highly dependent upon individual circumstance.

The second aspect of the problem was brought home to him by Reuther, who conveyed to the panelists the inhomogeneity of economic displacement. Reuther argued that if Buick closed a factory employing 5000 people in Detroit and opened a new automated factory in Tennessee needing substantially fewer workers, those new jobs in Tennessee would be of little benefit to the idled workers and wounded economy of Detroit.[179] Watson's experience on the panel and his natural instincts led him to the conclusion that something more than the "invisible hand" was needed to ameliorate the uneven effects of technological displacement. The panel paid particular attention to the cooperative programs between business, labor, and government in Sweden that facilitated the retraining of people in areas of high unemployment and moving them to places where new jobs were being created. Watson believed that Kennedy would have been willing to experiment with aspects of Scandinavian industrial planning had he been given the opportunity.[180]

After Jack Kennedy's assassination, Tom and Olive Watson remained close with the rest of the Kennedy clan. Bobby Kennedy was elected to the Senate from New York in 1966 and became deeply involved with the problems facing the black ghettos in New York City. Riots in Watts in the summer of 1966 revealed tinderbox conditions ready to ignite in the heart of America's largest cities. Kennedy worked with Mayor Lindsay and Senator Jacob Javits to establish a partnership between business leaders and community leaders from Brooklyn's Bedford-Stuyvesant neighborhood that worked to provide advice and access to capital for projects that created some jobs, made some cosmetic improvements, provided some social services, and gave some sense of progress. When riots erupted in dozens of cities during the "long, hot summer of 1967," New York's Bedford-Stuyvesant neighborhood was not one of them. IBM built on the success of this effort by opening a manufacturing plant in the Brooklyn neighborhood. The plant producing computer cables employed 500 people from the community, provided them with the same benefits and opportunities for advancement that other employees enjoyed, and ran profitably for the company.[181]

In 1967 frustration with the Vietnam War and lack of racial progress in the Northern cities was tearing at the fabric of society. Watson saw Bobby Kennedy as the one person who could bring the country together and promised to support him if he ran for president.[182] When Johnson dropped out of the race, that time-table for a Kennedy campaign was moved up to 1968.

Kennedy came to Watson for advice. In one of the last meetings the two men had together the conversation turned to Vietnam. Watson, like many other liberals, including Reuther, at that stage of the war, saw the disaster that was unfolding, but, trapped in the Cold War logic that provided the framework for public debate, he saw no honorable way out. When Watson asked him what he'd do about Vietnam, Kennedy replied "Tom, there is no sensible, easy solution. Just none. The only possible thing to do is to get our people out."

He went on to respond to the question "How?" "I'd get out in any possible way. I think it is an absolute disaster. Being there is much worse than any of the shame or difficulty one would engender internationally by getting out. So, with whatever kind of apologies and with whatever grace I could conjure up, I'd get us out of there in six months with all of the troops the U. S. has."[183]

Watson was not ready to accept Kennedy's conclusion at that time. None of the syllogisms developed from the Cold War axioms produced that conclusion. Two years later, the fallacies in the thinking of the time were more apparent. During his appearance before the Senate Foreign Relations Committee in 1970, Watson echoed the message Kennedy had passed on to him. Watson's testimony made front-page news in the *New*

York Times the next morning.[184] By then, however, the absolute disaster that Kennedy had foreseen was increasingly evident.

Stories without a proper ending invite the mind to finish the process—to take the narrative down the plot line each reader wants it to go. For an aging generation of Americans the Kennedys are like characters in a Romantic novel—part historical actors, part invention. How might the movie version have ended if the Zapruder film were just another home movie, if Bobby had taken the originally planned route back to the elevators? Had Kennedy lived and Johnson not become president, the Civil Rights Act might have stalled in Congress and Voting Rights, Medicare, and Medicaid might never have become law. Had Bobby lived and become president the country may have exited from Vietnam down one of many different paths—some, but not all of them, better than the one it eventually took.

Watson and the Kennedys came from similar backgrounds, traveled in similar social circles, enjoyed similar activities reserved primarily for the rich, and shared similar political beliefs. Watson and Reuther shared few of these common experiences, but the two became friends. More than their involvement in Democratic Party politics explains the mutual respect that Thomas Watson and Walter Reuther had for one another. On the surface one was the Chief Executive of the most prominent non-union company in America, and the other was the President of the nation's most influential labor union. Beneath the surface both men felt a similar obligation to contribute to the greater good. Both men used the organization they headed to promote the social change in which they believed. Watson considered Reuther to be "one of America's great men" and his loss "a tragedy for the country."[185]

In their official capacity, both men kept an eye on the labor contracts in each other's industry. Watson could give; Reuther had to coerce through bargaining and the threat of strikes. IBM had a legacy of generosity and good corporate citizenship. The auto industry had a very checkered history in its labor relations. It wasn't until 1950, when the Treaty of Detroit established a quasi partnership between the union and the industry that the agreements in the auto industry and the benefits awarded the workers at IBM began to shadow one another.

The 1950 agreement with General Motors reaffirmed the annual improvement factor and cost of living adjustment (COLA/AIF) that gave workers an annual increase as a percentage of the national productivity gain for the year and an escalator with a floor that adjusted quarterly wages according to the consumer price index. It also included a partially paid health plan and a pension of $125 per month for workers with 25 or more years with the company.[186] Shortly afterward IBM revised its pension plan from one based only on years of service that had a cap of $3300 per year to one that took into account salary as well as service time and increased the maximum pension to $25,000 per year. It also offered a new major medical plan.[187]

In 1955 the union won supplemental unemployment benefits (SUB) from Ford and GM after rejecting the companies' alternative offer of a stock purchasing plan that it dismissed as a "wheel of fortune plan." The first SUB plan provided workers with 60% of their take-home pay during a period of up to 26 weeks during a layoff.[188] Reuther regarded this agreement as the first step in securing a guaranteed annual wage. The SUB benefit was increased in subsequent contract agreements until in the 1967 contract with Ford, it was raised to 95% of take-home pay during a layoff period of up to one year. This was as close as the UAW came to its goal of a guaranteed annual wage.[189]

IBM, whose employment patterns were not geared to a yearly restyling of its product line, put all of its workers, whether in the factories, sales, or engineering, on salary in 1957.[190] One year later it announced a stock purchasing plan that allowed employees to obtain stock through a system of payroll deductions at 85% of its market value on the date of purchase.[191] The IBM plan was a variation on the "wheel of fortune" offer by the auto companies which would have matched an employee contribution dollar-for-dollar until the market price of a share was reached. The basic difference between the two offers was that the IBM plan was offered in addition to the security of a salary and employment stability. The auto workers did not have that stability of employment and needed the protection of the SUB more than a small share in the ownership of their company.

Watson considered corporate stock purchasing plans to be a key ingredient in the recipe for mixing capitalism and democracy that would keep the flavor of one from overwhelming that of the other. In a reflection on his vision of a more perfect union of corporation and state, Watson wrote:

> "I began asking myself whether our present form of capitalism is the best way to support American democracy in the long term. It didn't seem that way to me. I thought that the model corporation of the future should be largely owned by people who work for it, not by banks or mutual funds or shareholders who might have inherited the stock from their parents and done nothing to earn it. Entrepreneurs and capitalists would always have a key place—if you risk money by putting it behind Henry Ford you certainly ought to be able to enjoy the fruits of your investment. But there is enormous strength in proprietorship—people develop strong attachments to the things they own, especially if they can influence whether those things succeed or fail—and it seemed imprudent to let the ownership of a business rest with the people and institutions that are not directly involved. Remedying this situation would have to be an evolutionary process, but I imagined it, gradually, over two or three generations, a business would by law, shift into the hands of employees."[192]

The early returns on his vision of employee proprietorship were not encouraging. Watson found that despite his promotion of the benefit of long-term ownership many employees grabbed the quick profit their below-market purchase price provided and sold the stock soon after they acquired it. He came to realize that the average worker would rather use the profit from his or her stock transaction to help pay off the mortgage than keep it at risk in the market.[193] That situation prevailed to a greater extent with the auto workers whose work schedule was more volatile and whose cash emergencies more unanticipated.

The Anti-trust Suit

In 1963 the Control Data Corporation announced the 6600 supercomputer that would be faster than any machine on the market and faster than any of the processors in the yet to be announced IBM 360 series. The 6600 was the product of the legendary computer architect Seymour Cray who directed a laboratory team of 34 people—that included 14 engineers, 4 programmers, and one janitor.[194] Watson became incensed that IBM would not be known for having the fastest computer and that a laboratory as small as Cray's could produce a machine superior in performance to anything IBM had yet to produce. Watson's "janitor memo" pushed IBM into diverting some of its engineering resources away from work on the 360 processors and into an effort to beat Cray. When the 360 Series was announced in April, 1964, the company indicated it was also working on a supercomputer that would be faster than the 6600.[195] That information led prospective customers for high performance computers to hold off committing to Control Data. Ultimately four different versions of the supercomputer were announced, but none was ever delivered. IBM was never able to match the performance of the 6600. Finally Watson realized that there was a lot more money to be made in building Chevys and Cadillacs than in making Ferraris and gave up trying to compete with Control Data for what was a small niche market.[196]

The effect of IBM's announcements and the hold it had on customers willing to wait for its products cut deeply into Control Data's sales and forced it to lower its prices for the $7 million dollar machine. Its chairman, William Norris, decided to fight back. His salesmen compiled a dossier of IBM sales practices that abused the company's power in the marketplace.[197] When the Justice Department brought an anti-trust suit against IBM on the last working day of the Johnson Administration, Norris and several other smaller companies piled on and brought suits complementing the federal case. Against IBM's army of lawyers, the Justice Department was only able to muster a platoon, but Control Data had its own formidable legal team.[198] It requisitioned documents from sixty IBM departments and the files and memos of over one hundred IBM executives. In all, it reviewed over forty million documents, of which it found 80,000 key to its case.[199] It created a sophisticated computerized index of these documents that allowed an operator to assemble supporting evidence for various lines of inquiry. Control Data worked in tandem with the Justice Department and provided it with access to its collection of documents.

Control Data was suing IBM for damages that it caused to its business. The Justice Department was suing to break up the company. Control Data had the more formidable legal team, and Control Data was sharing its information with the feds. As the Control Data suit moved forward, IBM did the prudent thing: it settled out of court. IBM sold its Service Bureau Corporation to Control Data for a fraction of its real worth, gave its competitor $101 million in cash and contracts, and paid its $15 million legal fees.[200] In return IBM received the computerized index as part of the customary return of paperwork prepared by the two parties. The index was not entered into evidence in any proceeding and was merely property that now belonged to IBM. The first piece of advice that Watson received from his lawyers was to burn it, and that is what was done.[201]

The Justice Department sought to split IBM into as many as seven separate companies.[202] Its main complaint against the company was its practice of bundling the cost of systems, software, support, and training into a single price. The practice went all the way back to Hollerith, but it prevented smaller service and software companies from competitively bidding for pieces of an IBM customer's business. IBM voluntarily stopped bundling its products shortly after the Justice Department suit was brought to strip the federal argument of its most fashionable dress. Once the Control Data lawyers left the courtroom, the IBM legal team overwhelmed the out manned Justice team and the court that had to officiate a contest beyond the scope of anything it had seen before. The case dragged on for thirteen years until in 1981 the government drew in its chips and folded its hand.

IBM came out of the long proceedings intact, but the lawyers that could tie up a court room for over a decade could tie up a board room just as thoroughly. The lawyers were always looking over the shoulders of the executives or were there in their heads when they discussed new product ideas or responses to a competitor's initiative. The company became more bureaucratic as it grew and more tentative as it learned to speak in the new vocabulary mandated by its lawyers.

In 1970, in the midst of the company's legal problems and a fairly severe recession that battered its stock price, Watson suffered a heart attack. He was 57, three years short of the mandatory retirement age he had established for IBM executives, and there was no other Watson waiting in the wings to run the family business. Company president, Vin Learson, was himself only a couple of years from retirement. Watson was given the choice—his company or his health—and he chose to retire a few years early. Control of IBM passed to its next generation of leaders three years ahead of schedule.

The Watson Junior years marked a period of remarkable growth. At the end of his first year as Chief Executive, IBM passed the $1 billion mark in revenues and employed 83,588 people—about four times as many as it did at the end of World War II.[203] Ten years later, in 1967, revenues were $5.3 billion and the workforce had expanded to 221,858.[204] At the beginning of the post-Watson era in 1973, revenues had doubled again to $11 billion.[205] Over the next thirteen years, the company doubled again in size and more than doubled its annual revenue. The only thing growing faster than IBM was the pace of technological change.

As IBM was getting bigger and more bureaucratic, the technology was trending smaller and less centralized. People within IBM recognized the direction in which the industry was heading, but the success of its mainframe business made the corporation complacent and defensive in responding to the new realities of open system architectures and microprocessors with more processing power than the gigantic UNIVAC. Moves to enter the early desktop market were thwarted by interests that did not want to see a high end model compete with the company's minicomputers and a perception of the low end market as limited to a few hobbyists and computer geeks. When IBM made a first half-hearted attempt to produce a personal computer, it came out with a machine that was no better than the Tandy TRS 80, but many times more expensive.[206]

Small is Beautiful, But not for Big Blue

The sexy new kid on the block was Apple. The Apple II was introduced to the public along with the tale of how its inventors, Steve Wozniak and Steve Jobs, built their first models in the family garage. The story of the pair starting from scratch in a make-shift laboratory to create a product that extended the human reach placed them in a tradition that harkened back to Henry Ford and the Wright brothers. That two kids from the fringes of the counter culture could tweak the big blue bastion of the establishment in their ads and in their manner was particularly galling to the computer giant. IBM Chairman, Frank Cary kept prodding his executives with the question "Where is my Apple?"[207] Finally in July, 1980 he was presented with a plan for a machine that could compete with Apple in price and exceed its performance. Cary told the presenter, Bill Lowe, to find an off-site location, choose forty people to be the development group, and keep them isolated from the rest of the corporation.[208]

Lowe, and his successor, Don Estridge, looked outside of IBM to get their parts. They convinced IBM management that the only way they could produce a competitive machine in a year's time was to avoid the internal turf wars and development cycles that doomed earlier efforts. This was particularly true for software. IBM was not very good at writing software. Other companies were still learning their craft at the time as well, but the kids writing code at emerging companies developed their skills on machines like the Altair, Tandy, and Apple where hardware resources were scarce and concise, efficient code was a necessity. IBM programmers inhabited a world of resource abundance where their performance was graded in lines of code per hour. Despite the experience of smothering a software project under the weight of too many programmers that delayed the release and added to the cost of the System 360 operating system, IBM methodology still followed up a squad of analysts and software architects with an army of programmers stitching patches of code into an evolving pattern that needed to come together seamlessly at the end. Programmers spent more time communicating with one another and rewriting code than a smaller team working together from the beginning would require.[209]

One of the places IBM went looking for software was Microsoft. The company founded by Bill Gates and Paul Allen specialized in developing language compilers for the personal computers of the day. When IBM called in 1980 the company had 31 employees and was considered an established entity in the fledgling industry producing software for the home computer market.[210] IBM wanted to know if it could rely on Microsoft to produce computer language compilers for the machine it was developing, and, oh, by the way, it was looking for an operating system too. Gates was not interested in writing an operating system, but referred IBM to a company called Digital Research Intergalactic (DRI) whose operating system CP/M was a standard on the early personal computers. Gates and DRI founder Gary Kildall had an understanding that they would stay off of each other's turf.[211]

When IBM called on DRI, Kildall was off flying his new airplane.[212] His lawyer wife balked at signing the many non-disclosure agreements the computer giant required. IBM and DRI never came to terms, and Gates was told that he had to produce an operating system or the language deal was off.[213] Paul Allen knew of another Seattle software developer who had produced an operating system called QDOS (quick and dirty operating system). Allen determined that Microsoft could acquire QDOS, and Gates called IBM with the news, then asked the billion dollar question: "Do you want to buy it, or do you want me to buy it?" IBM wanted no part of repeating another operating system fiasco, and told Gates that he should buy the rights to the system. For $75,000 Microsoft purchased the rights to what would become MS DOS.[214]

IBM was willing to pay a big fee up front to license DOS to make sure that its supplier remained healthy and able to maintain a long-standing relationship, but Gates asked instead for a small royalty on each machine sold and that the license to use DOS be non-exclusive.[215] That arrangement soon propelled Microsoft to the top rung of the *Fortune Five Hundred* list and made Gates, Allen, and Steve Ballmer billionaires.

The IBM PC arrived one year after it was first proposed and was a huge success. It was developed and marketed by IBM, but there was little else intrinsic to IBM about it. It was produced outside of IBM proper; ran on an Intel microprocessor under Microsoft's operating system; was sold in ComputerLand stores; and featured software IBM bought or licensed from other vendors. The original PC was quickly followed by a more powerful model, the XT, aimed at the business office, and later the AT, which used the next generation Intel 80286 processor. PC sales during the first half decade of the 80s helped boost IBM profits to $6.6 billion in 1984, double what they were three years earlier.[216]

That success proved illusory. The IBM PC established a standard that developers flocked to, but there was very little of IBM inside the package besides the label on the front. Companies like Compaq and Dell sprouted up producing clones that ran all the software written for the IBM PC world. The personal computer became identified by the label *Intel Inside* and the version of Microsoft's operating system that it ran. The manufacturers of the clones proved more agile at adapting to the 18 to 24 month time table at which the component density on a chip doubled and machines using the old processor became obsolete. By the second half of the decade IBM compatibles leapfrogged over the IBM brand and grabbed the largest share of the market.

The decision by Cary's successor John Opel to abandon the traditional IBM practice of renting its systems and sell them instead artificially inflated the revenue figures for the period. The change meant that money that previously flowed in as a steady monthly income now poured in all at once each time a sale was made. However, once the market became saturated or the sales went someplace else, there was no monthly income stream to sustain the growth that the company was experiencing. That strategy change was not an aggressive push to shove IBM products into new businesses, but a defensive gambit to hold on to the territory already claimed. IBM had virtually eliminated all of its domestic mainframe competition, but it feared encroachment by the big Japanese firms that had lower operating costs. Opel saw the wave of Toyotas and Nissans replacing Chevys and Fords in American garages and feared that Fujitsus and Hitachis would replace IBM mainframes in American businesses. He figured that a rental machine could be replaced by a competitor's model with only one month's notice, but if the company made the big investment to purchase a large IBM computer, its business would be retained for at least the traditional seven year life cycle of a mainframe.

While Opel's IBM was focused on the threat from abroad to its high-end business, the exponential growth in computing power of the microprocessor was eating away at his core from below. Smaller machines came to do more-and-more of the jobs that previously needed a mainframe. The job of buying these smaller machines migrated further down the corporate hierarchy to younger, more tech-savvy mid-level managers who were not the people with whom the IBM salesmen had developed a relationship. As the profits and revenues climbed, the foundation supporting that growth was beginning to weaken. Opel chose to revel in the growth rather than repair the foundation, and continued to expand the company as if 13% growth per year were sustainable well into the future. When he handed the top job over to John Akers in 1985, the world-wide workforce had ballooned to over 400,000 people.[217]

The company Akers inherited was big and bloated, slow to move, but still with formidable human and financial resources and a reputation that won it more admiration than any other institution, public or private. Akers was unable to take advantage of the strengths the company still possessed and free them from the bureaucratic weight that handicapped the company's pace in responding to the competition. During the second half of the decade, the forces eating away at IBM's dominance—lack of agility in competing with the clones in the low-end market, inability to write software in a timely, cost-competitive manner, and erosion of its profit margin in its mainframe business—brought the company to the brink of collapse.

Akers' first response to the downturn in the company's fortune was to mint more sales people to drum up additional business. He took people from overloaded manufacturing and programming departments, put them through a training program, and sent them off to the hinterlands to sell IBM products.[218] Not surprisingly, the plan cost more to train and install the people than it returned in additional revenue. People educated in technical fields needed more than a few months of training and a blue suit and white shirt to be effective or eager sales representatives.

As the balance sheet moved from black to red, the company started to slash its work force. In the first round of cuts in 1987, Akers remained committed to the company tradition of no involuntary layoffs. He offered the domestic employees a voluntary severance plan that provided counseling services, job placement services, and use of company time and resources in finding a new job. The offer was open to any IBMer except those in a few "skills categories" that included programming. Ten thousand workers accepted the offer, including eight thousand with the highest performance rating. One third of the top rated IBM workers in the United States left the company[219] at a time when proper deployment of their skills might have stopped the slippage in the company's fortunes.

In 1987 there was still an opportunity for IBM to regain its footing in the desktop market. IBM and Microsoft had entered into an agreement to collaborate in writing the next generation operating system to sit on top of DOS and provide a graphic interface similar to the one on the Apple Macintosh, while running all of the programs written for the IBM compatible world. The operating system would be called OS/2 and Microsoft committed the bulk of its programmers to the joint venture. The initial version of its own graphic user interface, Windows, was only able to run small applications that used little memory. It had received a very cool reception in the marketplace. In 1987 Microsoft considered abandoning its Windows project and at times had less than a half dozen programmers working on it.[220] Major software companies such as Lotus were committed to writing applications to run on OS/2.

A timely release of OS/2 could have restored IBM's dominance of the PC market and limited Microsoft's growing control of the desktop. It never happened. During the summer of 1988, a University of Arizona physicist, Murray Sargent, came to Microsoft as part of an internship project for one of his students. Sargent finished his OS/2 assignment early and had some time to work on a problem of his choice before classes resumed in the fall. He began tinkering with Windows and found a fix for the memory limitation problem.[221] Sargent's work rekindled interest in Windows at Microsoft at a time when relations with IBM were becoming strained. By the time that IBM and Microsoft ended their collaboration in 1991, Windows 3.0 had been introduced, and it became entrenched on IBM and compatible PCs. Microsoft now not only owned the operating system of choice, but also possessed applications such as the Office Suite that ran on Windows at a time when other software producers were developing applications for OS/2. By the time that IBM finally delivered a version of OS/2, there were few customers waiting around to get it. In 1995, the new Chairman, Lou Gerstner, decided to kill the product despite the $2.5 billion dollars the company had sunk into its development.[222]

Throughout Akers years as Chairman, the culling of the workforce continued. Later severance plans were more targeted, less generous, and less voluntary. Employees were told to accept the offer or be fired. One group that was not targeted was upper-level management. Management was spared the pain they were inflicting upon the lower echelons of the company. After an apparent turnaround in 1990, Akers convinced the board to increase his salary and that of his top executives by 35% plus additional stock options.[223] One month after receiving his hefty pay hike, Akers had to announce first quarter losses in 1991 that foreshadowed the looming $3 billion loss for the year.[224] The next year was even worse. IBM suffered the largest corporate loss in history.[225] Finally, at the end of 1992 John Akers was given a severance notice of his own. IBM looked to the outside for its next chief.

Under New Management

The IBM board scoured Silicon Valley for a replacement, but found no one of stature in the industry willing to believe that taking on the leadership of IBM was anything other than a dead end road for their career. The new leader came from the tobacco and food conglomerate R. J. Reynolds Nabisco by way of American Express by way of the McKinsey Company Management Consulting firm. When Lou Gerstner was named the next IBM Chairman, reporters and analysts looked at his most recent post and joked about how his experience managing the production of potato chips and cookie wafers would help him produce computer chips from silicon wafers. In reality, the short time he spent at RJR Nabisco had little bearing on his new job at IBM. His most recent career stops would influence the style he brought to IBM, but the playbook for how he would restructure the ailing giant borrowed from heavily from his days at McKinsey.

When Gerstner left home to head off to Armonk for one of the first days on the new job, he found a passenger waiting in his car to join him. Tom Watson lived right around the corner from Gerstner in Greenwich, Connecticut and wanted to convey the message "save my company" directly to the new boss.[226] Gerstner heard a similar message a few weeks earlier when the announcement of his new appointment was widely anticipated by the media and known to most insiders. During a chance encounter with Nobel Prize winning geneticist Joshua Lederberg who he knew from his seat on the board of the Sloan Kettering Memorial Cancer Center, Dr. Lederberg asked if he was going to IBM. When Gerstner nodded yes, Lederberg told him "Don't mess it up. It's a national treasure."[227]

Despite its troubles, IBM remained the cornerstone of *the* industry. Data processing or information technology as it became known was the industry shaping the world economy. It was an industry the United States dominated, but one in which other countries like Japan, the European Union, and soon China and India were racing to take the lead. A strong IBM was vital in establishing and maintaining America's economic and political security.

IBM computers guided the Gemini capsules in orbit around Earth and piloted the Apollo missions to the moon. IBM was at the heart of national defense and intelligence gathering efforts, and its processors remained the key organ in the central nervous system of most large companies. More importantly to the future of the industry in America, IBM spent $7 billion a year on research in the early 1990s. That was one tenth of the total annual corporate research budget in America.[228] Scientists at IBM Research in Yorktown Heights, NY and Zurich, Switzerland garnered four Nobel Prizes and developed technologies ranging from the magnetic disk to the relational database that fueled the growth of not only IBM but also many of its competitors. In 1992, IBM contributed $120 million to higher education, but that figure was down from $189 million seven years earlier.[229] IBM support was key to the activities of computer science departments in many of the country's leading universities, and the company provided internships and jobs for many of their students and graduates. In a January 13, 1993 *New York Times* article James H. Morris, Chairman of the Computer Science Department at Carnegie Mellon University, warned "we're at a watershed. The restructuring of the computer industry has put computer science at a turning point."[230] IBM support was crucial to the continued health of the field of computing in America, and none of the new kids on the block were yet in a position to assume that role should IBM fail.

Gerstner did not have a technical background, but he needed to make prompt strategic decisions to put the company on a course of sustained profitability. He decided early on to keep the company together and not split it into several independent Baby Blues as the government intended in its anti-trust case and as the company was preparing to do when he arrived.[231] He ceded the desktop to Microsoft, Intel, and the various clones and shifted the emphasis away from the stagnant mainframe business and into services. IBM would enter into multi-year contracts with companies to manage their information technology needs through advice on how to integrate the various computing resources from many different sources into a cohesive system and how best to employ IT to serve the client's business objectives.[232] Gerstner believed that retaining the cohesiveness of a company that still had many areas of strength served its interest in moving into services better than breaking it up into a loosely tied collection of its divided assets.[233]

Just as the desktop era of the 1980s exposed IBM's weaknesses, the emergence of the Internet in the 1990s played to its strengths. Computers no longer just churned out payroll and inventory data for the accountants, supported the engineers with CAD/CAM applications, and crunched numbers for the scientists. They now became components in a new system of commerce that connected the home PC to the electronic store front. The arrival of e-commerce coincided with IBM's push into services, and reinvigorated the role of the mainframe. IBM staked out the ground between the home and office machines and the networks operated by the old telephone companies.[234] The territory became known as the *cloud* and IBM operated server farms and supplied software that allowed applications to access the resources stored on the mainframes concealed inside the virtual cirri-stratus. The confluence of good timing and stronger leadership lifted IBM out of its slide and back to a position of prominence in the industry.

IBM soared up into the *cloud*, but it retained its visibility to the general public with two public relations stunts worthy of the senior Watson. In 1997 an IBM computer called Deep Blue challenged reigning world chess champion Gary Kasparov to a match. In the previous year an earlier version of the Deep Blue program lost to Kasparov, but in the 1997 match a deeper Deep Blue defeated Kasparov in the deciding game and for the first time a computer was able to defeat the world champion in a competitively timed match. Deep Blue combined a brute force capability to evaluate 200 million positions per second, twice as many as its 1996 version, with an evaluation function that scored positions at various stages of a game according to information gleaned from a library of hundreds of thousands of grandmaster games.[235] Previous games of Kasparov were used to calibrate the evaluation function of the computer, but IBM denied Kasparov's request to allow him to study previous games played by Deep Blue so he might better understand the "thinking" of his opponent.[236] The victory of its chess playing machine provided IBM with some positive publicity at a time when it was trying to restore some of the luster to its brand lost in the PC wars, but it introduced no new product to its catalog. IBM denied Kasparov's call for a rematch and dismantled Deep Blue shortly after the publicity photos were published.

The Deep Blue-Kasparov chess match was reported widely in the media, but it was not shown live on television. The next publicity stunt, which the company pulled over a decade later, was a made for TV event with more lasting implications for the company and the future. During a prolonged stretch in 2004–2005 national attention was drawn to the winning streak of Ken Jennings on the quiz show *Jeopardy*. The TV audience built as Jennings progressed through 74 wins and amassed over two million dollars in earnings. Among the viewers was an IBM Research manager Charles Lickel who became intrigued with the idea of building a machine with the capability of rapidly recalling the same kind of trivia as a *Jeopardy* contestant.[237] Lickel was given permission to form a team and work on the project. The team headed by principal investigator David Ferrucci included artificial intelligence (AI) researchers at leading universities in addition to twelve IBM Research employees.[238] By 2011 the team had built a system that was ready to challenge Jennings and Brad Rutter, the two most successful *Jeopardy* contestants. The IBM system named WATSON was able to process and parse natural language, phrase queries to four terabytes of stored information, and evaluate possible answers in the context of other information in its storage.[239] In a well publicized two night match WATSON handily beat the two *Jeopardy* champs. Jennings later wrote of the encounter:

"IBM has bragged to the media that Watson's question-answering skills are good for more than annoying Alex Trebek. The company sees a future in which fields like medical diagnosis, business analytics, and tech support are automated by question-answering software like Watson. Just as factory jobs were eliminated in the 20th century by new assembly-line robots, Brad and I were the first knowledge-industry workers put out of work by the new generation of 'thinking' machines. 'Quiz show contestant' may be the first job made redundant by Watson, but I'm sure it won't be the last."[240]

Unlike for Deep Blue there is a life after Jeopardy for WATSON. The first place WATSON systems headed after the quiz show was to the Cleveland Clinic, Sloan Kettering, and other medical facilities to acquire and enhance their medical diagnostic skills. Their medical internship began by using patient data and medical knowledge to assist doctors and nurses in establishing an individualized treatment plan for clinic patients.[241] Medicine is only one of the fields where WATSON is expected to contribute in the future. IBM expects that by the 2020s WATSON will contribute $10 billion annually to its revenues.[242]

IBM's resurgence in the 1990s under Gerstner came at the expense of its cherished reputation for its working environment. The layoffs begun by Akers continued under Gerstner without any pretext masking the end of the company's long-standing claim of never resorting to the practice. Workers being fired were given short notice, given a brief time to clean out their desk under supervision, and escorted out of the building. The world-wide workforce dropped from a high of 407,000 in 1985 to 260,000 ten years later.[243] The country clubs were sold, no-cost medical insurance ended, and rounds of benefit reductions began. The culture that sustained IBM during the Watson years was now held responsible for its lethargy. The layoffs and benefit cuts were driven by more than economic necessity. They also came with a repudiation of the old cultural values.[244]

Gerstner decreed that the beat to which the company would march would no longer be drummed from within, but from the market. He described his philosophy by saying

> "I wanted IBMers to think and act like long-term shareholders—to feel pressure from the marketplace to deploy assets and forge strategies that create competitive advantage….In the past, IBM was both the employer and the scorekeeper in the game. I needed my new colleagues to accept the fact that external forces—the stock market, competition, the changing demands of our customers— had to drive our agenda, not the wishes and whims of our team."[245]

The people from whom Henry Ford rid himself early in the century were the ones Lou Gerstner courted in its last decade. The interests of the group that George F. Johnson called his parasites—people of selfish interest who reap where they have not sown—were placed before those of the employees who committed their skill and labor, above those of the community that shared in the company's success and shuddered with its failings, and even above the customers' loyalty to a brand and the reputation that stood behind it. When strains appeared within the enterprise, it was the employee and family that was uprooted, facing an uncertain future; it was the community that suffered an economic decline and shrinking tax base; while with the click of a mouse the investor was free of all previous ties and into a new and equally transient attachment with a more attractive corporate heartthrob. In truth the average investor, big and small, knew little of where his or her money was housed and what group of companies were part of that portfolio. Those decisions were left to the agents who moved their chips around the Big Board like high-rollers at a Las Vegas roulette table, collecting a commission on every bet they made while risking nothing of their own on the outcome. It was here where the strengths and weaknesses of the capitalist system were most clearly revealed—its ability to reconstruct the economy in real-time, and its inability to distribute the costs and rewards of that process between capital and labor in an equitable manner.

To amplify the drumbeat of the market in the ears of his staff, Gerstner tied compensation directly to it. He made stock options the largest component of executive pay. To qualify for the options, executives had to have some multiple of their own salary plus the incentive invested in the market. The multiple ranged from four for the CEO down to one for members of the Senior Leadership Group who were not in one of the higher categories.[246] For the top executives the amount of bonus would be tied to the performance of the overall company, not just the unit for which he or she was responsible.[247]

This stock-based compensation plan came right out of the McKinsey & Company playbook. It made the senior leadership attentive to the market's appraisal of their performance, but it also exposed them to the jitters that Wall Street went through when the economy caught a cold or ran a fever. Gerstner was critical of the Watsons for not holding a larger share of the company's stock and for making executive stock ownership such a small aspect of IBM's compensation package, but the senior Watson had reason to be cautious about giving his executives more incentive to acquire company stock. During the early days of the Great Depression, he spent so much time providing brokerage advice and financial help to the distraught members of his inner circle that it distracted him from the job of piloting the company through the rough waters it faced. Watson Junior wanted to encourage employee ownership and made his stock purchasing plan available to everyone in the company, but noted that morale in the office fluctuated with the price of a share.

The market can be more a distraction than a motivator. When stock performance dictates executive compensation there is an incentive to influence the price of a share by creative accounting practices or worse. One of McKinsey's star clients in the 1990s was Enron, where former partner Jeff Skilling was CEO. Enron was the darling of Wall Street before its house of cards collapsed, wiping away the jobs and retirement accounts of its employees and the investment of its shareholders. Skilling engineered the scams that concealed the true state of the company finances, was convicted of fraud and insider trading, and given a 24 year jail term.

In better days, when Skilling was roosting at the top of the corporate pecking order, he instituted a policy at Enron that he and the McKinsey people plucked out of the Harvard Business School.[248] All Enron employees were given a rating on a scale of 1 to 5. At least 10% of the workforce had to be given a rating of 5 on each review no matter how well in absolute terms they were performing. Workers with a 5 rating were fired.[249] The practice was not limited to Enron or the many companies with ties to McKinsey. It permeated much of corporate behavior. For mature companies like IBM it provided a means of regularly renewing itself with new people while not increasing the size of its workforce.

The "Skilling plan," or some variation on the theme is a feature of the corporate culture that has elbowed aside the paternalism of George F. Johnson and the Watsons and muted the voices of labor. The flexibility it provides management is wrung from the loyalty of its workforce. The ratings used to target underachievers are inherently subjective and influenced as much by politics and favoritism as by merit. In IBM, a large bureaucratic firm that continued to experience waves of firings after the company had recovered from its near death experience, the arbitrariness in the rating system used to reward, punish, and dismiss produced a toxic environment where the sense of community has disappeared and the workers offer the same loyalty to the company that it affords them.[250]

As Gerstner prepared to step aside in 2002, IBM abandoned its roots and moved all manufacturing out of Endicott. It left a skeleton staff of about 600 people behind along with a toxic spill of photo resist and degreasing chemicals that had seeped into the ground water.[251] From the days of Tom Junior the Southern Tier had become less-and-less central to the company's operation, so it was not surprising that the downsizing would hit particularly hard at the place where IBM grew up and reached maturity. The departure marked a symbolic closing of the door of the old IBM and the culture with which it was imbued. Visitors to Endicott are still greeted by a pair of stone arches on either end of route 17C proclaiming it the "Home of the Square Deal"—a pair of historical relics offering mute testimony to what once was there.

Gerstner spent nine years as the head of IBM. During that tenure he has been credited with turning the fortunes of the company around and restoring its financial health. The stock price doubled and redoubled.[252] The workforce added about 100,000 jobs through hirings and acquisitions.[253] The ledger book pages turned from red to black. With the patient returned to health, Gerstner received accolades for administering the cure.

The prescription he offered might be better described as providing a remission from a chronic illness that recurs from time-to-time and may eventually prove fatal. In the decade since Gerstner retired, symptoms of the old ailments caused by overweight and unhealthy ingrained habits have reappeared, and the internal defense system of a loyal, dedicated workforce has been seriously compromised. The new management has confronted sluggish growth with new rounds of layoffs and repeated rounds of stock repurchases using borrowed money to try to reach the optimistic earnings per share targets it projected to the market. IBM has become just another company—divorced from its past and reluctant to commit to a lasting relationship in the future.

The *cloud* has not been entirely an "ice cream castle in the [virtual] air"[254] for IBM or for the human element hidden in its vapors. IBM is forced to view the *cloud* from *Both Sides Now*—"*from up and down*"—a business opportunity that poses a threat to its legacy in the data centers of the big banks and insurance companies that have fueled its growth. Companies that grew up in the era of open systems have been more adept at providing cloud computing and e-commerce services than the giant who thrived by keeping its product base closed to would-be rivals. In the area of *cloud* services, Amazon has over five times the amount of computer capacity in use than its next fourteen closest rivals combined.[255] Amazon expanded its online bookstore into a virtual mall by providing "store fronts" on its *cloud* and linking orders to a network of vast distribution warehouses that pay poverty wages to their permanent workers and minimum wage to the many temps who retrieve and box the ordered merchandise on an assembly line that pushes them to the brink of exhaustion.[256] At the time of writing, IBM lags in *cloud* services, is shrinking its hardware business, and getting most of its income from the middleware software it produces. It is banking on its next WATSON to restore luster to the company image.

For much of the twentieth century IBM served as a role model for good corporate citizenship. It was not without its character flaws, as evidenced by its dealings with Dehomag and by its ignoring health hazards in its clean rooms, but it served its customers well, benefited its employees and its communities, and strengthened the foundations of the American industrial and scientific establishment. IBM culture together with the Treaty of Detroit provided the guidelines for personnel policies in the fifties and sixties when doors to the middle class swung open for a large number of Americans. The computer giant was a major force in shrinking the world and a major player in the global market that it enabled. But the technology it pioneered and the global market it helped produce combined with other forces to undercut the unions and render the IBM culture unsustainable. With the disappearance of that culture, and in the absence of a union presence in many sectors of the economy, employment practices have been left to the discretion of a generation of generically trained MBAs filtering through consulting firms into board rooms and government offices. Corporate wealth has been shared less equitably and the opening to the middle class has narrowed.

CHAPTER IX

Civil Rights

Detroit—City of grinding gears and axle grease.
Heart of pounding cylinders, an
Engine of internal combustion,
Driven by an explosive fuel of rednecks—
Up from the Black Belt with Bibles and bedsheets,
Poles, uprooted from the anti-Semitic soil
of the Silesian homeland; and rural blacks,
the unreconstructed refugees of the Reconstruction.
A treadmill town set to the metronome
beat of the assembly line.

The Civil Rights Struggle was waged in the 1950's and 60's on the buses of Montgomery, at the lunch counters of Greensboro, North Carolina, and on the hostile streets of Birmingham and Selma, Alabama. It was also fought in court rooms and board rooms, on playing fields and battlefields, on camera and behind closed doors. It was backed with financial and logistical support from a coalition of labor, religious, and business organizations. The alliance between the NAACP and the UAW was particularly instrumental in enabling the movement to realize its political goals. The union received help from the national rights organizations in overcoming the antipathy of black auto workers toward the union, and it committed its organizational expertise and political clout to the rights struggle. From its beginning, the leaders of each of the UAW factions were outspoken in their support of equal opportunity for all their workers. When Reuther gained full control of the union in 1947, he became the most recognizable white leader championing the campaign for equal rights and economic justice.

The autoworkers were not a natural constituency for a leader committed to the struggle for civil rights. The promise of the $5 a day paycheck in 1914 induced a northern migration of Southern whites who brought their racial attitudes north with them. The Ku Klux Klan became entrenched in Detroit. In 1924 the Klan demonstrated its strength in the city by running a write-in candidate, Charles Bowles, for mayor. Bowles received 106,679 votes and lost the election by just over 10,000 votes to the winner only because some 17,000 write-in votes were disqualified for misspellings and other technical errors.[1] In the mid '30s, when the struggle to establish the union presence within the plants was in its most confrontational phase, there were an estimated 200,000 Ku Klux Klan members in the state of Michigan. Between 1933 and 1936 over 50 murders were attributed to the Black Legion, a KKK offshoot.[2]

European immigrants, mostly from Poland also flocked to the automobile factories of Michigan. Poland had a tragic history of anti-Semitism, but no direct experience with racism. The new arrivals, and more particularly their native-born offspring, viewed the black man as a rival for the jobs they were seeking, and adopted the racial prejudices of the white society they were eager to join.

In 1910, blacks occupied just 569 of the 105,758 jobs in the automobile industry.[3] Black employment only picked up during periods of white labor shortage, chiefly the periods during the two World Wars. Blacks were concentrated in factories engaged in foundry operations and assigned to the least skilled manual jobs. Efforts to promote qualified blacks to skilled positions like tool and die maker usually lead to labor disputes and plant shutdowns. By the 1930s, blacks only comprised 4% of the workforce, and were most prominently concentrated in the Ford River Rouge plant.[4]

The former French fur trading fort on the Detroit River was well-suited to absorb the raw materials floated down the lake and river system from the mines and factories at their source and spew out the finished product to the marketplace that craved it. It was less able to absorb the disparate, often antagonistic populations that fed its factories. Housing was chronically in short supply, and living conditions for most were substandard. In 1944 the Detroit Housing Commission reported that "One fifth [of the city's housing] is so badly blighted that it is in need of complete rehabilitation and rebuilding. Over 90,000 families of our population are living in substandard living quarters."[5] City Council President, George Edwards, testified in 1948 that "Much of the city is a rotting slum[...] 70,000 families were living doubled up, 37,000 married veterans were holed up in rooms, cabins, shacks, trailer camps, or poaching on in-laws."[6]

Housing shortages exacerbated racial tensions in the city. Like most American cities, Detroit was a checkerboard of neighborhoods, segregated along racial, ethnic, and social lines. In the 1940s most blacks inhabited a neighborhood sarcastically dubbed "Paradise Valley" that was wedged between a predominantly Southern working class neighborhood to the south and east and the largely Polish enclave of Hamtramck to its north. Between 1940 and 1942 over 60,000 blacks, migrating North to find war-related work in the auto plants, crammed into the already overcrowded slum.[7] On the western side of the city there was another slum inhabited largely by poor Southern whites and social outcasts from various backgrounds that scratched out a living by day and relieved their misery with drink and brawling by night. It was fertile ground for Klan membership and fascist demagogues like Gerald L. K. Smith.

Social pressure and economic status usually enforced the demographic patterns of the city, but when upwardly mobile blacks tried to move into all-white neighborhoods, they were met with hostility and violence. When Dr. Ossian Sweet, a black gynecologist, purchased a home in a white neighborhood in July of 1925, the Klan held a rally drawing over 10,000 people and called for the establishment of neighborhood protection associations.[8] Dr. Sweet's announcement that he planned to move into his new home in September prompted residents of his new neighborhood to organize the Waterworks Park Improvement Association. When the day of the move arrived, a crowd reported variously from about thirty to over five hundred gathered outside his house.[9] It ranged from the openly hostile to the just curious. Dr. Sweet, his family, and seven friends and relatives arrived set for a siege. They brought with them a large supply of food, ten guns, and over 400 rounds of ammunition.[10] The Sweets were aware of the harassment and violence endured by other blacks who attempted to move into all-white neighborhoods, and were determined that they were not going to be intimidated or driven from their new home. As the day progressed, the crowd began to turn more violent. Shouted threats and racial slurs turned to rock throwing. Two African-Americans on their way home from work approached the area where the crowd was gathered and were set upon and beaten while police stood by and watched.[11] Shortly afterward a rock was hurled through one of the windows and bullets began piercing the side of the house. As the crowd began to advance a shot rang out from inside the house striking down one of the crowd of protesters. The police sprang into action. All eleven blacks and none of the whites were arrested.[12]

The trial that ensued was one of the landmark civil rights cases of the early twentieth century. The NAACP hired the noted lawyer Clarence Darrow to handle the Sweet defense. During the trial, Darrow convinced an all-white jury that speakers at a Waterworks Park Improvement Association rally a few days before the incident had urged the crowd to use violence to protect their neighborhood, and Dr. Sweet was justified in using force to protect his home and family from a hostile mob. Sweet was acquitted.[13] The maxim that "a man's home is his castle" even applied to a black man fortunate enough to receive top flight legal representation, but racial tensions in the city were not diminished.

The influx of blacks seeking jobs in the defense plants during World War II exacerbated Detroit's chronic housing shortage. With single rooms renting for $60 a month or higher in Paradise Valley at the outset of the war, the Detroit Housing Authority felt compelled to respond to an obvious need and proposed a black-only housing project that would be located in the black neighborhood.[14] Since the project was to be built as part of the war housing program, federal approval was needed. Social planners in the Federal Housing authority wanted to see the development integrated into a white neighborhood located just north of the Polish community of Hamtramck near a predominantly black enclave called Conant Gardens. Despite objections from both the black and white leadership of Detroit, who feared a racial confrontation, the federal government approved plans for a housing development, named for the black abolitionist Sojourner Truth, at the crossroads of Nevada and Fenelon just outside the Conant Gardens neighborhood.

Construction of the units proceeded with dispatch and the development was ready for occupancy by mid December, 1941. As the buildings were made ready for their new tenants, a dispute raged over whether those tenants would be black or white. Before a backdrop of simmering racial agitation in the surrounding white neighborhoods, the black and white power structures of the city lobbied Washington vigorously in support of their opposing positions. The federal authorities wavered under pressure from the competing interests and reversed their decision over which racial group would occupy the project several times. It was not until April 30, 1942 that, with protection from 1,000 Army troops, 300 state police, and 450 Detroit policemen, 300 black families moved into their new homes.[15]

The Sojourner Truth dispute occurred on the heels of the UAW victory in the Ford strike at the River Rouge plant, and marked an important chapter in the reorientation of the attitude of the black community toward the union. CIO support for black occupancy of the project was resolute and crucial in achieving the final outcome, and a basis for continued cooperation between the two groups was established.

The "victory" in the housing project dispute did little to dampen the racial animosities that permeated the city during the war years. Sojourner Truth was a prelude to some of the worst racial violence in mid-century America. During this period of often violently expressed intolerance, the union and the civil rights organizations stood together and forged an alliance that would ultimately write an obituary for Jim Crow in America.

Living in the Shadow of Ford

During the "roaring twenties" and "desperate thirties," the leadership of the black community in Detroit was decidedly pro-business and comfortably snuggled within the protective shadow of Henry Ford. The symbiosis between Ford and the black community of Detroit began one afternoon in 1919 when Charles Sorenson, Ford's Production Manager, invited the Reverend Robert Bradby of the Second Baptist Church to a luncheon meeting with Henry Ford. Ford expressed his desire to hire blacks in the River Rouge and Highland Park plants. Bradby agreed to recommend "very high type fellows" and "to acquaint the colored workers with the responsibilities of employment [...] telling them they should be 'steady workers' so as to prove the worthiness of colored industrial workers."[16] For the next 6 years Bradby would roam the production floors of the two plants, resolving racial conflicts and preaching good working habits to his black recruits. Another prominent minister recruited to Ford's service was Everard Daniel, pastor of the St. Matthews Episcopal Church. St. Matthews was Donald Marshall's congregation, and Ford, an Episcopalian, made it a point to attend services at St. Matthews at least once a year.

Ford was no liberal. He harbored the racial attitudes of his time. He believed in the superiority of the white race and in racial segregation, but he rallied to Kipling's call to "Take up the White Man's Burden." Ford's attitude on race paralleled Kipling's. "Dominance is an obligation," Ford wrote. "The solution of the race question as of every other, lies in the stronger serving the weaker, the abler serving the less developed. [...] The superior racial stream was equipped for the service of the other, not for exploitation and suppression."[17]

Ford wrote in the Dearborn Independent, that Anglo-Saxon-Celtic peoples were the only cultures capable of sustaining democratic institutions, and shared the suspicions of Henry Cabot Lodge and Henry Adams about recent immigrants from Eastern European and Mediterranean countries. Jews were viewed by Ford, and many of his contemporaries, as a particularly pernicious people that fostered alien doctrines and stirred unrest among the black population with ideas that were more clever than the black man would arrive at on his own.[18] Government was best left in the hands of those capable of running it—men like Ford, Lodge, and Adams.

The Urban League was the organization founded to promote black economic development. Its Detroit chapter was made up of businessmen and professional people whose livelihoods were dependent on the business they received from the Ford workers. It was founded in 1916 and received much of its funding from the Community Chest and the Employer's Association of Detroit.[19] Its long-time leader was J. C. Dancy, an outspoken critic of the AFL.

The NAACP chapter in Detroit was also sympathetic to the business interests in the city. Black clergymen like Bradby and Daniels, and black businessmen were prominent in the leadership of the chapter, and Edsel Ford and Mrs. Horace Dodge were among the organization's most notable supporters and financial contributors. The NAACP traditionally concentrated on legal challenges to discrimination and deferred to organizations like the Urban League to promote black economic development, but the NAACP, like the rest of the black leadership in Detroit, was solidly pro-management, anti-union, and beholden to Ford.

The Detroit chapter, the largest and best financed chapter in the NAACP, increasingly found itself at odds with its national organization during the labor struggles of the late thirties. The national organization recognized the inevitability of industrial organization, and realized that the black worker stood more to gain from being part of that effort than resisting it and earning the enmity of his white co-workers. The Detroit chapter remained avowedly anti-union and pro-Ford.

The emergence of the CIO under the tutelage of John L. Lewis in the mid-thirties, offered hope that the discriminatory practices of the AFL that had solidified black opposition to the union movement would not be continued in the industrial unions. The United Mine Workers under Lewis had a good record in combating discrimination and the CIO committed itself to non-discrimination in its charter. The schism between Lewis and the AFL leadership under William Green occurred after the 1935 AFL convention. A. Phillip Randolph of the Sleeping Car Porters Union organized a picketing effort at the previous convention and called for an investigation into discrimination by the AFL. A committee was formed to look into the charges. Expert Witnesses, like NAACP lawyer, Charles Houston, appeared before the committee and documented instances of discrimination by the union. The committee report was presented at the 1935 convention, but ignored by its delegates, prompting one of the members of the committee, John Brophy, a Lewis protégé, to denounce the union for its failure to combat discrimination.[20.] The same convention failed to approve a plan for organizing industrial workers, leading Lewis to form the Committee of Industrial Organizations. Within weeks of the close of the AFL convention, Brophy became a director of the new organization.

The depression and the New Deal policies to address its consequence brought changes to the black community in Detroit and elsewhere. Before the New Deal, blacks voted overwhelmingly Republican. After Roosevelt's term, blacks became a pillar of Roosevelt's Democratic coalition. Men coming of age during the depression developed a different world view from their elders. New voices like those of Horace White, Louis Martin, and Charles Diggs began to be heard in black Detroit.

In 1936 Horace White, fresh out of the Oberlin College Divinity School, became pastor of the Plymouth Congregational Church. White attracted a younger, more educated congregation to his services and became the spokesperson for a generation no longer content to squeeze out an existence by currying favor of the industrial plantation boss. The energetic young minister was immediately active in the civic affairs of the community and became a member of the executive board of the local NAACP chapter. White's article *Who Owns the Negro Churches* exposed the collusion between Ford and the back clergy and insisted that the black church was the one institution where all the voices of the community should be heard and issues affecting the community freely discussed.[21]

Louis Martin moved to Detroit to become the editor of the *Michigan Chronicle*, a subsidiary of a conservative black paper published in Chicago. Martin used the paper to air his pro-union sympathies. The *Chronicle* offered an alternative viewpoint from two other pro-Republican black papers in the city, and developed a sufficiently large readership to allow the conservative ownership of the paper to tolerate its divergent political orientation.[22]

Charles Diggs was elected to the Michigan State Senate from a racially mixed district that included the Polish enclave of Hamtramck. Diggs was a vigorous supporter of the CIO and Roosevelt's New Deal. His politics resonated with the auto workers living in his district, and he received sufficient white support to enable his election. Elected office provided Diggs a platform that elevated his voice within both the black and white communities of the city.

The other new voice being heard in Detroit and elsewhere in the country in the 1930's belonged to the Communist Party. The collapse of the capitalist economy during the depression drove intellectuals and desperate workers alike to embrace a collectivist alternative. The party identified the exploited factory worker and the marginalized black man as the revolutionary cadre that would overturn the system and wrest control from the capitalists whom it benefited. The Communist message resonated within the black community at the time, and Communists were very active within the industrial union movement. Blacks were not prominent in the labor movement, but the few that were either actively supported the Communist party or flirted with Communist ideology. Communist influence was a big reason why the CIO took a principled stand against discrimination in employment within the industries it represented.

Walter Hardin was the most prominent black labor leader during the sit downs and the battle with Ford. He had been part of the union movement from the days of the International Workers of the World. Hardin joined the Communist Party in 1929 and was active as an organizer of the Communist-led AWU.[23] Hardin later quit the party and got a job at Pontiac where Homer Martin made him an organizer in 1937. Walter Hardin had a commanding presence, spoke with a big voice, and was a gifted orator. He had earned the respect of workers of both races for the battle scars he had received in the labor wars of the period. A CIO feature story described Hardin as "Kicked and flogged, clubbed on the picket line, threatened with bodily violence a score of times and victim of other anti-labor uprisings […] His courage in refusing to be bullied by vigilante mobs symbolizes the driving spirit of the CIO."[24]

Hardin was later named to a position on the Ford Organizing Campaign Committee and made the head of a Committee charged with doing organizational work among blacks. Paul Kirk was employed by the union in 1938 to be the first black organizer at the Rouge, and William Nowell and Frank Evans were added to Hardin's staff. Both Kirk and Nowell had Communist ties, but Nowell like Hardin left the party by the time of the Ford campaign. Other notable blacks that were part of the Ford organizing drive included Leon Bates, Joseph Billups, and John Conyers, Sr.[25]

During the thirties, the Communists were able to work effectively with progressives in support of common goals. At about the same time that the CIO formalized its break with the AFL and became the Congress of Industrial Organizations, John Davis, who had strong ties to the Communist Party, formed the National Negro Conference (NNC). The NNC served as an umbrella organization for other groups combating racial and social injustice. It included among its supporters future Nobelist Ralph Bunche and A. Phillip Randolph, who served as the group's first national president. Among the financial backers of the NNC was the United Mine Workers of John L. Lewis.[26]

As the economy improved during the latter years of the thirties and New Deal programs blunted the appeal of Communist ideology, Communist party influence began to recede. Factional disputes within the party also winnowed its membership. After being denounced as a right-deviationist for supporting Bukharin in the succession struggle after Lenin's death, Jay Lovestone formed an opposition wing of the Communist Party that in a succession of steps deemphasized its affiliation with Communism in name and deed, eventually calling itself in 1938 the Independent Labor League of America.[27] Hardin and Nowell went through the same evolutionary process in their ideological development as Lovestone, and became identified with his movement.

Lovestone landed a position of influence on the staff of Homer Martin during the first phase of the factional struggle within the UAW.[28] Black unionists were caught in the crossfire. The Negro Department, created by Martin and staffed with his loyalists, was dissolved by his opponents on the Executive Board. Blacks were forced to choose sides. Martin rehired Evans and Nowell for his staff and created a Negro seat on the board for Evans, but despite his efforts, the majority of blacks attending the 1939 convention sided with the Unity caucus at the urging of CPUSA members Paul Kirk and Billups.[29] Martin was ousted from his leadership position and formed a splinter union affiliated with the AFL. Evans and other staffers from the Negro Department followed Martin into his exile. Martin's successor, R. J. Thomas, was faced with the task of reestablishing the apparatus for organizing black workers for the coming fight with Ford.

By the time of the McCarthy hearings in the early fifties, the Communist Party of the United States was an unpicked fruit shriveling on the branch. Worker representation in the plants and participation in the economic boom rendered the prospect of a post-capitalist America remote, and Stalinist repression had turned the dream of a worker's paradise into a nightmare. The hearings were a tool for stigmatizing a few old lefties for their youthful flirtation with an unchaste ideology and making an example of them to anyone straying off the well-marked trail in the future. The real objective of the far right was to slow and reverse the gains achieved by labor and minorities over the previous twenty years. McCarthy spread a chill over the cultural and intellectual climate in the country, but did little to stifle the demand for social and economic progress arising from the factories and ghettos across the land.

With the demise of the Soviet Union and the face lift the ideology has been given in China a more dispassionate examination of the role Communists played in American history is timely. There is no label "Made in Moscow" stamped on any of the progressive measures and movements coming out of the thirties and forties, but, whether through conviction or ideology, American Communists served as an accelerant in these movements. Individuals who also happened to be Communists risked their physical and economic well-being for civil rights and workers' rights. Without their contributions the history of the second half of the twentieth century might read far differently.

Black Detroit After the Overpass

A strike at Dodge in the fall of 1939 provided a preview of the coming battle with Ford. Dodge was the second largest employer of blacks in Detroit, most of whom were consigned to low-level, low-paying jobs. Most of the black workers at Dodge were suspicious of the union and willing to cross the picket line to remain working. On Friday, November 24, about 60 black workers brushed past the pickets and entered the plant to pick up their pay checks. The blacks were promised work if they returned Monday.[30] Over the weekend, Homer Martin, acting for his rival AFL affiliate, held a rally at which Frank Evans urged the assembled black workers to return to work on Monday. John Dancy was also working behind the scenes to advance the company position.[31]

Horace White was horrified by the prospect of a full scale racial riot resulting from a conflict between blacks and whites on the picket line, and hurriedly called a meeting of community leaders to try to head off the confrontation. White gathered liberals like Louis Martin, State Senator Diggs, and Hardin, and conservatives like Reverend William Peck and Wilbur Woodson together to plan a strategy to thwart the back to work effort.[32] White's group also contained two new faces in the black establishment: Malcolm Dade, who had recently arrived in the city, and Charles Hill, who had once served as Bradby's assistant pastor, but, when given a parish of his own, became an outspoken advocate of cooperation with the CIO. White's committee composed a pamphlet urging blacks not to report for work on Monday that was signed by White, Diggs, and Louis Martin, and was distributed to parishioners attending church services on Sunday morning.[33]

When Monday morning dawned a couple hundred blacks and a few dozen whites arrived at the company gates to report for work and were confronted by about 6,000 picketers. Over 1,000 Detroit policemen were on hand, ready to intervene if fighting erupted. Horace White tried with little success to persuade the blacks arriving for work to return home and not try to cross the picket line. White then worked with Richard Frankensteen and Samuel Fanroy to convince the pickets to allow the few hundred workers to pass and avoid a confrontation that would likely result in the National Guard being activated to halt the strike.[34] On Monday evening Martin held another rally to try to encourage more blacks to cross the lines, but again the strikebreakers were allowed to peacefully enter the plant, and the few hundred workers reporting were far too few to keep the plant operating. The AFL intervened to curtail the back to work effort of Martin and curb his strikebreaking activity.[35] With the plant effectively closed by peaceful assembly, an agreement brokered by federal mediator James Dewey was expeditiously achieved. The agreement stipulated that "rank on the seniority list shall not be affected by race [...] of the employee."[36]

Between the end of the Dodge strike and the revival of the Ford campaign, attitudes toward the union in the black community continued to moderate. During the period between 1937 and 1939, the local NAACP chapter conducted a spirited membership drive that increased its number to over 6,000.[37] A physician, Dr. James McClendon, became the chapter president and announced a militant program to increase black employment in civil service jobs. McClendon was personally conservative, but broadened the base of his organization by including people like Horace White, Malcolm Dade, UAW member Prince Clark, and NNC member Robert Evans on the executive board.[38] McClendon also started a Youth Division headed by Gloster Current and Horace Sheffield, a worker at the Rouge and part-time college student. The Youth Division, though loosely affiliated with the NAACP, worked closely with the NNC, often challenging its elders by taking militant positions and resisting the rights group's interference with their projects.

In preparation for the Ford campaign, UAW president R. J. Thomas named Emil Mazey, president of the Briggs local, to head the Negro Organizing Committee. Mazey was considered for the assignment because of his resolve in supporting black promotions at Briggs and for hiring a black secretary for his staff in the face of opposition within the office pool, but black unionists demanded that a black occupy the position. Thomas acquiesced to the demand from the blacks and recalled Hardin from an assignment in Chicago to fill the post.[39]

As the struggle at Ford neared a climax, much of black Detroit was still skeptical of the UAW and retained a reserve of support for Ford. Though the death of Reverend Daniel in 1939 deprived Ford of its most stalwart friend in the black community, the established leadership and the older clergy continued to advocate gradual change through cooperation with the industrialist. There was growing annoyance with this approach. The "new-crowd," affiliated with the NNC and the Youth Division of the NAACP, urged black workers to join the union. The younger generation was impatient with the slow rate of progress being achieved and favored direct action to demand equal opportunity as a fundamental right, not as a favor curried from a placated oligarch. Geraldine Bledsoe, a member of the Urban League Board, began attending NNC meetings in the late thirties and heard the message that blacks "had to be vigorous and uncompromising and demanding in order to find their place."[40]

The union victory at Ford began a period of courtship between the UAW and the black leadership of the city that ended in a stable, if not always harmonious, union. National NAACP Executive Secretary Walter White explained his support for the union during the strike by stating the alliance between the black community and organized labor was "the new order of things."[41] Blacks no longer received consideration in hiring by Ford and had to rely on the unions to advance their economic welfare, and the concentration of black workers in specific plants made the position of the union vulnerable without their support. The top leadership of the UAW, though fractured by factional rivalry, was united behind the goal of equal opportunity. The means for achieving the goal, however, was often dictated by the political posturing of the opposing caucuses, and the commitment of the leadership was frequently not shared at the local level or by the shop stewards on the factory floor.

Double V for Victory

The battle to organize the last major recalcitrant manufacturer ended as the country prepared itself for a different war that offered new challenges for labor and new opportunities for blacks. With the United States becoming increasingly committed to the battle for freedom on foreign soil, A. Phillip Randolph linked the struggle abroad with the struggle for equality at home. Under the slogan "Double V for Victory," Randolph, along with Bayard Rustin and A. J. Muste, organized a March on Washington Movement (MOWM) that threatened to have over 100,000 blacks descend on segregated Washington, and demand jobs in the rapidly expanding defense economy.[42] Faced with a potentially explosive racial confrontation, Roosevelt issued Executive Order #8802 barring racial discrimination in hiring and promotions in industries receiving government contracts. To enforce the order, a Fair Employment Practice Commission was established inside the Office of Production Management. The order was hailed as a second Emancipation Proclamation in the black community, and Randolph called off the threatened march.

The March on Washington Movement did not disband after the order was issued, but was fused into the Double V for Victory campaign. Randolph resigned from the presidency of the NNC in 1940, blasting its association with the Communist Party after the Hitler-Stalin nonaggression pact was signed, but he remained close to individuals within the group who were instrumental in developing the confrontational strategy to quicken the pace of racial progress. The MOWM restricted its membership to blacks. Whites were welcome to support the various activities planned by the movement, but the planning and organization of activities was to be done exclusively by blacks. It was felt by leaders of the movement that blacks were often too deferential to sympathetic whites and that whites exerted a moderating influence that steered the group away from confrontation toward a more gradualist approach.[43] The MOWM and the activities of the NNC in the 1940s created the first stirrings of a movement that resurfaced two decades later under the slogan of "Black Power."

With the advent of war, Government became more directly involved in the personnel decisions of the defense industries. The unions offered a no-strike pledge at the outset of hostilities, and a War Labor Board (WLB) was established to resolve labor disputes in the critical industries and maintain the relative status quo that existed between labor and management in 1941. It was composed of four representatives each from management, labor, and the general public. When the case load became too heavy, the Board was decentralized into twelve regional administrative boards and later reorganized nationally into subsections concerned with specific industries. War-time labor and production directives were enforced by military compliance officers who had broad latitude to resolve problems that threatened the prompt delivery of war materiel.[44] In Detroit, the military compliance officers included Colonel George Strong of the Army Air Corps, who played a prominent role in resolving the "hate strikes" that resulted from enforcement of Executive Order #8802.

The various government agencies created to deal with the war-time emergency were hastily composed and frequently reorganized. Robert Weaver, who had served as Chief of Negro Employment and Training in the Office of Production Management was named to head the Fair Employment Practices Commission (FEPC). The FEPC received little in the way of funding and little authority to take direct action to resolve cases of discrimination. It mainly acted by holding public hearings to embarrass companies that blatantly flaunted the executive order. When Weaver's commission was eventually placed under the supervision of the War Manpower Commission, headed by Paul V. McNutt, his field representatives were not transferred along with him. McNutt did not place a priority on fighting discrimination, and in one of his first decisions, canceled public hearings into discrimination in the railroad industry.[45] Only continued pressure from the black community made Executive Order #8802 an important milestone in the march to full equality.

War production required fewer foundry workers where many blacks were employed, necessitating layoffs for workers who were not transferred to positions requiring additional skills. In the summer of 1941, black workers at the Chrysler Dodge plant, walked out to protest the upgrading of whites with less seniority. Reliance on good relations with the auto executives provided little return for the black establishment. J. C. Dancy's old friend, Charles Winegar, the Personnel Director at Chrysler, was conspicuously insensitive to pleas from the Urban League on the workers' behalf.[46] The walkout at Chrysler Dodge was the first in a wave of racially-related wildcat strikes that troubled the factories during the war years. Black "victory" committees formed inside the locals and forced the pace of integration of the workplace faster than the union hierarchy and the government had intended.

The top UAW leadership was sympathetic to the demands of the black workers, but preferred the government take the main initiative in resolving the crisis. The job action at Dodge was halted when representatives from the Office of Production Management sat down with management and labor and negotiated a "Six Point Transfer Program" that provided for the upgrading of defense workers strictly on a seniority basis. The Six Point Transfer Program became the basis for an agreement to upgrade about 150 black workers at Kelsey Hayes.[47] Victor Reuther met with the white workers of local 174 and secured their support to win approval of the agreement.[48] Upgrading of black workers to skilled positions in the defense plants proceeded without significant problems in some industries, but triggered a racist counter response in others.

The union acted to counteract hate strikes when they occurred. At Curtiss Wright in Cleveland, management was willing to upgrade black workers, but a prejudiced union official stood in the way. R. J. Thomas intervened directly by removing the staff member and negotiating an agreement directly with the company. When a similar dispute at Hudson led to a walkout of about 10,000 white workers, Thomas wired the Local 154 president stating that the "display of vicious race prejudice" violated the UAW Constitution and would not be tolerated. Strikers would face expulsion from the union and the union would not intercede for anyone dismissed for these actions.[49] Frankensteen flew in from Washington to reinforce the directive and the strike was settled with four of the ringleaders dismissed.

The most serious hate strike occurred at Packard in 1943. The Ku Klux Klan made a concerted effort to infiltrate the UAW in the early forties and exert its influence in the councils of its leadership. Though R. J. Thomas strongly denounced the attempt ("If the KKK and the rest of the nightshirt boys want to fight the union on this issue, we are ready to take them on."[50]), it is estimated that as many as 200 delegates to the 1941 convention were members of the Klan. Klan presence was particularly strong in Packard Local 190. The racial bigotry prevalent inside the union local was also manifested by the company's management. Personnel Director C. E. Weiss was an unabashed racist. When a white FEPC investigator was accompanied by his black counterpart at meeting aimed at resolving the conflict, Weiss greeted him with the comment "You ought to know better than to bring a Negro in here to settle this thing."[51]

When three blacks were upgraded to the assembly line, several hundred whites put down their tools and refused to work. Efforts to get the men to resume their work proved unsuccessful, and the union proposed removing the three black workers from the line until a meeting could be held to resolve the situation. The removal of the three blacks caused the black foundry workers to walk out and shut down the foundry for three days. Colonel Strong promised the foundry workers that the three blacks would be upgraded and coaxed them back to work. Appeals by Thomas and Strong at a May 30th meeting to resolve the problems were greeted with boos and shouts of disapproval. Hundreds of members walked out while Thomas was speaking. Thomas vowed to enforce the UAW Constitution and shouted to the assembled "This problem must be resolved or it will wreck our union."[52]

Before the three blacks were returned to the assembly line as required by Executive Order #8802, they were warned by Weiss that they would only keep their jobs if it was acceptable to the white workers. Then he and other management officials circulated about the plant telling the whites that they would not be required to work alongside blacks if they objected to doing so. Management used the dispute to provoke hostility toward the UAW by telling the workers that they had no union and they should come back into the company union again.[53] The whites walked off the job and Packard again removed the blacks from the line.

With the situation spiraling out of control, Thomas asked the Labor Department to refer the dispute to the WLB and requested that the FEPC formally enter the dispute. When efforts in Detroit reached an agreement to restore the three blacks to the line, 25,000 white workers walked out. Thomas and Local 190 president Norman Mathews condemned the strike but were unable to stop it. Thomas flew to Washington to seek federal intervention. He urged officials at the War Department to take over the plant and to return Colonel Strong to Detroit from another assignment.

The Deputy Director of the WLB sent a blunt telegram ordering Packard workers to "resume production of vitally needed war material at once."[54] Colonel Strong was ordered back to Detroit, and he reinforced the WLB directive with a threat that anyone persisting in the strike would be fired. Thomas reiterated his threat of expulsion from the union for workers who did not return to work at once. He told a supportive conference of Ford union representatives "Some people in front of the Packard plant say that if they stay on the street long enough the International union must retreat. We will not retreat. I say to you if we take any other position our organization is lost."[55]

In the face of the determined stand of the WLB and the union leadership, the strike lost momentum and the workers trickled back to work. An investigation conducted by Colonel Strong identified thirty ringleaders who were suspended. Included among those suspended was Christopher Alston, the black union steward who led the walkout by the foundry workers during the initial phase of the confrontation. Strong had threatened to have Alston drafted into the Army if he persisted with his militancy. When the strike ended Strong made good on his threat.

Alston, a thirty-one year old father, was fired by Packard and drafted into the Amy.[56]

The strong stand taken by the union during the hate strikes and the Sojourner Truth housing dispute did much to win over the black community of Detroit. At the height of the Packard strike, Robert Bradby opened his church to the NAACP's Emergency Wartime Conference, where William White and Thurgood Marshall held Packard solely responsible for the troubles. Five years earlier, national NAACP leaders like White and Marshall, and UAW President R. J. Thomas were unable to find a venue in any black church in the city, much less Bradby's. With the strike concluded, Christopher Alston told the Conference "in the face of KKK opposition, UAW leaders had broken the strike."[57] J. C. Dancy too became a vocal supporter of the union. In writing his memoirs in later years, he conveniently forgot that he was ever anything but a proponent of the union movement.[58]

The Detroit Riot of 1943

The hate strikes in the plants ended with the forced acceptance of black upgrades to skilled and semi-skilled positions, but the racial animosity in the city did not diminish with the end of the walk out. On June 20th, two weeks after the strike at Packard ended, some long-forgotten incident occurred between whites and blacks enjoying a Sunday respite at Belle Isle Park. By that evening fighting had spread from the park over into the city. Rumors spread like a contagious disease. By evening upwards to 5,000 people were involved in the fighting including 200 sailors from the naval armory located near the bridge linking the park with the rest of the city.[59] As the rioting intensified, leaders of the black community asked the mayor and the governor to call in federal troops to restore order. Both refused.[60] On Monday afternoon, R. J. Thomas joined the black leaders in demanding a federal response to quell the riot. Thomas announced that he had alerted the shop stewards in all of the plants with union representation to keep the peace and reported that no fighting had occurred in any of these locations.[61]

By Monday evening gun battles erupted between the rioting mobs and with the police. The surge in violence finally prompted the governor to declare martial law and request federal troops. When the riot ended, 34 people were dead, 23 of whom were black, 800 people were injured, and 1,800 were arrested.[62] The United States Army had to be called upon to take possession of an American city during a time the nation was fighting a world war on two fronts.

J. C. Dancy lauded Thomas for the support he offered during the riot,[63] but the experience of the riot and the hate strikes rattled the leaders of the still-fledgling union. Thomas and Reuther became impatient with the "march behavior" of militants in the rank-and-file who initiated actions on their own without consent from the leadership. Hardin's relationship with Thomas became strained. He was seen to be frequently acting at cross purposes with the regional directors, and after the Packard strike the Inter-Racial Committee was dissolved.[64]

At the 1943 UAW Convention, Shelton Tappes, the Recording Secretary of Ford Local 600, introduced a proposal to establish a Minorities Department headed by an elected board member who would be black. Tappes's proposal stipulated that the Negro seat on the board would have thirty votes. (Votes allotted to members of the Executive Board were weighted according to the size of the constituency they represented.) The proposal was endorsed by Hardin and Sheffield and was championed by Communists in the Addes camp.[65] The proposal was interjected into the political struggle between the Reuther group and the group headed by George Addes and Richard Frankensteen. Reuther was supporting the Ford division leader Richard Leonard to replace Addes as Secretary-Treasurer of the Union. The Addes group, while genuinely supportive of the proposal, saw an opportunity to win crucial black support in the closely contested election battle. Reuther feared that the thirty votes assigned to the Negro seat would tilt the balance of the board decisively in the Addes camp's favor. He affirmed his support for a black on the board, but not for a reserved seat. Reuther did voice support for a Minorities Department with its own director.[66] The compromise position was unacceptable to the proposal's sponsors and Addes won re-election with the support of a large percentage of the black delegates. Reuther and Frankensteen were elected first and second vice president respectively.

The Tappes proposal was considered after the vote for the officers. It was amended to give the position only a single vote on the board, but Reuther remained opposed, arguing that reserving a special black seat was a hypocritical demand for reverse racism. Thomas sided with Reuther, and the proposal was defeated. Sheffield and Hardin broke ranks with the black block and voted against the proposal, claiming that the position with only a single vote was one of impotence. Their vote also indicated their disaffection with the Communist Party.[67]

The Tappes proposal was revisited in subsequent conventions, but never gained sufficient support for its approval. At the 1944 Convention, the UAW established a Fair Practices Commission headed by former labor lawyer, George Crockett. The Fair Practices Commission came under tighter supervision from the Executive Board than the previous Inter-Racial Committee. Both Thomas and the Reuther group were concerned that the autonomy of the black caucus groups could fracture the fragile unity of the labor movement.[68] Hardin was relegated to positions of less authority and ushered out of the union entirely in 1946 with the ascendancy of Walter Reuther.

UAW Civil Rights Policy Under Reuther's Leadership

By 1947 Walter Reuther had gained full control of the UAW leadership; the Russian winter had descended over Eastern Europe; and the Republicans had gained control of Congress. With Roosevelt dead and the country plagued by the many long strikes that followed the wartime moratorium on sanctioned job actions, conservatives sensed an opportunity to roll back gains achieved by labor under the New Deal. The Republican Congress, with Democratic support, passed the Taft-Harley Act over President Truman's veto. The act amended the Wagner Act to prohibit jurisdictional strikes, secondary boycotts, secondary picketing, and closed shops. The act granted states the right to pass their own right-to-work laws outlawing union shops. It prevented unions from contributing money to federal political campaigns, mandated a sixty day notification in advance of a strike, and granted the President the right to seek an injunction to prohibit any strike that would "imperil the national health or safety." In a blatant affront to the right of free speech, the Taft-Hartley Act required that union officers sign non-Communist affidavits with the government.

The union movement was under attack and anti-Communism was enshrined as a national religious belief. Blacks were specifically targeted. Many veterans of the MOWM had aligned with Communists or flirted with Communist ideology to one degree or another during the pre-war years. It became a tactic of the right to thwart the Civil Rights Movement by coloring it red.

Walter Reuther consolidated his control of the UAW by purging Communists and their allies from positions of leadership and restricting the autonomy of the black caucus. In 1946 the Fair Practices Committee was reorganized as the Fair Practices and Anti-Discrimination Department with 1% of the union dues allocated to its operation. Crockett was replaced by a Reuther ally, William Oliver, and Reuther assumed the role of co-director in a gesture to enhance the department's visibility, but also limit its autonomy. Black activists were either forced out of their union positions or accommodated to the new environment. Shelton Tappes went through a transformation from militant activist with Communist sympathies to cooperative witness before the House Un-American Activities Committee.

Reuther's opposition to the agenda of the black caucus and his effort to rid the union of Communist influence at the expense of some of its most capable organizers has led some on the left to consider him a social conservative who stalled the drive for equality in the workplace at a time when there was wind in its sails. Such a conclusion misreads the political and social context of the times and diminishes the character of the man and the pivotal role he played in the legislative and contractual victories of the movement. Reuther believed that securing better pay, employment opportunities, and benefits for all workers would benefit blacks more than a divisive emphasis on a militant black agenda. He subsumed the civil rights struggle into the larger class struggle and built a constituency for the former through education, coalition building, and legislative initiative.

Walter Reuther emerged as the leader of the winning coalition after a bitter factional fight. The faction he led was composed of various elements that agreed on their opposition to Communism, but differed on many other issues. As leader, Reuther had to maintain his coalition and unite the rank-and-file behind realizable goals. He faced personal danger as well as threats to his union and his leadership. The union movement faced a hostile Congress, a growing hysteria over Communism, and an increasingly unsympathetic public. The acrid smell of the 1943 Detroit riot lingered over every major city. The Red Scare haunting the post-war period frightened even George Addes and Richard Leonard into abandoning their former allies and endorsing the use of Section 8 of the Taft-Hartley Act to exclude Communists from holding union office.[69]

Pervasive anti-Communism produced a re-evaluation of strategy in the black community. Horace Sheffield and later Shelton Tappes were among the prominent blacks aligning with the Reuther group. The Michigan Chronicle endorsed Reuther's bid for the UAW presidency, albeit in lukewarm tone. The paper's editorial writers believed that the black autoworkers would benefit from the stability of a Reuther regime. The paper asserted "the so-called Negro issue had become such a political football in the union that no real, substantial gains for our workers was possible. While we do not regard Walter Reuther as another Abraham Lincoln or John Brown, we do believe that Mr. Reuther is best fitted [...] to advance our cause within and without the organization."[70] While not a ringing endorsement of Reuther, the editorial was a tacit admission that aggressive confrontation was likely to produce more backlash than benefit.

Walter Reuther was no reluctant recruit to the issue of civil rights. His empathy for the civil rights struggle was honed by his father, Valentine, while growing up in the steel town of Wheeling, West Virginia. In Reuther's youth, black workers from the South were transported through Wheeling in open rail cars to work in the auto factories of the North. One day Valentine caught some of the Reuther boys' playmates on a hill above the tracks throwing stones at the exposed blacks on the rail cars below. Reuther later recounted the incident to his daughter Lisa and told her "he came home white with rage. He gave us a tongue-lashing and said he had better not catch any one of us down there doing anything like that. We never had. But he gave us a tongue-lashing just in case."[71]

Reuther's earliest involvement in a civil rights cause occurred while he was a student at Detroit City University. Reuther continued his education during the day while working nights as a tool and die maker at Ford. On campus, he was active in forming a Social Issues Club and served as its president. During this time the college made arrangements with a nearby hotel to allow students to use the hotel pool. The arrangement did not include the school's black students. When Reuther learned of this exclusion, he organized club members to picket the hotel, carrying signs charging both the hotel and the university with discrimination. The student action drew the attention of the press, bringing unwanted publicity to the hotel and the university. When they started receiving angry letters from the community, the arrangement was terminated. Use of the pool was denied to all students, making Reuther very unpopular on campus.[72]

Walter Reuther was a vocal advocate for civil rights, but foremost he was president of a union and leader of a block that contained some of the more conservative members in the union hierarchy. He was in the forefront of marches and demonstrations for civil rights throughout the period of his leadership, but as an astute politician, he marched no faster nor farther than his membership was willing to allow him to proceed. Reuther maneuvered to consolidate rank and file support for his civil rights agenda by securing his leadership position with gains at the bargaining table and through educational programs that brought blacks and whites together in settings removed from the obligation of conforming to the pattern of behavior traced for them. Reuther believed that a favorable climate for black economic advancement could only occur in conjunction with a climate producing parallel gains for all workers.[73] Throughout his tenure as president of the UAW he fought for a national commitment to a full employment economy.

Reuther envisioned a full-employment economy as an offshoot of national planning that allied labor, industry, and government in a coordinated effort to expand consumer demand and direct production into satisfying the needs of this expanding consumer base. Despite the post-war retreat from New Deal and war-time programs favoring the evolution of such an alliance, he sought to fashion a more substantive partnership with industry than a purely adversarial deliberation on wages and working conditions. Union influence never did extend beyond personnel issues, but Reuther sought to build a base for the eventuality.

The contractual relationship between labor and management created a bureaucratic structure geared to minimize the areas of contention between successive negotiations. The channeling of worker militancy through a mechanistic structure was in part a natural maturation of the labor movement and in part the manifestation of Walter Reuther's management style.

Reuther's leadership style was demonstrated early in his presidency in the campaign to end discrimination in bowling. Bowling was a popular pastime of the working class with costs amenable to the working class budget. The sport was loosely regulated by the American Bowling Congress (ABC) which sanctioned leagues for all levels of competition and recognized bowling alleys that conformed to ABC standards. The ABC had a white-only policy in leagues they sanctioned. Bowling alleys, fearful of losing their ABC recognition and alienating their white clientele, excluded blacks during periods of non-league play as well as from sanctioned league activity. Blacks attempting to bowl were often confronted by hostile whites.[74]

During the war years, black caucus groups challenged the discriminatory practices of the ABC. Local 600, representing workers at the River Rouge plant and with strong Communist influence, voted to ban its membership from participating in ABC sanctioned leagues. Crockett, with backing from the NNC, urged the international leadership to do the same thing. He argued that if the union banned its membership from participating in ABC sanctioned leagues and established union-sponsored alternatives, local alleys would find it in their interest to allow mixed leagues even at the risk of loss of ABC affiliation.[75] The leadership was more concerned about the divisive affect a bowling restriction would have upon its rank-and-file, and instead ordered local 600 to lift its boycott. The union promised to complain to the ABC about its discriminatory policy, and secured the unsatisfactory concession of ABC sanction for segregated leagues.[76]

After Reuther's ascension to the presidency, the UAW renewed its attempt to get the ABC to change its discriminatory practice. The campaign was conducted in a manner characteristic of the Reuther approach. He continued to oppose a boycott that he argued would be divisive and drive members into company sponsored leagues. He channeled efforts into a legal and organizational engagement. He worked through the courts to present the ABC with a number of legal challenges that they were forced to defend and established a Fair Play in Bowling Committee of sympathetic clergy and lay people to reinforce the direct lobbying efforts of his Fair Practices Committee.[77] While the lobbying effort proceeded, the UAW sponsored its own integrated bowling tournaments. After a sustained effort of nearly a half dozen years, the UAW campaign helped convince the ABC to abandon its discriminatory policy.

In 1945 when still the head of the UAW General Motors Division, Walter Reuther flew to Atlanta to demand that Local 34 representing workers from the Fisher Body plant admit 120 black sweepers into the union and allow upgrades of black workers to production jobs. He met with a packed assembly of the rank-and-file and appealed to union solidarity, cajoled, and threatened the local with administratorship if they failed to uphold the UAW constitution. When he left the 120 sweepers were admitted to the union, but they all remained sweepers.[78] As the civil rights struggle intensified during the fifties, the local became hardened in its resistance to black advancement. Autoworker Elston Edwards, Imperial Wizard of the Georgia KKK, found the Fisher Body plant a hospitable place to find recruits for his extracurricular activities.[79]

GM had the worst record of the big 3 automakers in hiring and promoting blacks, and as it moved more of its manufacturing into the South it made no effort to change this reality. In 1957 the plant manager in Atlanta stated the GM position candidly and succinctly. "When we moved into the South we agreed to abide by local custom and not hire Negroes for production work. This is no time for social reforming [...] and we're not about to try it."[80] The UAW could not get GM to agree to an anti-discrimination clause in its contract talks, and between the demise of the FEPC after WW2 and the enactment of Title VII of the 1964 Civil Rights Act there was little government pressure brought against recalcitrant companies and unions over discriminatory behavior.

The Reuther approach achieved some measurable success. Gains at the bargaining table gave the UAW leverage to extract compliance with its anti-discrimination policy from some reluctant Southern locals during the fifties and sixties. Irving Bluestone recounted an incident in

Birmingham, Alabama when he stepped into a situation where local shop stewards were not permitting the upgrading of black workers to positions beyond the menial jobs for which they were originally hired. Bluestone gave the shop stewards an ultimatum: "You can have your paychecks or you can have your prejudice, but you can't have both."[81] Faced with that decision, the stewards chose paychecks and a roadblock to black advancement was removed. The union had the ability to force compliance and retain its influence with reluctant white workers because of the impact it made on the daily lives of its members.

The opposite sentiment was expressed by International Harvester workers in Memphis. When the company opened its Memphis factory in the late 1940s, it hired a substantial number of blacks to staff its new operation, but conflict between blacks and segregationist whites quickly devolved into a strictly enforced system of racial hierarchy. In the late fifties the segregationist Local 988 used money loaned by the international to construct a union hall with segregated restrooms and water faucets. As much as the international wished to ignore the situation and avoid a conflict with its rebellious local, the embarrassing dichotomy between its public posture and internal passivity forced it to take a stand. Douglas Fraser and Pat Greathouse were sent to Memphis to resolve the problem. The UAW stipulated in offering the loan that the facility would not be segregated. It got a court order that allowed it to take possession of the building, change the locks, and paint out the signs saying 'colored' and 'whites' on the restroom doors.[82] In response the local obtained a court order permitting it to reclaim the hall. This time the wording on the doors was changed to 'whites' and 'nigger'[83]. During a contentious meeting a white welder informed Fraser "we belong to Reuther's union, but we don't believe in Reuther's integration. When the showdown comes, we'll take segregation and leave you guys up in Detroit."[84] In Fraser's account of the incident, he related that the mood of the meeting turned ugly and he feared for his safety.

> "There was a cluster of tough guys waiting for me at
> the door and there wasn't any back exit. Well, George
> Holloway [leader of the black unionists of Local 988]
> came up to me and said 'Come over here, I want to show

you something.' He took me over to the side window. I looked out and saw a lot of cars parked over there. 'Those are our fellows. Just let me tell you something. We know it took a lot of guts for you to come down here. And we're going to see that you get back to Detroit safely.' And we won that battle [...] They knew we were firm in our commitment."[85]

In the auto factories of the North, the pace of black hiring and promotion was the issue, and critics of Reuther insisted he pushed the issue no further than was politically expedient. Without the FEPC machinery available to pressure the industry and the union, the pace of upgrading blacks to production jobs slowed and the percentage of blacks in skilled and semi-skilled positions remained at post-war levels for most of the next two decades.[86] The Treaty of Detroit surrendered a UAW role in production decisions for a package of benefits and scheduled productivity and cost of living increases. The contract restricted the role of seniority in departmental transfers and the right of the union to protest reassignments. When the economy went into recession later in the fifties, blacks bore the brunt of the layoffs and remained blocked from moving into the skilled positions. During the fifties the UAW faced an unsympathetic Congress, a diffusion of jobs away from its Midwestern base, and disaffection of its skilled craftsmen for a vertically organized industrial union. Reuther tempered his support for equal rights with the need to advance the union and his authority within it.

The Struggle for Civil Rights Moves from the Court House to the Streets

Reuther was elected to the executive board of the NAACP in 1949, and his union made substantial contributions to the organization. The NAACP concentrated its legal attack on the structures of segregation, and in 1954 convinced a unanimous Supreme Court to declare "separate but equal" school segregation unconstitutional. The NAACP effort was led by Thurgood Marshall, who later would become the first African-American justice seated on the Court, but much credit also belongs to

Associate Justice Hugo Black. Black was a Senator from Alabama when he was appointed to the Court by Roosevelt, and he had once been a member of the Ku Klux Klan, which he joined as a precursor for seeking public office in the state. Black was regarded as a New Deal liberal during his time in the Senate, but as part of the Southern block, led a filibuster against anti-lynching legislation. Black was the senior Justice on the Court at the time of Brown vs (Topeka, Kansas) Board of Education, and he used his influence to help Chief Justice Earl Warren secure the unanimous ruling.[87]

The Supreme Court ruling struck down the concept of "separate but equal" in education but did not provide a time frame for accomplishing the task or guidelines for how to proceed. The first test of enforcement of the law occurred in Little Rock, Arkansas in 1957. The Little Rock School Board reluctantly devised a plan for desegregating the city's schools in stages. The first stage was to be the token integration of all-white Central High by nine carefully chosen black students from the all-black Horace Mann High School. Integration of the junior highs and elementary schools was to occur in separate stages in subsequent years. The day before school was set to re-open, Arkansas Governor Orval Faubus called out the National Guard and refused entry to the nine blacks trying to attend the first day of classes. NAACP lawyers Thurgood Marshall and Wiley Branton obtained an injunction ordering Faubus to desist from his efforts to deny entry to the "Little Rock Nine." Faubus drew back and allowed an angry mob to take over. By noon the city police had lost control of the situation at the high school and escorted the black students out of the building through a back entrance.

President Eisenhower answered the challenge to federal authority by nationalizing the Arkansas guard and sending elements of the 101st Airborne Division into Little Rock to enforce the court order. The troops went in, the press descended on the city, the nine were able to begin attending classes, and the immediate crisis was resolved. The troops returned to their base, the press went home, and the black students were left to suffer the abuses hurled at them by their fellow classmates. With the spotlight turned off, the folks in Arkansas conducted a campaign of delay and intimidation for the next two years. The students faced constant harassment from their classmates and some of their parents lost their jobs and had to leave the state.[88] The persistence of the relatively few black families in the face of constant hostility helped inspire students sitting in at lunch counters in North Carolina and riding the buses on the dusty highways of the South.

Shortly after the historic Supreme Court ruling, Rosa Parks refused to give up her seat on a Montgomery Alabama bus to accommodate a white passenger. Parks was actually not the first black woman to refuse to yield her seat on a bus in the South, nor the first in Montgomery,[89] but her act of refusal and arrest spurred a black boycott of the Montgomery bus system that brought a young minister into national prominence. Dr. Martin Luther King, Jr. became the face and voice of a movement germinating in the soil of the old Confederacy. King was telegenic, courageous, and a gifted orator. His message of nonviolence appealed to white liberals, and his early focus on the trappings of segregation in the South, like rest rooms, lunch counters, and preferential seating on buses and trains, did not threaten any of their own interests. King set the tone for the movement and established its strategy of nonviolent confrontation, but he had to rely on other organizations, most notably the Student Nonviolent Coordinating Committee (SNCC), that adopted nonviolence as a tactic rather than a philosophy, to supply the ground troops.

To stay ahead of the movement and to push it forward, King needed to demonstrate the moral imperative of his crusade to sympathetic whites and achieve some tangible successes to maintain the resolve of awakened blacks. He needed the right script to attract his audience and the right actor to recite its lines. He found both in Birmingham, Alabama and its police chief Bull Connor. King intervened in a black boycott of Birmingham businesses aimed at eliminating segregated facilities and drinking fountains in the stores and the hiring of blacks to noncustodial positions. His intervention was not particularly welcomed in the city at the time, but King was looking to confront segregation on a wider scale and Birmingham provided the appropriate setting. King's Southern Christian Leadership Council (SCLC) organized demonstrations and sit-ins designed to provoke Connor and fill the city's jails. King himself was arrested on Good Friday and chose to forgo bail and remain incarcerated over the Holiday period. News of King's arrest and fears for his safety drew the attention of the world back to Birmingham. President Kennedy interceded to voice his concern for King's safety and telephoned his wife, Coretta Scott King, that she would soon be receiving a phone call from her husband. King used the time in jail to write an answer to a group of eight moderate local clergymen who were critical of his tactics and urged him to call off the demonstrations.

By the time King was released from jail, the demonstrations were losing steam. The population of adult volunteers was running low and the attention of the media was drawn elsewhere. James Bevel, the SCLC's Director of Direct Action and Nonviolent Education persuaded King to use high school and elementary school students to swell the ranks of the protesters and the population of the jails. Bevel argued that students who had spent years together in common circumstances were the most cohesive group in the community and were more receptive to the call for direct action than most adults.[90] King was to receive much criticism for approving of the tactic, but after prayerful reflection authorized Bevel to proceed with a program of instruction for the students into the dangers they would face and the nonviolent response they would employ. On May 2, 1963, the "Children's Crusade" began. The jails quickly filled, but the demonstrators kept marching. Bull Connor played his role in the script that the SCLC had written for him to perfection. He turned the fire hoses on the young demonstrators and sicked his police dogs on anyone not quick enough to beat a retreat. The scene was captured on camera and stung the conscience of the nation. President Kennedy told reporters that he was sickened by the photos he saw in the papers. The black community of Birmingham that had been lukewarm toward King's involvement in their affairs consolidated behind his leadership. Fissures developed between the business community of Birmingham and the city's political leadership. Bull Connor's term in office abruptly ended and an agreement to end the demonstrations was reached. The agreement produced little more than token improvement in employment opportunities for blacks, but Jim Crow was hit by a blast far stronger than the force of Bull Connor's water cannons.

Part of the agreement to end the demonstrations in Birmingham was that the AFL-CIO, principally the UAW, would put up the money to bail the demonstrators out of the city's jails. When called by Robert

Kennedy to request the bail money, Reuther was genuinely curious as to why the Attorney General was calling him about this problem. "Because we don't know anyone else we can call" was the reply on the other end of the line.[91] The contribution by the UAW of bail money for gaining the release of black civil rights activists was used in Southern factories to rally workers against voting for the UAW in representational elections.

UAW support for Dr. King and his Civil Rights Movement was made far more explicit on June 23rd of the same year when King journeyed to Detroit to take part with Reuther, Randolph, and several Michigan politicians in Walk to Freedom Day that commenced with a march down Woodward Avenue and ended with speeches in Cobo Hall. The Detroit march was in many ways a prelude to the March on Washington event being planned for later in the summer. King electrified the Cobo Hall crowd with a version of the "I Have a Dream" speech he would deliver before a national audience during the Washington event.

The events in Birmingham, together with the violence greeting the Freedom Riders and the attempts to integrate Southern Universities, pressured a politically cautious John F. Kennedy to introduce Civil Rights Legislation to Congress. Kennedy announced the move during a nationwide address on the evening of June 11, 1963, the same day George Wallace stood in the doorway to the future at the University of Alabama as a symbol of the old intransigent South. On the next night, Medgar Evers, the Field Secretary for the NAACP in Mississippi, was shot in the back returning home from a late meeting with NAACP lawyers.

The Evers murder put an exclamation mark at the end of the narrative spewed out by Bull Connor. Evers was buried with full honors at Arlington Cemetery while his assassin enjoyed decades of freedom under the protection of Jim Crow justice. The murder left a deep wound in the national conscience. Phil Ochs sang "It struck the heart of every man when Evers fell and died." Eudora Welty sought the rational of the killer in her short story *Where is the Voice Coming From?* Bob Dylan identified the killer of Evers as *Only a Pawn in [the] Game* of white politicians and community leaders needing to establish a social hierarchy to secure their own place of privilege. One of those white politicians, Mississippi Governor Ross Barnett, paid a friendly visit to the killer, Byron De La Beckwith, during his first trial that resulted in a hung jury.[92]

Kennedy's legislation faced a huge obstacle in the form of a Southern filibuster, and he feared his political future would be jeopardized by a deteriorating interracial climate. He had been reluctant to push the issue of civil rights, but events in Birmingham and throughout the South forced his hand.

The planned March on Washington had the potential to derail his presidency. Washington was as segregated a city as any in the South. Its location was determined by a compromise between the financial interests of Hamilton and the North and the agrarian interests of Jefferson and the slave-owning aristocrats of the South. It was still a rather sleepy Southern town, risen from a swamp, that everyone who could vacated during the oppressive summer heat. Racial attitudes were as deeply felt and strongly expressed as they were in Birmingham. The potential for trouble stirred the nightmares of the administration.

Randolph never canceled his March on Washington Movement after Roosevelt issued Executive Order #8802, he only put it on pause. Instead of marching to the capital to pressure the president, Randolph's marchers paraded into the union halls and city halls to demand fair employment and adequate housing. After the war the marchers retreated to safer ground to defend against a red scare and a white backlash. By 1963 the time was right for the march to go forward.

Randolph had always insisted upon black-only organization of black civil rights initiatives. The 1963 March was to be no different. Randolph structured an organizing committee consisting of himself and the leaders of the five main civil rights organizations: Roy Wilkins of the NAACP, Martin Luther King of the SCLC, Whitney Young of the Urban League, James Farmer of CORE, and John Lewis of SNCC. Reuther had a good deal of influence within this group because the UAW was a principal source of funding for several of the groups and because of the rapport he had with many of the leaders. Reuther was able to persuade the organizing group, with the support of Wilkins, to expand the organizing committee to include members of his "coalition of conscience." The original group of six was increased by four non-voting members to include Reuther, the Protestant cleric Eugene Carson Blake, rabbi Joachim Prinz, and Catholic layman Matthew Ahmann. Robert Kennedy set up a Justice Department task force to work with the organizers to ensure the event was orderly, peaceful, and well-attended with white participants also evident within the crowd. Kennedy sought to shift the focus of the event away from the Capitol and ensure the rhetoric would not sting the ears of the TV audience.[93]

Just as Randolph feared, the whites influenced the committee to moderate the tone of the March. The original plans called for a two day event with the rally at the Capitol occurring on the second day after a day of civil disobedience and sit-ins at Congressional offices. King was cool to the idea of civil disobedience and there was little opposition from the committee to calls for limiting the event to a one-day rally.[94] Jack Conway, Reuther's representative to the March organizers, convinced Randolph and the rest of the committee that the mall in front of the Lincoln Memorial was better suited than the area around the Capitol for accommodating the more than 200,000 people expected to attend the rally. The promise that the UAW would pay for the sound system needed to penetrate the length of the long corridor surrounding the reflecting pool secured Randolph's approval of the change in venue.[95]

Reuther worked inside the organizing committee to direct the focus of the rally toward passage of Kennedy's Civil Rights Legislation. The Kennedy bill did not contain a Fair Employment Practices Commission and was considered too weak by Randolph and Lewis. Reuther and the Civil Rights leaders continued to lobby Kennedy for inclusion of a FEPC in the bill, but muted their reservations at the public rally. The original focus of the rally was to be for jobs and justice, but specific demands such as a full employment economy—a central theme of Reuther's—and a $2 per hour minimum wage were watered down to become a vague call for jobs.[96]

Outside the committee Reuther lobbied within the house of labor for a strong endorsement of the March. Meany demurred. The AFL President was in Europe when planning for the March occurred, and Reuther phoned him when he returned to arrange a meeting of the AFL-CIO Executive Council to get labor's endorsement of and participation in the March. When Meany informed him that the next meeting of the Executive Council was scheduled for August 12th, only two weeks before the August 28th event, Reuther replied the time would be too short for organizing a meaningful display of labor support. Meany agreed to hold an emergency meeting on July 18th but abruptly called it off three days before it was to occur.[97] A five-person task force consisting of Meany, Reuther, Randolph, and two others was hastily formed to consider the AFL-CIO stance. At its August 2nd meeting, Reuther stressed the need for a broad cross section of white Americans to show support for the causes dramatized by the March. Meany was not convinced. He disliked mass protests and feared violence. He said that others on the Executive Council shared his concerns and doubted there would be a majority in support of the march. He lobbied to ensure that was the case. At the August 12th meeting of the Executive Council, only Reuther and Randolph voted to endorse the March. After the meeting, Meany drafted a statement restating AFL-CIO support for a comprehensive civil rights bill that Reuther claimed was so weak it needed a blood transfusion. Meany prevented the parent organization from endorsing the March, but allowed individual unions within the organization to participate as they saw fit. James Carey's Electrical Workers, David Dubinsky's ILGWU, and Jerry Wurf's State and County Municipal Workers joined the UAW in providing active support for the event.[98]

The UAW put a major effort into assuring the success of the event. It shifted a sizeable portion of its staff to Washington to help plan for the event. The union rented two hundred hotel rooms, printed over 2,000 hand-held signs, and engaged trains and buses to bring over 5,000 of its members to Washington. Victor, Roy, Mildred Jeffrey, Irving Bluestone, Horace Sheffield, and William Oliver were among the marshals assigned to ensure the march would proceed without incident. The UAW contingent was the single largest group attending the event.[99]

As the day of the march approached, concern within Washington increased. Tourists abandoned the city; the Washington Senators baseball team postponed two games while the marchers were in town; and many of the elected Washington Senators and Congressmen left town or holed up at home with hired protection. The right fired a barrage of criticism at the March and warned of possible violence. They focused their attack on March organizer Bayard Rustin to sow fears about Communist involvement in this event and the rights movement in general. Rustin was a soft-spoken intellectual who had tutored King on nonviolent resistance. He was also someone who had been identified with Communism in the past and was a homosexual that had a conviction for engaging in proscribed sexual behavior.

Rustin was attracted to nonviolence through his Quaker upbringing. During World War II he served a prison term as a conscientious objector. In 1948 He traveled to India to study first-hand Gandhi's use of a strategy of nonviolence in a liberation movement. Rustin worked with King from the time of the Montgomery Bus Boycott and was valued for his organizational skills and his counsel. Both King and Randolph valued Rustin for his capabilities and did not yield to the innuendos raised by enemies.

The appointed day dawned sunny and warm. A festive crowd of 250,000 people began to gather at the Washington Monument to hear Joan Baez, Bob Dylan, Odetta, Peter, Paul & Mary, and others sing anthems of the movement like *Blowin' In the Wind, If I Had a Hammer, Only A Pawn in Their Game,* and *We Shall Overcome.* Charlton Heston read from a speech by James Baldwin, and actors and entertainers like Ossie Davis, Ruby Dee, Marlon Brando, Lena Horne, Paul Newman, Diahann Carrol, Harry Belafonte, Sammy Davis Jr., and Sidney Poitier lined up behind him, adding the aura of their celebrity to the occasion.

Behind the scenes a different drama was unfolding. John Lewis had prepared a speech that, if delivered, would be the story coming from the March and define the conversation in the days and weeks to follow. Lewis called Kennedy's Civil Rights Bill "too little and too late." He planned to declare:

> "We will take matters into our own hands [...] If any radical social, political, and economic changes are to take place in our society, the people, the masses must bring them about.[..] We will march through the Heart of Dixie the way Sherman did. We will pursue our 'scorched earth' policy and burn Jim Crow to the ground—nonviolently."[100]

A late bargaining session the night before was unable to dissuade Lewis from delivering his planned address. Reuther recalls that the SNCC leader pounded on his chest with great emotion and challenged "do you realize we have five of our leaders in prison in the South charged with sedition? They could be executed!"[101] The Archbishop of Washington, Patrick O'Boyle, who was scheduled to give the opening invocation, threatened to pull out unless the speech was altered. When the day ended, the unity of the March and the message it would convey were very much in doubt.

On the morning of the event, Reuther persuaded Rev. O'Boyle to wait in the White House to see if a last minute settlement could be reached that would enable him to participate as planned. The Archbishop agreed to give the invocation if Protestant cleric Eugene Carson Blake could give assurances that Lewis's speech was acceptable to him.[102] With no time for further bargaining, Reuther assembled the organizers and demanded:

> "Six weeks ago we formed a coalition. Now John Lewis has written a speech. [...] We have no right to tell him what he has a right to say in America, but we have a right to say that if you want to use this platform which this coalition made possible, you are morally obligated to speak within the policy framework around which the coalition came into being. [...] If John Lewis feels strongly that he wants to make this speech, he can go someplace else and make it, but he has no right to make it here because if he tries, he destroys the integrity of our coalition."[103]

Lewis said nothing, and Randolph polled the other organizers who voted unanimously to deny Lewis a platform unless he changed the speech. Lewis submitted to the will of the committee, and went off with King and Blake to rewrite his speech. The archbishop was alerted and driven to the Lincoln Memorial by the Secret Service to deliver the invocation.

The revised Lewis speech still struck a militant note that might have drawn more attention had it not been made a footnote by the "I Have a Dream Speech" of Dr. King.

The revolution is at hand, and we must free ourselves from the chains of political and economic slavery. The nonviolent revolution is saying, "We will not wait for the courts to act, for we have been waiting for hundreds of years. We will not wait for the President, nor the Justice Department, nor the Congress, but we will take matters into our own hands, and create a great source of power, outside of any national structure that could and would assure us victory." For those who have said, "Be patient and wait" we must say, "Patience is a dirty and nasty word." We cannot be patient, we do not want to be free gradually, we want our freedom, and we want it now. We cannot depend on any political party, for the Democrats and Republicans have betrayed the basic principles of the Declaration of Independence.[104]

The Lewis speech conveyed the tone the rights struggle would strike in later years, but seemed too bold and too atonal for the audience of 1963 to appreciate. Reuther was scheduled to follow John Lewis to the podium, and he worried about the setting into which he might be placed. He followed Lewis's remarks with a spirited call for full employment "if we can have full employment for the negative ends of war, then why can't we have a job for every American in the pursuit of peace?" He challenged the hypocrisy of a government that touts freedom abroad while denying it at home: "We cannot defend freedom in Berlin so long as we deny freedom in Birmingham." Reuther closed with a warning that proved too prescient several years later:

"If we fail, the vacuum of our failure will be filled by the Apostles of Hatred who will search for answers in the dark of night, and reason will yield to riot and brotherhood will yield to bitterness and bloodshed and we will tear asunder the fabric of American democracy."[105]

The day ended with the poetry of Martin Luther King resonating through the mausoleum honoring the man who had begun the March for Freedom one hundred years earlier. The assembled left carrying the individual seeds disbursed from the collective experience they had just shared. The event whose critics decried as provocative and likely to spawn violence and rioting in the nation's capital ended peacefully with a feeling of "good vibrations" The tide for sweeping out Jim Crow continued to swell.

Jim Crow was sustained by a climate of intimidation, violence, indifference, and a prevalent belief in the superiority of the white race. It lived in the shadows of the night and behind the dark glasses of the law. In the glare of the spotlight, with a generation refusing to be intimidated, and the pseudo-science behind old racial theories exposed, Jim Crow had little time to live. White supremacists countered the nonviolent tide running against them with a last outburst of violence. In September of 1963, four little black girls were murdered in Birmingham when a bomb exploded during their Sunday school lessons. In the spring of 1964 three civil rights activists, Andrew Goodman, Michael Schwerner, and James Chaney, two white and one black, were murdered by "law enforcement officers" sworn to protect them. Mississippi burned, and the nation was revolted. A Southern filibuster could not withstand the tsunami sweeping over it. The Civil Rights Act of 1964 was passed into law as an enduring legacy of the slain President who first proposed it and the son of the old Confederacy who steered it through Congress.[106]

The next stage of the battle was to turn the words on the page into the reality on the ground. It was the young activists of SNCC who went into places like Selma, Alabama to attempt to register blacks to vote that risked their lives in this fight. Attempts to register black voters and enforce the provisions of the Civil Rights Act were thwarted by Sheriff Jim Clark. Within a week of passage of the landmark legislation, Alabama Judge James Hare issued an injunction forbidding the gathering of more than three people under the sponsorship of civil rights organizations at any one time. SNCC organizer Amelia Boynton appealed to the SCLC to become involved in Selma.

On February 18, 1965, a march to the Perry County Courthouse in Marion, Alabama was organized by the two groups to protest the lack of compliance with the new law. Governor Wallace ordered a line of state troopers to block entry to the courthouse. When the marchers approached, the street lights suddenly went dark and the troopers charged with billy clubs into the marchers. One in the group, Jimmie Lee Jackson, fled from the scene with his mother and ducked into a nearby cafe to seek refuge from the onslaught. Jackson was followed into the cafe by one of the troopers who drew his gun and shot him dead while he was trying to shield his mother.[107]

The Jackson murder triggered the events of the day now remembered as *Bloody Sunday*.[108] On Sunday, March 7 a march of about 600 protesters led by John Lewis and Hosea Williams of the SCLC set out to walk from Selma to Montgomery and confront Governor Wallace about his role in the Marion violence. When the march crossed the Edmund Pettis Bridge it was confronted by a wall of State Police and local volunteers that Sheriff Clark had deputized for the day. The marchers were told to disperse, and when they failed to comply, they were set upon with night sticks, tear gas, and mounted charges. The photograph of a badly beaten and gassed Amelia Boynton appeared on the front page of newspapers worldwide.

King rushed to Selma to plan for a second march to begin on the coming Tuesday. Before heading to Selma, he sent out a call to clergymen and other citizens across the country to join him. Walter and May Reuther were among the citizens who responded to that plea. King sought a court order preventing the police from interfering with the rights of the protesters to voice their grievances to their elected officials. Instead Federal District Judge Frank Johnson issued a restraining order against further protest until he could conduct hearings later in the week. Judge Johnson had been one of the few Southern justices who had shown sympathy for the cause of the SCLC in the past and King did not want to alienate him. He was sure that the judge would rule in their favor later in the week.[109]

The Tuesday march had gained a momentum of its own, and the people who journeyed to Selma from around the country were determined to make their voices heard. King arranged a symbolic march that would step out to the bridge, hold a brief prayer session, and turn back to the small black church where the march originated for an evening of speeches and song. May Reuther told her daughter about the "victorious" feeling she experienced inside the cramped, sweltering church,[110] but outside the church a Unitarian minister from Boston, James Reeb, and two colleagues were beaten by a white mob. Reeb was denied admission to the public hospital in Selma and had to be rushed to the University Hospital in Birmingham where he died a day later.

As King expected, Judge Johnson ruled in favor of the SCLC petition, saying that the First Amendment rights of the protesters could not be abridged by the State of Alabama. On March 21st King led a group of 8,000 demonstrators across the Edmund Pettus Bridge toward the State Capitol in Montgomery. The trek to Montgomery required several days to complete, and the bulk of the original group returned by bus to Selma after the first day to leave a more sustainable number of about 300 to complete the middle portion of the trip. When this group reached Montgomery the crowd of marchers swelled to 25,000.[111] King addressed the assembled from the steps of the State Capitol and told them:

> "The end we seek is a society at peace with itself, a society that can live with its conscience. I know you are asking today, 'How long will it take?' I come to say to you this afternoon however difficult the moment, however frustrating the hour, it will not be long."[112]

It was not long after King's speech before a car load of KKK members, including FBI informer Gary Rowe, pulled up alongside the car of Mrs. Viola Liuzzo, a Detroit housewife compelled by a sense of moral duty to come to Selma. Mrs. Liuzzo fought her fear by singing *We Shall Overcome* at the top of her lungs as the smirking Klansmen put a bullet through her head.[113] It was not long before President Johnson reacted to the events in Selma by introducing a Voting Rights bill. And it was not long before the usually deliberative Congress passed the Voting Rights Act into Law. The practice of Jim Crow had no legal leg to stand on, and the Justice Department was uncommonly vigorous in enforcing the new edicts.

The elimination of sanctioned segregation and the enfranchisement of blacks allowed a new generation of leaders to emerge in the South. Bull Connor and Jim Clark had no role to play in the new order. They were expendable poisoned pawns in a game where white supremacists had to repackage their message to appeal to a younger generation ready to move beyond the iconic past and embrace a less provincial future.

The face of the new South was most visible in its principal city. Atlanta was governed by two progressive mayors, William Hartsfield and Ivan Allen, for most of three decades and was the home base of Martin Luther King's SCLC. Under their leadership Atlanta became a commercial and aviation hub and grew from a pre-war population of about 100,000 to a metropolitan area of over one million. Atlanta avoided the unrest troubling many other Southern cities during the civil rights campaign and became known as "the City Too Busy to Hate." Allen testified before Congress in 1963 in support of the Civil Rights Legislation proposed by President Kennedy. Atlanta Congressman Charles Weltner broke ranks with his Southern Congressional colleagues and voted for the 1964 Civil Rights Act. In casting his vote he declared "We can offer resistance and defiance [...] or we can acknowledge this measure as the law of the land."[114] *Newsweek* profiled Weltner as "a prototype of the articulate young congressman—the 'new breed' on whom so many southern moderates stake their hopes for the future."[115] Weltner surrendered his Congressional seat in 1966 when he refused to sign a Democratic Party loyalty oath supporting the Democratic ticket that was headed by the segregationist Lester Maddox. In resigning his seat, Weltner declared "I love the Congress, but I will give up my office before I give up my principles. I cannot compromise with hate. I cannot vote for Lester Maddox."[116]

Maddox came to national attention when he supplied his white clientele with pickaxe handles to confront a group of black activists trying to dine in his Pickrick Restaurant. Maddox vowed to close his restaurant before submitting to the decree of the 1964 Civil Rights Act, and sold the restaurant in 1965 to become a martyr to the new legislation. As governor, Maddox left a legacy that did not easily conform to his public persona. He presided over a period of rapid growth in the state and invested heavily in education. Maddox appointed more African Americans to state positions than any previous governor, and named a black to head the State Department of Corrections. He commissioned the first black state trooper and ordered troopers to desist from using the words "boy" and "'nigger" and to address African Americans as "Mr."[117] Maddox was limited to one four-year term by the state constitution, but left office with an extremely high favorability rating when he was succeeded by Jimmy Carter.

Carter was one of the "new breed" that *Newsweek* touted years earlier—a Southern politician in tune with the national attitude on race. He became the fresh Southern face chosen to clear the stench of Watergate from a stagnant Washington atmosphere. Andrew Young, the man who cradled the dying Dr. King in Memphis, was selected by Carter to represent the United States to the World at the United Nations. Behind in Georgia, Maynard Jackson was serving as the first African American mayor of a major Southern city. Black and white issues remained, but the Carter election marked a transition to the post-civil rights era in American race relations.

The legal battle against segregation secured basic human rights for blacks in the South, but did little to change the situation for blacks in the North. They still faced discrimination in employment and housing and attended disadvantaged neighborhood schools. King's organization was based in the South. It had little organizational structure in the North,. When he came to Chicago and its neighboring city of Cicero to march for housing, he ran into counter demonstrations by American Nazis, angry taunts from the residents of Cicero, and intransigence from an entrenched political machine. Changing housing patterns is a lot more difficult and less immediate than changing seating regulations on a bus. King left Chicago with only vague promises and no tangible results.

Since the influence of the SCLC was not strong in the North, its message of nonviolence was muted. Other voices urged a different route to the "Promised Land." Malcolm X and Elijah Muhammad drew converts to a philosophy of black supremacy that advocated black self-determination, self defense, and separation of the races. Malcolm X was a compelling figure whose message resonated in the black community and frightened many in the white. It was Malcolm X, not Elijah Muhammad, who became the public face of the sect. It was he who brought wider recognition to the religion through the recruitment of heavyweight champion Cassius Clay (now Muhammad Ali). Malcolm's celebrity grated on Elijah Muhammad and Elijah's infidelities troubled Malcolm. Malcolm outgrew the custom tailored brand of Islam fashioned by Elijah and broke with the Nation of Islam. It signed his death warrant.

After Malcolm's death the advocates of Black Power grabbed a greater share of public attention. As from the sound and fury of an electrical storm, their background static scratched across the fading voice of non-violence. The decade of the sixties ended in a convulsion of violence. Riots erupted in scores of cities including Detroit. The 1967 Detroit riot left 43 people dead, 347 injured, 3,800 arrested, and over 5,000 homeless. It left a scar on the face of Detroit which never vanished.

The movement for civil rights that galvanized the youth of the nation in the early sixties splintered into the women's movement, the gay rights movement, the Causa for farm workers' rights, the Black Power movement, and the anti-war movement. By the end of the decade King was dead; the Kennedys were dead; Reuther was soon to take an ill-fated trip to Black Lake, and Edward Kennedy an ill-considered drive on Martha's Vineyard. The Civil Rights Movement became an orphaned child, left to grow up on its own under the foster care of affirmative action.

A program of affirmative action designed to correct two hundred years of slavery and one hundred years of discrimination attempted to extend opportunity to blacks without depriving whites of opportunities they deserved. Affirmative action created a labyrinth of vaguely worded directives and established targets that were not to be considered quotas. It infuriated those whites whose children were bused out of neighborhood schools or were denied entry to colleges of their choice to accommodate blacks with weaker credentials. It also failed to mollify blacks who still found the road to equal opportunity strewn with potholes. Like foster care, affirmative action was a poor substitute for parental care, but its child managed to grow up to become a functioning adult.

Civil rights advanced through direct action and legal initiatives during the fifties and sixties, but it also received a big impetus from Truman's integration of the military in 1948 and Jackie Robinson's integration of major league baseball one year earlier. At the end of World War II, Randolph's MOWM focused upon integration of the military. From the time that "Colonel Shaw and his bell-cheeked Negro infantry" lost half the regiment "two months after marching through Boston"[118] during the Civil War to the days the Tuskegee Airmen escorted bombers over the factories and rail lines of Hitler's Reich, black soldiers served with distinction but without proper respect in a segregated service. Only the efforts of Walter White and A. Phillip Randolph and the support of Eleanor Roosevelt provided a limited number of African-Americans the opportunity to train to fly, and only pressing manpower needs led to their deployment. Despite the reputation of the buffalo soldiers on the plains and the "immunes" in the fevered swamps of the Caribbean, most black soldiers during World War II served in supply units. Black servicemen built the trans-Alaska highway on the permafrost of the Arctic and raced to supply Patton's 8th Army on its dash through France.

After heavy losses sustained during the Battle of the Bulge, manpower levels of some units were so low that General Eisenhower ordered black support troops to pick up a gun and join some of the depleted white regiments. This decision so incensed his Chief of Staff, General Walter Bedell Smith, that he complained the American public would take offense at the integration of these military units.[119] Even during a war-time emergency, maintaining separation of the races was more important than maintaining an effective fighting force to some of those charged with defending the country.

After the war, President Truman appointed a Committee on Civil Rights which issued a report in October of 1947 condemning segregation and recommending immediate administrative action to end the practice in the military. Randolph seized upon the report and formed a Committee Against Jim Crow in Military Service and Training. He subsequently testified before Congress and in a letter to the President that unless the President issue an executive order ending segregation in the military, African-American youth would "have no alternative but to resist a law [Selective Service Act], the inevitable consequences of which would be to expose them to the un-American brutality so familiar during the last war."[120] Truman faced a difficult re-election campaign and was confronted with pressure from both wings of his party. At the Democratic Convention the delegates led by Hubert Humphrey voted to reject a watered down civil rights plank and endorse a platform that included a call for desegregation of the armed forces. Two weeks after the convention, Truman signed Executive Order # 9981 ending segregation in the military. He managed to survive the disaffection of a Dixiecrat block supporting Strom Thurmond and the premature pronouncement of the *Chicago Tribune* on election day and win a second term.

The Navy and the Air Force indicated their willingness to implement the order. Under the prodding of Eleanor Roosevelt, the Navy began integrating one of its ships, the USS Mason, during the latter days of the war. It now indicated it was continuing this war-time policy. The Army and Marines were not willing to comply. Army Secretary Kenneth Royall argued that "the Army was not an instrument for social evolution."[121] Ultimately it was the Korean War that forced integration upon the Army. The surprise North Korean offensive pushed the American and South Korean defenders back to the Pusan Perimeter at the tip of the peninsula and inflicted heavy casualties. As with Eisenhower earlier, war-time expediency required the Army to fill its depleted ranks with any troops available, regardless of race. Truman's Executive Order was reluctantly implemented.

The integrated military provided a generation of young men an occasion to work and socialize with soldiers of another race that previous generations did not have. Separation of the races allowed prejudice to develop and metastasize. For many white youth, particularly Southern youth, military service was the first time in their life that they encountered blacks in a situation in which they were equals sharing a common experience. People of the two races may not have always liked one another or respected one another, but they learned how to deal with the situation where they worked and lived together, and this helped create a climate for adapting to the new reality after the Civil Rights legislation was passed.

Cultural Barriers Lifted

Sports also played a significant role in changing the attitudes of whites, particularly younger whites whose racial attitudes were more malleable. Jackie Robinson may have done as much to lower racial barriers as anyone directly connected to the civil rights movement. Robinson not only integrated the sport, he reinvigorated it. Robinson only led the league in stolen bases twice in his ten year career, but he was probably the most intimidating presence on the base paths since the era of Ty Cobb. He did not simply take a lead, he pulsated about the base, generating an electric current through the stadium. First base was never his destination in sport or life, merely a way station on the road to home—a base he stole a remarkable nineteen times during his career.

Robinson may have begun his career as a pawn in a "noble experiment" but he quickly proved to be much more than that. In 1949, his third year in the major leagues, he led the National League in batting and stolen bases, finished second in hits and RBIs, and third in runs scored. For his achievements he was named the league's most valuable player. His level and style of play won him fans to whom the color of his skin meant far less than how he could hit and field and help his team to win ball games. The decision to bring Jackie to the major leagues may not have been very popular when it was first announced, but once he was there he was voted to the All-Star game six times.

By the time the Dodgers finally beat the Yankees and won the World Series in 1955, Robinson had become a complimentary player. He had only 317 at bats for the year and his average had dropped to 256. His hair was turning white and his once proud frame was becoming stooped and bloated by the ravages of diabetes. The strain of carrying the expectations of his race through nine grueling seasons had taken its toll, but the country had fundamentally changed. Young fans grew up cheering black stars like Robinson, Willie Mays, and Hank Aaron and dark-skinned Latino players like Roberto Clemente. The concept of blacks and whites playing on the same field had transcended the context in which it was first realized.

On February 19, 1948, ten months after Jackie Robinson broke the color barrier in baseball, 17,823 people, black and white, showed up on a cold winter night in Chicago to witness an exhibition basketball game between the Minneapolis Lakers, champions of professional basketball, and the Harlem Globetrotters. The Lakers were led by the powerfully built 6-10 center, George Mikan, who was proclaimed the greatest basketball player of the half century by the sportswriters of the day. The Trotters star, Goose Tatum, was best known for his huge hands that could grasp a basketball like a grapefruit, enabling him to flash and distribute the ball as the centerpiece of the weave the team employed to stage its trick plays. Tatum gave up several inches and more than a few pounds to the gigantic Mikan. The game matched the deliberate half court offense of the Lakers against the speed and fast-break approach of the Globetrotters. The game was tied at 59 all as time ran down with the Trotters holding the ball. Dribbling artist Marques Haynes controlled the ball drawing the defense away from Ermer Robinson who got the ball for the last shot. Robinson launched a one-handed push shot, a scorned variant of the two-hand set shot practiced in Mikan's day, that swished through the net as time expired.[122] The Globetrotters defeated the champions of white professional basketball and ushered in a new era for the sport.

The current professional league, the NBA, was started in 1950 with the consolidation of two earlier leagues. The new league accepted black players. Sweetwater Clifton and Earl Lloyd were signed from the Globetrotters to play for New York and Washington. After several years the fledgling NBA stabilized into an eight team league with franchises in Syracuse and Rochester New York, Fort Wayne, Indiana, Tri-Cities, Iowa, as well as Minneapolis, Boston, New York, and Philadelphia. The NBA came of age in the mid fifties with the arrival of Bill Russell in Boston to team with Bob Cousy and Bill Sharman. Cousy brought the playground to the NBA with his behind the back dribble and no-look passes. His up-tempo approach to the game was complemented by the defensive and rebounding skills of Russell and the outside shooting of Sharman. The Boston Celtics fast-break offense swept the flat-footed, deliberate style of play that characterized the Mikan era off the court and brought thousands of new fans to the sport.

Once professional basketball was integrated, the question became how many black players could any one team start without losing support of its largely white audience? By the late fifties, black players were coming to dominate the sport. The 1958 All-America team featured five black starters including Oscar Robertson, Elgin Baylor, and Wilt Chamberlain. In baseball, Robinson was to be joined on the Dodgers by Roy Campanella, Don Newcombe, Sandy Amoros, Joe Black, and Junior Gilliam, but in basketball the court was closer to the stands, the players wore shorts and T-shirts, and only five players were on the court at a time. There was always room for a black star like Russell, Baylor, or Robertson, but lesser skilled blacks were victimized by a defacto quota system.

The Celtics were able to blur the issue of too many black players by gradually increasing the playing time of Sam and K. C. Jones as Sharman and Cousy aged. By the time the career of the two white stars was ending, the Celtics were usually playing four blacks at the same time. The team kept winning, the fans kept cheering, and the transition from a mostly white to a mostly black team proceeded seamlessly.

The question of racial balance shadowing the sport was highlighted in the college championship game of 1966. An all-white Kentucky team that included future NBA player and coach Pat Reilly played a team from a little-known school in El Paso that started five blacks. Kentucky was coached by the legendary Adolph Rupp, but Texas Western was not daunted by the reputation of its rival and won a hard-fought victory. The pace of integration was well underway by 1966, but the loss by Kentucky was deeply felt in the South.

The lesson of the 1966 basketball defeat by the SEC was pounded home four years later by Sam 'Bam' Cunningham and his USC Trojans. Southern California humiliated Bear Bryant's Alabama football team in front of a stunned partisan crowd in Birmingham. Bryant had wanted to recruit black players for several years, and the sight of Cunningham shredding the Alabama defense convinced the University and its supporters that Alabama would not compete for national honors unless it opened its doors to black athletes. Bryant's assistant coach Jerry Claiborne later remarked that "Cunningham did more to integrate Alabama in 60 minutes than Martin Luther King did in 20 years."[123]

When professional sports were being integrated in the late forties and early fifties, they were largely played within the geographical confines of the Northeast. Until 1958, professional baseball was played only as far west as St Louis and south as Washington. Professional basketball and hockey were confined to the same general area. Professional football, with a more limited schedule of games, supported two West Coast teams, but none from the country's middle or south. Population density and the speed of rail travel limited the area conducive for sports franchises, and the north-south divide, persisting since the Civil War, was reflected in the location of sports teams.

Integration of sports began in the Northeast where discrimination in employment was less pronounced. By the time that population migration and jet travel made expansion of professional sports to wider markets feasible, television had promoted the product to a receptive public. Cities in the South and Southwest were eager for their own franchise and were no longer uncomfortable with the prospect of accepting black athletes.

Atlanta had been something of an oasis in the racial desert of the segregated South when the Braves arrived in 1966 with their star player, Hank Aaron. The Braves had a number of other black and Latino players on their roster during their first years in Atlanta, but everyone else played in the shadow of Aaron, and he played away from the spotlight more than any other superstar in sports. Aaron was not as flashy as Willie Mays, nor did he exude the same electric energy as Robinson and Clemente. He did everything well, but without flair or excessive emotion. He was the lunch box superstar who showed up for work every day, consistently did his job better than most everybody else, and went home to a private family life. He was a role model that a parent of any race would want for his children.

Aaron was able to maintain his consistent level of performance well into the latter years of his career. In his twentieth season, he still managed to bat .300 and hit 40 home runs. As he neared Babe Ruth's career home run record, he received threats from people who did not want to see one of the most revered records in sports surpassed by a black man. The Northern press pictured this as a Southern phenomenon, but in reality there existed racial bigots in all parts of the country who would vent their hatred in the same manner. When the record was surpassed, Atlanta celebrated, and most people felt proud that the most cherished record in sport was now held by a player from their team and their generation.

Acceptance of blacks in professional sports hastened the acceptance of black actors in leading roles on the large and small screen. Sidney Poitier was cast as the Jackie Robinson of Hollywood—the first black actor to play in leading roles that did not conform to racial stereotypes. Like Robinson he was asked to represent the exemplar of his race. While Robinson was required to turn the other cheek to the racial taunts and sharpened spikes he had to endure to play a kid's game, Poitier was typecast in roles of heroic dimension, devoid of sexuality and lacking character flaws that might give his repertoire more range. Like Robinson, he excelled at his craft and became the first African-American to win a Best Actor Oscar in 1963.

In 1967 Poitier was the top box office draw, starring in two films that explored the changing racial attitudes of the times. In "*Guess Who's Coming to Dinner?*" the sensitive subject of interracial marriage was broached. Miscegenation was the ultimate affront to proponents of racial superiority. It was still illegal in 17 Southern states when the movie began production. Poitier played a prospective son-in-law meeting the parents of his future bride for the first time. Poitier's character—an accomplished doctor of high moral standards—was the man any set of parents would want their daughter to marry except for the color of his skin. The film presented a stylized morality play in which the parents, played by Spencer Tracy and Katherine Hepburn, worked through a conflict between their liberal beliefs and attitudes honed in the social order of the world in which they belonged. The doctor's parents and the white couple's black maid added their own discomfort over the disturbance of the established order the marriage would provoke.

In his next film, *In the Heat of Night,* Poitier expressed the attitude of the proud black man of 1967 when he replied to the disdainful question of Rod Steiger's rural Mississippi sheriff "What do they call you up there in Philadelphia, Virgil?" "They call me MISTER Tibbs." Virgil Tibbs, with the backing of new money coming into the old South, ignored every stop sign the culture erected to keep uppity blacks from venturing too far into the white only world. Emmett Till and countless others were lynched for less presumptive acts in the documentaries from the same period. During one dramatic scene, the black theater audience of the day, and some of the white, broke into applause when Poitier returned a slap in the face to the condescending white plantation owner who sat atop the antebellum social pyramid. By the end of the film, the characters portrayed by Poitier and Steiger found they had more in common than could be seen from opposite sides of the racial divide.

Poitier's success at the box office proved to skeptical movie producers that even in the South there was an audience for movies with black actors and actresses playing a leading role. The popularity of the *I Spy* series playing on television in the mid sixties also opened new opportunities for blacks in dramatic roles. When blacks demanded to see more black faces reading the news and appearing in commercials, there was little resistance from the bean counters at the networks. There was no evidence to suggest the audience would change the channel. African-Americans in prominent roles in sports, the arts, entertainment, and politics did much to erase the old misconceptions about race and open doors that in the past had been marked Whites Only.

Walter Reuther was the white face of the Civil Rights Movement. He shared the platform with Hardin during a war-time rally in Detroit for equal employment opportunity. He marched with King in Detroit and Washington, and again in Selma and Memphis. He testified before Congress numerous times on behalf of civil rights legislation. His union contributed generously to the Civil Rights organizations, and he served on the Executive Board of the NAACP. He was vilified by the right and dismissed by his critics on the left. The pace of his march was dictated in part by the pace of his membership, but also by his need "to play the lead in any orchestra he was in." Just as Stanley Kramer in directing *Guess Who's Coming to Dinner?* was compelled to create an idealized black character to narrow white reaction to his movie to the question of race, Reuther was predisposed to direct the tone of the rights movement to appeal to a white audience. Like the director, he was trying to script the black actors to convey the message he wanted his white audience to hear.

The man Reuther may have wanted to cast in a leading role in his union was James Farmer of CORE.[124] As early as 1952, Reuther realized that "Singin' Sam" Oliver lacked credibility with blacks in the shops and had been given too small a supporting role. (Oliver got the disdainful nickname Singin' Sam from many in the black workforce because of his participation in a black singing group formed in the thirties for a Ford advertising campaign.) Reuther sought to bring Farmer to Solidarity House as head of the Fair Practices Department and prepare him for an elected position on the board. Just as the Poitier character, Farmer had all the right credentials. He was a respected activist, a dynamic speaker, a committed anti-Communist, and a man comfortable with the social-democratic leanings of the Reuther inner circle. The plan was abandoned when it met with stiff opposition from the Executive Board, due as much to Farmer's marriage to a white woman as his socialist and pacifist politics.[125]

The white liberal Reuther was more sensitive to white reaction to the pace of black advance than black sensitivity to the hand of white control. Like Hepburn and Tracy's couple in the film, the mid-century white liberal was the product of a culture that separated him from meaningful contact with blacks during his formative years, surrounded him with messages of his racial superiority, and imbued him with an obligation to speak for those he deemed less fortunate. He or she was as much a product of their times as tail fins, sock hops, and 45 rpm records.

Reuther had argued against establishing a Negro seat on the Executive Board during the factional struggles of the mid-forties, claiming it would be a case of reverse Jim Crow racism. He avowed support for a "qualified" black, but selecting a man because of the color of his skin would be just as bad as excluding him for the same reason. As the years went on and no "qualified" black was elevated to the Board, its lily-white complexion became an embarrassment for the progressive-minded union. In the 1959 convention Horace Sheffield and Buddy Battle insisted at a caucus before the opening session that Reuther put a black on the Executive Board.[126] The need for black voices in the councils of labor became more urgent weeks earlier when George Meany publicly dismissed A. Philip Randolph with the jibe, "Who appointed you to be the guardian of all the Negroes in the United States?"[127] Sheffield and Battle argued that white labor leaders could no longer presume to be able to adequately address the concerns of their black membership. Reuther felt ambushed by the demand and fell back on his stale defense. Reuther avowed "the UAW is part of America" and could do little more than reflect the racial mores of the society. He compounded his gaff with a repetition of his condescending promise "There will come a time when a Negro will be qualified, and…at such a time a Negro will be placed on the board."[128] Sheffield took the issue to the convention floor when he rose to nominate Willouby Abner for the position of one of the Vice Presidents. Sheffield reminded the Convention that in 1943 he had voted against a reserved Negro seat, but now, when the UAW was insisting that blacks be represented at all levels of government, how could it not have black representation in its own leadership? Sheffield acerbically countered

Reuther's caucus remarks with the observation, "Negroes are sick and tired of the matter of qualifications being raised [...] because I think it is fairly evident to everyone here that it is not necessary to be a Rhodes Scholar to sit on the International Executive Board."[129] Abner declined the nomination as planned, but a clumsy attempt to put through a routine civil rights resolution on the last day of the Convention led to a walkout of black delegates while Reuther presided over the closing session.

Sheffield and Battle organized the Trade Union Leadership Council (TULC) in 1957 to, in Sheffield's words, "interpret the Negro community to the labor movement [...] from the inside, speaking up as a member of the union with all the rights and privileges that go with membership."[130] Sheffield was affiliated with the Reuther majority within the union, but saw the need to provide a counterweight to the union's hesitancy to confront the racism within its membership. The TULC forged links with the NAACP and the black churches in Detroit. In the 1960 mayoral election, the TULC backed candidate, Jerome Cavanaugh, defeated the more conservative incumbent, Louis Miriani, who was backed by both the business community and the UAW leadership.[131] In subsequent years Detroit politics elevated veterans of the MOWM like Coleman Young, John Conyers, Jr., and George Crockett to elected office. When Herbert Hill, the NAACP labor secretary, published his 1961 report, *Racism within Organized Labor: A Report of Five Years of the AFL-CIO*, it was not only the old AFL trade unions that came in for censure, but the Steel Workers and the ILGWU were particularly singled out for harsh criticism within the industrial unions.[132] Criticism of institutionalized racism in the union movement was hitting close to home. Reuther was compelled to act and add an African American to his Executive Board.

Reuther finessed his long-standing opposition to a Negro seat on the board in 1962 by creating three new at-large positions and allocating one to a Canadian and another to an African American. Once the long-awaited Negro seat was created, it became a question of who should fill it. Sheffield and Abner were the most immediate candidates, but both had independent constituencies that could claim their loyalties. Emil Mazey frequently voiced the concern of the Executive Board to Sheffield when he admonished him with the charge "You have to be either a trade unionist or a civil rights leader!"[133] This advice reflected the stance of the leadership. They were committed to the cause of civil rights, but foremost they were trade unionists. Reuther and his inner circle had an ambitious social agenda, but they realized the union was their "orchestra". Without the "orchestra" the music playing in their heads would never reach an audience.

The TULC lobbied for Sheffield and made it known that if he were not selected, it would need to be one of their own that got the nod. Reuther may have been amenable to Sheffield, but the full board was skeptical that Sheffield could be a "team player." He could not get a majority of the Board to support his candidacy.[134] Instead the Board selected Nelson Edwards as its candidate to fill the Negro seat. Edwards worked with the UAW to dilute the influence of the TULC in the councils of the city and state Democratic party. Black appointments to the UAW staff increased during the remainder of the decade, and in 1968 Reuther pushed through the appointment of a second African-American on the Board.

When the Civil Rights movement took a left turn in the late sixties away from the direction charted by the NAACP and Martin Luther King, Reuther was no longer able to influence the speed or direction it was heading. Discordant notes were now sounding in his own orchestra. In some plants like, the Dodge Main Assembly plant in Hamtramck, the workforce was predominantly black, but the shop stewards, foremen, skilled tradesmen, and upper management in both the boardroom and Solidarity House were almost all white. Blacks, tuned to the militant chord resonating within the community, challenged the white authority that was smothering their ambitions. A group of activists in the Dodge plant formed an insurgent movement within Local 3 called the Dodge Revolutionary Union Movement (DRUM) and showed their strength by halting plant production for two days with a brief wildcat strike.[135] DRUM subsequently picketed the UAW convention that was formulating preparations for the pending tough round of contract negotiations with the industry, causing the convention to adjourn and embarrassing the Reuther leadership.[136]

Similar black caucuses sprouted in other plants in the Detroit region. ELRUM formed at the Eldon Avenue Gear and Axle plant and FRUM at Ford. In 1968 these caucuses coalesced into The

League of Revolutionary Black Workers, a self-proclaimed Marxist-Leninist organization. While the League sought to color its black nationalist appeal with a red class-struggle tinge, its success in building a constituency in the plants was based on the voice it gave to local shop floor grievances. The Treaty of Detroit had erected a bureaucratic structure for dealing with local grievances that eviscerated the role of the Shop Steward in the process.

By the late sixties, the golden age of the American automobile industry was approaching its end. The companies sought to maintain their profits through automation and an increase in worker productivity. These efforts led to layoffs and a speedup of the production process that disproportionately affected blacks in the lower skilled jobs. The union was hamstrung by its previous agreements to effectively address the workers' most immediate concerns. Black caucuses like DRUM filled the void by giving voice to worker frustration.

DRUM showed its strength within Dodge Local 3 in a 1968 election for the local governing board. DRUM activist, Ronald March received the largest vote total in a field of 27 candidates in the first round of voting. The union hierarchy reacted to the challenge by bringing the full weight of the establishment down on the dissident movement. The Local 3 magazine, *Battleline*, lambasted DRUM as a "racist, Communist group which was attempting to destroy the automobile industry through internal subversion."[137] Solidarity House mailed 300,000 leaflets to its membership warning that the militants "stood for the complete separation of the races in the shop and the destruction of our union through the tactics of violence, fear, and intimidation."[138] Even the AFL-CIO put aside its animosity toward Reuther and the UAW to pile on its own criticism of this rank-and-file militancy. When the runoff election was held, legions of mostly Polish retirees were driven to the polling stations to boost the loyalist slate and crush March and the DRUM insurgency.[139]

The union neutralized the threat posed by the dissidents. The League, mesmerized by its own rhetoric, lost credence with the black workers it sought to represent. America in the 1970s was not in revolt against the capitalist system, and the majority of African-Americans were demanding their share in that system, not trying to overthrow it. The League lost its cohesion and evaporated into the post New Left Diaspora.

During the sixties, Reuther and his closest associates realized that they were aging and their organization had lost the vitality it possessed in the early days of the sit-downs. Younger workers who joined the union after the Treaty of Detroit had little appreciation for the struggles of the earlier days and took their current situation for granted. Their ties to the union became more and more tenuous. It was the younger black workers, whose sense of militancy was stirred by the struggle for civil rights, who most closely imbued the qualities of the men and women who built the union and confronted the oligarchs in the thirties and forties. Ironically, the aging leadership was no longer comfortable with this younger, darker version of their former selves. The time was too soon to contemplate a black vanguard in a revitalized labor agenda and too late to shake the foundation of the structure shaped by the bargain made in 1950.

After the March on Washington, Irving Bluestone told Reuther that he overheard two black participants discussing the people in the front row of the march. One nodded toward Reuther and asked the other who that man was. The other told her friend "that's the White Martin Luther King."[140] Reuther was flattered, but the reality was more complicated. There was no "White Martin Luther King." The Civil Rights Movement had white allies, but it was led by blacks and more importantly sustained by the courage and sacrifice of blacks who had to live in the towns and cities of the South after the demonstrations were over and the organizers went home. Reuther was a prominent figure at the events highlighting the movement. His image, his organizational talents, and the financial and political support of his union were significant in securing passage of the Civil Rights Act of 1964. No other white official with a political constituency or business enterprise to maintain took a more public or more forceful stand on the issue than Reuther did for the three decades he was in the public eye. He was not without his limitations, nor did he lack for critics. From a separation of over four decades it becomes fashionable to dismiss Reuther for what he did not do and not celebrate what he did. If Reuther's foot was too lightly on the accelerator in steering his union through the course of the civil rights struggle, it is not clear that a heavier foot would not have caused his vehicle to spin out of control. In the three decades during which Reuther was prominent in the labor movement, African-Americans made their most significant gains since emancipation. He played a secondary, but not insignificant role in that drama.

PART 3

Heading in Different Directions

CHAPTER X

The Cold War

Heretofore, in our history, we had to take the world pretty much as we found it. From now on we will have to take it pretty much as we leave it when the crisis is over.

George F. Kennan, 1944

In America the end of World War 2 was like the dawn of a new day—an awakening from a horrible nightmare to the reassurance of a sunny sky and a chorus of birds. The country set about enjoying the fruits of its victory and trying to ignore any cloudy post-war realities gathering on the horizon. There was hope that the "Big Three" powers would maintain their war-time alliance and be the guarantors of a stable peace. The defeated Germany was still more mistrusted than the victorious Soviets.

In war-torn Europe the end of hostilities only brought continued scarcity and uncertainty. The peace was policed by the conquering armies, and the structure of a new Europe quibbled over by ideologically irreconcilable diplomats. The United States, Britain, and the Soviet Union had been allied by a common enemy, not a common purpose. The Yalta and Potsdam talks between the three leaders finessed the post war problems to preserve battlefront unity. With the war ended and with little agreement at the conference table, Europe became frozen into competing zones of influence delineated by the forward advance of the converged armies.

While America was more inclined to retreat behind its ocean, British voices expressed concern about the emerging totalitarian tide washing over Europe. On March 5. 1946, Winston Churchill, now out of office, came to Westminster College in the small Missouri town of Fulton, and, with President Truman in attendance, warned his audience that "from Stettin in the Baltic to Trieste in the Adriatic, an iron curtain [had] descended across the continent." He impressed upon his listeners that "The Sinews of Peace" required the combined military and diplomatic muscle of the United States and the British Commonwealth. He asserted a belief

> "that Soviet Russia [does not desire] war. What they desire is the fruits of war and the indefinite expansion of their power and doctrines [...] From what I have seen of our Russian friends and Allies during the war, I am convinced there is nothing they admire so much as strength, and there is nothing for which they have less respect than weakness, especially military weakness."[1]

The American left was not yet ready to abandon the hope that post-war difficulties could be resolved by the former allies working through the United Nations. James Roosevelt called upon "every peace-loving man and woman in the world to stand up now and repudiate the words, schemes, and the political allies of the Honorable Winston Churchill."[2] Victor Reuther drafted a resolution supported by the majority at the UAW convention three weeks after Churchill's speech that responded to James Roosevelt's call, stating: "We join with all peace-loving people throughout the world in denouncing the recent speech of Winston Churchill calling for an American-British military alliance against the Soviet Union."[3] Victor's resolution criticized all three of the war-time allies for "deliberately circumventing" the United Nations and for preferring the "old imperialist, war inciting methods of power politics and military alliances."[4]

Victor Reuther's resolution was similar in tone to a minority resolution proposed by Nat Ganley. Both denounced the Churchill speech, but Ganley's made no specific criticism of any of the major powers. The majority resolution contained praise and criticism for specific actions taken by each of the three parties.[5] Both resolutions cited the U. N. as the body for resolving differences between the powers. The 1946 convention that elevated Reuther to the presidency pitted Communists and non Communists against one another for control of the union. Neither side won a complete victory. The non-aligned delegates were not willing to let either faction have total control. The popular front was in disarray, but not yet in disrepute. In 1946 Communists and other leftists still banded together on issues of common concern.

Official United States policy toward the Soviet Union began to develop about the same time as the Westminster College speech. In February, 1946, the Treasury Department, troubled by lack of Soviet support for the International Monetary Fund (IMF) and the World Bank, cabled the American embassy in Moscow for an explanation of Russian behavior.[6] In the ambassador's absence, his deputy, George Kennan, responded with a 5500-word message that became known as the "Long Telegram." Kennan attributed Russian behavior to a "traditional and instinctive sense of insecurity."[7] He claimed that Stalin needed the perception of a hostile world to legitimize his autocratic rule. Marxist-Leninist doctrine became

> "justification for their instinctive fear of the outside world, for the dictatorship without which they did not know how to rule, for cruelties they did not dare not to inflict, for sacrifice they felt bound to demand. In the name of Marxism they sacrificed every single ethical value [...] Today they cannot dispense with it."

He recommended a policy of "firm containment designed to confront the Russians with unalterable counterforce at every point where they show signs of encroaching upon the interests of a stable and peaceful world."[8]

Kennan's letter drew the attention of Secretary of the Navy James Forrestal, and he was brought back to Washington to serve as first deputy for foreign affairs in the National War College.[9] His containment policy served as the intellectual framework for the Truman Administration's approach to U. S.-Soviet relations. He was encouraged to publish his doctrine of containment anonymously in the July 1947 issue of *Foreign Affairs*. The article entitled "Sources of Soviet Conduct" was attributed to X, but it quickly became common knowledge that the author of the "X Article" was Kennan. In the article Kennan envisioned that victory would not be won on the battlefield but by the ultimate implosion of the Soviet system. In an amazingly prescient analysis he contemplated that at some point in a history of futile efforts to advance their expansionist policy, some Soviet leader would be compelled to seek popular support from the politically immature masses. If such a situation were to arise and "the unity and efficacy of the Party as a political instrument" so disrupted, "Soviet Russia might be changed over night from one of the strongest to one of the weakest and most pitiable national societies."[10]

Kennan realized that the United States and the West were dealing from strength in confronting Soviet expansionism, and that in the age of nuclear weapons the way to exploit that strength was to refrain from direct confrontation and frustrate improper Soviet ambitions by strengthening Western institutions and maintaining Western resolve. Kennan's personality flaws precluded his advancement to a position higher than deputy, and he was never in a position charged with implementing his program. As his ability to influence the policy he set in motion declined, he became more critical of those responsible for its implementation.

Truman began implementation of containment in February, 1947 with announcement of the Truman Doctrine. He pledged $400 million dollars to aid the Greek royalist forces battling a Communist insurgency.[11] Truman framed the conflict as a struggle between free people and totalitarian regimes. He accused the Soviet Union of conspiring against the wishes of a free people to expand their influence even though the bulk of the Communist support came from their neighbor Marshall Tito of Yugoslavia.

The Marshall Plan

On June 5, 1947, Secretary of State George Marshall delivered the commencement address at Harvard in which he provided rationale for a major commitment of American aid to war ravished Europe. In his speech Marshall said

> "It is logical that the United States should do whatever it is able to do to assist in the return of normal economic health to the world, without which there can be no political stability and no assured peace. Our policy is not against any country, but against hunger, poverty, desperation and chaos."[12]

The speech provided few details about how the plan might be implemented.

The plan outlined by Marshall and developed by Kennan and William Clayton called for the European countries to submit proposals for how aid money would be utilized to rebuild the continent. The United States would then fund the European plan, or at least some substantial part of the plan. No country was excluded from the offer. The Soviet Union and the Eastern European nations under its influence were eligible for funding. Stalin was initially inclined to accept the offer, but changed his mind when he learned that it entailed economic cooperation and that Germany would be a recipient of Marshall Plan funding. Czechoslovakia and Poland expressed interest in participating in the plan but were dissuaded by Soviet pressure. In rejecting Marshall Plan aid, the Soviet Union accused the United States of being the "center of world-wide reaction and anti-Soviet activity."[13] It countered the apparent willingness of some of its client states to participate in the plan by cracking down on the non-Communist parties in the internal politics of its Eastern neighbors and by setting up its own economic recovery plan, originally named for Foreign Minister Molotov.

The 1948 coup in Czechoslovakia, bringing that county under strict control of Moscow, and the Berlin blockade of the same year confirmed the view of a world polarized into two antagonistic camps.

George Orwell envisioned such a division years earlier and had given the resulting standoff a name. In an essay titled "You and the Atomic Bomb" that appeared in the October 19, 1945 edition of the British newspaper *Tribune*, Orwell wrote:

> "looking at the world as a whole, the drift for many decades has not been towards anarchy but towards the reimposition of slavery. We may be heading not for general breakdown but for an epoch as horribly stable as the slave empires of antiquity. James Burnham's theory has been much discussed but few people have yet considered its ideological implications—that is the kind of world-view, the kind of beliefs, and the social structure that would probably prevail in a state which was at once unconquerable and in a permanent state of '*cold war*' with its neighbors."

Orwell explored the nightmarish ideological implications of such a state in his novel *1984*.

European workers were critical to the success of any plan to buttress Western institutions against Communist pressure. Communism had sunk deep roots in the European "Popular Front" and held a strong influence within European labor. Communists were in the forefront of opposition to the rise of Fascism in the pre-war years, and suffered in the Nazi prisons and death camps during Hitler's reign of terror. Communists were prominent in the French Resistance and among the Greek and Yugoslav partisans fighting German occupation. They had secured a place in the political framework of the societies reemerging from the ruins of war.

In anticipation of the war's end, several hundred trade union delegates from allied countries gathered in London in 1944 to formulate goals for "winning the peace."[14] Plans were made at the London conference for another meeting in Paris in October, 1945 for the purpose of founding a World Federation of Trade Unions (WFTU). The CIO participated informally in the London conference and sent official delegates to Paris.

The AFL, citing the presence of Soviet and Eastern European government controlled unions at the Paris meeting, did not send representatives to the conference and declined to join the WFTU.[15]

The WFTU was born during a spell of fair weather that followed the storms of war. There was no illusion that the Soviet trade unions were other than government controlled bodies, but hope prevailed that the spirit of cooperation between allies that had defeated Hitler's armies would continue to forge a sustainable peace. The hope soon proved illusory. There was no real change of political climate. The prevailing winds carried the same chill mistrust and national ambition that stunted cooperation in the past. The WFTU became a vehicle to promote Soviet ambitions and frustrate the establishment of stable governments in Italy and France.[16] In 1949, after the WFTU refused to support the Marshall Plan, the CIO pulled out. It was joined by the free trade unions of Western Europe except those dominated by the Communists in Italy and France. Later that year, the AFL joined the CIO and the major European unions not following the Moscow line in forming the International Confederation of Free Trade Unions (ICFTU).

Philip Murray chose Victor Reuther to be director of the CIO's Paris Office and serve as its liaison with the ICFTU. Victor was an ideal choice for this mission. During his pre-war travels around the continent, he and Walter met many of the people prominent in their country's labor movement, and gained first-hand knowledge of the challenges facing the various national organizations. During the war, Victor broadcast messages for the Office of War Information to German-speaking workers within the shrinking Nazi empire urging them to believe that the postwar years would bring a return to freedom of expression and a rebirth of democratic trade unionism.[17] At the close of hostilities he visited Germany and Austria at the request of the War Department and General Lucius Clay, who was in charge of the American occupation forces in Germany, to help identify and recruit local labor leaders for roles in the military government. With his fluency in the language, Victor Reuther was instrumental in providing the Independent Trade Union Federation in West Berlin with the technical support and equipment they needed to stave off a takeover by the Communist trade unions at a time when there was no other civil authority in place in the Western

Zone.[18] General Clay later admitted that he was doubtful the American military could have maintained a presence in Berlin without the show of support from the workers.[19] Victor's experience as the director of the Education Department of the UAW proved particularly germane to the requirements of his Paris office.

Victor stipulated to Murray that the CIO should provide assistance to democratic trade organizations in carrying out their own policies. It should avoid appearing like the "rich American" throwing its money and weight around in Europe, trying to dictate how others should act.[20] In keeping with its modest aims and limited funding, he moved the CIO office from Boulevard Haussmann to a less upscale neighborhood near Les Halles market. By contrast, the AFL office was situated on Rue de la Paix, the bright blue Boardwalk on the French Monopoly board.[21]

The AFL came to Paris with an agenda and with cash, some provided by the CIA. It tried to foist its own policy of refusing to have any dealings with Communists upon its European counterparts. It pressured Léon Jouhaux, the co-general secretary of the Confédération Générale du Travail (CGT), to break from the large union he had founded after World War I and helped reconstitute after the Second World War because it was becoming increasingly dominated by the Communists.[22] Jouhaux and a few other non-Communist leaders of the CGT broke from the parent organization and formed the CGT-Force Ouvrière. The CGT-FO advocated freedom from political control, action to advance the status of labor, and it sought a United States of Europe. It drew membership from the CGT, but not in substantial enough numbers to compete in influence with the parent organization. The break left the CGT under unchecked domination of the Communists.

Jouhaux came to regret the break with the CGT as premature and poorly planned. It diminished his influence in the French labor movement.[23] Jouhaux was a giant in the international labor movement for many years. He helped to found the International Labor Organization (ILO) after World War I, and was a founder of the ICFTU after the free trade unions split from the WFTU. He championed arms control and opposed Fascism and Communism. During the war, the CGT was dissolved by the Vichy government, and Jouhaux was placed under house arrest. In April, 1943, he was handed over to the Germans and spent twenty-five months in Buchenwald. In 1951 he was awarded the Nobel Peace Prize.

The split between the CGT and the FO was engineered with American encouragement and financed with American money. The AFL representative in Paris, Irving Brown, was the agent promoting the clumsy efforts of his union and government to make the French more like ourselves. His activities were resented by Jouhaux, and when he called the French masses "indifferent, cynical, and inert"[24] during an AFL convention, Jouhaux reacted by declaring:

> "We are happy that in our debonair republic there is enough freedom for Mr. Irving Brown, welcomed as an American citizen without the need for a visa on the soil of France, to attack with powerful means a movement of ideas and action that is honored by the support of many distinguished Frenchmen. We are determined to fight against the setting up in Paris of an Un-French Activities Committee on the model of the Un-American Activities Committee in Washington."

He went on to suggest that if such a committee were to exist it might investigate the activities of Mr. Brown.[25]

While overtures to the non-Communist French left by prominent elements of American labor, management, and the foreign service were often short-sighted and insensitive to French culture, relations with a defeated Germany scratched raw nerves and required particular skill and understanding. After the war, the French received American technical and financial assistance, but elected their own leaders and governed their own affairs. The Germans were governed by an occupation force that selected German citizens for leadership roles, and regulated their authority. The first question was whether these leaders were to come out of Hitler's prisons or from the ranks of those who facilitated his rise.

Sentiment was strong in the United States after the war, and after the horrors of the Holocaust became widely known, to turn Germany into an agrarian state that could not again threaten its neighbors. Treasury Secretary Henry Morgenthau, Jr. proposed dismantling Germany's heavy industry and shipping much of its industrial capacity to its European neighbors in reparation for wartime damages.[26] This proposal was strongly supported by the Soviet Union, and a large-scale removal of East German industrial equipment to Russia was undertaken. The Morgenthau position was endorsed by R. J. Thomas and other CIO leaders who urged President Truman to punish Germany economically.[27] Truman was initially receptive to the Morgenthau plan, but as the wartime alliance soured, concern over Soviet actions modified his thinking.

At the end of the war the British and Americans were as eager to strip Germany of its industrial war potential as their Soviet ally. German steel production was capped at 25% of its pre-war capacity.[28] And for the first three years German importation of raw materials was severely limited. The first influential voice raised against this policy was that of ex-President Herbert Hoover. Hoover wrote in March, 1947 that

> "The whole economy of Europe is interlinked with the German economy through the exchange of raw materials and manufactured goods. The productivity of Europe cannot be restored without the restoration of Germany as a contributor to that productivity."[29]

The experience of the occupying forces in Germany led the military to reconsider its earlier determination to strip Germany of its industrial base. In 1947 the Joint Chiefs reversed their previous policy and declared, "the complete revival of German industry, particularly coal mining, [was now of] primary importance" to American security.[30] Walter Reuther echoed these sentiments in a May 1949 letter to President Truman urging him not to go ahead with the dismantlement of six steel and three chemical plants earmarked for reparations by a Three Power agreement reached in Washington. Beyond the specifics for maintaining the plants in question, Reuther argued that "Establishment of vital democracy in Western Germany is crucial to [the goal of preventing the spread of Communism]. Needless dismantlement of German plants will deprive German workers of employment and will drive them, out of desperation, into the arms of Communism."[31] Within months the United States called a halt to its dismantlement of German industry.

The revival of coal mining in Germany highlighted the struggle for the soul of the new Germany, and the Army's ability to adjust its strategic objectives to the tactical situation on the ground. The man chosen by the Military Government to get the coal mines back into production was an industrialist who had collaborated with the Nazis in implementing their industrial regime. The German miners were determined that their country was not going to fall back into the hands of the people who had facilitated Hitler's rise to power. Hans Böckler, head of the Mine Workers Union, told the American general in charge that the man appointed was not acceptable to his workers and they would strike if he were not removed.[32] The general reacted to this as a challenge to his authority, and told Böckler that any strike would not be tolerated, and he would be arrested if one were called. Böckler merely offered his outstretched arms across the table for the general to cuff, and replied "Herr General, you may arrest me, but I doubt there is anything in your jails which I have not already seen in Hitler's prison."[33] The manager was replaced shortly afterward.

The disrepute of much of the German industrial class after the war allowed the workers and their political allies to push for *Mitbestimmung* or co-determination. *Mitbestimmung* in its most extensive form allowed workers up to one-half the seats on the company supervisory board, but not the chairmanship which carried two votes in the event of a tie. It applied to companies with 2,000 or more employees. It was first instituted in the coal and steel industries in 1951, and later spread in various lesser forms to other industries.[34] It has proved most useful in providing workers with advance notice of company production plans, allowing them an opportunity to acquire the necessary new skills to adapt to changes in the nature of their employment. The relationship established between labor and management during the reconstruction period has served the country well. Germany remains an exporter of high quality manufacturing products, and German union membership has remained at above 30% of its workforce at a time it has fallen below 10% of the U. S. workforce.[35]

By the end of 1949, the Marshall Plan was in place and the rehabilitation of Germany underway. The emergence of leaders like Konrad Adenauer on the right and West Berlin Mayors Ernst Reuter and Willy Brandt on the left with strong anti-Nazi credentials helped reshape the image of their country. The 1949 Berlin Blockade elevated the citizens of the former Nazi capital into heroic defenders of freedom on the front lines of the Cold War.

Preventive War

The Truman Doctrine and the Marshall Plan were the first steps in implementing the policy of containment. They were soon reinforced by the first of a number of military pacts—NATO. Four decades of uneasy coexistence followed. Winston Churchill questioned the wisdom of containment. He feared the psychological strain of an endless strategic stalemate. Churchill became the most prominent proponent of a more confrontational approach.[36]

In August, 1949, the Soviet Union tested an atomic bomb. The United States no longer possessed a monopoly on this "Destroyer of Worlds,"[37] but it still possessed a huge advantage in the number of bombs in its arsenal and in its ability to deliver them to a target. Later in the same year, Communist forces under Mao Zedong gained complete control of China, driving Chiang Kai-shek's Nationalists to seek refuge on the island of Taiwan. A year later North Korean armies swept south in an attempt to reunify the peninsular nation under a single red flag. As the Cold War heated up, a crescendo of voices began calling for a preemptive war.

The first prominent figure to make such a suggestion publicly was Bertrand Russell. The mathematician-philosopher was a pacifist who had spent six months in jail during World War I for promoting his antiwar views. In 1920 he visited the Soviet Union and was profoundly disturbed by the totalitarian nature of the Bolshevik state. The experience left him with a deep hatred of the Soviet system. He wrote to a friend that "I hate the Soviet Government too much for sanity."[38] Days after Hiroshima, Russell wrote:

> "There is one thing and one only which could save the world, and that is a thing which I would not dream of advocating. It is, that America should make war on

Russia during the next two years, and establish a world empire by means of the atomic bomb. [but] This will not be done."[39]

Two months later he began to advocate the thing of which he would not dream. He proposed that the Western Allies form a world federation and give the Russians the option of joining. Refusal to join would be a cause for war.[40]

Russell, like many of the scientists that actually worked on the bomb, lived with a visualization of a post-atomic world. He once told the House of Lords, "As I go about the street and see St. Paul's, the British Museum, the Houses of Parliament, and other monuments of our civilization, in my mind's eye I see a nightmare vision of those buildings as heaps of rubble with corpses all around them."[41] Richard Feynman later wrote of the time:

"my first impression was a very strange one...I felt it very strongly then. I sat in a restaurant in New York, for example, and I looked out at the buildings and I began to think...about how much the radius of the Hiroshima bomb damage was and so forth...How far from here was 34th Street?...all those buildings, all smashed—and so on. And I would go along and I would see people building a bridge, or they'd be making a new road, and I thought they're crazy, they just don't understand, they don't understand. Why are they making new things? It's so useless."[42]

The most persistent advocate for "preventive war" within the American scientific community was John von Neumann. The Hungarian-born mathematician brought a hatred of Communism with him when he immigrated to the United States in the 1930's. Like many others, he felt war with the Soviet Union was inevitable after the defeat of Hitler, and he advocated a first strike before the Soviets came into possession of the bomb themselves.[43] Von Neumann's advocacy of a first strike was of particular significance, because he was the founder of the mathematical field intimately involved in assessing Cold War options—Game Theory.

An early war-time application of game theory was assessing bombing targets. An evaluation of how an opponent might array its air defenses in anticipation of the likely cities its adversary would choose to target, was used to select a site that a single airplane would have the best chance of successfully reaching. A notepad dated May 10, 1945 with lists of Japanese cities in von Neumann's handwriting now resides in the Library of Congress. One list reads Kyoto, Hiroshima, Yokohama, Kokura. Kyoto was spared because of its cultural and historic heritage.[44]

Unlike many of the scientists who worked on the Manhattan Project, von Neumann did not recoil from the implications of what he had done and retreat back into academia. He devoted a good deal of his time and considerable intellectual prowess consulting for private companies like IBM and for the defense-related agencies, most notably the Rand Corporation. In 1954, von Neumann was appointed to the Atomic Energy Commission by President Eisenhower. After his confirmation, the von Neumanns moved to Washington, and he became a more public figure. Shortly after his appointment, he was stricken with bone cancer and spent the last year of his life confined to a wheel chair. This image of von Neumann may have served as a model for Dr. Strangelove, the heavily accented, wheel chair bound consultant from the Bland Corporation that advised the President's War Council in the 1963 black comedy.[45]

If von Neumann were a model for the fictional Dr. Strangelove, then the movie's General Jack Ripper had a real-life soul mate in SAC Commander, General Curtis LeMay. When warned in 1957 that his planes were vulnerable to a Soviet attack, he replied that he relied upon U2 reconnaissance flights to give him advance warnings of Soviet preparations. He boasted to his visitors "I'll knock the shit out of them before they get off the ground." When told that first use of nuclear weapons was not national policy, LeMay retorted "No, it's not national policy. But it's my policy."[46]

The Soviet nuclear test and the onset of the Korean War renewed earlier calls for "preventive war." On August 25, 1950, the Boston Naval Shipyard celebrated its 150th anniversary. Secretary of the Navy Francis

Matthews was a featured speaker at ceremonies commemorating the occasion. Matthews closed his address by asking the nation to consider "a war of aggression for peace."[47] He stated:

> "To have peace we should be willing, and declare our intention to pay, any price, even the price of instituting a war to compel cooperation for peace. Only the forces who do not want peace would oppose our efforts to transform the hostile nations embroiled in the present international conflicts into a tranquil world...We could accept [their] slander with complacency, for in the implementation of a strong affirmative, peace-seeking policy, though it cast us in a character new to a true democracy—an initiator of a war of aggression—it would win for us a proud and popular title. We would become the first *Aggressors for Peace*"[48]

Matthews's speech ignited a firestorm. Secretary of State Acheson emphasized that the speech had not been cleared beforehand and did not represent the policy of the United States.[49] Matthews was denounced by many for the ideas that cooperation could be compelled and aggression could produce peace. Many other letters arrived supporting Matthews.

Religious belief informed many of the opinions expressed by both groups. Matthews was an extremely devout Catholic who had constructed a chapel in his home and he prayed there daily.[50] His visceral hatred of Communism was colored by his own religious interpretation. He claimed Communism "[...] is the fatal mischief of man's fallen nature exerting its nefarious influence in a new and falsely alluring garb. Beneath the sophistry of its superficial philosophy, however, are visible the familiar devices to deceive men's minds and corrupt their will that have been the Devil's handmaidens throughout his foul career."[51] The reaction to Matthews' remarks divided according to the biblical emphasis that best justified an individual's disposition.

Among Matthews supporters were members of Congress, including the influential Georgia Democrat Richard Russell, and several generals who were willing to discuss the topic openly.[52] The national press was largely opposed. *Time* ran an editorial that discounted the feasibility of preventive war.[53] It concluded "[...]In such a situation the question of the morality of preventive war, which troubles many Americans, may not even arise. Whether or not preventive war is morally bad, the facts of 1950 make it military nonsense." Those facts were that the United States did not have a sufficient arsenal of nuclear weapons and capability of delivery that by itself would ensure success, and it could not ensure that Soviet bombs would not strike American and European cities. The November 11, 1950 edition of *Collier's* magazine stated the case against what Air Force General Carl Spaatz called "gangster reasoning."

> For several months we have been reading and hearing about something called "preventive war." We have examined the arguments in its favor. We have listened to them and thought about them. And in the end we haven't even learned what the term means. "Preventive war." What would it prevent? It wouldn't prevent war. It wouldn't prevent the atomic bombing of the United States. It takes an incredible optimism to believe that the Russians have collected all their atomic weapons in one vulnerable place, and that the U. S. Air Force knows exactly where that place is, and that our bombers would surely and inevitably get through on their first strike and destroy all the Soviet bombs on the first day of war.

The Cold War mentality produced a sizable constituency for the concept of "preventive war," but whether from ethical restraint, lack of assurance of success, or lack of a compelling argument to justify such horrific an action, the world made it through this most dangerous period of the confrontation. By the middle of the 1950's the balance of power was restored and the danger of either side launching an unprovoked attack was reduced. The policy of containment, with the avoidance of direct conflict between the two parties reinforced by a threat of "mutually assured destruction," was embraced in the United States by a bipartisan consensus.

The Dulles Brothers

In 1952 the "Republic summoned Ike."[54] The old soldier ensured his election by promising during the campaign to go to Korea and lend a personal hand in bringing the war to a close. Negotiations were begun, and soon after Ike's inauguration the war ended in a tenuous draw. After his initial foray into personal diplomacy, Eisenhower retreated back into an executive oversight role, leaving the new Pattons and Bradleys and Montgomerys to manage the details of his grand design. In his administration, foreign policy was the province of the Dulles brothers— John Foster as Secretary of State and Allen at the CIA. John set about building alliances with any questionable despot willing to take the anti-Communist pledge in exchange for American dollars to sustain his regime. Allen was the "bad cop" who used his agency to tip the balance of power in the unstable oligarchies in favor of the side willing walk the American line. Two countries became the particular foci of Cold War intrigue in the early days of the Eisenhower presidency: Guatemala and Iran.

An early target of the Dulles brothers was Jacobo Árbenz Guzmán, the democratically elected president of Guatemala. Árbenz became the object of American concern because he allowed the Communists to participate freely in the country's political process, as stipulated by its constitution, and he was implementing a land reform program that distributed unused prime farmland owned in part by multinational corporations, principally United Fruit, to landless peasants. United Fruit owned 42% of the arable land in Guatemala, and was unwilling to relinquish claim to any of their reserve holdings.[55] They pressed the U. S. Government to remove Árbenz and the threat he posed to their Central American operations.

To reinforce his appeal, United Fruit President Sam "the Banana Man" Zemurray hired Edward Benarys, one of the best-connected public relations agents in the country, to sell the company line on Guatemala. Benarys viewed his calling as something much more than that of a company shill. He once wrote that "The conscious and intelligent manipulation of the organized habits and opinions of the masses is an important element in democratic society. Those who manipulate this unseen mechanism of society constitute an invisible government, which is the true ruling power of the country"[56] Benarys was a liberal who traveled in elitist circles and knew most of the important publishers, editors, and journalists on a social as well as a professional basis.[57] He bombarded these friends and acquaintances with press releases, visits, and phone calls to spread alarm about the situation in the Central American country. Benarys arranged two week tours for journalists to visit Guatemala, meet with opponents of the Arbenz government, many of whom were on the United Fruit Company's payroll, see the side of the country the company wanted to show, and enjoy the hospitality of their host in a pleasant tropical setting.[58] When they returned, articles defending the American company and warning of Soviet penetration into Central America appeared in the major newspapers such as *The New York Times, The New York Herald Tribune, The Christian Science Monitor,* and *The San Francisco Chronicle, and in* the weekly magazines *Time, Newsweek, U. S. News & World Report,* and the liberal *New Leader.*[59]

The domesticated press was content to accept a relationship with their handlers and consume a message full of artificial colors and flavors that they were being fed. Concern over the course of events in Guatemala arose at the height of the McCarthy era when national hysteria over Communist plots, real or imagined, was at a peak. The United States was not about to see a Communist beachhead established within its hemisphere. It needed little prodding from United Fruit to launch a clandestine operation, code named PBSUCCESS, against Árbenz. The fact that both Dulles brothers had long-standing connections with United Fruit only added to their enthusiasm for the project.[60]

Details of the Guatemala operation released by the CIA in 1997 reveal that assassination of government loyalists was one of the options being studied. A list of targets prepared by rightist military officers was included in the released material, but the names were blacked out, preventing any attempt to determine the identity and fate of the designated victims.[61] Other tactics employed by the CIA included intimidation of government officials, staged provocations, rumor campaigns, and sabotage. The agency recruited and armed a private army of 480 mercenaries under the command of Colonel Carlos Castillo Armas that it trained in neighboring Honduras.[62] The threat of invasion led the Guatemala military to compel the resignation of President Árbenz in

June 1954, and Colonel Armas was named as his replacement. The CIA reveled in what it termed an unblemished success. It was not troubled by the inconsistency of an "army of liberation" composed of paid mercenaries deposing a newly minted democracy. Nor did it give second thought to the fact that operation PBHISTORY, launched subsequently to the coup, failed to confirm its belief that the Árbenz government harbored pro-Soviet agents or was subject to Soviet influence.[63] It determined that the relatively few Guatemalan Communists were nationalists taking no direction from the Soviet Union.

The CIA playbook for operation PBSUCCESS read like a script for its campaign against Fidel Castro a decade later. Guatemala was used then as the training ground for the exile army recruited, armed, and trained by the CIA, and Howard Hunt, the Watergate "plumber" of a decade later, was prominently linked to both operations.[64] There were assassination attempts, propaganda campaigns, and assorted efforts to intimidate and destabilize the Castro government. This time, however, it was far from an unblemished success. The Bay of Pigs fiasco derailed the start of the Kennedy Administration, and the varied attempts to assassinate Fidel exposed the nefarious connection between the agency and organized crime.

Like with later CIA operations, the blemishes on the Guatemala coup began to appear after the initial flush of success. The coup leaders provided little relief for the country they liberated and began fighting among themselves. Armas was assassinated by his presidential guard and a succession of military rulers followed. A four-decade long civil war ravaged the country. Anti-Communism provided a pretext for igniting underlying ethnic divisions within the society. The American trained military unleashed a brutal counterinsurgency campaign against a predominantly Mayan peasant population it accused of having Communist sympathies.[65]

Iran

The coup in Guatemala followed swiftly on the heels of a CIA engineered coup in Iran. Iran was the most strategically important prize of the Cold War competition. It lay between Russia and its centuries-old dream of a warm water port on the Indian Ocean. Whereas Guatemala exported bananas, Iran was awash in oil. The long-term consequences of the coup in Guatemala were disastrous for the people of that country, but had little effect upon the United States.[66] The repercussions to the United States of the coup engineered by the CIA in Iran are still reverberating.

Both the British and Russians schemed for most of a century to achieve hegemony in Iran. Prior to the First World War, a weak Qajar Shah in Tehran granted the British concessions in the oil-rich south and asked the Russians to help police the ethnically-distinct northern provinces.[67] The Russians formed a gendarmerie force known as the Cossack Brigade that superimposed a Russian officer corps on the ranks of native privates and NCOs.[68] At the outbreak of the first war, Russian and British forces moved into their respective Persian enclaves to ensure that the resource-rich kingdom did not fall into the hands of the Ottoman Turks and their German allies.

After the Russian Revolution, the Russians went home. The Cossack Brigade was left in the hands of its Persian NCOs. The most forceful and ambitious of these men was Reza Mirza, who added the title Khan to his surname after he became an officer in the brigade. The departure of the Russians only increased the influence of the British who hastened to fill the power vacuum in the north. Reza Mirza Khan was named deputy commander of the brigade, now safeguarding British interests in the country.[69] From this base of power, Reza Khan took over first the brigade, and then the country. In 1925, Reza Mirza Khan became Reza Shah. The illiterate, self-educated peasant leapfrogged the strata of Persian society to sit on the Peacock Throne.

Reza Shah set out immediately to build his dynasty. To emphasize his break from the recent Qajar past, he renamed the country Iran, a title from its distant past, and called his family dynasty Pahlevi, the name of the pre-Muslim era language of the region.[70] He committed himself to the task of grooming his son to be a worthy successor.

Reza Khan married a woman from the landed aristocracy shortly after he became an officer in the Cossack Brigade, who bore him twins in 1919—a boy, Mohammad Reza and a girl named Ashraf. From the early age of his offspring, Reza Shah thought nature had played a mean trick upon him. Ashraf had the strong personality and toughness of her father. Mohammad Reza was "by nature a creature of indecision, beset by formless doubts and fears" as described in a 1952 CIA report. The father reinforced the boy's poor self image with his frequently expressed disdain.[71]

In 1941, Reza Shah ran afoul of the foreign powers deeply involved in Iranian affairs by his declared admiration and support for Nazi Germany. Immediately after Germany invaded the Soviet Union, Russian and British troops were back in Iran, and Reza Shah was forced to abdicate in favor of his son. Reza Shah ended his days in exile in South Africa.

During the war, a new power began to gain influence in Iran. Britain and Russia were preoccupied with the defense of the homeland and empire. The United States was less encumbered with a defensive war and eager to gain a foothold in this emerging theater of global competition. Iran became a back door delivery port for arms headed to the Russian front, and within months there were 28,000 American troops in the country handling the delivery of war materiel to the Soviets.[72] American advisers were involved in every aspect of Iranian society.

With most of the senior Iranian politicians and influence peddlers bought and paid for by the British and Russians, the Americans targeted the young Shah as their most likely conduit into the decision making councils of the country. The Shah was distrustful of the senior Iranian politicians, who had little regard for him.[73] He was suspicious of the British and Russians and the designs they had on his country's resources. He welcomed the American presence as bringing a source of stability to a situation in which he had few trusted associates and few means of control. He came to be particularly close to the American Ambassador Leland Morris and Colonel, later General, Norman Schwarzkopf, the father of the Desert Storm commander, who was an adviser, and later director, of the rural military police force.[74]

Tehran was the site of the 1943 meeting of the Big Three wartime leaders. The meeting was held in the Atabeg Palace, part of the sprawling Russian Embassy compound that included several other palaces and smaller houses, a wood inhabited by a herd of gazelles, and a small picturesque lake with swans and recreational rowboats.[75] The American presence in the city was still modest. Roosevelt chose to stay in the Atabeg Palace as a guest of Stalin. Churchill stayed nearby in a suitably grand

British Embassy and walked across the street to attend the conference sessions.[76] Tehran was the first of several meetings where the three leaders met to determine the shape of the postwar world. In the general communiqué released at the end of the conference, the leaders pledged to provide Iran with assistance after the war, and promised all foreign troops would be withdrawn within six months of the defeat of Germany and her 'associates.'[77]

When the war ended, the six month deadline came and went—first six months after the Germans surrendered, then six months after the Japanese. The Russians showed little inclination to withdraw from the northern sections of the country. Instead they appeared ready to annex the province of Azerbaijan into the ethnically similar soviet inside their own territory. The Azerbaijan issue threatened to become the first test of the ability of the United Nations to resolve an international crisis. The Iranian Prime Minister Qavam es-Sultaneh correctly realized that the Russians were more interested in oil than they were land, and, after a pattern of appeasement, induced them to withdraw from Iranian territory in turn for new Iranian elections that promised to return a Majlis (Parliament) favorable to granting the oil concessions.[78]

The Russians withdrew, and the Shah's army moved in to occupy the provincial capital of Azerbaijan, Tabriz, but the new Majlis voted almost unanimously not to rescind the war-time ban it imposed on granting new oil concessions.[79] The Russians had been duped by Qavam, but with the strong American and British presence in Iran, they could only complain of Iranian treachery.

The post-war period was a time of real democracy in Iran. The National Front Party of Mohammad Mossadegh had strong public support. It contested the Royalists and other more conservative parliamentarians, many of whom were in the employ of the Anglo Iranian Oil Company and other foreign interests.[80] Another major voice in the national dialog was the Communist Tudeh (Masses) Party. It covered its support of Russian interests in Iran with a nationalist veneer. One of the concessions Qavam granted the Soviets during his negotiations to get them to withdraw their troops was to allow the Tudeh Party to participate freely in Iranian politics. Its internal discipline and organizational strength made it a force in Iranian politics well beyond its level of support in the electorate.[81] The strongest voice supporting extension of the ban on granting additional concessions to foreign companies and nationalizing the existing oil concessions belonged to the 70 year old Mossadegh. On April 19, 1951 he became Prime Minister. Within two weeks a law nationalizing the Anglo Iranian Oil Company was passed by the Majlis and signed by the Shah. The move precipitated a crisis with Britain over compensation for their appropriated assets, and opened rifts within the Iranian political fabric.

Mossadegh was a curious public figure in the West—old and frail, his oratorical skills uniquely tuned to an Iranian audience. He would be drawn to tears by his description of the suffering of the Iranian people, work himself up into a coughing fit and collapse, only to be revived by his supporters and continue with the speech.[82] In the Shi'ite faith, grief over the martyrdom of Ali, son-in-law of the Prophet, and his son Hussein casts a pall of sadness over the faithful. Its rituals feature self-flagellations and lamentations over the death of Hussein, hearkening back to a "Good Friday" without a compensating "Easter Sunday." Mossadegh played on these national sensitivities to bolster his appeal. He was a skilled parliamentarian, but proved to be a poor administrator.[83]

The British were eager to see Mossadegh ousted to retrieve their oil revenues. The Americans were fearful he was heading the country toward ruin, opening the way for the Tudeh Party to swing the country into the Soviet orb.[84] The Dulles brothers were more willing to contemplate a joint Anglo-American effort in Iran than their predecessors in the Truman Administration had been.[85] In May, 1953, Dr. Donald Wilber of the CIA Iran desk met with his British counterpart in Cyprus to plan a coup. An officer loyal to the Shah, General Zahedi, had approached American Embassy officials in March indicating his willingness to lead an anti-Mossadegh putsch, and Allen Dulles had set aside $1 million to fund the effort.[86] The plan called for a CIA sponsored propaganda campaign to turn public opinion against Mossadegh and staged disruptions and acts of vandalism that would be attributed to the Tudeh Party. When the situation in the streets appeared to be deteriorating toward anarchy, Zahedi would move to secure the Tehran garrison and communication centers within the city. Crowds of loyalists recruited by agents in the employ of the CIA would flock to the streets to give the coup a semblance of popular support. The Shah would be required to sign documents relieving Mossadegh of his duties as Prime Minister and appointing Zahedi to the post to clothe the effort in a threadbare cloak of legality.[87]

The British and American planners did not fully trust each other's Governments, had a Kiplingesque disdain for the ability of the "[Oriental] Iranians to plan or act in a thoroughly logical manner," and had severe misgivings about the cooperation they would get from the Shah.[88] It was the "forceful and scheming twin sister"[89] Princess Ashraf that was selected to be the principal contact between the CIA and the house of Pahlevi. Princess Ashraf was to meet with her brother, assuage him of his "pathological fear of the UK hidden hand" in Iranian affairs, and, like Marley's ghost, appraise him of two other visitations to follow that would reinforce her message and outline the role he was expected to play.[90]

The first of these visitors was the British agent in Iran, who asked the Shah to choose one of several phrases that would be included in the Persian language broadcasts of the BBC at a set time on successive days to indicate that he was speaking directly for the British government.[91] The second visitor was General Schwarzkopf, who the Shah knew and admired for his work with the rural gendarmerie. The Shah, fearful that the palace might be bugged, escorted Schwarzkopf to the grand ballroom where he dragged a table to the middle of the floor. He then got up on the table and requested the general to do the same.[92] From this platform the general assured the monarch that the United States was committed to the continuation of the Pahlevi dynasty as the bulwark of national sovereignty; told him Mossadegh was leading the country to ruin, and there would be no increase in U. S. aid as long as he was in power; said a suitable oil agreement would be offered but not foisted upon the country once Mossadegh was removed; and warned if the Shah failed to align with the anti-Mossadegh forces, he would be responsible for the collapse of the country and loss of its independence.[93]

By early June, the initial phase of the operation was in progress. Kermit Roosevelt, grandson of the Rough Rider, sneaked into Iran to take charge of the effort on the ground. Back in Langley, artists were busy drawing cartoons with unflattering caricatures of Mossadegh that were destined for the farsi language papers.[94] The owners of leading newspapers were paid to open up their pages to the CIA generated articles.[95] The effort to discredit Mossadegh in word and image was advancing, but repeated efforts to get the Shah to commit and sign the needed documents only met with indecision and reluctance. He told the British agent, Asadollah Rashidian, that he heard the phrase in the broadcasts, but needed more time to assess the situation.[96]

By the time he did sign the decrees, knowledge of the coup planning was widespread. On the day of the event, word passing down to Zahedi's co-conspirators leaked to General Riahi, Mossadegh's chief of staff, who was able to place loyal brigades in front of the Prime Minister's house and at other crucial locations in the city.[97] General Riahi's counter moves interrupted the coup in progress and caused key members of Zahedi's group to abandon the effort and go into hiding. By the morning, radio Tehran was broadcasting news of the failed coup attempt. The Shah fled to Baghdad.

General Zahedi and some other key officers escaped arrest and got word to Roosevelt that they were still interested in going ahead with the original plan.[98] Officials in Washington and London concluded that the plan had failed and advised Roosevelt to come home, but he remained convinced that the plan to oust Mossadegh was still viable. He was able to install Zahedi and a top lieutenant in a safe house and sneak them in and out of the embassy in the false bottom of a car for planning sessions.[99]

The plotters got a break when the forces loyal to the Prime Minister felt secure enough to relax their grip on the capital and move their forces back to their barracks. CIA assets posing as Tudehists resumed their intimidation of religious leaders, including the bombing of the home of one prominent cleric, to inflame public anger against the Communists and their protector Mohammad Mossadegh.[100] The Shah paused long enough in Baghdad on his way to Rome to broadcast a message stating that he had relieved Mossadegh of his duties and nominated General Zahedi to form a new government. Roosevelt's operatives worked the media channels left open to them to get the Shah's message to the public.

Mossadegh's popularity had diminished significantly in the wake of the recession precipitated by his nationalization of the foreign oil company and the media campaign directed against him from both the left and right. Iran was not ready to operate the industry by itself yet, and the British induced other suppliers to boycott Iranian oil. The reduced oil revenues sapped the entire economy of its vitality. With Mossadegh's legitimacy now in doubt, the public was receptive to efforts to remove him.[101]

What happened next came as a surprise to Washington and Moscow and even to Roosevelt and his colleagues in the embassy in Tehran. The claques organized by Roosevelt took to the streets spontaneously, but they were joined by larger segments of the population who marched on the radio station and the Majlis demanding Mossadegh's ouster and crying "the Shah is victorious." Officers who were part of the original plot appeared with tanks and troops and occupied the main squares of the city.[102] As Radio Moscow was broadcasting news of the failure of the American attempt to change the government in Iran, Radio Tehran fell to the pro-Shah crowd, and it began announcing the success of the counter coup and reading the royal decrees.[103]

The Shah returned from Rome to sit on his Peacock Throne. He told Roosevelt on next meeting him that "I owe my throne to God, my people, my army—and you."[104] More properly, the order of indebtedness should have been reversed. The loyal officers were given their rewards. Fazlullah Zahedi was named Prime Minister; his son was given the hand of the Shah's daughter Shahnaz and later became Ambassador to London and Washington; Colonel Nassiri, who delivered the message to Mossadegh dismissing him as Prime Minister, was promoted to general and put in charge of Savak, the internal security agency; Captain Khatemi, who had piloted the Shah to Baghdad and Rome, was made commander of the air force. When the new oil deal was signed a year later, American oil companies gained a 40% stake in what had been exclusively a British company.[105] Kermit Roosevelt received more than the gratitude of the Shah. He was named adviser to a number of oil companies.[106]

The successful counter coup in Iran was partly CIA inspired, part popular sentiment, and part serendipity. Once the Shah was back on his throne, the Iranian government for the next twenty-six years came with the label, "Made in America." The Shah met for two hours every Saturday morning with the CIA officer in charge of the Tehran operation.[107] Every Iranian military officer of the rank of Colonel and above was trained, usually for a two or three year assignment, in the United States. Many junior officers and NCOs went for shorter periods.[108] Savak came into existence more-or-less as an extension of the CIA. The secular opposition that formed the base of support for Mossadegh's Nationalist Party and the Tudeh was targeted by the Shah's police. Prominent individuals were either silenced by arrest, or driven into exile, or in some instances executed, leaving religious fundamentalists as the only well-established opposition to the monarchy.[109] The modest American presence at the time of FDR's visit grew into an Embassy compound covering sixty-five acres in the heart of Tehran, rivaling the Russian compound in size, but lacking the gazelles and swans.[110]

John Foster Dulles used the change of events in Iran to fashion a belt around the sagging underbelly of the Soviet bear to keep its appetite in check and prevent it from crushing its smaller southern neighbors. In Baghdad in 1955, he orchestrated the creation of the CENTO Pact. It aligned Britain with the military dominated governments of Turkey and Pakistan, the Hashemite kingdom in Iraq—a leftover from the days of British hegemony, and the increasingly autocratic Shah. The United States became an associate member two years later after budgetary issues that prevented its initial membership were resolved.

A Passage to India

Walter Reuther was a leading critic of this American reliance on military pacts with autocratic regimes to contain Soviet ambitions. As early as 1948, he warned that "The chief weakness of American foreign policy is the predilection of our State Department for dealing with anybody who will promise to hate Communism. It is fatal to resist Communism by courting reaction." He recognized that the revolutions sweeping through the emerging nations in Asia, Africa, and Latin America were the struggles of "hungry men to get the wrinkles out of their bellies."[111] The Communists were simply "riding its back." Reuther's position was not only counter to the thrust of State Department policy, it also put him at odds with his new partner, George Meany.

Days after the AFL-CIO merger, George Meany berated a largely liberal gathering at a National Religion and Labor Foundation luncheon for the "stone silence" of liberals in the face of Soviet human rights abuses and the destruction of the national independence of hundreds of millions of people in Europe and Asia. He went on to echo the sentiment of John Foster Dulles that nations not aligned with us are against us. Meany told his audience "no country, no people, no movement can stand aloof and be neutral in this struggle. Nehru and Tito are not neutral. They are aides and allies of Communism in fact and in effect if not in diplomatic verbiage."[112]

Meany's comments received front page coverage in both the United States and India. His comments strained already difficult relations between the two countries. In Dulles's containment strategy, the southern belly of Russia and the flanks of China were surrounded by countries starched with military agreements to present a formal appearance of anti-Communist solidarity. A key member of both SEATO and the Baghdad Pact nations was India's rival, Pakistan. India, located at the buckle of this hypothetical belt, remained outside the alliance structure that delineated friend from foe in the simplistic calculus of Cold War politics.

India resisted pressure to toe the American line and maintained friendly relations with both of its Communist neighbors. Soviet leaders Bulganin and Khrushchev had been welcomed to India by Nehru shortly before Meany's speech. In the United Nations, India's flamboyant ambassador Krishna Menon often tweaked American public opinion with denunciations of neo-colonial imperialism and racism. Few Americans had an appreciation of the internal complexities of India that governed its foreign policy, and few Americans had influence within a broad spectrum of Indian public opinion.

The leaders of both of the world's two largest democracies wanted to repair the damage caused by Meany's remarks, and worked to arrange a visit to India by a prominent American. The names of the two individuals that Indian ambassador G. L. Mehta referred to his government as best symbolizing the common values of the two countries were Walter Reuther and Chief Justice Earl Warren.[113] When Chester Bowles was Ambassador to India in the last years of the Truman Administration, he urged Reuther to accept an invitation from the Indian National Trade Union Congress (INTUC) and visit the country as part of a leadership exchange program he was promoting. His successor, John Sherman Cooper, personally appealed to Reuther to accept the standing invitation that was now seconded by an official invitation from the Nehru government.[114]

Walter Reuther arrived in New Delhi on April 4, 1956 for the start of a twelve-day visit. He was greeted by Prime Minister Nehru, and after a formal ceremony, he joined his host for a wide ranging discussion During the meeting Nehru expressed his deep concern over the drift in Indo-American relations "because obviously we need you, just as in the long run, you need us." Nehru came away from his discussion impressed by the range of knowledge of his guest. "What a remarkable, amazing, stimulating fellow this Reuther is," he told his Congress Party executive committee.[115] Reuther returned the compliment during a New Delhi address calling Nehru "truly one of the great statesmen of the world."[116] He delighted his hosts by revealing "Like many Americans, I have felt that U. S. foreign policy in Asia has placed undue emphasis upon military pacts, and military alliances. This [...] has in my opinion, tended to trade reliable democratic friends for dubious military alliances."[117]

Reuther spent the next ten days touring the vast subcontinent, meeting with trade union leaders, workers, and the Indian elite. He donned the native "Nehru cap" and was festooned with garlands on each stop of his tour. His schedule called for as many as sixteen speeches in a single day.[118] As his travels took him through eight different language regions, he grew to appreciate how the linguistic and religious cleavages within the newly independent nation necessitated its neutralist stance internationally.[119] The black and white view screen of John Foster Dulles and George Meany did not have sufficient resolution to represent the multiple shades of the Indian political landscape. Moraji Desai, Chief Minister of the Bombay State, characterized the psychological gulf separating the two cultures when he told Reuther

"You Americans have the complex of a successful people who cannot bear contradiction. You cannot tolerate the thought of being wrong once. For us to live together, you have to learn to live down your success, and we—we have to live down our frustration."[120]

Reuther's visit to India was a huge triumph. He arrived with established credentials as a critic of the Cold War emphasis on military alliances and as a spokesman for African-American rights at home. He had a credibility with Indian audiences that provided him a receptive hearing for his explanation of American post-war policy and of the "different backgrounds of experience" leading Indians and Americans to contrasting world views.[121] The Indian Press gave the visit prominent coverage and generally effusive praise. The *Hindustan Times* called Reuther's visit "a welcome whiff of fresh air" that revived Indian faith in the United States.[122]

One person less enthralled with Reuther's mission was George Meany. The trip highlighted the philosophical and personality differences of the two men. Inside the AFL-CIO Meany was the top man with solid organizational support, but on the world stage he was eclipsed by his more dynamic junior partner. The publicity given to Reuther only made Meany more determined to assert his authority as the spokesperson for labor. Upon Reuther's return Meany sent a letter to the *New York Times* reaffirming his previous position that "Americans and liberty-loving people everywhere have a right, indeed a duty to oppose nations that sat on the sidelines in the struggle against Soviet expansion."[123] Meany reasserted his primacy as foreign policy spokesman for American labor by telling Reuther "if I don't speak for the labor movement, then who does?"[124] For the 1957 convention of the INTUC Meany tapped Irving Brown, not Walter Reuther, to represent the AFL-CIO.

Meany relied on Jay Lovestone for foreign policy advice. The former mentor of Homer Martin and the "Progressive Caucus" had wormed his way into the hierarchy of the AFL. The once upon a time Communist caterpillar emerged from the chrysalis as a right-winged moth that flitted about the head of George Meany and pointed him in a direction he was all too willing to go. Meany channeled Lovestone in his foreign policy pronouncements, and Meany made it clear that he spoke for labor.

Americans in the fifties had an insatiable appetite for cowboy movies. Roy Rogers, Gene Autry, and Hopalong Cassidy rode off the big screen and onto the small screens filling American homes. The networks filled their time slots with Westerns—Gunsmoke, Bonanza, The Rifleman, and many more. Western epics replaced the Saturday matinee vignettes. Alan Ladd, Gary Cooper, and John Wayne came to embody the American self-image—tough, courageous, resourceful, and noble. Western movies were the mid twentieth century morality plays. The good guys wore white hats and rode pretty horses. The bad guys wore the black hats and had no redeeming qualities. At the end of the movie, the heroine was rescued from either physical harm or psychological torment, only to watch the hero ride off into the sunset. Sex was neither explicit nor implicit in the typical Western. Black cowboys were common in the real West, but all the Hollywood cowboys, good and bad, were white.

Americans lived in a world of black and white hats. We saw our country as virtuous, and our adversaries as evil. While we weren't always sure what we were for, we became convinced we knew what we were against. The Shah and Colonel Armas didn't really wear white hats, but they were just part of the posse rounded up by the hero to chase the bad guys. The funny little white cap that Nehru wore was no hat at all, only a pretentious ruse to make him look like one of the good guys.

Tail Gunner Joe

Driven by fear of a nuclear armed adversary, unsettling changes in the emerging post-colonial landscape, and a Hollywood version of the American identity, politics swerved sharply to the right. The Republican class of 1946 included Richard Nixon and a rather nondescript junior Senator from Wisconsin, Joe McCarthy. McCarthy eked out a narrow primary win over the Progressive Party stalwart Robert La Follette, Jr. by accusing the incumbent, who was forty-six years old at the time of Pearl Harbor, of shirking his duty to enlist in the war effort and making a profit from investments during the conflict.[125] McCarthy billed himself as "Tail-Gunner Joe" and asserted that the Senate needed a tail-gunner in its midst. Tail-Gunner Joe neglected to mention that his own stock investments during the war netted him profits comparable to those La Follette made from his investment in a radio station.[126]

McCarthy benefited from the support of Harold Christoffel's left-wing local 248 and the Communist controlled United Electrical Workers Union during the primary.[127] Support from these segments of labor, that favored McCarthy over the avowedly anti-Communist La Follette, may have been decisive in an election where a difference of one percent of the vote cast separated the two candidates.

For his first three years in the Senate, McCarthy was a back-bencher with little influence within his own party. One newspaper survey found him to be the worst Senator in the chamber. Then, in an appearance before a Wheeling, West Virginia Republican Women's Club on February 9, 1950, he brandished a sheet of paper he claimed contained the names of 205 known Communists working in the State Department.[128] The speech was not recorded, and the number read into the Congressional Record several days later was 57, a number that seems to be taken from the label of a Heinz ketchup bottle.[129] Suddenly "Tail-Gunner Joe" was no longer an anonymous junior Senator from the Dairy State.

The Democrats responded to McCarthy's attacks upon the Truman Administration State Department by dragging the Wisconsin Republican before a televised hearing of the Senate Foreign Relations Committee chaired by Millard Tydings of Maryland. McCarthy used the hearings to charge nine people with having Communist connections. Most of the nine no longer worked for the State Department, or never did, and all had faced similar accusations of dubious validity previously.[130] McCarthy was forceful and colorful in his denunciations, but produced no evidence to substantiate his charges. The Democratic attempt to discredit the Senator degenerated into a partisan standoff, with the majority report labeling McCarthy's charges a "fraud and a hoax," and Republican Senator William Jenner accusing Tydings of "the most brazen whitewash of treasonable conspiracy in our history.[131]"

In the 1950 Congressional elections, McCarthy campaigned vigorously against Tydings and several other liberal Democrats. He accused Tydings of "protecting Communists" and "shielding traitors."[132] McCarthy's staff provided a nucleus of campaign aides for Tydings Republican opponent John Marshall Butler. With their assistance, the Butler campaign produced a flyer featuring a doctored photograph of Tydings appearing to be in a confidential discussion with Communist Party leader Earl Browder.[133] The Maryland Senate campaign was noted as one of the dirtiest in history.

When the votes were counted, Tydings and the other Senators targeted by McCarthy were all defeated. McCarthy's anti-Communist rants had a resonance with the electorate that every politician noted.

For the next three years voices of moderation were intimidated. Even President Eisenhower, who detested the Senator, was dissuaded from coming to the defense of his mentor, George C. Marshall, for fear of the electoral repercussions it may have caused.[134] McCarthy attacked Marshall in print and in speeches for the 'loss of China.' He did not frame his criticism of Marshall as merely the author of a policy failure, he suggested the General was part of "a conspiracy so immense and an infamy so black as to dwarf any previous venture in the history of man."[135]

McCarthy had his strongest base of support in the Catholic community. The Church hierarchy long voiced strong disapproval of Communist ideology, and the ACTU was the organizational base within the CIO for efforts to purge Communists from the ranks of the labor movement. The Catholic press gave McCarthy's campaign the blessing of the clerical establishment.[136] The most visible Catholic in national politics, Joseph Kennedy, also embraced the anti-Communist views of his coreligionist. McCarthy was a frequent guest of the Kennedy clan at Hyannisport, and was named the godfather of Robert Kennedy's daughter, Kathleen.[137] Robert Kennedy was first introduced to national politics as assistant counsel for McCarthy's Senate Permanent Subcommittee on investigations.

With his critics intimidated, McCarthy fed the national hysteria over Communism. His constant warnings that Communists were embedded like moth larvae in the very fabric of American government recalled the witch hunts of a superstitious colonial past. He flailed away at the State Department, then turned his attention to the Voice of America and finally the United States Army. He embarrassed Army General Ralph Zwicker, a World War 2 hero on the battlefield, during one of his hearings because a soldier with left-wing political allegiances was given an honorary discharge rather than a court-martial.[138] When Army Secretary Robert Stevens intervened to protect his officer, a confrontation between Stevens and Republican Senators including McCarthy ensued that ended with Stevens issuing a "memorandum of understanding" that capitulated to McCarthy on most of his demands.[139] The *Times of London* editorialized on the affair that "Senator McCarthy achieved today what General Burgoyne and General Cornwallis never achieved—the surrender of the American Army."[140]

McCarthy was allowed to run roughshod over the civil rights of American citizens for three years with impunity. It probably led him to become increasingly reckless, and precipitated his downfall. With the encouragement of President Eisenhower, the Army retaliated against him by charging that his chief counsel, Roy Cohn, used undue influence to secure favorable treatment for his friend, private G. David Shine.[141] The televised hearings were held before McCarthy's investigations subcommittee with Republican Senator Karl Mundt in the chair. The viewing public was treated to McCarthy's bluster and bullying for thirty-six days. His negative ratings soared. The highlight of the hearings occurred on the thirtieth day when Army counsel Joseph Welch asked Cohn to provide the Attorney General with the list of 130 Communists or subversives McCarthy claimed were working in the defense industry. McCarthy rushed in to deflect the request, charging that if Welch was so interested in people aiding the Communists he should check out a man named Fred Fisher working in his Boston law office. Welch responded by telling McCarthy "until this moment, Senator, I think I never really gauged your cruelty or your recklessness." When the Senator persisted with his attack, Welch interrupted and said "let us not assassinate this lad further, Senator. You've done enough. Have you no sense of decency, sir, at long last? Have you no sense of decency?" The gallery erupted with applause.[142] McCarthy was finished.

McCarthy's fall was as rapid as his rise. Just prior to the Army-McCarthy hearings Edward R. Murrow aired an examination of McCarthy's investigations on his news journal, *See It Now*. The program showed clips of McCarthy making wild accusations, haranguing witnesses, and berating General Zwicker.[143] Murrow concluded the broadcast with a monologue:

> We proclaim ourselves, indeed we are, the defenders of freedom, wherever it continues to exist in the world, but we cannot defend freedom abroad by deserting it at home. The actions of the junior Senator from Wisconsin have caused alarm and dismay amongst our allies abroad, and given considerable comfort to our enemies. And whose

fault is that? Not really his. He didn't create this situation of fear; he merely exploited it—and rather successfully.

McCarthy was now a liability to his party and to the good name of the institution. On December 2, 1954, the Senate voted to "condemn," not "censure" McCarthy for abusing the members of his subcommittee and his failure to cooperate with the Subcommittee on Rules and Administration. All of the Democratic members present and voting sided with the majority. Senator Kennedy was in the hospital for back surgery at the time of the vote and never revealed how he would have declared. The vote was a literal death sentence for McCarthy. His presence in the Senate was ignored by his colleagues.[144] He began to drink more and more heavily, and on May 2, 1957, he died of acute hepatitis.

Senator McCarthy stole the spotlight with his theatrics and wild accusations, but the sustained conservative assault on the American left came from the House Committee on Un-American Activities (HUAC). HUAC was made a permanent House investigating committee in 1945. One of its most outspoken members, John Rankin of Mississippi, set the parameters for the committee's investigations when he declared that slavery was "the greatest blessing that the Negro people ever had."[145] Racial discrimination and lynchings were not sufficiently un-American to warrant the scrutiny of the committee. More often it was the people fighting these injustices who were dragged before their Congressional interlocutors. "After all," said Congressman Rankin, "the Klan is an old American institution."[146]

The committee targeted leftists in Hollywood and academia who were in a position to influence opinion, and civil rights leaders who had been aligned with the Popular Front. It sought to diminish the influence of labor by identifying it with Communists in its ranks. It used the Cold War hysteria of the period as a cover to conduct an Inquisition. People summoned to appear before it were not charged with any particular crime other than holding to a heretical belief or associating with people espousing such beliefs. They were not permitted to confront their accusers; their attorneys were not permitted to address the committee; and hearsay was given the appearance of fact.[147] The sole purpose of the hearing was to single out the accused as an un-American—to be shunned by employers and ostracized by former friends and colleagues, fearful of sharing a similar fate.

The target of the investigation may have been a member of the Communist Party, past or current, or a "fellow traveler"—a person who worked closely with Communists during the time of the Popular Front. The first question addressed to the witness was always "Are you now, or have you ever been a member of the Communist Party?" If the person admitted his or her association with the party and attempted to defend the conjunction of their political beliefs and their patriotism, they would be required to answer requests to divulge the names of their associates or face contempt of Congress charges. If they asserted their Fifth Amendment rights, they would be labeled in Joe McCarthy's words as "Fifth Amendment Communists," and suffer the consequences accompanying the stigma of such a perception. The HUAC hearings ruined the reputations of both those who stood behind the shield of the Fifth Amendment and those who cooperated with the Committee and testified against their friends and colleagues.

The case of the "Hollywood Ten," a group of writers and directors cited by HUAC in 1947 for their left-wing affiliations, was the first major public hearing of the permanent committee focusing on Communist influence in the common culture. In 1940, a temporary committee of the same name under chairman Martin Dies, had briefly looked into charges by a former party member John Leech that Communism was pervasive in Hollywood. Dies summoned leading actors named by Leech, including Humphrey Bogart, James Cagney, and Frederic March, to meet privately with him to clear their names of charges of Communist connections.[148] Dies cleared all cooperative witnesses. Only actor Lionel Stander failed to get the Dies seal of approval, and he was fired immediately by his studio. Spurred by charges from Walt Disney that a strike by his animators was Communist inspired, California State Senator Jack Tenney formed a state version of the House committee in 1941 and began his own quixotic effort to tilt at Communist windmills on the Hollywood landscape.[149]

The Dies committee was formed in the late thirties during the "first red scare." It was a time when the appeal of Communism during the depression had been greatly diminished by the Moscow show trials and the Molotov-Ribbentrop pact. The disfavor with which the public viewed the Russian state at the time provided conservatives an opportunity to isolate Communist influence at home. Anti-Communist fervor diminished during the war years when the Soviet Union was seen as a valiant ally in the struggle against Hitler. By 1947 the wartime alliance had devolved into the early Cold War period, and a conservative Congress was eager to grab the anti-Communist cudgel again to beat back the liberal advances of the New Deal.

It was as much the promise of a right wing bias in the entertainment industry that drove the 1947 probe of Hollywood as fear of the exploitation of the industry by the left. The Motion Picture Alliance for the Preservation of American Ideals (MPA) co-founded by Walt Disney cautioned against the inclusion of "subtle communistic touches" in films. To avoid these "touches" it told the industry "don't smear the free enterprise system [...] Don't smear wealth [...] Don't smear the profit motive [...] Don't deify the "common man" [...] Don't glorify the collective."[150]

During the hearings, there was little attempt to produce evidence of Communist sentiment appearing in the films of the witnesses or in Hollywood movies in general. The Committee produced no evidence to substantiate a claim made by Congressman Rankin in a press conference that Hollywood was home to "one of the most dangerous plots ever instigated for the overthrow of this government."[151] It was purely an inquisition. The witnesses were made to recant their apostasy or face damnation by the apparatus of the state. The "Ten" refused to cooperate, citing their First Amendment rights of freedom of speech and assembly. All ten were cited for contempt of Congress by the full House and sentenced to prison terms ranging from six months to a year.[152] The Supreme Court allowed the convictions stand. HUAC had carte blanche to press ahead with its inquisitorial style of attack.

The Hollywood Ten became the first set of movie makers blacklisted by the industry. Subsequent hearings added additional names to that roster. The industry endured a decade of self-censorship after the initial HUAC hearings. Even a movie like It's A Wonderful Life would have run afoul of the MPA proscriptions. The community went through its own form of self-censorship. Movie personalities shunned fund raising drives for humanitarian causes and were reluctant to lend their name to civil rights campaigns and efforts to stop nuclear testing lest they draw the attention of HUAC.

Behind the efforts of the committee lurked J. Edgar Hoover. People willing to defend the rights of the accused and lawyers representing them were dubbed "Communist sympathizers" and subjected to FBI scrutiny. Bartley Crum, a lawyer for some of the "Hollywood Ten" had his mail opened, his phone tapped, and was under constant surveillance. Old friends and clients drifted away and Crum became dependent on barbiturates. After enduring a decade of harassment, family tragedy, and career reversals, Bartley Crum had had enough. In 1959 he committed suicide.[153]

The ADA

The anti-Communist hysteria generated by the sensational claims from McCarthy and the drum-beat cadence with which the press kept the public in step with his campaign, created a crisis on the left. The Popular Front, the anti-Fascist coalition through which Liberals, Socialists, and Communists cooperated in promoting mutually held goals, had been fraying for years. In the face of this offensive by the right it disintegrated. By the end of the decade, Communists no longer had a voice in the national dialog, and elements of the left were as vigorous as the right in exorcising them from the national scene.[154] Communists were now "not nice to know," and liberals, seeking the approval of the body politic, made a show of avoiding them.

At the outset of the Cold War progressives were united in calling for an expanded New Deal and protection of civil liberties, but split over foreign policy issues and the means for promoting a liberal agenda. Shortly after the Democratic election defeat of 1946, the Progressive Citizens of America (PCA) was formed by many of the same people that attended a CIO-PAC sponsored conference of progressives earlier in the year. The PCA sought to unite progressives regardless of "race, creed, color, national origin, or political affiliation."[155] It was open to any of the components of the Popular Front that supported its agenda. The PCA was unhappy with the Truman Administration's lack of commitment to the New Deal and was in general agreement with Henry Wallace's criticism of administration foreign policy. It was sympathetic to calls for a third party, and enlisted Wallace to give the keynote address at its convention.[156]

A week after the PCA was formed, a second group of liberals formed the Americans for Democratic Action (ADA) to compete with the PCA for the legacy of Franklin Roosevelt's presidency. The ADA was essentially a rebranding of the Union for Democratic Action (UDA) that spoke for the anti-Communist left during the war years. The UDA formed in 1940 to promote social democracy at home and an interventionist policy abroad. It urged deeper involvement in the war in support of England, but regarded the Soviet Union with suspicion and barred Communists from its membership.[157] The guiding force in the UDA was the theologian Reinhold Niebuhr. Niebuhr came to espouse a pluralistic democracy that delicately balanced the conflicting interests of the "moral cynicism" of *the children of darkness* and the utopian idealism of *the children of light*.[158] Liberal idealism was tempered by real-world pragmatism.

The UDA never attracted a wide following in the progressive camp. Most liberals found the group's effort to disassociate itself from the Popular Front as divisive, and once the United States and the Soviet Union were allied in the struggle against Fascism the mood of the country toward Communism softened. During the war years, the *children of light* clung to the hope that the marriage of convenience necessitated by the war would settle into a marriage of mutual regard once the conflict ended.

The Republican election gains in 1946 and the hardening posture of the two former allies precipitated a resurgence of anti-Communist militancy at war's end. Prominent liberals came to believe that they would never be in the ascendancy while the progressive community continued its self-denial of Soviet imperialism.[159] They regarded the stance of the PCA as not only naive, but inimical to the pursuit of a progressive social agenda.

One hundred and thirty people committed to a revitalized UDA gathered at the Willard Hotel in Washington on January 4, 1947 to form an organization on the left that was both progressive and anti-Communist. Among those gathered were stalwarts of the UDA such as Niebuhr and executive director James Loeb; Walter Reuther and James Carey came from the CIO, and David Dubinsky from the ILGWU of the AFL. Other notables included Walter White of the NAACP, economist

John Kenneth Galbraith, Minneapolis Mayor, Hubert Humphrey, and actor Ronald Reagan. Joining Loeb as primary organizers of the meeting were attorney Joseph Rauh and scholar-writer Arthur Schlesinger, Jr. The assembly included a scattering of former New Deal luminaries, but staked its claim to the late president's legacy by the participation of his widow, Eleanor, and son Franklin D. Roosevelt, Jr.[160]

Two issues dividing the gathering were how closely to associate with the Democratic Party and how vigorously to proclaim its anti-Communism. Franklin Roosevelt, Jr. believed that "the surest way to make the Democratic Party a liberal party is to go into the Democratic Party." Leo Lerner cautioned "politics is like poker. If we announce we are going to work within the Democratic Party, they will hold us at arm's length or actually push us out, as has been the experience with some before. The best thing is to hold back." Loeb agreed with Lerner stating that the role of the organization should be to make it "wise for parties to be liberal."[161]

Another debate at the conclave centered on the emphasis the group should place on its anti-Communism. Some members wanted to condemn Fascism in Spain and Latin America as forcefully as they condemned the actions of the Soviet Union. UDA board member Louis Fisher countered, justifying the primary focus of the organization on U. S.-Soviet relations as the central problem facing civilization. In a construction that would gain adherence as the Cold War winter settled in, he stripped away the separation between Communism and Fascism as if they drank from the same stream and "wash[ed] one another's hands."[162]

Some voices at the convention worried that excessive anti-Communism could inhibit other liberals from joining the ADA. Former OPA director Chester Bowles refused to join the organization for over a year because he felt its harsh anti-Communistic tone prevented reconciliation with non-Communists in the PCA. Bowles lamented later that he "thought that the ADA was concentrating too much of its time on opposing Communism and not enough in opposing the Republican Party, which is the major threat in this country."[163]

These and other differences precluded the group from formulating a specific agenda during the two-day conference. Following the advice of Walter Reuther, it issued a statement of general principles to the press at the close of the conference. The six principles enunciated could be summarized succinctly as an extension of the New Deal at home and promotion of democracy abroad. The communiqué stated the group's opposition to both Fascism and Communism, claiming both were "hostile to the principles of freedom and democracy on which the Republic has grown great."[164]

To emphasize that it was undertaking a new initiative, the organization was given a new name. The gathering decided that the old name, UDA, provided neither cash nor cachet, and settled on the title Americans for Democratic Action as encompassing the broadest constituency while being devoid of any negative connotation that a term Liberal, Populist, or Progressive may convey to segments of the public.[165]

The momentum of the Cold War rendered the question of excessive anti-Communism moot. By 1950, few in the progressive community dared defend the rights of Communists to have a voice in the national conversation. The PCA withered away. It lost its labor constituents as anti-Communism spread through the CIO. Phil Murray attended the formative conference of the PCA and was named a vice president of the organization, but quickly divorced himself from any active role in its affairs.[166] He recognized the formation of rival bodies vying to speak for progressives as a threat to the unity of the CIO and to his leadership. In March, 1947, the CIO Executive Board at Murray's initiative passed a resolution recommending CIO officers participate in neither of the two organizations. Murray resigned his post in the PCA and Reuther and Carey suspended their participation in the ADA.[167] After Murray's departure and the decisive defeat suffered by Wallace in the 1948 presidential election, the PCA faded into oblivion.

The ADA survived to define Cold War liberalism, but it never resolved its relationship with the Democratic Party. True to Lerner's contention, The Democrats held the ADA at arm's length. Besides the young Hubert Humphrey, there were few elected representatives and party officials at the Willard during the January inaugural session, and few others joined in later years.[168] More tellingly, the secondary labor leaders in the locals and on the shop floor did not fill out the ranks of the organization. The New Deal intellectuals, labor bosses, and academics at the core had a limited constituency. The party had no reason to "think it was wise to be liberal."

The ADA secured a small place in the suburbs of the Democratic establishment, but it failed to move into the actual suburbs where a burgeoning white middle class was putting distance between the activism of their earlier days and the comforts they had now secured. The growing disconnect between the intellectuals at the liberal core and their natural constituency on the periphery signaled a problem that has yet to be satisfactorily addressed.

In 1952, HUAC came to Detroit. Their targets were the Detroit Civil Rights Congress (CRC) and UAW-Local 600, the large local representing the Ford River Rouge plant.[169] They were fishing for Communists, but by 1952 the streams they were trawling had been over-fished and not restocked. The few active Communists remaining with significant influence that might be netted could not justify the cost of the expedition. The real purpose of the visit was not to catch Communists, but to dampen black activism and extinguish the dying embers of the Popular Front.

The 1952 visit occurred at the height of the red scare. The Korean War was raging abroad and Joe McCarthy was raging about an ever-changing number of Communists in high places at home. Preemptive war had been proposed and was still debated. The bomb that obliterated the city of Hiroshima short years earlier was about to be made obsolete by a weapon three orders of magnitude more powerful. The climate of fear prompted a search for easy answers and convenient villains. The Detroit papers, reliably conservative and pro-industry, were wired and tuned to amplify the charges coming from the hearings, signal and noise alike.

Among the people subpoenaed to appear before the committee were Art McHale, Executive Director of the CRC, the Reverend Charles Hill, Coleman Young, and Stanley Nowak.[170] Twenty-six of the thirty-five leaders summoned were represented by George Crockett, former Fair Practices Director of the UAW, and Ernest Goodman, counsel for Local 600. The committee was now chaired by Congressman John Wood from Georgia and its chief counsel was Frank Tavenner of Virginia. The defense counsels were allowed to advise their clients in confidence, but were not permitted to make any public statements on their behalf.

The proceedings began in the usual fashion with the witnesses being forced to skirt between the Scylla of candor at the expense of colleagues and friends and Charybdis of silence and be dragged into a whirlpool of perceived guilt. It was the defiance of Coleman Young that distracted HUAC from its prepared script. When asked the standard first question, if he were now or ever had been a Communist, Young shot back that he would not answer "since I have no purpose being here as a stool pigeon."[171] That began an exchange between Young, a self-assured black man, and Tavenner, a Southern white, that anticipated the tone of the coming Civil Rights struggle the committee was trying to forestall.[172]

Tavenner:	You were the executive secretary of the National Negro Congress…
Young:	That word is Negro, not Niggra.
Tavenner:	I said "Negro." I think you are mistaken.
Young:	I hope I am. Speak more clearly.
Wood:	I will appreciate it if you will not argue with counsel.
Young:	It isn't my purpose to argue. As a Negro, I resent the slurring of the name of my race.

Coleman Young had grabbed the initiative, and when the Georgian Wood made the same pronunciation mistake, he jumped to the attack.[173]

Young:	I would inform you, also, the word is Negro.
Wood:	I am sorry if I made a different pronouncement of it, it is due to my inability to use the language any better than I do. I am trying to use it properly.
Young:	It may be due to your Southern background.
Wood:	I am not ashamed of my Southern background. For your information, out of the 112 Negro votes cast in the last election in the little village from which I come,

I got all 112 of them. That ought to be a complete answer of that...

Young: I happen to know in Georgia Negro people are prevented from voting by virtue of terror, intimidation, and lynchings. It is my contention you would not be in Congress today if it were not for the legal restrictions on voting on the part of my people.

The committee's Southerners were confronted by a black man speaking to them in a tone they had never heard from such a source before. Every attempt to question the activities of the CRC and the National Negro Labor Council provided Young with an opportunity to point out how these organizations forced Sears to hire black saleswomen in Congressman Jackson's California and fought for voting rights in Tavenner's home state of Virginia.[174] At every chance he pointed out that the committee should be focusing on the real un-American activities being perpetrated on black people throughout the country every day.

When he finished testifying, he had become a hero in the black community. The white papers gave their version of the committee's work, but the black papers told a much different story. Coleman Young spoke the words every black person felt in his or her heart. It was Local 600 and the CRC that had their backs against the forces represented by the members of the committee. A phonograph record of his testimony was produced and became a big seller on the East side of the City.[175] Coleman Young was able to walk the streets of the Black Bottom district of Detroit and be treated like the mayor of the city[176]—a position he would attain twenty years later.

The triumph of Coleman Young was soon followed by the tragedy of Shelton Tappes. Tappes was the first Recording Secretary of Local 600. He had been a leader of the black caucus, a force behind the effort to establish a black seat on the Executive Board, and a former president of the Metropolitan Detroit Negro Labor Council. He was pushed out of his leadership positions when, according to McPhaul, he refused to join the Communist Party.[177] Tappes felt betrayed and made his peace with Reuther, who appointed him to a staff position as an international representative. His appearance before the committee, along with that of former Local 600 vice president Lee Romano, may have been arranged as part of a deal between Reuther and the committee to limit the scope of the investigation to the one local in exchange for his cooperation.[178] Tappes later said that he was in the process of divorcing his first wife at the time and was afraid of losing custody of his children if he did not cooperate with HUAC.[179]

Tappes and Romano named names. The Detroit papers and radio stations sensationalized the news coming out of the hearings. Representative Donald Jackson proclaimed during Romano's testimony that it was time to "take some of these Communists by the seat of the pants and throw them out of the unions," regardless of their rights under the UAW's "bylaws and constitution."[180] Despite Romano's objection that that would "use the same methods they do in Russia," Jackson was unconcerned. He repeated his call that "loyal Americans in the Union should see that it is done."[181] This call unleashed a week of lawlessness in the plants. Jackson's "loyal Americans" took it upon themselves to conduct plant "runouts" of people named in the committee testimony. The UAW Executive Board condemned the vigilante tactics, but none of the leaders came to the plants to forcefully confront the situation.[182] Shop stewards and local committeemen were threatened with violence for trying to enforce the union position.

When the committee left town and the violence abated, eighteen people had been forcibly removed from the plants. People named in the hearings were evicted from public housing, fired from positions in the public schools, and expelled from Wayne University.[183] Still, nobody was charged with a crime. The committee came and went, leaving a stain on the lives of many of those it left behind.

The McClellan Hearings

With Communists ferreted out of UAW and CIO leadership positions and the CIO safely tucked into bed with the staid old AFL, Reuther and his Union now stood on the extreme left side of the American political stage. Republicans looked for any opportunity to push him over the edge. They sensed the televised hearings of the Senate Select Committee on Improper Activities in Labor and Management chaired by Senator

John McClellan of Arkansas provided a unique opportunity to attack their target in a venue where they held a distinct home field advantage.

The Select Committee consisted of four Republicans and four Democrats. Three of the Republicans—Goldwater, Curtis, and Mundt—were extremely hostile to labor in general and Reuther in particular. The Democratic members at the time of the UAW hearings were not known to be particularly friendly to labor either, though John F. Kennedy was planning a run for the White House and was solicitous of Reuther's support. The Committee's lead counsel, Robert Kennedy, was no longer the kid who served as a minority counsel under Joe McCarthy and not yet the man who championed the poor and disenfranchised in his ill-fated presidential campaign.

The UAW proceedings followed on the heels of hearings into corruption in the Teamsters Union. Those sessions uncovered links between organized crime and top officials of the union. Teamster President Dave Beck, a man who looked like he walked off a movie lot to play a shady labor boss, invoked the fifth amendment 65 times when grilled about $300,000 he misappropriated from the union treasury.[184] The viewing audience was treated to weeks of testimony about Beck's financial transgressions and his union rival Jimmy Hoffa's ties with mobster Johnny Dio. Beck was forced to resign the presidency of his union and plead guilty to misuse of Teamster funds, but Hoffa avoided conviction on a witness tampering charge, and his continued sparring with Robert Kennedy kept his own and his union's name in the news for years after the McClellan Committee had finished its investigations. Corruption was so endemic in the Teamsters Union that shortly after its extent was exposed in the hearings it was expelled from the AFL-CIO.

The Republicans now thought the stage had been set to associate Reuther with Beck and Hoffa in the public mind and deliver a knockout blow to organized labor in general. They zeroed in on a long, bitter dispute between the UAW and the Kohler Company.

The Kohler Company, a manufacturer of bathroom and plumbing fixtures, was an old-line industrial firm with a history of violent resistance to efforts at unionization. A 1934 attempt to organize the company ended in a confrontation between stone-throwing pickets and armed company guards that left forty-five strikers wounded and two dead.[185]

The company tried to mollify their workers with a company sponsored union that provided entertainment, and social and sporting events, but kept wages fifty to eighty cents an hour less than their competitors. In 1952 the workers voted to affiliate with the UAW. When the contract came up for renewal in 1954, the union asked for a twenty cent an hour pay increase, a union shop, a dues check off system, an arbitration clause for resolving shop floor disputes, a revised layoff policy, and a longer lunch hour.[186] The company refused every demand. By the time the union struck they had dropped most demands, but the company remained intransigent. It was resolved to rid itself of the union.

At the time of the hearings, the strike was two years old. The small company town of Kohler outside of Sheboygan, Wisconsin was bitterly divided. The company kept the plant open by importing scabs and fostering a division of the workforce into strikers and non-strikers. The strikers lost their jobs and watched their families struggling to put food on the table. Neighbor was set against neighbor. The potential for violence was great.

By the end of the first month, the union realized the strike was lost and dropped all demands except for a face-saving seven cent an hour raise.[187] The company sensed it was winning a complete victory and spurned the offer. The union was backed into a corner. It did not unleash goons on Kohler as the company charged, but it did send in about a dozen organizers who took it upon themselves to counter company pressure with intimidation of their own[188] Early in the strike they held nightly "house parties" where a group of strikers, sometimes accompanied by UAW officials, would gather outside the home of a non-striker to chant insults and yell cat-calls at the people inside. There was no evidence that top UAW officials orchestrated or condoned these tactics, but no evidence they did anything to prevent it.[189]

Two of the organizers were brutish men with short tempers who brought the union into the cross hairs of their Congressional critics. Two hundred forty pound Albert Vincent got into a fight with a non-striker in a Sheboygan bar one evening, and beat his much smaller opponent unmercifully. Vincent went to jail for the assault.[190] On another evening, John Gunaca and two colleagues got into an altercation at a gas station with an older man and his son. The older man was severely beaten. He died eighteen months later of causes unrelated to the beating, but never fully recovered from the assault. Gunaca fled back to Michigan after the attack where Governor G. Mennen Williams refused his extradition to Wisconsin.[191]

Committee Republicans used these incidents as examples of UAW thuggery, and demanded Kennedy investigate Walter Reuther and the UAW with the same vigor that he displayed in going after the Republican inclined Teamsters. Senator Mundt publicly doubted that the Democrats would look into the Kohler strike because of the close association between Walter Reuther and the Kennedys.[192] The Teamsters, eager to shift some of the attention from themselves to their labor foe, abetted the calls for an inquiry into the affairs of the UAW by circulating rumors that the investigation into their affairs was hatched at a secret meeting between Reuther, Adlai Stevenson, and Robert Kennedy aimed at discrediting Reuther's enemies in organized labor.[193] In fact Robert Kennedy never met Reuther until just prior to his testimony a year and a half later, and Reuther supported Estes Kefauver over John Kennedy for the Vice Presidential nomination at the 1956 Democratic Convention. There was no particular affinity between Reuther and the Kennedys at the time.

Responding to the criticism he was receiving, Kennedy dispatched staff investigator Vern Johnson to Sheboygan to learn if there was sufficient evidence to warrant a Senate investigation. An NLRB inquiry had produced thousands of pages of testimony that criticized the union for importing outsiders to reinforce Kohler workers on the picket line, and charged the company with failing to bargain in good faith. It cited the company for numerous unfair labor practices. Johnson reported to Kennedy that he found nothing beyond the NLRB report to warrant another probe.[194]

Kennedy relayed this information to McClellan, but suggested that because of the charges of political cover up that were being raised, the committee should go ahead with its investigation.[195] A recent issue of *Newsweek* had featured an article stating "Counsel Robert Kennedy has ignored continued demands for investigation of Walter Reuther, GOP members say privately."[196] It went on to quote from "reliable sources" that the Kennedys did not want to embarrass their political ally Walter Reuther.

McClellan gathered the Republican members of his committee together to ascertain the source of this leak and determine whether they believed that the counsel was not conducting a proper investigation of the Kohler strike. Senator Ives stated categorically that he was not the source of the leaks and was satisfied with the way the investigation was being handled. His colleagues denied in turn that they were talking to reporters and expressed their satisfaction with the counsel's handling of the investigation. Senator Goldwater proclaimed that "so far as this Republican member is concerned, I'm as happy as a squirrel in a little cage." Not to be out done, Senator Mundt added "I'm as happy as a South Dakota pheasant in a South Dakota cornfield." Senator Curtis didn't admit to a level of satisfaction of a caged squirrel or a hunted pheasant, but joined the happy GOP chorus about the way the investigation was being conducted.[197]

At Goldwater's request, the Committee hired Jack McGovern for its investigative staff.[198] Kennedy put McGovern, a Republican political appointee, in charge of the Kohler investigation and sent him along with Johnson to Sheboygan in July of 1957 to see what they could learn that might warrant further investigation by the Senate Committee. Nothing was heard from the pair until December. McGovern claimed he was keeping Kennedy out of the loop for fear he would pass any information they uncovered to Reuther.[199] Finally, in December McClellan received a report from McGovern and Johnson that selectively plagiarized the NLRB findings, excluding any portion that was unfavorable to the company.[200]

Kennedy informed Goldwater of the basic dishonesty of the McGovern report and expressed his reluctance to become directly involved in the investigation because of the political characterization of his handling of the inquiry.[201] The conservative media was again beating the drum for the Republican attack on Walter Reuther. *The Wall Street Journal* ran a story claiming that McClellan's reluctance to go after Reuther stemmed from his fear that hearings on the UAW could cost Democrats Senate seats in Michigan and Wisconsin in the fall elections that could result in their losing control of the chamber.[202] The editor did not fact check the story sufficiently to realize the only Senate seat contested in those two states in the fall was held by a Republican. After

McGovern told a press conference in Detroit that he had uncovered "sensational developments" in his investigation of the union, radio commentator Fulton Lewis Jr., the Rush Limbaugh of his day, regaled his nightly audience with stories that Kennedy was so upset by the explosive new information on Walter Reuther being unearthed by McGovern that he was doing everything in his power to stop the hearings.[203]

The UAW told the Committee to "put up or shut up." It was tired of being slandered in the media and welcomed an investigation into its affairs. John Kennedy pressed for a start of the UAW-Kohler hearings during the first week of February, 1958. The Republican members appeared flustered and lobbied for more time to pursue other investigations into UAW activities.[204] McGovern and Johnson indicated they were ready to begin hearings into the Kohler dispute by February 1.

The "sensational developments" McGovern ballyhooed to the press turned out to be a missing $100,000 from the union treasury and a large expenditure for knockwurst at a Sheboygan deli that McGovern and Johnson figured must have involved a kickback.[205] The Committee's financial investigator Carmine Bellino was sent to Sheboygan to audit the union and Kohler books. Bellino found the missing $100,000 in a column for expenditures overlooked by the previous pair. The large purchase of knockwurst also had a ready explanation. The striking German and Slavic workers simply loved their knockwurst.[206]

Bellino's examination of the company books revealed that it had made sizable purchases of firearms and ammunition just prior to the strike. The committee learned that the company conducted target practice at the plant just before the strike started using human-like figures as targets. Bellino also discovered large expenditures for spies who not only infiltrated the union, but also probed the NLRB investigator on the scene.[207]

McGovern's key witness turned out to be a petty crook named Francis Drury who was caught burglarizing the offices of a rival union to the UAW. Drury, who had a record of twenty previous arrests and ten convictions for burglary, first admitted that he was after stamps and money in the union office. A few days later he changed his story and claimed he had been sent to the office of the Mechanics Educational Society of America [MESA] by the UAW to burglarize their files.[208] Drury told the investigators that he had worked for the UAW off-and-on for years as a paid goon, and that he had been sent to Kohler by a man named McCluskey to terrorize non-strikers.[209] McCluskey was his immediate contact in the union who paid him for his strong-arm services.

The tip to explore the association between Drury and the UAW came from Jimmy Hoffa in an interview with a Washington reporter.[210] Drury changed his account of the motivation for his crime from petty theft to soldiering for the UAW after firing his original lawyer and meeting with three lawyers close to Hoffa. Three weeks were spent looking for McCluskey. There never was a McCluskey working for the UAW. Johnson held on to the belief that Drury's story was true. He wrote a memo claiming that a man named Brotz had made the arrangements with McCluskey to bring Drury and other goons to Kohler at the outset of the strike in 1954.[211] The problem with this account was that Brotz died in 1951.

With the hearings looming and their case against the UAW disintegrating, McGovern and Johnson made a last desperate attempt to get the "sensational development" the Republican Senators sought and they had promised. At eleven o'clock one evening just before the hearings were scheduled to open, the pair of investigators picked up a high-level UAW official and drove him around town for hours threatening to expose his left-wing leanings if he didn't turn informer on Walter Reuther.[212] The escapade did not elicit any damaging information about the UAW president, but it did threaten to tarnish the reputation of the Senate Committee. Robert Kennedy got the union to reluctantly agree not to bring the matter up at the hearings for the sake of the good name of the Committee.

Reuther prepared for his appearance before the committee in the way he prepared for a tough labor negotiation. Like a good general, he took the initiative and prepared the battlefield before the hostilities began. Jack Conway delivered the complete union records of the Kohler dispute to Kennedy's office with the message "that we were going to be open and aboveboard and direct and that if he was the same way that we'd have no trouble."[213] Reuther requested that Committee financial investigator Carmine Bellino examine his personal accounts to establish a sharp distinction between himself and Dave Beck. The UAW officials sensed that Kennedy was skeptical of their claims about the company's efforts to rid themselves of the union and dubious of their picture of conditions in Kohler and Sheboygan. They encouraged Kennedy to go to Sheboygan and see the situation himself.

Kennedy's January 3rd visit to Kohler made him more sympathetic to the union claims. He met with the Kohler currently heading the family business and the company lawyer, Lyman Conger, who was the man really in charge. Conger was defining the company negotiating strategy, and "[Conger] made no secret of his deep and abiding hate for the union. It was all-consuming hate—a thing unpleasant to see."[214] Kennedy was given a tour of the enamel plant where even in the middle of January the temperature was over 100 degrees. The UAW was trying to win a twenty minute lunch break for these workers who could not leave their posts and had to gulp down bites of lunch in the two to five minutes that they had to remove their masks and gloves and eat while the piece they were preparing was in the oven. Conger said this had been the procedure for the twenty-six years he had been with the firm and saw no reason why the current workers could not do it.[215]

The trip to Sheboygan also gave Kennedy an opportunity to meet with the local UAW leaders running the day-to-day strike support operations. He was not in complete agreement with their methods, but came to a better understanding of the challenges they faced. The UAW officials in Sheboygan showed him another face of Labor. He recounted later that "I was impressed with the difference between these officials of the UAW and the men Jimmy Hoffa and Dave Beck surrounded themselves with in the Teamsters Union. These men wore simple clothes, not silk and hand-painted ties; sported no great globs of jewelry on their fingers or their shirts; there was no smell of the heavy perfume frequently wafted by the men around Hoffa."[216]

Kennedy's trip to Sheboygan was an important step in his own development. Reuther had not yet met Kennedy, but by the conclusion of the hearings he "came to feel more rapport with Robert [than Jack], sensing the younger brother was less detached, more committed, more of an activist." Jack once told Reuther "You fellows are Educating Bobby."[217] Sheboygan started Robert Kennedy on the path to Delano, where he embraced Cesar Chavez and the cause of the disenfranchised farm workers; to Indianapolis, where he calmed revengeful black emotions on the night of Martin Luther King's assassination; and to Los Angeles where an all too short moment of triumph came to a tragic end.

The last vulnerability that Reuther shored up before the hearings was the letter from Gorky, or at least Hoover's version with the words "for a Soviet America" added to the closing "Keep up the fight." Reuther's friend Hubert Humphrey prodded the committee to interview Melvin Bishop and Reuther's associates from his days in the Socialist Party. There was no one able to testify that the original draft contained the disputed phrase. Bishop, who went to work for the Teamsters after his ouster from the UAW, could not produce a copy of the original and gave such contradictory testimony that he had no credibility as a witness. None of the Republican Senators felt comfortable walking into the swamp surrounding the letter during the hearings, and Joseph Rauh was able to get McClellan to sign a letter to Humphrey stating "the established unreliability of Mr. Bishop and the fact that the existence and text of the letter were so questionable, no member of the committee saw fit to ask Mr. Reuther about it."[218]

The Republican Senators realized they had a very weak case and were no longer anxious to have Reuther testify at all. They saw much more advantage in attacking him by innuendo in the press than confronting him directly before a television audience. The four Republicans threatened to walk off the committee if Reuther was called as the first UAW witness as was customary in these proceedings.[219] Two months into the hearings Goldwater announced in a closed committee meeting that he saw no reason to call Walter Reuther to testify at all.[220] McClellan was dumbfounded by the sudden reluctance of Reuther's principal critic to confront his adversary, but he refused to deny Reuther an opportunity to answer the charges floating through the media. Walter Reuther took the stand on March 27th for three days of testimony.

Before Reuther appeared, Carmine Bellino had detailed Reuther's personal finances for the Committee. He was paid a salary of $20,902.14 in 1957 and earned an additional $11,290.96 from speaking and writing that he donated to charity.[221] Bellino described how Reuther meticulously separated out even the smallest personal expenses from those reimbursed by the union. In Reuther's one foray into the stock market he invested

$1000 in Kelvinator stock in 1948 and sold it for $1001.26 in April of 1956, prompting one of the reporters covering the hearings to slip a note up to the witness table reading "Reuther, the fox of Wall Street."[222]

At the start of his testimony, he admitted the union had made a mistake in not giving more affirmative leadership and direction to the organizers it sent to Kohler. He called Vinson's actions "reprehensible and a disservice to the union."[223] He agreed that Gunaca should be extradited to Wisconsin, but after a change of venue to a less inflamed environment. Once he acknowledged the union's errors, he was home free. The discussion turned to labor philosophy, and the Republican Senators were no match for him. Robert Kennedy described him as, "a smart, confidant, articulate witness." Kennedy went on to explain "The reason was he was talking about something he knew far better than any of us—unionism. Once he admitted the union's mistakes, the general philosophical questions asked of him gave him no concerns."[224]

At one point in the hearings he challenged Goldwater on a statement he had made on television where he said "Kohler had a right not to have a union if he could win a strike." Reuther told the Senator, "This is a fundamental question. Only the employees under the law of these United States can make a decision whether they want a union and which union. An employer cannot make that decision without violating the law." He then questioned the Senator on the matter:[225]

> Reuther: I would like to know whether you think under the Taft-Hartley law a Company can decide not to have a union and destroy that union? I maintain they can't.
>
> Goldwater: I will tell you what, someday you and I are going to get together and lock horns.
>
> Reuther: We are together now and I would like to ask you right now—
>
> Goldwater: You save that.
>
> Reuther: I am asking a fundamental question.

Goldwater: Wait a minute, Mr. Reuther. You are not asking the questions. I am asking the questions. If you want to save that someday—

Reuther: I am seeking advice.

Goldwater: You come out to Arizona and enjoy the bright sunshine and clean air and save it for then.

Backed into a corner, Goldwater retreated to the terrain where he felt most secure—behind the lines of a media barrage. At one of the sessions he railed against violence associated with the CIO and made a claim that thirty-seven people had been killed in CIO strikes. The mainstream press trumpeted the Goldwater charge without critical scrutiny. An examination of the claim by Senator Paul Douglas revealed that the thirty-seven people killed had been strikers and none of the deaths had occurred at UAW labor disputes.[226] When Senator Curtis tried to portray the UAW as one of the nation's most violent labor organizations in subsequent questioning, Reuther sprang to the attack.[227]

Reuther: Why did you associate it with the UAW? This is part of the smear campaign. Our union has had less violence than most unions. That is why none of these 37 people who were killed were in our union. This is the attempt—the decision is: Reuther has got to be destroyed because his union is active in politics, and let's find some way. We know Reuther did not steal any money. We know Reuther hasn't got gangsters running his union. We know they kicked out the Communists. Now let's fabricate this theory of violence.[...] The facts are that this union has worked hard to avoid violence. We have done everything in our power to discourage it.

Curtis: All right. (Reuther continued, not allowing the Senator to regain floor.)

Reuther: But that doesn't change the fact that sometimes people being human are carried away by their emotions and they do things that are wrong, and we condemn that.

When you say we are trying to obstruct justice, I am here to tell you are wrong, and you can go on doing it. But you are wrong. And if you think it will get you political votes, go ahead because you are fooling yourself. The people of this country are going to look at you and say: What are you doing about unemployment, what are you doing about farmers, what are you doing about schools? And these are the things that will determine the election issues in 1958 and 1960.

Reuther framed the questioning in its real context—politics. The Republicans needed an issue to draw voters to their platform. Anti-communism no longer held the same partisan appeal. By now it was firmly embedded in a bipartisan national catechism. They needed a new issue, a new villain, and that was to be Walter Reuther. He became the embodiment of the Democratic Party and all the things the right-wing was against. The Republican national campaign committee published a 216-page treatise entitled, "The Labor Bosses—America's Third Party," over half of which was devoted to an attack on the UAW and its president, Walter Reuther.[228] In Indiana, Republican advertisements declared that the election of Democrat Vance Hartke would render the state "legally annexed to Walter Reuther's socialist empire."[229] In California, a GOP election poster entitled "Know Your Opponents" showed a picture of Walter Reuther as the Democratic choice for each of the top ten elected offices in the state.[230]

Like the UAW hearings, the GOP election tactics failed miserably. The Republicans suffered their biggest election defeat since the Roosevelt landslide of 1936. Labor mobilized its base as it hadn't done since FDR's time. The Democrats picked up 42 seats in the House and held a 64-34 majority in the Senate. The right-to-work initiatives that Republicans placed on the ballot in six states all went down to defeat except in agrarian Kansas.[231] If the election of 1958 was a verdict on the UAW hearings in the Senate, it was a vindication for Walter Reuther.

The altered composition of the Congress did little to melt the frozen politics of the fifties. It merely reinforced the consensus politics of the moderate Republicans under Eisenhower and the majority Democrats aligned with Lyndon Johnson. The New Deal would not be dismantled, labor would see no additional infringement upon its rights, but civil rights, health, and social spending legislation would remain bottled up in interminable debate.

The time McGovern and Johnson spent searching for the mythical McCluskey was time they wasted by not delving into the affairs of Toledo area boss Richard Gosser. Gosser had faced an internal investigation in 1951 into conflict of interest charges involving his half interest in a Toledo hardware business and its dealings with the Toledo local he headed. He was acquitted of the charges at the time, but whisperings of his "flower fund" and other questionable practices persisted. When it became evident that Gosser was going to be a target for the next phase of the McClellan Committee probe, the UAW Executive Board gave him a medical leave and placed him on inactive status. Gosser was not an ideological soul mate of Walter Reuther, but he had been an extremely effective organizer in the Toledo area. The Reuther group contained relatively conservative people like Gosser who once were aligned with Martin or were affiliated with the Association of Catholic Trade Unions movement. Reuther was protective of their union positions and they did not interfere with his advocacy of social causes they would not have supported. Before securing Gosser's effective retirement, Reuther defended him before the McClellan Committee. "I happen to know Dick Gosser and I know he has made a great contribution to this union. He has made a great contribution to the city of Toledo. He is a decent, honorable citizen and I know he would not take a dishonest penny from anyone or any source."[232]

Had the investigators done a more thorough job of investigating Gosser that endorsement may have come back to haunt Reuther. As it was, the "Gosser hearings" bled into the start of the quadrennial election cycle. John Kennedy was preparing his presidential run, and Robert Kennedy was anxious to leave his work with the committee and manage his brother's campaign. The hearings raised suspicions about Gosser but no conclusive evidence of his guilt.

When Reuther finished his testimony, Goldwater confided to Robert Kennedy "you were right. We never should have gotten into this matter. This investigation was not one in which we should have become involved."[233] At the end of the Gosser hearings, Kennedy resigned his chief counsel position. When he heard that Goldwater had accused him of running out on the Reuther investigation, he called the Senator and asked if there was more he wanted him to do. Goldwater replied no, he was eager to get back to Arizona. Responding to Kennedy's question of why he told the press what he did, Goldwater gave the rationale for the whole affair "that's politics."[234]

One year later, the Kohler strike ended after the NLRB found the Kohler Company guilty of unfair labor practices and failure to bargain in good faith. Most of the strikers were offered their old jobs back and the company agreed to reimburse them $4.5 million in back pay.[235] All of the issues were not resolved until 1965, more than ten years after the strike began. The Kohler strike cost the union more than $12 million, but the UAW considered it a victory.[236]

Meeting with Mikoyan and Khrushchev

Early in 1959, shortly after the McClellan Committee closed its investigations into Reuther and the UAW, Soviet Deputy Premier Anastas Mikoyan made an official visit to the United States. Mikoyan's schedule was crowded with meetings with bankers, businessmen, politicians, and State Department officials, but he expressed a desire to visit the AFL-CIO headquarters across from the White House and meet with representatives of American labor. George Meany reflexively refused to allow Mikoyan into his building, claiming that he represented a country that stifled free trade unionism.[237] Meany's personal policy of containment was one of strict quarantine, as if Communism were a communicable disease that might be caught by exposure to a Communist leader. He made clear his wishes that other federation officers observe the same policy. Walter Reuther, International Electrical Workers president James Carey, and a few other leaders felt strongly that there was much more to be gained by meeting with high Soviet officials and speaking frankly to them so that they were under no illusion as to where labor stood on important issues of the day. Carey phoned the Soviet embassy and arranged a luncheon meeting with the Deputy Premier in the IEU headquarters building. George Meany was invited to attend, but declined, rebuking Reuther with an attack on "Americans who feel they can meet the Soviet challenge at the conference table."[238]

Mikoyan was a survivor of the intrigues and leadership battles that went on behind the Kremlin walls. He was the Stalin associate who was the principal Soviet negotiator in securing the Ford technology transfer in the early thirties, and he remained the one constant in the party hierarchy from Stalin through Brezhnev. He rose to the position of number two man in the Kremlin by knowing how to navigate the currents and never aspiring openly to be number one. He got along by knowing how to get along. The businessmen and bankers he met during his visit were often people like himself, who rose through the organization by making the right connections and recognizing the right opportunities. They were generally deferential to Mikoyan and muted in their criticism of Soviet behavior.

Reuther, Carey, and the other labor leaders advanced through a different path. They had not ascended to the highest levels of the ruling commercial-political "Capitalist Party," but sat across the table from these people and voiced the demands of the workers frankly and sometimes bluntly. They were no less frank in addressing their Russian visitor. At the luncheon meeting the usually unflappable Mikoyan was drawn into heated debate with his hosts, who would not be deflected from a denunciation of Soviet actions in Hungary and criticism of unrepresentative Soviet labor unions. Reuther issued a statement at the end of the meeting with the high official of the "Worker's Party" expressing the sentiments of the workers of America. It concluded "The Soviet Union has made great industrial progress and the Soviet workers have won more bread, but they have not won more freedom. We in the free world want both bread and freedom."[239]

Meany remained upset that the meeting took place at all, but John Sherman Cooper, now a Republican Senator from Kentucky, called Reuther's forthright discussion with Mikoyan a "major service for peace."[240]

Mikoyan's visit set the stage for Premier Nikita Khrushchev's extended fall tour of the United States. His schedule called for a speech at the United Nations, a meeting with President Eisenhower, a courtesy call on Eleanor Roosevelt, a visit to a large farm in Iowa, and meetings with bankers, businessmen, and politicians at stops around the country.

Reuther wanted to add a meeting with "free labor" to that agenda. Meany remained adamant about not giving any form of recognition to Communist leaders. He rammed through the Executive Council a resolution condemning the anti-union practices of the Soviet Union.[241] The resolution had the intent of embarrassing Reuther for his attempt to arrange a dinner meeting with Khrushchev in San Francisco, but the UAW chief went ahead with his plans.

At precisely eight o'clock in the evening of September 20th the Russian delegation of Premier Khrushchev, Foreign Minister Andrei Gromyko, Ambassador Mikhail Menshikov, and others including the editor of Pravda arrived in the Golden Empire Room of the Mark Hopkins Hotel. The first person to meet the Soviet leader was Victor Reuther who greeted him in Russian. The surprised Khrushchev was told by Victor that he had spent two years in his country. When asked when and where, Victor replied, "in 1933–1934 [..] at the Gorky Automobile Plant named in honor of Molotov." He then impishly asked the Chairman "Tell me [...] is the Gorky plant still named in honor of Molotov?" [Molotov, Malenkov, and Kaganovich had conspired to wrest control of the party apparatus away from Khrushchev in 1957 and had been reassigned to minor duties far from Moscow.] Khrushchev turned white with rage, and blurted out a loud "nyet. Today we call it only the Gorky Auto Works!" The Soviet leader then turned away to meet the other guests.[242] A tone for the remainder of the evening had been set.

Besides Walter and Victor Reuther, the labor representatives consisted of the host, James Carey, President of the International Union of Electrical Workers (IUE); George Weaver of the IUE; Joseph Curran, President of the National Maritime Union; Karl Feller; President of the International Union of Brewery Workers; O. A. Knight, President of the Oil, Chemical, and Atomic Workers International; Paul Phillips, President of the United Paperworkers of America; and Emil Rieve, President Emeritus of the Textile Workers Union of America.[243] After some initial pleasantries, the discussion turned to the part of Khrushchev's speech to the U. N. General Assembly dealing with disarmament. In that speech he said

"In contrast to the 'let us arm' slogan still current in some quarters, we put forward the slogan 'Let us completely disarm!'" "Let us compete in who builds more homes, schools, and hospitals for the people; produces more grain, milk, meat, clothing, and consumer goods; and not who has more hydrogen bombs and rockets. This will be welcomed by all peoples of the world."

He believed the United Nations was the forum through which such a dream was possible.[244]

Carey complimented the Chairman on comments he made at the Lincoln Memorial and for the sentiments he expressed at the U. N., but asked what specific implementation he had in mind to enforce any disarmament agreement. When pressed on what he had difficulty understanding in the speech, he pointed out that each country was spending $40 billion a year on the military and that with disarmament a meaningful portion of that money could be devoted to third world development.[245] The conversation then bounced between verification of arms reduction and cooperation in the delivery of aid.

As was his wont, Reuther talked too long and too often. At times the Soviet contingent was another audience to be won over by the logic of his argument:[246]

Reuther: I think we can all agree that the most pressing problem is how we can preserve the peace. We all understand that the United States and the Soviet Union have produced the kind of weapons that make war inconceivable, that make war now a question of human survival. The question today becomes, what will we do in a practical sense. The only war America wants to fight is war against poverty, hunger, ignorance, and disease. It is the only war mankind can win. The Chairman has said repeatedly that he believes in no interference in the internal affairs of the United States and the kind of government we prefer to live under, and we share that feeling about the kind of government the Russians may prefer to live under. We think the people of Russia have a right to choose their own government and all people should have the same right. Therefore, as we see it, the "cold war" is not an attempt to change each other's systems of government, but to influence those that are uncommitted. Therefore, I want to ask the Chairman, is the Soviet Union prepared to contribute to the ending of the "cold war" by joining the United States and other countries through the United Nations in a cooperative effort to aid the underprivileged nations to abolish poverty and ignorance.

Khrushchev: In our proposal…it is made clear that the outlays on armaments would be greatly reduced and a certain percentage of the reduction switched from the amount saved to the underprivileged nations.

The Russian response gave Reuther an opening to tout his 1950 proposal that was the precursor of the Peace Corps, and he passed a copy he happened to have with him across the table to the Russian delegation. He told his guest "It seems to me that if we wait for disarmament to start we lose great opportunities. Our proposal would create the better climate in which disarmament could be carried forward faster and more effectively.[247]

At other times the Soviet leader was seen as a recalcitrant boss who had to be persuaded in negotiations to abandon an indefensible position.[248]

Reuther: There is no value in this, just going around the barn as we seem to be now. I am familiar with the steel plant in India and other enterprises When you do it, it's part of the "cold war." When we do it, you charge it's capitalist imperialism. Why can't we do it together? Through the U. N.? Do it together for their benefit, not for our separate advantage.

Khrush.: We don't agree.

Reuther: Why not?

Khrush.: America has now surrounded us with military bases, alliances such as NATO and SEATO, and by these means the United States wants to obtain world domination. In the United Nations we are always outvoted. Thus it would be up to the United States to decide how the money would be used.

Reuther: How about a U. N. commission with equal representation? Equal representation of Russia and the United States and U. S. friends and Soviet friends.

Khrush.: That would already be progress, but it won't be accepted.

Reuther: Why not expose the two positions to public air? That's what we do with unreasonable employers.

Khrush.: So long as we are surrounded by U. S. bases, we can have no agreement on this.

Khrushchev was not Charlie Wilson, who shared some common experience and could relate to Reuther's idealistic vision, even if he could not accept it. In a negotiation with GM, Reuther had his own "army" ready to deploy, and he spoke from a position of strength. In this discussion, he had no leverage over missile deployment or U. N. governance. Khrushchev recognized that his hosts had no power to affect such recommendations. He did not rise to the top of the Kremlin hierarchy by chasing after idealistic visions.

As the evening progressed, Reuther's tone became more that of a prosecuting attorney questioning a hostile witness.[249]

Khrush. The United States exploits the wealth of other countries, underdeveloped countries, for profits. England and France do the same. They exploit the wealth of countries that need aid. We do not exploit any country—we only engage in trade.

Reuther: You exploit the workers of East Germany.

Khrush.: Where did you dream that up?

Reuther: If you don't exploit them, why should 3 million of them cross the border into West Germany?

Khrush.: You are feverish.

Reuther: The workers in West Germany are free.

Khrush.: We are free too.

Reuther: Do you have credentials to speak for the workers of the world?

Khrush.: Do you have credentials to poke your nose into East Germany?

Carey: (Intervenes to change the subject.)

By this point in the evening Khrushchev had developed a real animosity toward the pesky Reuther. Reuther's persistent questioning was making some of the other labor leaders uncomfortable as well. James Carey had ordered a generous supply of whiskey and cognac to compliment the dinner, and there were frequent toasts and refilling of glasses. The labor representatives displayed the same fondness for this cultural exchange as their Russian guests, but not the same capacity. Khrushchev noticed that Reuther would observe the toast by raising his glass to his lips, but not sip its contents. "Gospodin Valter" (a term of address like Mister that did not convey the level of respect of comrade) he called across the table "what is this? You are giving only lip service to the toast." Irritated as much by the behavior of his fellow unionists as by the Chairman's contemptuous comment, Reuther responded in a solemn voice "Mr. Chairman, I think you should know that when the revolution comes to America, there will be at least one sober trade unionist."[250]

The combination of Hungary and alcohol proved particularly volatile, and Khrushchev defended Soviet intervention against what he termed "thugs and hooligans." "The government asked us for aid and we gave it, and we're proud of it [...] There would be Fascism there if we had not [intervened]."[251] Khrushchev indicated that they had exhausted the Hungarian question, and the discussion turned to Soviet jamming of Radio Free Europe and Voice of America.[252]

> Reuther: You advocate more trade. How come you oppose a free flow of ideas?
>
> Khrush.: (Still standing after a previous outburst.) As head of the working class I will protect workers from capitalist propaganda.

Khrushchev had visited a Hollywood studio the previous day where they were filming the movie *Can-Can*. He found the dance the chorus line was practicing to be vulgar, and offered his hosts a demonstration. He turned his back to the table, bent downward, flipped his coat up, and gave an imitation of the can-can. "This is a dance in which girls pull up their skirts," he panted. "You're going to see that, we are not. This is what you call freedom—freedom for the girls to show their backsides. To us it is pornography."[253]

The cultural divide was too wide. Reuther was determined to assert his anti-Communist credentials and ensure that Khrushchev hear the resolve of working America. The Chairman was equally determined not to be humiliated by his American hosts and not to have himself or his country treated as an inferior. The exchange of insults that marked the event was demeaning. Meany felt vindicated in his refusal to meet with the Soviets. Reuther drew criticism from admirers like Murray Kempton and antagonists like Jay Lovestone.[254] Lovestone, probably speaking for Meany, said "I think Walter is his own worst enemy [...] This was a mistake, and for Khrushchev, a bonanza [...] I don't think Reuther knew he got screwed until he was eight months pregnant."[255] Khrushchev got his revenge in the pages of the Communist trade union paper *Trud* which printed "reminiscences" of Reuther's time in Gorky from old acquaintances in an obvious attempt to discredit him. John Rushton remembered him as stingy and self-absorbed, and Lucy claimed she was betrayed and abandoned by a husband to whom she was supposedly wed.[256] The clumsy attempt at character assassination gained little credence in the mainstream press that was prepared to believe that Reuther was an agent of the devil, but not a bigamist.

Reuther and Meany represented two approaches toward Russia in the immediate post-McCarthy era. Meany was not prepared to talk or listen to representatives from the Communist World. The Iron Curtain served Meany's purposes as much as it had served the needs of the Kremlin. Reuther was prepared to talk, but not really listen. For years before Khrushchev's visit, the two countries hurled accusations back and forth across a cultural divide, but the leaders of the two powers never met or had any first-hand knowledge of life on the other side of the divide. Common citizens had even less access to one another. It was little wonder that in the first encounter between a Soviet leader and American citizens there were moments when there was neither a common language nor a common vocabulary for meaningful dialog.

Khrushchev was accompanied to America by his family including his adult son Sergei who later moved to the United States and became a Senior Fellow of the Thomas Watson Institute at Brown University. Dr. Sergei Khrushchev remembered the day his father told him he was going along to visit America. "It was not just going abroad; it was going to America, in our imaginations a fantastic country which had gripped our curiosity all through the preceding years. Now I was to see everything with my own eyes."[257]

The invitation to visit America came after a flurry of diplomatic activity, including Mikoyan's earlier visit, surrounding Khrushchev's November 27, 1958 ultimatum that "either the Western powers sign an [East] German peace treaty and agree to turn West Berlin into a demilitarized 'free city' within six months, or the Soviets would turn control of access over to East Germany."[258] The leader admitted to his son that the move was just a gambit to get negotiations rolling on an eventual settlement of the German question. He reassured his concerned son that, "nobody would start a war over Berlin."[259]

The ploy worked. Khrushchev was received as an equal in Washington, and he established a working relationship with President Eisenhower. The trip was hailed in the United States as a tremendous success in breaking the ice that had frozen Cold War relations between the two countries. On his return to Moscow he was greeted with a triumphant reception.[260] Both capitals were eager to normalize relations and move from Cold War rhetoric to productive negotiations. Eisenhower's return visit to the Soviet Union was eagerly awaited.

Unfortunately that visit never occurred. The opportunity to relieve Cold War tensions was shot down with Gary Powers U2 plane. The lack of trust, symbolized by a risky spy plane flight on the eve of an important summit, doomed chances for a normalization of relations between the two world powers. After the U2 incident, the two sides retreated behind their familiar positions. The years immediately following the canceled presidential visit marked one of the darkest periods of the Cold War. The Berlin Wall was erected and became the physical manifestation of the iron curtain separating East from West. A year later the world teetered on the brink of nuclear war during the Cuban Missile Crisis. The Spirit of Camp David was relegated to a footnote in the unfolding saga of the Cold War.

Berlin was the epicenter of Cold War tremors in 1959. Nikita Khrushchev sought to swallow the city inside a reunified, neutral, demilitarized state strongly influenced by a deeply entrenched Communist party. The western half of the divided city was an island plunked in the middle of a red sea. It survived by the perseverance of its people and the resoluteness of the West.

West Berlin in 1959 was the bastion of Willy Brandt, the dynamic young mayor who was positioning his Social Democrats (SDP) to challenge the conservative Christian Democrats (CDU) of Konrad Adenauer under a banner of *Ostpolitik*—extended dialog with the Soviet Union and Germany's East-block neighbors. Brandt was eager to demonstrate Western resolve to confront the Soviet threat to his city and at the same time convey to the German electorate his support within an influential segment of the American labor movement.[261] He invited Walter Reuther to be a principal speaker at a huge May Day rally in front of the Brandenburg Gate.

Brandt had known both Walter and Victor Reuther for years through their involvement with the Independent Trade Union Federation and their many visits to West Berlin. He felt the message Walter Reuther had delivered to Mikoyan during their luncheon meeting needed to be repeated in Berlin to remove any misconceptions the Soviets may have had about Western commitment to a free West Berlin. Victor Reuther had addressed a May Day rally during an earlier period of confrontation and told his brother of the exhilaration he experienced being part of that crowd at that moment of history.[262]

Walter wanted to deliver his speech in German, but, despite being raised in a family where German was a second language and despite the time spent with his German relatives waiting for the Soviet visas, he did not feel comfortable speaking the language at a public gathering. Walter Reuther had a keen eye and a quick mind for assimilating detail, but he did not have an acute ear for language. Perhaps his propensity to speak overwhelmed the receptors provided for listening. It was Victor who accompanied him on his visit to Lucy's family in Gorky to expatiate his limited Russian, and now it was Victor who coached him on the speech he was to give in German.[263]

Reuther told a crowd of 600,000 people in their own language, "We shall stand with you in Berlin no matter how strong and cold the Soviet winds blow from the East."[264] He spoke of his first visit to Berlin after the Reichstag fire, his efforts to halt the dismantling of German industry after the war, and his recent confrontation with Mikoyan. He ended with a familiar staple of the Reuther "speech"

> "The only war in which the American people wish to engage is the war against poverty, hunger, ignorance, and disease. The promise of a world at peace, dedicating its combined resources to the fulfillment of human needs everywhere, will kindle the same hopes and warm response in the hearts of the Russian people as among the people of the free world."[265]

The tone of the speech was one of resolve, not confrontation.

The visit to Berlin served a dual purpose. It delivered a message of Western commitment to the city to the German audience assembled in the square and the Russian audience inside the Kremlin walls, and Reuther's appearance with Brandt provided the mayor with an endorsement of his policy of *Ostpolitik* from an influential American public figure. Chancellor Adenauer had strong backing from George Meany and from the National Association of Manufacturers in his opposition to opening dialog with the Communist governments of the East.[266] Adenauer sought to convey to the German electorate that he alone had the stature in Washington to guarantee the continued flow of American aid. Reuther's presence in Berlin permitted Brandt to claim some influential American support of his own.[267]

The Reuthers were greatly admired in Germany for the support they provided the country during the post-war years and for the values they expressed. Adenauer recognized the debt the country owed to Walter Reuther for his intervention in the dismantling of German steel and chemical plants by awarding him the *Bundesverdienstkreuz*, the highest civilian honor awarded by the state. In making the award, Adenauer too sought to associate the union leader with him in the minds of the German public.[268]

The Peace Corps

The phrase that Reuther included in his speech at the Brandenburg Gate about the only war America was interested in fighting was one he repeated frequently at home. It expressed his own interest more than that of his country. For years he was among the most vocal critics of a strategy to contain the spread of Communism that relied so heavily on shadowy alliances with reactionary elements in the developing world. He stressed at nearly every occasion that the battle to contain Communism was really a battle to combat hunger, disease, and ignorance, but the government was unwilling to devote the resources to this fight that it was allocating to maintain its foreign clients in power.

In the closely contested presidential election campaign of 1960, Walter Reuther's active support in energizing the labor base for Senator Kennedy was crucial for the candidate's success. Given an occasion to flex his political muscle, Reuther's ideas received more consideration. Kennedy was enlisted to fight the war on poverty, hunger, ignorance, and disease.

In 1950, Reuther urged President Truman to fight Communism on a positive basis with a "Total Peace Offensive." The "Reuther Plan" called for the appropriation of $13 billion dollars per year for a period of 100 years, a total amount equal to the cost of World War 2 to the United States, to mount a similar effort to secure the peace. According to the plan, the money would be channeled through the United Nations, but not through the established U. N. bureaucracy. Reuther proposed a special assembly of citizens from participating countries that would be filled like "Noah's Ark" with a two-by-two selection process from the various layers of society—labor, management, agriculture, academia, medical, legal, and professional, including both men and women. Each participating country would send eighteen people to the deliberative body that would evaluate the aid proposals, and allocate the funds.[269]

The proposal highlighted several of Reuther's priorities: citizen involvement in the decision making process, a prominent role for the U. N. in the post-war world, and the importance of alleviating hunger and ignorance in achieving peace and stability. The proposal won applause from supporters like Eleanor Roosevelt,[270] but was largely ignored by the general political and diplomatic establishment. The thirteen billion dollar yearly price tag was about the total amount spent on the Marshall Plan during its four year span.[271] That amount and more could be spent on the implements of war, but there was no constituency for spending that kind of money on social programs in this or any other country. Neither was there any government willing to concede that large a role to an international forum like the U. N.

Reuther modified his original proposal several times. In an address to an NEA group in Cleveland in December, 1956, he outlined a program that anticipated the Peace Corps and VISTA. Reuther proposed a federal aid to education program that would help fund classroom construction, teacher's salaries, and a competitive scholarship program. Recipients of the federal scholarships would be obligated to a period of national service in return. Reuther proposed,

> "that if a young person is willing to sign up in one of these federal scholarship programs, that, after graduation, they would have the choice of enlisting in the teaching professions – or in some other fields where they are needed—for a period of one year longer than, and in lieu of, their military service." He continued, "Perhaps we

could enlist these young people as technical missionaries whom we ought to be sending around the world to fight poverty, hunger, ignorance, and disease, which is the positive aspect of the struggle against tyranny."[272]

Cleveland wasn't the first place he made these suggestions. He told a UAW-CIO Full Employment Conference three years earlier that, "The more young Americans are sent to the places in the world where people are hungry, and sent with slide rules and textbooks and medical kits…the fewer of our sons we will have to send with guns to fight Communism on the battlefields of the world."[273] He also was not alone in proposing some form of voluntary service. His brother Victor proposed training at least one hundred thousand promising young graduates to serve as "a human reserve from which the underdeveloped countries of the world could draw in their efforts to fight poverty, hunger, ignorance, and disease."[274] Hubert Humphrey echoed the Reuthers in calling upon the Eisenhower Administration to establish a corps of "Volunteers for Peace."[275]

After John Kennedy was nominated to run for president in 1960, Reuther was invited to Hyannisport to secure his active support and solicit ideas. He urged the Senator to lay before the public a plan for waging peace to compliment the "missile gap" rhetoric defining his campaign. He suggested the alternative service program he had proposed in Cleveland and elsewhere as an example of a non-military initiative for securing the peace.[276] Kennedy showed interest in the idea, and, after the meeting, Reuther sent him copies of statements he and Victor had made on the subject. The concept of a voluntary army for peace began to slip into the stump speeches,[277] and after the election the Peace Corps became a signature accomplishment of the Kennedy presidency.

The Thaw

The Soviets did not move militarily against West Berlin as Brandt feared. They isolated it behind a barrier. The Berlin Wall became the symbol of the Cold War. It was a penitentiary wall for which the inmates were the people on the outside trying to escape the workers' paradise to which they had been sentenced by war-time judgments. It symbolized the failure of Soviet-style Communism, and it became the backdrop for American presidents and Western leaders visiting Berlin to trumpet Soviet failure and Western superiority.

By the time the Wall was erected, the Cold War was into its second decade. A new generation of leaders was emerging on both sides of the divide. In the democratic West the transition from one generation to the next, from one world view to another, followed a natural progression. The opposition parties were not invested in the policies of the governing party, and election defeats allowed new leadership to emerge. The single party states were far more rigid. They were ruled by a gerontocracy—a clique of old men heavily invested in the past, zealous in maintaining their grip on power. When the third generation raised under Communism finally came to the fore, the system had atrophied and devotion to Marxist orthodoxy was more a Sunday morning obligation than an expression of real faith. The Wall shut in the frustration felt in the East, but it did not keep out the currents drifting across from the West. It was not the Wall around the Western section of Berlin that came to define the future course of Europe, but the economic agreements signed in Rome in 1957 between West Germany, France, Italy, and the Benelux countries.

Early efforts to forge a more comprehensive European Union from the original six-member Economic Community were hampered by the extreme nationalism of French President Charles de Gaulle and the political instability of Italy. De Gaulle blocked the entry of Britain, along with Ireland, Denmark, and Norway, into the EEC, and thwarted efforts to cede areas of national sovereignty to a European parliament. Although de Gaulle envisioned a "Europe, from the Atlantic to the Urals," maturation of the European Union was stunted until his retirement in 1969.

De Gaulle reemerged in French public life during a period of political chaos and incipient revolt and left a stable, functioning democracy as his legacy. In Italy the political system was as dysfunctional as it had been in pre-de Gaulle France. Government tenures were measured in weeks and months, rarely years. The conservative Christian Democrats held the largest number of seats in parliament, but not enough to govern without coalition partners. An alignment of the Socialists and Communists formed a strong opposition that forced the Christian Democrats into alliances with incompatible fringe parties on their left and right. The Communist dominated Italian trade union confederation (CGIL) conducted frequent strikes aimed at keeping the political process in a state of turmoil.

The Socialist leader Pietro Nenni became increasingly unhappy in this marriage of convenience with the Communists. The Reuthers knew Nenni from their time in Europe in 1933, and knew he was looking for an opportunity to break with the Communists and join a center-left coalition with the Christian Democrats. In the Vatican and in Washington Nenni was type cast in the role of Communist "fellow traveler," and these bodies exerted their influence with the Christian Democrats to keep him and his party out of any role in the government.

The elevation of a new, more liberal pope, John XXIII, softened official church opposition to Nenni, and the Reuther brothers worked with Averell Harriman and Arthur Schlesinger Jr. to alter the American position. Robert Kennedy arranged for the Reuthers to make a presentation before the National Security Council to lobby for a change in the nation's policy toward Italy.[278] The CIA with support from some in the foreign service and Meany and Lovestone in the labor movement resisted these efforts,[279] but President Kennedy signaled his willingness to adopt a new American attitude toward the Socialist leader during a 1963 visit to Italy when he singled out Nenni for a long private chat and invited him to visit the United States.

The formation of a center-left coalition in Italy stabilized the political situation in the country and solidified the EEC. The Common Market delivered tangible benefits to the six original participants that dulled the appeal of Communism in the West and whetted the appetite for a European homeland in the East. The "spectre haunting Europe" in the century after Marx was not Communism but free market capitalism with a social democratic hue.

Reuther was part of a social democratic discussion group that met yearly at Harpsund, the country home of Swedish Prime Minister Tage Erlander. The "group of friends" that gathered at the first meeting in 1963 included Reuther, Erlander, British Labor Party leader Harold Wilson, Willy Brandt, Hubert Humphrey, and several European labor leaders. The discussions ranged from Keynesian monetary policy to stimulate the global economy, to plans for strengthening the International Monetary fund, to ways of establishing cooperative efforts between American and European labor unions to prevent multinational corporations from exploiting wage and working condition differences in the various countries in which they operated.[280] The gatherings only occurred three times, but by the end of the decade these European leaders had come to power in their countries and were actively engaged in cementing the framework of the European Economic Community.

In 1970 Willy Brandt became Chancellor in West Germany and initiated the policy of *Neue Ostpolitik* that normalized relations between the government in Bonn and its eastern neighbors. This initiative matured into an era of detente that ushered in a more pragmatic world view. The warming climate between the two sides brought about an expansion of contacts that created small fissures in the rigid orthodoxy of the authoritarian regimes. The fundamental weakness of the underpinning ideology allowed these fissures to grow beyond repair and brought about the sudden collapse of the whole structure of the Soviet Empire.

The Cold War ended much as George Kennan anticipated forty-five years earlier. The strengthening of Western trading blocks and institutions contained the expansion of Communism. Unable to grow and nurture itself on new soil, it withered and died. A few patches of Communism are still tended by the old hands like the Castro brothers, but most of those still calling themselves Communists have long since given up on Communism.

CHAPTER XI

Vietnam

"First we didn't know ourselves. We thought we were
going into another Korean War, but this was a different
country. Secondly, we didn't know our Vietnamese
Allies...And we knew less about North Vietnam. Who
was Ho Chi Minh? Nobody really knew. So until we
know our enemy and know our allies and know ourselves,
we'd better keep out of this kind of dirty business. It's
very dangerous."

General Maxwell Taylor,
Chairman, Joint Chiefs of Staff, 1962–1964
US Ambassador to South Vietnam, 1964–65

All men are created equal. They are endowed by their Creator with
certain unalienable rights, among these are Life, Liberty, and the pursuit
of Happiness (September 2, 1945, Hanoi, Vietnam). Citing these
immortal words from the proclamation of American Independence
nearly two hundred years earlier, Ho Chi Minh began his address
declaring the people of Vietnam independent from nearly a century of
French colonial rule. He continued his speech by listing the abuses that
the French Colonial Government inflicted upon the Vietnamese during
this span, and describing the role that the Vietminh League played in

helping the Allies to evict the Japanese from Vietnam during the just-completed Pacific War. He concluded by expressing a conviction that the Allied nations that acknowledged the principles of self-determination and equality at Tehran and San Francisco would not refuse to acknowledge the Independence of Vietnam.[1]

Thirty-three years earlier, Nguyen Sinh Cung, the son of an actively anti-colonial mandarin father, left Vietnam working as a cabin steward on a steamship bound for Marseilles. His period of self-imposed exile took him to places like New York, London, and Paris where he worked at odd jobs and refined his political philosophy from the cultural influences he experienced in these different locations. Nguyen moved to London at the outset of World War I and worked as a kitchen hand in the Carlton Hotel. During the War years he also worked for a period of time in New York. At the end of the War in 1919, Nguyen moved back to Paris. In Paris there was a large contingent of Vietnamese expatriates and an intellectual affinity for the Socialist agenda. Nguyen wrote nationalistic articles for Socialist publications under the pseudonym Nguyen Ai Quoc – Nguyen the Patriot. At the end of the Great War, Nguyen was the most prominent Vietnamese nationalist to attend the Peace Conference at Versailles. He lobbied unsuccessfully for an audience with President Wilson to press his demands for recognition of Vietnamese rights. This was the first of several occasions when Nguyen affirmed the rights granted in the US Constitution and looked to America to endorse self-determination for Vietnam. Nguyen submitted an eight-point plan that called for elected representation in the French Parliament, freedom of speech, the press, and assembly, and equality under the law with French nationals.[2] He regarded this proposal as a last chance for France to retain Vietnam within a French Confederation.

In 1920 Nguyen grew disillusioned with the tepid support that the French socialists accorded to the cause of Vietnamese Independence, and joined with other radicals within the movement to become one of the founding members of the French Communist Party. In 1924, he moved to Moscow where he received training in organizing a revolution. Two years later he became a liaison with the Russian representative in Canton, China. Nguyen spent most of the next 14 years shuttling between Moscow and various Chinese cities. It was during this time that he adopted the pseudonym by which the rest of the world would come to know him: Ho Chi Minh.

Colonial repression became particularly pronounced during the Great Depression. Vietnamese farmers were squeezed between low prices for their produce and high taxes and rents by the Colonial regime. On September 30, 1930, about 6,000 peasants from the town of Nghe An congregated for a peaceful march on the regional capital of Vinh to protest the high taxes. The protest was met with a French air strike that killed 117 of the marchers. When relatives came to retrieve the bodies of their kin, the French provincial authorities ordered a second strike.[3] The Nghe An massacre ignited the hostilities between the French and Vietnamese Nationalists that persisted off and on for the next twenty-four years.

It wasn't until 1939, at the eve of the outbreak of World War II, that Ho met up with Pham Van Dong and Vo Nguyen Giap in China. Pham Van Dong was arrested shortly after the Nghe An revolt, and spent most of the intervening years in French prisons. Ho was sentenced to death in absentia. He was arrested in Hong Kong in 1931 during a crack-down on revolutionary activity in the colony, but managed to escape extradition with the help of his British lawyer and British officials in Hong Kong, who smuggled him into Shanghai rather than acceding to the French request for his extradition. Giap managed to elude capture and directed guerrilla operations against the French regime, but his wife and infant child were imprisoned and subsequently died in 1940 while in French custody.[4] The gathering of the leadership of the Vietnamese resistance movement offered the opportunity to coordinate political leadership and strategy within a liberation movement they named the Vietminh.

After the French defeat at the hands of the Germans in 1940, the Japanese took control of the northern province of Tonkin but permitted the Vichy French to exercise formal administrative authority within the two southern provinces of Amman and Cochin China. The Vietminh viewed these events as their opportunity to identify with the aspirations of their people. After nearly thirty years away from the country he left in 1912, Ho returned to a cave in the densely-forested, mountains of Cao Bang Province to launch a resistance movement against the Japanese occupation and ultimately against French colonial rule.

During the Japanese occupation, Ho established a working relationship with the OSS, the World War II precursor of the CIA. The Vietminh received radio equipment and some small arms and ammunition from the United States. In return, the Vietminh supplied intelligence to the OSS, coordinated sabotage against Japanese targets, and rescued some downed Allied airmen. The war-time collaboration between the OSS and the Vietminh provided Ho's movement with support for its political agenda within the agency. President Roosevelt too was open to the nationalistic objectives expressed by the Vietminh. Roosevelt detested Charles de Gaulle and, to the chagrin of Winston Churchill, expressed his sympathies for the nationalist ambitions of the people under colonial rule in Asia. He envisioned a trusteeship leading to eventual independence for Vietnam. The Vietminh indicated it would be open to such a program and proposed their country be given a status similar to the Philippines for some undetermined period.[5]

As the war progressed, the Japanese extended their direct control to include the two southern provinces. When news of their impending surrender circulated throughout Vietnam in August of 1945, Giap issued an order for general insurrection throughout the country. The Vietminh guerrillas attacked and cut off the retreating Japanese troops, and, with support from the OSS, took control of the major cities within ten days of the official surrender. The Vietminh liberated their land not from the French, but from its most recent colonial occupier. On August 24th the hereditary emperor, Bao Dai, abdicated and was granted the title of Supreme Advisor to the new government. On September 2nd, Ho issued his Declaration of Independence in Hanoi.

The allied powers redrawing the post-war map did not recognize the principles of self-determination and equality of nations they acknowledged at Tehran and San Francisco as Ho requested in his address. One hundred and fifty thousand Nationalist Chinese troops entered the north of the country to process the surrender of the Japanese. The British, with operational control of the Southeast Asian theater of the war, encouraged the French to reestablish control of their colony below the 16th parallel. The new Truman administration in Washington was not as committed to the self-determination of the former French colony as its predecessor, and, with the deterioration of relations between East and West, they were more concerned about weakness of a left-leaning France in the heart of Europe than a colonial war in a remote corner of Asia. After the communist victory in China and the start of the Korean War, US policy backed the French war effort in Indochina and looked for a nationalist alternative to Ho Chi Minh.

Finding a popular alternative to Ho, proved to be a difficult chore. The Emperor Bao Dai was more temperamentally suited to a leisurely retirement on the Riviera than an active role as a constitutional monarch in Hue. He was only used by the French to put his seal of legitimacy on the non-communist alternatives to the Vietminh. In May, 1948, Bao Dai appointed General Nguyen Van Xuan to lead a new central government. One month later, Bao Dai, Xuan, and French Consul, Emille Bollaert, met on a warship in Ha Long Bay and signed an agreement establishing an independent Vietnam within the confines of the French Union. French citizens were to be protected by the Vietnamese government, and French technicians and advisors were to be given priority in hiring decisions. After the agreement was signed, Bao Dai headed off to the Riviera, leaving Xuan to face the storm of protest generated by the accord. The agreement was denounced as a sham by the Vietminh, but it proved equally unpopular with non-communist nationalists as well. One member of the royal family who had participated in previous negotiations with the French lamented

"The former Imperial family of Vietnam regards with profound sadness the spilling of blood which is taking part in Vietnam because of the refusal of the French authorities to negotiate with the National Government of president Ho Chi Minh. There will be no end to this fratricidal war while the French authorities continue the policy of creating and supporting artificial governments without any roots in the Vietnamese people."[6]

Prodded by the United States, and supported by US aid that reached as much as $500 million a year in 1953,[7] the French continued the war to regain their former colonial holdings in Southeast Asia with a decreasing amount of success. In 1953, the conservative Joseph Laniel, became the latest 4th Republic premier to pass through the revolving door of Ellysee Palace. Hoping to reverse the deteriorating French fortunes, Lanier and his Army Chief, Henri Navarre, determined that their best hope for defeating the Vietminh was to draw them into conventional battles where the superiority of French armaments could be used to advantage. The Navarre plan called for sending an additional 331,000 troops to the conflict over the next three years. The troops were to be drawn mostly from the French colonial empire and funded by the United States.[8]

Navarre needed to draw the Vietnamese into a major battle. The site he chose for the first test was the hamlet of Dien Bien Phu in western Tonkin Province. Navarre expected the Vietnamese would use human wave assaults, similar to the tactics used by the Chinese in Korea. Dien Bien Phu was located in a wide valley surrounded by mountains, and was in a spot that threatened the reserve forces of the Vietminh in the north and their contingents that had invaded Laos. It was also positioned to cut off their lucrative opium trade. Navarre established an airbase at Dien Bien Phu and assigned command of the operation to Colonel Christian DeCastries, an artillery officer for the Free French during World War II. DeCastries selected the location for nine artillery bases around Dien Bien Phu and named them for his three current mistresses, Isabelle, Beatrice, and Gabrielle, and six former lovers.[9] The remoteness of the hamlet and the difficult terrain of the surrounding mountains were assumed by the French to prevent the enemy from deploying artillery to support their attack. Thirteen thousand French paratroopers were dropped into Dien Bien Phu to await the expected battle.[10]

The only problem with the plan was that Giap did not follow Navarre's script. In a feat reminiscent of the transfer of the heavy guns from Ticonderoga through the snow-clogged Berkshires to Dorchester Heights by General Knox during the American Revolution, the Vietminh disassembled artillery pieces and had porters on bicycle and on foot carry them up the mountains. Throughout the winter of 1953–54, Giap used the labor of 100,000 peasants, many women, young boys, and old men, to carry supplies for the 50,000 combat and 50,000 support troops moved to the area.[11] Bad weather and the use of large numbers of peasant repair crews limited the ability of the French air force to disrupt the Vietminh buildup.

As preparations for the battle were being made by the two sides, momentum for an international peace conference was building, and both sides were eager for a decisive victory to strengthen their position at the bargaining table once it began. On March 12, 1954, Giap's forces began the assault and within 48 hours had overrun fire bases Beatrice and Gabrielle.[12] The Vietminh next turned their artillery on the airfield and rendered it incapable of permitting supply planes to land. The French position immediately became precarious. The paratroopers at Dien Bien Phu were surrounded and could only be supplied by drops from the air. On March 20th the Chief of Staff of the French Army, Paul Ely, arrived in Washington to seek American help.

The French wanted continued US logistical support and threats of air strikes should the Chinese enter the fray, but they did not want American combat troops. The French did not yet regard their position with the same degree of pessimism that was felt by their American counterparts. Admiral Radford, Chairman of the Joint Chiefs of Staff, felt the French position was extremely precarious and lobbied for air strikes, possibly using nuclear weapons, against the Vietminh. The Radford plan had the support of Vice President Nixon, but was vociferously opposed by Army Chief of Staff, Matthew Ridgeway.[13] On April 3, Secretary of State, John Foster Dulles, and Admiral Radford met with eight Republican and Democratic Congressional leaders to request Congressional authority to use United States air and sea power in Vietnam if it were necessary in the interest of national security. The Congressional delegation balked at the request. The United States had just concluded a bloody, indecisive war in Korea, and there was little appetite in the country for a new conflict in a land most Americans had never heard of. The Congressional delegation told Dulles that they would support the resolution only if three conditions were met: the United States would be part of a multinational force participating in the operation; the French would promise to accelerate the granting of independence to all of its Associated States; and the French would have to commit to remaining in Vietnam until the war was won.[14] The catch-22 in these conditions was that none of the European allies would commit their forces until the Americans committed first.

British Prime Minister, Winston Churchill, made it clear that Britain had no plans to join a multinational coalition in Vietnam. He told Radford that since Britain had recently given up its far more valuable colony, India, the British people would not stomach using British forces to enable the French to keep control of theirs. Churchill thought that the only way to "save" Vietnam would be to use that "Horrible thing" against it.[15] Without additional help from its allies, the French position at Dien Bien Phu continued to deteriorate.

The Geneva Conference to discuss the future of Vietnam was to begin on May 8, 1954. On May 6–7 the Vietminh forces began their decisive assault on the French stronghold. The defeat at Dien Bien Phu was followed in short order by the fall of the Lanier government in Paris. Lanier was succeeded in office by the Radical Socialist Pierre Mendes France, who promised to resign on July 20th if a cease-fire had not been achieved by that time in Vietnam.

The Geneva Conference was co-chaired by Great Britain and the Soviet Union, and included delegations from France, China, the Vietminh, Cambodia, Laos, and observers from the quasi-autonomous State of Vietnam established by the French. The United States attended only as an interested party. Each of the main participants had their own reasons for bringing the conference to a successful conclusion. The British wanted to play the role of peacemakers, so long as they were not required to supply any of their troops as peacekeepers. An amicable solution to the conflict would enhance the image of the Russians as peacemakers. The Chinese were eager to demonstrate to the world that they were a responsible international player, and they were determined to maintain a French role in Indochina to forestall the possibility of an American presence on their southern border.[16] The French needed a settlement, and the Vietminh expected to be rewarded at the table for their victories on the field. Only the United States came to the conference with no expectations and no desire to be there.

The start of the conference created an awkward moment for John Foster Dulles. Since the United States didn't recognize China, he refused to shake hands with Chinese Premier, Zhou En Lai. Dulles sat uncomfortably through the opening session, uncertain where to focus his glance, and beat a hasty retreat to the airport as soon as the day's proceedings were finished. Dulles's departure left the US conference chairs filled with a more junior delegation. President Eisenhower summarized the predicament of the US to his press secretary, Jim Hagerty, in these words:

> "The trouble, Jim, with this whole situation is that the French will try to get us, if we are physically there with Dulles or Bedell, to approve the terms of the settlement. We don't think it is going to be a good one and it certainly isn't one we can support."[17]

Eventually Ike thought there was more to be gained by having Under Secretary of State Bedell Smith present at the conference than not to have high-level representation there at all. The United States would not sign any agreement reached at the conference, because doing so would be an implicit recognition of the government in China, but it did pledge to respect the agreement that the conference produced.

The United States was not to be the only party dissatisfied by the final accord. The Vietminh won far less territory at the conference table than they did on the battlefield. The Chinese were more interested in establishing their credibility as a responsible international power broker and keeping the United States out of their back yard than in continuing to support the Vietnamese insurrection, and acceded to an agreement that divided the country at the 17th parallel, not the 16th.[18] This division left the imperial capital of Hue and the port of DaNang outside of the territory awarded to the Vietminh. The State of Vietnam was not happy with the agreement either, and refused to sign the accords.

This division of the country was to be temporary with elections providing for its unification promised within 24 months. An immediate cease fire was affected and an International Supervisory Commission, consisting of Canada, Poland, and India, was established to oversee the agreement. The Vietminh harbored a simmering resentment of what they considered a sell-out by their Chinese allies that boiled over into a brief conflict in 1979 after the reunification of the country had been achieved.

Ngo Dinh Diem Becomes "Our Guy"

With the signing of the Geneva accord, the French role in the southern part of the country was diminished and became subordinated to that of the United States, whose immediate objective was to build the State of Vietnam into a viable nationalist alternative to the Vietminh. The search for a credible leader led them to Ngo Dinh Diem. Diem was a true nationalist who had spurned an offer of the premiership by Bao Dai in 1950 because he believed that France had not offered real independence, and he refused to be a figurehead. After rejecting the offer and spurning efforts by Ho to become part of his nationalist coalition, Diem fled Vietnam under threat of a Vietminh death sentence and a lack of commitment by the French for his protection. With little success in promoting his "third force" non-communist-non-colonial path for Vietnam, he settled into the safety of a Catholic seminary in Lakewood, New Jersey. While there, he attracted support from an influential group of "Friends of Vietnam" that included Cardinal Spellman, Senators John F. Kennedy and Mike Mansfield, and Supreme Court Justice William O. Douglas.[19] When the need to find a credible leader for what was to become South Vietnam again arose, Diem was the Americans' man.

The State of Vietnam that Diem was appointed to lead had lacked strong central authority for years, and, in that absence, the province of Cochin China was the fiefdom for several religious and political sects with their own armed militias. The area north and south of Saigon was controlled by the Cao Dai and Hoa Hao sects. The opium, gambling, and prostitution trade, largely centered in the Cholon district of Saigon, was controlled by the Binh Xuyen, a criminal gang with its own militia of thugs and street-toughs. Bao Dai relied on bribes paid by the Binh Xuyen to support his luxurious lifestyle in Cannes. Diem precipitated the first challenge to his authority by including no representatives from these sects in his government.

President Eisenhower appointed one of his most trusted aides, General J. Lawton "Lightning Joe" Collins to assist Diem in providing internal order and economic security for the people of South Vietnam. Collins found Diem to be a true nationalist with great tenacity and personal honesty, but soon soured on his ability to be an effective leader. Besides being a Catholic in a predominantly Buddhist country, Collins found that Diem lacked the personal skills needed for effective leadership. Collins reported to his superiors that

> "Diem has valuable spiritual qualities, is incorruptible, is a devoted Nationalist, has great tenacity. However, these very qualities, linked with his lack of practical political sense, his inability to compromise, his inherent incapacity to get along with other able men, and his tendency to be suspicious of the motives of anyone who disagrees with him, make him incapable of holding the government together....He pays more attention to the advice of his brothers Luyen and Nhu than he does to General Ely or me."[20]

Collins' report caused consternation in Washington. Dulles sent a letter back to Collins stating "we backed him 100% because (a) nobody better appeared on the horizon, and (b) because no one can survive without wholehearted backing."[21] The 100% backing began to waiver, and on April 27, 1955, the State Dept cabled the embassies in Saigon and Paris that it was withdrawing support from Diem and his brothers, and looking to replace them with Phan Huy Quat and Tran Van Do, two officials with wider appeal to the Buddhists. Six hours later they rescinded the original communication. In the interval between the two communiqués, perhaps tipped by CIA operative, Edward Lansdale, that a coup was about to take place, Diem launched an offensive against the Binh Xuyen, and his army appeared to have gained the upper hand.

Collins reluctantly supported his bosses' decisions, but the successful offensive did nothing to change his opinion about Diem. In his final cable from Saigon he wrote

> "I still feel that even if Diem manages to suppress the Binh Xuyen, this will not change his own basic incapacity

to manage the affairs of government. His present success may make it harder for us to persuade Diem to take competent men into government, to decentralize authority to ministers, and to establish sound procedures for the implementation of reform programs. I am still convinced Diem does not have the knack of handling men nor the executive capacity truly to unify the country and establish an effective government. If this should be evident, we should either withdraw from Vietnam because our money will be wasted, or we should take such steps as can legitimately be taken to secure an effective new Premier."[22]

Diem's CIA confidant, Colonel Edward Lansdale, was a pivotal figure influencing American Cold War strategy during the 1950s. He first came to prominence in the Philippines, where he worked effectively with Philippine Defense Minister Ramon Magsaysay to suppress the Hukbalahap insurgency. The Huks were a Communist-led guerrilla movement that was one of several resistance groups that formed to fight the Japanese occupation during World War II. The name Hukbalahap is a contraction of a Tagalog phrase roughly translated as "People's Army Against the Japanese". When the Philippines received their full independence in 1946, the Huks felt they did not get representation in the new government commensurate with their contribution during the war, and retreated to the jungles of central Luzon to conduct a resistance movement. The initial government response to the revolt was to match the terror tactics of the revolutionaries in kind, indiscriminately raiding villages and killing civilians. These heavy-handed tactics only succeeded in creating more support for the Huks within the local population. In 1950, at the urging of the United States, Magsaysay was named Defense Minister, and he undertook a reorganization of the army and developed with Lansdale a new strategy that turned the tide against the rebellion. Magsaysay and Lansdale created several guerrilla-hunting special forces battalions, and used these and other army units to deliver aid and relief supplies to the largely peasant population where the insurgency was located. These measures changed the perception of the Philippine Army in the minds of the locals and made them more inclined to work with the government, especially when the terror tactics of the Huks increased as their situation became more desperate. The pair also employed psychological warfare, propaganda, bribes, and reward payments to undermine the resistance. Magsaysay offered amnesty, re-education, and economic assistance to Huk fighters who abandoned their cause, and instituted land reforms that included clearing portions of the jungles in Mindanao to build settlements for former Huk fighters and other peasants who were encouraged to resettle on the less densely populated island.[23] In 1954, after Magsaysay was elected President of the island chain, the Huk revolt effectively came to an end with the surrender of its leader, Taruc.

Magsaysay became the poster boy for the anti-communist, nationalist leader the United States wanted to see installed in the other post-colonial Southeast Asian countries. His success was saluted by the American press. Even the *Weekly Reader*, a newspaper freely distributed to schoolchildren, trumpeted his success and his virtues in an article titled, "Magsaysay, Rhymes with Our Guy".[24] Unfortunately, shortly after the *Weekly Reader* feature, "Our Guy" was tragically killed in a March 17, 1957 plane crash.

With success against the Huks becoming apparent, Lansdale was moved to Vietnam in 1953, first as an advisor on counterinsurgency to the French, and after 1954, as advisor to President Diem. Lansdale's attempt to replicate the success he had in the Philippines in his new assignment ran into difficulties, not the least being that Diem was no Magsaysay. The two men could not have been more different. Magsaysay was the son of a blacksmith father and a school teacher mother. Diem's father served as a mandarin in the court of Emperor Than Thai during the French colonial period. Magsaysay served as Captain of a guerrilla unit resisting the Japanese occupation. The religious Diem retired to a seminary after refusing an offer to lead a colonial government. Magsaysay was charismatic; Diem, uncomfortable around people. Magsaysay authored several land reform measures. Diem dragged his feet on meaningful land reform. Magsaysay enjoyed popular support that Diem lacked.

The Geneva Accord provided for a brief period of free movement between the two zones. Lansdale exploited the opportunity this period offered by sending agents north to disseminate rumors of an impending Chinese invasion and that the Americans were planning to use nuclear weapons against the North. Catholics, in particular, were encouraged to move south with slogans such as "Christ has gone south" and "The Virgin Mary has departed the north", and with allegations of impending persecution of Catholics by Ho's regime.[25] Up to one million people, mostly Catholics, were cajoled, frightened, or preinclined to board a flotilla of US Navy ships in Haiphong Harbor and head south. Besides the propaganda triumph that "Operation Passage to Freedom" accorded the West, Lansdale realized that the influx of Catholics from the north would strengthen Diem's base of support within the south and increase support in the overall population in advance of the referendum on reunification scheduled for 1956. Agents from the north also used this opportunity to enter the south.

The reunification vote stipulated by the Geneva Agreement was never held, but in October of 1955 a referendum was held to determine the governmental structure of the South. As Prime Minister, Diem served at the pleasure of a constitutional monarch, Bao Dai, who disliked him and frustrated many of his initiatives. The referendum gave voters a choice between a restoration of the monarchy and a republic headed by a president. Diem's brother, Ngo Dinh Nhu, supervised the election, denying Bao Dai the right to campaign, and intimidating his supporters in the precincts. When the votes were "counted," Diem had won with a resounding 98.2 % of the vote. In the City of Saigon alone Diem received 605,025 votes from the 450,000 registered voters. Similar super majorities were reported in provincial cities.[26] Lansdale, suggested a 60 % win would be sufficiently convincing and more believable, but this advice was ignored.

With Bao Dai dispatched back to the Riviera, Diem set about consolidating his rule by relying primarily on members of his family. His brother Ngo Dinh Nhu was leader of the Can Lao political party whose militia served as the Ngo family's secret police. Nhu, an alleged opium addict, was an admirer of Adolf Hitler and not averse to using Nazi-like tactics in dealing with dissenters.[27] Another brother, Ngo Dinh Can, was put in charge of the imperial city of Hue. Can was widely believed to be heavily involved in the black market trade, selling rice to the North and distributing opium throughout Southeast Asia. Diem's older brother, Ngo Dinh Thuc, was the archbishop of Hue, but lived mainly in the Presidential Palace in Saigon with Diem, Nhu, and Nhu's wife. It was the beautiful Madame Nhu, not the shy, reclusive Diem, that became the public face of the regime. She became identified in the press as the Dragon Lady after the seductive, but sinister, Asian woman in Terry and the Pirates comic strip.

After successfully dismantling the private militia of the sects, Diem and Nhu went after people they suspected of being communists. Nhu's secret police killed an estimated 20,000 to 50,000 people and jailed over 75,000 others in a campaign that not only targeted communist insurgents, but also suspected northern sympathizers, anti-government dissidents, and anti-corruption whistle blowers.[28] The harsh tactics alienated important segments of the population and spawned a low-grade insurrection, but they did take a toll on the communist cadres operating in the south. These units petitioned the northern politburo for help, and in January, 1959, it responded with a secret decision to support armed struggle in the south. On December 20, 1960, the National Front for the Liberation of South Vietnam was established. In an effort to portray the NLF as a nationalist movement, non-communist opponents of the Diem regime were included in the group's leadership, but policy decisions were dictated by the communist majority. The date of the coming out party for the NLF marked the formal beginning of a civil war that would soon involve the United States in what was to become at the time the longest, most-divisive foreign conflict in the country's history.

Diem further weakened his position in South Vietnam by antagonizing the majority Buddhist population with policies that favored his Catholic co-religionists. Military promotions went to Catholics. US aid was distributed primarily to the Catholic villages, and weapons for village defense militias were only given to Catholics. To secure aid or avoid mass resettlement, some villages converted to Catholicism en masse.[29] In some areas forced conversions and looting and demolition of pagodas occurred. Buddhist resentment boiled over in Archbishop Thuc's home city of Hue in 1963 when a display of religious flags during celebrations commemorating the anniversary of the birth of the Buddha was forbidden by the government although religious flags were prominently displayed during a Christian festival a few weeks earlier. A protest led by Thich Tri Quang provoked a violent response from the government in which nine protesters were killed. Diem rejected Buddhist demands for religious equality and justice for the victims of the massacre, prompting a June 3rd march in which tear gas and attack dogs were turned on the demonstrators.[30] Later that month Thich Quang Duc became the first of several Buddhist monks to sit down at a busy intersection in Saigon, douse himself with gasoline, and light himself on fire before a stunned crowd of onlookers and a horrified, world-wide television audience.

The government reacted by further intensifying its repression of the Buddhists. Madame Nhu referred to the self-immolations as "monk barbecues," and her husband vowed to supply the gasoline if the Buddhists wanted another barbecue. With the discomfiting images on the evening news disturbing the dinner hour of the American television viewer, support for Diem within the Kennedy administration was exhausted. On November 1, 1963, with the acquiescence of the United States government, a coup in Saigon replaced Diem with the first in what was to become a sequence of military leaders. Diem and his brother Nhu were both killed.

As flawed a leader as Diem was, he was respected inside the country as a true nationalist. None of his successors shared this mantle. They were all regarded as little more than American puppets. Ho Chi Minh was reported to have remarked upon learning of the coup "I cannot believe the Americans would be so stupid."[31] The politburo was more prophetic in their reaction to the news when it stated in its communiqué

> "Among the anti-communists in South Vietnam or exiled in other countries, no one has sufficient political assets and abilities to cause others to obey. Therefore the lackey administration cannot be stabilized. The coup d'etat on 1 November, 1963 will not be the last."[32]

America's War

When the coup occurred there were 16,000 American special forces advisers supporting the South Vietnamese Army (ARVN). As the situation deteriorated in the south these advisers became more-and-more actively engaged in the fighting. At the time of the coup, President Kennedy was reportedly rethinking his commitment to an inept South Vietnamese government that was unwilling or unable to make the reforms necessary for winning popular support, and had begun a limited recall of some of the advisers. How Kennedy's policy toward Vietnam may have evolved will never be known. Three weeks after the brothers Diem and Nhu were murdered in the back of an armored personnel carrier in Saigon, Kennedy was assassinated in Dallas.

Kennedy's successor, Lyndon Johnson, ascended to the presidency with an ambitious social agenda that the war threatened to derail, but he was also a believer in the doctrine of containment of communist expansion and accepted the validity of the domino theory – that a communist victory in Vietnam would precipitate the fall of neighboring non-communist governments. During the election year of 1964, he sent additional troops to support the government of South Vietnam, while campaigning on the promise that he wouldn't "supply American boys to do the job that Asian boys should do [for themselves]."[33]

On the nights of August 2nd and 4th in 1964 incidents occurred in the Gulf of Tonkin, off the coast of North Vietnam, that escalated the US involvement in the war. Since 1961, covert operations code named "Operation Plan 34-Alpha" were conducted by South Vietnamese naval personnel against coastal targets in the north. The specific targets and approval for each mission was given by Admiral U. S. Grant Sharp, the CINPAC commander in Honolulu. On August 1st, an Operation Plan 34-Alpha attempt to land an infiltration team into the north was launched, but resulted in the immediate capture of the agents. On the next night a CIA-sponsored fighter-bomber attack, using Laotian planes piloted by Thai mercenaries, was directed against border outposts in the north. During these activities the destroyer USS Maddox was conducting electronic eavesdropping activities in the gulf as part of a separate, but not totally unrelated, operation code named DESOTO. On August 2nd the Maddox was approached by three North Vietnamese torpedo boats while patrolling in international waters. It is not clear from the testimony whether the Maddox first fired a warning shot at the approaching boats, but one of the boats fired a torpedo that the Maddox maneuvered to avoid, and then returned fire at the attackers. Planes from the aircraft carrier Ticonderoga were called in and one of the retreating torpedo boats was sunk and another heavily damaged. The Maddox suffered only minor damage from a single machine gun bullet and no casualties. It retreated to South Vietnamese waters where it was joined by a second destroyer, the USS Turner Joy.

On August 4, the Maddox and Turner Joy were ordered back into international waters off the coast of North Vietnam on another DESOTO mission and to show the flag in response to the earlier attack. Freak weather conditions may have contributed to misleading radar signals that caused the Maddox to think it was about to be attacked. The crewmen maneuvered the ship and fired their artillery at the radar ghosts that floated over the empty sea. Initial reports of an encounter were soon tempered by the captain of the Maddox who radioed

> "Review of action makes many reported contacts and torpedoes fired appear doubtful. Freak weather effects on radar and overeager sonar men may have accounted for many reports. No actual visual sightings by Maddox. Suggest complete evaluation before further action taken."[34]

No complete evaluation occurred before the incident was used by President Johnson to request from Congress the authority to conduct military operations in Vietnam without a formal declaration of war. Only Wayne Morse spoke forcefully against the resolution and questioned the official account of the episode. On August 7th, the US Congress voted to give the president the authority to "conduct military operations in Southeast Asia without the benefit of a declaration of war." Only Morse and Alaska Senator Ernest Gruening voted in opposition.

Johnson used his authority initially to only order a retaliatory bombing raid against the North. He was in the midst of an election campaign where he was trying to convince the voters of his intention to avoid a wider war. The mainstream media rallied behind the president's request by exaggerating some of the details in the administration's account of the incident and attesting to the fact that there was no debate or confusion within the administration about the incident. The vote on the Gulf of Tonkin Resolution placed a final exclamation mark upon the post-World War II foreign policy consensus.

After the election in 1964, the situation in Vietnam continued to deteriorate, and Johnson was forced to use the authority granted him by the Gulf of Tonkin resolution to steadily increase the combat role of American troops. Johnson presided over a nation that had been nurtured on almost two decades of anti-communist fervor and had a strong belief in its national virtue and national strength. It entered the war to the accompaniment of Barry Saddler's paean to the Green Berets and the spectacle of John Wayne leading these special forces to their inevitable triumph.

For the first two years of his full term, Johnson tried to keep the events in Vietnam on the back burner while he passed historic social legislation like Medicare, Medicaid, and other Great Society measures, but the war would not go away. The optimistic assessments of Cabinet Secretaries and battlefield commanders were shattered on January 31, 1968, when the Viet Cong and North Vietnamese regulars conducted a massive Tet offensive that captured the imperial city of Hue, threatened many of the provincial capitals, and attacked strategic and symbolic targets within Saigon. The offensive failed to spark a general uprising within the south or encourage mass defections of ARVN troops as its proponents in the northern politburo had hoped, but the images of American soldiers battling to dislodge Viet Cong troops that had breached the walls of the US embassy compound in Saigon and pictures of the Viet Cong flag flying over the citadel in Hue undermined support for the administration's handling of the war. The country was divided between the doves who wanted to get out of Vietnam and the hawks who wanted to carry the fight directly to the North. The events surrounding Tet robbed Johnson of support from both groups and made the gulf between them all the wider. On March 31 in a televised address to the nation, Johnson announced that he would not seek reelection.

Tet and Johnson's withdrawal from the presidential race were only the first of the traumatic events that shook the nation in 1968. In May, Martin Luther King was assassinated and riots in cities across the country ensued. The flames of Washington burning were visible only blocks away from the Capitol. In August, moments after Robert Kennedy had celebrated his victory in the California primary in a hotel ballroom filled with his supporters, he was gunned down as he was making his way back to his room after delivering a victory speech. The Democratic Convention that followed degenerated into an angry exchange of words and a few punches inside the hall, and a riot between Chicago police and demonstrators outside. Richard Nixon, with a secret plan to end the war, was the beneficiary of the chaos inside the Democratic Party and inside the country as a whole. He became the 37th President of the United States, and inherited a divisive war and a deeply divided country.

Nixon's War

Nixon had always been a polarizing figure, and he made little effort to lower the fever burning in the nation. He appealed to his "silent majority," while his Vice President, Spiro Agnew, derided the "nattering nabobs of negativism." The secret plan remained secret while the American and Vietnamese death toll continued to mount. One dirty little secret kept hidden was that Nixon used Anna Chenault, widow of the Flying Tiger commander during World War II, as an intermediary urging South Vietnamese President Nguyen Van Thieu to stonewall negotiations during the last months of the Johnson administration and hold out for a better deal that he would get from Nixon.[35] The American presence in South Vietnam would drag on for another four years.

In June of 1968, the commander of US forces in Vietnam, General William Westmoreland, was promoted to Army Chief of Staff and replaced in the field by General Creighton Abrams. Abrams commanded a tank battalion in Patton's 3rd Army during World War II, and had distinguished himself in the rugged fighting to drive the Germans from their entrenched positions in the Lorraine. Now he was being called upon to wage a more defensive campaign against guerrilla units while he prepared the ARVN for the eventual withdrawal of American forces. The

Abrams-Nixon strategy was labeled Vietnamization and the key to its success rested in the ability to stem the flow of men and supplies entering the country through Cambodia.

With a stalemate looming in Vietnam, the focus of the war turned increasingly toward Cambodia. The 1954 Geneva Agreement called for a neutral Cambodia and required the local Communists to integrate into Prince Sihanouk's political structure. The Indochinese Communist movement was primarily a Vietnamese movement. Cambodian Communists operated under Vietnamese direction and, after 1954, most moved north with the Vietminh. As the years passed they became more-and-more removed from the affairs of Cambodia and more-and-more irrelevant. The Cambodian Communists that remained in the country retreated to the remote jungles where they had carried on guerrilla operations against the Japanese. These fighters felt they had been sold out in Geneva by the Vietminh and operated outside of their control. Until 1970, their numbers were small and their resistance, little more than a nuisance.

The mercurial Sihanouk tried to navigate the currents that were swirling around the region by aligning with neither the left nor the right. When free elections in 1966 returned a right-wing parliament with Lon Nol as Prime Minister, Sihanouk formed a counter government of the left that included Khieu Samphan.[36] The next year, a peasant revolt broke out in Battambang Province. The revolt was likely a spontaneous uprising, but Sihanouk blamed Chinese agents and ordered Lon Nol to liquidate the rioters. Lon Nol willingly complied by burning villages and having peasants clubbed to death.[37] Many villagers fled to the resistance along with Khieu Samphan and other leftists in the counter government. The Battambang revolt marked the beginning of a three year period of civil war. The brutality of the Khmer Rouge has been well publicized, but horrific acts of brutality were standard features in Cambodia throughout the Sihanouk and Lon Nol years as well. Khmer Rouge prisoners often had their stomachs slit and were then hung in trees to die slowly.[38] Both sides intimidated peasant villages by killing the elders and beating villagers to death.

In March of 1969, Abrams was able to convince Nixon to initiate a secret bombing campaign against the enemy sanctuaries in eastern

Cambodia.[39] The bombing, code named Operation Menu, dropped over 100,000 tons of explosives during the 14 months that it was in operation. By the fall of 1969 Abrams and the Joint Chiefs realized that the Menu bombing had failed to disrupt the Viet Cong supply lines and destroy the Central Office for South Vietnam (COSVN) command headquarters believed to be located in eastern Cambodia. The bombing had only succeeded in driving the Viet Cong and North Vietnamese forces deeper into Cambodia, putting more pressure on the Sihanouk government.

In August of 1969, Sihanouk appointed a far right government with Lon Nol serving as Prime Minister. At the end of the year he departed for Paris to receive medical treatment, leaving his cousin, Prince Sirik Matak as acting head of state. Sirik Matak's family had been by-passed by the French when Sihanouk was crowned king in 1941, and he harbored resentment against Sihanouk that only deepened because of the Prince's initiatives to collectivize the economy. In January, government sponsored demonstrations against the Vietnamese also encouraged anti-Sihanouk students and businessmen to voice their displeasure at his policies. Pressed by Sirik Matak, On March 18, 1970 the Cambodian National Assembly deposed Sihanouk and named Lon Nol as the Provisional Head of State.

In February of 1970, Abrams lobbied Defense Secretary Melvin Laird to authorize an invasion of Cambodia.[40] Laird refused, but did authorize clandestine raids by South Vietnamese troops. After Sihanouk's ouster, events moved rapidly. On April 14th Lon Nol requested military aid and assistance from the United States. On the same day, ARVN forces began their clandestine cross-border raids. On April 23rd Secretary of State Rogers testified before the House Appropriations Subcommittee that "the administration has no intentions [...] to escalate the war. We recognize that if we escalate and get involved in Cambodia with our ground troops that our whole program [of Vietnamization] is defeated."[41] One day previous, Nixon had authorized a South Vietnamese incursion into the "Parrot's Beak" region of Cambodia as a confidence builder for the ARVN and a demonstration of the success of Vietnamization. Plans to add an American operation in Cambodia were supported by Kissinger, but strongly opposed by Secretaries Rogers and Laird and by several of Kissinger's staff members.[42] On April 20th, Nixon had gone on national TV to announce a planned withdrawal of 150,000 troops from Vietnam by the end of the year. On April 25th, he gathered with Kissinger and his friend Bebe Rebozo to watch his favorite movie, *Patton*, for the 6th time. On the next day, he approved hastily drawn up battle plans for a joint American and South Vietnamese incursion into Cambodia. The invasion of Cambodia began on May first.[43]

The reaction at home was just as Rogers and Laird had predicted. Demonstrations erupted on college campuses across the country. As violence escalated ROTC buildings on 30 campuses were burned or firebombed. National Guard units were mobilized in 16 states and assigned to 21 campuses.[44] On May 4, a confrontation between protesters and guardsmen on the campus of Kent State in Ohio led to the shooting death of four students. Late on the night of May 14th, police opened fire on students demonstrating at the historically black college of Jackson State in Mississippi, killing two people and wounding 12 others. Student strikes shut down many campuses all over the country. Hastily organized demonstrations drew 100,000 people to Washington and 150,000 to San Francisco on May 8th. In another demonstration in New York on that date, pro-Nixon construction workers violently attacked the student marchers. On May 20th about 100,000 construction workers and other labor union members staged their own pro-Nixon rally in New York. The nation was divided by generations, by race, by educational level, and by region over the war, with a majority still supporting the president. The turbulent response of the American people to the Cambodian invasion caused President Nixon to limit the time and scope of the incursion to two months and an advance of no more than thirty kilometers inside the country.

The Cambodian invasion proved little more than an interruption in the Communist's supply chain for its forces in the south. COSVN headquarters were never found, and were probably never at a single centralized location to begin with. The North Vietnamese had prior knowledge that an invasion was being planned and relocated many of their units north and west of the Parrot's Beak and Fishhook areas of Cambodia where the joint American and South Vietnamese operation occurred. The only parties surprised by the incursion, besides the American public, were the Lon Nol government and the American Embassy in Phnom Penh, who found out about it from news reports on the radio.[45] The invasion pushed the Communist forces deeper into Cambodia, and the constraints placed on the operation by Nixon left Lon Nol's army over matched against a growing Khmer Rouge insurgency backed by more closely aligned Vietnamese units.

The events in the spring of 1970, brought the war that had been intruding on Cambodia's border areas into the heart of the country. The proximity between the coup that ousted Sihanouk in March and the American and South Vietnamese invasion that began on the first of May begs the question of American complicity in the coup. There is no evidence that Nixon or National Security Advisor, Henry Kissinger, sanctioned any direct US role in the ouster of the Prince, but neither did the administration signal its support for his government.[46] In the absence of any clear directive from Washington, agents in the region were not constrained from taking their own initiatives. General Abrams was lobbying for an invasion of Cambodia and was not too upset that the Menu bombing campaign was destabilizing Sihanouk's left-right balancing act.

CIA involvement in Cambodia at the time was later revealed by two former agents, Frank Snepp and Drew Swain, Snepp was a strategic analyst in the Saigon office in 1970 from where many of the CIA operations in Cambodia were organized and directed. Snepp has since asserted that the Agency believed in 1970 that if Sihanouk were replaced by Lon Nol, he would welcome the US with open arms, and that all the American objectives in Indochina would be accomplished.[47] Swain, the son of missionaries, had lived in Indochina since 1947 and had worked for the CIA in the Central Highlands of Vietnam since 1960. He has claimed to have met with Sihanouk in Paris in early 1970, and that the Prince asked him to arrange a meeting with someone from CIA headquarters. Swain claimed to have reported his conversation with Sihanouk to his superior, Gilbert Layton, but was told that the Agency had decided against closer involvement with the Prince, and was instructed to inform Sihanouk he should instead speak to the US ambassador in Paris. The Prince was furious at this slight, and refused the offer.[48]

As events in Pnomh Phen unfolded in the spring of 1970, Snepp claimed that the CIA exacerbated the crisis with a disinformation campaign and that the Agency had persuaded the Queen Mother to reassure the

Prince that things in the country were not so desperate as to necessitate his immediate return. Snepp asserted that throughout the spring the CIA was in close contact with Lon Nol, Sirik Matak and their associates.[49] One of the CIA links to the anti-communist element in Cambodia was through Son Ngoc Thanh and his Khmer Serei forces. The Khmer Serei, or "Free Khmer," was an anti-monarchist, anti-communist militia that had been conducting clandestine operations against the Sihanouk regime from sanctuaries in neighboring Vietnam and Thailand since independence in 1954. In late 1969, a group of Khmer Serei fighters "defected" and were incorporated into the Cambodian Army. Sihanouk later regarded this defection as a ruse that created a Trojan Horse inside his defense forces.[50] After the coup, Son Ngoc Thanh became a minister in the Lon Nol government. Snepp asserted that the CIA was using the defectors to assure Lon Nol that he had US support for his hard line against the communists.[51] General William Roston, Abrams' deputy, has confirmed that US commanders were informed a few days beforehand that a coup was being planned and their support was solicited.[52]

Regardless the actual role of the United States in facilitating the coup, leaders in the military and the administration were not displeased that it had occurred. General Abrams was quoted later in the *New York Times* as saying "the ouster of Sihanouk and the change in Phnom Penh really did an awful lot to assist the orderly withdrawal [of American troops from Vietnam]."[53] Elliot Richardson told Congressmen privately that it was only Sihanouk's overthrow that allowed the invasion to be considered.[54] Less than two months later, an invasion was authorized, and American ground forces were fighting inside Cambodia.

Withdrawal and Genocide

At the time of the coup, Khmer Rouge guerrillas were estimated to number no more than 4000 men. Vietnamese sources have since claimed the number was substantially less.[55] It was only after the coup, that they became a significant concern for the government in Phnom Penh. After his overthrow, Sihanouk was urged by Beijing to form a government in exile based in the Chinese capital. On March 23, 1970, he recorded a broadcast to the people of Cambodia announcing his new National

Unity Front of Kampuchea government in exile and urging resistance against the Lon Nol regime. His appeal was immediately welcomed by Khieu Samphan and Hou Yuon broadcasting from Hanoi. Lon Nol and Sirik Matak had used widespread discontent of urban businessmen and intellectuals against the Prince's autocratic rule to oust him, but Sihanouk remained popular in the countryside. Immediately after the Prince's broadcast, rioting erupted throughout the countryside and in Kompong Cham, the country's second largest city. Rioters in Kompong Cham burned down the house of the new governor, and were stopped from marching on Phnom Penh by a military roadblock at which the marchers were fired upon and 90 people killed. The rioters then took their revenge on Lon Nil, one of Lon Nol's brothers who was murdered by the crowd and had his liver cut out, cooked, cut up, and eaten by some of the vengeful demonstrators.[56]

Lon Nol tried to compensate for his lack of support among the peasantry, by turning their vengeance on the Vietnamese community in Cambodia. After the 1954 Geneva accord partitioned Vietnam and established neutralist governments in Cambodia and Laos, about 400,000 Vietnamese living in Cambodia decided to remain. Many were merchants and were well-established in the local economy. Lon Nol decided to stir up ethnic hostility by claiming that all the Vietnamese living in Cambodia were actively or passively supporting the Viet Cong. To reinforce the propaganda campaign, the government put on a pageant showing the beautiful Khmer people killing the evil, knavish Vietnamese.[57] With such official encouragement, Khmer villagers took it upon themselves to murder their Vietnamese neighbors. In the village of Chrui Changwar about 800 Vietnamese men were taken from their homes, marched to the Mekong River, put on boats, murdered, and left to drift down the river where their bloated bodies were snagged in the nets of local fishermen. The same scene was repeated for several days.[58] When rumors of a massacre prompted journalists to visit the village of Takeo, they found a schoolyard filled with dead and dying bodies supervised by a handful of young Cambodians, insensitive to the suffering of those who were not yet dead.[59] Faced with protests from foreign diplomats and the press, Lon Nol toned down his anti-Vietnamese propaganda campaign, but part of the rationale for the ARVN incursion into Cambodia was to repatriate some of their unfortunate countrymen.

The atrocities that occurred under the Sihanouk and Lon Nol regimes were just a foretaste of the genocide committed by the Khmer Rouge once they came to power, but they underscored the warning issued by French archaeologist, Bernard-Phillipe Groslier, some years earlier when he observed "beneath a carefree surface [of the Khmer people] there slumber savage forces and disconcerting cruelties which may blaze up in outbreaks of passionate brutality."[60] The extension of the neighboring war into Cambodia unleashed such an outbreak.

The deep animosity that Cambodians harbored for their Vietnamese neighbors was not understood by the senior American war planners and not factored into their narrative of the dynamics of the forces shaping Cambodia. When Kenneth Quinn, a young vice counsel stationed in the provincial Vietnamese city of Chau Doc near the Cambodian border, noticed villages burning over the border and refugees streaming into Vietnam, he composed a long fifty-page, single-spaced report about the results of his investigations.[61] He circulated his findings widely within the State Department and to relevant embassies. The report described the brutal attempt by the Khmer Rouge to eliminate all vestiges of previous institutions and completely remake Khmer society along the revolutionary ideals they espoused. Quinn stressed to his readers that the Khmer Rouge were not allied with the Vietnamese Communists, but strongly opposed to them and committed to driving them out of their country.[62]

When Quinn's long "airmail" reached its intended audience, the senior diplomats paid little attention to his warnings but took great umbrage over a junior diplomat overstepping his station and presuming to question basic tenets at the core of American foreign policy. Quinn was admonished and silenced; his report was filed away; and the war planners from Nixon and Kissinger on down persisted in seeing the world as described in Cold War orthodoxy.

As Quinn reported, the people of the two countries had little regard for each other and their leaders had little in common. Whereas the leaders of the Vietminh were the product of post-World War I and depression era radicalism, the leaders of the Khmer Rouge honed their political philosophy in the French universities of the 1950's. Saloth Sar, later known to the world as the infamous Pol Pot, was an engineering student in Paris that spent more of his time forwarding the cause of revolution than analyzing the current flow in a circuit diagram. He failed his exams three times and returned home to mark time in his revolutionary career as a history and geography teacher and journalist as he began his rise in the Communist Party hierarchy.[63]

Khieu Samphan was remembered by associates during his university years in Paris as a serious and studious young man who devoted all of his time and energy to study and politics. He had no time for socializing.[64] Khieu Samphan studied political science at the University of Paris, and his 1959 thesis, "Cambodia's Economy and Industrial Development," served as a blueprint for the forced depopulation of the cities that characterized Khmer Rouge rule. Khieu argued that even though the majority of Cambodian peasants owned parcels of land and their own animals, this independence was illusory because they lacked the capital to exploit their ownings. To prosper peasants needed capital that could only be borrowed from money lenders at exorbitant interest. To make matters worse, large landowners and city dwellers were spending more-and-more of their income on imported goods. Luxury goods accounted for 49% of the imports, but were purchased by fewer than 10% of the population. Cambodian industry could only be developed after agriculture was properly developed, and only when more of the wealth remained in the country would the multiplier effect benefit the economy at large.[65]

The generational gap between the two countries' leadership groups, and the feelings of a betrayal at Geneva created a difficult relationship between the Khmer Rouge and their Vietnamese counterparts. Only after the coup and subsequent American and South Vietnamese incursion into Cambodia did the Khmer guerrillas receive active North Vietnamese assistance and cooperation. Initially, the provisional government established by Sihanouk in Beijing had the strong support of the Chinese, particularly of Zhou EnLai. Conversations between Zhou and Sihanouk, and between Zhou and French Ambassador Etienne Manac'h convinced both men that Zhou wanted to see Sihanouk return to lead a neutralist Cambodia.[66] When this information was relayed to Washington, it was met with skepticism. Henry Kissinger had only contempt for Sihanouk and regarded him as "yesterday's man."[67] This missed opportunity for a compromise solution may have been the last chance to save Cambodia from the fate that waited. Reluctantly, the Chinese transferred their support from the Prince to the Khmer Rouge.

By 1973, rebel strength had increased to over 50,000 fighters who were more than a match for Lon Nol's army.[68] When the Paris Peace accords were signed, the North Vietnamese were able to enforce a cease fire in Laos, but Le Duc Tho informed Kissinger that his government had little control over the Khmer Rouge and could not make the same commitment for Cambodia.[69] As a condition for getting South Vietnamese President Nguyen Van Thieu's agreement to the accord, the anti-communist Lon Nol regime was not to be replaced by a neutral compromise government. With the American withdrawal from Vietnam, Lon Nol was left to fend for himself. After a brief pause in the hostilities in the wake of the Paris agreement, the Khmer Rouge renewed their offensive. The US responded with B-52 bombing raids over Cambodia, but the maps that were in use were dated and did not reflect the mass population displacement occurring inside the country. Targets suggested by the Cambodian high command paid little regard to the risks to civilians in the area.[70] The bombing did little to turn the tide of battle, but much to garner the ill will of the people in the countryside. The end came in April, 1975 after Lon Nol was incapacitated by a stroke, and his government reduced to a few urban islands in a vast sea of red.

Two weeks later, on April 30, 1975, Saigon fell to the North Vietnamese. Communist led or dominated governments were in control of all of the former French colonies in Indochina. The end of hostilities did not signal a return to tranquility for the people of Cambodia. The Khmer Rouge government liquidated the educated and the middle class and emptied the cities of everyone else. Perhaps two million people died in the Cambodian killing fields during their reign of terror. After the United States washed its hands of its debacle in Indochina, Cambodia became a pawn in the power struggle between its Communist friends and neighbors. As the Sino-Soviet split became more antagonistic, other Communist States were forced to choose sides. On November 3, 1978, Vietnam signed a 25-year mutual defense pact with the Soviet Union.

Vietnam became a key component of the Soviet drive to contain China. In the meantime, hostilities between Vietnam and Cambodia broke out almost as soon as both Communist movements achieved their national objective. The Khmer Rouge claimed the Mekong delta as their own and launched a number of bloody raids into Vietnam to emphasize their determination to exercise their claim. Finally, in 1979, the Vietnamese reacted to the provocations by invading Cambodia and dislodging the Khmer Rouge from the urban centers. The Khmer Rouge retreaded to their old guerrilla haunts in the jungles, but declined in strength and influence as they faded into oblivion.

The Chinese reacted to the invasion of their Cambodian client state by massing up to 200,000 troops on the border with Vietnam and launching an invasion to "spank" their recalcitrant former ally. The Chinese drive on Hanoi stalled when it encountered stiff local resistance after bloody house-to-house fighting in the capture of the towns of Cao Bang and Lang Son. The Chinese were content to claim that the door to Hanoi was now open and that a lesson had been taught. The invasion revealed that the Cultural Revolution had weakened Chinese industry and produced military equipment of inferior quality. The Chinese were hampered by poor communications, logistics, and transportation. The invasion revealed weaknesses in the Chinese military and did not succeed in causing the Vietnamese to withdraw their forces from Cambodia. The Chinese retreat marked the final act in the forty year drama that focused the world's attention on the former French Colonies in Indochina.

The carnage that the American war in Vietnam wrought on both countries was staggering. Over three million American servicemen and women served in Vietnam during course of the conflict. Of these, 58,198 were killed and over 150,000 wounded of whom more than 20,000 were permanently disabled.[71] The North Vietnamese claimed that their forces suffered 1.1 million killed and over 600,000 wounded. The United States estimated the ARVN death toll at between 200,000 to 250,000. The death toll for civilians in the two sections of the partitioned country ranged to as high as two million.[72] There are no precise figures for the casualties suffered by the people in Cambodia and Laos, but the Cambodian genocide that followed the Khmer Rouge victory is believed to have claimed between 1.5 and 2 million lives.

The end of the war did not bring an end to the casualties. Over 830,000 American military men and women suffered from some degree of post traumatic stress disorder.[73] The lingering effects of exposure to dioxin laced defoliants have inflicted disease and death on veterans on both sides of the conflict, and genetic mutations on children and grandchildren of some of the exposed. Over six million gallons of toxic herbicides were sprayed over 13 percent of the South Vietnamese countryside. In some areas of the south in Vietnam today, dioxin levels are still 100 times higher than internationally accepted safe standards. Defoliants were not only used to strip away the jungle canopy from enemy combatants, but 43 % of the total used in the war was directed at food crops in an effort force the peasants away from Viet Cong controlled areas and into government controlled strategic hamlets. Vietnam claimed in 2006 that four million of its citizens are victims of dioxin poisoning.[74]

The cost to the United States in its treasury, its cohesion, and in lost opportunity was also enormous. Over the ten-year period from 1965 to 1975 the United States spent the equivalent of 738 billion in FY2011 dollars.[75] The military was plagued by a growing problem of dissension, drug use, and desertion as the war dragged on. About 50,000 servicemen deserted during the course of the conflict, and another 125,000 young Americans fled to Canada to escape the draft.[76] Differences over the conduct of the Vietnam War have colored American politics for the last forty years. The fracturing of the electorate over the issue of Vietnam effectively brought to an end the period of liberal ascendancy in American politics.

The analysis and recriminations about what went wrong in Vietnam have concentrated on the way the war was fought and whether the goals were too modest or too optimistic. Most of the analysis assumes that since the war was not won, it ended with an undesirable outcome. Given the sacrifice of life, limb, and treasure that was devoted to the war effort, anything short of victory can be viewed as dishonoring that sacrifice. But if we can manage to dispassionately examine the reasons that we entered the war, and the outcome that the war produced after the fighting ended, a different picture emerges.

American foreign policy since the Truman administration rested on the belief in the need to contain Communism. If the Communist movement was not monolithic, it was at the least believed in Washington to be tightly controlled by the Kremlin. The need to contain Communist expansion in Vietnam was given particular import by the popularization of the Domino Theory: that if the one shaky domino of Vietnam should fall, the other countries in the region would be toppled one-by-one like a chain of dominoes. Senator John F. Kennedy gave voice to this concern in a June 1956 speech to the Friends of Vietnam when he stated "Burma, Thailand, India, Japan, and the Philippines and obviously Laos and Cambodia are among those whose security would be threatened if the Red Tide of Communism overflowed into Vietnam."[77]

When Kennedy became President in 1961, he faced several international crises following a meeting in Vienna with Soviet Premier Khrushchev that went badly. Khrushchev immediately challenged Kennedy by erecting a wall around the Soviet sector of Berlin. The fait accompli of the Berlin Wall following closely after the Bay of Pigs fiasco and a negotiated settlement in Laos that brought the Pathet Lao into coalition with the pro-Western government of that country damaged Kennedy's reputation as a leader, and he perceived that another failure to contain the spread of Communism would damage the reputation of the United States in the eyes of the world as well as his own reputation at home. Vietnam became important not so much for itself, but as an example of American resolve to "pay any price, bear any burden, meet any hardship, support any friend, oppose any foe, in order to insure the success and survival of liberty."[78] The case of Vietnam as an exemplary war was reiterated by Secretary of State Dean Rusk in his March 13, 1968 testimony before the Senate Foreign Relations Committee when Senators began to challenge the precepts that took the country into a war that was looking more problematic after the Tet offensive.

America marched off to war under the belief that Communist aggression in Southeast Asia was being instigated and directed from Moscow; containing Communism in Vietnam was essential to keep the dominoes from tipping throughout the region; and the war would provide an example of American resolve and commitment to friend and foe alike. The egos of three different Presidents also figured into decisions to escalate the war.

None of these assumptions proved true after the Communist victory in Vietnam. Laos came under Pathet Lao control, and the Cambodian domino was toppled by the clumsy boot of its American protector as much as it was by the Red Tide washing across its border, but none of the other countries mentioned by Kennedy fell to Communism. Burma lapsed into a military dictatorship of its own origin, but the others plus Malaysia, Singapore, and Indonesia have developed thriving economies.

The perception of a unified Communist block taking marching orders from the Kremlin was shattered by the open Sino-Soviet split and the Communist neighbors of Vietnam, Cambodia, and China doing battle with one another. Rusk's assertion that persisting in the war effort was essential for demonstrating American resolve to friend and foe alike was seriously flawed. The Soviets were only too happy to see their adversary bogged down in an endless war that was draining its treasury and sowing discord among its citizens. They had much more to gain in prolonging the conflict than adding the burden of another dependent client state on their own overstretched economy. Defeat in Vietnam did little to alter the balance of power between the two sides in the Cold War.

And what if the outcome had been different and the war ended with Vietnam remaining divided at the 17th parallel? Would this have been a preferable outcome? Probably not! All of America's other 20th century wars, except World War I, ended with American bases and a residual American military force remaining in the host or occupied country. American troops still patrol below the demilitarized zone in Korea, and American bases in Okinawa are a source of contention with the local population more than a half century after the end of World War II. American forces remained in Kuwait and Saudi Arabia after Desert Storm, fueling the anger of Osama bin Laden, and even though the United States has no diplomatic relations with the Communist government of Cuba, it retains a naval base at Guantanamo Bay more than a century after the Spanish American War. Events of 1975 revealed that South Vietnam would require an American military presence indefinitely if it were to survive.

An American victory would have resulted in a costly, long-term commitment to South Vietnam to achieve regional goals that resulted anyway without the same expenditure. In the long run, the region would probably be less stable with a divided Vietnam than it is today with a united country. A divided Korea, sixty years after the armistice was signed, remains a global flash point. Ho Chi Minh was known to his people as "Uncle Ho," not as a "Dear Leader" seeking to impose a dynastic rule, but in a divided Vietnam, revolutionary struggle would likely trump economic reform and introduce a measure of instability into the region. The American rapprochement with China may also have taken a different course had Vietnam remained an issue of contention between them.

If in retrospect the United States can live with the situation that has existed in Vietnam for the past forty years, could that result not have been achieved without the disastrous war that preceded it? Had successive administrations viewed the situation in Vietnam as it was instead of how they wanted to see it or how it was perceived through the window of a few speculative theories, the conflict may have been shortened or avoided. Maxwell Taylor was a principal architect of the strategy employed in that war, so his advice comes only with the wisdom of hindsight. *"So until we know our enemy and know our allies and know ourselves, we'd better keep out of this kind of dirty business. It's very dangerous."*[79]

CHAPTER XII

Aftermath

Turning and turning in the widening gyre
The falcon cannot hear the falconer;
Things fall apart; the centre cannot hold;
Mere anarchy is loosed upon the world,
The blood-dimmed tide is loosed, and everywhere
The ceremony of innocence is drowned;
The best lack all conviction, while the worst
Are full of passionate intensity.
The Second Coming

William Butler Yeats

As the turmoil of the depression years of the 1930's had once ushered in the New Deal and a thirty-year span of liberal gains, the turbulent 1960's buffeted the eroding coalition that FDR had pieced together to create the Democratic electoral base. Just after the progressive movement reached a postwar zenith with Johnson's landslide defeat of Barry Goldwater in the 1964 election, and the passage of landmark civil rights and Great Society legislation in 1965, a perfect storm began brewing off the South China Sea and in the neglected inner cities of the North and on the nation's campuses. When the separate pressure gradients coalesced and the full ferocity of the storm struck later in the decade, the Great Society was marooned off the coast of distant possibilities, the political landscape was drastically rearranged, and familiar voices were silenced or stilled.

The New Left

The decade began promisingly with a charismatic young President inspiring a generation of young people to "ask what [they] could do for [their] country." A freedom struggle, playing out nightly to a sympathetic television audience, provided an answer. The pictures of Bull Connor's police dogs and fire hoses turned on peaceful demonstrators in Birmingham, Alabama, and news of the murder of three civil rights workers in Philadelphia, Mississippi caused profound shame and revulsion in the country. The new medium gave a glimpse into the ugly face of racism that for so long was hidden behind a bed sheet or lurking on an unlit road in rural Mississippi. Jim Crow separatism in the South could no longer be tolerated. A vanguard of young people were inspired by Kennedy to service in the nameless villages of the third world or compelled by the TV images to confront injustice at home.

During the 60's, the Baby Boomers came of age and headed off to college in record numbers. In 1950 just over 2.28 million students were enrolled in the nation's colleges. By 1964 that figure had climbed to 5.28 million and by the end of the decade it had increased further to 8 million.[1] The college population was swelled with middle class kids, many the first in their family to attend college, who had experienced only the security of the post-war bounty. The urgency of the social issues troubling America transcended worries about the future for many of these students. The prospect of a good job and continued prosperity after graduation was taken for granted. The only obstacle threatening this future was the war. African Americans were also being admitted to college in greater numbers. Many of these kids did not share in the post-war prosperity and did not regard their future assured. The lesson they learned from the civil rights struggle was that opportunity only arose by fighting for it.

The colleges and universities were places where young people were gathered in number away from parental and community influence. The students did not share the same adolescent experience as their parents.

They appropriated a pop culture of which many parents did not approve, and were not constrained by the mores professed by the older generation. The colleges were home to a distributed community that found much in common with one another and less in common with the ideals and aspirations of their parents.

Walter Reuther and the UAW executive board saw the civil rights demonstrators and student activists as the heirs of the progressive labor movement of the thirties. The black youth who risked life and limb to sit down at all-white lunch counters in the South were reminiscent of the sit down strikers of the early CIO days that braved company goons and local authorities to win union recognition in the automobile plants. In a few short years the movement had galvanized public opinion behind civil rights legislation that had lain dormant for decades. Reuther was impressed by the vitality of the movement and recognized an opportunity to advance the social agenda he had championed for the preceding two decades. He moved aggressively to amplify the voice of the UAW in the councils of both the civil rights and campus reform movements.

The UAW had long-standing ties with the older civil rights organizations such as the NAACP and the Urban League that Reuther used to mobilize a "Coalition of Conscience."[2] He lobbied tirelessly to convince the coalition that fundamental economic change was essential for black empowerment and racial harmony and must be part of a larger agenda if true integration were to be achieved.[3]

The UAW also worked to establish a liaison with the New Left movement germinating on college campuses. The campuses were beginning to awake from a troubled sleep haunted by the specter of Joe McCarthy. A new generation who did not experience the trauma of seeing reputations ruined, colleagues blacklisted and hounded out of the academy, and strong voices become circumspect was arising to color the muted frequencies of the political spectrum. The University of Michigan, home to a number of highly politicized children of people in the UAW hierarchy and their friends and sympathizers, was in the forefront of campus ferment. The union had long supported a moribund socialist organization called Student League for Industrial Democracy (SLID) that Alan Haber, the son of an economics professor and UAW confidant, now directed. Haber changed the name of the organization to Students for a Democratic Society (SDS) and sought to revitalize it into a vehicle for channeling campus activism into a coherent force for fundamental reform. Haber's organization attracted many of the offspring of UAW leaders on campus. Sharon Jeffrey, the daughter of UAW staffer Mildred Jeffrey, worked through her mother to introduce Haber to Victor Reuther and helped him secure organizational and financial backing from the union.[4] Victor Reuther was impressed with Haber and the program he outlined, and wrote to Irving Bluestone that, "This kind of program would contribute to the strengthening of the democratic political activities in this country. It could also become a valuable source of leadership in the decades ahead."[5]

With the younger union members becoming more securely middle class and more-and-more disassociated from the activities of their union, the UAW leadership was eager to find a new generation of socially-aware activists to whom they may pass the torch. By the 1960's the universities, with their burgeoning population of students and their expanded research role in a more technologically complex society, had replaced the shop floor as the locus of growth and change in the American economy. The UAW was eager to cement its relationship with similarly-minded campus groups and became a primary backer of SDS.[6]

The union offered its summer camp at Port Huron, Michigan for the pivotal SDS conference in 1962, after which the group published its statement of purpose. The Port Huron Statement began with a catalog of ills with American society and inconsistencies between American precepts and practice. It listed racial injustice and Cold War militarism with its threat of annihilation the principal disquieting issues stirring them from comfortable middle class complacency into a critical assessment of American culture and policy.[7] The foreign and domestic policy changes it recommended were essentially the same as those advocated by the UAW, although the labor movement was not immune from its criticism and Reuther was regarded by many of the delegates as being as much a part of the establishment that needed to be changed as Meany and Kennedy.[8]

The Port Huron Statement ended with recognition of the university as the central institution in the economic framework and as the institution that was accessible to grass roots reform. The academy became the battleground for much of the organization's later initiatives.

The closing paragraphs of the Port Huron Statement outlined the venue in which the organization would concentrate its effort most profitably.[9]

"First, the university is located in a permanent position of social influence. Its educational function makes it indispensable and automatically makes it a crucial institution in the formation of social attitudes. Second, in an unbelievably complicated world, it is the central institution for organizing, evaluating, and transmitting knowledge. Third, the extent to which academic resources presently is used to buttress immoral social practice is revealed first, by the extent to which defense contracts make the universities engineers of the arms race. Too, the use of modern social science as a manipulative tool reveals itself in the 'human relations' consultants to the modern corporation, who introduce trivial sops to give laborers feelings of 'participation' or 'belonging,' while actually deluding them in order to further exploit their labor. And, of course, the use of motivational research is already infamous as a manipulative aspect of American politics. But these social uses of the universities' resources also demonstrate the unchangeable reliance by men of power on the men and storehouses of knowledge: this makes the university functionally tied to society in new ways, revealing new potentialities, new levers for change. Fourth, the university is the only mainstream institution that is open to participation by individuals of nearly any viewpoint."

"These, at least, are facts, no matter how dull the teaching, how paternalistic the rules, how irrelevant the research that goes on. Social relevance, the accessibility to knowledge, and internal openness—these together make the university a potential base and agency in a movement of social change."

Buttressed by a new wave of activism and a "Coalition of Conscience" that drew its strength from diverse elements within the society, the UAW was poised to exercise its political muscle on a reluctant Kennedy Administration to break decisively with the Dixiecrats and pass strong Civil Rights legislation along with meaningful economic reform. Then on November 22, 1963, President John F. Kennedy was murdered in Dallas. The shock of Kennedy's murder to the UAW leadership was compounded by the realization that Lyndon Johnson, the architect of consensus politics in the fifties, was now President of the United States.

A Rumble of Distant Thunder

Johnson was a strong believer in the Cold War policy of containment and a New Deal populist who as Senate Majority Leader strived to keep controversial issues like Civil Rights off the Senate agenda in order to preserve the Democratic electoral base, maintain the bipartisan foreign policy agenda, and avert any efforts to roll back New Deal entitlements. He was unsympathetic to the UAW legislative agenda in the Senate, and his selection as Kennedy's Vice President was strenuously opposed by the union leadership. Johnson, however, was an astute politician with an impeccable sense of timing. He realized his legitimacy as President would be undermined if he alienated the liberal wing of the party and that the tide for a Civil Rights Bill was at its crest. The day after the assassination, Johnson phoned Reuther and asked for his help in the trying days to come. "My friend, I need your friendship and support now more than ever," Reuther recalled Johnson telling him, and the phone call ended with Johnson asking Reuther to send him a list of his national priorities.[10]

Johnson was a complex man and consummate politician, but the role into which he was thrust may have provided him an opportunity to pursue the ideals that led him to public service in the first place. Whatever the motivation, Johnson affirmed in his first televised national address on November 27 that he was fully committed to passage of the strong Civil Rights Bill that the union and Civil Rights groups supported. In his State of the Union Address the following January he championed many of the ideas that Reuther had sent him in giving a broad outline of his

Great Society programs. Johnson became the one politician willing to revisit the unfinished agenda of the New Deal.

With Johnson's leadership, the Civil Rights Act of 1964, banning discrimination in employment and public accommodations, passed with over 80% of Republicans in both Houses joining Northern Democrats to support the measure.[11] One Republican who did not vote for the bill was Barry Goldwater, the Party's 1964 Presidential candidate.

In 1952, in one of the first party conventions to be televised, the contest between the Eastern business interests and Midwestern conservatives for control of the Republican Party was highlighted by Taft supporter, Everett Dirksen, standing at the podium pointing down at Thomas Dewey and chiding "You have taken this party down to defeat twice before. Don't take us down the path to defeat again." In the final voting, however, Dewey's candidate, General Dwight D. Eisenhower, out polled the conservative Taft, and the Party Moderates maintained control of the Republican agenda for the next twelve years. In 1964, with the Party out of control of the White House, the Conservatives were poised to wrest control of the Convention once again. After a spirited struggle in one of the last political conventions that was not a staged infomercial, the party nominated Goldwater. Two nights later, Goldwater reinforced the country's fears about his candidacy with his proclamation that "Extremism in the defense of liberty is no vice, and [...] moderation in the pursuit of justice is no virtue." The nation that had anxiously endured the Cuban Missile Crisis and been traumatized by the assassination of its President, overwhelmingly opted for the reassuring figure who had led them through its difficult hour. The Johnson landslide not only buried Goldwater, but swept aside many Republicans in the House and Senate as well. The stage was set for a liberal resurgence with the aspirational theme of building a Great Society.

Nevertheless, A few clouds appeared in the otherwise sunny post-election skies. Goldwater carried only six states: his own state of Arizona, and the deep-South states of Louisiana, Mississippi, Alabama, Georgia, and South Carolina. He thus became the first Republican since Reconstruction to break the Democratic stranglehold on the solid-South. The 1964 election presaged a change in the political calculus for elections to come, and began the realignment of the political parties on purely ideological grounds. The UAW leadership was not unhappy to see the Dixiecrats beginning to leave the Democratic fold. They reasoned that a more coherent Democratic Party would be a more effective vehicle for sponsoring and passing a progressive agenda.[12] They also felt that with enactment of a Voting Rights Bill, the Thurmonds and Eastlands that symbolized the old South would be replaced by a less conservative generation of new leaders.

Another speck on the horizon appeared in the final weeks of an otherwise lackluster Goldwater campaign. On October 27th, only a week from Election Day, Ronald Reagan delivered to a nationally televised audience a transcribed version of a stump speech he had been giving for Goldwater. The speech raised 8 million dollars for the candidate, but was too-little-too-late to revive his sagging fortunes. The *A Time for Choosing* speech as it has become known did, however, launch the political career of Reagan, and helped carry him to the State House in California and ultimately to the White House. The speech is still a pilgrimage site for conservatively-minded Internet tourists visiting the public shrines and historical artifacts of cyberspace.

The final cloud that would not blow over was the war in Vietnam. Armed with the Gulf of Tonkin Resolution, Johnson contented himself with a brief retaliatory bombing strike on coastal military installations in North Vietnam in response to the 1964 incident involving two US warships. The hope that the North would be intimidated in the face of American military might and that ARVN resistance would stiffen with increased American aid proved illusory. Ultimately, when Johnson was forced to choose between guns and butter, he hedged and chose a little bit of both. That choice displeased both ends of the political spectrum.

In 1965 the nation was experiencing an economic boom, fueled to a large extent by the tax cut passed three months after President Kennedy's assassination, and the Asian war was still playing "off Broadway." The election returned a President with a populist past and the most liberal Congress in the nation's history. If a war was to be waged, it was a "War on Poverty" that the nation mobilized to fight

The Great Society

The Johnson landslide left the Democrats with a 68 -32 majority in the Senate and a 295–140 margin in the House. Having more than a two-thirds majority in both chambers of Congress permitted Democratic Congressional leaders to revise rules that in the past had diverted legislation to committees chaired by Dixiecrats, whose long seniority resulting from uncontested elections enhanced their control over the legislative process. The Johnson administration sent 87 bills to the Eighty-ninth Congress which passed 84 of them.[13]

Johnson launched his Great Society Program during a Commencement Address at the University of Michigan on May 22, 1964. In it he proclaimed "I intend to establish working groups to prepare a series of conferences and meetings—on the cities, on natural beauty, on the quality of education, and on other emerging challenges. From these studies, we will begin to set our course toward the Great Society."[14] Johnson's speech writer, Richard Goodwin, borrowed the term "Great Society" from Adam Smith, who wrote that

> "government has only three legitimate functions: protecting society from foreign invasion, establishing a system of justice and protecting citizens from harm or oppression from one another, and "the duty of erecting and maintaining certain public works and certain public institutions, which it can never be the interest of any individual, or any small number of individuals, to erect and maintain; because the profit would never pay the expense to any individual or small number of individuals, *though it may frequently do much more to repay it to a great society*."

Though Smith clearly meant great to signify large, Johnson used the term to convey a noble purpose.

Immediately after the Michigan speech Johnson established fourteen different study groups composed largely of government workers and academicians. Recommendations proposed by each of the study groups were submitted to the White House program coordinator, Bill Moyers, and reviewed by affected government agencies and experts on Congressional relations before being forwarded to the President. By January 4, 1965, Johnson was ready to include a recitation of specific Great Society initiatives in his State of the Union Address.

The Economic Opportunity Act of 1964 created an Office of Economic Opportunity (OEO) to oversee community-based anti-poverty programs, and Johnson selected John Kennedy's brother-in-law, Sargent Shriver, the Peace Corps Director, to be in charge. The OEO organized its programs around a Community Action Plan (CAP) that required local governments to create their own poverty boards that would develop community-based initiatives and administer programs within their area. Shriver asked UAW official Jack Conway to serve as his deputy director in charge of the Community Action Program. Conway agreed to accept the appointment with the understanding that he would return to the union once CAP was in place. Conway developed the poverty boards along the UAW concept of forming a tripartite structure with representatives from local government, private agencies, and the affected poor providing the local initiative. Conway later explained,

> "I had spent so many years in the labor unions that I had a fairly good concept of how you organize people into action groups. I developed a three-cornered stool concept, which was that the best community action organization had very strong representation from local government, from [...] private agencies, and from the people themselves. If you could figure out how you could get this kind of three-cornered stool stability [...] that's what we strove for."[15]

To complement the administration's poverty program, Reuther sketched out a plan to incorporate the Coalition of Conscience into the poverty struggle in a Citizen's Crusade against Poverty (CCAP). Civil Rights groups, their allies in the religious organizations, labor unions, student activists, old-line liberal organizations like the ADA, and the poor themselves would be enlisted to "implement the federal program and supplement that with private action." CCAP would encourage coalition members to participate on local boards, work with the administration to transform locally sponsored initiatives into funded programs, and train representatives of the poor to become effective advocates for their community. The 1964 UAW Convention set aside one million dollars for the CCAP project, and exercised tight control over its operation. The organizational structure of CCAP consisted of an annual convention to which member groups would send delegates and elect a national chairman. The chairman would appoint an executive director, set salaries, approve staff work, and exercise effective control over the organization. Not surprisingly, the first, and only, national chairman was Walter Reuther. Reuther briefed the President in April on the project, and found him "very excited about what we are doing."[16] OEO and CCAP worked closely together, exchanging ideas, funding, and personnel. Conway named Brendan Sexton to be the head of CAP's first training program. Sexton held the job for a year, before leaving to head CCAP's training effort. Reuther named Richard Boone, one of the architects of the Community Action Program in OEO, to be the first executive director of CCAP.

So even before Johnson's 1965 State of the Union Address, the framework for implementing the Great Society initiatives was well-established. The most difficult piece of legislation, the 1964 Civil Rights Act, had already been passed; the tax cut had stimulated the economy, producing low unemployment and increased government revenues; and the organizational structure for fighting the War on Poverty was already in place. The legislative triumphs followed in quick succession. In 1965, Congress passed

- the Voting Rights Act that abolished discriminatory practices which prevented blacks from registering to vote and authorized federal examiners in areas that did not meet voter-participation requirements,

- the Immigration and Nationality Services Act that abolished the national-origin quotas of the 1924 Immigration Act,

- the Social Security Act of 1965 that created Medicare for the elderly and Medicaid for welfare recipients,

- the Elementary and Secondary Education Act that provided federal aid for public education and established the Head Start Program for preschool children from disadvantaged neighborhoods,

- the Higher Education Act which increased monies given to universities and established a low-interest student loan program,

- the National Foundation on the Arts and Humanities Act which established the National Endowment for the Arts and National Endowment for the Humanities, and a number of other significant pieces of legislation in the areas of public health and safety, the environment, and public broadcasting.

As the Great Society gathered momentum, Walter Reuther became more enmeshed in its gears. During 1965 alone, he met individually with the President thirteen times.[17] The differences that separated them in the fifties had dissipated, and Reuther expressed a real affinity for the new President. "[John Kennedy] and I were on the same wavelength," he told a reporter. "I think I am equally close to Lyndon Johnson, but I approach him differently. He was poor. I too know poverty. Lyndon Johnson and I came out of the same family background."[18] Whether the two had warm feelings for one another or not, the pair became entwined in a marriage of convenience. Reuther needed Johnson to further his vision for society, and as the war increasingly isolated LBJ from his former allies, Johnson needed Reuther's loyalty.

The aspect of the Great Society with which Reuther was most actively involved was the revitalization of urban centers like Detroit. He recognized the divisive potential inadequate housing posed for a labor-civil rights coalition. Gains won by workers during the post-war period had enabled many to join the middle class and flee the decaying cities for the mostly-white suburbs. Their homes were the biggest investment made in realizing this dream, and their greatest fear was that black families moving into their neighborhood would drive down the value of that investment. Unscrupulous real estate practices that targeted certain neighborhoods for block busting encouraged these fears. African-Americans were locked into deteriorating neighborhoods from which the whites had fled or warehoused into poorly constructed public housing projects.

In May of 1965, Reuther sent Johnson a four-page letter proposing "an urban TVA to stop the erosion of cities and people." He suggested that the federal government be enlisted in a campaign to "create architecturally beautiful and socially meaningful communities" that would not only build and restore housing, but would also build schools, parks, and senior centers to create a neighborhood that would be attractive to black and white alike. In his proposal, neighborhood renewal teams consisting of government officials, business and labor representatives, prominent citizens, and neighborhood residents from six selected cities would formulate proposals for approval, and the government would channel grant money back into the community through the renewal teams.

Reuther formally presented his proposal to the President in a White House meeting on May 20th. He recommended that if Johnson liked the concept, he should appoint a task force to develop the idea more fully. Johnson embraced the proposal, and later wrote in his memoirs that, "The sense of home runs deep in me, and better housing would automatically appear on any list of priorities."[19] Johnson turned the project over to his aides, Richard Goodwin and Joseph Califano, who formed a task force of progressive thinkers from academia, business, labor, civil rights organizations, and the public sector. Walter Reuther was asked to be the representative from labor. Califano informed the group that it was responsible for not only developing the Demonstration Cities plan, but also creating the organizational structure for the new Department of Housing and Urban Development (HUD). The task force was to complete its work by late December to enable the President to incorporate their recommendations into the 1966 budget request.

Reuther and the liberal industrialist Edgar Kaiser with the assistance of Jack Conway directed the Demonstration Cities part of the initiative. The group poured a great deal of effort into their assignment, meeting in Califano's office every weekend from mid-October until the December deadline. Johnson aide Harry McPherson reported to the President that "this is the hardest working group of volunteers I have ever seen." He credited the task force's academicians with providing important knowledge of the problems involved, but went on to stipulate that

"Reuther has supplied the vision, drive, and sometimes mere rhetoric that has kept us moving."[20] The group decided that demonstration sites should be selected through competition rather than fiat. The Secretary of HUD was to receive proposals from interested cities and evaluate the proposals on the basis of how well they incorporated the several voices of the community, how extensively they proposed to employ innovative housing technology, and how adequately they addressed the intent of closing the gap in the living conditions between the disadvantaged and the rest of the community.[21] Smaller urban centers also became eligible to receive grant money to make the program more attractive to legislators from states and districts without a major city.

Reuther proposed to the task force that the Community Action Program (CAP) be transferred from the OEO to HUD where it would offset the more conservative Federal Housing Authority that was slated to be housed in the new department. He suggested that it would also strengthen CAP if it were moved to a department with cabinet status. There may have been a more compelling reason he had for relocating CAP inside of HUD. There was support within the administration for naming Reuther as the first Secretary of HUD, and he let it be known that he would accept the position if it were offered.[22] If Reuther were to be named to the position and he could engineer the transfer of CAP to HUD, he would effectively become the field general for the War on Poverty.

The offer was never made. Johnson fulfilled his promise to civil rights leaders to place an African-American in his cabinet by naming Robert Weaver as the first Secretary of Housing and Urban Development. Johnson may never have wanted a headstrong Reuther in his cabinet, or he may have been dissuaded by the realization that a Reuther nomination would have been subjected to a back stage smear campaign led by J. Edgar Hoover, who had used selective leaks and disinformation to thwart every previous presidential effort to name Reuther to some office, however small or temporary the role. Robert Weaver would experience a much smoother confirmation process than Walter Reuther and share a much smaller spotlight with his boss. Reuther remained in his post in the UAW and CAP remained under the auspices of OEO.

Despite the disappointment of not being offered the cabinet post, Reuther was optimistic that the Demonstration Cities Program he had championed, now renamed Model Cities, would provide a springboard for launching additional social reform. He set about the task of preparing the Model Cities application for Detroit. Immediately after the White House task force had submitted its recommendations to the President, Reuther urged Detroit Mayor Cavanaugh to set up a nonprofit development authority to prepare the city's proposal for federal support.[23] Cavanaugh promptly created the Metropolitan Detroit Citizens Development Authority (MDCDA) to oversee redevelopment of a blighted nine square mile section of the central city, and named Reuther as its Chairman. Seats on the Authority were allocated to the city's labor and business leaders, public officials, and leaders of its academic and civic institutions. Reuther contributed $100,000 of UAW money to launch the initiative, and promised another $1 million more if the Big Three automobile companies would pledge the same. *Fortune* magazine hailed the collaboration between the business community and its erstwhile adversary as a "remarkable synthesis."[24]

The one component missing from the MDCDA synthesis was representation from the affected neighborhood. The UAW did not hear any leadership voices in the northern ghettos that were ready to participate effectively in the deliberations of the development authority, and, as in the factional battles of the nineteen forties, it opposed token representation. It did, however, assume responsibility for creating effective leaders from the ranks of the disadvantaged and set up education centers in Watts, Chicago, the greater New York/New Jersey area, Mississippi, and, for the farm workers, in Delano, California. [25]

It is not that there was a lack of leadership voices in the black inner city. There was a chorus of voices ranging from separatists like the Black Muslims and the increasingly more militant SNCC to the black churches and veterans from the civil rights struggle. This chorus did not produce a harmony, and did not take direction from a guest conductor on the podium. When these voices were not heard inside the MDCDA, they made themselves heard outside of its corridors.

Flashes of Lightning, Bursts of Thunder, Torrents of Rain

On the morning of July 25, 1967, Walter Reuther received a phone call from Lyndon Johnson.[26] The city that Reuther wanted to make into a laboratory for urban development that all the world might see was in flames and street battles were breaking out in the neighborhoods. Johnson was committing troops to quell the riot, and he wanted the people of Detroit to know that the troops he was sending were the same ones sent to Little Rock by Eisenhower to enforce a school desegregation order in the first test of the Supreme Court Brown vs. [Topeka] Board of Education ruling and later by Kennedy to allow James Merideth to enroll at the University of Mississippi. Johnson was sensitive to the anti-war chant of "Hey, hey LBJ, how many kids did you kill today?" and he did not want to give credence to the notion that he was indifferent to the suffering his actions at home or abroad might be causing.

The task for Reuther now was to help save the old city, not shape the future of a new one. Detroit would never recover. The MDCDA Novi City plan for an integrated community never left the drawing board. A Renaissance Center, built by the business community under the direction of Henry Ford II, with hotels, shopping malls, and corporate office space replaced community housing as the city's priority and stands today as an island of faded opulence in a sea of decay.

Reuther and auto executives belatedly met with neighborhood representatives to try to calm tensions in the city, but their influence was minimal. One of the young men in the audience pointed at Henry Ford II and GM president, John Roche, and said "You fat cats don't know what's going on." Ford and Roche said nothing, but Reuther shot back "You listen to me. We're going to need help and its going to have to come from these men you're calling 'fat cats'." The youth was not impressed. After the meeting he told the press "Reuther doesn't dig me and I don't dig him."[27]

The disconnect between Reuther and black youth may have been exacerbated during a struggle at the 1964 Democratic Convention to seat the Mississippi Freedom Democratic Party (MFDP) delegation in place of the all-white party regulars. The Student Nonviolent Coordinating Committee with some assistance from SDS worked tirelessly throughout the spring and summer to form a multiracial delegation that would claim the right to represent the state. Robert Moses, the MFDP director, was advised to seek support from the UAW, and he found a sympathetic ear from Joseph Rauh, Mildred Jeffrey, and William Dodds. Dodds channeled UAW funds to the MFDP and Rauh agreed to serve as its counsel.[28]

The prospect of a floor fight that would further alienate the South at the Democratic Party National Convention troubled Johnson, and he indicated to Reuther that he would not be able to name Hubert Humphrey as his running mate if the regular party delegation were unseated. Reuther pressured Rauh to withdraw as MFDP counsel, and, when sentiment for the challengers remained strong on the convention floor, was himself pressured by Johnson to work out a deal to prevent an open fight that might benefit the chances of Barry Goldwater in November. Reuther left a negotiating session with General Motors to fly to Atlantic City only to learn that a compromise within the leadership had been achieved that awarded the MFDP two seats at the convention and a promise that no segregated delegations would be seated in any future convention. It became Reuther's task to sell this compromise to the inter-racial group from Mississippi. The MFDP wanted the two seats to go to Aaron Henry and a sharecropper named Fannie Lou Hamer, but LBJ's representative, Texas Governor John Connally, insisted that they go to his nominees: Henry, the head of the Mississippi NAACP, and a white college chaplain named Ed King. The MFDP would not accept this dictate. During a hastily arranged meeting between Humphrey, Reuther, Henry, Martin Luther King, Andrew Young, and Bob Moses, strong pressure was brought by Reuther to make the group accept the deal. When Moses refused, Reuther turned to King for support. King replied that he had no right to tell the MFDP what to do and Reuther exploded, reminding King of all the financial support the UAW had given him over the years.[29] None of the black leaders was willing to back down, and when word reached the room that the Credentials Committee had accepted Connally's compromise delegation, Moses walked out. The MFDP was outraged at being presented with a fait acompli, and at a caucus the next day it rejected the seats it had been offered.[30]

The UAW leadership got its man Humphrey nominated to run with Johnson, and a divisive floor fight was averted; but Reuther underestimated the lasting effects that the brokered compromise would have on the union's relationship with the emerging new civil rights leadership and the tensions that were surfacing within his governing coalition of the UAW. The relationship between Reuther and his friend of twenty years, Joseph Rauh, was never the same, and the door Robert Moses slammed on Hubert Humphrey and Walter Reuther remained closed as the new and old left went their separate ways.[31] Reuther and Humphrey remained shut inside the confines of a political apparatus that provided a presence at court but demanded their acquiescence.

As the intoxicating days of 1965 drew to a close, the future seemed bright for progressive forces. Voting Rights, Medicare, Medicaid, and other important legislation had been passed, and the challenge of blighted and segregated neighborhoods was about to be addressed. The sound of rolling thunder off in the distance was not close enough to forgo the picnic in progress, and, with any luck, might pass by entirely. Riots in Watts and Harlem were treated as isolated storms and not harbingers of bad weather to come. Johnson's courtship of Reuther had drawn him deeper into the political process, but the opportunity to affect change seemed never greater.

All of this began to change when the new year started. As the leadership of the UAW contemplated its role on center stage in a Great Society being lavishly produced in the corridors of Washington, public attention was diverted to the drama unfolding in the rice paddies of Vietnam. With each new escalation, draft calls expanded, casualties increased, and opposition voices grew louder. The war in Vietnam was accompanied by an increasingly bitter battle being waged on the campuses, in the union halls, and in the Congress of the United States over the wisdom, morality, and conduct of the war.

Cold War orthodoxy prevailed at the outset of the war, with an overwhelming majority of Americans agreeing with the necessity of preventing a Communist takeover of another Asian land. Reuther long argued for a parallel, non militaristic strategy to assist developing and newly independent countries evolve their own structures outside the orbit of big-power alliances, but he publicly supported the war initially as staunchly as the hawkish George Meany.

Opposition to the war first surfaced on the college campuses. Within a month of Johnson's launching a bombing campaign against the North in February of 1965, more than 3000 University of Michigan students and professors staged a day long "teach-in" against a simplistic, Cold War view of the struggle. Similar events occurred in subsequent weeks on thirty-five other campuses and were culminated by an Easter march on Washington.[32] The student activists had committed allies within the UAW, but Walter Reuther was not among them. On the day that Johnson initiated the bombing campaign, Reuther was in the White House meeting privately with the President and urging him to support the Voting Rights Bill.[33] Two months later he was pressing his Demonstration Cities proposal. Reuther needed Johnson to advance his social agenda, and Johnson required loyalty in return.

Walter Reuther was a man of extraordinary vision coupled with physical vigor and meticulous preparation. His success in winning and maintaining control of the UAW and building it into an effective force for economic advancement of working-class people rested in his personal attributes and his ability to forge coalitions in support of a common agenda. As the Great Society took shape throughout the first two years of Johnson's presidency, Reuther was the man with the vision of what it might achieve, the tireless organizer who fashioned a Coalition of Conscience around a broader social-economic agenda, and the leader of a team with years of negotiating and lobbying experience geared to see it through Congress. All the pieces were in place for a successful struggle against the anticipated resistance from the usual adversaries. The ferocity of the building storm stalled these efforts and put Reuther in the tenuous position of straddling a widening breech between his commitments to the administration's social agenda and his reservations, and those of his executive board, over its Vietnam policy. After the summer of 1966, the forward advance in the War on Poverty turned into a defensive struggle to preserve the progressive coalition and recapture the lost initiative.

The activities of the Coalition of Conscience partners were loosely coordinated under an umbrella organization called the Leadership Conference on Civil Rights (LCCR), a group the NAACP and UAW originally helped to form in the 1950s. The LCCR contained representatives from the various Civil Rights organizations, organized labor, religious groups such as the National Council of Churches, and campus organizations. By the end of 1965, as the civil rights struggle moved from the legal to the economic and social sphere and the war continued to escalate, tensions began to surface not only within the LCCR, but within the member organizations themselves.

At the 1965 AFL-CIO convention, George Meany proposed a draft resolution supporting the administration's Vietnam policy and condemning "a tiny but noisy minority" opposed to the war. Reuther objected to the tone of the resolution and managed to insert a paragraph praising the administration's effort to secure a negotiated settlement into the final resolution. When a few of the "noisy minority" seated in the balcony created a disturbance during discussion of the resolution, Meany ordered the sergeant-at-arms to remove the "kookies" from the hall. Emil Mazey received a rebuke from Meany when he defended the protesters' right to question the war and got no support from his boss, who reported after the convention that "the protesters should be demonstrating against Hanoi and Peking [...] they are responsible for the war."[34] Eight months later the federation's executive council drafted a stronger resolution, over Reuther's objections, that condemned the anti-war protesters for "aiding the Communist enemy of our country" and omitted any mention of a negotiated peace.

As the war escalated, prominent citizens stepped forward to voice their opposition. William Sloane Coffin, the Chaplain at Yale University, and Dr. Benjamin Spock, the pediatrician and author of popular baby care books, were among the early critics of the administration's Vietnam policy. Spock became a particular target of conservatives, who contended that his permissive child-rearing prescriptions were responsible for raising a generation of campus radicals. One of the more surprising public figures who was becoming disillusioned with the war was Chicago mayor, Richard Daley. Daley would become the bête noire to the anti-war movement with his police assault on demonstrators at the 1968 Democratic Convention, but he was privately expressing his reservations about the war to Lyndon Johnson. Part of Daley's disillusionment with the war may have been based on the divisive effect it was having upon his coalition in Chicago, but he was also affected by the deaths of Chicago area servicemen. The death of Joseph McKeon, the "bright kid" from his

Bridgeport neighborhood, had a particularly sobering effect on Daley's enthusiasm for the war. McKeon was a friend of Daley's son Michael who had attended Harvard and then, surprisingly to his friends, joined the Marine Corps. Within three weeks of his deployment to Vietnam he was killed. Daley did not make his feelings known publicly, but as early as a 1966 visit to the White House, he was asked by the president what he thought about Vietnam. He took a minute to compose his answer and replied, "Well, Mr. President, when you've got a losing hand in poker you just throw in your cards." When Johnson pressed him about the loss of American prestige, he replied, "You put your prestige in your back pocket and walk away."[35]

As one-by-one civil rights leaders, such as Martin Luther King, and New Frontier liberals, like John Kenneth Galbraith, Arthur Schlesinger, Jr., and ultimately Robert Kennedy, broke with the administration over its conduct of the war, Reuther became more isolated. Within the UAW the voices of Emil Mazey, Mildred Jeffrey, Paul Schrade, and Walter's brother, Victor, grew more reluctant to support even a tepid endorsement of the administration's war policy and less constrained to express their differences with the official union position.[36] Reuther's position on the war was even being challenged at home.

By 1967, the generational divide that was straining family bonds across the land threatened to disrupt an annual Passover Seder gathering, celebrated with the Reuthers by UAW official Irving Bluestone and his family. Bluestone's son, Barry, and his girlfriend, Leslie Woodcock, substituted readings of excerpts from speeches by Martin Luther King and anti war verses from World War I poets for the traditional reading from the Haggadah. When they had finished, Reuther remarked "I take it that was aimed at me." He expressed reservations about the war, but explained that he could not afford to break with LBJ during contract talks.

Barry Bluestone later recounted the reaction that this comment sparked in Leslie Woodcock:

> "[Leslie] turned to Walter and said, "You really said that didn't you?" And Walter said, "what did I say?" And Leslie became just as angry as I ever saw her. Her face

was flushed with anger. "You really said that. You really said that." And Walter, frustrated, asked again, "What did I say?" Leslie turned to him and said, "what are you trying to do, maybe get eighty cents an hour in the pay envelope, five cents here, five cents there? You're telling me that you are unwilling to make a statement that may save fifty thousand lives or one hundred thousand lives or maybe a million lives because you want fifty cents more in your goddam fucking contract…that's the most inhumane thing I have ever heard in my life."[37]

Victor Reuther explained his brother's situation as head of an organization with responsibilities to the members of that organization.

"Walter never really believed this was a war we should have entered. But as the head of an organization, you really hesitate to break openly with the President of the United States on a foreign policy issue. Whether you like it or not, you don't always have the luxury of a personal opinion. I talked to Walter enough about the Vietnam War privately to know he thought it was one of our greatest tragedies. And I think that if there were any way he could have manipulated Johnson to pull out, he would have."[38]

Not only was the war drawing Reuther farther apart from his colleagues and his coalition partners, it was also drawing Johnson farther apart from Reuther. As the war came to dominate Johnson's agenda and the defections of former allies mounted, he became increasingly concerned that Reuther might support a Kennedy challenge to his leadership and was receptive to false rumors about Reuther's activities delivered by his aide, John Roche.[39] After the summer of 1966, Reuther's private meetings with Johnson at the White House ceased.

The war was not the only issue dividing the LCCR. As the civil rights movement moved from a legal struggle in the South to an economic struggle nationwide, new, and more militant, leadership emerged and discomfited many of its Old Left and labor allies. After the Mississippi Freedom Democratic Party lost its battle to be seated in the credentials fight at the 1964 Democratic National Convention, SNCC began a process of reassessing its strategy culminating in 1966 with the replacement of its long-time leader, John Lewis, by Stokely Carmichael.

Carmichael burst into national attention that summer during the completion of James Meredith's quixotic "March Against Fear" from Memphis to Jackson, Mississippi. Shortly after Meredith crossed into Mississippi he was felled on a lonely stretch of highway 51 by a shotgun blast fired by someone hiding in ambush beside the road. Meredith was hospitalized, and mainstream Civil Rights Organizations including SCLC and SNCC rushed into Mississippi to support him and complete his lonely trek. During the march, Carmichael was arrested and briefly held in Greenwood, Mississippi on a charge of trespassing when he defied an order not to pitch his tent in a restricted area. When he was released on bail later that evening, he thundered to a receptive crowd of supporters "this is the twenty-seventh time I have been arrested, and I ain't going to jail no more! The only way we're gonna stop them white men from whuppin' us is to take over. What we gonna start saying now is Black Power!" For the remainder of the march, the old chant of "Freedom Now" was drowned out by a chorus of "Black Power."[40]

King rushed back to Mississippi from a campaign against segregated housing in Chicago, to persuade the marchers to adhere to nonviolence as the cornerstone doctrine of the struggle for equal opportunity and justice. He pleaded with Carmichael to abandon the divisive slogan of "Black Power," but was rebuffed with the response that "Power is the only thing respected in this world, and we must get it at any cost."[41] The only concession King was able to wrest from Carmichael was that the slogan "Freedom Now" would be chanted along with "Black Power" for the rest of the march. King was also able to dissuade the SNCC leaders from expelling whites from the remainder of the trek to Jackson, but SNCC later voted to oust whites from its membership, charging them with the task of working for justice and raising consciousness within their own community. Carmichael confided to King that he raised the issue of Black Power during the march to force him to take a stand on the issue. King replied, "I have been used before. One more time won't hurt."[42]

What the rise of black militancy in the wake of riots in Watts and Harlem did hurt was the appetite for additional Great Society programs. Northern whites who supported efforts to end legal segregation in the South were resistant to efforts to end defacto segregation of their schools and neighborhoods. The rise of black militancy only hardened racial attitudes. As events in Vietnam, campus unrest, and urban riots polarized society, Washington battened down to ride out a storm. Reuther was like a well-prepared football coach who had assembled a talented squad of players, analyzed his opponent, developed a sound game plan, and expected a crowd of supporters filling the stands at game time, only to arrive at the game and find a whole different opponent waiting on the field and his cheering section empty save for a few diehard fans. Planning, organizational skills, and lobbying expertise were useless in the new environment.

Republican gains of 44 seats in the House and 3 in the Senate in the 1966 midterm election put the Great Society on hold, rioting in Reuther's Model City, Detroit, in the summer of 1967 became a Waterloo in the War on Poverty. As 1967 came to an end, the Summer of Love turned into the Winter of Our Discontent.

The Deluge

The full fury of the storm struck early in 1968. Administration assurances of progress in the war were shattered by the North Vietnamese Tet offensive. What turned out to be a tactical defeat for the North on the battlefield was a strategic triumph in the larger struggle to shape American perceptions about the duration, costs, and chances for success in the war. Frustration with the war was vented in numerous directions, but Johnson was the common denominator when adding up the blame. Shortly after Tet, voters in the New Hampshire Democratic primary gave the president a narrow 49–42 percent victory over the relatively unknown anti-war candidate, Eugene McCarthy. In the parlance of expectation politics, that narrow victory was pronounced a defeat, and the outlook for Johnson in the upcoming Wisconsin primary appeared even bleaker.

Four days after the New Hampshire results were announced, Robert Kennedy declared his candidacy. Three weeks later, on March 31, Johnson went on national television to announce that he had ordered a limitation on bombing targets in North Vietnam, to express his willingness to begin negotiations to end the war, and finally to declare that he would not seek nor would he accept his party's nomination for president. Lyndon Johnson's political career and his vision of a Great Society became a casualty in what had become known as "Johnson's War".

Four days later Martin Luther King was assassinated in Memphis. King had embraced the idea that only with policy that promoted full employment, could assimilation of blacks into middle class society proceed.[43] He became an early critic of the war, not only on moral grounds, but also because it was diverting resources and energy needed to sustain a growing economy at home and because it was being fought disproportionally by young black men. He came to Memphis, during preparations for a Poor People's Campaign in Washington, to support striking sanitation workers. The night before his death he told a crowd of the workers, "I have been to the mountaintop." "I have seen the Promised Land. I may not get there with you. But I want you to know tonight, we as a people will get to the Promised Land."

The strongest advocate for non-violent resistance was now silenced. Days of violent rage erupted in cities across the country, most prominently in Washington, D. C., where fires burned within sight of the Capitol. With no other leader having the stature of Dr. King to command the public spotlight, angry voices from the fringe of the movement received greater amplification from the media. The difficult task of assuaging white fears and black anger as integration moved from the public space in the South to the neighborhoods, workplaces, and community schools throughout the country was to proceed without the presence of the movement's most prominent leader.

Before the end of the same month in which Dr. King was murdered, students at Columbia University seized control of several campus buildings and demanded that the administration sever ties with the Institute for Defense Analysis (IDA) and halt plans for a gymnasium in Morningside Park. The gymnasium was to be built on land owned by the City and made available for use by residents of nearby

Harlem. The original plan called for a lower-level, back entrance that neighborhood residents could use to avoid having to negotiate a steep incline that separated the University atop Morningside Heights from Harlem below. As militancy in the community grew, opposition to the plan hardened, and the lower, back entrance ceased to be regarded as a convenience and instead was looked upon as a discriminatory vestige of "Gym Crow." Students from the Student Afro Society (SAS) aligned with neighborhood activists to protest any appropriation of park land by the university. The Columbia SDS chapter echoed their opposition to the gym project, but also protested the university's support for the war effort through its unpublicized association with the IDA. When the strike began, black students occupying Hamilton Hall, a classroom and administration office building, demanded that whites leave. Their protest was directed against the gym project, and they did not want to diminish that emphasis by placing it into any broader context. The SDS members then occupied the Low Library, which housed the President's office but no longer collections of books, and three other campus buildings. There was little further communication or solidarity between the two groups.

The university was cautious in its handling of the strike, aware of the support the students had in the surrounding community and sensitive to the racial climate in the wake of King's murder. Negotiations between the NYPD and students occupying Hamilton Hall led to a peaceful evacuation of that building, but the SDS members occupying Low Library and the other campus buildings were violently assaulted. About 150 demonstrators were admitted to hospitals and over 700 arrested. After the buildings were cleared, the university capitulated to both of the student demands. All military presence was removed from the campus and the controversial gymnasium was never built. The cost of the confrontation to the university was steep. Applications for admission declined in quantity and quality and alumni donations dropped substantially. Columbia estimated that it took twenty years to recover from the riots.[44]

Confrontations between students and administrations occurred on other campuses throughout the two-year duration of the storm. SDS had become less ideological and more confrontational as a progression of each cycle of leaders moved the organization farther, from its roots in labor and awareness of its antecedents in the "old left." Most SDS activity was confined to campuses, but Mark Rudd, the campus SDS leader at Columbia, and several of the more militant members of his group joined with some members of the New York Black Panthers to form the Weatherman underground: a group, named from a line in Bob Dylan's *Subterranean Homesick Blues*, that resorted to violence in its efforts to overthrow the establishment.

The election campaign of 1968 played to a backdrop of the war going badly and neighborhoods and campuses in turmoil. The Republicans, unwilling to relive the Goldwater disaster, coalesced around the familiar figure of Richard Nixon. The "new Nixon," repackaged after a loss to Pat Brown in the California gubernatorial race, courted the "silent majority" who were turned off by the protesters more than by their cause and sought a return to traditional values. Nixon correctly gauged that the country did not want to see the Great Society dismantled, but neither did it want to see it expanded. He campaigned touting a secret plan to end the war.

After Johnson left the race and Kennedy entered it, the Democratic nomination was up for grabs. Eugene McCarthy retained much of the support he had garnered on the campuses and in liberal circles by being the one Democrat willing to challenge a sitting president over the continuation of the war. Kennedy's late entry seemed opportunistic to many anti-war partisans who were enthusiastically committed to McCarthy's cause as much as to the candidate himself. Kennedy was strongly backed by black and Latino voters, and represented a nostalgic return in the hearts of many of the electorate to a Camelot that was prematurely ended by an assassin's bullet. Kennedy did the most to establish his credibility as a candidate when, against the wishes of Mayor Richard Lugar and his own security detachment, he ventured into a tense inner-city neighborhood of Indianapolis on the evening of Martin Luther King's assassination and delivered a brief, impromptu message that defused a powder keg of anger ready to explode. Indianapolis was not one of the many cities that erupted in rioting on that tragic night, and Kennedy seemed the one leader capable of bridging the racial divide in the second phase of the civil rights struggle.

The labor and party apparatus that backed Johnson and his war policy transferred its support to his vice president, Hubert Humphrey. Humphrey announced his candidacy too late to enter the primaries, so his campaign was waged among the governors and party leaders like Mayor Richard Daley, Sr. of Chicago, who controlled the selection of delegates to the national convention. Meany and much of the AFL-CIO hierarchy backed Humphrey. Paul Schrade, Mildred Jeffrey, and others in the UAW leadership actively supported Robert Kennedy, but Walter Reuther and the official UAW position remained uncommitted to any of the candidates.

Kennedy needed to demonstrate his popular appeal in the primaries if he were to convince the party leaders that he was the only Democrat who could win in November and cause them to back away from committing to Humphrey. His loss to McCarthy in the Oregon Primary made victory in California two weeks later essential if he were to have any chance of securing the nomination. His support of Cesar Chavez and the United Farm Workers Union in their struggle against the grape and lettuce producers in the state gave him an enthusiastic base of support among California's large Latino population, but he had very limited success in wooing away the anti-war vote from the candidate that it had rallied around from the beginning. After a spirited campaign, the closely contested election went to Kennedy, who announced in a ballroom packed with his ebullient supporters. "Now it's on to Chicago." Moments later he lay dying on the floor of the hotel pantry with a gunshot wound to the head.

The decade that had begun with a new generation of leaders ready to receive the torch passed to them was ending with repeated tragedy. The burdens that the nation was asked to bear and the price it was required to pay proved far greater than the rhetorical flourish suggested on that cold January afternoon in 1961. The family central to the political life of the 1960's was fated to bear a heavy share of that burden. While the lives cut short left open an idyllic vision of what was and might have been, a return to the legendary land of Camelot was precluded for good one year after Robert Kennedy's death when the youngest Kennedy brother, Ted, drove his car off a bridge in Chappaquiddick Harbor and left his passenger alone to drown.

The death of Robert Kennedy assured the Democratic nomination would go to Hubert Humphrey, but the convention became the eye of the storm that was buffeting the land. Anti-war activists, unwilling to acquiesce to a continuation of Johnson's Vietnam policy, black militants, protesting the practices of local police, and Yippees, using street theater to protest against the war and the capitalist system that it was alleged to serve, all gathered in Chicago to voice their grievances in the spotlight of the media coverage. Mayor Daley was determined that demonstrations would not detract from the convention that he brought to his city. Violent confrontations between the Chicago police and protesters camping out in Grant Park without a city permit occurred throughout the week culminating in the clash witnessed by TV viewers around the world when the demonstrators attempted to march to the convention site during the nomination process. The scene inside the hall was almost as tense as the confrontation taking place outside. Senator Abraham Ribicoff of Connecticut deplored the "Gestapo tactics" of the Chicago police during his nominating speech for Senator McCarthy, causing Mayor Daley to fire back into the din "Fuck you, you Jew son of a bitch, you lousy motherfucker go home."[45]

On the final night, a tribute to Senator Robert Kennedy preceded the acceptance speeches of the presidential and vice presidential candidates. When the tribute ended, Kennedy and McCarthy delegates would not relinquish the floor, with the large California delegation, led by the booming baritone of *Fiddler on the Roof* star, Theodore Bikel, joining with other delegations in non-stop choruses from the *Battle Hymn of the Republic*. "Glory, glory Hallelujah Glory, glory Hallelujah Glory, glory Hallelujah His truth is marching on!" Humphrey only got to experience his triumph after the singing died down and the mood of the floor was angry.

Walter Reuther urged Humphrey to adopt a peace plank that included an immediate cease fire, an international peace keeping force, land redistribution in South Vietnam and free elections, but Humphrey refused to break with Johnson and stake his own position on the war. Victor Reuther was blunter in telling Humphrey "We have been friends for a long time and I have the greatest affection for you, but, quite frankly, Hubert, if you don't have the courage to come out now against the Vietnam War, you don't deserve to be elected."[46]

When the nation went to the polls in 1968 to choose a leader to steer it through the storm, it was offered a choice of a compromised, and vacillating Hubert Humphrey, a retooled and slickly re-marketed Richard Nixon, and a segregationist governor standing in the doorway to national reconciliation. Lyndon Johnson offered his own assessment of the leading candidates when he pointed to his head and groin saying Nixon has it here and here, but not sure he has it here, pointing to his heart. Humphrey had it in the head and heart, but Johnson wasn't sure if he had it down here, pointing to his groin.[47] Reuther worked tirelessly to swing the UAW membership behind Humphrey and to blunt the appeal of Wallace among working class voters, but disaffected McCarthy and Kennedy supporters were unenthusiastic about the choice of Humphrey. By the time Democratic voters started to swing to Humphrey, it was too late, and Nixon won a close election.

Reuther was shaken by the assassinations of King and Kennedy. In November of 1967 his father, Valentine Reuther had died, and two months later his brother Roy, the head of UAW political activities, suffered a massive heart attack and died on route to the hospital. The subsequent murders of his friends and political allies caused him to reflect upon his own fate. Walter Reuther was now 61 years old, and had been the target of more than one assassination attempt. He viewed the storm battering the United States through the lens of memories experienced during his time in 1933 Germany when trade unionists were singled out for interment in concentration camps, or worse. He expressed his concerns for America to the UAW Executive Board:

> "This is where we are in America." "American society is coming apart…I am not going to be put in a position where my own conscience—if I ultimately end up in a concentration camp—where I am going to be charged in my own mind with having twaddled and twiddled my thumbs when real decisions were made."[48]

The election of Nixon freed Reuther to voice his opposition to the war, and a final break with George Meany and the AFL-CIO removed constraints on his social activism. But America after 1968 sought a firm hand on the rudder rather than a fixed eye upon a star. Behind the turmoil obscuring the broader picture lurked fundamental problems facing American manufacturing. Reuther's power base within the automotive sector was being eroded by climate changes in a new economic environment. The labor force was changing, and black militancy was raising a voice in opposition to the Reuther establishment within the UAW. Complacency was putting the whole industry at risk.

The first hints of trouble for the auto industry came in the arrival of cheap little Japanese imports dotting the American roadways and with Ralph Nader's condemnation of the safety and quality of American made automobiles in his book *Unsafe at Any Speed*. The national thirst for oil exceeded the capability of the domestic wells to produce it, and would lead to price hikes and shortages that accelerated the Japanese and European penetration of the domestic market with more fuel efficient cars. Reuther's successors would be forced to accept cuts and concede gains while manufacturing jobs hemorrhaged out of the country.

Reuther remained a forceful advocate for social, racial, and economic justice, but with many of his old associates dead or retired and regarded as an anathema by the Republican administration, a racist by the Black Power movement, and a toady of the establishment by the New Left, he was an increasingly isolated figure in what was once a bright liberal firmament. Reuther devoted much of his energy in what were to be his last two years to overseeing the construction of the UAW Educational Center at Black Lake, Michigan and priming it to house a conference of ecologists.

Reuther was an avid naturalist and early environmentalist, creating within the union in 1965 a Department of Conservation and Resource Development, headed by board member Olga Madar. The UAW worked with Wisconsin Senator Gaylord Nelson in establishing the first Earth Day, and followed up the April 22, 1970 event by inviting over 200 local organizers to their newly opened Black Lake Center to try to mold the fledgling environmental campaign into a cohesive national movement.[49] In one of his last public appearances, Walter Reuther served as the keynote speaker for the Earth Day celebration at his daughter Lisa's Oakland University.

The storm reached a crescendo in 1968, but persisted throughout the Nixon presidency. The revelations of a massacre in the hamlet of My Lai and its subsequent cover up by the military stained the national image. The moral superiority the United States claimed over its adversary was reduced from absolute to relative terms by the images coming from the conflict zone. The cover up extended high up the chain of command,[50] but the only person convicted of a crime was a junior lieutenant, who was subsequently released and pardoned by the President. The standard of conduct America demanded from its adversaries at Nuremberg and Tokyo was not to be applied to its own forces in Vietnam.

The Cambodian invasion in May, 1970 unleashed the next spasm of violent confrontation on the campuses. The crisis was heightened when National Guard troops, ordered to the campus of Kent State University in Ohio after an ROTC building had been burned during the previous day's protest, fired on the demonstrators, killing four and wounding nine others. Four hundred colleges shut down across the country, and a week later a similar confrontation between police and students at the predominantly black college, Jackson State, in Mississippi led to the shooting death of two more students. Reuther was outraged by the Kent State shootings and immediately drafted a telegram to the White House in what was to be his last public pronouncement.

Days later Walter Reuther was dead. Messages of tribute poured in to the UAW and Reuther family from world leaders like Willie Brandt, Golda Meier, and Swedish Prime Minister Tage Erlander who had developed close personal friendships with the labor leader. Richard Nixon noted in his message that "even those who disagreed with him had great respect for his ability, integrity, and persistence." Henry Ford II called him "a central figure in modern industrial history." Even the Engineering Workers Union of the Soviet Union wired its "deep sorrow at Walter Reuther's passing."[51] The memorial service, attended by world and national leaders like Erlander, Hubert Humphrey, and Edward Kennedy, auto executives like Ford and George Romney, who once called Reuther the most dangerous man in Detroit, and members of his union, was held in the Ford Auditorium, thirty-three years after Reuther had been kicked and beaten by Harry Bennett's goons in the Battle of the Overpass.

Assessing the Damage

The remaining years of the Nixon administration were troubled by the final stages of the war and the political scandals that brought down the Vice President, Spiro Agnew, and ultimately led to the resignation of the President. The administrations of Gerald Ford and Jimmy Carter proved to be a transition between the turmoil of the late 60's and early 70's to the new political dynamic of the Reagan years. The accomplishments of Ford and Carter have been dismissed in the common wisdom dispensed by the talking heads populating the airwaves, but the era provided a period of healing and a return to civil discourse.

When the storm ended, Walter Reuther, Martin Luther King, and Jack and Robert Kennedy were dead. Edward Kennedy was fatally compromised. Lyndon Johnson had retired to his ranch, and Hubert Humphrey was weighed down with the baggage of Johnson's Vietnam legacy. John Lindsay had the look of a Hollywood star, but he was marginalized in the Republican Party, and made the career ending choice of trying to govern New York City in the 1960s. The nihilistic New Left produced no leaders capable of stepping into the void. The Civil Rights Movement produced young charismatic leaders like Andrew Young, Jessie Jackson, and Julian Bond, but the nation was not ready yet to grant them a chance to play a leading role in the political drama. Unfortunately, there was no candidate on the left with the star power to cast in the lead role.

Passage of the Civil Rights and Voting Rights Acts effectively ended the Democratic monopoly in the South. Old line Dixiecrats like Senators Eastland and Stennis of Mississippi moderated their opposition to racial integration somewhat to appeal to newly empowered black voters and served as long as age permitted them, to be succeeded by ideologically sympathetic Republicans. Others, like Strom Thurmond and, opportunistically, John Connally changed their party affiliation. The realignment of political affiliation in the two parties, which was originally welcomed by the UAW, swung the balance of power in the Republican Party firmly away from the Northeast and industrial belt moderates to rural, Western, and Southern conservatives.

Demographics strengthened the hold of the conservatives on the Republican Party and enhanced their power nationally. In 1952, Dewey's

New York was the most populous state in the union and the industrial heartland states of Pennsylvania, Ohio, Michigan, and Illinois trailed only California in the weight of electoral votes they cast. By the end of the twentieth century, the industrial heartland had become the rust belt, and the Northeast and Great Lakes regions had lost population to the Western and Southern states. Texas and Florida joined California as the new heavyweights of the Electoral College.

As conservative control of the Republican Party increased, they grew not simply content to out vote their moderate colleagues within the party caucuses, but became determined to define what it meant to be a Republican along strict ideological guidelines. Republican liberals and moderates were termed RINOs (Republicans in Name Only) and targeted for extinction in party primaries. The party of Lincoln, Teddy Roosevelt, and Dwight Eisenhower came to trace its ancestral roots no farther back than Ronald Reagan.

The debacle of the 1968 National Convention caused the Democrats to revise the delegate selection process for future conventions. A commission headed by South Dakota Senator George McGovern shepherded to approval a new set of rules for delegate selection that reduced the influence of party insiders like Mayor Daley, increased the number and importance of primaries and caucuses, and mandated quotas for blacks, women, and youth representatives in each state's delegation.[52] The new rules had the unintended effect of narrowing the Democratic base to its most passionate ideologues who were no less committed to establishing the intellectual purity of their party than were the conservative Republicans. When the white, middle-class voter tuned in to the Democratic Convention, he or she was to see the face of America in its true diversity, but she didn't see her face in the panorama or hear her concerns articulated.

After 1968, primaries had an increasingly important role in selecting a party's nominee. In 1912, Theodore Roosevelt won all of the Republican primaries contested that year, but was denied the party's nomination. In 1968, Hubert Humphrey did not run in a single primary, but secured his party's nomination on the first convention ballot. In 1964, seventeen states conducted primaries, by 1976, the total was up to thirty-one.[53] Even then, primaries did not always provide for a direct choice between the candidates. "Favorite Son" candidates were sometimes used to allow the state party apparatus to control the delegate selection process. In other states like New York, voters chose between rival delegate blocks that needed not to be identified with any particular candidate. In the 1976 New York Democratic primary, party regulars lined up behind an "uncommitted" slate that was backing Hubert Humphrey against the insurgent campaign of Jimmy Carter. When the Onondaga County party regulars picked their slate, they included among the familiar names of prominent local officials the name of Syracuse University basketball coach Roy Danforth, who had just taken the Orangemen to the NCAA final four. The strategy of capitalizing on the popularity of the college basketball program backfired, however, when Danforth accepted a position at Tulane before the primary was held. When Danforth's successor, Jim Boeheim, was asked for whom he was campaigning, he astutely named Roosevelt Bouie, a seven foot center he was recruiting to play at Syracuse.[54]

The increased prominence of primaries have lengthened the election process and increased the cost of running for office. The party nominating process is now contested on the public airways, not in the private back rooms of the party elite. Candidates are required to identify with the voters well in advance of the early contests. The next round of the election process begins within two years of the last election, and with the interruption of the midterm Congressional elections, a sitting president has less than a year and a half to enact his or her legislative agenda before the distraction of political electioneering renders additional achievements unlikely. Cable media feeds on partisan discord and political speculation to bolster ratings, and the electoral process has come to supersede the governing process in the demands of public office.

The old arrangement where coalitions within the Democratic and Republican parties and the Dixiecrat block would align with one another over particular issues has been replaced by two ideologically polarized parties. In 1964–65, 80% of the Republicans in the House and Senate voted for the Civil Rights and Voting Rights Acts. Thirteen Republican Senators voted for Medicare and Medicaid with seventeen opposed and two not voting, and seventy of the one hundred forty Republican House members voted for the legislation.[55] Congressmen George H. W. Bush and Donald Rumsfeld cast two of those Republican no votes.

In 2010, a health care bill not too dissimilar from one supported by Richard Nixon in 1970 and one passed by Massachusetts Governor Mitt Romney in the 1990s passed Congress without a single Republican vote. Only three Republicans in the Senate voted for the 2009 stimulus bill that most liberal and conservative economists credited with preventing a much deeper recession. The collapse of the broad tent that formerly accommodated a diverse assembly from the electorate has resulted in a disputatious and largely dysfunctional Congress.

Consensus politics thrived during the complacent fifties, but proved unsustainable during the turbulent sixties. The civil rights struggle tipped the balancing act staged by the national Democratic Party and its Dixiecrat partner. Later efforts to lower barriers to full integration of society alienated segments of the working class base from its traditional champion, the Democratic Party. Enactment of Great Society legislation expanded the role of the federal government beyond the boundaries negotiated during the New Deal, and awakened conservative resistance to the renewed liberal offensive. Consensus on foreign policy was a casualty of the Vietnam War.

Foreign policy consensus was, in part, a legacy of the Second World War. The country was unified by the Japanese attack on Pearl Harbor and its Nazi enemy was the embodiment of evil. When the war ended it was not difficult to cast Soviet dictator Joseph Stalin in the same mold as Adolph Hitler and restage the same morality play. The enemy being confronted was evil and the American cause was righteous. With this belief deeply ingrained in the national conscience, it was easy to demonize voices on the left and forge a broad agreement on the policy of containment. As the Vietnam War dragged on beyond the patience of the American public, limits to the policy of containment and the veracity of its domino corollary came in for scrutiny. Congress, like the country, divided into hawks and doves and argued over who was to blame for the situation in Vietnam.

United States foreign policy suffered from bipolar disorder. The two-dimensional model for understanding a multi-dimensional world led to policy blunders that the simplified equations could not predict. Regional conflicts and popular uprisings were all viewed through a bipolar lens. Foreign aid was dispensed as a reward for compliant behavior as much as for the urgency of the need, and military aid to questionable governments consumed a greater share of the total aid package. Support for despotic rulers like the Shah of Iran and destabilization of the democratically elected government of Chile to allow imposition of a harsh military dictatorship stained the reputation of the United States in the eyes of the developing world. America lost much of the luster that had surrounded it after World War II. My Lai rather than Omaha Beach came to symbolize the American effort to reshape the world in its own image.

As late as the 1980s Ronald Reagan was still referring to the Soviet Union as the "Evil Empire," but that did not stop Reagan and his predecessors from forging deals with it that recognized each side's sphere of influence. Stalin's successors, while no less totalitarian, were regarded as less demonic and "Peaceful Coexistence" under Kennedy and Khrushchev became "Detente" under Kissinger and Brezhnev. The Vietnam War era ended with Nixon dining in Beijing with Zhou En Lai, the man his mentor, John Foster Dulles, snubbed twenty years earlier.

One thing that got lost in the storm blowing in from the Pacific was trust in the government. The federal effort to end the depression, provide social security, and win the war, followed by a post-war period of prosperity, had created a positive impression of government. It was not seen as intrusive by most people, even though the top tax rate was as high as 90%. This impression was undermined by inflated claims of success in Vietnam and the inability to quiet disturbances in the cities and on the campuses. The Pentagon Papers revealed a pattern of government lies and disinformation about our involvement in Vietnam dating as far back as the Truman administration. Revelations of malfeasance during the Watergate scandal further diminished public perception of the government. The bill for guns and butter charged to the Johnson and Nixon administrations came due during Carter's tenure in the form of double-digit inflation. When Ronald Reagan pronounced that "government was not the solution; it was the problem," he had a ready audience of believers.

When the storm ended, it was time to write an obituary for the Great Society. Its supporters and critics cherry picked statistics from the low-hanging branches to buttress claims about the success or failure of the program. Like with most political debate, the numbers were offered as singular exhibits of evidence with little effort made to account for other factors that may also have affected the measurements. The Great Society legislation was enacted in a time of divisive and costly conflict, during a period when a large cohort of the population was at an age when it was entering college and the job market and into the age group most responsible for violent crime. It was a time when the old social order changed too fast for some and not fast enough for others; a time when more opportunities for women were opening outside of the traditional nursing and teaching fields, and it was a time when automation and globalization were already changing the American workplace.

Conservative critics like the columnist Thomas Sowell blamed the Welfare State for creating a climate destructive to the African-American family by subsidizing unwed pregnancies and fostering a culture of dependency, but didn't consider that social patterns within the white society were also changing, leading to a decline in multi-generational living, increased divorce rates, and more single parent families.[56] An increase in the murder rate during the 1960's was attributed by conservative writers to permissive liberal attitudes toward criminals without acknowledging that violent crime tends to correlate best with the number of teenagers and young adults in the population.

Johnson's aide, Joseph Califano, countered the conservative critique by noting that Johnson wanted to change the "outmoded" welfare program first enacted in the thirties, by creating "a work incentive program, [providing] incentives for earning, day care for children, child and maternal health, and family planning services," but Republicans and Democrats in Congress did not approve these changes. Califano noted that the percentage of Americans living in poverty dropped from 22.2 percent in 1963, when Johnson became president, to 12.6 percent in 1970. The decline in the percentage of blacks living in poverty was even more dramatic, falling from 55 percent in 1960 to 27 percent in 1968. Califano credited programs like Medicare and Medicaid for a reduction in the infant mortality rate and an increase in life expectancy, but failed to take into consideration the effect that improvements in medical technology and health delivery that had occurred during the same period of time may have also contributed to these statistics.[57]

Much of the criticism of the War on Poverty was directed at the Office of Economic Opportunity (OEO), which housed the controversial Community Action Program (CAP). CAP became a focal point of conservative criticism following the 1967 riots.[58] It was accused of fostering class struggle and held responsible for fomenting some of the violence. After the riots the program was targeted for cuts amid claims it rewarded criminal behavior. Conservatives, who railed against government infringement upon personal liberty, were equally vocal in condemning this effort aimed at empowering the poor.

CAP was no more popular with some big city mayors like Richard Daley of Chicago, who did not want to cede any control over development plans within their city or miss any opportunity to channel federal dollars into patronage appointments. Daley flaunted the OEO dictum of "maximum feasible participation" of the affected poor by loading the Chicago Committee on Urban Opportunity (CCUO) with Daley machine loyalists. Of the ninety CCUO board members only seven were residents of poor neighborhoods. As a token gesture at demonstrating compliance with maximum feasible participation, the Daley machine created a panel of one thousand salaried community representatives who were selected by the ward bosses. Daley dismissed criticism of the selection process with the comment "What's wrong with a Democratic committeeman sending a capable man or woman when the test is on the person's qualifications and not who sends him?"[59] Other mayors were as concerned as Daley that real participation of the poor in determining the allocation of federal funds would undermine their authority in the city and empower voices of activist opponents within the poorer neighborhoods. In June, 1965, the U. S. Conference of Mayors formed a new War on Poverty Committee to address their concerns about enactment of OEO programs and named Daley to be its chairman. After the riots of 1967 increased the opposition to CAP, Chicago machine representative Roman Sierpinski was able to shepherd through Congress an amendment to the Economic Act of 1967 that reinterpreted the maximum feasible participation clause of the earlier act along the lines of Daley's Chicago Concept.

In 1974 the Office of Economic Opportunity was disbanded by Richard Nixon, and its programs placed inside of HUD. HUD Secretary

George Romney, when addressing community participation mandated by the Model Cities program, stated bluntly that "it will be up to the mayors how they spread the money." In Chicago, that meant it mostly went to sweetheart contracts for Daley cronies, and "administrative expenditures" in the form of patronage.[60]

Neither Reuther's Detroit nor Daley's Chicago had adequate community participation in formulating their Model Cities proposals. Whereas Daley was unaccommodating to any program that compromised the mayor's authority in his Chicago, Reuther sought to provide training to equip community representatives with the skills needed to make a meaningful contribution to the development plans. The Reuther position smacks of paternalism, but the only chance that community participation could overcome resistance from local power brokers was having representatives able to work effectively within the establishment. The advent of the Black Power movement, spreading urban unrest, and opposition from local officials did not afford time for the UAW to nurture the community representatives able to provide its conception of this "third leg of the stool." With the emasculation of CAP, Reuther's vision of national planning, in which representatives from management, labor, government, and affected citizen groups jointly formulated economic and social policy objectives, would not be realized. Rather than a coordinated statist approach, the Great Society was a patchwork of programs with separate appeal to various interest groups.[61] The poverty war focused primarily on the problems of urban blacks, and did not create a constituency among marginalized whites. When it came under attack, there were too few soldiers to sustain an advance.

The ascendancy of the liberal era in American politics was bracketed by two turbulent decades. In the 1930's the depression and dust bowl created legions of unemployed and dislocated workers who were angry at a system that had exploited their labor and impoverished them. Conditions in the factories led them to sit down and rebel. The workers were encouraged by a sympathetic government and supported by a range of left-leaning social activists who supported their strikes and helped organize their unions. The movement led to a coalition that defined the politics of the next thirty years.

By contrast, the movements of the sixties occurred during one of the most affluent decades in American history. Social, rather than economic, issues were central to the ferment. The civil rights struggle in the early years of the decade drew wide support from the greater population, but once the legal struggle was won and the battle for social and economic advancement moved into the neighborhoods and schools of the North, support steadily waned. Black militants seized the spotlight from the heirs of Martin Luther King and frightened away many once sympathetic whites and moderate blacks. The movements at the end of the decade were viewed by many in the middle class as the product of privileged youth and affluent suburbanites who were immune to the consequences of the actions they advocated. It was not their kids who were being bused to achieve school integration and drafted to fight in Vietnam. The youth revolt showed its disdain for middle class values in its behavior, language, and dress. The movements of the sixties became so engrossed by the virtue of their own causes that they made no effort to open a dialogue with those deemed less enlightened. Bob Dylan put those sentiments to verse when he warned fathers and mothers not to "criticize what you can't understand" and to "get out of the new [road] if you can't lend a hand."[62] Though much of middle America had grown disillusioned with the war and was predisposed to right historic wrongs against African-Americans, they had little affinity for the people espousing these causes. When Nixon gave them an identity as the silent majority, they were ready to see liberals as part of the other, and it became fashionable for Republicans to use liberal as a term of disparagement.

Ronald Reagan proclaimed "Morning in America" when he entered the White House. The storm clouds were parted, and the stereo tuned to George Harrison's, *Here Comes the Sun*. The public was all too ready to believe the extended forecast of sunny skies and fair weather. The solar panels on the White House were torn down; the thermostat was turned up; the sweater was discarded; and only the good news was proclaimed. Family values were extolled. Greed was good, government programs bad, and the media liberally biased. Liberals were deemed to have pointy-heads, be out of touch, and were afflicted with bleeding hearts. When the progressive era ended the evil it was alleged to have caused lived after it, the accomplishments, interred with its memory.

CHAPTER XIII

The End of an Era

> The sequel of today unsolders all
> The goodliest fellowship of famous knights
> Whereof this world holds record. Such a sleep
> They sleep—the men I loved. I think that we
> Shall never more, at any future time,
> Delight our souls with talk of knightly deeds,
> Walking about the gardens and the halls
> Of Camelot, as in the days that were.
>
> From Idylls of the King
> Alfred Lord Tennyson

Before the last American troops had left Vietnam, the world stage rotated a quarter turn, and the drama switched to a new theater. On October 6, 1973, Egypt and Syria launched an attack on Israel during its observance of Yom Kippur. The surprise assault met with initial success. Israel suffered heavy losses in territory and equipment during the first days of the conflict leaving it more vulnerable than it had been during any previous Arab-Israeli war since its founding. Within days the United States initiated an airlift to resupply Israel, while the Soviet Union rushed military equipment to its Arab clients. As tensions between the two Cold War adversaries rose, the Arab oil exporters countered America's support of Israel by initiating an embargo. The people who had been colonized, marginalized, and denigrated by Western nations for over one half century were asserting their new importance in an energy dependent world. The oil embargo was the first act in a drama that would supersede the Cold War in the years ahead.

The oil crisis of 1973 had its origins some years earlier. By the seventies American demand for oil had exceeded the capacity of its domestic production. The U. S. economy had grown increasingly dependent upon foreign commodity suppliers from less stable regions of the globe. In 1971 Richard Nixon ended the Breton-Woods monetary arrangement that pegged the dollar to the price of gold, and allowed the dollar to float. The depreciated dollar effectively reduced the income of the oil producers, whose product was priced in the U. S. currency. To regain lost purchasing power and reduce the ability of the big oil companies to dictate the price of crude, they formed the Organization of Petroleum Exporting Countries (OPEC) cartel. The Yom Kippur War provided the cartel the opportunity to leverage their new unity to exercise greater control over their product and the price they would receive for it.

Israel soon regained the initiative in the conflict, and, with both superpower patrons eager to avoid the possibility of further escalation, the war came to a quick end. The embargo lasted six months longer, driving up the cost of gasoline and causing long lines at the pump. The oil shock accelerated the inflation in the United States that had been rising steadily since the mid sixties. President Nixon reacted to the economic crisis by instituting price controls on oil from previously developed wells while allowing oil from newly explored sites to sell at the higher market price.[1] The move had the predictable effect of giving the oil companies the incentive to hold back delivery of the old oil until the price controls were lifted, causing a further shrinkage of supply.

Nixon's attempt to halt inflation with price controls had little success. His successor Gerald Ford's attempt to cajole inflationary expectation out of the public mindset with his WIN (Whip Inflation Now) button provided fodder for the late-night talk show hosts but little practical ammunition for combating the problem. When a second interruption of oil supplies occurred in 1979 due to the Iranian Revolution, inflation soared above 10% a year.

The Iranian Revolution changed the dynamic of the global ideological battle from a secular struggle between Communism and Capitalism to a confrontation between religious fundamentalism and liberal humanism. Before the revolution, political grievances in the Middle East were expressed through secular groups like the Communist Tudeh party in Iran, the Baathists in Iraq and Syria, and the PLO of Yasser Arafat. The rise of the Ayatollah Khomeini and his Islamic Republic inspired others in the region to voice their aspirations in the guise of religion. Hamas and Hezbollah became a religiously based counterforce to PLO inclinations toward moderation. The Chechen independence movement was appropriated by religious extremists, and the fight against the Soviet invasion of Afghanistan became the radicalizing experience for Islamic youth throughout the region.

The downfall of the Shah and the rise of the Ayatollah was an unanticipated setback for American foreign policy. Part of Nixon's Vietnamization strategy was to establish strong local leaders throughout the Middle East and South Asia who would be able to withstand Communist pressure without the need for direct American involvement. The Shah, awash in oil revenue, was the ideal client, eager to purchase U. S. military hardware and able to pay for it. The new regime resented the United States for its role in establishing and maintaining the reign of the Shah, and was deeply antagonistic toward Israel. When the United States admitted the deposed ruler for medical treatment, the Iranians demanded his return, and seized the U. S. embassy and held its occupants hostage when the demand was refused.

Skyrocketing inflation and the inability to end the Iranian hostage crisis doomed Jimmy Carter's presidency. Ronald Reagan secured the Republican nomination with primary victories over the establishment insider George H. W. Bush, then selected Bush as his running mate, despite Bush's characterization of his supply-side agenda as 'voodoo economics'. Reagan was the darling of conservatives, but neither major party candidate generated much enthusiasm in the general electorate. *Newsweek* magazine captured the public mood during the campaign with a cartoon showing an open voting booth listing the two choices for president above the caption "abandon hope all ye who enter here."[2] During the campaign there was a flirtation in the electorate with third party candidate John Anderson that was more serious than his final vote total indicated. In the debates, the affable Reagan was able to brush aside charges of extremism from a dour Carter and emerge victorious. The electoral verdict was more a rejection of the "malaise" that surrounded the Carter presidency than an affirmation of the economic prescription offered by Reagan, but with the election of Reagan the transition from the Great Society of Johnson to its conservative opposition was completed.

Ronald Reagan had a very simple prescription for the malaise of stagflation and the perceived impotence to counteract the new challenge to American supremacy: cut taxes, reduce regulations, and appeal to American exceptionalism. At the end of Reagan's tenure in office, the prescription seemed to have worked. The economy was growing. Inflation was cured. The malaise had dissipated in the warmth of a new "Morning in America." Neither the Democratic opposition nor the "liberal" media bothered to seriously question whether the country benefited from the prescribed treatment, or whether it had been slipped a placebo and recovered through the workings of its own immune system. The medicine prescribed had a pleasant taste and a narcotic effect that induced in the electorate an addiction for continuing doses of the same cure. Reagan left the presidency eight years later far more popular than when he arrived.

Supply Side Economics

The centerpiece of the Reagan economic program was the Kemp-Roth tax plan that sought to lower personal income taxes in three installments of 10% each and to accelerate the time period for corporations to depreciate their plant, machinery, and vehicle assets to ten, five, and three years respectively. Jack Kemp, the old Buffalo Bills quarterback, became the offensive coordinator of the Reagan team's domestic agenda. Prior to the primaries, Kemp had made a deal with Reagan that he would not compete with him for the conservative vote if he were given a prominent role in the formulation of economic policy in a Reagan administration.[3] Kemp introduced Reagan to economist Arthur Laffer and author Jude Wanniski, the two principal advocates of supply-side economics. Their assertion that a significant reduction in the marginal rates for the top income groups would spur enough economic growth to offset the perceived loss in revenue to the treasury resonated with the candidate. Reagan remembered from his Hollywood career during the war years, when the top rate was 90% on all income over $200,000, actors would limit themselves to four films a year. After reaching the $200,000 threshold, there was little incentive for additional work.[4] He heard what he wanted to believe. The anecdotal experience from his past crystallized his support for the concept whose finer details remained clouded in the arcane jargon of economists.

Supply-side economics was not the product of mainstream conservative economists such as Milton Friedman and Robert Lucas, but was the prescription of a group of policy entrepreneurs whose platform was the editorial page of the Wall Street Journal.[5] Supply-siders discounted the importance of monetary policy in regulating the business cycle and preached that the only proper role for government was to promote business growth by reducing regulation and encouraging investment through reduced taxes on capital gains, corporations, and the well-to-do.[6] They cherished a *Field of Dreams* faith that if you build it, they will come. Tax savings would be invested in capital projects. Demand would follow an increase in industrial capacity much the way the heroes from the memories of Kevin Costner's father came from the other side of the cornfield to play for the love of the game in the field his son built for them. The benefits offered the rich would "trickle down" to the middle class and the poor in the form of greater economic opportunity, and the larger economy would more than compensate the public coffers for the nominal loss of revenue due to the tax cut.

Kemp was the leader of a group of committed true believers in the House. After recruiting Reagan to the supply-side ideology, Kemp pushed for the appointment of his young congressional colleague David Stockman as Budget Director in the new administration. Only Stockman in the Reagan inner circle was a committed supply-sider who understood the budgetary implications of the economic program they were advocating. The youthful-looking, bespectacled wunderkind was the public face of the administration's economic agenda, and his role was magnified by the unorthodox approach to budgeting used by the administration to advance its economic priorities. Instead of projecting expenses and determining the revenue needed to cover those expenses, the Reagan team started with a tax cut of 30% over three years and a growth of the military budget by 7% in real terms over the amount proposed by the outgoing Carter administration and then determined the size of the non-defense portion of the budget that could be sustained by these requirements. In a climate of decreasing inflation, a savings of $100 billion per year would have been needed to have been wrung from social welfare and non-discretionary spending in order to bring the budget into balance.[7] Stockman became the grinch that threatened to steal Christmas as he toured the halls of Congress with his flip charts and briefing books looking for ways to justify the loss of tax revenue with deep cuts in spending.

There was sufficient appetite in Congress for passing most of the Reagan tax cuts and increasing the defense spending, but very little for making drastic cuts in popular domestic programs. Within the administration worry about the deficit was tempered by unrealistic expectations about revenue projections promised from the "Laffer curve" and a propensity to vastly overestimate the amount of fraud and waste that could be painlessly trimmed from the budget. With Defense, Social Security, Medicare, and debt repayment off limits, there was very little room for making any substantive cuts. Even powerful conservatives who favored trimming social spending had their own government programs they held inviolable. Jesse Helms prevented any cuts in tobacco subsidies. Howard Baker insisted upon funding for the Clinch River Breeder Reactor. Orin Hatch vigorously defended the Job Corps facility in Utah. The Southern Democrats resisted attempts to eliminate farm subsidies and fought to preserve the oil depletion allowance.[8] The only constituency without a politically important advocacy in Congress was the poor.

Congress passed Kemp-Roth in July of 1981 with only slight modification. The first cut, reduced to 5%, was scheduled to take effect on October 1 of the same year. Additional cuts of 10% were to follow in each of the next two years. The top rate was reduced from 70% to 50%, and the lowest rate was cut by 3% to 11%.[9] The accelerated business depreciation schedule was also voted into law. With the tax cut legislation passed, Congress acquiesced to the substantial increase in defense spending and passed the budget, making only modest cuts in the least protected social programs. The deficit in 1982 increased by $50 billion dollars over the previous year and nearly doubled again in 1983, reaching a value of $212 billion.[10] Reagan was forced to modify his original tax plan several times to find additional revenue to slow the growth of the deficit. The 1986 Tax Act reduced the top rate to 28%, but closed loopholes and prevented millionaires from sheltering all of their income from the tax collector.[11] In 1991, when George H. W. Bush was confronted by an increasing deficit, he was forced to break his campaign pledge of "Read my lips. No new taxes!" The top rate was raised to 31%, and Bush was fatally compromised in his reelection bid. By the end of the Reagan-Bush years the deficit stubbornly hovered around $200 billion per year, and the national debt had quadrupled to over $4 trillion.[12]

While the budget was working its way through the Congress in 1981, Federal Reserve Chairman Paul Volcker was raising interest rates to tighten the money supply and wring inflation out of the economy. Volcker had been appointed to his post in 1979 by Jimmy Carter, and began during the latter months of his administration to aggressively combat double-digit inflation by tightening the rate at which the Federal Reserve lends to its member banks. By June of 1981, the prime rate peaked at 21% and a steep recession was induced. Once the inflation rate began falling below 5%, Volcker reversed his policy and began pumping liquidity back into the economy.[13] The recession was very steep with unemployment peaking at over 10%,[14] but short-lived, and by 1983 a sharp, sustained recovery was in progress. Since Volcker's monetary policy and Reagan's fiscal policy were independently applied to the economy in parallel, credit for the economic expansion that followed was subject to partisan interpretation.

Besides encouraging investment by cutting the top rate for the well-off, the supply-siders sought to encourage production by reducing regulations on industry. Deregulation began in the Carter years with the relaxation of restrictions placed on interstate commerce during the depression days.[15] During the 1930s, many rural Plains and Western communities were served by a single railroad line, leaving them vulnerable to price manipulation on shipment of their produce by an effective monopoly. By the 1970s the interstate highway system and regional airports provided sufficient competitive alternatives to negate the need for the earlier regulations. The Reagan supply-siders turned their deregulating zeal on the Environmental Protection Agency, the Occupational Safety and Health Administration, and the Consumer Product Safety Commission: three offices established by the Nixon administration.[16] Whenever they were unable to gut the environmental and safety statutes, they achieved a similar end through indifferent enforcement and reduced funding for the regulators.

The zeal for deregulation reversed more than a half century of government enforcement of standards of conduct in the economy it was charged with promoting. That capitalist economy is a contest that rewards talent and hard work, but can be capricious and favor pedigree, connections, and circumstance or penalize the lack of such. The Great Society sought to improve the game for everyone by leveling the playing field. Legal, structural, and cultural barriers that inhibited women, racial minorities, the disabled, and the disadvantaged from achieving their full potential were attacked with legislation, regulation, and palliative programs. The Reaganites were antipathetic to government intervention in the economy, and thought the game was better played by taking the whistle away from the referee. The shirts and skins competing on the Big Board were left to call their own fouls where the prize for which they were competing was not prestige on the playground but billions on Wall Street.

The most serious consequences of ill conceived deregulation occurred in the financial industry. During the high inflation of the 1970s, Savings and Loan Institutions were squeezed by the need to pay higher interest to attract investment than they were receiving on their older mortgages. Instead of allowing the Federal Reserve to shut down insolvent S & Ls, the Reagan administration loosened the regulations on the types of investments they were permitted to make and the capital requirements to which they were forced to adhere.[17] Since deposits were insured by the Federal Savings and Loan Insurance Corporation (FSLIC), unscrupulous bankers were freed by deregulation to gamble with depositors' money on high-risk-high-reward bets. When many of these bets failed, it was the taxpayers, not the bankers, left holding the bill. The Savings and Loan crisis began during the Reagan administration and was hidden for a time by creative accounting gimmicks, but it was the succeeding

Bush administration that inherited the mess. Twenty years later a similar scenario was repeated on a global scale with the commercial banks.

Myth and Reality

The growth of the economy during the Reagan-Bush era did not meet the expectations of the supply-siders. The average annual growth of the GDP during twelve years of the two administrations (1982–1993) was 3.025%. This is about the same as the 2.933% average growth from the period from 1973–1981, and less than the 3.65% average growth during the Clinton years.[18] There were three years of high growth from 1983–1985 as the economy recovered from recession, but, buffeted by the Savings and Loan crisis, the economy slipped back into recession during the Bush years.

Since recessions and recoveries are cyclical and distort economic performance over the short term, a more appropriate way of judging that performance over a period of time is to look at the average potential growth during that time period. Potential growth averages out fluctuations in the business cycle by estimating how much the economy would grow each year if unemployment remained constant from the previous year. Growth in potential output was 2.3% per year in the decade from 1979–1990. During the previous decade growth in potential output was a slightly more robust 2.8% per year.[19]

Other measures of economic performance dispel the notion that the Reagan years were marked by exceptional economic gain. The supply-side dogma dictated that lower taxes would spur investment, but private investment during the years from 1980 -1992 was only 17.4% of GDP, compared with 18.6% during the 1970s.[20] Private savings was 9.1% of disposable income in 1980, but fell to 5.1% in 1987.[21] The overall national savings rate, both public and private. fell from 7.7% in the 1970s to an average of just 3% in the years from 1988–1990.[22] Capital spending by all levels of government continued its decline from 3% of GDP in the 50s to 1% during the Reagan-Bush years.[23] The disappointing numbers are not necessarily entirely attributable to Reagan era economic policies. Other long term economic trends such as a two decade long decline in productivity gains and the lasting effects of previous economic policy may have influenced economic performance as much as administration policy, but the numbers do not give conservatives evidence for validating the success of their policy.

If the tax savings did not go into additional investment, where did it go? One obvious answer is into the pockets of the corporate elite. From the mid-seventies to 1990, CEO pay more than tripled. In 1992 the average Fortune 500 CEO was making over $3 million per year. Salaries and benefits paid to CEOs increased from an average of 30 times the average annual salary of their employees in 1980 to over 130 times the average salary of their employees in 1991.[24] By 1987 the corporate elite had increased their slice of corporate profits to 61%, up from the 22% share that went for executive compensation in the 1950s.[25] Had the corporate chiefs believed in supply-side theory, as their political counterparts, they would have reinvested these profits and benefited from the growth of their enterprise more than from the increased "taxes" they extracted from its coffers. The continued disparity of executive compensation in 2010 is highlighted by the pay package of $87.1 million awarded to Gregory B. Maffei, CEO of Liberty Media, which was about $3 million more than the payroll of the Atlanta Braves baseball team that his company owns.[26]

Reagan era policies exacerbated the trend toward income disparity that began after 1973. During the boom years from 1947–1973, all quintiles of the population, from the lowest 20% to the highest, saw their income rise at about the same 2.5% annually.[27] After 1973, and particularly during the 1980s, income growth was progressively higher for the highest income groups than for the middle group, and the lower two quintiles actually saw their income decline. Much of the growth in the high income group came from the top 1% of the population. The very rich saw their income double over the 12-year period from 1977–1990. This translates into a 6% annual growth in income over the period when the average income growth for the population at large was less than 1% annually.[28] The average weekly earnings for non-supervisory workers reached a peak in constant dollars in 1973 that it has not achieved since.[29]

During the twenty year period between 1973 and 1993, productivity, which had been growing at the rate of 3% annually throughout the boom years, declined to a 1% yearly growth rate.[30] The most consistent explanation for the decline is that the country was changing from a manufacturing based to a service based economy, and the technology for increasing the productivity of workers in the service sector was not yet ripe. The 1970s and 80s saw the birth of the microprocessor, the personal computer, the local area network, and the Internet, but these technologies did not fundamentally change the paper flow model of the workspace until the mid-nineties.

The Decline of the House of Labor

The decline in manufacturing brought about a similar decline in membership and influence of the CIO unions that had been catalysts for the New Deal and Great Society and vehicles with which workers drove their way into the middle class. After Reuther's death, the UAW was led until 1986 by his two lieutenants: Leonard Woodcock and later Douglas Fraser. The pair shared Reuther's commitment to the social, economic, and environmental causes that he had championed for the previous four decades, but lacked his stature and his stage. The UAW now spoke with the diminished voice of an aging institution. There were no new Treaties of Detroit to negotiate. The union now presided over the slippage of gains previously won in order to salvage the jobs of its members.

The first oil shock generated a demand for fuel efficient Japanese automobiles to which Detroit was slow to respond. Reagan's "morning in America" reaffirmed the industry's commitment to chrome, size, and horsepower, but it became increasingly unable to compete with the imports on quality and price. Chrysler was the most vulnerable of the Big Three automakers, and the first to require a bailout from the Federal Government in 1979. Lee Iacocca, the father of the Mustang at Ford and the man that asked the nation's school children to contribute their pennies and dimes to keep the Statue of Liberty from rusting away in New York harbor, had recently assumed the leadership of Chrysler. He had inherited a company on the verge of bankruptcy that had already shed about one quarter of its workforce. His reputation and promotional skills were enough to secure a $1.5 billion loan guarantee over the objection of critics that included GM chairman Thomas Murphy. Murphy called the bailout "a basic challenge to the philosophy of America," prompting UAW chief Douglas Fraser to call Murphy a "horse's ass."[31] Murphy may have tempered his remarks somewhat had he a crystal ball to glance into the future of his own company. Chrysler survived to beg another day, but the domestic industry was at an increasing disadvantage against its foreign competition.

Had Reuther not died in the plane crash in 1970, it is doubtful he would have made a difference in the influence of his union or the lives of its members. Walter Reuther was 62 years old at the time of his death. His political rivals were occupying the seats of power. His generation was being ushered into the pages of history by generations born to different circumstances. In many respects he was like Housman's *Athlete Dying Young*, taken at the peak of his triumph and not fated to grow old and watch his skills erode and his edifice crumble. Victor Reuther, however, survived the organizing wars at Flint, an assassination attempt, and an altimeter failure to live to an age of 92 and witness the dismantling of many of the gains that the union had won during its heyday. In the mid 80s, Victor sided with the Canadian Autoworkers (CAW) when they split from their US counterpart because of the concessions that the UAW was giving to the companies. Victor became an outspoken critic of the UAW leadership and never acquiesced to the givebacks they felt necessary to sustain the industry.[32]

In January 2010, the union placed the Black Lake Education Center up for sale. The Center was the vision of Walter Reuther and Swedish architect Oskar Stonorov. It was to be a place where workers could come and increase their horizons or just experience the tranquility of the landscape. It was to be the setting for the first global environmental conference, and it was the destination to which the Reuthers and Stonorov were heading on the night of the fateful crash. It is the final resting place for the ashes of Walter and May Reuther amidst a memorial grove of trees collected from around the world. In August 2010, Black Lake won a reprieve when the new UAW board pulled the property off the market.

With the decline in influence of the old industrial unions, conservative and business interests marshaled their resources to minimize union activity in the emerging technology and service sectors. In 1981 the air traffic controllers union, PATCO, struck for higher wages, shorter hours, and a recognition that the extremely stressful nature of their work should allow them to retire after 20 years of service. In one of the defining moments of his presidency, Ronald Reagan ordered the strikers to return to work within 48 hours or face termination. When they refused, he fired them. Much to PATCO's dismay, the air transport system was able to withstand the absence of the striking controllers by reducing volume and using non-striking controllers and military controllers until an enlarged group of new applicants completed training. Reagan's action emboldened management and had a numbing effect upon all union activity.

While labor's influence in national affairs declined, business voices grew louder and clearer. Business leaders led by Thomas Murphy of GM, Reginald Jones of GE, Irving Shapiro of DuPont, and William Writson of Citibank formed the Business Roundtable in the early 70s.[33] The group was instrumental in defeating a consumer protection agency advocated by Ralph Nader and the common site picketing bill endorsed by organized labor.[34] The Business Roundtable also exerted its influence in securing a reduction in the capital gains tax despite a lack of support for the measure from the Carter administration.

Court decisions in 1974 and 1975 made it legal for government contractors to have political action committees (PACs). According to Fred Werthheimer, President of Common Cause "[this decision] opened the door for the creation of PACs and institutionalized the role of PAC money to buy influence."[35] The number of PACs grew from 608 in 1974 to 4,157 by mid 1987, and their contributions to political campaigns grew by a multiple of fifteen between the congressional races of 1974 and 1986. In 1974 total spending on the House and Senate races was $72 million with only $8.5 million of that total contributed by PACs. By 1986, total spending on congressional races increased to $450 million dollars with over 1/4 of that total coming from PACs.[36]

Corporate lobbyist flocked to Washington, and the number of corporations opening a Washington office increased tenfold over the period from 1968–1986. By 1992, corporations formed two-thirds of the PACs and contributed 79% of all PAC money.[37] Most of that money favored Republican candidates, but Democratic candidates who toned down their liberal rhetoric and voted for legislation favored by the corporations also received some of this largess.

As Congressional seats became more expensive to "buy" and PAC money more instrumental in securing them, a new breed of legislator arrived in Washington. This new breed was telegenic, adept at using the media, and either independently wealthy or dependent on funds contributed directly to the candidate, not funneled through the political party. The new breed was characterized by political staffer and later reporter Chris Matthews as "having no imprint of their districts." "They are people who have gone away to college and may have settled in localities other than the one in which they grew up." Matthews went on to claim:

> "The old-breed guys [like Tip O'Neill and Dan Rostenkowski] are very hierarchical. They keep their friendships. They keep their alliances. They dance with the girl they came with. The new-breed guys play one night stands. They're always forming new coalitions. They are always worrying about their image and how to position themselves. They decide what image they want to project, and they position themselves to project that image."[38]

Chuck Schumer, then a young Representative from New York, explained the lack of party discipline in Congress with the metaphor of an ideal gas.

> "Congress has become atomistic. In the House we are 435 little atoms bouncing off each other, colliding and influencing each other but not in a very coherent way. There used to be much more structure. But now there is no bonding that holds the atoms together."[39]

In the new Congress, seniority could be skirted by skillful manipulation of the media, and party loyalty was not essential for securing the necessary funds to finance a campaign.

The three-legged stool, so central to the Reutherite concept of participatory democracy, had become a one-pronged crutch, supporting the full weight of the republic. Labor was diminished. Community participation was unsolicited and actively discouraged. Only the voice of business was amplified through the political sound system with sufficient decibels to resound within the halls of Congress. As the balance tilted in one direction, wealth slid toward the heavy end. Reuther never achieved his goal of national planning where capital, labor, and consumers would work together to outline common objectives. This represented too great a whiff of socialism for even liberals to endorse, but the government during the boom period between 1947 and 1973 was responsive to pressures from all three groups. Union money and union political organization was able to compete for seats and influence in Congress on similar terms with its corporate counterpart. Both groups required support from the general population to move their agendas. Muckrakers from Upton Sinclair and Rachel Carson to Ralph Nader had been able to rally support for health, environmental, and safety regulation. As a single leg of the stool began to grow like Pinocchio's nose, the government became less responsive to the needs of the worker and the poor.

Much of the business of business during the 1980s involved companies shedding their declining domestic manufacturing components to reposition themselves in the new service and technology economy. The 1980s was the decade of mergers and acquisitions. Financial deregulation and the maturation of computerized transaction processing allowed the big commercial banks on Wall Street to grow rich selling off the accumulated wealth of industrial America. Huge fortunes were made overnight by young traders creatively marketing new financial products of dubious value to underwrite the sale of formerly great American companies. The money being made in the boardroom and on the Street attracted many of the brightest students away from careers in science, engineering, or education and into business and finance. The motto for the go-go 80s was coined by the fictional Gordon Gecko: "Greed is good." Ivan Boesky and Michael Milken were two of the real-life lions of Wall Street who became fabulously rich profiting from inside information like the Michael Douglas character in *Wall Street*.

The United States entered the 80s clinging to a trade surplus and ended the decade with the world's largest balance of payments deficit. The profits made on Wall Street came indirectly at the expense of the steelworkers in places like Bethlehem, Pennsylvania, and the autoworkers in Detroit. In the 1962, *Look Magazine* named Bethlehem's nearby neighbor Allentown, Pennsylvania one of its All American Cities.[40] Allentown was home to the Hess Brothers Department Store, the epitome of a regional marketing giant that attracted shoppers from a three state area and sponsored parades and community activities for the city residents. Allentown symbolized the growth of a middle class American Dream. In 1981, Billy Joel questioned the durability of that dream in his song *Allentown.*

> We're living here in Allentown
> And they're closing all the factories down
> Out in Bethlehem they're killing time
> Filling out forms
> Standing in line

The middle-aged factory workers were trapped: not having the education to compete for the good new economy jobs, and disadvantaged by age and family obligations to be able to return to school to get the credentials needed to try to compete with younger, more-valued graduates. Cities like Allentown and Detroit never recaptured their previous promise. During the 70s and 80s Hess's went through the corporate dance of expansion, acquisition, merger, consolidation, and finally closure. In 1996, the Allentown store closed its doors for good. The Hess building was demolished in 2000 to make room for an office complex.

On a hill above the old steel plant in Bethlehem stands Lehigh University. Lehigh was known throughout the East as an engineering school whose graduates populated the workplaces of the Lehigh Valley and well beyond. Its sports teams were nicknamed the Engineers reflecting the University's primary distinction. Today it has gone out of its way to divorce itself from its previous identification. Its teams are now known as the Mountain Hawks, and it lists its College of Engineering and Applied Science last after the colleges of Arts and Science, Business and Economics, and Education in its on-line catalog. Enrollment in science and engineering curricula across the country is well down from the post-Sputnik peak of the 1960s.[41] Only the most elite programs like MIT and Cal Tech can afford to identify themselves in the recruitment wars for the post-baby boom student population as primarily colleges of engineering and science. Without an influx of foreign students to provide the necessary enrollment in graduate science and engineering programs, it would become difficult to maintain the viability of these programs at many American universities. If and when these students realize comparable educational experiences and employment opportunities in their home lands, the quality and preeminence of American science and technology will be seriously jeopardized.

Union membership declined from 33% of the workforce at the time of the AFL-CIO merger in 1955 to 12.1% in 1990s, but the declining bargaining power of the workforce was only one factor in the decline in constant dollar wages for non supervisory personnel from its peak in 1973.[42] The supply of labor increased dramatically during the 70s and 80s with baby boomers and women streaming into the labor market. The supply-siders point with pride to the 18 million new jobs created during the 80s, but this was 25% fewer than the 24 million created during the 70s. Unemployment averaged 6.36% during the post-recession years of 1984–1991, remaining stubbornly above the 5% considered normal during the 1960s.[43] The influx of new workers into the labor market created a surplus that kept the cost of labor for lesser skilled positions down.

Women attended university in greater numbers in the 50s and 60s, and these women were no longer content to restrict their horizons to the home or the "women's professions" of teaching and nursing. The diploma, the washer and dryer, the dishwasher, and the microwave, all freed women from their traditional role in the home. During the 70s and 80s, professional women entered the workforce by choice and many others by necessity. For many households, a second income was essential for maintaining the family's former lifestyle. Women entering the workforce in numbers diluted the labor pool, but the new source of talent also boosted the economy.

The emergence of women in the business and professional world created a crisis for the old "women's professions" of teaching and nursing that were no longer assured a monopoly on the services of educated women. With better opportunities open to the most talented women, fewer chose a relatively low paying career in education. The best and the brightest of both sexes concentrated on other fields of study. During the depression, teaching jobs were relatively secure and coveted by extremely able men and women alike. By the 80s, this generation of teachers was retired, and a captive population of career women was no longer available. Just as the economy was requiring a greater level of skilled workers, the American educational system was experiencing stress in maintaining the quality of instruction needed to produce them.

An educational system heavily reliant on property taxes has produced an uneven level of funding that has left many districts with deteriorating buildings, inadequate resources, and uncompetitive salaries for teachers. A Conservative effort to weaken teachers' unions and to privatize the responsibility of educating the nation's youth fails to address either the problem of attracting more talent to the teaching profession or the inadequacies and discrepancies in which the system is funded.[44] A lack of qualified workers to fill the knowledge-based jobs has been muted by immigration, but threatens to put a brake on the forward momentum of the economy. The educational system is just one more component of an infrastructure whose maintenance has been deferred to finance tax cuts and military spending.

When a second income wasn't enough or wasn't available to a struggling family, there was the credit card. Before the mid sixties, credit was largely restricted to an individual retailer, who offered approved customers a delayed payment option on merchandise purchased in the particular store. Buying on time was not done casually during the fifties. Jackie Gleason's character, Ralph Kramden, ridiculed the practice in an episode of *The Honeymooners*. Ralph's wife, Alice, complained to Ralph that their upstairs neighbors, the Nortons, had a new TV, and she wanted one too. She wanted to see Liberace! Ralph retorted that the Nortons bought that TV on lay away. The Nortons were in debt, whereas the Kramdens had $75 in the bank. The Kramdens had financial security![45] The comedy struck a note with a middle class America that had recently survived the depression and the war time scarcity. The public was tempted to consume by the visual advertisements appearing on television, but was cautious, and brought up on the advice of Polonius to, "neither a borrower nor a lender be."

The credit card changed that psychology. The first credit card to appear in the 1950s was the Diners Club card. The card was a metal plate with the customer's information embossed on the surface. When making a payment, the card was laid in the recess of an imprinter with a transaction slip placed on top. The imprinter was moved across the top of the slip producing an inked copy for the restaurant and a carbon copy receipt for the customer. Diners Club was accepted only at participating restaurants. Two other cards, Carte Blanche and American Express, appeared shortly after Diners Club. All three were technically charge cards, not credit cards, since the entire balance was due with each statement. The first card with revolving credit was BankAmericard, issued in Fresno, California in 1958. BankAmericard experienced difficult growing pains and eventually evolved into the Visa system. In 1966 a consortium of California banks created what became the Master Card system.

Once established, the banks vigorously pushed the cards on their customers. Credit worthiness of the card holder became less a concern as banks began charging usurious interest rates on the unpaid balance and hefty penalties for late payment. As memories of the depression faded and a new generation of baby boomers, who knew only prosperity, reached adulthood, the population became less-and-less restrained by the admonishment of Polonius. In the time of declining purchasing power of many working and middle class salaries, the credit card became the means of preserving one's previous lifestyle. The 80s became a decade of burgeoning national and personal debt.

Ironically it was demand, not supply, that drove the economy in the 80s. Investment and savings were below their 70s level. Public and private debt financed the Reagan revolution. Once Volcker had wrung inflation from the economy, he abandoned any pretense of monetarism and began pumping money back into the system.[46] The country recovered rapidly from "Volcker's planned recession", and the pent-up demand for a range of new products spurred a three-year period of strong growth.

When OPEC solidarity crumbled in the wake of the Iran-Iraq War, falling gasoline prices gave Detroit a reprieve, but old habits died hard. Smaller cars meant smaller profit margins, and the automobile industry remained committed to a formula of horsepower, size, and accessories. Despite the falling birth rates and declining family sizes, Detroit ushered in the era of the SUV, and found an enthusiastic market for its product. "Morning in America" was a time of denial—denial that 1973 had marked a turning point in the post-war world, denial that gasoline supply shortages were chronic, denial that climate change was real and placed limits on the growth of the carbon-fueled economy. "Morning in America" was the black-and-white world of dusty old Kansas transformed into Technicolor in the magical land of Oz.

The New Economic Engine

Detroit settled into its "golden years"—its vitality ebbing, its step slowed, its once imposing stature stooped, but still commanding the deference for what it once was and what it still represented. The driver of the new economy was the technology sector centered on the West Coast in the Silicon Valley around the research center of Stanford University and along the route 128 corridor around Boston and MIT. In 1971, Intel, the company responsible for putting the silicon in the Silicon Valley, constructed the first microprocessor—a simple central processing unit on a single silicon chip. By the end of the decade the microprocessor was powering game consoles manufactured by companies with names like Atari and Nintendo and computers by the likes of Commodore, Apple, and Radio Shack. In 1981 IBM entered the home computer market. Despite its own pioneering efforts in the development of the integrated circuit and its long experience in creating operating systems, IBM powered its PC with the Intel 8088 processor and bought its operating system from a fledgling little company named Microsoft before that company actually had a product to sell. With the imprimatur of IBM, the personal computer moved from the realm of the hobbyist to the general public and began to appear in the business office. The PC became a standard platform, attracting software developers with applications that extended the machine's appeal, but IBM was as wedded to the high profit margin, "big iron" mainframe as Detroit was to the gas guzzler. Its decision to outsource the guts of its micro computer made the PC a commodity with multiple manufacturers, and made the suppliers, Intel and Microsoft, the masters of the new technological universe.

The public was enthralled by the array of new products that emerged by the beginning of the 80s. Every kid had to have a game console, and there was always another new game or game box with superior graphics that topped the Christmas and birthday wish list. The VCR became a standard accessory to the family TV set, only to be rendered obsolete by the next wave of technology. By the middle of the decade the personal computer could be used to do word processing, generate spreadsheets, and play video games. By the end of the decade it had become a staple of the middle class home.

As predicted by Moore's Law, the density of integration doubled every eighteen months, and by the end of the decade the desktop machine acquired many of the capabilities of the more expensive minis. The pace of technological change led to rapid emergence and demise of companies and whole industries. Names like Atari, Commodore, Lotus, WordPerfect, and VisiCalc had their hour to step onto the stage and then be heard no more. The pace of change was particularly devastating to the industries scattered around route 128. Massachusetts boomed during much of the 80s, based largely upon the success of the minicomputer, particularly the 32-bit super-mini VAX produced by Digital Equipment Corporation. Digital Equipment (DEC) pioneered interactive computing in the early 60s with the introduction of its PDP-1. Later models of the PDP line, particularly the PDP-11, were the favored platform for computer enthusiasts who used DEC machines to construct the earliest video game, Spacewar!, the first text editor, and the first word processor. DEC was also a pioneer in the field of computer networking, and along with Xerox and Intel promoted the Ethernet local area network (LAN) standard, that has continued to evolve into the dominant local network technology in the office and campus environment today. DEC coupled its networking expertise with its VAX to create the VAXcluster, a strategy allowing companies to incrementally increase their computing capacity with moderately-priced minis and obtain performance comparable to a standalone mainframe. By 1986, DEC was challenging IBM's leadership of the computer industry. But while DEC was attacking IBM's dominance of the high end market, the micro was rapidly becoming competitive with the more expensive minis. In 1977, DEC founder and chairman, Ken Olsen, dismissed the microcomputer with the comment "There is no reason for any individual to have a computer in his home."[47] DEC was slow to enter a market it should have dominated, and only reacted hastily after IBM achieved an early success. DEC negated superior engineering with poor marketing and myopic management and never became a significant force in the microcomputer market.

Much of the rest of the route 128 industry was similarly based on the mini. DEC's primary competition for the mini computer market came from two other Massachusetts based companies, Data General and Wang. Data General was started by three DEC engineers who became frustrated with Olsen's management. The Data General Nova was temporarily a serious competitor with the DEC line until the introduction of the PDP-11 reestablished the older company's dominance. The next Data General challenge to the VAX was celebrated in Tracy Kidder's best seller, The *Soul of the New Machine*, but the MV8000 never threatened the dominance of the VAX. The other large employer in Massachusetts was Wang Computers. Founder An Wang smarted from a slight he felt he received in a patent battle with IBM in the 50s and resolved to supersede the computer giant before the end of the century.[48] Wang started building high-end office calculating machines and later word processors. His word processing machines evolved into more general purpose minis. Wang did achieve some brief success in undercutting IBM in certain of its corporate markets, but could not outpace the technological change that was racing against his own product line.

While route 128 was challenging IBM with a new computing model, Massachusetts thrived. Governor Michael Dukakis trumpeted the "Massachusetts Miracle" and launched his 1988 presidential campaign on his accomplishments as the state's executive officer. Unfortunately for Dukakis, the clock was striking midnight on the miracle just as the general election campaign began. The deteriorating state of the Massachusetts economy, however, drew little attention during the campaign. The Dukakis candidacy was doomed by an ad featuring the menacing face of Willie Horton, a black man sentenced to life without parole, who raped a Maryland woman after using a weekend furlough to escape from a Massachusetts jail.

The Massachusetts Miracle created a housing bubble that collapsed when route 128 began hemorrhaging its workforce. Before the end of the century all three of the minicomputer giants were either bankrupt or subsumed into a competitor. Dukakis was at best a minor actor in the Massachusetts story. Ken Olsen and An Wang were much more responsible for the growth and demise of the region's leading employers. With the collapse of the Massachusetts computing industry, the Silicon Valley became the single pole of the American technological sector. Regional centers exist around university research sites in places like Cambridge, Raleigh-Durham, Austin, and Redmond, Washington, but the Silicon Valley is the nexus of the industry in much the way Detroit was the nexus of the automobile industry. The vulnerability of this industry to new products and new paradigms was vividly demonstrated in Massachusetts. Without a constant infusion of talent, cash, and new ventures, the entire region rests precariously on the continued vitality of its legacy firms.

The Gipper and the Second Bush

The Reagan presidency occurred during an era of transition from a manufacturing based to a service and technology based economy. It was a period when the fruits left over from the effort to win the Second World War were starting to turn and the fruits produced from the effort to win the Cold War and the space race were not quite ripe. Productivity gain during this period was at a post-war low. It was a period of dislocation in the workforce, and a period of narrowing competitive advantage, as the nations of Europe and Asia, recovered from the devastation of the war, had emerged with more modern factories and infrastructure. It was a period of chronic supply and demand imbalances in critical commodities such as petroleum. Supply-side economics, deregulation, or any other prescription for the economy could do little to alter these historical trends, but could only affect their future trajectory. An assessment of the economic performance during the Reagan and Bush years must view that performance in the context of these larger trends.

Economic growth was not exceptional during these years, and was slightly less robust than the pattern observed in the years immediately preceding and following when the fluctuation of the business cycle is factored out.[49] The new wealth was distributed disproportionately to the more affluent members of the population. Growth in income disparity had roots in the changes occurring within the workplace, but it was exacerbated by administration tax and social policy. Increases in payroll taxes for social entitlement programs raised the tax burden slightly for the lower income taxpayer while reductions in the capital gains tax and the highest bracket rate reduced the burden on upper income people. Overall, the average federal tax rate remained at the 19.4% it had been when Reagan entered the White House.[50]

The growth of the deficit can be attributed directly to Reagan economic policies and the failure of the Laffer curve to generate the promised revenue return to the Treasury. The correlation between tax reduction and economic growth has become Republican dogma, but there is little evidence to support it. Conservatives point to George Bush's apostasy in raising taxes in 1991 for derailing the Reagan revolution, but Bush was confronted with a new spike in the deficit caused by the Savings and Loan bailout that was part of the legacy of the Reagan years.[51] Recovery from the recession during the latter half of the Bush administration began *after* the tax increase was enacted. A quick scan of the economic record of the past four administrations reveals that under Reagan and Bush taxes were cut, the deficit quadrupled, and economic growth averaged 3.025% per year; under Clinton the top tax rate was increased to 39%, the deficit was reduced, and the economy grew at an annual 3.65% rate; under George W. Bush the top rate was reduced to its pre-Clinton level, the deficit ballooned, and the economy grew at an anemic 1.625% per year.[52] During the post-war years when the economy was robust and the American Dream was becoming a reality for middle class families, the top tax rate was a confiscatory 88%. There is more to the story of economic performance during these periods of time, but the raw statistics provide no justification for the Republican doctrine of faith.

Reagan benefited from the one essential thing that every successful leader needs: luck. This does not diminish from Reagan's ability to project strength and communicate with the electorate, but he occupied his office during an unusually propitious decade. OPEC's solidarity disintegrated under the pressure of conflicting national interests, and gasoline prices returned to near their pre-1973 levels. Volcker's attack on inflation caused a steep recession at the beginning of his administration, but by his third year in office, the economy experienced a robust recovery and inflation returned to more manageable levels. The Soviet Union suffered through a disastrous Afghan war and was experiencing symptoms of what proved to be a terminal condition of arteriole sclerosis throughout its empire. A new leadership in China was quietly rewriting the Little Red Book of Chairman Mao in the language of the "capitalist roaders" and their "running dogs." The hostage crisis ended during Reagan's inauguration, and the revolutionary regime in Iran and Saddam's brutal dictatorship in Iraq were soon engaged in a long bloody stalemate that distracted any challenge they would pose to American interests for the duration of his presidency. Even the most unfortunate event of his presidency—the assassination attempt—had a silver lining. He survived and received an outpouring of sympathy and admiration that extended the traditional honeymoon period for the new president. Reagan's aide, Richard Darman, emphasized the importance of the reaction to the assassination attempt in the passage of the administration's legislative priorities.

> "That whole episode was crucially important. I think we would have been way out of the normal presidential honeymoon at the time of the crucial votes on the budget and tax cuts if there hadn't been a 'second life.' The shooting and Reagan's recovery was not only a second life for Reagan but a second life for Reagan's honeymoon. Sheer chance—and extraordinarily important. In fact, I think we would have had to compromise on the tax bill without it."[53]

Most of the international events that surrounded the Reagan presidency were not attributable to any influence of his. He was fortunate that a third and fourth generation of leadership had come to power in the Soviet Union during his tenure in office, and this leadership was committed to confronting the stagnation of the Soviet economy by allowing a new level of openness. The Soviet economy needed closer cooperation from the countries of Western Europe, and the restless satellites of Eastern Europe provided little benefit to Mother Russia. Reagan's military buildup may have had some influence on Gorbachev's decision to quiet the arms race and seek an arms limitation treaty with the Americans, but his decision in 1989 to renounce the Brezhnev Doctrine and let the countries of Eastern Europe determine their own destinies followed a progression of internal events emanating from the policy of glasnost and perestroika.[54] Reagan, Bush, and the world were fortunate that an empire built over centuries by the Tsars and Commissars disintegrated almost overnight without a violent explosion. Reagan and Bush were the last custodians of the policy of containment formulated by George Keenan and others during the Truman administration. Overzealous prosecution of the policy sometimes led to disastrous decisions like Vietnam and support for regional dictators like Augusto Pinochet and the Shah of Iran, but containment created a cocoon about the Soviet state that allowed it time to morph into a more responsible adult.

David Stockman claimed that Reagan conceptualized things in terms of anecdotes.[55] His stories were sometimes apocryphal like the one about a Chicago welfare queen collecting checks totaling $150,000 under a variety of names, but they confirmed the reality of the world view he had formed. In this regard Reagan was not unlike the electorate that had elevated him to office. Their conception of his presidency was rooted in a set of images pasted in the album of collective memory. There was the angry Reagan rebuffing the editor of the Nashua Telegraph with the words "I'm paying for this microphone, Mr. Green," when he attempted to shut off Reagan's microphone during a debate in New Hampshire. Then came a smiling Reagan passing off the assassination attempt by telling his wife "Honey, I forgot to duck." An unflinching Reagan carried through with his threat to fire striking air traffic controllers when they failed to return to work, and, as leader of the western alliance, he stood before the Berlin Wall and called upon his Soviet counterpart "Mr. Gorbachev, tear down this wall." Gorbachev did not tear down the wall. The citizens of Berlin did that on a November night in 1989 after George Bush had succeeded Reagan in office, but Reagan is popularly pictured as winning the Cold War.

Reagan charm, Reagan fortitude, and Reagan luck combined to produce a nostalgic era of American history. In many respects the legend is bigger than the man. Some things got better, some things got worse during Reagan's tenure, but the looming challenges posed by automation, globalization, and climate change just got kicked down the road. Reagan's aide, David Stockman, extracts the man from the mythical aura that surrounds him with the following assessment:

> "[Ronald Reagan] was a consensus politician, not an ideologue. He had no business trying to make a revolution because it wasn't in his bones. He leaned to the right, there was no doubt about that. Yet his conservative vision was only a vision. He had a sense of ultimate values and a feel for long-term directions, but he had no blueprint for radical governance."[56]

Reagan railed against big government and "tax and spend" liberals, but when he left office, the size of the government was bigger than when he arrived, the average federal tax rate was virtually unchanged, and the deficit had more than tripled.[57]

George W. Bush had a presidency with similarities to Reagan's—A tax cut aimed primarily at the high earners, did not produce the promised economic growth, but exploded the deficit. Deregulation of the banking industry, begun under Clinton, led to questionable lending practices and a financial crisis requiring a huge government bailout. The trade deficit widened; infrastructure investment was deferred; and energy and climate change issues were ignored. Both leaders were aloof from the details of governance.—But the second George Bush lacked Reagan's rapport with his audience. The anecdotes were different. The photos pasted into the collective memory were not always flattering. The picture of the defiant young president donning a hard hat and promising retribution to the cleanup workers at ground zero, was followed by an image of the commander-in-chief landing in a fighter jet on board an aircraft carrier beneath the banner "Mission Accomplished." It was not. Ten years after, both the mission, and how to accomplish it are as uncertain as the thoughts that were racing through the mind of the young president on September 11, 2001, as he was sitting in the third grade classroom contemplating how to extract himself from the smaller and the larger moment with which he was confronted. As the pages of the album turn the photos become less-and-less flattering. There is the image of George Bush standing in the hurricane ravaged Gulf Coast with his FEMA director, telling him, "Brownie, you're doing a heck of a job." The other photos on that page tell a different story. They show a major American city suffering from the disorganization of the disaster relief effort—an image that hitherto only appeared in the news coverage of a disaster in a remote third world country. The last page shows the Treasury Secretary emerging from an emergency weekend meeting, warning that the whole financial house of cards was about to collapse unless the tax payers ponied up a trillion dollars. George W. Bush was Reagan Reddux, without the veneer, without the command, and without the luck.

The Reagan Legacy

A lasting legacy of the Reagan era is the low esteem in which much of the public holds its government. During the period between the Second World War and the Vietnam War, the public overwhelmingly regarded their government favorably. It was the government that navigated the country through the depression and the war, and the government that was an ally in creating a framework for a growing middle class. Vietnam, Watergate, and urban riots shattered this "era of good feeling." Politics became more contentious following a period of revolutionary social change and during a period of nascent insecurity in the workplace. Reagan crystallized the growing disillusionment with government when he proclaimed that "government is not a solution, it is the problem." That has become the mantra for every Republican politician and some Democratic politicians ever since.

Conservative politicians demean government and extol private enterprise at every opportunity. It is government that collects information on its citizens and seeks to limit their freedoms, not the private companies like Google and the credit bureaus that collect far more information on far more people, and use that information to steer or limit their economic activity. Government involvement in decisions affecting the health and welfare of its citizens is to be feared more than private determination over which citizens have far less recourse. Government is deemed bloated and inefficient. Since government is scrutinized by the media and by hordes of self-appointed watchdogs, there is no shortage of its foibles to document the claim. Private enterprise receives much less scrutiny, and revelations of private malfeasance and waste only come to light when a major scandal breaks. As a result there is no obligation for the politician to justify the claim of government ineptitude, and little basis to refute it. Government is not suited to compete in the marketplace of consumer products like cell phones, video games, and automobiles. Its role in this market is to ensure fair competition. Much of government is by nature bureaucratic, but it is not clear that government is ill-suited to compete against other bureaucratic institutions like insurance companies in markets such as health care. In fact, health care systems that are either managed by the government or heavily regulated by it in the rest of the developed world have produced outcomes that are as good as or better than ours at substantially lower cost. The health care argument devolves into one of almost religious conviction where doctrine is not to be challenged by evidentiary inquiry.

A window into the comparative capability of well-run public and private endeavors is provided by three of the most significant engineering programs of the 50s and 60s. Two of the programs are government managed: the atomic submarine program of the 50s and the manned moon mission of the 60s. The third project was the IBM 360 program where the company bet heavily on a project that secured its position in the industry for another twenty years. The atomic submarine program was remarkable because it came in on time and under budget.[58] It produced some management tools, like the PERT chart, that have since become industry standards.[59] Its feisty director, Admiral Hyman Rickover, became such a legend with the Congress that he was granted an active duty status for life, to the dismay of some of his colleagues whose funding requests he regularly challenged.

The manned lunar mission and the development of the 360 system were the first large projects where software issues were as critical to the timeline as the hardware. Early in his presidency, John F. Kennedy responded to Soviet space successes by announcing a program to put a man on the moon by the end of the decade. That goal was met in the summer of 1969 when Neil Armstrong took "one great leap for mankind." Unfortunately neither of the Kennedy brothers who launched the effort were around to see it accomplished.

The IBM project came in over a year late and one billion dollars over budget. Software problems that delayed release of the system were detailed in a book entitled *The Mythical Man Month, an Apology to Thomas Watson* by Fred Brooks, the project leader. Despite the overruns, the project was a huge success. Computer programming matured during the course of these two efforts. At the start it was a craft honed by a relatively small group of skilled artisans, by the end of the decade it was becoming a science practiced by software engineers, and part of the curriculum of a growing number of colleges and universities.

The best model for public-private cooperation is the creation of the Internet. After the Soviet launch of Sputnik, President Eisenhower created the Defense Advanced Research Projects Agency (DARPA) to coordinate the Pentagon's research funding. The agency was given an acronym and a big mission but a small budget and little direction. DARPA spent several years trying to define its mission. In 1967 DARPA's director, Larry Roberts, focused on building a distributed packet switched network that would be less vulnerable than the centrally switched AT&T phone network during wartime. The Cambridge, Massachusetts consulting firm of Bolt, Beranek, and Newman was awarded the contract to build the subnet. The original network, known as ARPANET, grew from four sites to over thirty in the first three years, but participation was limited to universities and laboratories with Defense Department contracts.[60]

As ARPANET demonstrated the impact it could have on collaboration between researchers, the National Science Foundation decided to build a backbone network to connect six supercomputer centers. It also funded regional networks that connected universities without Defense Department contracts to the NSFNET backbone. As the network continued to grow, and to be able to accommodate commercial organizations that were prevented by charter from connecting to the NSFNET, the NSF prevailed upon their network operator MERIT, along with MCI, and IBM to form a nonprofit corporation, ANS (Advanced Network Services) to prepare to turn the network over to commercial interests. ANS made substantial upgrades to the NSFNET backbone. The NSF awarded contracts to four telecommunications companies to establish access points to their backbone in San Francisco, Chicago, Washington, and Pennsauken, New Jersey, just over the river from New York City. Any commercial provider that wanted to be part of the backbone had to connect to all four of the access points.[61] This established competition for the business of carrying each packet that entered the backbone. When the government ended its involvement in the project, it had created a competitive, commercially-operated Internet that has become the information highway attracting companies such as Yahoo, Amazon, Google, and Facebook to set up shop along its exit ramps.

From its role in building the canals and railroads of the nineteenth century to the interstate highway system and Internet of the twentieth, government has been a catalyst for promoting growth, not an impediment. Effectively managed government projects have been as efficient as the best run private projects, and have produced seeds from PERT charts to digital computers and integrated circuits that have flowered in the private economy.

The conservative image of America feeds on nostalgia for a mythical past. The American right would have us revere the Constitution but demean the institution that it created. The symbolic reading of the document at the start of the 2011 Congressional session had all the appearance of a strict teacher making an uncooperative pupil write one hundred times on the blackboard "I will not misbehave in class!" A return to an eighteenth or nineteenth century interpretation will not address the problems that the country faces in the twenty-first century. The country does not need less government, but good government; a government capable of providing twenty-first century infrastructure— higher bandwidth, efficient transport, an educated citizenry, and a healthy middle class.

By the end of the era of liberal ascendancy the American landscape had drastically changed. Working families had become part of the middle class and witnessed their sons and daughters become the first in their families to attend college. African Americans had a pathway to first-class citizenship. Women were beginning to crack the glass ceiling. Social Security, Medicare, and company pensions lightened the worries about retirement for the elderly. Childhood labor had been abolished and the forty hour work week was standard. Factories were safer, bank deposits insured, and public health better protected. Food stamps and unemployment insurance were part of the safety net for those less fortunate. The Clean Air and Clean Water Acts began to reverse the effects of decades of industrial pollution. The ability of conservatives to persuade the American public that despite these accomplishments, government was an impediment to their well-being, not an ally in improving their standard of living speaks to the media megaphone at the disposal of the right and the timidity of the left in defending its legacy.

CHAPTER XIV

The Enduring Struggle for Health Care

> We have relied primarily upon the market place to satisfy
> our health needs. But our experience has demonstrated
> clearly that the market place is much more responsive to
> our needs for gadgets and our material requirements than
> it is responsive to satisfying essential human services. I
> share the view that the right to good health is a basic
> human right; that comprehensive, high-quality health
> care must be made available to every citizen as a matter
> of right.
>
> Walter Reuther November 14, 1968

On the night of November 14, 1968, Walter Reuther announced to the
members of the American Public Health Association the formation of the
Committee of 100 for National Health Insurance. He would chair the
committee, and the heart surgeon Michael DeBakey, medical researcher
Mary Lasker, and the civil rights leader Whitney Young would serve as
vice chairpeople.[1] In a characteristic Reuther assemblage, the remainder
of the committee was to be chosen from the ranks of the medical
profession, industry, farm, labor, social services, education, church

groups, civil rights organizations, and consumers—representatives from all segments of the society, but representatives filtering through the sieve of a selection process overseen by Reuther.

Reuther underscored the need for a program of national insurance coverage by citing the deficiencies in the existing approach: 24 million Americans with no health insurance, 35 million with no surgical insurance, 61 million with no hospital coverage, and 108 million with no prescription coverage.[2] Despite the fact that "three quarters of all Americans [had] health insurance of one description or another, two thirds of the cost of personal health in America [was] uninsured."[3] The ramifications of this constrained access to care in the nation with the highest per-capita income were reflected in its world rankings in measures such as male and female life expectancy—21st and 12th respectively, and infant mortality 16th. The nation was spending 6.5 percent of it GNP for health care in 1969 and witnessing hospital costs tripling and doctor's fees more than doubling over the previous two decades.[4]

Reuther's announcement was well-received. The time seemed ripe for a major initiative to enact a national health insurance plan. In the earlier fight to pass Medicare and Medicaid, the AFL-CIO had created the National Council of Senior Citizens to mobilize union retirees in a lobbying effort to counter anticipated actions of the AMA that had thwarted previous attempts to pass meaningful health care reform. The senior campaign quickly expanded to include other retiree groups. The grandmothers and grandfathers relaying stories of their struggles to afford the care they desperately needed as they aged reached a sympathetic public and thwarted efforts by the AMA and other business groups to wage an effective attack on the measure. Even after the passage of Medicare, senior groups provided a constituency for broader reform.

The committee for National Health Insurance (CNHI), as it came to be known as its membership expanded beyond the initial target of 100, was intended to provide focus for the various different plans that were being suggested by reformers and to counter the diversionary measures floated by the entrenched beneficiaries of the status quo. Meaningful reform of the healthcare system would require measures to extend coverage and contain costs. Physician and industry groups adopted the tactic of steering the discussion toward cost containment as the necessary first step in the reorganization of American healthcare, even though none of them were willing to support meaningful steps that would cap doctor's fees, drug company profits, or administrator's salaries. Reuther argued that a national health insurance system was the only way to acquire the economic leverage to make basic changes in the delivery system.[5]

Reuther's announcement came shortly after the 1968 presidential election—some say deliberately timed to avoid making it an issue in the campaign. His old adversary Richard Nixon was soon to occupy the White House, but that did not appear to be a major impediment to achieving significant reform. Shortly after taking office Nixon warned of an imminent health care crisis. His warning reflected the concern of the business community which financed much of the existing system through employer-provided insurance plans. Business was feeling the pinch from the escalating cost of these plans and was no longer willing to march to the beat of the AMA drum.

Nixon has been called by later historians the last president to govern from a liberal framework—a designation neither Nixon nor most liberals would apply at the time. He would be the last president to declare that, "We are all Keynesians now."[6] Political calculations much more than political philosophy dictated Nixon's domestic agenda, and he sensed an opportunity to wrest significant segments of labor from the Democratic base. He continued to fund many of the Great Society programs and even expanded some. The Occupational Safety and Health Administration (OSHA) and the Environmental Protection Agency (EPA) were both established during the Nixon Administration. He would have preferred limiting healthcare reform to cost containment, but would have been willing to sign a broader bill.

One of the first people Reuther approached when he was forming the Committee of 100 was Senator Edward Kennedy. Kennedy later described in an interview how Reuther first approached him in 1969 and delivered a passionate account of the need for comprehensive healthcare reform in America and urged him to take a leading role in this effort.[7] Kennedy told Reuther of his keen interest in healthcare issues, but that he had been focused on serving on the Education sub-Committee and that his friend Claiborne Pell of Rhode Island seemed lined up to chair the Senate Health sub-Committee. A short time after the meeting with Reuther, Pell decided to switch and chair the sub-Committee on Education, where he sponsored the act setting up Pell Grants, enabling students of limited means to attend universities. Pell's switch of preference left the Health sub-Committee chairmanship open for Kennedy.

Kennedy's commitment to this issue deepened after his 12 year old son Teddy lost his leg to bone cancer. Teddy suffered from an aggressive case of the disease that was arrested by a new experimental chemotherapy treatment. During the course of the clinical trial, the treatment methodology was declared a success and the trial discontinued. Parents who had already depleted their savings and mortgaged their house were desperate to find the means to continue the treatment needed to save the life of their child. Kennedy realized how different his situation would be if he didn't have the means and insurance coverage to pay for the special care Teddy required.[8]

Reuther's own commitment to the campaign for universal health care coverage strengthed after a 1948 assassination attempt left him clinging to life and his right arm dangling uselessly at his side. Though his chances of ever regaining use of the arm were deemed very small, he underwent successful surgery to repair nerve connections and began a tedious rehabilitation regimen. During his hospital visits for whirlpool treatments he met and befriended a 28 year old man who had been paralyzed for nine years. One day when he came to visit, the young man was overcome with joy. He told Reuther he had been reborn that morning and asked the nurse to pull back his sheet so he could show Mr. Reuther that he was able to wiggle his big toe. A few days later Reuther stopped by to visit again and the man was crying. When Reuther asked the nurse if the man had suffered a setback in his treatment, she said no; he hasn't any more money; he goes home tomorrow.[9]

At about the same time an article appeared in the *Detroit Free Press* about GM president Charlie Wilson's bull.[10] It seems the bull had developed a back problem that was interfering with his ability to perform the duties expected of him. Wilson spared no expense to make sure the bull got the best care available. General Electric flew out a 140,000 volt x-ray machine on a special chartered flight. When the x-ray machine reached Wilson's farm, the power line was not adequate for operating it, so Wilson had Detroit Edison run a high voltage line out to his property.

After the x-ray pictures were taken, medical specialists from around the country were brought to the farm to provide the bull with the best treatment options.[11] The bull had cost Wilson $16,000 and therefore merited this special attention.

Reuther was appalled that the young man was sentenced to a life of confinement with no hope of "being reborn" again while no expense was spared in caring for the prize bull. The juxtaposition of the two stories became a fixture in every Reuther speech on the subject of health care. Walter Reuther was not a very religious man, but he had a deeply ingrained sense of moral responsibility. He considered the many instances of people like the young, paralyzed man who were denied the care they needed because they lacked the money to pay for it to be morally wrong and a condemnation of the country that permitted it. He would tell his audience:

> "No nation that has an ounce of self-respect or human decency, no nation that can spend four hundred billion dollars for war, can stand idly by and tolerate a continuation of that kind of double standard…"[12]

On February 18, 1971 President Nixon proclaimed that this would be "health year" when the nation would tackle the massive crisis of spiraling costs and over-strained medical resources. The plan he outlined to confront the "massive crisis" amounted to cosmetic surgery on the existing delivery system. The majority of working Americans would be covered through employer-based plans that would require employers to pay 75% of the cost of the coverage. Medicaid would be replaced by a private insurance plan with the government assuming the cost for the very poor and offsetting the amount people making over $3000 per year paid for insurance with a supplement declining in value with salary. People who were self employed or in domestic service would be offered the opportunity to participate in a group plan. Nixon's proposal was estimated to only cost the government an additional $2 billion per year and would leave more than half of the average patient's medical bill uncovered.[13]

On the same day Nixon announced his plan, Senator Kennedy countered with a plan generated primarily by the CNHI. Kennedy proposed universal coverage funded by additional social security taxes. His plan placed no cap on coverage and was to be administered by an appointed presidential board instead of the private insurance companies. The Kennedy plan would cost the government an additional $60 billion per year by assuming much of the cost then born by individuals and businesses. Over 70% of medical costs would be covered under the CNHI-Kennedy plan.[14]

There was a huge difference between the contending proposals. Several other bills were introduced during the legislative debate—some entered specifically by the AMA and insurance industry to create a traffic jam and prevent any meaningful legislation from moving forward, others attempted to bridge the differences between the Nixon and Kennedy plans. It remained until 1974 for the political process to sort out and point toward a possible resolution. By then Kennedy had realized that a single payer, universal coverage plan was unattainable and had moved in the direction of modifying the existing employer-based insurance system. The Kennedy-Mills bill would require all citizens to have insurance coverage largely funded through the Social Security system with employers continuing to pay $3 for each dollar the individual employee paid in additional Social Security tax.[15] The Nixon Administration greatly expanded its initial proposal, but continued to rely on private insurance provided through employer plans with the same 75/25 percent contribution ratio paid by employer and employee. In the Nixon plan, participation was not mandatory. Younger, healthier people and those less affluent who were not covered by company plans would not be required to buy insurance. The Administration proposal had higher deductibles for both medical bills and major illness than the Kennedy-Mills plan.[16]

A major difference between the two parties existed over the role of the federal government in managing the program. Under Kennedy-Mills the system would be managed by the Federal Government, much as the existing Medicare program, with private insurers playing a lesser role. The Nixon Administration insisted on private insurers managing the system. Both plans were estimated to cost all parties about $40 billion per year.[17]

Kennedy's retreat from universal coverage was not followed by most of the other participants in the CNHI. They were still adhering to a plan funded from general tax revenues that would cover all Americans for all illnesses, and would cost about $80 billion per year.[18] In the same NBC news broadcast that reported the differences between the Nixon and Kennedy-Mills proposals, Leonard Woodcock, Reuther's successor as UAW president, was pictured insisting on universal coverage. Woodcock cited polling data showing that the American public believed health care was a right that he contended could only be achieved through a system of universal coverage, He was quoted saying, "compromises that throw away universality are unacceptable and we prefer to see nothing come out of this Congress than that kind of compromise."[19]

Despite Woodcock's stance, expectations were high that a compromise would be reached and a bill would be passed by that Congress. The positions between Nixon and Kennedy had narrowed, and the question seemed to be not whether a healthcare bill would pass, but what form the final measure would take. By 1975 those expectations were dashed. Watergate sapped the life out of the Nixon presidency and buried the legislative process under its weight. The political maneuvering needed to squeeze an acceptable compromise through a legislative process designed to protect traditional practice from sudden whims and big departures frayed the liberal coalition around its edges until the critical mass needed to secure a deal was no longer present.

Meaningful health care reform may have suffered its most damaging loss in May of 1970 when Walter Reuther died. The skills that distinguished Reuther over his long career as a labor leader and public advocate were critical for shepherding a meaningful reform package through each of the phases of the legislative process. He was an idea man whose fingerprints were all over the initial proposal. He was an organizer who put together the "coalition of conscience" to support the efforts of the Civil Rights Movement to pass the Civil Rights and Voting Rights Acts. He was a tough bargainer who knew the parameters of the best deal that could be reached and had the stature to enforce the discipline from within his ranks needed to achieve it.

In announcing the formation of the CHNI, Reuther indicated members would be drawn from across a broad spectrum of American life, but when it was described in the media, its position was only identified as that of labor. Either in fact or impression the CNHI never achieved the broader appeal required for it to become an effective advocacy group. Reuther's biggest battles were always marked with a catchy slogan and an effective use of the media. In his absence, this one featured neither.

Reuther made the same point in his address to the Public Health Association in 1969 as Woodcock made on the news snippet five years later: that "the right to good health is a basic human right, [and] that comprehensive, high quality health care must be made available to every citizen as a matter of right."[20] In the same speech he also said that the purpose was not to borrow a health care system from any other country but

> "to create a system of national health insurance that will be uniquely American and that will harmonize and make compatible the best features of the present system with maximum freedom of choice within the economic framework and social structures of a national health insurance system."[21]

In reality, accommodating the economic structures supporting the existing health insurance system in a model providing comprehensive universal coverage is as uniquely American as the complexity of its tax code. It requires contortions that leave the body politic stiff and in pain and not eager to repeat the same exercise anytime soon. The plan coming out of the CNHI may have had some American relatives, but it spoke with a heavy European accent.

It would have required all of Reuther's skill and stamina to build an effective public campaign in support of universal coverage, and then to hold that coalition together during the negotiations and compromises that would follow. In his absence the CNHI lacked the vision and vitality it seemed to promise when first introduced.

After the "health year" stretched farther into Nixon's term in office and ended with his presidency, the forces pushing for national health insurance legislation would wait for the next Democratic president, who they felt would see the goal to its completion. That president was expected to be a sympathetic Hubert Humphrey. But at the beginning of America's third century politics was not that predictable. The insurgency against the old party regulars begun in 1972 produced a relatively unknown governor from the New South who promised a return to a common touch from the imperial trappings of the previous Nixon administration. Jimmy Carter ran as an outsider coming to Washington to clean up a system grown remote from its roots and corrupted by the company it kept. When he entered the White House, he had to deal with this system as an outsider.

Health care was not part of Carter's original agenda. Pushed to respond to the sentiment within his party, he offered a rather tepid piecemeal approach that focused on cost containment rather than extending coverage. His first major piece of health care legislation was the Hospital Cost Containment Act of 1977. In his message to Congress he proposed to contain the growth of hospital costs by limiting the rate of increase in reimbursements to hospitals from all sources—Medicare, Medicaid, private insurers, and individuals—to a yearly amount set by a formula. With run-away inflation picking the pockets of Americans in the late 1970's and medical costs outpacing the rest of the field, Carter was fixated on controlling costs.[22] In the same message he wrote "I am determined, for example, to phase in a workable program of national health insurance. But with current inflation, the cost of any national health insurance program the Administration and the Congress will develop will double in just five years."[23]

Carter's step-by-step approach in health care policy infuriated Ted Kennedy. Kennedy continued to push a plan similar to Kennedy-Mills that addressed cost and coverage in the same measure. Relations between the two men became testy, and Kennedy decided to challenge Carter for the party's nomination in 1980. The internecine battle insured no health care legislation would pass until it was settled. Kennedy faced long odds trying to unseat a sitting president and he was fatally compromised by Chappaquiddick. Carter won the nomination and the subsequent battle at the national convention over the health care plank in the party platform. But Ronald Reagan won the White House and the health care debate was muted for the next twelve years.

The Earlier Efforts to Provide Healthcare Coverage

The issue of health care coverage dates to the beginning of the twentieth century. In those early years, loss of wages due to illness was a bigger concern than the cost of medical care. The average life expectancy was much shorter, and the lifestyle of the people much more active. Illnesses associated with age and excessive weight like heart disease, diabetes, cancer, and dementia that consume a large share of health cost today were less common and less treatable when they occurred. Infectious diseases accounted for a much higher percentage of deaths, but were not chronic illnesses that required extensive treatment after recovery.

Call for a social safety net "for the protection of home life against the hazards of sickness, irregular employment, and old age through the adoption of a system of social insurance adapted to American use," appeared in the 1912 platform of Teddy Roosevelt's Progressive Party. The old "Bull Moose" was asking the country to borrow the system of social protection recently provided in Germany and other European countries and adapt it for use in America.[24] The platform also called for women's suffrage, limits on campaign contributions, fixing of occupational health and safety standards, and standards of compensation to families of workers killed or injured in industrial accidents. The Progressive Party provided a last hurrah for Teddy and a preview of issues that would fuel political debate for much of the rest of the century.

The platform plank calling for social insurance was left purposely vague for a political campaign. Details of a health care policy were provided by the American Association for Labor Legislation (AALL) three years later. The details of the proposal, borrowed liberally from German and English models, are less relevant today than the way in which it was presented. The AALL was comprised of academics who drew up their recommendations without any input from the workers their plan was to benefit.[25] They suffered from the delusion that with their expertise they could convince Congress with logic, absent pressure from an aroused public.

This doomed any chance of success they had. The 1912 election revealed a sizable potential reservoir of supporters. Roosevelt finished second with 27 percent of the popular vote and the Socialist candidate Eugene Debs received another 6 percent of the total. It was a time when women were marching for the vote and labor was raising its voice in the sweatshops and the mines. Instead of tapping into this source, the AALL saw their constituency as the medical profession—the group that proved to be the most resistant to any change that might affect their income or independence.[26]

The group's failure to involve labor in drawing up its proposal cost it a chance of picking up an important source of support. AFL chief Samuel Gompers denounced the AALL for ignoring labor's opinion and told his members to oppose the plan he considered an example of elitist paternalism.[27] Gompers committed labor instead to a for members only policy of negotiated benefit packages.

The same pattern has come to define the health care push each time the issue is addressed. The CNHI tapped into the leadership of the various interest groups, but did little to involve their membership. Many of the high profile members of the group lent their names to the effort, but did little other than endorse the recommendations developed by the paid staff. The public that Leonard Woodcock claimed supported comprehensive, universal health care as a fundamental right was uninvolved in the fight to obtain it.[28]

Two decades later President Clinton followed the AALL script like an actor unfamiliar with the history of his role. He designated his wife, Hillary, and aide, Ira Magaziner, to produce a finished product layered with the complexity needed to fit the existing health care infrastructure into a new package for delivery. The presumed beneficiaries had little involvement with the planning. Neither did the Congress that was asked to approve it. The measure did not satisfy many liberals holding out for universal coverage, nor did it win the favor of the American Medical Association (AMA).[29] There was no constituency bombarding Congress with demands to pass "Clintoncare," but there was the medical and insurance lobby pouring campaign contributions and advertising cash into the effort to defeat it.[30] The general public had only the vaguest idea of what was in the health care bill other than what Harry and Louise told them on the TV commercials run by the insurance companies. The effort died in committee.

The one constant underlying the health care debate from the early efforts of the AALL to the Clinton years has been the opposition of the

AMA to any change in the medical delivery model that might affect the way in which doctors structured and were compensated for their practice. Successor organizations to the AALL in the twenties and thirties proposed a model of group practice and private individual insurance similar to the HMO of today. The AMA lobbied against the idea, labeling it socialism, and pressured doctors not to participate.[31]

Walter Reuther told the audience of his November, 1969 speech how the UAW negotiated its first health benefit from General Motors in 1940. The workers were responsible for the entire contribution; the company only agreed to a payroll deduction to reduce administrative costs. To provide affordable care, the union signed a contract with Blue Cross when such contracts were still rare. In the city of Flint, the epitome of a company town, eighty percent of the GM workers signed up for the Blue Cross plan, but the union was able to get only one doctor to participate in the program. After two weeks that doctor asked out. He and his wife were being ostracized socially, and he was threatened with the loss of his hospital privileges. The union then went to the Genesee County medical society and flexed its economic muscle to overcome their resistance. Years later, the head of the doctor's group who had called the plan socialism testified before members of President Truman's Committee on the Health Needs of the Nation and called Blue Cross and Blue Shield wonderful.[32]

The experience described by Reuther was not isolated. Through the depression years the AMA attempted to prohibit its members from working for the nascent HMOs. This restraint of the free exercise of trade was deemed a violation of the Sherman Anti-Trust Act and led to a conviction upheld by the United States Supreme Court in 1943.[33]

Running afoul of the antitrust law did not inhibit the group's lobbying efforts or diminish its clout on Capitol Hill. During the Great Depression there were hunger marches and people in the streets calling for relief and justice. The victims of the calamity were focused on trying to regain something of what they once had and have some security from loss of a job and the poverty of old age. New health benefits were a less immediate concern. The Roosevelt administration's approach to health care reform was tentative and done almost surreptitiously, as if the AMA were looking over its shoulders. In the absence of significant public support for health care reform, Roosevelt avoided a confrontation with the doctors' organization and left health care out of his New Deal agenda.[34]

The first real attempt to provide universal, comprehensive health care came during the Truman Administration. Truman scored an improbable come-from-behind victory over Thomas Dewey in 1948 by promising the working man a *Fair Deal*. By 1948 fears of renewed depression had receded and a landscape of abundance stretched out before the nation that was bathing in its recent triumph and hearing the jingle of new coins in its pocket. Truman's ambitious domestic agenda included universal health care, aid to education, slum clearance, the repeal of Taft-Hartley, and extension of the Fair Employment Practices Commission. But the narrowness of his victory margin betrayed the scope of his vision.

In some respects the time was right for a major health care initiative. Labor was now a well-established force in American life with an ability to mobilize support from a membership numbered in the millions. Advances in health care were beginning to more effectively treat costly illnesses like cancer, heart disease, and stroke which were becoming more prevalent as the average life span increased. The family doctor practicing in the spare rooms of his home and making after-hours house calls was heading toward obsolescence, and the medical industry at the heart of the current system was not yet entrenched. Medical care was becoming more expensive as the promise of its benefits became more-and-more desirable to have.

Despite these favorable circumstances, universal health care may not have been attainable at a time the House Un-American Activities Committee conducted its witch hunts for Communists festering in the fabric of society. Anything deemed socialist was immediately suspicious enough to cause potential supporters to shy away. Defeat was inevitable when the opponents not only got to prepare the battlefield, but also waged a more effective campaign. The coalition of labor and liberal policy experts never deployed the forces at their disposal.[35] Labor leaders discouraged rank-and-file participation and never considered a mass mobilization of supporters. The medical professionals, academics, and public interest groups supporting the legislation lacked the funds to organize an outpouring of public support independently.[36]

The AMA was not hesitant about augmenting their million dollar advertizing campaign with letters to patients from their own doctor and visits to congressmen from their personal physician.[37] In 1950 the outbreak of the Korean War shifted budgetary priorities from domestic programs to defense and fanned the epidemic spreading from the virus carried by Joe McCarthy and his counterparts in the House. Many of the Congressional supporters of comprehensive health care targeted by the AMA in the midterm elections, were defeated. The opportunity for enacting comprehensive health care reform was missed.

After the Truman years, the next attempt to expand health care coverage came during the Kennedy-Johnson effort to pass Medicare. The architects of the Truman proposal recognized the futility of passing a comprehensive bill as a single legislative act and settled on a strategy of expanding medical coverage by a series of piecemeal measures.[38] They took into account opponents' objections to providing benefits to people able to provide for themselves and ducked the formidable opposition of the AMA lobby in crafting a limited plan to provide help with only hospital costs to the elderly.[39] Statistics showed that people sixty-five and older were more likely to be poor, had twice the average medical expense of those in other age groups, and were either uninsured or covered by policies that covered less than a tenth of a typical hospital bill.[40] An eldercare program funded through the Social Security system mitigated most of the objections raised against comprehensive coverage and garnered support not only from the elderly beneficiaries but also younger family members who would bear much of the brunt of a catastrophic illness to an aged relative. The original Kennedy initiative was presented as the King-Anderson bill to the 1961 legislative session. It covered only part of the hospital costs and none of the doctors' fees.

The first hurdle faced by the bill was the House Ways and Means Committee. Before a bill could be released to the full House for debate, it had to be approved by this influential committee chaired by Wilbur Mills. The committee assignment carried a great deal of prestige and was typically reserved for the more senior members of the House— preponderantly Southern Democrats and rural Congressmen who represented districts with uncontested elections. [41]

Despite the 65% favorable polling numbers from the public at-large, Mills and the other Southern Democrats on the Committee joined with the Republicans to keep the bill bottled up in committee for the next three years. The AMA responded to Kennedy's proposal by launching *Operation Coffee Cup*. Doctor's wives were instructed to organize social gatherings among their friends and relay the organization's objections to the Kennedy proposal. The AMA produced an LP with Ronald Reagan voicing concerns about what he called socialized medicine that the wives would bring to these gatherings and play for the guests before putting the same concerns in their own words and encouraging their friends to write their Congressmen. This time the cry of Socialist wolf did not generate the same sense of alarm that it had a decade earlier. Senior participation in the lobbying effort to support the measure drowned out the sour notes coming from the Great Communicator.[42] After the 1964 election, the AMA recognized that this was a fight it was not going to win.

When the 1965 legislative session convened, it was clear that a Medicare bill would be approved. The King-Anderson bill rose to the top of the legislative agenda, but it was accompanied by two other alternative measures. The Republicans, smarting from their electoral thrashing, did not want to appear an intransigent opponent to health care for the elderly and proposed an alternative that would cover doctor fees in addition to hospital costs, but would make the plan voluntary with a senior's share of the premium scaled to his or her social security benefits.[43] The AMA backed a third plan that would provide federal support for the states to institute insurance coverage for people meeting a state-determined eligibility criteria.[44] Mills realized that the full House would force a bill out of committee if he did not act and abruptly changed from an impediment of the legislation to the champion of a much broader bill than the one originally proposed by Kennedy. Mills suggested to representatives of Health Education and Welfare (HEW) that the three bills be combined with the coverage proposed in the Republican Byrnes bill retained but the funding method made consistent with the Democratic King-Anderson approach. Mills did his homework on the budgetary ramifications of the new bill and made a persuasive presentation to the full House to approve almost intact the measure that came out of his committee. The King-Anderson and Byrnes bills became Medicare parts A and B and the AMA bill became known as Medicaid. Mills skillfully steered a more expansive program through the legislative minefield, but with the intention of putting a fence around future attempts to expand the program.[45]

Employer Provided Coverage

Failing to achieve universal, comprehensive health insurance during the Truman years, labor concentrated on winning health coverage at the bargaining table. Employer provided health insurance plans became the backbone of the American medical delivery system. In the early fifties the cost of medical care was not yet inflated by the availability of expensive medications and the proliferation of sophisticated diagnostic tools. Company plans locked employees into their place of employment to retain their health insurance. Employers found that providing insurance plans was cheaper than the cost of higher turnover of its workforce or the cumulative cost of more generous wage increases.[46] Employers, but not employees, were able to write off their contributions as tax deductions.

Employer-based health insurance plans left a large segment of the population uncovered—forced to buy an individual insurance policy or go without medical insurance entirely. There was also a disparity between the cost to the individual employee and the amount of coverage the various corporate plans offered. The system of relying on employment circumstances to provide access to health care was neither universal nor fair. If two friends raised in the same environment went to work for two different employers—one for a company like General Electric that provided generous benefits at little cost to the individual, the other for a local small business that could not afford a benefits package at all, the second individual either had to pay for her own coverage or go without, but she also contributed toward her friend's coverage at GE every time she purchased a light bulb or toaster oven. Higher salaried employees generally worked in situations that provided premium coverage at little individual cost. Lower wage earners were more likely to have inferior plans for which they paid more out of their own pocket or have no plans at all.

Once employer-based health insurance was broadly established, the urgency for political action on health care was greatly diminished. A majority of the population had insurance coverage with which they were satisfied. The health care debate shifted from universal need to individual worry about losing elements of the coverage already afforded. The health industry lobby has been skilled at exploiting that worry.

In the fifties, when employer-based insurance became established, employment mobility was fairly low and medical costs were relatively modest. People, particularly those in manufacturing and production tended to stay their whole working life with one company. People changing jobs were usually attracted by better pay and a better benefits package. The employer-based insurance model revealed its limitations when these conditions changed.

The period of rapid technological change that has accelerated ever since the fifties has benefited the health-related fields as much or more than any other. The family doctor making house calls at the end of World War 2 had little in his bag besides his stethoscope. Penicillin and aspirin were the best weapons available for fighting disease. There were no drugs for lowering blood pressure and cholesterol, no effective drugs for treating most cancers, and nothing to prevent pregnancy or treat erectile dysfunction. The hospital in which doctors operated had few diagnostic tools other than the x-ray and the only surgical implement was the scalpel.

The advances in medicine over the past sixty years have radically changed the service the medical profession provides. Treatment options are now available that did not exist in the fifties. Diseases that were inevitably fatal are now treated with improved success rates. The stethoscope has been augmented by an array of diagnostic tools; the scalpel, ignored for the arthroscope in most procedures. The improvements in the level of care have come with a rapidly escalating cost for the service.

As medical technology improved and attracted a larger percentage of the nation's GDP, the industries supporting the delivery of medicine—pharmaceutical, insurance, and equipment supply—grew and matured around it. In 1950 the *Fortune Five Hundred* list was dominated at the top by companies producing automobiles, steel, oil, and chemicals. Today, many of those same rungs on the list are occupied by finance, pharmaceuticals, insurance, and technology. Medicine has become a cash cow for which there are many willing hands ready to milk. In 1969 the latest available figures cited by Reuther showed that health care consumed 6.5% of the country's GDP and its costs were rising at more than double the rate of inflation.[47] In 2005 the World Health Organization listed the total health expenditures by the United States to be 15.2% of GDP.[48]

The growing influence of the Drug Companies is readily observed by tracing the evolution of television commercials over the years. Dispensing advertising money is like casting bait into a pond where the fish are likely to be hungry and plentiful. The changing display of products and messages from one decade to the next reveals cultural and economic trends running through society. Certain ads are effective and linger in memory because of a catchy jingle or memorable character, but the relative frequency of ads for a particular kind of product, the time slots that are targeted, and the image an industry portrays are markers on the trail of where the money has been and where it is headed.

Breakfast cereals, beer, and soft drinks have maintained a relatively constant presence on the TV screen since it became a household fixture in the fifties. All three of the products contribute to the increase in obesity and diabetes that threatens the health care system with insolvency. Sugar coated cereals first appeared in the fifties and were heavily advertised by appealing cartoon characters on programs aimed at young children. Tony the Tiger and Captain Crunch have gradually ascended the time slots to maintain the relationship they established with these kids as they grow and have families of their own.

In the fifties tobacco companies used the new medium to portray their product as sexy and part of the life style of the rugged outdoors man. The Marlboro Man rode into our living rooms, appeared on billboards, and later showed up on anti-smoking ads, dying from lung cancer. Tobacco's message did not always end with the commercial. Mike Wallace pointedly puffed away on his Parliament during his entire *Mike Wallace Interview* with Walter Reuther, despite Reuther's aversion to the smoke.[49] In the sixties, before tobacco advertising was banned on TV, Big Tobacco endorsed the Women's Liberation Movement by marketing a new cigarette, *Virginia Slims*, with the message "You've come a long way baby."

Household appliances were prominent television advertisers in the fifties. The move to the suburbs was accompanied by the acquisition of labor saving appliances. Betty Furness showed off the technology advances of the day with big self-defrosting refrigerator-freezers from Westinghouse. The lonely Maytag repairman made us believe that his despair would be our source of happiness with the product he never had to service. He was last reported on his way over to China with the rest of the Maytag factory.

Autos and oil remain a fixture of TV advertising. General Motors has told us that America is "hot dogs, baseball, apple pie, and Chevrolet." More recently we have been persuaded to buy a car because it is the product of German engineering and Italian styling. Big Oil used to try to differentiate its product. We watched a chorus line of gas station attendants sing the song that "You can trust your car to the man who wears the star: the big red Texaco star." A rival jingle told us that "Atlantic keeps your car on the go." Esso, before changing its name domestically and later merging with Mobil, told us to put a tiger in our tank and showed the real thing springing to life under the hood of the car on the screen. Today, mergers and acquisitions have reduced the competition. The commercials no longer sell a product, but an image. The message Big Oil conveys is that their drilling is environmentally sound, and that they are reducing the nation's dependence on foreign oil. When they make a boo boo, like polluting the shoreline of the Gulf with black, sticky goo, we are shown sandy beaches and happy bathers and made to believe that everything's the same as if it had never happened.

By the seventies, the microprocessor entered our daily lives. Companies like Atari, ColecoVision, Commodore, and Compaq flashed across the TV screen and quickly faded away. The poor old commodore slunk off into retirement carrying a portable the size and weight of the average suitcase. What started as toys and clunky old curiosities went through generations of development faster than fruit flies. The personal computer became the Westinghouse refrigerator and the Maytag washer of the nineties—the appliance every household needed to have. IBM and Apple offered competing platforms. The casual Mac portrayed himself as the cool alternative to the buttoned-down PC until the devices shrank and the advertising dollar chased the sexiest cell phone with the most killer apps.

Within the last two decades the financial muscle of the insurance, banking, and pharmaceutical companies has elbowed its message onto the no longer small screen. The effervescent Flo competes with a cute little gecko and a fun-loving pig for auto and home insurance dollars. The companies compete over price, but are silent about comparing their service records. The banks keep feeding our appetite for credit and the pharmaceutical companies promise relief from our ills in a bottle. Over the counter remedies have been hawked on television for years, but lately prescription medications are touted just as frequently. The consumer can't run out and buy these products, so the message suggests they "ask your doctor (or euphemistically, health care provider) about whether the product is right for you." Freely translated, it says go bug your doctor into prescribing this drug for you. A favorite slot for these advertisements is the network news time where the story being reported is frequently about the ravages caused by abuse of the latest fad drug. America fights a war on drugs by filling up its jails with small-time users and feeds it with the message—if there's a problem, there's a pill for that.

During the period of escalating medical costs, the life span of the individual has increased significantly, but with the rapid pace of technological progress, the life span of the average corporation has shrunk as firms adjust too slowly to the obsolescence of their product line. Polaroid, DEC, Sun Microsystems, Palm, Nokia, and Blackberry are among the familiar names that no longer dot the corporate landscape. Former Wall Street stars like Kodak and IBM have shrunk in size and stature. Short-lived companies cannot provide long-term security. Ailing firms are cutting both staff and benefits. The rising cost of providing health insurance has placed a burden on companies that they have lightened by increasing employee contributions, cutting back on plans offered to new hires and retirees, and making greater use of part-time and temporary hires.[50] Employer-based insurance is a much more fragile benefit now than when it became established in the fifties, but it remains the centerpiece of the health care system.

Obamacare

After the failure of the Clinton initiative, problems with the health care system continued to mount. The number of uninsured rose to 45 million in 2008 and to a projected total of 54 million people by 2019.[51] Many other people found that high deductibles and caps on coverage left them with huge bills when family illness revealed the limitations of their policy. The financial meltdown in 2008 threw many people out of work and made many more feel vulnerable to the threat that they would not only lose their job, but also the insurance coverage that went with it.

Republicans were not blind to the problems troubling the health care system. The individual mandate requiring the uninsured to purchase insurance coupled with subsidies to help the poor meet the requirement that became a centerpiece of President Obama's health care plan was originally the core of a 1989 recommendation by the conservative Heritage Foundation as a market-based alternative to a Medicare for all approach to universal coverage.[52] The idea was picked up by Senate Republicans including Orin Hatch and Charles Grassley and introduced in 1993 as an alternative to the Clinton plan.[53] There was no questioning the constitutionality of the mandate when it surfaced as a Republican backed proposal. Mark Pauly, who developed a plan for President George H. W. Bush that contained an individual mandate, remarked later "I don't recall [its constitutionality] being raised at all. The way it was viewed by the Congressional Budget Office in 1994 was, effectively, as a tax."[54]

After the failure to pass a federal comprehensive health care plan, the activity switched to the states. The most significant advance with national implications occurred in Massachusetts in 2006. The state Legislature passed an Insurance Extension Act with both an individual mandate and an insurance exchange where residents could select from a list of approved private plans. Governor Mitt Romney initially vetoed the individual mandate, but when the bill was approved by the legislature over his veto he signed the measure. Senator Kennedy was not directly involved in state government, but worked behind the scenes to help shape and shepherd the bill through to passage.[55]

The successful debut of the "Health Connector Exchange" and the implementation of the individual mandate made Governor Romney a GOP rising star, vaulting him onto the national stage. During his

2008 presidential primary campaign, the future Tea Party champion, Representative Jim DeMint praised Romney for his ability to "take some good conservative ideas, like private health insurance, and apply them to the need to have everyone insured."[56] Romney reveled in his accomplishment stating "I'm proud of what we've done. If Massachusetts succeeds in implementing it, then that will be the model for the nation."[57]

The individual mandate was part of Hillary Clinton's plan during the 2008 Democratic primaries. Barack Obama was opposed to it.[58] After he was elected, he was convinced by his advisers, who included Jonathon Gruber, an architect of the Massachusetts plan, that the individual mandate along with a community rating (a requirement for insurance providers within a given territory to offer coverage to all persons at the same price regardless of their health status) were essential to insure that a sufficient number of healthy young people participated in the plan to be able to extend coverage while maintaining the rate structure for those currently insured. The plan seemed to have bipartisan appeal that more comprehensive measures like "Medicare for all" lacked.

The plans that emerged from the Senate and House were very similar to the Massachusetts plan and not too dissimilar from the plan offered by Nixon in 1974. Insurance companies were required to provide coverage to all applicants regardless of the person's health status. They were prohibited from charging different rates based upon a person's sex or prior conditions. The bill established minimum standards for acceptable insurance plans and set up health exchanges where those plans could be compared and a selection made. Employers of fifty or more full-time workers were required to provide insurance for their employees or be charged a surtax of 8% on their worker's wages. Medicaid eligibility was expanded to 133% of the Federal Poverty Level, and other low income individuals would be provided a subsidy on a sliding scale. Young people were allowed to remain on their family's plan until age 26.[59]

Not a single Republican supported the bill. Senators Grassley and Hatch were backers of the similar Republican plan in 1993, and many of the Republicans that backed a 2007 bill that contained an individual mandate and state based regulated insurance markets were still in Congress during the 2009–2010 debate. Many accommodations were made to Republicans and conservative Democrats. The public option—a plan to offer insurance through a government program as one of the alternatives on the insurance exchange—was dropped. Medicaid eligibility expansion was left to the discretion of the individual states. Despite these and other concessions, no Republicans budged from their solid opposition.

The Republican game plan was established two weeks before Barack Obama was inaugurated. Senate Minority leader Mitch McConnell gathered his colleagues and outlined a strategy that would erode the popularity of the new President and boost the sagging fortunes of his dispirited party. It was purely politics. The overwhelming Democratic victory aside, the Democratic Administration would have to adhere to a strict Republican policy agenda or face obstructions that would prevent them from governing at all. McConnell would use the Senate operating procedures to slow things down, deny the opposition any Republican support, and make the Democrats dicker between themselves to make any progress in moving key legislation toward enactment. McConnell, the Louisville University basketball fan, stressed the importance of "team ball." The team in this case being the Republican Party, not the country at large. During the health care debate McConnell told an interviewer, "It was absolutely critical that everybody be together, because if the proponents of the bill were able to say it was bipartisan, it tended to convey to the public that this is OK."[60]

McConnell got some immediate help in keeping his caucus in line. Almost as soon as the crowds packing the Mall to hear Obama deliver his inaugural address dispersed and went home, Tea Party activists arrived and took their place. Ostensibly angered by the TARP bank bailout passed in the waning days of the Bush Administration and the economic stimulus bill the Obama Administration crafted to confront the crisis left in the wake of the sinking of Lehman Brothers, the movement appeared as if on cue before the Presidential honeymoon period had even begun. It showed itself to be much more than a reaction to a piece of legislation. The activists saw themselves as part of a revolution—a revolution of the haves against the have nots—a revolution to overturn the results of the recent election. The revolutionaries did not lack for contemporaries of Madame DeFarge knitting the names of any Republican showing a hint of cooperation with the new president into a scarf to pull around the culprit's neck in the next primary election.

Republican politicians fed the fury of their partisans with rumor, exaggerations, and lies. The boldest lie was spread by former Vice Presidential candidate Sarah Palin. She claimed that a provision in the bill that would provide reimbursement to physicians for consulting with elderly patients about their end of life treatment options while they were capable of making their own decisions would lead to death panels deciding which patients were eligible for care and which were not. A Pew Research Survey found that 85% of the public was aware of the claim and 30% believed it was true.[61]

The McConnell strategy worked better than even he might have suspected. None of his caucus broke ranks; the President's favorable ratings slipped rapidly; and the Republican brand rebounded in the polls. The public grew disgusted with the mess in Washington, but that suited the Republican narrative that government was the problem not the solution. For the strategy to work so well, it needed the acquiescence of an uncritical media. Bipartisanship was not on display on Capitol Hill, but it was the prime directive for network news. Blame for government dysfunction had to be apportioned equally or not assigned at all. Sound bites of Republican politicians decrying the lack of input they had in formulating the health care legislation were played without examination. Previous Republican positions were never mentioned. Republican complaints and Tea Party shenanigans stirred viewership more than Democratic rebuttals. A political mugging was in progress, but the public's cop on the beat just looked away and treated it like business as usual.

The Democrats had one brief window to steer the legislation through the Senate. Al Franken won the closely contested seat in Minnesota and Arlen Specter switched party affiliation shortly after siding with the Administration on the stimulus package. The Democrats had the 60 votes needed to break a filibuster. Senator Kennedy, the long-time champion of health care legislation, died on August 25, 2009, before he could see the bill become law. He was replaced in the Senate by Democrat Paul Kirk until a special election would be held later in the year. While the Democrats still had their veto-proof margin, Majority Leader, Harry

Reid worked quickly to satisfy the Democratic holdouts. The public option was dropped from the Senate bill to satisfy Senator Lieberman,[62] and Senator Ben Nelson of Nebraska was won over with a modification of the language on abortion coverage to require consumers to pay for the coverage out of their own pocket, and he received a special kickback to his state in the form of a higher Medicaid reimbursement that became known as the "Cornhusker Kickback." With all 60 Democratic votes lined up, the Senate Bill was passed on Christmas Eve by a vote of 60 to 39 with the old Tiger and Phillies right-hander Jim Bunning sitting in the bullpen. Three weeks later, Republican Scott Brown was elected to fill Kennedy's old seat and the Democrats lost their filibuster proof majority.

The loss of Kennedy's seat left one option open to the Administration: The House could pass the Senate bill unamended except for budgetary changes that could be put in a reconciliation amendment that would not be subject to a filibuster. Scott Brown's victory sent a chill through the House Democratic caucus as members sensed their own vulnerability in the upcoming midterm elections. Support for passing any health care legislation began to waver. Chief of Staff Rahm Emanuel advised the President to settle for a weaker bill and retrieve some measure of success from what was shaping up to be a humiliating failure.[63] House Speaker Nancy Pelosi pressed for moving ahead with trying to win House approval of the Senate measure.[64] The President also insisted on comprehensive reform.[65]

Securing the needed votes in the House to accept the Senate version came down to satisfying the concerns of a group of pro-life Democrats led by Congressman Bart Stupak who felt the language in the Senate version left open the possibility of federal money being used to pay for abortions. Substantive changes could not be made to the bill without returning to the Senate and opening the door to a filibuster. The Stupak group was adamant about not agreeing to the Senate version's language, but was ultimately persuaded to give up its opposition by President Obama issuing an executive order reaffirming the principles in the Hyde Amendment that no federal tax dollars be used to fund abortions.[66]

The first comprehensive health insurance bill was signed into law by Barack Obama on March 21, 2010—98 years after support for some vague government role in providing for the health of its citizens first appeared in the platform of the Progressive Party of Teddy Roosevelt. The final act fell short of providing full universal coverage as a right of every citizen as Walter Reuther demanded fifty years earlier, but it was, as Vice President Biden was overheard telling the President at the signing ceremony, "A big fucking deal."

Republican Reaction

One day after the bill that came to be known as Obamacare was signed into law, the Republicans vowed to repeal it. The legislative process was not open to them with Democrats in charge of the Senate and a Democrat sitting in the oval office, so their best opportunity to sabotage the act was to attack it in the courts. Republican state and local officials brought suit in federal court that the individual mandate that Republicans embraced during the Bush and Clinton years was, on second thought, unconstitutional. The argument quickly found its way to the Supreme Court where Chief Justice Roberts broke ranks with his conservative colleagues and cast the deciding vote in ruling that the mandate constituted a tax that was within the powers granted to the Legislative Branch by the Constitution to levy. Court reporters speculated that Roberts wanted to avoid drawing the Court into another political controversy like Bush vs. Gore that might lower public respect for the institution.[67]

After failing to fatally wound Obamacare in the Court, the 2012 election provided the Republicans their next opportunity to repeal it. They campaigned under the slogan "repeal and replace." Mitt Romney voiced his antipathy for the measure as if his fingerprints were not on the original document. Republicans were insistent upon the repeal and vague about any plans they had for a replacement. In truth there was no substantially different market-based alternative that offered almost universal coverage. Opposition to Obamacare proved a winning formula for the Republicans in the 2010 midterm elections, and they were confident that it would sweep them back into power in 2012. Romney was so sure he was going to win that he had no concession speech prepared when it didn't happen. People who vote in the general election don't always vote in the midterm elections. The Republicans failed to see the changing face of America. Barack Obama was handily reelected and Democrats gained seats in both houses of Congress.

The Republicans did not give up their effort to roll back Obamacare. Their disruptive tactics became more desperate with the realization that once the law took full effect people might find in it more of what they like and fears of death panels and loss of current benefits would fade. The law would become less-and-less possible to repeal. Of course the need to repeal might be less pressing than the need to keep the issue alive to weaken a Democratic administration.

The debate over Obamacare turned the playing field upside down. The usual opponents—the AMA, the drug companies, and the insurance companies—were sitting in the stands on the President's side of the field.[68] The Democrats' game plan centered on a strategy drawn up by the conservative Heritage Foundation, and the Republicans relied on the courts to throw a yellow flag and declare that formation to be illegal. The calls of "single payer plan" and "Medicare for all" coming from the far end zone seats were drowned out by chants of "socialism" from the cheering section behind the Republican bench. When the game ended the Democrats limped off the field leaving their supporters to wonder if and what they had just won. The other team refused to leave the field and denied the game had ended.

The Affordable Care Act set parameters for insurance companies on coverage and eligibility, but it allowed them to retain the right to "manage care"—dictate to physicians the limits on the tests and treatments that would be covered by insurance. The law authorized the Secretary of Health and Human Services to establish a set of "essential health benefits" to which all approved insurance plans must adhere. Insurers were prohibited from imposing yearly or lifetime caps on essential benefits, that included ambulatory services, hospitalization, prenatal and maternal care, pediatric care, rehabilitation treatment, mental health care, and management of chronic illness. Preventive care was emphasized as a means of controlling costs. Vaccinations and screening for diseases such as breast and colon cancer, HPV, and HIV were deemed "essential health benefits" for which there were to be no co-payments or deductibles. These and other stipulations formed a broad guideline of essential services established by Secretary Sebelius in accordance with the provision in the law.[69] The scope of standard benefits provided within these guidelines was required to equal that of the typical employer provided plan. It was left to the individual states to identify the benchmark plan for their market.

The law established four categories of coverage named for a progression in the value of precious metals: brass, silver, gold, and platinum. Each category was required to provide the same essential health benefits, the difference being the cost of the plan to the consumer and the percentage of out-of-pocket costs for which that consumer would be responsible. For the subscriber to a brass rated policy, out-of-pocket costs are expected to average about 40% of his or her medical bills. Holders of platinum plans will pay only about 10% in the uncovered cost of their medical services. The Affordable Care Act also required insurance companies to spend 80–85% of the money they collect in premiums on health costs and claims.[70]

The Affordable Care Act permitted states a lot of latitude in managing the delivery of the prescribed services. States were offered the opportunity of setting up the insurance exchange within their borders for plans that met the federal guidelines. States setting up their own exchange could determine which plans, meeting federal guidelines, were offered on the website, negotiate prices, and impose higher standards than mandated by the federal guidelines. Residents of states not providing their own exchange would use an exchange provided by the federal government, and responsibility for managing all aspects of the service defaulted to the federal government.

The lack of state participation in establishing their own exchanges proved to be a major factor in the troubled roll out in October, 2013 of the requirement for individuals to meet the individual mandate and purchase insurance on an exchange.[71] Thirty-six states, twenty-nine controlled by Republican legislatures, failed to set up a state exchange. This produced an unanticipated burden on the federal exchange that was never supposed to be the focal point for marketing health insurance and was not provided with the funds necessary for the task. Again the Republican role in what was reported as a disaster for the president and his party was ignored in the coverage.

The Supreme Court ruling that upheld the individual mandate also removed the penalty for states not increasing Medicaid eligibility to 133% of the federal poverty level. A number of Republican controlled states have refused to increase the eligibility limit. About half of the uninsured population at the time the law was passed lived in these states.[72] In some, the eligibility cutoff for Medicaid was well below the national poverty line. In Kansas Medicaid eligibility cut off at 32% of the national poverty line. A family of three living in Kansas with an income between $6,250 and $19,530 in 2013 would not be covered under Medicaid and would not be eligible for federal subsidies that start at the federal poverty limit. Individuals or couples without children in Kansas are not eligible for Medicaid at all.[73] Other states that have a Medicaid eligibility cutoff close to the federal poverty line have refused to increase the eligibility limit despite the fact that the federal government will cover 100% of the increased cost for the first three years of the program and gradually reduce it to 90% of the additional cost by 2020. As a result of the court ruling and states' decisions not to expand the limit for Medicaid, it is estimated that about 6.4 million Americans will fall into the gap of being both ineligible for Medicaid and the federal subsidies to offset the cost of insurance.[74]

The roadblocks to enrollment erected by critics of the law are intended to undermine popular acceptance of the act when it takes full effect. The cost of adding substantial numbers of people with pre-existing conditions or cautionary family health histories to the insurance rolls can only be balanced by adding large numbers of healthy young people as well. If enough of the uninsured are discouraged from enrolling in the program because of difficulties in navigating the website, ineligibility for stipends, or lack of information about available benefits, the additional cost for extending coverage will be borne by existing policy holders. Higher insurance bills to millions of subscribers would likely generate an avalanche of opposition to the law and the party that produced it.

Should these hurdles be surmounted, the law provides states with an "innovation waiver." If an individual state devises a different plan that provides the same level of coverage at similar or lower cost and does not increase the federal deficit, then the state could apply for a waiver after 2017 and be exempt from the implementation requirements in the federal law such as the individual and employer mandates. A state granted an innovation waiver would continue to receive the equivalent federal compensation to which it and its residents would be entitled under the terms of the Affordable Care Act. The innovation waiver provides Republican critics an opportunity to develop their own market-driven plan that provides the same level of coverage. It is likely, however, that Obamacare, or a close relative such as Romneycare, is the only market-driven approach that extends insurance coverage to a substantial segment of the uninsured and prevents people from being denied coverage because of their previous medical history. The Republican election slogan of "repeal and replace" offered no suitable replacement and showed a lack of concern for the millions of uninsured and under-insured Americans for whom illness is a more frightening reality than a terrorist attack.

The waiver may prove to be the most salient feature of the law. It provides a laboratory where individual states can experiment with minor or major modifications of the original document. Vermont explored the possibility of requesting an innovation waiver to enact a single payer plan, but found the market forces too entrenched for a small state to radically alter the established model.[75] Political realities make it almost impossible to create a new health delivery system in one great "Big Bang" approach, but incremental changes percolating through the various states provide an alternate path toward universal, comprehensive, high-quality health care that Reuther regarded as an individual right in his address to the Public Health Association.

The Affordable Care Act relies on employer-provided, private insurance plans and free market competition on the exchanges to control costs. The weakness in the approach is that for the entities involved—the businesses and the insurance companies—providing low-cost, quality healthcare is a secondary concern. They are in business to make money. For businesses healthcare is an expense that can be reduced by skirting the mandate. Small businesses can avoid the mandate to supply insurance coverage for their employees by keeping their full-time work force below fifty, the number that triggers their obligation to "play" and provide an insurance plan or "pay" the fine instead. Companies can also hire more part-time workers for whom they are not obligated to provide insurance coverage. Once a small business adds a fiftieth worker, it is responsible for either providing health care for its entire full-time workforce, or paying a tax to cover the government subsidy for each of its low wage workers. The size of the tax increases with the size of the subsidy for low wage earners with a family.

Employer-based coverage for the majority of the public remained a cornerstone of Obamacare, because the majority of those insured through their employer were happy with their plan. Changing the model risked alienating a large portion of the public. An attempt to force a switch to a different model of group coverage was one of the factors that doomed the earlier Clinton effort. But extending the role of the employer in providing for the health care of the nation also has negative consequences. It has a dampening effect upon employment, wages, and workforce mobility. There are Liberal and Conservative health policy experts that argue for a mechanism for organizing group coverage plans outside of employment that would be more portable and more stable for the insured and less intrusive for businesses.[76] They just don't agree on what that mechanism should be.

America and the World

For the majority of Americans, particularly the majority of the more politically active, the employer-provided health insurance delivered adequate coverage at reasonable personal expense. They were generally satisfied with the American system as it affected them and were receptive to the medical establishment's warnings about the rationing of services in the Canadian and British National Health Services. During the 2009 health care debate a significant segment of the population believed that the United States had the best health care system in the world.[77]

The truth is much more nuanced and far less flattering. In 2001 the World Health Organization (WHO) issued a list of national rankings based on a set of metrics that measured the fairness, responsiveness, and performance of the various national health systems. The United States ranked 37th immediately behind Costa Rica and two rungs above Cuba.[78] France ranked first in the overall standings, with all of the European countries of the old Western Alliance, the Scandinavian countries, the Middle Eastern oil states, and Canada, Japan, Colombia, Chile, and several smaller nations ranking ahead of the United States. In performance measures the United States ranked 24th in healthy life expectancy—about 4.5 years less than in Japan and over 3 years less than in France.[79]

In the same survey the United States came out first in the responsiveness of its health care system. Responsiveness was rated on the respect for the individual—the promptness and dignity with which an individual was treated and the autonomy with which he or she had in selecting a physician and method of treatment. Responsiveness was also graded on the resources available to the patient during convalescence and the quality of these basic amenities.[80]

The reason for the low overall ranking was the fairness with which health benefits were distributed across all sectors of the population. The large number of uninsured in the United States contributed to the fact that gains in health care delivery went largely to those already enjoying better health care opportunities. Access to care in the United States is limited by the high cost to many individuals. The individual contribution to health care in the developed, industrial countries averaged about 25% at the time of the report. The big exception was the United States where the average was 56%, and the disparity between the mean and median suggested that the highest individual costs were borne by those least able to afford them.[81]

Critics of the report dispute the methodology used in conducting the study and the weights attributed to the various components of the ranking scheme. Much as with the case of ranking college football teams where different polling organizations use different judges, and put different emphasis on factors like strength of schedule, margin of victory, reputation of the program, and team statistics, another approach by a different committee might jiggle the national rankings slightly, but leave the basic conclusion unchanged. The United States' health care system restricts access to its services because of high individual cost that is born unequally by its citizens.

A second study examining the number of preventable deaths per year of people under seventy-five years of age in nineteen developed countries produced another poor evaluation for American health care. The list of countries consisted of all the countries of what former Defense Secretary Donald Rumsfeld once called "Old Europe," the Scandinavian countries, and the United States, Canada, Japan, Australia, and New Zeeland. Preventable deaths were deaths from those illnesses which early detection and proper intervention should have been able to deter. Deaths from treatable conditions like hypertension, routine surgeries like appendectomies, and illnesses like cervical and colon cancer that are not usually fatal if detected early and treated in a timely manner draw attention to deficiencies in a health care system that require corrective action. The study supported by the Commonwealth Fund was first done in 1997–1998 and repeated five years later in 2002–2003. In the first study the United States ranked fourteenth with 115 preventable deaths per every 100,000 people.[82] In the second study, the US reduced this number to 110 for every 100,000 people but fell to last place in the rankings. The other eighteen countries had reduced their numbers by an average of 16% over this period compared with the modest 4% decline in the United States. France again finished first in this measure of health care outcomes in both years the survey was conducted. In 2002–2003 it registered only 66 preventable deaths for every 100,000 of its people.[83]

The one category where the United States far and away leads the rest of the world is in the cost of its system. In 2005 it spent 15.4% of its GNP on health care.[66] In the same year France spent 11.2% of its GNP to obtain better rated results. France had one of the costliest systems in Europe—only Switzerland spent slightly more. The UK, Japan, and Spain spent 8.2% of GNP on health care, and Canada spent 9.8% of its GNP, and all produced better overall outcomes than the United States.[84]

When the WHO rankings were released in June of 2000, the story received prominent coverage in Britain. Prime Minister Tony Blair was grilled by the Tories in Parliament on why the United Kingdom was in 18th place below, among others, ten European countries.[85] The attention given the report may be partially responsible for tighter government focus on steps to improve outcomes in the country's lower performing hospitals. Government making health care delivery improvement a national priority is cited as a big reason for the higher than average decline in preventable deaths in the UK in the second Commonwealth Fund survey.[86]

In the United States, the WHO report received scarcely a mention. Its reception was in marked contrast to the results of international comparisons of educational outcomes. Every time some sample of the nation's students brings home a bad report card, the offending document is pasted on the TV screen and the teachers are taken out to the woodshed and spanked. Politicians and business leaders are always available to add their comments to the news coverage, and are quick to place the teachers' unions at the root of the problem.

When the nation's health establishment received a bad report card from an international panel of judges, it was slipped into the home unnoticed. There was not the same force pushing this story forward that there is behind the message about American schools. Media coverage was scant, and there was no politician eager to grab headlines by attacking the nation's doctors or the organization that represents them. The doctors were above reproach and their "union," a pillar of the establishment.

The American Medical Association (AMA) is a guild more powerful and influential than any union. Its lobbying resources dwarf those of other unions and professional organizations.[87] As a professional organization it is a vehicle for promoting advances in the practice of medicine. It publishes the *Journal of the American Medical Association* (JAMA) where new treatment methodologies and best practices are disseminated to the medical community. But as a guild protecting the interests of its members it has opposed efforts to reform the nation's health delivery system since before the time of FDR, and it has used its influence to limit the supply of new doctors by fixing the number of enrollments in medical schools.[88] Members of state medical societies affiliated with the AMA dominate state licensing boards that control the number, curriculum, and size of medical schools within the various states. Within the past ten years, that control has been relaxed somewhat in recognition of the severe shortage of doctors in many rural areas.

While protecting the interests of its members, the AMA has had more influence in shaping the health delivery system of the country than any other group or set of individuals. Its efforts on behalf of its members are not dissimilar to those of the National Education Association (NEA) and the American Federation of Teachers (AFT) in support of theirs, nor is it unreasonable for a guild or union to advance the interests of its own. Then why is the tone of coverage of the shortcomings of America's schools so different from that of its health care system?

One big reason is that education is largely public and health care predominantly private. Conservative critics are quick to jump at any opportunity to highlight a poor performance by the public sector. In education policy they have an alternative plan in privately run charter schools and a favorite whipping boy in the union. Charter schools have had mixed results in improving student performance,[89] but satisfy the free marketer's impulse to strip away tenure and union representation safeguards from the teachers. By contrast the health care report compares the American system unfavorably to national systems where there is a much greater public role in the delivery of health services. This is a message the free market advocates find more convenient to ignore than to defend.

The deficiencies in both the education and health care systems disproportionally affect the poor and minorities. The poor quality of inner city schools is part of the indictment of public education, but lack of health insurance for the poor is not pinned on the tail of the privately financed health care donkey. It is not likely that conservative politicians have a greater concern for the education of disadvantaged youth than the health of disadvantaged families. Philosophical considerations determine the response to both issues. It is the strict adherence to their belief in unfettered capitalism that feeds right wing zeal to dismantle the public institutions and the labor unions that blossomed during the catastrophic collapse of the free market in the 1920's.

The American media hardly ignores the health care issue. It has been at the center of political debate since Harry Truman's administration. But there is little international dimension to the discussion. It is the quantity rather than the quality of the care provided that is in question. Conventional wisdom allows that the American model may need a tune up, but not a new transmission. The virtue of the private sector is beyond reproach. It is upheld by its many defenders pointing fingers at the loose habits of the neighbors, where supposed infringement on individual freedom produces alleged delays in treatment and rationing of care. The conversation ends when the dark curtain of Socialism is drawn across the open window.

France may or may not deserve its number one ranking in the polls, but its health care system provides quality service and universal coverage at a lower percentage of its GDP than the United States. France is a country with an aging population and a relatively large number of immigrants from its former colonies in Africa and Indochina. It has a demographic profile that is very similar to that of the United States, and many social issues are common to both countries. The French system may not fit the tastes of the American market, but with a little tailoring and more choice of fabric, it would likely find no shortage of willing buyers.

The French system might be described as "Medicare for all" on steroids. It is a mixed public-private system that has evolved in stages since its legislated debut in 1928. The system preserves individual choice. People are free to choose their own doctors and to see specialists without having to first go through a gatekeeper. Doctors are free to choose their own location and structure their practice as they prefer. All legal residents of France are covered by National Health Insurance (NHI) which pays for the bulk of the cost of medical and hospital services. Ninety percent of the population also has private supplemental insurance which pays for the portion of the bill not covered by the NHI.[90]

Medical care in France is on a fee for service basis. The patient pays for the doctor or hospital visit out of his or her pocket and is then reimbursed by the NHI and supplemental insurance. Fees exceeding about $100 are paid directly by their insurance.[91] Long hospital stays, chronic illness, and long-term care are covered fully by NHI. Individuals with an income below the poverty level are also fully covered by NHI.[92]

Health care in France operates like a public utility. The legendary French bureaucracy regulates doctors' fees, hospital revenues, and the private insurance market. Yearly negotiations between representatives of the physicians and the NHI determine the fees that general practitioners and specialists may charge.[93] About 20% of the physicians, mostly specialists in the major cities engage in a practice of extra billing. If individuals choose to use one of these doctors, the NHI only compensates them for the negotiated fee. Any additional amount must come from the supplemental insurance according to the stipulations in the plan or be the responsibility of the individual.[94]

French doctors average about one third the net yearly income of their American counterparts, but don't face the same financial hurdles in establishing their practice.[95] Medical education in France is free, whereas the average American medical school student in the year 2000 was faced with a debt of $140,000 upon graduation. After four years of residency this figure rose to $220,000.[96] Doctors in the United States also pay higher malpractice insurance premiums.

The United States relies on the (semi) free market to regulate medical costs. Insurance companies establish provider networks and negotiate a price structure that will satisfy enough doctors to make their policy attractive to customers seeking the broadest coverage at a competitive cost. The insurance companies act as both a middleman, that banks its clients' health dollars to be drawn upon by their providers as the need arises, and the regulator motivated to hold down costs to stimulate demand by its customers, increase profits for its shareholders, and provide large salaries for its executives.

This arrangement has not succeeded in controlling medical costs which have risen faster than inflation since the fifties. The debate over which goal to pursue first—extending coverage or reducing costs—has lingered since the time of Reuther's initiative without any resolution until the passing of the Affordable Care Act. Obamacare extends coverage to millions of the uninsured, but leaves millions of others in states unwilling to extend Medicaid eligibility to 133% of the poverty limit ineligible for either Medicaid or the government stipend to offset the cost of insurance. It encourages efficiencies in medical practice that would reduce costs, but leaves the current delivery system to accommodate these recommendations.

There are only three ways to cut the nation's health care bill: reduce administrative overhead, reduce the amount of money that goes to doctors, drug companies, hospital administrators, and other politically favored groups, and reduce the cost of treating chronic illnesses by early detection and preventive care. The main initiative in the Affordable Care Act to control administrative costs and reduce errors was to require that medical records be stored electronically and be accessible to all of the physicians responsible for an individual's care. At the time the act was passed it was still too often the billing department that had computerized records available at a keystroke and the medical staff that sifted through slips of paper in a manila folder. The uneven embrace of the technology provided anecdotal examples like that of the family vet pulling up a display of the pet's medical history on the monitor in his treatment room and the family primary care physician fumbling through his folder to recall the information from a previous visit.[97]

The Affordable Care Act made little effort to curtail the fees and profits of the various service providers. The Obama Administration secured its flanks at the beginning of the debate by soliciting the support of the AMA and the drug companies for its proposal. Health maintenance and prevention were to be the main ingredients in the recipe for curtailing the rising cost of health care. Accessibility to the system and managed care were key to realizing that goal.

Managed Care

The alternative to a fee-for-service model for delivering health care is through a pre-paid contract with a group of salaried physicians. This became the model for the Health Maintenance Organizations (HMO) that evolved in the 1930s. One of the earliest HMOs was started by Dr. Sidney Garfield in 1933 in the remote town of Desert City, California. Garfield was lured to the Mojave Desert by the Indemnity Insurance Company founded by the Industrialist Henry J. Kaiser and several associates to meet the worker's compensation obligations for the 5000 construction workers building the Colorado River Aqueduct. The small hospital facility Garfield established for tending workers injured on the project ran into immediate financial difficulty until Indemnity Insurance executives Harold Hatch and Alonzo Ordway proposed a prepayment scheme with contributions from the Insurance Company for work-related injuries and from the workers for non work-related health concerns.[98] The commitment ended when work on the project was completed, but Garfield was enlisted by the Kaiser consortium to provide a similar service when they took over the completion of the Grand Coulee Dam.[99]

After the start of World War 2, Kaiser became heavily engaged in ship building. He again asked Garfield to set up an insurance plan for the workers in his Richmond, California shipyard. The Permanente

Health plan was established in June 1942. It soon spread to other centers of the Kaiser industrial empire on the West Coast and became Kaiser-Permanente. After the war, Kaiser continued the plan and opened it to the general public.[100]

By the mid-fifties, there was widespread dissatisfaction with the Blue Shield insurance coverage available to UAW members through employer benefit plans.[101] Walter Reuther summarized the problems with Blue Shield that his members were experiencing:

> "Many of the benefits are hedged in by cash limits that leave the patient with large bills for services he thought were covered. Gross overcharges for doctors' services are commonplace. Contrary to basic precepts of modern medicine, few plans make any provision for preventive care or encourage early diagnosis of illness [...] They overemphasize hospitalization and surgery [...] At best they cover half of the average family's medical bill."[102]

He began looking for an alternative plan and told his associate Jim Brindle to "go work on it, especially the Kaiser plan."[103] When presented with data on the Kaiser plan, Reuther decided to fly to San Francisco and visit the hospital Garfield and Kaiser had established. His visit attracted a bevy of reporters, and when he and Brindle emerged from touring the hospital and its associated clinic, he demonstrated his prodigious ability to assimilate the details of information he had received only hours earlier and relay it authoritatively to the press.[104]

When he returned to Detroit, his staff located a run-down old tuberculosis hospital that was purchased and renovated with the help from a loan by the Nationwide Insurance Company.[105] The hospital was renamed Metropolitan and converted into a general hospital with three floors devoted to out-patient care. Reuther adopted some features of the Kaiser-Permanente plan, added features of his own, and established the Community Health Association (CHA) plan in Detroit. The plan was open to anyone in the Detroit metropolitan area. Reuther was named the president of the fifteen member board elected by the membership.

Salaried positions in managed care organizations were attractive to depression era physicians like Sidney Garfield, but the HMO model was vigorously attacked by the AMA throughout its early growth period. Physicians like Garfield experienced increased pressure from the doctors' organization as public acceptance of the managed care approach grew. The AMA threatened Garfield with loss of his license and closure of the Kaiser-Permanente facilities.[106] The Community Health Association was viewed as socialized medicine by the Michigan medical establishment, and its doctors were banned from hospital admitting privileges.[107] The AMA vigorously promoted Blue Cross and-Blue Shield preferred provider networks to stem the growth of managed care plans.[108] AMA affiliated groups were instrumental in passing laws restricting HMO development in a number of states.[109] By the early seventies there were only about forty surviving managed care plans in the country.[110]

The picture began to change in the seventies with passage of the Health Maintenance Organization Act of 1973. The act, signed into law by President Nixon, provided grants and loans to start an HMO, established a federal certification program, and removed state restrictions from federally certified HMOs. The act required employers of twenty-five or more people who offered health insurance plans to their employees to offer a federally certified HMO plan as an option alongside their traditional indemnity plan. Nixon's enthusiasm for managed care was sparked by conversations with Dr. Paul Ellwood, who headed the group of advisers looking for ways to curb the rise of health cost, and Edgar Kaiser, Henry J's son.[111] He was intrigued by the cost reduction possibilities he saw in the HMO approach. His domestic policy adviser John Ehrlichman was heard on the oval office tapes explaining the Kaiser-Permanente philosophy to his boss. He told Nixon "All the incentives are toward less medical care, because the less care they give them, the more money they make.[112]"

The Health Maintenance Organization Act established the HMO as a major component of the health delivery system and attracted marketeers to the action, but the new attention given managed care in the marketplace did not enhance its public perception. HMOs became notorious for the excessive constraints placed by administrators upon the independence of their doctors and the restrictions they placed on access to specialists outside the group.[113] Ellwood later confessed, "I've also had the disappointment of seeing the country embrace only part of what I had hoped it would. The whole HMO thing was perverted by the desire for maximizing profits."[114] In his documentary, *Sicko,* Michael Moore put on a proverbial rubber glove, telling the audience that this exploration into the bowels of the for-profit HMO industry might hurt a little. He proceeded to document the evidence that corroborates Ehrlichman's assessment of the industry's prevailing philosophy.

The health care system Michael Moore documented in his film was the product of the medical-industrial complex that emerged in the wake of the Health Maintenance Organization Act of 1973. Major hospitals began buying up smaller hospitals and medical practices.[115] An AMA survey conducted in 2012 found a "majority of doctors under forty are employees, no longer independent practitioners."[116] Representative Jim McDermott, himself a doctor, charges that "the medical-industrial complex is putting itself together so that the docs will be the least of our problem […] They will simply be serfs working for the system."[117] These serfs will be well compensated, but their labor will be for the benefit of the lords of the fiefdom in which they serve. AMA market research reports that "hospitals focus on employing primary care physicians in order to maintain a strong reference base for high-margin specialty service lines."[118] Big hospitals with expensive equipment need a reliable level of patients to remain profitable. This situation echoes back to the 1950s when Walter Reuther complained about Blue Shield because it over emphasized hospitalization and surgery and did not place enough emphasis on prevention. The specialist brought in to cure the problem ended up catching the same disease.

The AMA sat on the sidelines during much of the debate over the Affordable Care Act. Its previous legislative battles had taken a toll. Its politics has alienated a segment of its constituency, and its membership has declined over the past several decades. It now represents less than half of the nation's physicians.[119] The health care industry that has grown and matured over the same period has other well-financed voices that do not always share a common interest with the AMA.[120] In drawing its defenses against the Socialist wolf it depicted huffing and puffing at its doorstep, the AMA has found itself in the embrace of a corporate bear that is no less restrictive on its members' freedom to define their role in the delivery of medical services than one administered by a federal bureaucracy.

The full story of American health care cannot be told in black and white. The mixture of market incentives and social obligation has proved a difficult alchemy to master. Neither managed care nor fee for service comes without a warning on the label about the side effects the patient might experience. When generics are substituted for the original formula in the HMO model, the effect upon individual subscribers is much more pronounced and the anecdotal tales are more poignant.

The HMOs provide a cautionary note on systemic reform. Islands of low entropy left unsustained by their creative impulse will dissolve into the ambiance of their surround.[121] The American health care model, in whatever format it is presented, is the province of powerful financial interests. Efforts to curb the appetite of this lobby have had limited impact. If Obamacare survives the Republican assault, the glitches in its roll out, and the sticker shock on the early models in its line, it will be an important advance in extending coverage, but will likely have limited impact in controlling cost. It is unlikely to be the last health care initiative in the elusive struggle for comprehensive, high-quality, affordable health care for all Americans.

PART 4

Epilogue

CHAPTER XV

The Post-American Century

I went through this Ford plant three years ago—One of the management people, with a slightly gleeful tone in his voice said to me, 'How are you going to collect union dues from all these machines?' And I replied, "You know, that is not what's bothering me. I'm troubled by the problem of how to sell automobiles to these machines.

> Walter Reuther
> Address to the National Conference
> for Social Studies of the NEA
> Cleveland, November 23, 1956

The twentieth century began with a competition between stronger national economies exploiting the resources and markets of colonial dependencies in Africa and Asia to promote the welfare of their homeland. Such a competition was inherently unstable. Conflicting national interests were regulated by a patchwork of treaties and alliances, and colonial ties were enforced by gunboats. National self-interest proved too strong for these flimsy constraints; two disastrous wars and colonial rebellions brought the old world order to an end.

The one national economy destined to prevail in the new environment was that of the United States. It was blessed with abundant deposits of iron and coal and a lake and river system that facilitated their delivery to the factories of the Midwest. Liquid gold gushed from the derricks of Texas and Oklahoma and flowed plentifully from gas pumps sprouting across the landscape. America had the skilled mechanics and machinists needed to appropriate the nascent automobile industry from its German and French roots and an internal market big enough to consume the ever increasing supply of its product. The US came late to the colonial land grab by the European powers at the end of the nineteenth century and only picked up a few crumbs that dropped from the table of the more rapacious nations, but it alone was self sufficient in resources and market to prosper disproportionately. The destruction of Europe and Japan at the end of World War II left the United States with a singular place on the world stage for the next thirty years.

By the last quarter of the century the natural and man-made advantages enjoyed by the United States began to erode. Europe and Japan had recovered and began to challenge American industry for markets at home and abroad. American industry, in turn, recognized the emerging markets and shifted more-and-more of its production to foreign shores. The abundant resources began to play out, and wages sustained in a closed economy came under assault in the global market place that emerged. The end of the Cold War marked a triumph of American industrial and military might, but diminished the relevance of that power in the "hot, flat and crowded"[1] environment that ensued.

The post-American century does not necessarily mean American influence in the twenty-first century will be eclipsed, nor suggest that China or any other nation will come to dominate it in the way that the United States dominated the previous century. How the country fares in the coming decades will depend on how well its political system is able to recognize the real challenges that are faced and marshal the will to confront them.

Twenty-first century challenges include climate change, population migration, nuclear proliferation, the fair distribution of wealth, and the fragility of democracy in the grip of an interconnected global corporate superstate. These challenges will not be recognized and adequately addressed while they are eclipsed by the unresolved issues from the past. Much of the nation's energy is expended re-fighting the philosophical, cultural, and military battles of the proximate past. In election-after-election the candidates sound the same notes, reprise many of the same issues, run the same old attack ads, and hit on most of the same big donors seeking many of the same favors. The world keeps changing faster than the political system seems able to accommodate.

By the start of the new century the transition from a collection of mostly self-contained national economies to a global marketplace was well under way. Countries like China, India, and Brazil that had been largely peripheral to the old economic order were more flexible in adapting to the new. In established countries like the United States, globalization has been accompanied by an agglomeration of wealth in fewer hands and an abrupt change of circumstance for many in the middle class.

The United States has struggled to define its place in the new environment. Accustomed to regarding itself the "leader of the Free World," it clings to this conception long after the bipolar alignment of the Cold War has diffused into a variety of conflicted national identities. It is more-and-more a leader with fewer, less willing followers. The American claim of global leadership is reinforced by a powerful but bloated military fed with a Defense budget larger than that of the next fourteen countries combined.[2] The United States has chosen to become the cop on the international beat, policing neighborhoods far different from its own, unfamiliar with and suspicious of the people it is charged to protect, and earning only resentment for its efforts.

The cost of maintaining this expression of national pride has siphoned public expenditure away from infrastructure improvements, education, and programs to help the disadvantaged and vulnerable. The belief in a strong international presence contrasts with efforts to minimize the public presence in domestic affairs. The fight between the forces trying to roll back the New Deal and those trying to preserve it has paralyzed the legislative process and obscured the nation's vision for its future. With a fraying safety net providing scant protection, it is left to the *Invisible Hand* of the market to provide security from the worries of daily life—illness, job insecurity, income erosion, and the loss of dignity in old age. With *Life* and *Liberty* so narrowly focused on military deterrence, the question of America's place in the twenty-first century will be answered by how well it affords its citizens the *Pursuit of Happiness.*

For Lyndon Johnson a Great Society could not ignore the pockets of poverty festering in its cities and rural hamlets while it was reaching for the moon. His *War on Poverty* tapped into the idealistic tenor of the times. He enlisted into his army the Volunteers In Service to America (VISTA) recruits that Reuther envisioned in his 1956 speech to the NEA.[3] Johnson's poverty war funding provided nutritional supplements and Head Start to disadvantaged tots and a military-style boot camp for enlistees in the Job Corps. He was a confident and accomplished general with a string of legislative victories that emboldened the scope and urgency of his campaign. He attacked the slums with a wrecking ball and a "Picket's Charge" approach that numbered more casualties than territory secured.

While the *War on Poverty* was being fought at home, the war on a second front abroad was going badly. Johnson exuded the hubris of a nation convinced of its *Manifest Destiny* and intoxicated by its post-War affluence. He thought it could have both guns and butter, but waging both hot and cold war abroad and fighting poverty at home proved too much. Johnson lost the support of many of his allies in the poverty war because of the other war he couldn't win and couldn't stand to lose. In the end the country won neither.

The loss of the war in Southeast Asia had no lasting effect upon the United States. The dominoes did not fall. Communism did not prevail in the global struggle. Relations between the two adversaries are still strained but more normal; and Capitalism is alive and well in Communist China. The American military is as formidable a deterrent to aggression initiated by another nation state as it had been previously.

Retreat from the *War on Poverty*, however, has left previously held terrain unclaimed and largely uncontested. The country no longer aspires to become a *Great Society*, but rather to encourage individuals to become great, usually meaning wealthy, within the society. It has lost its appetite for big national projects, and its concern for citizens left behind in the race to the top. The nation that won the race to the moon now sends its astronauts up to the International Space Station in Soyuz rockets,

Commuters into New York City crawl along the roadbeds Cornelius Vanderbilt laid out in the nineteenth century while bullet trains speed passengers between cities in Europe, Japan, and China. The Large Hadron Collider reveals secrets of the universe beneath a field outside of Geneva instead of beneath the Dallas-Fort Worth Metroplex in Texas.

In its rush to get out of the way of the private sector, the country has lost sight of the fact that the corporation only exists to make money. Its officers may have strong ethical standards and a sense of obligation to the community, but their prime responsibility is to their shareholders. They will benefit from the health and education of their labor pool, the infrastructure for transporting their goods and services, and the affluence of their customer base, but it is not their obligation to provide for it.

Since the focus has shifted from building a *Great Society* to allowing freer rein to the market forces, the country has seen income disparity balloon. The cost of higher education has left college graduates drowning in student debt, and has caused many qualified youngsters to question the value of continuing their education. The I 35W bridge collapse sending cars plummeting into the Mississippi River near Minneapolis in 2007 highlighted the deteriorating state of the nation's infrastructure after years of deferred maintenance and delayed replacement. South Korea has built the world's most-up-to-date information highway system, not the country that launched its massive interstate highway system in the 1950's. The Invisible Hand may allocate resources efficiently in a well-prepared environment. It does not find rabbits in a hat that are not already there.

The Progressive legislation enacted during the first seventy years of the twentieth century produced significant advances in family income, equality of opportunity, avenues for personal fulfillment, and security from the vagaries of illness and age. Educational opportunities were expanded for middle class youth, providing a ladder to the upper stories of society. Racial discrimination was made illegal. Private enterprise flourished with government supporting its infrastructure and regulating its excesses. The political dynamic worked to adjust the balance between public and private initiative for the benefit of the many. For America to become a more competitive, more just, and less aggressive society, it must aspire to a higher purpose than the pursuit of individual wealth and reestablish the principle enunciated by Abraham Lincoln that government should "do for the people whatever they need to have done, but which they cannot do at all, or cannot do, so well, for themselves."⁴

The end of a century and the birth of the (blue collar) blues

Walter Reuther was sixty-two years old on when he boarded the plane for Black Lake on Mother's Day in 1970. He was only a couple of years from retirement. If he were to reflect back upon his life on that last voyage, Reuther might see the young radical, turned union insurgent, turned establishment figure. Each time something was gained, something was lost. The assassination attempts prompted a move from a middle class neighborhood in the city to a guarded compound in the countryside that removed him from the everyday experiences of a typical American. As he moved up the union hierarchy, he drifted away from old colleagues in struggle like George Edwards, Frank Winn, and Genora Johnson and surrounded himself with technocrats like Jack Conway, Nat Weinberg and Irving Bluestone. The confrontational relationship he had with auto executives like GM president William Knudsen in the early days of the CIO grew into a scripted bureaucratic ritual between stakeholders in a common enterprise. As his influence in Democratic administrations grew his degrees of freedom of action became more constrained.

Reuther was watching the tide of history ebbing from him in 1970. His brother Roy had died of a heart attack in 1968, and that death was closely followed by the deaths of his father Val and of Martin Luther King and Robert Kennedy. His old antagonist Richard Nixon was in the White House and he was diminished by the absence of colleagues, family members, and friends. He was increasingly out-of-step with the new generation of workers for whom the CIO struggles at Flint and the River Rouge were ancient history. The black members of his union were impatient with the pace of economic advancement, and the white workers resentful of their loss of station. Both found the union bureaucratic and aloof. The marriage between Reuther's UAW-CIO and Meany's AFL had ended in divorce and his affair with the Teamsters was a desperate gambit to cling to his dream of organizing the many unorganized workers in the South, in the oil fields, and in the urban ghettos.

The spring of 1970 was a very pivotal time in the history of the labor movement.[5] The American worker was frustrated with his job and angry about social changes that were unsettling his sense of community. The white male laborer was resentful of the special efforts introduced to achieve integration. It was his kids who were being bused away from their neighborhood schools, his neighborhood targeted for blockbusting by predatory realtors, and his kids who were being drafted to fight in Vietnam. He resented the children of privilege who protested the war his kids had to fight and who thumbed their nose at the labor he had to perform. At the same time his income was being eaten away by inflation, and he was finding his workplace more dispiriting as the forces of automation and globalization shaped his job and shaved his earnings outlook. Many turned to George Wallace to express their anger at an establishment that had marginalized them.

Forces were pushing Reuther in several directions that spring. His membership was being squeezed between inflation and the Nixon administration's attempt to wring inflationary pressures out of the system with a planned recession. Black workers wanted more economic progress and a greater voice in union affairs. White workers wanted early retirement—"thirty and out." Skilled tradesmen who had seen the differential between their earnings and those of their unskilled counterparts narrow over the years were questioning the relevance of belonging to a union that benefited them less than what they considered their skills were worth. The union was preparing for a strike at General Motors that neither party was able to afford.[6]

Shortly after the UAW convention in Atlantic City closed, as the cherry blossoms along the Potomac began to fade and fall with the arrival of May, the nation was told that American and South Vietnamese forces had invaded Cambodia. The news sparked protests on campuses across the country. At Kent State University in Ohio, a confrontation between students and a National Guard detachment ended with the guard firing a volley of shots that left four students dead and nine wounded. The dead included two students who were part of the protest gathering and two others who were passing nearby on their way to class. The Kent State Massacre precipitated a nationwide student strike that closed 450 campuses and involved over four million students.[7] In his last public act,

Walter Reuther reacted to the invasion and the killings at Kent State by drafting a public letter to Nixon condemning the widening of the war and reminding him that it was "your responsibility to lead us out of the Southeast Asian War—to peace at home and abroad."

> Your decision to invade the territory of Cambodia can only increase the enormity of the tragedy [...] in that area. Widening the war merely reinforces the bankruptcy of our policy of force and violence in Vietnam. Your action, taken without the advice and consent of Congress, has created a serious constitutional crisis at a time when there is growing division in our nation. The bitter fruits of this growing alienation and frustration among America's youth are now being harvested on the campus of Kent State University [...] the problem, Mr. President, is that we cannot successfully preach nonviolence at home while we escalate mass violence abroad. It is your responsibility to lead us out of the Southeast Asian war—to peace at home and abroad.[8]

After Reuther's death, the "growing division in our nation" that he warned about in his telegram was highlighted on the nightly news. A group of youthful demonstrators protesting the war and the Kent State Massacre in front of the New York City Federal Building was set upon by a counter demonstration of construction workers organized by Peter Brennan, head of the New York building trades. The "Hard Hat Riot" grabbed the attention of Richard Nixon, who sensed an opportunity to wean the working class vote away from its Democratic breast. Nixon invited Brennan and other New York labor leaders to the White House and received a hard hat and a flag pin for his lapel as tokens of endorsement from his guests. Brennan was later rewarded with the position of Secretary of Labor in the Nixon cabinet.

The hard hats represented the not-so-silent face of the Silent Majority that Nixon portrayed as the real America. The Republican president courted labor by appealing to their conservative instincts on social issues. He fashioned a pseudo-liberal domestic agenda that lured working class voters into his coalition by not threatening their collective bargaining rights and not moving to dismantle popular New Deal and Great Society programs like Social Security and Medicare, but neither by doing anything to advance labor's economic interests. Nixon did shepherd the Occupational Safety and Health Act (OSHA) through Congress, to the dismay of many traditional Republicans and business leaders, but his more typical tactic was to propose a weakened version of progressive legislation that liberals could not endorse then blame them for the failure to get it enacted.[9] Nixon was the consummate political animal who considered the appearance of action to hold as much value as the action itself. His appeal to labor was an appeal to a testosterone laced sense of patriotism. His flag pin symbolized the virility of the leader embracing an expansive world view faithful to the Cold War tradition. It quickly became a required wardrobe accoutrement that no aspirant to public office could be without.

Nixon's courtship of labor was not limited to the rank-and-file. George Meany and his executive council were also wooed by the Republican president on the links and at a Labor Day dinner in the White House. Nixon's advances did not result in a formal engagement, but did win a pledge of neutrality from the AFL-CIO leadership in the 1972 presidential election campaign.[10] The old Cold Warrior Meany was more comfortable with a pro-business Republican than the youthful insurgents who elbowed their way into the Democratic Party leadership councils. Meany, the guardian of the status quo, may have assumed that a Democratic bloodbath in the 1972 elections would return him and his labor allies to their former prominence in party affairs, but he ignored the clock ticking away the minutes of his era and the economic order he symbolized.

The veterans of the Civil Rights movement, activists from the anti-war and social movements of the sixties, and labor never coalesced into a coherent force to sustain the gains that each had won separately. Race, age, gender, and experience were barriers too formidable to surmount. The New Left was no more willing to find common ground with George Meany than he was to sit down with them. At the end of the UAW convention weeks before his death, Walter Reuther met informally with a group of mostly young editors of union publications and offered his listeners the chance to be part of "this great organization called the UAW."[11] "Here is an opportunity," he continued, "for a young fellow to get in there and help us to do these things he's so impatient about." He mentioned ending the war, fighting for black economic advancement, building more livable cities, and striving for one America. "[...] don't try to do it outside of here, as though we were part of the Establishment and we're hopeless," he implored. "Come in here and get your teeth into it and get with us because here is a chance." Reuther may have been too chauvinistic, too white, and too late to the anti-war movement to attract a new generation of organizers who themselves were too impatient and too out of touch with his membership to use the union as a vehicle for social change. His untimely death removed the last prominent bridge between the New Left, the Civil Rights Movement, and the blue collar labor unions.

The strike for which Reuther was preparing when he died occurred at the end of the year. It lasted two months and resulted in the last major victory for the union. The workers won substantial increases in wages and benefits, restoration of the COLA protection against a high rate of inflation, and the "thirty and out" early retirement plan designed to open up more employment opportunities for younger workers. The strike was more costly than either side could afford. General Motors lost $1 billion in profits at a time when the revitalized European and Japanese manufacturers were whetting the American appetite for smaller, cheaper, more fuel efficient vehicles. The union treasury was depleted to the verge of bankruptcy.[12] The two decades of growth and prosperity for the industry and its workers alike was coming to an end.

By the second decade of the twenty-first century, Walter Reuther had faded into the pages of the historical record—his name unfamiliar to the younger generations, his union seen as set in a period of tail fins and wrap-around windshields. The causes Reuther embraced remain pertinent, but have been steadily eased off the agenda of both political parties. The influence of big corporate donors on both parties has narrowed the concerns of government and steered the benefits of the system toward the affluent and well-connected. Decades of declining middle class expectations has stemmed the appetite for big public initiatives like the space program, model cities, public transport, and a renewed war on poverty.

An Unfinished Liberal Legacy

At the memorial service for Walter and May Reuther, Senator Philip Hart of Michigan told the assembled that they were there "not so much to discuss [Reuther's] life, but to read his will—that unwritten document he spent a lifetime composing, [to which] everyone here today is an heir."[13] It is up to the beneficiaries of that legacy to ensure that it is not squandered but increased and available to future beneficiaries. At his death, Reuther was actively supporting several causes and touting a number of new "Reuther Plans." The Committee of 100 that he formed and charged with developing an affordable health care coverage plan for all Americans was readying its report. His "Swords into Plowshares" proposal to Congress in December of 1969 suggested a means of promoting an orderly transition from defense to civilian production without creating an economic upheaval in the community in which defense plants were located. He was an early supporter of Senator Gaylord Nelson's Earth Day and was readying Black Lake to house a UN sponsored conference on the environment when he went on the ill-fated inspection trip. He was a champion of the Model Cities initiative of the Great Society and continued to put affordable housing, slum clearance, and neighborhood empowerment high on his list of priorities. The program he presented to the National Education Association (NEA) in 1956 echoes in the twenty-first century debate about the state of America's schools, and his Congressional testimony in the 1950's about planning to spread the benefits of automation remains relevant as more skill sets are performed by increasingly "intelligent" machines.

Reuther the Environmentalist

Reuther began the last couple weeks of his life addressing the first Earth Day celebration at his daughter's college and readying Black Lake to host an international conference of ecologists that would be preparatory for the first UN sponsored conference on the Environment. His concern for the environment was longstanding and included both the urban environment that shaped its inhabitants and the pristine spaces that needed their protection. The Reuthers found solace in nature, and the sylvan beauty of Black Lake was intended to be a palliative for UAW families with troubled marriages scarred by the stress and monotony of the assembly line.

The Reuthers' childhood contained little in the way of material pleasures. The boys found their amusement in the fields and waters that stretched out beyond their Wheeling homes. When the family moved to a farm on Bethlehem Hill beyond the city center, their summer table featured the fruits and vegetables picked and grown on their own acres. The Reuther boys grew up in close proximity to nature and retained a love for retreating into its embrace for the rest of their lives. During their quest to "study the economic and social conditions of the world," the young Walter and Victor enjoyed the diversion of climbing high in the Swiss Alps while waiting for their visas to enter the Soviet Union and hiking the military highway through the Caucasus in Georgia on their journey back home.

Years later, while in Italy attending a conference of the International Metalworker's Federation, the two brothers visited Florence, a city that radiated through the dark cloud of Fascism hanging over their first Italian trip. The Florentine Mayor had invited the pair to meet with him in his office, and the Reuthers were enjoying a cappuccino at an outdoor table in the square reigned over by Michelangelo's David while waiting for their appointment. Suddenly a rush of traffic belching fumes and blaring noise invaded the square. The frenetic afternoon rush paid little court to the Biblical king and made no accommodation for tourists bathed in the city's Renaissance splendor.

Walter jumped up out of his chair, motioned his brother to follow, and barged into the Mayor's office exclaiming before he was formally presented "Mr. Mayor, why don't you do something about that terrible traffic? It's destroying the whole character of this lovely city!" The Mayor was taken aback by this brash Yank telling him how to manage his city, but then began to laugh when he realized the irony of the situation.

He looked straight at his guest and said "Mr. Reuther, aren't you the president of the Automobile Workers Section of the International Metalworker's Federation? How can *you* make such a suggestion?"

Reuther acknowledged the incongruity, but responded that "automobiles are made to meet man's needs, not to destroy his environment." Eventually, whatever the effect Reuther's outburst may have contributed, the automobile was recognized as an invasive species in the milieu of the Medici and weeded from the Piazza della Signoria and other historic parts of the city,[14]

Back home in industrial Detroit, the auto was nourished with government highway spending and allowed to choke out the native bus and trolley service that stitched the city into a cohesive fabric. Rivers of concrete sliced the city into islands of neglect and ferried the more affluent off to more alluring suburbs. When the economic climate changed much of the city reverted back into an urban wilderness.

Globalization Brings Change to Detroit

The first signs of trouble for the domestic auto industry were the little "punch buggies" puttering down the highway, briefly distracting the kids on a long family trip. As more and more punch buggies appeared on American roads, Detroit continued to dismiss its lightweight challenger. Reuther regularly prodded the industry to build smaller, safer, more fuel-efficient cars with little effect. In 1949 the UAW promoted a *Small Car Named Desire* that would be more accessible to the budget of the average American worker.[15] The industry considered marketing strategy to be solely a management prerogative and never diverted its focus from the high-profit gas guzzling models of the fifties and sixties.

By the mid-sixties the European and Japanese competitors were flooding the American market with the smaller, fuel-efficient cars Detroit had refused to build. Reuther proposed to President Johnson in 1965 that the American auto industry be permitted to set up a joint venture to meet this challenge by pooling their resources to build a single model American challenger to the Volkswagen bug and the wave of foreign imports washing ashore in its wake.[16] Such a plan would limit the commitment of the individual companies to the production of a small car and dispel their concerns about starting a new line of competition between them. This *Small Car Named Desire* would represent a patriotic gesture from the industry that would save American jobs, provide the consumer with an affordable American-made automobile, and help the nation reduce its growing trade imbalance.

Johnson was intrigued by the idea and ordered a top-level review of the proposal. The push to build an American *Small Car Named Desire* stalled after Attorney General Nicholas deB. Katzenbach told the President that the joint venture would dissolve in the courts under the scrutiny of the Clayton Antitrust Act.[17] It would be five more years before Detroit would introduce the Chevy Vega and the Ford Pinto—the badly timed, badly built, and badly received domestic answer to the foreign invasion.

General Motors planned to meet the challenge of the lower labor costs of its overseas rivals by re-engineering the production process at its Lordstown, Ohio plant to create the fastest assembly line in the world. Company reorganization created the General Motors Assembly Division (GMAD) to consolidate its management of the new assembly regimen and planned for one hundred Vegas an hour to roll off the line. It was an industrial engineer's dream. In a response that could have been uttered by Henry Ford sixty years earlier, GM officials claimed "the concept is based on making it easier for the guy on the line. We feel that by giving him less to do he will do it better."[18] Management expected the workers would match their enthusiasm for the project by snatching up the first Vega *Dream Cars* themselves.

The guy on the line felt otherwise. In 1971 he was younger, better educated, and more attuned to the cultural influences resonating through society around him. Trivializing his task removed all sense of job satisfaction. He reacted not by doing the job better, but by high absenteeism, drugs and alcohol, and shoddy workmanship. Management responded by enforcing harsher discipline. Grievances skyrocketed; turnover soared; and the workers voted overwhelmingly to strike.[19]

The Lordstown strike was not about money or benefits. It was a challenge addressed to both management and the union. The Treaty of Detroit no longer defined the mutual interests of the two parties. It needed to be renegotiated. Under terms of the treaty, management had been ceded domain over the workplace environment, and now the workers wanted more from their job than a paycheck. The young Lordstown workers had wider horizons than their immigrant and depression era fathers who were happy to have a job that kept them fed and sheltered.

They were the beneficiaries of the American Dream that promised each new generation better opportunities than the previous.

The strike at the Vega assembly plant reflected a national angst over the nature of blue color work at a time when automation and globalization were limiting the opportunity for growth and self-fulfillment on the factory floor. The national press labeled the alienation of the working class "the blue collar blues" and explored its roots and depth in numerous articles.[20] The Nixon Administration convened a national commission to study the problem and generate a report titled *Work in America*. The report recognized that "many workers at all occupational levels feel locked in, their mobility blocked, the opportunity to grow lacking in their jobs, challenge missing from their tasks."[21]

The Lordstown strike lasted only three weeks. It ended with the working environment restored to the pre-GMAD conditions in effect at the time of the 1970 contract between GM and the UAW. The speed of the line was reduced to sixty cars per hour; the jobs eliminated by GMAD were reinstated; and the 1400 workers dismissed for disciplinary action were recalled.[22] Reuther's heirs retreated back within the familiar confines of the Treaty of Detroit to win concessions on the immediate issues that precipitated the strike, but the quality of work life remained governed strictly by the determination of management.

The concessions granted by GM at Lordstown in 1972 represented a last hurrah for the UAW. By the end of the decade the treaty that governed labor relations for thirty years was in tatters. The worker was no longer sharing in the expansion of a healthy industry, but suffering in the decline of an ailing one. The moment for workplace reform had come and gone with the agreement at Lordstown. One may speculate whether the situation would have played out differently had Reuther lived. The ingredients were in place for the renewal of the labor movement he had been seeking. The activism fermenting on college campuses had diffused into the factories. The young workers were not divided by race or tamed by need like their immigrant and depression era forebears. The importance of planning to ameliorate the side effects of automation and to humanize the workspace that Reuther stressed in his many public appearances was central to the national discussion surrounding the strike. Labor was still a formidable force in American life in 1972, and work place reform was an issue that galvanized support from a broad expanse of the working public. Would he have deemed the moment favorable to renegotiate the terms of the treaty that framed post-war labor-management relations and find a mechanism for including the concerns of the worker in production planning? Or was Walter Reuther a spent force at the time of his death—a man out of favor with the new administration in Washington, out of touch with the young activists, and out of step with the larger union hierarchy?

Reuther witnessed the Big Three auto giants acquiring European companies during the sixties and beginning to move some of their production overseas. He warned of the need for labor to respond with coordinated global initiatives of its own, "The dominant economic characteristic of this decade (1960s), and in all likelihood, the very hallmark of the next decade, has been the emergence of the multinational corporation. It is also, conceivably, a very grave danger to the world labor movement…The sooner, and the more vigorously, we set about building an international source of worker power commensurate with the global power now uncontested in the hands of the macro-corporations, the safer and saner the world's future will be."[23]

The competition between labor and the macro-corporation proved an unequal struggle that labor was unlikely to win. The corporations were monolithic, rich, and well-connected. The labor movement was multicultural, multilingual, and ideologically diverse. The various international components of the corporation answered to a single management but the workers were represented by independent nationally-based unions. The national focus and varied strength and traditions of the individual unions weighed against a "macro-labor" counterweight to the multinational's exploitation of differences in pay and workplace regulations from country to country. The vulnerability of labor in the new environment grew more pronounced when globalization reached into emerging markets with little history of union representation.

Before his death, Reuther was instrumental in establishing a World Auto Council composed of delegates from the fourteen countries in which the Big Three auto makers had manufacturing facilities. The Council members exchanged contract information and bargaining positions at the various locations, but the different pay scales between the European and North American economies in the sixties made the eventual goal of equalization of wages a distant prospect. Instead, globalization gnawed away at the wage and benefits package of American auto workers and culled the domestic workforce.

During the first flush of globalization at the end of the sixties, the world was still divided into East and West with little in the way of commerce flowing between the two antagonistic blocks. The most fertile ground for capitalist cultivation remained Western Europe, North America, and Japan. China was Red and forbidden; the Third World, still largely peripheral to the heavy industries of steel, automobiles, and machinery. The period witnessed the large American firms expanding into Europe to tap the potential of a skilled workforce and an economy fully recovered from the devastation of war. The threat to American jobs in the new environment came not only from domestic companies moving production overseas, but from the smaller, more fuel-efficient European and Japanese cars appearing on the American roads. First a trickle and soon a flood of imports challenged the Big Three on their own turf.

The Japanese companies were particularly aggressive in penetrating the American market. Their domestic demand could not sustain the scope of their industrial ambition. The Japanese government promoted an export-driven strategy of rapid economic growth.[24] Japanese unions were part of a paternalistic industrial system, and did not have the same close ties with their U. S. counterparts that most of the major European unions had formed. Walter Reuther was honored by world leaders, unionists, and the citizenry on his many visits abroad, but got a rude reception on both of his official trips to Japan. Communists, who were influential in the Japanese labor movement, resented Reuther for his anti-Communism. On his first visit to the country after the war, a pickup truck followed the car in which he and Victor were riding from the airport into the city of Osaka, trying to force it off the road over a steep embankment. When the brothers reached the city, they were met by a crowd of protesters using their picket signs as clubs to beat against the car and threatened the passengers inside.[25] On his second visit in 1962, he was heckled by party members during a speech at Tokyo University and jostled by a group of Communist protesters in Kyoto. When Japanese automakers justified their export-driven strategy by claiming that their domestic market was too small, Reuther pointed to the rows of bicycles lined up in the parking lot and told his audience that "Workers find it difficult to buy automobiles on bicycle wages. Your best market is in your own back yard."[26]

One Japanese unionist who appeared impressed by Reuther's message was Ichiro Shioji. Shioji had attended a speech by Reuther at Harvard and later claimed the American labor leader as his hero. Shioji was a fervent anti-Communist, but was willing to compromise the interests of his membership for his own personal benefit. He was simultaneously a vice president of Nissan and the head of its union, Shioji used his position at Nissan to consolidate his power and run a pliable company union.

Shioji assured Reuther's successors that when Nissan opened auto plants in the United States, it would recognize the UAW as its bargaining agent. UAW president Douglas Fraser lobbied the government hard to encourage the Japanese auto maker to open factories in America to save industry jobs, only to be double crossed by the company when it refused to recognize the union in its plants.[27] The arrival of foreign manufacturers using non-union labor created a two tier wage structure within the industry that handicapped the Big Three manufacturers and depressed the wages of the workers.

Climate Change

The American economic climate was not the only ecosystem experiencing change at the end of the century. The wastes of years of industrialization in the West and accelerated industrialization in the developing nations of the South and East were accumulating faster than nature could recycle them. Smog, toxic landfills, and polluted waterways represented the visible scars on the environment, affecting the health, recreational activities, and ambiance of people living in close proximity. Greenhouse gasses leaching into the atmosphere at an unsustainable rate pose a largely hidden risk to populations on a global scale.

Climate change is regarded by some people as an existential threat to the survival of human civilization in its present state and to others as a hoax perpetrated by liberals with a political agenda. The impact of human activity upon the climate is a question that only science can address with any authority, but, because of the ramifications that accepting a causative link would have for established industrial enterprises and deep-rooted behavioral patterns, its denial has become a litmus test of conservative political orthodoxy. Some of the deniers place a greater faith in the corrective power of the invisible hand than in the ability of science to distinguish between man-made and natural effects on the climate. Others find a liberal conspiracy to extend the sway of the federal government more unsettling than the warnings from an elite beneficiary of government and institutional largess. Some may just cover personal misgivings with political expediency. Since the early signs of a possible oncoming crisis are most visible in the remote polar regions, in the depths of the oceans, and in the glacial fields of the sparsely settled mountainous areas, the urgency of taking expensive preventive action against a threat experienced mainly on the nightly news is not compelling to a segment of the population wedded to a culture of abundance. The question of who is right in the debate between two sides with deeply held convictions and with little respect for the views of the other will not be settled before the possible consequences of inaction become too great to ignore and perhaps too late to mitigate. In the current climate it is the wrong question to ask. The question each side needs to ask the other is *suppose you are wrong*? What are the consequences of making a wrong choice now?

The best way to picture the problem is to take a plain sheet of white paper and draw a vertical line down the middle of the page. The area to the right of the line will represent the truth of the claim that human activity is contributing to an unsustainable increase in the temperature of the earth. The area to the left depicts the opposite truth. Next draw a horizontal line across the page and let the area above the line indicate the situation where no action is taken to combat the perceived threat and the area below to indicate effective measures are undertaken. The page is divided into four quadrants—the upper left is no human cause and no action taken; the upper right indicates the situation where no action is taken to avoid a real threat; the lower left depicts the case where action is taken to combat a threat that does not exist; and the lower right represents actions taken to address a real concern.

Now in each quadrant list the costs and benefits that result. In the upper left there is no redirection of the economy and no early migration to more environmentally friendly technologies. There is no disruption of existing practices, but perhaps a risk of ceding profitable new markets to countries that take a different approach to the problem. In the lower left quadrant money is spent to confront a non-existent problem, but health benefits accrue from a reduction of pollutants associated with burning carbon-based fuels and new industries and jobs emerge more quickly. In the lower right quadrant the initial costs are the same, but the benefit of avoiding the consequences of inaction to a real threat is substantial.

The choice of making no investment to confront a real problem, as depicted in the upper right quadrant, would have huge, perhaps catastrophic, consequences. The cost of postponing action until the effects of human activity on the climate can no longer be denied will be many times higher than they are today and may occur too late to save the planet from some of the worst-case scenarios offered by climate scientists.

The political argument in developing a game theory analysis of this admittedly simplified construction arises over assigning probabilities and costs to each of these quadrants. Since only scientists directly involved in climate research have an independently acquired basis of knowledge of the subject, the percentage of these scientists asserting carbon emissions as the principal source of global warming serves as a good way of affixing a probability to the left and right-hand side of the diagram. Well over 90% of climate scientists believe human activity is driving the current phase of global warming and this number will represent the area to the right of the vertical line on our page. The probability that timely action sufficient to confront the situation will be taken by the United States and other world governments is much more problematic. Assigning 50% to the area above and below the horizontal line is perhaps too generous a belief in the collective wisdom of our species. The probability that effective action is taken to reduce greenhouse gases during any set period such as a year depends on the percentage of people in the general population that favor strong measures to confront the problem and the extent to which this sentiment translates into a political imperative for their leaders. This probability will change with time, but the costs will only increase over the same period.

There is more disagreement among climate scientists over the extent of the reduction in carbon emissions needed to slow and eventually reverse the temperature rise and over the severity of the effects that a delayed or inadequate response would entail. Costs and penalties to assign to each of the four quadrants reflect these assessments. The cost of taking action depends on the target value set for carbon emissions reduction and the time frame over which it is to be achieved. The penalty for taking no action or insufficient action is the cost of drought, flooding, population displacement, disease, extinctions, severe weather, and unrest envisioned in one or several of the scenarios depicted by climatologists. Whether one takes the best case, worst case, or some consensus assessment, the cost in dollars, lives, and instability would likely dwarf the cost of previous wars and economic upheavals.

Once costs and benefits are assigned to the four quadrants an average or expected cost is obtained by multiplying the cost in each box by the probability associated with that quadrant and adding the results. In our model there is a 0.45 probability associated with the upper right hand quadrant and an enormous penalty so the expected cost will be heavily weighted by this term. If national and world leaders commit to aggressively reduce greenhouse gases, only the bottom half of the page applies and the high penalty associated with the failure to protect against the reality of human-caused warming is avoided. If no action is taken or too long deferred, only the two alternatives on the top half of the page remain and there is a high probability that the extreme penalty will be assessed.

The above argument reformulates the debate over climate change from an interpretation of scientific data to a rationale for buying insurance. If no action on climate change is taken or if action is deferred for too long, then policy makers will be betting on the long odds that the consensus of scientific opinion is wrong and the world will avoid the consequences of losing that bet. If the leaders of this generation make the wrong bet, it is their children and grandchildren who will pick up the tab and suffer the consequences. The climate change denier is presented with a situation that is not dissimilar from that of a parent who needs to protect his family until his children are grown and his financial situation secured. The responsible parent takes out an insurance policy even if the probability of needing it for an emergency is fairly small. Whether one accepts the scientific explanation for climate change or not, it is beyond irresponsible not to "buy the necessary insurance."

The cost of this "insurance" will not be cheap. It will result in higher energy bills and higher taxes, and will necessitate some lifestyle adjustments. It will require an honest presentation of the costs and benefits from its proponents and examples of statesmanship by responsible conservatives. It will be difficult to sell to a population that has been encouraged to resist any government effort to promote the public good at the expense of individual prerogative by many of the same voices loudly denying the science today.

Climate change is not an issue affecting any one country. It affects every country whether they are influential or weak, developed or developing, and whether they are major contributors of carbon to the atmosphere or strictly limiting their own greenhouse gas emissions. Effective action to limit emissions will require a degree of international cooperation rarely, if ever, exhibited by the "international community." The United States often claims to speak on behalf of this amorphous collective and proclaims itself the leader of this coalition or that. If it is to retain this voice into the twenty-first century it must exhibit its leadership on this issue, by example more than by exhortation. Failure of the United States to show mature leadership will likely lead to an inadequate or untimely global response and diminish its influence in the world forum, particularly with those of the more forward-looking nations that have been its traditional allies. The alternative to cooperation is very likely a more feverish world separating into contentious blocks, each looking out for their self-interest.

Nuclear Power

Back in the '50s industrial and government energy planners envisioned a far different future for the American power grid. By the year 2000 they expected to replace coal burning power plants with over a thousand nuclear plants.[28] Climate change was only the concern of a few scientists working in labs far removed from the political theater. Nuclear power was sold to a receptive public as cheap, clean, and safe.

Walter Reuther embraced technological progress but cautioned that planning was necessary to fairly distribute its benefits and limit its disruptions. Harnessing the energy of the atom for the benefit of mankind was a prospect the former skilled craftsman applauded. He supported building nuclear power plants to generate electricity when appropriate safety standards were applied and public concerns were addressed.[29] But in 1956, when Walker Cisler, Chairman of the Detroit Edison Company, proposed building the Fermi fast-breeder reactor at a location thirty miles south of Detroit and twenty miles north of Toledo, Reuther was convinced that public safety was being compromised. Over three million people were within a danger zone should radioactive elements escape from the plant.

The Fermi I fast-breeder was not like other nuclear plants under construction by the domestic power industry at that time. Most reactors used pressurized water in the containment vessel to serve as both a coolant and a moderator to slow the neutrons produced during fission and increase the efficiency with which the fuel was "burned." Nuclei of the fissionable uranium isotope U235 have a greater cross section for capturing neutrons that have been slowed to the ambient temperature of the boiling water in the reactor's containment vessel. Neutron capture causes the heavy uranium nucleus to split, release energy, and produce two or more neutrons to continue the chain reaction that powers the generation of electricity.

U235 constitutes less than one percent of naturally occurring uranium and must be enriched to a concentration of at least three percent for use as reactor fuel. The more abundant isotope U238, which constitutes the bulk of the fuel rod, will also capture some neutrons and go through a decay process that produces a fissionable plutonium isotope. A boiling water reactor "breeds" about six plutonium nuclei for every ten U235 nuclei it burns.[30]

A breeder reactor produces more fissionable fuel than it burns. It operates at a higher ambient temperature than that of boiling water because U238 nuclei capture fast-moving neutrons more efficiently. It compensates for the less efficient capture of fast neutrons by the U235 nuclei by starting with a more highly enriched fuel to sustain a chain reaction sufficient for commercial power generation. A breeder must use a coolant that remains liquid at temperatures higher than that for which boiling water is safely maintained. The Fermi I reactor was cooled with liquid sodium pumped through the reactor by a system of pipes that transferred heat from the reactor to water in a secondary vessel producing steam for driving the turbines generating electricity.

At a time when uranium for commercial use was relatively scarce and expensive,[31] the fast-breeder had the attraction of being able to produce additional quantities of its own fuel. Breeding made all of the naturally occurring uranium a potential fuel source, not just the relatively scarce isotope in its composition. But it also posed a higher risk. The liquid sodium coolant used in the breeder reacts violently and catches fire if it is exposed to water or oxygen. The higher ambient temperature and greater volatility of its coolant introduced additional risk factors into the emergency shutdown procedures in the breeder above those encountered with boiling water reactors.

Fermi 1 was the country's first commercial fast-breeder reactor. Nuclear power was in its infancy, and despite the rosy picture painted by the industry, numerous accidents at research prototype facilities indicated that serious growing pains might be experienced before the industry matured.[32] Walter Reuther was alerted to the haste with which this project was being pushed forward and challenged the location of such a potentially dangerous power plant so close to major population centers. Backed by the International Union of Electrical Workers, the United Paper Workers of America, and the UAW, Reuther demanded a public hearing on the safety of the reactor[33]

Reuther urged the commercial backers of the project to build a prototype reactor in a more remote location that would not expose the public to as much danger. He cited the example of the United Kingdom where nuclear power plants were being built on the remote Scottish coastline at Dounreay and at Windscale near the Lake District.[34] Detroit Edison countered with an impressive group of scientists including the Nobel Prize winner Hans Bethe to attest to the safety of the fast-breeder. Reuther cited a study by the Advisory Committee on Reactor Safeguards of the Atomic Energy Commission that alerted the AEC about safety concerns surrounding the Fermi reactor.[35] But the AEC had the dual responsibility of promoting the commercial use of atomic energy and ensuring the safety of the public. It was structured from the start to be an advocate for the power industry. The AEC established a pattern of obscuring information about problems at experimental reactor sites such as Idaho Flats, minimizing safety concerns, and downplaying the more pessimistic figures on the consequences of a major accident.

The construction permit was granted on August 4, 1956—six months before the public hearings were convened. Construction at the site continued as the hearings and subsequent court proceedings dragged on. In March of 1960 Reuther's group won a battle in the U. S. Court of Appeals that ordered the construction stopped within 15 days. The dispute eventually ended in the United States Supreme Court which decided 7 to 2 for the power company.[36] A last attempt by Reuther and his co-petitioners to deny the plant an operating license failed and Fermi 1 began operation in December, 1965.

Reuther's concern was validated months later when a partial meltdown occurred. The reactor was operating at limited capacity at the time and radiation was contained within the structure, but the anxious times at the plant continued for a month while engineers struggled to bring the situation under control and determine the cause of the accident. Months later the problem was determined to have arisen from one of the five triangular pieces of zirconium, that were grafted to the original design as an added safety measure to protect the cone-shaped flow guide. It had dislodged and blocked the coolant from reaching a number of sub-assemblies in the core. The part that caused the partial meltdown was not even pictured on the original blueprints[37]

The plant was plagued by a series of problems for the next several years. By 1971 when its license came up for renewal, the cost of the plant to the rate payers and investors in the utility was under scrutiny by the Michigan Public Service Commission. Many of the corporations that Cisler had enlisted in his Power Reactor Development Corporation were backing out. On August 27, 1972 the AEC rejected Detroit Edison's application for license extension and the Fermi I power plant was decommissioned. The final cost of the project was $132 million (in 1972 dollars).[38] Over its ten years of operation it functioned at its licensed capacity for fewer than thirty days. It produced negligible electricity and bred scarcely any plutonium.

Walker Cisler was as passionate in his belief in the potential of nuclear power to solve mankind's future energy needs as Walter Reuther was in his commitment to social justice. The two men argued their views in public hearings and court proceedings and engaged in public debates and discussions during years of hearings and litigation. Despite their disagreement on an issue of fundamental importance to both, the two men established a friendship based on mutual respect. When Walter Reuther was honored in 1969 by the Weizmann Institute in Rehovot, Israel with the establishment of a Walter Reuther Chair for the peaceful uses of atomic energy, Walker Cisler traveled at his own expense to be present at the dedication.[39]

The decommissioning of Fermi I in 1972 did not deflect the AEC from their goal of developing a national electrical grid supplied by nuclear energy, and the breeder reactor was critical to that vision. Without the breeder, only a tiny fraction of the scarce uranium extracted from the earth was usable as fuel, severely limiting the economic potential of this power source. Even as Fermi I was slipping into its eventual demise, a new breeder reactor project was being planned for a site adjacent to the Clinch River near Oak Ridge Tennessee. The project was conceived as a joint public and private enterprise, and many of the consortium partners that Cisler had enlisted into his Power Reactor Development Corporation jumped aboard this new effort. It was authorized by Congress in 1970 and deemed to be "the nation's highest priority research and development effort" in 1971 by President Nixon.[40]

But the mood of the public had dramatically shifted from the blind, exuberant acceptance that greeted the promise of cheap, clean power back in the 50s. Faith in authority, whether civil or scientific, had been battered by the turbulent 60s, and promises were regarded with much more skepticism. As the costs of the Clinch River project soared from the original estimate of $400 million into the billions,[41] the skeptics became more numerous and more vocal. In 1977 President Carter vetoed additional spending for the project he called "large and unnecessarily expensive [which] when completed would be technically obsolete and economically unsound."[42] The funding was routinely continued by Congress over his vetoes, but the 1979 partial melt-down accident at

Three Mile Island poisoned attitudes toward nuclear power. In 1983 Congress cut off funds for the Clinch River breeder project.

Diminished public support for nuclear power provided cover for Congress to stop seeing each new raise on the project and fold its hand on a pot that it had already enriched with taxpayer dollars beyond its likely return. When the project was terminated in 1983, the Congressional General Accounting Office estimated that its total cost would run to $8 billion, nearly twenty times the original estimate.[43] The vote to kill was also made easier because breeder reactor investment had lost its most important constituency—the power companies. Breeder reactors were now twice as expensive to build as the more conventional light water reactor plants, and uranium was less scarce than originally anticipated. The 1981 price of $25 per pound of processed uranium would have to increase over six-fold in terms of 1981 dollars for a breeder to be competitive with the light water alternative.[44] With the cancellation of Clinch River, Fermi I remains the last breeder plant ever built and completed in the United States.

Reuther's challenge to the licensing of Fermi I had little public support at the time. The power industry conducted an effective public relations campaign to sell the concept that nuclear power was safe and clean, and seduced the residents of lower Michigan with promises of jobs and economic growth. The press played up these benefits and ignored safety concerns stemming from accidents at nuclear facilities in Idaho Flats, Chalk River in Canada, and Windscale in the UK.[45] Reuther's efforts did create a precedent for public hearings as part of the license approval process, and such scrutiny exposed the regulatory structure within the AEC to be compromised by the agency's directive to promote the commercial use of nuclear energy.

In 1974 Congress recognized the incompatibility of the dual charge given the AEC and reorganized the agency into two new entities. The Energy Research and Development Administration (ERDA) was given control of the nuclear weapons program and responsibility for the development and promotion of commercial nuclear power; and the Nuclear Regulatory Commission (NRC) was created as a separate organization charged with license approval and renewal, and monitoring safety and security at nuclear plants. In 1979 the Department of Energy was created by expanding the role and status of ERDA. Reorganization freed the NRC from an obligation to promote the technology it was charged with regulating, but did not shield it from the influence the nuclear industry wielded over its appointments and deliberations.

After Three Mile Island and the cancellation of the Clinch River project, nuclear power fell out of favor with both an apprehensive public and utilities weighing the costs and benefits of their investments. Major accidents at Chernobyl and Fukushima-Daiichi reinforced opposition and seemed to relegate nuclear power to the fringes of the spectrum of energy alternatives under discussion in the United States. But its adherents are still holding some high trump cards in their hand.

Concern about global warming has reintroduced nuclear power as *Pandora's Promise*[46] for an energy-rich tomorrow without the carbon emissions that threaten the sustainability of a habitat supporting the current numbers and economic activity of our species. Climate science is dismissed by a well-funded lobby of interest groups that have blocked effective measures to reduce carbon emissions and lessen our dependence on fossil fuels, but many of the same people would not be averse to citing it as a reason to further a nuclear power agenda.

In the 2012 campaign, Republicans seized upon the stimulus money given to the bankrupt solar panel company Solyndra as their battle cry against Obama's betting public money on a favorite horse in the energy derby. But long before Solyndra, government was picking winners in that race. Soon after President Eisenhower's Atoms for Peace speech to the U. N. General Assembly in 1953, the United States opened its Pandora's Box of nuclear expertise and encouraged the private sector to enter what was being called at the time "The Atomic Age." The AEC forecast that one thousand nuclear reactors would be generating the nation's electricity by the year 2000,[47] and the government pushed the technology with grants to research groups, processed uranium at bargain prices for the power companies, and offered catastrophic insurance coverage that private insurers would not assume.[48] Nuclear power consumed the bulk of the research and development money devoted to exploring fossil fuel alternatives, and government partnership with private industry created entrenched interests committed to the success of their enterprise.

It has been fifty years since Fermi I was licensed to begin operation. Present day reactors represent the fourth generation in the evolution of the technology. These new reactor plants are engineered to minimize or avoid the problems that plagued earlier designs like Fermi I and Three Mile Island. The centerpiece of a nuclear powered electrical grid is still the fast reactor—the breeder that produces more new fuel than it burns in generating electricity and solves the nuclear waste disposal problem by burning the long half-life actinides produced in the decay cycle of trans-uranium elements. After fifty years of development, nuclear power represents an "off the shelf" technology that is capable of sustaining the world's appetite for electrical power without adding greenhouse gases to the atmosphere.

Nuclear power still carries substantial risk. Engineers, and the businessmen who employ them, regard risk as a problem with an engineering solution. Substantially all of the money invested in reactor research over the years has been allocated toward finding these solutions. The far greater danger lies in mankind's ability to manage the risk beyond the reinforced containment shell of the power plant.

Plutonium is the most toxic substance on the planet. If the "plutonium standard" is adopted as the energy currency of the realm, tons of plutonium would be in circulation throughout the world. This supply would have to be safely monitored in perpetuity. A strict accounting of the world's ever changing plutonium supply would need to be kept during all phases of the fuel cycle. Plutonium would be another commodity of great value that would attract the interest of unscrupulous dealers eying the profits it represents. It would be a target for terrorists and a temptation for regimes seeking nuclear weapons. India, Pakistan, and North Korea used the reprocessing of plutonium to hasten the date they acquired nuclear weapons.[49]

A more attractive nuclear option has gathered dust on the shelf since the 1970's. A reactor using thorium as its primary fuel source alleviates the danger of catastrophic meltdown and is unsuitable for generating products during its fuel cycle that can be extracted and used for making weapons. Thorium is estimated to be three to four times more abundant than uranium and does not have to be enriched before it can be used in a reactor. Thorium itself is not highly radioactive and not fissile, but undergoes a transmutation cycle that produces fissile U233 when exposed to a neutron flux inside a reactor.

Thorium can be used in a number of different reactor designs, but the one generating the most interest is the liquid fluoride thorium reactor (LFTR). A molten fluoride salt solution containing naturally occurring Th232 and some initial fissile starter serves as both the fuel and the coolant. Unlike the liquid sodium coolant used in the Fermi 1 breeder, the molten salt does not react violently when exposed to oxygen or water. Molten salt reactors are not pressurized like boiling water reactors, and there is no water or hydrogen in the reactor core to cause a pressure build up and explosion like occurred at Fukushima-Daichi. The liquid fuel in an LFTR can be reprocessed online, removing the fission by-products without having to shut down the reactor and reprocess spent fuel rods off-site, as is the case with solid fuel uranium-plutonium reactors. Almost all the fissile material produced in the core burns, alleviating much of the waste disposal problem plaguing the enriched uranium fueled reactors currently in use.[50]

Molten salt reactors are not a new concept. They were pioneered by Alvin Weinberg at Oak Ridge National Laboratory in the 50s and 60s. Weinberg demonstrated the fueling of an experimental reactor using a liquid thorium-fluoride salt mixture containing U233.[51] He lobbied for making thorium the centerpiece of the nation's civilian nuclear power effort, but ran into stiff resistance from advocates of the uranium-plutonium breeder project that enjoyed a head start and received substantially all the allocated funding.[52]

At a time when uranium was scarce and the Cold War arms race dictated the course of the nation's civilian nuclear program, there was a willingness to uncritically accept AEC assurances about the safety of the technology. Weinberg described to science writer Richard Martin a conversation he once had with Congressman Chester Holifield of California, the Chairman of the Joint Committee on Atomic Energy.

> "Chet Holifield was clearly exasperated with me, and he finally blurted out, 'Alvin. If you are concerned about the safety of reactors, then I think it may be time for

you to leave nuclear energy.' I was speechless. But it was apparent to me that my style, my attitude, and my perception of the future were no longer in tune with the powers within the AEC."[53]

The government terminated all thorium-based nuclear research in 1973, and Weinberg was forced into retirement

Interest in thorium reactors has revived in recent years. India, with perhaps the largest reserve of thorium in the world, plans to have sixty-two thorium reactor power plants operational by 2025.[54] It plans to use its abundant thorium deposits to become energy independent. Other countries announcing intentions to pursue the development of thorium reactors include China, Norway, Israel, Brazil, and Canada.[55] In the United States research activity on thorium-based reactors has been suspended for forty years. Uranium fueled reactors have had forty years to develop and mature while no thorium reactor prototypes were being investigated, and they had forty years to build an influential constituency promoting their use.

In the United States private initiative remains poised to advance and commercialize a technology that has been nurtured and developed by government research grants. One of the private American companies pushing nuclear power is TerraPower, chaired by Bill Gates. TerraPower refers to itself as an innovation house whose only product is the patents it secures. It provides venture capital to clients fleshing out its designs and partnering in its research. TerraPower is primarily pushing a Traveling Wave Reactor, a new design for a liquid sodium cooled fast breeder that converts depleted uranium into plutonium without requiring refueling over the life of the power plant.[56] The Gates group is also investigating molten salt thorium reactors, but expects the Traveling Wave Reactor to obviate the need for an alternative. There are other "innovation houses" in the United States concentrating on thorium reactors, but they lack the star power and resources available to TerraPower. If thorium is to replace uranium and plutonium as the fuel in the nuclear furnace, it is likely that standard will be established by countries and groups outside of the United States.

The recent exploitation of vast quantities of domestic oil and natural gas that new drilling techniques have made accessible mitigates against an early exodus from a carbon fueled economy. The energy lobby envisions a near-term transition from coal to natural gas and a longer-term reliance on nuclear power to supply the electrical power demands of the economy. The politics of abundant oil and gas favor this scenario.

Military Spending

Since the end of World War 2 the United States has fought five major wars and conducted over a half dozen other brief incursions into countries deemed either unstable, unreliable, or unfriendly. Two years of war in Korea ended in a stalemate with twenty-five thousand American troops still in the country sixty years later. The Vietnam War began with special forces *advisers* being dispatched to Laos and South Vietnam in the early sixties. It turned into a major commitment of forces after the Gulf of Tonkin resolution in 1965, and ended with withdrawal of US forces in 1973 and defeat of our client state two years later. The war in Afghanistan began after the terrorist attack of 9, 11, 2001 and is projected to end thirteen years later with a residual component of non-combat special operations forces of unspecified size remaining in the country. The Afghan war bracketed an eight year struggle with a larger commitment of forces in Iraq. Since the departure of American troops from that country, the weakness and sectarian agenda of the Iraqi government has allowed the Al Qaeda affiliate, rebranded as ISIS, to capture major cities in the Sunni heartland and bring the United States back to a battlefield that has metastasized to new sites throughout the world. Only *Operation Desert Storm,* in which U. S. forces drove an over-matched invading Iraqi army from Kuwait and returned the country back to its ruling family, could be considered a military triumph.

The stalemate in Korea has produced a modern economic powerhouse in the South living beneath the shadow of its feudal, family-run neighbor to the north. The intervention prevented a Communist takeover of the South and provided its people the space to evolve into a democratic, economically strong state. The success in Korea was not repeated in Vietnam, and there is little indication of it in the Middle

East. The sacrifice of life and treasure poured onto the parched sands of Iraq and Afghanistan has born only a stubble crop of representative government and stability. The total cost of the effort, including indirect costs such as interest on war-related debts and long-term medical care for the 33,000 wounded veterans of the wars, is expected to exceed 3.7 trillion dollars.[57] Only one year of the combined twenty years of fighting in the two wars involved fighting a conventional army of a nation state.

In addition to the five major conflicts, there were interventions in Lebanon (twice), the Dominican Republic, Haiti, Panama, Grenada, Cambodia, Somalia, Bosnia, and Kosovo, and drone strikes announced in Pakistan and Yemen. The United States intelligence services supported the Contras in Nicaragua, the United Fruit Company in Guatemala, secured the throne for the Shah in Iran, destabilized Chile, and supplied missiles to the mujahedin fighting the Russians in Afghanistan, a group of fighters that included Osama bin Laden and Islamists who came to fill the ranks of Al Qaeda and the Taliban.

Some of the interventions stabilized the situation in the country, others resulted in unanticipated side effects with serious consequences. A bombing of the Marine compound in Lebanon and the downing of a Black Hawk helicopter with a subsequent humiliation of its crew member in Somalia hastened the withdrawal of American forces from those two engagements. Efforts to check Soviet expansion on the periphery of the Cold War battle lines in Iran and Afghanistan have shaped events in those countries and made them the central focus of twenty-first century concern.

In 2012 the United States budgeted $711 billion for the Department of Defense.[58] This figure was larger in dollar amount than the next fourteen countries combined, most of whom were U. S. allies. If the figure for defense related expenditures including homeland security, veterans affairs, pensions, and interest on past war debt were included the total would exceed $1 trillion.[59] The $46.9 billion allocated to Homeland Security alone would rank it eighth on the list of the world's top military spenders, just ahead of India and Germany.[60] The 4.7 percent of GNP that DoD spending represents is exceeded only by Israel, Saudi Arabia, a couple of Gulf States and two small countries in Africa.[61]

The expenditure of so much blood and treasure has done little to increase our sense of security in the post Cold War era. Fear of Soviet bombs has given way to fear of terrorist plots. The amount budgeted for "defense" far exceeds the requirement for protection of the homeland. Defense has come to mean the enforcement of a Pax Americana that justifies preemptive wars such as in Iraq and interventions in numerous countries. Having the world's most powerful military has made policy makers more prone to flex military muscle to resolve international disputes.

In the nineteenth century, it was said that the sun never set on the British Empire. In the twenty-first, it never sets on American military bases scattered throughout the world. The "Upstairs Downstairs" world of Edwardian England that the empire sustained died in the trenches of the Somme and later in the bomb shelters of London. Even before the Great War, the price of empire had become too high to sustain. The Britain that emerged from the blitz was more egalitarian, more compassionate, and more comfortable with its place in the family of nations. In contrast, appropriation of the trappings of empire has made the United States less egalitarian, less open, and less comfortable in a world that increasingly resents its intrusion into the affairs of cultures it barely understands.

American militarism has inflicted "collateral damage" on its own society. Seventy years of nearly continuous hot and cold war has solidified a militaristic culture that devours funds otherwise available to be spent on education, social programs, and infrastructure improvement. It has created a constituency for its ambitious agenda in the many towns and states that depend upon defense plants and military bases for their livelihood. It feeds the common culture with movies and video games that glorify "black ops" inside countries with whom we are not in a formal state of war. It sustains, or is sustained by, a culture of gun violence that claims more casualties in a single year than the combined death toll of the decade long conflicts in Iraq and Afghanistan.[62] It seeps into our institutions under a cloak of official state secrecy. It pollutes our language with euphemisms like collateral damage and terminate with extreme prejudice to sanitize civilian deaths and targeted assassinations. It mesmerizes us with technology that distances us from its consequences.

For most Americans war has become something of a spectator sport. The numbers fighting in Iraq and Afghanistan are small by historical measures. The burden of combat is borne unevenly. The ranks of the all-volunteer army are filled by members of fewer than five percent of American families. The men and women who enlist for patriotic or economic reasons are asked to serve multiple tours of duty in the war zones. The rest of the population experiences the "shock and awe" on CNN. George Bush dispatched the troops to the Middle East and told the rest of the country to go shopping with a fresh tax cut in their wallets. There was no war tax, no shortages, no sacrifice asked of the public. Life went on as before with a pause for tributes to the troops and a chorus of *God Bless America* during the seventh inning stretch.

Collectively, we have composed and frequently repeated the lyrics of a national tribute to the men and women of the military. Their bravery and sacrifice are worthy of the honor they receive. But in recognizing individual heroism, we must also ennoble the cause it serves. The chorus repeats that "they are fighting for our freedom." The certitude with which this declaration is repeated mutes discussion of the efficacy and morality of the wars and the role of military power in our foreign policy. There is no space given to the discussion of whether our freedom is at risk from our adversaries or curtailed by the forces of cultural imperialism at the root of their hatred.

The weapon of choice in the asymmetric wars of the early twenty-first century has become the drone. Nothing depicts the asymmetry of these conflicts more than the signature weapons of the two parties—the suicide vest and the drone. One, the product of a fundamentalist faith in the certainty of an idyllic afterlife. The other, created by a culture that puts a premium on life—its own life. One combatant wears body armor, the other, a lethal vest. The drone is an antidote to the poison of terrorism—a swift vigilante justice meted out on the frontier of civilization.

Today drones patrol the skies over Pakistan and Yemen. Tomorrow they will secure the borders and survey the mean streets of the homeland. Soon warfare by remote control will proliferate to the armies of the eager powers great and small that strut across the world stage. The new weapons of war embrace a technology that measures its growth in shrinkage, its capacity in terabytes, and its robustness in the distributed architecture of its brain. It will become cheaper and easier to acquire with fewer constraints on its use. The very size and extent of American military might encourages rivals to assert their own national identity in similar fashion. The nation is no more secure under the aegis of imperial ambition than it would be under a more modest umbrella adequate for its own defense.

President Eisenhower warned in his farewell address to the nation about the dangers of a military-industrial complex that had become the byproduct of a perpetual war-footing environment.

> "Our military organization today bears little relation to that known by any of my predecessors in peacetime, or indeed by the fighting men of World War II or Korea. Until the latest of our world conflicts, the United States had no armaments industry. American makers of plowshares could, with time and as required, make swords as well. But now we can no longer risk emergency improvisation of national defense; we have been compelled to create a permanent armaments industry of vast proportions. Added to this, three and a half million men and women are directly engaged in the defense establishment. We annually spend on military security more than the net income of all United States corporations. This conjunction of an immense military establishment and a large arms industry is new in the American experience. The total influence—economic, political, even spiritual—is felt in every city, every State house, every office of the Federal government. We recognize the imperative need for this development. Yet we must not fail to comprehend its grave implications. Our toil, resources and livelihood are all involved; so is the very structure of our society. In the councils of government, we must guard against the acquisition of unwarranted influence, whether sought or unsought, by the military industrial complex. The potential for the disastrous rise of misplaced power

exists and will persist. We must never let the weight of this combination endanger our liberties or democratic processes. We should take nothing for granted. Only an alert and knowledgeable citizenry can compel the proper meshing of the huge industrial and military machinery of defense with our peaceful methods and goals, so that security and liberty may prosper together"[63]

The *rise of misplaced power* in the military industrial complex has continued, despite Eisenhower's warning. It has survived the Cold War and is impervious to the decline in middle class fortunes in the budget battles of the new century. Defense jobs in key Congressional districts have proved an effective brake on efforts to curb military spending. Companies like General Dynamics, LTV Aerospace, and North American Rockwell that cater almost exclusively to the needs of the Defense Department and NASA emerged during the Cold War. Divisions of these companies were encouraged to locate in regions of low industrialization where they would be the main source of employment and economic activity. Loss of government contracts would create massive dislocation in these communities, ensuring strong Congressional support to keep the spigot open.

In December of 1969, six month before his death, Walter Reuther presented a proposal to Congress he titled *Swords into Plowshares* that addressed the problem of conversion from military to civilian production. Reuther presented his proposal during testimony before the Senate Committee on Labor and Public Welfare that was considering a bill proposed by Senators McGovern (Dem. SD) and Hatfield (Rep. Ore.) that anticipated the problems of reconversion at the end of the Vietnam War. He was sympathetic with the plan to establish a National Economic Conversion Commission contained in the bill, but skeptical that the requirement for the defense contractor to merely define his capability for converting to civilian production to this board would have any real effect on its behavior.[64]

The defense contractors had little interest in converting to civilian production. They enjoyed a symbiotic relationship with their counterparts in the Pentagon. They made little effort and experienced little success in the less constricted civilian market. They relied instead on a continuing demand for weapons and military hardware. Washington Post reporter Bernard Nossiter cited a study by the Electronics Industry Association in a December 8, 1968 article that revealed "the document forecasts that arms control agreements 'during the next decade are unlikely,' the 'likelihood of limited war will increase' and 'thus for the electronics firms, *the outlook is good in spite of* [the end of hostilities in] *Vietnam.*'" Peace was a dirty word to the industry marketing folks who generated geopolitical assessments reinforcing a world view consistent with their business model. It was not only the military that defined its needs. The companies courted their military clients and whet their appetite for new weapons systems with marketing campaigns for the next generation of products on their drawing boards.

Reuther testified that the only way to get the defense contractors to take reconversion seriously was "with the strongest practical financial motivation." He argued companies needed a financial incentive to plan seriously for reconversion and face a penalty for failing this obligation. In his proposal companies would be required to submit a reconversion plan with the National Economic Conversion Commission when they were awarded a defense contract. A fraction of company profits would be held in a reserve fund to finance its reconversion plan. (Reuther used 25% for purpose of the discussion.) The plan would specify the civilian product the firm would produce, the marketing analysis performed to indicate the viability of the enterprise, the machines that could be converted, the additional machinery that would be needed, the time needed for conversion, and the cost. The Commission would have the authority to review the plan for compliance with the filing requirements and ensure sequestered funds would be used only for conversion to civilian production and paying employee benefits. It would not be able to alter a properly formulated plan, but would make its review available to the contractor and offer its resources to correct deficiencies or alert the company to additional opportunities.

The Reuther proposal stipulated that interest on the sequestered profits would accrue to the company's conversion fund. It also provided the contractor an ability to borrow money from its reserve fund to finance a conversion project if it could find a private lender willing to share at least ten percent of the risks of that investment. Interest on the money borrowed from its reserves would go back into the company's reserve fund. Under such an arrangement, the company would be paying interest to itself.[65]

Companies that made an honest commitment to reconversion and prepared in advance for a transition to non military production, would minimize the disruption to its workforce and reclaim the bulk of its sequestered profits. Companies delaying conversion efforts would see more of their reserve fund spent on benefits owed to their employees when their defense work declined or terminated. Failure to comply with the reconversion plan would lead the Commission to contract with another company to convert and operate the facility and pay for the conversion expenses and rent out of the original contractor's reserve fund.

The civilian market that a defense contractor chose to enter upon reduction or termination of its military work was at its own discretion by the terms of the proposal, but Reuther pointed to housing, transportation, and air and water pollution as neglected social issues that would provide opportunities for the defense contractors to target. He retained a faith in Fordism to provide the abundance that would deliver mankind from want and free it to grow spiritually, intellectually, and culturally. He cited the launch vehicles for the Apollo program that had recently landed Neil Armstrong on the moon as among the most sophisticated systems built by man, but the workforce producing these vehicles was fifteen percent skilled and eighty-five percent unskilled. By contrast, the workforce building a house, which he characterized as "a box with some holes punched in it," was ninety percent skilled.[66] In the first case the sophistication was in the tools that required little skill of the operator, whereas the more primitive tools of the construction trades required a greater competence from the person using them to produce the finished product. Reuther preached that the need for low cost housing was enough to induce the builders of cylinders filled with sophisticated electronics into the market for boxes with holes.

Nothing came of Reuther's proposal. Congress was more inclined to the appearance of a reconversion strategy that would provide few carrots and no sticks than even a watered down version of Reuther's plan. The military spending continued unabated after the Vietnam War as stagflation settled like smog over the country and the factories emptied out.

By the end of the century the Cold War was over. The Soviet Union collapsed under the weight of its military spending, a hemorrhaging of blood and rubles in Afghanistan, and fractures in the old Tsarist empire as the heel came off the throat. The end of the Cold War produced only a burp in the feeding of the military-industrial complex. Addiction to the habit of a quick military fix was too long-standing in the body politic. New threats emerged. Some like Saddam and his weapons of mass destruction were exaggerated. Each was fanned by an uncritical media and industry lobbying.

In 2003 the New York State Transit Authority requested bids to supply a fleet of new cars for the New York City subway system. Not a single bid was received from an American company. Contracts of more than 3 billion dollars were awarded to Kawasaki of Japan, Bombadier of Canada, and Alstom of France.[67] A modern railcar is much more than a box on wheels with holes punched in it. It contains some of the same electronics found in the cylinders built by the defense contractors. A factory producing six cars a week for New York would allow the city to turn over its entire stock on a twenty year cycle. Add in the dozens of other cities with a subway or light rail system and thousands of American workers would be busy building for the transport infrastructure.

The needs of war frequently require measures that circumvent individual liberty and blur moral guidelines. A half century of war and war readiness has institutionalized many of these measures into public consciousness. We have become accustomed to a blanket of official secrecy covering more-and-more government operations. The concept of a liberal democracy conducting raids, assassinations, and drone strikes inside a sovereign state with which it is not formally at war has been validated in the entertainment we watch and the video games our kids play. We have been mesmerized by the technology of the war machine and become callous to its consequences.

The wars of the first half of the twentieth century were fought against conventional armies. Success was measured in towns captured and ground gained. Since Vietnam the metric for success against an unconventional foe has been the body count. In Vietnam it was reported weekly like a football score—some hundreds of them, some dozens of us. We were killing our way to victory. The pressure from the generals at the top worked its way down to the unit commanders in the field. The trappings of morality were dropped. My Lai may not have been the rule during the conflict, but neither was it the exception.[68] With the focus on body count, atrocities were committed all too often.

In the later wars, mention of the body count has been muted. It surfaces in the reports of drone strikes and with the names of high-profile targets who have been "eliminated." It was seen in Iraq as a deck of cards with tricks that were captured and points accredited in the effort of the United States to make its bid. In Afghanistan it was a ten most wanted list of the top Al Qaeda leaders where every X on one list was replaced with a new face on the next. The progression of names and faces appeared like mutations in a pathogen that develops a resistance to each new drug with which it is treated. Body count is used more selectively, but it remains a metric of success in wars with few other concrete measures to report.

The extent to which the violence and the glorification of violence on the battlefield has seeped into the rhythms of civilian society cannot be ignored. In the past patterns of violence were associated with Reconstruction, territorial expansion, labor unrest, assertions of white supremacy, Prohibition, and Depression era desperation. Schools, theaters, and houses of worship were rarely listed as scenes of carnage. Today, many violent acts are not associated with previous patterns and do not spare places of nurture and relaxation. The abundance of guns, the availability of military style weaponry and ammunition clips, the glorification of violence in film and video games, and the lack of opportunity in neglected corners of the land all play against a background of national machismo that filters through the news and politics of the day to create an atmosphere that breeds a level of violence unparalleled in the democracies of the developed world. Despite the increasing frequency with which highly publicized mass shootings have occurred, a numbed acceptance of the situation permeates the mood of the country that only an event as horrific as the Newtown school massacre could momentarily penetrate. Gun control and background checks are only a partial response to the problem and taken alone deter a more incisive discussion into the conditions that foster such an elevated scale of violence in this society.

The Last Chapter—

The last chapter of the book records the last chapter of life—the shadow life that lingers after the ashes are scattered to the wind; after the tangible is dust to dust. The intangible lives in the ambitions of those on whom the shadow is cast. What is built during a lifetime suffers the ravages of neglect and vandalism. What is not maintained crumbles and falls to ruin. What is planted in dreams is nourished and tended to sprout anew in another spring. The last chapter in a story about Walter Reuther is not about a death, a funeral, or the decay of "[his] tremendous organization called the UAW."[69] It is not about what has been left behind, but what force that life retains in going forward.

The decade after Reuther's death began with revolt and ended with Reagan. It was not the aspirational revolt of the denied in the sixties, but an angry cry of the discomfited against a world seen falling apart. The post-war boom was losing steam. Jobs were diffusing offshore at the same time the baby boomers and newly liberated women were flooding into the labor force. As competition from foreign imports in the seventies ate into the profits of the automakers, they responded with a more automated and faster assembly process. Workers reacted to the pace and drudgery of the job with high absenteeism, alcohol, drugs, and occasionally sabotage. There was disaffection with the job, with the company that viewed them a cog in the automated production machine, and with the union they did not build and which they regarded as remote from their daily concerns.

The pace of change was also felt outside the factory gates. Workers who were supportive of granting African-American equal access to public facilities and equal protection of civil and voting rights were less inclined to accept them as equal competitors for the skilled and unskilled jobs that were growing scarce. Northern blacks received few direct benefits from the Civil Rights Movement of the sixties but felt a sense of liberation, fueling the feeling of growing frustration over the limited opportunity for economic and social mobility that remained their reality. Black demands for economic as well as social justice were delivered with a new tone of militancy Whites who supported laws outlawing segregation in the schools were not willing to see their children bussed out of their neighborhood to achieve it.

Blacks and other minorities achieved equality under the law, but few blacks and whites lived in the same neighborhood, worked at the same jobs, belonged to the same clubs, or attended the same church. The patterns of segregation that had been molded for hundreds of years could not be broken in the space of a decade. The attempts to right hundreds of years of wrong were often clumsy and always contentious. The disaffection of working class whites, who felt the effect of mandated desegregation efforts most immediately, played against the backdrop of a controversial war.

Much of "middle America" retreated behind the safety of traditional values. Social issues trumped economic concerns and race trumped class in the politics of the day. As in the movies, the sequel to *The New Hope* was *The Empire Strikes Back*. After the debacle of the 1972 election in which labor, youth, minorities, and women battled uncompromisingly for the soul of the Democratic Party, the corporate elite mounted an offensive against the remnants of the liberal establishment. Better organized and better funded corporate PACs wrestled political influence away from labor and dictated the tone and agenda of the debate.

Between *The New Hope* and *The Empire Strikes Back,* Hollywood produced *Norma Rae.* The character played by Sally Field led an organizing campaign in a Southern textile factory that, despite intimidation from company management, led to the union winning an NLRB jurisdictional vote to represent the mill's workforce. The film fairly faithfully chronicled the struggle of the real-life Norma Rae, Crystal Lee Sutton, who was a leader in the effort to win union representation at a J. P. Stevens factory in Roanoke Rapids, North Carolina. Like in the movie, the campaign crossed the racial divide in the workforce and won a jurisdictional vote in the factory. Here the movie script ended and there was no Academy Award forthcoming for Crystal Lee and her fellow workers. The company simply refused to negotiate. It was content to pay the fines and wear the label of "the nation's number one labor law violator."[70] In the fragile job market of the seventies, companies no longer reasoned that cooperation with the union was preferable to a rebellious workforce and the prospect of lengthy strikes. The threat to close the plant and move to a low-wage alternative hung over labor like a shadow on the x-ray of a chronic smoker. There was no sequel to *Norma Rae.* Crystal Lee Sutton's union succumbed to the legal costs and intimidation that J. P. Stevens inflicted upon it.

Labor made an effort during the Carter Administration to maintain the compact that existed with management since the 1950s. It pushed for passage of a rather tepid labor reform act that would streamline the NLRB certification and judicial process and stiffen the fines for violators of NLRB rulings. The bill easily sailed through the Democratic House but lingered in the Senate under the threat of a Republican filibuster. While the bill stood in line behind the controversial Panama Canal Treaty measure, the business lobbyists applied all of their muscle to engineer its defeat. A weakened old George Meany could only plead in an open letter to *The Wall Street Journal*, "Why should law-abiding companies seek to continue a system that allows some employers to break the law with impunity?…Do you secretly seek a death sentence for the collective bargaining system you so often hail in public forums?" Meany recognized that what he faced was "an all out attack on the American labor movement…by every anti-union group in America to kill the labor movement."[71]

The bill never left the queue. The Administration was never able to get the votes to bring it to the Senate floor. Senator Orin Hatch, one of the key opponents of the legislation, recognized "a starting point for a new era of assertiveness by big business in Washington."[72] An exclamation mark was put on Hatch's assessment four years later when Ronald Reagan summarily fired striking air traffic controllers, casting a chill on labor activism with little sign of a thaw thirty years later.

Reuther's protégé, Douglas Fraser, the UAW president at the time the labor reform act lay moribund in the Senate, reacted to the defeat by drafting an angry public letter of resignation from his seat on the Labor Management Group, an advisory panel established during the Nixon Administration. In his letter Fraser complained that the bill had been "an extremely moderate, fair piece of legislation that only corporate outlaws would have had needed to fear." Affirming his Reutherite roots, Frazier vowed, "I would rather sit with the rural poor, the desperate children of urban blight, the victims of racism, and working people seeking a better life than with those whose religion is the status quo, whose goal is profit and whose hearts are cold. We in the UAW intend to reforge the links with those who believe in struggle, the kind of people who sat-down in the factories in the 1930's and who marched in Selma in the 1960s."[73]

Frazier's letter conveyed his frustration tinged with a bit of petulance, but ignored the reality with which he was confronted. The kind of people who sat-down in the thirties and marched in the sixties were not around in the seventies. The conditions that provoked people to act in the previous era could not be manufactured or conjured up from the past. Neither could Frazier coax the support his mentor enjoyed from a membership with short-term memory that was bored with its job, worried about its future, and disillusioned with its union. The UAW had neither the money nor the vigor to be the engine for social change it had been since its inception.

With labor wrestled to the canvas, the face of liberalism became the academics, the feminists, the veterans of the movements of the sixties— the other—the elites that were dismissed by the right as condescendingly lecturing others how they should feel and act while immune to many of the same circumstances themselves. Of course the people pointing fingers at the left were also an elite who were not asking for a generosity of spirit, but were tacitly requiring a generosity of means.

By the end of the decade Reuther's union was in retreat, his agenda scrapped, and many of his ambitions unfulfilled. Yet the challenges he addressed persist. Had he lived to enjoy retirement he would have called himself an educator in his second career. He would have enjoyed coming to Black Lake to inspire a new generation of leaders. There would have been new Reuther plans and passionate testimony for many of the old ones. Even with a diminished voice and a smaller stage, he would never stop trying to convince an audience with his logic, or abandon his faith in the essential goodness of mankind. He lived with the belief that, "There is no greater calling than to serve your brother. There is no greater satisfaction than to have done it well."[74] That is the legacy he leaves his heirs.

BIBLIOGRAPHY

Abrahamian, Ervand, *A History of Modern Iran*, Cambridge University Press, New York, 2009.

Alinsky, Saul, *John L. Lewis: An Unauthorized Biography*, G. P. Putnam's Sons, New York, 1949

Altgeld, John Peter and Spies, August, The Chicago Martyrs:The Famous Speeches by the Eight Anarchists in Judge Gary's Court, October 7–9, 1886, c1899, reprint from Kessinger Publishing, 2009

Ayres, David M., Anatomy of a Crisis: Education, Development, and the State in Cambodia: 1953–1998, University of Hawaii Press, 2000.

Baldwin, Neil, Henry Ford and the Jews: The Mass Production of Hate, PublicAffairs, New York, 2001.

Ball, Howard, *Hugo L. Black: Cold Steel Warrior*, Oxford University Press, New York, Oford, 1996.

Belden, Thomas Graham & Belden, Marva Robins, *The Lengthening Shadow: The Life of Thomas J. Watson*, Little, Brown and Company, Boston-Toronto, 1962.

Bernstein, Mark, Grand Eccentrics: Turning the Century: Dayton and the Inventing of America, Orange Frazier Press, Wilmington, Ohio, 1996.

Black, Conrad, *Franklin Delano Roosevelt: Champion of Freedom*, Public Affairs, New York, 2003

Black, Edwin, *IBM and the Holocaust*, Random House, New York, 2001.

Bosworth, Patricia, *Anything Your Little Heart Desires*, Simon & Schuster, NewYork, 1997

Boyle, Kevin, The UAW and the Heyday of American Liberalism, 1945–1968, Cornell University Press, 1998

Bowser, Eileen, *The Transformation of Cinema: 1907–1915*, Scribner, New York, Toronto, 1990.

Brinkley, Joel, *Cambodia's Curse: The Modern History of a Troubled Land*, Public Affairs, a member of Perseus Books Group (paperback), 2012.

Brooks, Frederick P., *The Mythical Man Month (Anniversary Edition)*, Addison Wesley, 1995.

Burns, James MacGregor, *Roosevelt: The Lion and the Fox*, Harcourt, Brace & World, Inc., New York, 1956.

Carlson, W. Bernard, *Tesla: Inventor of the Electrical Age*, Princeton University Press, Princeton, NJ, 2013.

Carroll, Paul, *Big Blues: The Unmaking of IBM*, Crown Publishers Inc., New York, NY, 1993.

Cashin, Herschel V. and others, *Under Fire with the Tenth U. S. Cavalry*, Arno Press and The New York Times, New York, 1969.

Catton, Bruce, *The War Lords of Washington*, Harcourt, Brace and Company, New York, 1948.

Caute, David, The Great Fear: The Anti-Communist Purge Under Truman and Eisenhower, Simon and Schuster, New York, 1978.

Chapman, Peter, Bananas: How the United Fruit Company Shaped the World, Canongate, New York, NY, 2007.

Chomsky, Noam, Rethinking Camelot: JFK, the Vietnam War, and US Political Culture, South End Press, Boston, 1993.

Cohen, Adam & Taylor, Elizabeth, American Pharaoh: Mayor Richard J. Daley—His Battle for Chicago and the Nation, Little Brown, 2000.

Conwell, Russell H., *Acres of Diamonds*, John C. Winston Company, Philadelphia & Toronto, 1959 (From the book *Russell H. Conwell and His Works* by Agnes Rush Burr, © 1905, 1933 and revised editions © 1917, 1923, 1926)

Cormier, Frank & Eaton, William J., *Reuther*, Prentice-Hall, Edgewood Cliffs, N. J., 1970.

Cowie, Jefferson, Stayin' Alive: The 1970's and the Last Days of the Working Class, The New Press, New York, 2010.

Crosby S. J., Donald, God, Church, and Flag: Senator Joseph R. McCarthy and the Catholic Church 1950–1957, The University of North Carolina Press, 1979.

Crouch, Tom, First Flight: The Wright Brothers and the Invention of the Airplane, Division of Publications, Harpers Ferry Center, National Park Service U. S. Department of the Interior, Washington, D. C., 2002.

Crowther, Samuel, *John H. Patterson Pioneer in Industrial Welfare*, Doubleday, Page & Company, Garden City, Long Island and New York, 1923.

Cullather, Nicholas, Secret History: The CIA's Classified Account of Its Operations in Guatemala, 1952–1954, Stanford University Press, Palo Alto, California, 2006.

Cullather, Nicholas, *The Political Economy of United States-Philippine Relations, 1942–1960*, Stanford University Press, Stanford, California, 1994.

Dalton, Kathleen, *Theodore Roosevelt: A Strenuous Life*, Alfred A. Knopf, New York, 2002.

Deac, Wilfred, *Road to the Killing Fields: The Cambodia War of 1970–1975*, Texas A&M University Press, College Station, Texas, 1997.

Debouzy, Marianne, editor, In the Shadow of the Statue of Liberty: Immigrants, workers, and Citizens in the American Republic, 1880–1920, University of Illinois Press, Urbana and Chicago, 1992.

Dickmeyer, Elisabeth Reuther, *Putting the World Together—My Father Walter Reuther: The Liberal Warrior*, Living Force Publishing, Lake Orion, Michigan, 2004

DiNunzio, Mario R., editor, Theodore Roosevelt: An American Mind, A Selection From His Writings, St. Martin's Press, New York, 1994.

Doody, Colleen, *Detroit's Cold War: The Origins of Postwar Conservatism*, The University of Illinois Press, Urbana, Illinois, 2013.

Dunlap, Orrin E, Jr., *Marconi: The Man and His Wireless,* The MacMillan Company, New York, 1937

Dubofsky Melvyn, We Shall Be All: A History of the Industrial Workers of the World, Quadrangle Books. Chicago, 1969

Dubofsky, Melvyn & Van Tine, *John L. Lewis, A Biography,* Quadrangle/ The New York Times Book Company, New York, 1977.

Eisenhower, Dwight D. *The White House Years: Mandate for Change 1953– 1956,* Doubleday & Company, Garden City, New York, 1963.

Fall, Bernard, Hell in a Very Small Place: The Siege of Dien Bien Phu, J. B. Lippincott Company, Philadelphia, New York, *1967.*

Feynman, Richard P. & Leighton, Ralph, *"Surely You're Joking, Mr. Feynman!",* W. W. Norton & Company, New York, 1985.

Fine, Sidney, *Frank Murphy: The Washington Years*, University of Michigan Press, Ann Argor, Michigan, 19xx.

Fine, Sidney, *Sit-Down: The General Motors Strike of 1936–1937*, University of Michigan Press, Ann Arbor, Michigan, 1969.

Fine, Sidney, Laissez Faire and the General-Welfare State: A Study of Conflict in American Thought 1865–1901, The University of Michigan Press, Ann Arbor, Michigan, 1956.

Fireside, Bryna, The Haymarket Square Riot Trial: A Headline Case, Enslow Publishers, Berkeley Heights, NJ, 2002.

Foner, Philip, S., History of the Labor Movement in the United States, vol. 2—From the Founding of the American Federation of Labor to the Emergence of American Imperialism, International Publishers, New York, NY, 1955.

Foner, Philip S. & Lewis, Ronald L., editors, *Black Workers: A Documentary History From Colonial Times to the Present*, Temple University Press, Philadelphia, 1989.

Ford, Henry in collaboration with Samuel Crowther, *My Life and Work*, Doubleday, Page & Company, Garden City, New York, 1926 (c 1922).

Fredrickson, George M., *The Black Image in the White Mind: The Debate on Afro-American Character and Destiny, 1817–1914*, Wesleyan University Press, Published by University Press of New England, Hanover, NH, 1987.

Fried, Albert. editor, *McCarthyism: the Great American Red Scare*, Oxford University Press, New York, Oxford, 1997.

Fuller, John G., *We Almost Lost Detroit*, Reader's Digest Press, New York, 1975

Gaddis, John Lewis, *George F. Kennan: An American Life*, The Penguin Press, New York, 2011.

Gasiorowski, Mark and Byrne, Malcolm, editors, *Mohammad Mosaddeq and the 1953 Coup in Iran*, Syracuse University Press, Syracuse, NY, 2004.

Gatewood, Willard B., Jr., *Black Americans and the White Man's Burden 1893–1903*, University of Illinois Press, Urbana, Chicago, London, 1975.

Georgano, G.N., *Cars, Early and Vintage 1885–1930*, Grange-Universal, London, 1985.

Gerstner, Louis V., *Who Says Elephants Can't Dance?*, Harper Business, Harper Collins Publishers, New York, 2002.[HD 9696.2. V64 i2545 2002]

Geschwender, James A., Class, Race, and Worker Insurgency: The League of Revolutionary Black Workers, Cambridge University Press, 1977.

Gillon, Steven M., *Politics and Vision: The ADA And American Liberalism, 1947–1985*, Oxford University Press, New York & Oxford, 1987.

Goodwin, Doris Kearns, The Bully Pulpit: Theodore Roosevelt, William Howard Taft, and the Golden Age of Journalism, Large Print Edition, Thorndike Press, GALE CENAGE Learning, 2013.

Gordon, Colin, Dead on Arrival: The Politics of Health Care in Twentieth-Century America, Princeton University Press, Princeton and Oxford, 2003.

Gould, Jean & Hickok, Lorena, *Walter Reuther, Labor's Rugged Individualist*, Dodd, Mead & Company, New York, NY, 1972.

Grant, Madison, *The Passing of the Great Race*, 4th Revised Edition, Charles Scribner's Sons, New York, 1921.

Halperin, Martin, *UAW Politics in the Cold War Era*, SUNY Press, Albany, 1988.

Hammer, Ellen J., *The Struggle for Indochina, 1940–1955*, Stanford University Press, Stanford, California, 1955.

Hayward, Stephen F., The Age of Reagan: The Fall of the Old Liberal Order 1964–1980, Three Rivers Press, New York 2001

Hedges, Chris, *Death of the Liberal Class*, Nathan Books, New York, NY, 2000.

Heikal, Mohamed, *Iran: The Untold Story*, Pantheon, New York, NY, 1982.

Hendricks, Rickey, A Model for National Health Care: the History of Kaiser Permanente, Rutgers University Press, New Brunswick, New Jersey, 1993.

Hersh, Seymour, *The Dark Side of Camelot*, Back Bay Books, 1998

Hicks, John D., The Populist Revolt: A History of the Farmers' Alliance and the People's Party, A Bison Book, University of Nebraska Press, 1961.

Hoffman, Paul, Wings of Madness: Alberto Santos-Dumont and the Invention of Flight, Theia, Hyperion, New York, 2003.

Howe, Irving & Widick, B. J., *The UAW and Walter Reuther*, Random House, New York, 1949

Israel, Paul, *Edison: A Life of Invention*, John Wiley & Sons, New York, 1998.

Jonnes, Jill, Empires of Light: Edison, Tesla, Westinghouse and the Race to Electrify the World, Random House, New York, 2003.

Josephson, Matthew, *Edison: A Biography*, Francis Parkman Prize Edition, History Book Club, New York, 1959.

Karnow, Stanley, *Vietnam: A Huistory*, Penguin Books, New York, c. 1983.

Kelly, Fred G., *The Wright Brothers (Biography authorized by Orville Wright)*, Harcourt, Brace & Company, New York, 1943.

Kennedy, Robert F., *The Enemy Within*, Harper & Brothers, New York, 1960.

Kiernan, Ben, How Pol Pot Came to Power: Colonialism, Nationalism, and Communism in Cambodia, 1930–1975, Yale University Press, New Haven and London, 2nd Edition, 2004.

Kolko, Gabriel, Anatomy of a War: Vietnam, the United States, and the Modern Historical Experience, Pantheon Books, New York, 1985.

Krugman, Paul, Peddling Prosperity; Economic Sense and Nonsense in the Age of Diminished Expectations, Norton & Co., 1994

Khrushchev, Sergei, *Nikita Khrushchev and the Creation of a Superpower*, The Pennsylvania State University, University Park, Pennsylvania, 2000.

Lacey, Robert, *Ford: the Men and the Machine*, Little Brown and Company, Boston-Toronto, 1986.

Lane, Ann J., *The Brownsville Affair: Naional Crisis and Black Reaction*, National University Publications, Kennikat Press, Port Washington, NY and London, 1971.

Lewis, David L., *The Public Image of Henry Ford*, Wayne State University Press, Detroit, 1976.

Lewis-Colman, David M., *Race Against Liberalism:Black Workers and the UAW in Detroit*, University of Illinois Press, Urbana and Chicago, 2008.

Levy, Peter B., *The New Left and Labor in the 1960's*, University of Illinois Press, 1994

Lichtenstein, Nelson, The Most Dangerous Man in Detroit—Walter Reuther and the Fate of American Labor, Basic Books, New York, 1995.

Maney, Kevin, The Maverick and His Machihne: Thomas Watson, Sr. and the Making of IBM, John Wiley & Sons, Hoboken, New Jersey, 2003.

Marmor, Theodore R.with Jan S. Marmor, *The Politics of Medicare*, Aldine Publishing Company, Chicago, 1973

McCullough, David, *Truman*, Simon & Schuster, New York, 1992.

McDonald, Duff, The Firm, The Story of McKinsey and its Secret Influence on American Business, Simon & Schuster, New York, 2013

McGovern, George and Guttridge, Leonard, *The Great Coalfield War*, Houghton Mifflin Company, Boston, 1972.

McNamara, Robert S. and James Blight, Robert Brigham, Thomas Biersteker, Col. Herbert Schandler, *Argument Without End: In Search of Answers to the Vietnam Tragedy,* Public Affairs, New York, 1990.

Meier, August & Rudwick, Elliott, *Black Detroit and the Rise of the UAW,* Oxford University Press, New York, 1979.

Moyar, Mark, *Triumph Forsaken: the Vietnam War 1954–1965,* Cambridge University Press, Cambridge and New York, 2006.

Murphy, Brenda, Congressional Theatre: Dramatizing McCarthyis, on Stage, Film, and Television Cambridge University Press, New York, 1999

Musser, Charles, *The Emergence of Cinema: The American Screen to 1907,* Scribner, New York, Toronto, 1990.

Nelson, Daniel, *American Rubber Workers & Organized Labor, 1900–1941,* Princeton University Press, Princeton, New Jersey, 1988

O'Neill, John J., *Prodigal Genius: The Life of Nikola Tesla,* Ives Washburn, Inc., New York, 1944.

Oshinsky, David M., *A Conspiracy So Immense: The World of Joe McCarthy,* The Free Press, A Division of Macmillan, Inc., New York, 1983.

Phillips, Kevin, Wealth and Democracy: A Political History of the American Rich, Broadway Books, New York, 2002

Poundstone, William, *Prisoner's Dilemma,* Doubleday, New York, 1992.

Pringle, Henry F., *Theodore Roosevelt: A Biography,* Harcourt, Brace and Company, New York, 1931.

Ravitch, Diane, Reign of Error: The Hoax of the Privatization Movement and the Danger to America's Public Schools, Alfred A. Knopf, New York, 2013.

Reeves, Thomas C., *The Life and Times of Joe McCarthy: A Biography,* Stein and Day, New York, 1992.

Reuther, Victor, *The Brothers Reuther and the Story of the UAW: A Memoir,* Houghton Mifflin Company, Boston, 1976.

Reuther, Walter P., Education and the Public Good—The Challenge to Education in a Changing World, Harvard University Press, Cambridge, Massachusetts, 1964

Reuther, Walter P., *Selected Papers,* Macmillan, New York, 1961.

Salvatore, Nick, *Eugen V. Debs: Citizen and Socialist*, University of Illinois Press, Urbana and Chicago, 1982.

Schlesinger, Jr., Arthur M., *Robert Kennedy and His Times*, Houghton Mifflin Company, Boston, 1978

Schlesinger, Stephen and Kinzer, Stephen, *Bitter Fruit: The Story of the American Coup in Guatemala*, Harvard University Press, Cambridge, Mass., 2005 (Revised and Expanded Edition)

Schulzinger, Robert D., *A Time for War: The United States and Vietnam, 1941–1975*, Oxford University Press, New York, 1997.

Shaplen, Robert, *The Lost Revolution*, Harper & Row, New York, 1965.

Shawcross, William, Sideshow: Kissinger, Nixon, and the Destruction of Cambodia, Simon & Schuster, 1979.

Smith, Hedrick, The Power Game: How Washington Works, Ballantine, 1988.

Sorensen, Charles with Williamson, Samuel, *My Forty Years With Ford,* W. W. Norton & Company, New York, 1956.

Spiro, Jonathon Peter, *Defending the Master Race: Conservation, Eugenics, and the Legacy of Madison Grant*, University of Vermont Press, Burlington, Vermont and University Press of New England, Lebanon, New Hampshire, 2009.

Stanton, Mary, *From Selma to Sorrow: The Life and Death of Viola Liuzzo*, The University of Georgia Press, Athens, Georgia, 1998.

Stockman, David, The Triumph of Politics: Why the Reagan Revolution Failed, Harper & Row, 1986

Stromquist, Shelton, editor, *Labor's Cold War – Local Politics in a Global Context*, University of Illinois Press, Urbana and Chicago, 2008.

Sugar, Maurice, *The Ford Hunger March*, Meiklejohn Civil Liberties Institute, Berkeley, California, 1980.

Swanberg, W. A., *Norman Thomas: The Last Idealist*, Charles Scribner's Sons, New York, 1976.

Sward, Keith, *The Legend of Henry Ford*, Rinehart & Company, Toronto and New York, 1948.

Taft, Philip, *The A. F. of L. in the Time of Gompers*, Harper & Brothers, New York, 1957.

Tanenbaum, Andrew, *Computer Networks*, 4th ed., Prentice-Hall, Englewood Cliffs, NJ, 2002.

Tedlow, Richard S., *The Watson Dynasty*, HarperCollins, New York, 2003.

Theoharis, Jeanne F. & Komozi, Woodard, editors, *Freedom North – Black Freedom Struggles Outside the South, 1940 – 1980,* Palgrave Macmillan, 2003

The Pentagon Papers, Published by *The New York Times,* Quadrangle Books Inc., New York, 1971.

Tonnesson, Stein, The Vietnameses Revolution of 1945: Roosevelt, Ho Chi Minh, and DeGaulle in a World at War, Sage Publications, Newbury Park, California, 1991.

Treckel, Karl F., *The Rise and Fall of the Alliance for Labor Action (1968–1972),* Center for Business and Economic Research, Graduate School of Business Administration, Kent State University, Kent, Ohio, 1975.

Turse, Nick, *Kill Anything That Moves: The Real American War in Vietnam,* Metropolitan Books, Henry Holt and Company, New York, 2013.

Watson, Thomas J. Jr. and Petre, Peter, *Father, Son & Co.: My Life at IBM and Beyond,* Bantam Books, 1990.

Warren, Donald, Radio Priest—Charles Coughlin, the Father of Hate Radio, The Free Press, New York, 1996.

Weinberg, Alvin, *The First Nuclear Era: The Life and Times of a Technology Fixer,* AIP Press, American Institute of Physics, New York, 1994.

White, Walter, *A Man Called White*, The Viking Press, New York, 1948.

Widdick, B. J., *Detroit: City of Race and Class Violence*, Revised Edition, Wayne State University Press, Detroit, 1989.

Wilentz, Sean, *The Age of Reagan: a History 1974–2008*, Harper Perennial, New York, 2008.

Williams, Juan, Eyes on the Prize: America's Civil rights Years, 1954–1965, Viking Penguin Inc., 1987.

Williamson, Harold F., Andreano, Ralph, Daum, Arnold, and Klose, Gilbert, *The American Petroleum Industry: The Age of Oil 1899–1959*, Northwestern University Press, Evanston, Ill. 1963.

Woodward, C. Vann, *The Strange Career of Jim Crow*, Second Revised Edition, Oxford University Press, New York, 1966

Wolff, Leon, Little Brown Brother: How the United States Purchased and Pacified the Philippine Islands at the Century's Turn, Doubleday & Company, Garden City, NY 1961

Yellen, Samuel, *American Labor Struggles*, c1936, published by S. A. Russell, the Harbor Press by arrangement with Harcourt, Brace and Company, 1956.

Zahavi, Gerald, *Workers, Managers, and Welfare Capitalists*, University of Illinois Press, Urbana and Chicago, 1988. [HD 9787 .U6 E654 1988]

Zinn, Howard, *A People's History of the United States—1492–Present*, Harper Perennial Modern Classics edition, New York, 2005.

Zwerdling, Alex, Improvised Europeans—American Literary Expatriates and the Siege of London, Basic Books, New York, 1998.

Articles

Avik Roy, "The Torturous History of Conservatives and the Individual Mandate," *Forbes* February 7, 2012.

Beichman, Arnold, "The Politics of Personal Self-Destruction," *Policy Review*, Issue 135 (Feb-Mar, 2006) pp 63–74

Bernstein, Mark, "John H. Patterson—John Patterson rang up success with the incorruptible cashier," *Dayton Innovation Legacy*, http://www.daytoninnovationlegacy.org/patterson.html (retrieved 3/24/2014)

Bork, William, "Massacre at Republic Steel," *The Illinois Labor History Society*, 28 E. Jackson, Chicago, Illinois.

Boudreau, Jay, "The American Breeder Reactor Gets a Second Chance," *Los Alamos Science*, vol. 2, no. 2, summer/fall 1981 pp 118–119

Boyle, Kevin, "Why Is There No Social Democracy in America?," *International Labor and Working Class History*, 74.1 (Fall, 2008) pp 33–37.

Cohn, Jonathon, "How They Did It," *The New Republic*, May 21, 2010. (History of enactment of the Affordable Care Act)

Collins, Joe, two letters to the Secretary of State published in *Foreign Relations of the United States*, 1955–1957:1 retrieved at http://history.state.gov/historicaldocuments/frus1955–57v01/ U. S. Department of State, Office of the Historian

Halperin, Martin, "I'm fighting for Freedom: Coleman Young, HUAC, and the Detroit African American Community," *Journal of American Ethnic History*, vol. 17, No. 1, Fall 1997. pp 19–38

Harrison, Selig S., "Reuther in India," *The New Republic*, May 21, 1956.

Hearings Before the Committee on Un-American Activities House of Representatives Eighty-Second Congress 2nd Session, United States Government Printing Office, Washington 1952
—February 25, 26, 27, 28, and 29 1952 (HUAC Detroit Hearings Part 1)
—March 10, 11, 12, and April 29, 30 1952 (HUAC Detroit Hearings Part 2)

Hans H. Helbling & James E. Turley, "Oil Price Controls: A Counterproductive Effort," *Federal Reserve Bank of St. Louis*, November, 1975

Hoffman, Beatrix, "Health Care Reform and Social Movements in the United States," *American Journal of Public Health*, January 2003, 93(1) pp. 75–85

Hoover, Herbert, "The President's Economic Mission to Germany and Austria," Report 3, March, 1947 – The Harry S. Truman Presidential Library, Truman & The Marshall Plan.

Kordon, Kyle A., "Khrushchev Comes to America: The Advent of Mutual Understanding," *Voces Novae*, Chapman University Historical Review, Vol. 1, No. 1, 2009.

Levenstein, Aaron, "Satisfaction at General Motors," *The Nation*, June 17, 1950.

Lindsey, Almont, "Paternalism and the Pullman Strike," *The American Historical Review*, Vol. 44, No. 2, January 1939. pp 272–289. Published by: Oxford University Press on behalf of the American Historical Association, Stable URL: http://www.jstor.org/stable/1839019

Lizza, Ryan, "Romney's Dilemma," *The New Yorker*, June 6, 2011

Loth, Wilfried, "Moscow, Prague and Warsaw: Overcoming the Brezhnev Doctrine," *Cold War History*, 1, no. 2, 2001: 103–118.

Mandel, Bernard, "Samuel Gompers and the Negro Workers," *The Journal of Negro History*, vol 40, No. 1, January 1955, pp 34–61.

Melman, Seymour, "In the Grip of a Permanent War Economy," *Counterpunch*, March 15, 2003.

Record, Jeffrey, "Nuclear Deterrence, Preventive War, and Counter proliferation," *Cato Institute, Policy Analysis* No. 519, July 8, 2004. http://www.cato.org/pubs/pas/html/pa519/pa51900001.html (retrieved 1/20/2015)

Reuther, Walter P., "The Challenge to Education in a Changing World," in *Education and the Public Good*, Harvard University Press, Cambridge, Mass. 1964

Reuther, Walter P., *Swords Into Plowshares: A Proposal to Promote Orderly Conversion From Defense to Civilian Production*, Statement and Testimony of Walter P. Reuther, President of the UAW, To the Senate Committee On Labor and Public Welfare, December 1, 1969.

Risen, James, "Secrets of History: The CIA in Iran," The New York Times on the Web, 2000, www.nytimes.com/library/world/mideast/041500iran-cia-index.html. (Retrieved 2/21/2013)

Robbins, Leonard; "A Short History of the Modern Struggle for National Health Insurance," *Journal of Health and Human Resources Administration*, Vol 5, No. 3, Winter 1983, pp. 252–265.

Rodwin, Victor G., "The Health Care System Under French National Health Insurance: Lessons for Health Reform in the United States," *American Journal of Public Health*, January 2003, Vol. 93, No. 1 pp 31–37.

Swank, Emory, "The Land in Between: Cambodia Ten Years Later," *Indochina Issues*, Vol. 36, April, 1983, pp 1–7.

Wilber, Donald, CIA Clandestine Service History, "Overthrow of Premier Mossadeq of Iran, November 1952–August 1953," March 1954.

ENDNOTES

Chapter I

[1] Victor Reuther, *The Brothers Reuther and the Story of the UAW*, Houghton Mifflin Company, 1976 p 463; Dickmeyer, Elisabeth Reuther, Putting the World Together—My Father Walter Reuther: The Liberal Warrior, Living Force Publishing, Lake Orion, Michigan, 2004 p 363

[2] Lichtenstein, Nelson, The Most Dangerous Man in Detroit—Walter Reuther and the Fate of American Labor, Basic Books, New York, 1995. pp 17-18; E. R. Dickmeyer op. cit. p 25

[3] *Time*, December 7, 1998, "The 100 Most Influential People of the Century," written by Irving Bluestone – Reuther family credo

[4] Lichtenstein op. cit. p 33—Reuther claimed he was fired, but Ford records indicate he was still classified as a first-class worker

[5] Locke, John, *Two Treatises of Government*—The Second Essay defines natural rights

[6] Madison, James, *The Federalist Papers* #10 on property rights

[7] Hedges, Chris, *Death of the Liberal Class*, Nathan Books, New York, NY, 2000. pp 68-86

[8] Schlesinger Jr., Arthur, "Liberalism in America: A Note for Europeans", in *The Politics of Hope* (Boston: Riverside Press, 1962).

[9] Gillon, Steven M., Politics and Vision: The ADA And American Liberalism, 1947-1985, Oxford University Press, New York & Oxford, 1987. p 103

[10] From Robert Frost's poem *Acquainted With the Night*

[11] Gillon op. cit. p 94

[12] Anthony Lewis, *The New York Times*, Aug. 13, 1956

13   Richard Amper, *The New York Times,* Aug 3, 1956

14   Lichtenstein op. cit. p 436

15   Lichtenstein op. cit. p 437; E. R. Dickmeyer op. cit. p 337

16   E. R. Dickmeyer op. cit. p 337

17   E. R. Dickmeyer op. cit. pp 344-345

18   Lichtenstein op. cit. 435-436

19   E. R. Dickmeyer op. cit. p 344

20   Victor Reuther op. cit. pp 365–367

21   Lichtenstein op. cit. p 241

22   Victor Reuther op. cit. p 319—*Folks Magazine,* Month?, 1948, vol ?, issue ?

23   Victor Reuther op. cit. pp 372-373

24   Louis Aguilar, *Detroit News.* Jan 14, 2010

25   E. R. Dickmeyer op. cit. p 311-312; Gould & Hickok, *Walter Reuther: Labor's Rugged Individualist,* Dodd, Mead & Company (New York, 1972) p 370

26   Gail Collins, *The New York Review of Books,* June 21, 2012—How Texas influences the content of nation's textbooks; Resolution Opposing Restriction of Access to Materials and Open Inquiry In Ethnic and Cultural Studies Programs in Arizona, OIF Blog, January 24, 2012.— Office for Intellectual Freedom of the American Library Association. Rheana Murray, New York Daily News, Jan 16, 2012, *Ethnic book ban in Arizona school* district includes all books about Mexican-American History even Shakespeare's 'The Tempest.' (also includes Thoreau's On Civil Disobedience and Howard Zinn's People's History of the United States among others)

Chapter II

1   John H. Lienhared, www.uh.edu/epi2402.htm (retrieved 2/12/2014)

2   Ibid.

3   Reich Patent No. 37435

4   Georgano, G.N., *Cars, Early and Vintage 1885-1930*, Grange-Universal, London, 1985 p 17

5   Ibid. p 21

6   Ibid. p 25

7   www.ideafinder.com/history/inventions/assbline.htm (retrieved 2/12/2014)

8   www.bpmlegal.com/wselden.html (retrrieved 2/12/2014)

9   Hoffman, Paul, Wings of Madness: Alberto Santos-Dumont and the Invention of Flight, Theia, Hyperion, New York, 2003. p 16

10   Ibid. pp 256-262

11   Kelly, Fred G., The Wright Brothers (Biography authorized by Orville Wright), Harcourt, Brace & Company, New York, 1943. pp 81-83

12   Bernstein, Mark, Grand Eccentrics: Turning the Century: Dayton and the Inventing of America, Orange Frazier Press, Wilmington, Ohio, 1996. p 77

13   Crouch, Tom, First Flight: The Wright Brothers and the Invention of the Airplane, Division of Publications, Harpers Ferry Center, National Park Service U. S. Department of the Interior, Washington, D. C., 2002. p 61; Kelly op cit. p 99 puts camera in hand of one of the Kitty Hawk Kill Devil Life Saving Station and Daniels running alongside the wing of the plane.

14   Kelly op cit. p 143

15   Ibid. pp 123-124

16   Bernstein, *Grand Eccentrics* p 95 as reported in the autobiography of James Cox, publisher and future Senator and Presidential Candidate.

17   Hoffman op cit. p 267

18   Kelly op cit. pp 209, 213

19   http://www.centennialofflight.net/essay/Dictionary/Archdeacon/DI49. htm—Archdeacon admits he did the Wrights an injustice. Kelly op cit. p 237 before demo Archdeacon explains why plane won't fly well, Edouard Surcouf, a balloonist in the Aero Club, proclaimed that doubts were the greatest error of the century. Bernstein, *Grand Eccentrics* p 112 quotes French avator Rene Gasnier, "We are all children compared to the Wrights."

20   Kelly op cit. p 230; Hoffman op cit. p 272; Bernstein, *Grand Eccentrics* p 114

21   Bernstein, *Grand Eccentrics* p 125

[22] Hoffman op cit. p 288; Kelly op cit. pp 288–296

[23] Hoffman op cit. p 274

[24] Ibid. p 274

[25] Williamson, Harold F., Andreano, Ralph, Daum, Arnold, and Klose, Gilbert, *The American Petroleum Industry: The Age of Oil 1899-1959*, Northwestern University Press, Evanston, Ill. 1963. p 16

[26] Ibid. p 16

[27] Ibid. p 20

[28] Ibid. pp 21-24

[29] Jonnes, Jill, Empires of Light: Edison, Tesla, Westinghouse and the Race to Electrify the World, Random House, New York, 2003. 46-47

[30] Israel, Paul, *Edison: A Life of Invention*, John Wiley & Sons, New York, 1998.p 188, Jonnes op cit. pp 61-62

[31] Carlson, W. Bernard, *Tesla: Inventor of the Electrical Age*, Princeton University Press, Princeton, NJ, 2013. p 69

[32] Jonnes op cit. pp 129 -130

[33] Ibid. p 156

[34] Ibid. p 166

[35] Jonnes op. cit. pp 171-173; Josephson, Matthew, *Edison: A Biography*, Francis Parkman Prize Edition, History Book Club, New York, 1959. pp 344-350

[36] Jonnes op. cit. p 176

[37] Jonnes op. cit. pp 211-212; Josephson op cit. p 349

[38] Jonnes op cit. p 168

[39] Carlson op cit. pp 75, 77

[40] Jonnes op cit. pp 155-159

[41] O'Neill, John J., *Prodigal Genius: The Life of Nikola Tesla*, Ives Washburn, Inc., New York, 1944. pp 79-82; Carlson op cit. p 113 puts the deal at $200,000 for the patents and $2.50 per hp for every generator in use

[42] O'Neill op cit. pp 79-82

[43] ibid. pp 83

[44] Jonnes op cit. pp 241-242

45   Carlson op cit. p 173

46   Ibid. pp 182, 188

47   O'Neill op cit. p 165

48   Carlson op. cit. p 180; O'Neill op cit. p 126

49   Carlson op cit. pp 377-378

50   Carlson op cit. p 375; O'Neill op cit. pp 228-229 Has 1912 rather than 1915 as the year when Tesla and Edison were rumored to be co-recipients. O'Neill states that Tesla refused to share with Edison—He considered Edison an inventor of useful appliances while he was a discoverer of new principles. He opens up new fields of knowledge and to share the prize with Edison would diminish his achievements.

51   Carlson op cit. pp 402-403

52   Musser, Charles, *The Emergence of Cinema: The American Screen to 1907*, Scribner, New York, Toronto, 1990. pp 62-72——Edison and Dickson were quick to apply for patents in the United States for their kinetograph and kinetoscope. Their failure to apply for the same patents in Europe indicated that they recognized that challenges to the priority and originality of their work would be successful.

53   Ibid. p 81

54   Ibid. p 418

55   Bowser, Eileen, *The Transformation of Cinema: 1907-1915*, Scribner, New York, Toronto, 1990. pp 13-15

56   Bowser op cit. pp 4-6

57   36

58   Bowser op cit. pp 224-225

59   Ernst Mach was a logical positivist who believed that physical laws were a way of expressing sensory perceptions, but did not describe a reality beyond what was actually perceived by the senses. Since atoms and molecules were too small to be observed and their introduction into classical physics presented some inconsistencies with the theory, they did not represent the simplest and most economical expression of observable facts. Mach famously pronounced. "I don't believe that atoms exist!" to Ludwig Boltzmann after the latter's 1897 lecture to the Imperial Academy of Science in Vienna. Boltzmann suffered from depression that was exacerbated by the resistance of Mach and others to the atomic

model underlying his presentation of statistical mechanics. Boltzmann committed suicide in 1900 just as his important contribution was about to be widely recognized.

60   36b

61   Goodwin, Doris Kearns, The Bully Pulpit: Theodore Roosevelt, William Howard Taft, and the Golden Age of *Journalism*, Large Print Edition, Thorndike Press, GALE CENAGE Learning, 2013. pp 358-365, 370-371

62   D. K. Goodwin op cit. pp 386-387—T. R. "would rather welcome a foreign war" "No merchant, no banker, no railroad magnate, no inventor of improved industrial processes, can do for any nation what can be done for it by its great fighting men." Roosevelt encouraged Secretary Long's absence from the capital while he "had immense fun running the Navy."

63   Ibid. p 359

64   McKinley's instructions to U. S. negotiators on Sept. 16, 1898—"the United States cannot accept less than the cession in full right and sovereignty of the island of Luzon." *Annals of America vol. 12* pp 231-233. This instruction was later amended in November of 1898 to demand cession of the whole archipelego—"to accept merely Luzon, leaving the rest of the islands subject to Spanish rule, or to be the subject of future contention, cannot be justified on political, commercial, or humanitarian grounds. The cessation must be the whole archipelago or none. The latter is wholly inadmissible, and the former must therefore be required."—Wolff pp 169-170. Ultimately the Islands were purchased for $ 20 million. *Annals of America vol. 12* p 235 Speech by Charles Denby, former ambassador to China—"Dewey's victory is an epoch in the affairs of the Far East. We hold our heads higher. We are coming to our own. We are stretching out our hands for what nature meant should be ours. We are taking our proper rank among the nations of the world. We are after markets, the greatest markets now existing in the world. Along with these markets will go our beneficent institutions, and humanity will bless us."

65   Wolff, Leon, Little Brown Brother: How the United States Purchased and Pacified the Philippine Islands at the *Century's Turn, Doubleday &* Company, Garden City, NY 1961 pp 199-200—McKinley proclamation to Filipinos—"the future control, disposition and government of the Philippine Islands are ceded to the United States [which would determine] the private rights and relations [of its new wards]" Cooperation would be secured by "firmness if need be." Local offices may be held by natives who "accept the authority of the United States by taking the oath of allegiance."

But America would take over "all the public property and the revenues of the state." McKinley proclaimed this mission to be "one of benevolent assimilation...sedulously maintained [by] the strong arm of authority." The treaty ceding the Philippines to the United States was being hotly debate in the Senate at the time the proclamation was issued and was still two votes short of what was needed for ratification.General Otis, the military governor of Philippines, realized the firestorm the proclamation would provoke and took it upon himself to edit the document before posting it, softening its more provocative tone and granting natives a larger role in local governance than McKinley intended. The revised copy did little to quell the anger of the Filipinos and when the original was posted elsewhere in the Islands by a second general, the full intent of the American occupation was revealed and war between the islanders and its new colonial masters commenced.

66   E. San Juan, Jr., "U. S. Genocide in the Philippines" March 22, 2005 cites the Philippine death toll reported by various authors. The 600,000 figure reported in William Pomeroy's *American Neo-Colonialism* (1970) represented the death toll in Luzon alone by 1902. Gabriel Kolko writes in *Main Currents in American History* (1976) "...during the protracted conquest of the Phillipines from 1898 until well into the next decade, when anywhere from 200,000 to 600,000 Filipinos were killed in an orgy of racist slaughter..." A figure of 1.4 million was derived by Filipino scholar Luzviminda Francisco (*The Philippines: the End of an Illusion*, London 1973). Wolff op cit. p 360 cites the 200,000 figure that is the low end of most accounts. Wolff p 358 describes the orders of General J. Franklin Bell to all station commanders in the rebellious provinces south of Manila: "There were to be no more neutrals: inhabitants were to be classified either as active friends or enemies. The latter, regardless of age or sex, were to be killed or captured. Everyone had to live within designated military zones and nowhere else. The municipal police were disarmed. Outside the concentration zones all food supplies were to be confiscated or destroyed. An eight o'clock curfew was in effect. Any Filipino found on the streets after that hour was to be shot on sight. Whenever an American soldier was killed, a native prisoner would be chosen by lot and executed. Native houses in the vicinity of telegraph lines cut by insurgents would be burned."

67   Record, 56 Congress 1 Session. pp 794-812

68   Zwerdling, Alex, Improvised Europeans—American Literary Expatriates and the Siege of London, Basic Books, New York, 1998. p 26; Kipling to

TR, 23 September 1898, Theodore Roosevelt Papers, Library of Congress, reel 2.

69 *Annals of America, vol 12*, pp 345-352; Official Proceed. Of the Democratic National Convention held in Kiansas City, Mo., July 4,5,6, 1900 (pp 205-227)

70 Annals of America vol. 12, p 429

71 Zwerdling op cit. pp 99–101

72 ibid. p 53; Henry Cabot Lodge, "The Restriction of Immigration," *North American Review* 151 (1891) pp 30-36

73 Zwerdling op cit. p 55

74 *The Letters of Henry Adams, vol. 4*, p 405. ed. J. C. Levenson et al, Harvard University Press, Cambridge and New York, 1988

75 H. C. Lodge, "The Distribution of Ability in the United States"—*Historical and Political Essays*, Boston and New York, Houghton Mifflin, 1892, pp 147, 159

76 Zwerdling op cit. p 53

77 Fredrickson, George M., The Black Image in the White Mind: The Debate on Afro-American Character and *Destiny, 1817-1914*, Wesleyan University Press, Published by University Press of New England, Hanover, NH, 1987. p 230—"At some future period, not very distant as measured by centuries, the civilized races of man will almost certainly exterminate and replace the savage races throughout the world." Darwin in *The Descent of Man*, 1871. After emancipation, prominent Social Darwinists expected African Americans, freed from their "protected" circumstances, to lose out in the struggle for survival with their superior Caucasian rivals and gradually disappear and the race problem with them. An anomaly in the 1880 census caused by an under count of Blacks in the previous census seemed to contradict this expectation by showing the Black population increasing faster than the white and leading to fears of a future marginalized white society. These fears were abated when the 1890 census showed the African-American population in the South increasing slower than the white, primarily due to a higher death rate. Frederickson op cit. pp 236–245 The 1896 book *Race Traits and Tendencies of the American Negro* by Frederick L Hoffman was purported to lend the credence of "science and exact inquiry" to the conclusion that it was not discrimination and lack of opportunity that limited "the moral progress of the race," but basic hereditary characteristics that produced a higher mortality rate,

more crime, and immorality. He condemned the efforts of philanthropists to improve the circumstances of blacks as interfering with the natural struggle for existence by artificially attempting to preserve an unfit specie. Frederickson op cit. pp 249-252

[78] Zwerdling op cit. pp 33-34; Agassiz, Louis, "The Diversity of Origin of the Human Races", *Christian Examiner* 49, (July 1850) pp 142, 144

[79] Grant, Madison, *The Passing of the Great Race,* 4th Revised Edition, Charles Scribner's Sons, New York, 1921. p 49.

[80] Ibid. p 51

[81] Spiro, Jonathon Peter, Defending the Master Race: Conservation, Eugenics, and the Legacy of Madison Grant, Univ. of Vermont Press, p 357

[82] ibid. p 176—Fitzgerald had Tom reading a book titled *The Rise of the Coloured Empires* by a man named Goddard—an amalgamation of Grant and Lothrop Stoddard, author of *The Rising Tide of Color.* Tom Buchanan proclaims that, "[It's] all scientific. This fellow has worked out the whole thing. It's up to us, who are the dominant race, to watch out or these other races will have control of things." Fitzgerald, F. Scott, *The Great Gatsby,* Scribner, New York, (paperback edition 2004) pp 12-13

[83] ibid. pp 158-159—Roosevelt's original letter to Grant is lost except for the portion referenced here that was excerpted out to appear in Scribner's promotional materials. Positive reviews appeared in newspapers like *The New York Herald* and *The Sun,* the liberal weekly *The Nation,* and scientific journals. The main reservation expressed by the scholarly reviewers was the lack of footnotes and attributions to previous work in the first two editions. This was partially addressed in the fourth edition with the inclusion of a documentary supplement that cited later supporting works as much or more than the previous "research" upon which Grant built his thesis. (Spiro p 166) Roosevelt modified his racial views late in life when he dismissed Grant's assertion that soldiers from old-stock New England roots displayed better fighting skills in World War 1 than soldiers from other ethnic backgrounds. Roosevelt called the man providing Grant with such evidence "an addled ass."—Dalton, Kathleen, *Theodore Roosevelt: A Strenuous Life,* Alfred A. Knopf, New York, 2002 p 523

[84] Zwerdling op cit. p 55

[85] "America in 1900," *American Digest,* March 31, 2004—http://americandigest.org/mt-archives /2004_03 (retrieved 9/27/2008)

86   Frederickson op.cit. p 275

87   Gatewood, Willard B., Jr., *Black Americans and the White Man's Burden 1893-1903*, University of Illinois Press, Urbana, Chicago, London, 1975. pp 28-34; John Mitchell, editor of the *Richmond Planet*, raised the cry "Remember the murder of Postmaster Baker," a Black civil servant in Lake City, South Carolina, whose house was burned down and Mitchell opposed an imperialistic was with Spain while the country was unwilling to protect its citizens at home. The ambivalent attitudeof many Blacks was expressed by R. B. Montgomery, a Black editor in Milwaukee who wrote, "It is the Negro's business to be on the safe side."—urged blacks not to get involved in Spanish War

88   ibid. pp 24-28; Booker T. Washington wrote that Negroes could render a service to the country that no other race could because they were accustomed to the peculiar and dangerous climate; Other African-American voices argued that Black participation in the war would either bring about the rise of the Negro in the estimation of the Anglo Saxon or conversely unpatriotic utterances were being used by whites as evidence that Negroes were incapable of functioning as responsible citizens— opportunity for blacks to win respect

89   Powell, Anthony, An Overview: Black Participation In The Spanish-American War

90   ibid.; Gatewood op cit. p 44

91   Cashin, Herschel V. and others, *Under Fire with the Tenth U. S. Cavalry*, Arno Press and The New York Times, New York, 1969.

92   Cashin op cit. p 159 (from *New York Mail & Express*)

93   Powell, Anthony, An Overview: Black Participation In The Spanish-American War—testimony of one Rough Rider; Gatewood p 59; Cashin p 160—attributes the quote to a Washington Post reporter who goes on to say "I am not a Negro lover. My father fought with Mosby's Rangers and I was born in the South, but the Negroes saved that fight, and the day will come when General Shafter will give them credit for their bravery." Gatewood p 106 attributes this quote to one of the Rough Riders

94   Powell op cit. pp 5-6

95   Cashin op cit. p 131; Powell op cit. p 6

96   Zwerdling op cit. p 52

97   DiNunzio, Mario R., editor, Theodore Roosevelt: An American Mind, A Selection From His Writings, St. Martin's Press, New York, 1994. p 332; Feb. 1905 Lincoln Day address to New York City Republican Club

98   D. K. Goodwin op cit. p 552; Pringle, Henry F., *Theodore Roosevelt: A Biography*, Harcourt, Brace and Company, New York, 1931. pp 247-248

99   Theodore Roosevelt, Sixth Annual Message to Congress, December 3, 1906

100   Ibid.

101   Lane, Ann J., The Brownsville Affair: Naional Crisis and Black Reaction, National University Publications, Kennikat Press, Port Washington, NY and London, 1971. p 14; Report on Brownsville Affray p 1610 (U.S. Senate, 59th Cong., 2nd Sess., Doc. 155, pt. 1, Vol. XI, ser. no. 5078, *Report on Brownsville Affray*)

102   Lane op cit. pp 19-20

103   ibid. pp 41-52; from the minority report issued by Senators Foraker and Bulkely in the Report of Senate Committee on Military Affairs.—The exculpating evidence produced by Foraker was challenged and partially rebutted by Major Blocksom and other government sources, but the men of the 25th Cavalry were subject to summary dismissal without due legal process. Pringle, Henry F., *Theodore Roosevelt: A Biography*, Harcourt, Brace and Company, New York, 1931. pp 462-463—Among Foraker's evidence of a frame was the fact that the cartridges were all found within a 10 inch area, an unlikely occurrence if they had been rapidly fired

104   Lane op cit. p 42

105   Dalton op. cit. p 321; Pringle op cit. p 460

106   Lane op cit. pp 46-51

107   "America in 1900," *American Digest*, March 31, 2004—http://americandigest.org/mt-archives /2004_03 (retrieved 9/27/2008)

108   Ibid.

109   http://www.census.gov/compendia/statab/hist_stats.html—shows 60% of a population of 79.5 million was considered rural in 1900

110   www.presidency.uscb.edu/ws/index.php?pip=29630—Republican platform of 1900

And while the American people, sustained by this Republican legislation, have been achieving these splendid riumphs in their business and commerce, they have conducted and in victory concluded a war for liberty and human rights. No thought of National aggrandizement tarnished the high purpose with which American standards were unfurled. It was a war unsought and patiently resisted, but when it came the American Government was ready. Its fleets were cleared for action. Its armies were in the field, and the quick and signal triumph of its forces on land and sea bore equal tribute to the courage of American soldiers and sailors, and to the skill and foresight of Republican statesmanship. To ten millions of the human race there was given "a new birth of freedom," and to the American people a new and noble responsibility.

[111] www.presidency.uscb.edu/ws/index.php?pip=29587—Democratic platform in 1900

We declare again that all governments instituted among men derive their just powers from the consent of the governed; that any government not based upon the consent of the governed is a tyranny; and that to impose upon any people a government of force is to substitute the methods of imperialism for those of a republic. We hold that the Constitution follows the flag, and denounce the doctrine that an Executive or Congress deriving their existence and their powers from the Constitution can exercise lawful authority beyond it or in violation of it. We assert that no nation can long endure half republic and half empire, and we warn the American people that imperialism abroad will lead quickly and inevitably to despotism at home.

[112] www.presidency.uscb.edu/ws/index.php?pip=29630—Republican Platform of 1900

The American Government must protect the person and property of every citizen wherever they are wrongfully violated or placed in peril. We congratulate the women of America upon their splendid record of public service in the volunteer aid association and as nurses in camp and hospital during the recent campaigns of our armies in the East and West Indies, and we appreciate their faithful co-operation in all works of education and industry.

[113] www.presidency.uscb.edu/ws/index.php?pip=29587—Democratic Platform of 1900

We favor the continuance and strict enforcement of the Chinese exclusion law, and its application to the same classes of all Asiatic races.

Chapter III

1   Zinn, Howard, A People's History of the United States—1492–Present, Harper Perennial Modern Classics edition, New York, 2005. p 253

2   ibid. p 253

3   Yellen, Samuel, *American Labor Struggles,* c1936, published by S. A. Russell, the Harbor Press by arrangement with Harcourt, Brace and Company, 1956. p 10; Zinn op. cit. 247

4   Yellen op. cit. p 10

5   Zinn op. cit. p 251

6   Yellen op. cit. p 16; Zinn op. cit. *York Times,* July 22, 1877 reported that the Philadelphia Hussars boasted that they were going to clean out Pittsburgh

7   Yellen op. cit. p 17

8   Ibid. pp 31-32

9   Zinn op. cit. p 251

10 I*n the Shadow of the Statue of Liberty*, Nick Salvatore, "Some Thoughts on Class and Citizenship in America in the Later Nineteenth Century" p 215—Nature of republicanism, Eric Foner—republicanism presupposed a preindustrial economy organized around commercial and artisinal activity. Artisan's control of the workspace assured a sense of economic activity and time to engage in political activity. Such activity was not to advance the concerns of a particular class which was considered inimical to the republican experience.—Tom Paine – the public good as the good of every individual collected.

11 Salvatore, Nick, *Eugene V. Debs: Citizen and Socialist*, University of Illinois Press, Urbana and Chicago, 1982. pp 26-27

12 Salvatore op. cit. p 23

13 "The Growth of Corporate and Decline of Governmental Power," *The Nation*, May 15, 1873. "Corporations to a certain extent take the place in American society of the privileged classes in aristocratic Europe; for they constitue a feudal system which exacts service, if not homage, from an influential portion of every community, and which dcarries on a disguised warfare with the Government...in which warfare concentrated wealth and power are arrayed against the wishes and, in some cases, interests of society at large.

14   ibid.—with corporate wealth accumulating and "the efficiency of American government constantly lessening, it is apparent that a time might, indeed *must*, come when Government would be really too ineffective to maintain the rights of society by duly restraining their aggressive powers." *In the Shadow of the Statue of Liberty*, Nick Salvatore, "Some Thoughts on Class and Citizenship in America in the Later Nineteenth Century" p 218– Immigration incompatible with self-government

15   Yellen op. cit. p 34; *The Nation*, "The Late Riots," August 7, 1877 an editorial (E. L. Godkin)

16   Fine, Sidney, Laissez Faire and the General-Welfare State: A Study of Conflict in American Thought 1865-1901, The University of Michigan Press, Ann Arbor, Michigan, 1956. p 319

17   Taft, Philip, *The A. F. of L. in the Time of Gompers*, Harper & Brothers, New York, 1957. pp 16-17

18   Taft op. cit. pp 17, 63

19   Foner, Philip, S., History of the Labor Movement in the United States, vol. 2—From the Founding of the American Federation of Labor to the Emergence of American Imperialism, International Publishers, New York, NY, 1955. p 105 Fireside, Bryna, The Haymarket Square Riot Trial: A Headline Case, Enslow Publishers, Berkeley Heights, NJ, *2002.* p 12 gives a newspaper account of 6 killed

20   Foner op. cit. p 106 footnote; Zinn op. cit. pp 270-71

21   Foner op. cit. p 106; Fireside op. cit. pp 15-16

22   ibid. (Foner op. cit. p 106; Fireside op. cit. pp 15-16)

23   Zinn op. cit. p 271

24   Foner op. cit. p 106 footnote; Fireside op. cit.p 12; Zinn op. cit.pp 270-71

25   Altgeld & Spies, *The Chicago Martyrs*, Address of August Spies, p 3

26   Ibid. Altgeld's reasons for Pardoning, pp 132, 153-154

27   Foner op. cit. pp 257-258; Salvatore, *Eugene Debs* pp 119-122

28   Foner op. cit. p 261; Zinn op. cit. pp 279-80; Lindsey, Almont, "Paternalism and the Pullman Strike," *The American Historical Review*, Vol. 44, No. 2, January 1939. pp 272-289. Published by: Oxford University Press on behalf of the American Historical Association, Stable URL: http://www.jstor.org/stable/1839019Pullman created a town for his workers that at its height had a population in excess of 12,000 people that provided

decent accommodations, parks, recreation, and services. Pullman retained ownership of all of the dwellings and other properties in the town and charged rents in excess of the rates in neighboring towns. He charged premium prices for gas and water and controlled the entertainment and discussion presented in the public theater. After the Panic of 1893, Pullman lowered wages and cut hours, but did not reduce his rents or the price of his utilities.

29   Zinn op. cit. p 280

30   Salvatore *Eugene Debs* p 128

31   Lindsey op. cit. p 287; Foner op. cit. p 262

32   Zinn op. cit. p 255

33   Ibid. p 257

34   Ibid. p 257

35   Ibid. p 258

36   Ibid. p 259

37   Foner pp 273-74 (footnote)—Gompers going to the funeral of the ARU remark *The Chicago Times* 8/6/1894 – printed the retraction of the charge by Thomas J. Morgan after he accepted the word of Gompers over that of the capitalist press, but the charge persisted from other voices and appeared in 'Big' Bill Haywood's autobiography many years later. Foner op. cit. pp 274-275—The Railroad Brotherhoods welcomed the demise of the ARU which did not share their philosophy and attracted many of their members during the strike

38   Foner op. cit. p 277

39   Salvatore *Eugene Debs* p 150

40   Hicks, John D., The Populist Revolt: A History of the Farmers' Alliance and the People's Party, University of Nebraska Press, Lincoln, Nebraska, 1961. pp 84–85

41   Faulkner, William, *The Hamlet,* Vintage Books Edition (paperback) 1956. p 3

42   Hicks op. cit. pp 87-93; Zinn op. cit. p 284

43   Zinn op. cit. p 286

44   Hicks op. cit. pp 133-137; Zinn op. cit. p 287

45   Zinn op. cit. p 260

46 Ibid. p 260

47 Fine, *Laissez Faire* p 295; Z inn op. cit. p 273

48 Zinn op. cit. p 273

49 Foner op. cit. p 339

50 Henry F. Pringle *Theodore Roosevelt*, New York, p. 164. (see also footnote in notes)

51 Foner op. cit. pp 339-40

52 Ibid. pp 339-340

53 Zinn op. cit. p 340

54 Ibid. p 340

55 Salvatore *Eugene Debs* pp 264-265; Zinn op. cit. p 368

56 Zinn op. cit. p 351

57 Ibid. p 355

58 Ibid. p 328

59 Ibid. p 325

60 Howard Sachar, "The International Ladies Garment Worker's Strike," *MyJewishLearning.com*(accessed April 14, 2015)—Garment workers joined on picket lines by fashionable sympathizers

61 Zinn op. cit. p 326

62 Howard Sachar, "The International Ladies Garment Worker's Strike," *MyJewishLearning.com* (accessed April 14, 2015)—There were no indoor bathroom facilities in the factory. Workers needing to use a bathroom were required to get permission from a foreman to have the door unlocked for them to use the outside toilets.

63 Zinn op. cit. p 327

64 Ibid. pp 327–328

65 Zinn op. cit. p 262 from *Acres of Diamonds* published in 1915 by Harper & Row; Conwell gave versions of the same lecture 6100 times over a period of many years. In a 1959 issue of the lecture by the John C. Winston Company of Philadelphia and Toronto, the quote about his disdain for the poor who are made so only by their own sins does not appear. In pages 11-13 of this version, Conwell argues the virtues of seeking wealth and the vice of remaining poor. "Well when a man could have been rich

just as well, and he is now weak because he is poor, he has done some great wrong; he has been unfaithful to himself; he has been unkind to his fellow men. We ought to get rich if we can by honorable and Christian methods" McGovern, George and Guttridge, Leonard, *The Great Coalfield War*, Houghton Mifflin Company, Boston, 1972. pp 195-196—NYU Professor John Stevenson wrote an essay "Capital and Labor" in the spring 1914 issue of *Popular Science Monthly* in whcih he dismissed the need for a man to be paid wages adequately to support his family and stated that if his "services were not worth enough to secure wages that would support a family, he should not marry." Then, like the pre-reformed Ebeneezer Scrooge, he went on to say that if the claims that 200,000 women each year were forced to sell their bodies and 700,000 children perished from malnutrition were true, then "their deaths are a blessing to themselves and to the community. Such children should not have been born…Unskilled labor is merely animated machinery for rough work and adds very little value to the final product." John D. Rockefeller initially praised the article and recommended it as a defense of his company's labor stand in the 1913-1914 Coal Field Wars

66 Reuther, Victor, The Brothers Reuther and the Story of the UAW: A Memoir, Houghton Mifflin Company, Boston, 1976. p 4; Dickmeyer, Elisabeth Reuther, *Putting the World Together—My Father Walter Reuther: The Liberal Warrior*, Living Force Publishing, Lake Orion, Michigan, 2004 p 14

67 E. R. Dickmeyer op. cit. p 14

68 Zinn op. cit. p 328; Taft op. cit. p 93

69 Bernard Mandel, "Samuel Gompers and the Negro Workers," *The Journal of Negro History*, vol 40, No. 1, January 1955, pp 60-61 in a Jacksonville, Florida address as first reported in *The Metropolis*. May 25, 1907 Gompers to the south on blacks

70 Salvatore op. cit. p 206—At the founding convention of the IWW in Chicago during June 1905, Big Bill Haywood, in his opening remarks, stressed that, unlike the AFL, the new union would "open wide its doors to every man that earns his living either by his brain or his muscle." Haywood recognized a class struggle and vowed that the IWW has "but one object and one purpose and that is to bring the workers of this country into the full possession of the full value of the product of their toil."

71 Zinn op. cit. p 330

72   Dubofsky Melvyn, We Shall Be All: A History of the Industrial Workers of the World, Quadrangle Books. Chicago, 1969 p 159; Zinn op. cit. p 331

73   Zinn op. cit. p 331; Dubofsky op. cit. pp 165-166

74   Dubofsky op. cit. pp 86–87

75   Yellen op. cit. p 172; Zinn op. cit. p 335

76   Yellen op. cit. p 176; Zinn op. cit. p 335

77   Yellen op. cit. p 183; Dubofsky op. cit. p 242; Zinn op. cit. p 336

78   Yellen op. cit. pp 185-186; Dubofsky op. cit. pp 247-248; Zinn op. cit. p 336

79   Yellen op. cit. p 186; Zinn op. cit. p 336

80   Yellen op. cit. pp 190-191; Dubofsky op. cit. p 252; Zinn op. cit. p 336-37

81   Dubofsky op. cit. p 253; Yellen op. cit. pp 196-197; Zinn op. cit. p 337

82   Yellen op cit. p 201 15,000 rally for Ettor and Giovannitti at start of trial Vecoli, Rudolph, "'Free Country':The American Republic Viewed by the Italian Left, 1880-1920," *In the Shadow of the Statue of Liberty*, p 35—The leftist Italian-American paper *Il Proletario* called for mass demonstrations to "liberate the hostages of the Battle of Lawrence" An Italian Defense Committee called for simultaneous protests throughout the country

83   Yellen op. cit. p 204; Zinn op. cit. p 336

84   Salvatore *Eugene Debs* p 264; Zinn op. cit. p 365

85   Dubofsky op. cit. p 165

86   Zinn op. cit. p 341

87   Zinn op. cit. p 354; McGovern op. cit. p 102—Striker's demands include: recognition of the union, 10% wage increase, an eight hour day, pay for "dead" work, an elected weight check man at all mines, the right to trade at any store and choose their own boarding place, enforcement of Colorado laws and the elimination of the notorious guard system

88   McGovern op. cit. p 134

89   Ibid. p 126—Linderfelt assembles a force for CFI;. pp 167-168— Linderfelt was part of the American force that brutally suppressed the native Filipinos during Aguinaldo's revolt. He later served as a mercenary in the army of Francisco Madero in a revolt against Mexican President

Diaz. In disobediance to Madero's orders he led a premature assault on the city of Juarez and was under an arrest warrant for robbery and looting when he slipped back across the border to the United States.

90 ibid. pp 138-139—Chase arrives at Ludlow; p 146—Baldwin-Felts agents being enlisted into the National Guard

91 ibid. pp 143

92 ibid. pp 173-174

93 ibid. p 128

94 ibid. p 186

95 ibid. pp 142, 147

96 Yellen op. cit. p 226; Zinn op. cit. p 355

97 McGovern op. cit. p 205

98 ibid. pp 213-215

99 Yellen op. cit. p 234; Zinn op. cit. p 355; McGovern op. cit. pp 213-226

100 Zinn op. cit. p 355

101 Yellen op. cit. pp 234-235

102 Yellen op. cit. p 234; Zinn op. cit. p 355

103 Yellen op. cit. p 237; Zinn op. cit. p 356

104 Zinn op. cit. p 356—demonstrations erupt in Denver & NY; Yellen op. cit. p 237—Upton Sinclair and four women arrested for picketing Rockefeller's New York office

105 ibid. pp 355-356

106 80

107 Zinn op. cit. p 357

108 ibid. p 367

109 McGovern op. cit. pp 339-340

110 W. E. B. Du Bois. "The African Roots of War," *Atlantic Monthly,* May, 1915.

111 Zinn op. cit. p 362

112 ibid. p 362

113 ibid. p 363

[114] ibid. p 362

[115] Zinn op. cit. p 364; Hedges, Chris, *Death of the Liberal Class*, Nathan Books, New York, NY, 2000. pp 75-76

[116] *The New York Times* March 8, 1917; Hedges op. cit. p 75

[117] Dos Passos, *Mr. Wilson's War*, p 301; Hedges p 74

[118] Hedges op. cit. p 76

[119] ibid. p 77

[120] ibid. p 77

[121] www.infoplease.com/t/hist/state-of-the-union/127.html   (retrieved 7/21/2015)

[122] Zinn op. cit. p 365

[123] firstworldwar.com   https://history.state.gov/milestones/1914-1920/fourteen-points (retrieved 7/24;2015)

[124] Zinn op. cit. p 369

[125] Hedges op. cit. p 78

[126] Zinn op. cit. p 371

[127] Dubofsky op. cit. pp 404-410; Zinn op. cit. p 373

[128] Dubofsky op. cit. pp 436-437; Zinn op. cit. p 373 Harsh sentences handed down by Judge "Kenesaw Mountain" Landis better known for his role as baseball commissioner in wake of the Black Sox scandal

[129] Salvatore, *Eugene Debs* pp 291-293; Zinn op. cit. p 367

[130] Salvatore, *Eugene Debs* pp 294-296; Zinn op. cit. p 368

[131] Salvatore, *Eugene Debs* p 325

[132] Zinn op. cit. p 365

[133] U. S. Department of State, Offi`ce of the Historian https://history.state.gov/milestones/1914-1920/fourteen-points

[134] Victor Reuther op. cit. p 12

[135] Ibid. p 13

[136] Ibid. p 13

[137] Ibid. pp 11–12

[138] Ibid. p 12

139 Ibid. p 17

140 Ibid. p 9

141 Ibid. p 32

142 Ibid. p 19; Gould, Jean & Hickok, Lorena, *Walter Reuther, Labor's Rugged Individualist*, Dodd, Mead & Company, New York, NY, 1972. pp 13-14

143 Victor Reuther op. cit. pp 19-20

144 ibid. p 28

145 Ibid. p 29

146 Victor Reuther op. cit. p 30; Gould & Hickok op. cit. pp 18-19; Lichtenstein op. cit. pp 10–11

147 ibid. p 39

148 Ibid. p 23

149 Ibid. p 21

150 Salvatore, *Eugene Debs* p 329

151 Victor Reuther op. cit. pp 29-30

152 Ibid. p 31

153 Ibid. p 30

154 Ibid. p 39

155 127

156 Gould & Hickok op. cit. pp 33-34; Lichtenstein, Nelson, *The Most Dangerous Man in Detroit: Walter Reuther* and the Fate of American Labor, Basic Books, New York, 1995. p 12

157 Gould & Hickok op. cit. p 34; Lichtenstein op. cit. p 12

158 Victor Reuther op. cit. p 40

159 Ibid. pp 35–36

160 Ibid. p 37

161 The Detroit Free Press, April 5, 1942

162 Victor Reuther op. cit. p 44

163 Ibid. p 44

164 Ibid. p 46

165 Ibid. p 46

[166] Ibid. pp 46–47

[167] Ibid. p 47

[168] Ibid. p 48

[169] Gould & Hickok op. cit. p 49

[170] Lichtenstein op. cit. p 17

[171] Ibid. p 23

[172] Ibid. p 23

[173] Victor Reuther op. cit. p 56; Lichtenstein op. cit. p 26

[174] Cormier, Frank & Eaton, William J., *Reuther*, Prentice-Hall, Edgewood Cliffs, N. J., 1970. p 17

[175] Lichtenstein op. cit. p 26

[176] Ibid. p 28

[177] Ibid. pp 29–30

[178] Ibid. p 23

[179] Ibid. p 23

[180] Ibid. p 7

[181] Ibid. p 19

[182] Gould & Hickok op. cit. pp 49-51

[183] Ibid. pp 49–50

[184] Ibid. p 49

[185] ibid. p 52; Lichtenstein op. cit. p 33

[186] Lichtenstein op. cit. pp 31-33

[187] Cormier & Eaton op. cit. p 22; Lichtenstein op. cit. p 33

[188] Victor Reuther op. cit. p 66

[189] Lichtenstein op. cit. p 34

[190] Gould & Hickok op. cit. p 56

[191] ibid. p 57

[192] Victor Reuther op. cit. p 70; (Lichtenstein op. cit. p 34 tells of the brothers meeting a social democratic organizer on the train from Hamburg to Berlin who gave them the names of the students in Berlin)

[193] Victor Reuther op. cit. p 70

194   Ibid. pp 70–71

195   Ibid. p 71

196   Ibid. p 73

197   Ibid. pp 73–74

198   Ibid. p 76

199   Ibid. p 76

200   Ibid. pp 77-78

201   Ibid. p 78

202   Cormier & Eaton op. cit. p 25; Gould & Hickok op. cit. p 60

203   Victor Reuther op. cit. p 80

204   Ibid. pp 80–81

205   Ibid. p 81

206   Ibid. p 85

207   Ibid. p 86

208   Ibid. p 87

209   Ibid. p 88

210   Ibid. p 89

211   Lichtenstein op. cit. p 39

212   Cormier & Eaton op. cit. pp 35-36 in an interview by a reporter from the *Moscow Daily News*

213   Victor Reuther op. cit. pp 94-95

214   Ibid. p 107

215   Ibid. p 108

216   Ibid. pp 113–114

217   Gould & Hickok op. cit. p 80

218   Cormier & Eaton op. cit. p 132-133; A version of the Letter from Gorky that first appeared in a hostile biography of Walter Reuther by Eldorous Dayton is reprinted on pages 132-136 of *Reuther by* Cormier and Eaton

219   Ibid. p 133

220   Ibid. pp 134-136

221   Ibid. p 135

[222] Victor Reuther op. cit. p 109

[223] Cormier & Eaton op. cit. p 43; Victor Reuther op. cit. pp 108-109

[224] Victor Reuther op. cit. pp 109-110

[225] Ibid. p 102

[226] Lichtenstein op. cit. pp 167-168; Cormier & Eaton p 132

[227] Cormier & Eaton op. cit. p 136

[228] Victor Reuther op. cit. pp 90-92

[229] Ibid. p 90

[230] Ibid. p 91

[231] Ibid. p 112

[232] Ibid. p 115

[233] Ibid. p 114

[234] Ibid. p 114

[235] Ibid. p 114

[236] Ibid. p 116

[237] Ibid. p 117

[238] ibid. p 118

[239] ibid. p 119

[240] ibid. pp 119–120

[241] ibid. p 120

[242] Ibid. pp 120–121

[243] ibid. p 121

[244] Ibid. p 122

Chapter IV

[1] Lichtenstein, Nelson, The Most Dangerous Man in Detroit—Walter Reuther and the Fate of American Labor, Basic Books, New York, 1995. p 51

[2] Ibid. p 53

[3] Ibid. p 51

4   Ibid. p 51

5   Reuther, Victor, *The Brothers Reuther and the Story of the UAW: A Memoir*, Houghton Mifflin Company, Boston, 1976. p 126; Lichtenstein op cit. p 51

6   Dubofsky, Melvyn & Van Tine, *John L. Lewis, A Biography*, Quadrangle/The New York Times Book Company, New York, 1977. p 219

7   Hanna, Mark, *Mark Hanna: His Book*, Chapple Publishing, 1904. p 10

8   Zinn, Howard, A People's History of the United States—1492–Present, Harper Perennial Modern Classics edition, New York, 2005. p 325

9   Paul Simon, Parsley, Sage, Rosemary, and Thyme album

10   Dubofsky & Van Tine op cit. p 220, Alinsky, Saul, *John L. Lewis: An Unauthorized Biography*, G. P. Putnam's Sons, New York, 1949 p 74

11   Dubofsky & Van Tine op cit. p 220, Alinsky op cit. pp 76-77

12   Dubofsky & Van Tine op cit. p 222

13   Dubofsky & Van Tine op cit. p 228, Alinsky op cit. pp 89-90; Nelson, Daniel, *American Rubber Workers & Organized Labor, 1900-1941*, Princeton University Press, Princeton, New Jersey, 1988. p ???

14   Nelson op cit. pp 175-176, 183-184

15   Fine, Sidney, *Sit-Down: The General Motors Strike of 1936-1937*, University of Michigan Press, Ann Arbor, Michigan, 1969. p 124

16   Victor Reuther op cit. p 126

17   Victor Reuther op cit. p 126; Lichetnstein op cit. pp 51-52

18   Cormier, Frank & Eaton, William J., *Reuther*, Prentice-Hall, Edgewood Cliffs, N. J., 1970. p 61

19   Cormier & Eaton op cit. p 61, Lichtenstein. op cit p 56

20   Cormier & Eaton op cit. p 61, Lichtenstein op cit. p 56

21   Cormier & Eaton op cit. p 61

22   Victor Reuther op cit. p 124

23   Cormier & Eaton op cit. p 60

24   Lichtenstein op. cit. p 57

25   Ibid. p 58

26   Victor Reuther op cit. p 129

27   Victor Reuther op cit. p 129

28   Cormier & Eaton op cit. p 63

29   Ibid. p 64

30   Ibid. p 66

31   Gould, Jean & Hickok, Lorena, *Walter Reuther, Labor's Rugged Individualist*, Dodd, Mead & Company, New York, NY, 1972. pp 103; Victor Reuther op cit. p 127

32   Dickmeyer, Elisabeth Reuther, Putting the World Together—My Father Walter Reuther: The Liberal Warrior, Living Force Publishing, Lake Orion, Michigan, 2004. p 37

33   Gould & Hickok op cit. p 104; Cormier & Eaton op cit. p 66

34   Lichtenstein op cit. p 94

35   Cormier & Eaton op cit. p 67

36   Ibid. p 67

37   Ibid. p 67

38   E. R. Dickmeyer op cit. p 37

39   Lichtenstein op cit. p 60; Cormier & Eaton op cit. p 66

40   Cormier & Eaton op cit. pp 67-68, Lichtenstein op cit. p 60

41   Lichtenstein op cit. pp 60-61

42   Cormier & Eaton op cit. p 55

43   Lichtenstein op cit. p 61, Cormier & Eaton op cit. p 69

44   Cormier & Eaton op cit. p 66

45   Ward's Reports—Lichtenstein op cit. p 63

46   Cormier & Eaton op cit. p 70

47   Victor Reuther op cit. p 134

48   Lichtenstein op cit. p 64

49   Ibid. p 64

50   Ibid. p 64

51   Ibid. p 65

52   Victor Reuther op cit. p 136

53   Lichtenstein op cit. p 65

54 Ibid. p 65

55 Ibid. p 67

56 Victor Reuther op cit. p 136

57 Ibid. p 136

58 Victor Reuther op cit. pp 136 (Danzig); Lichtenstein op cit. p 68 (DeMong)

59 Victor Reuther op cit. pp 136-37 (Danzig); Licht p 68 (DeMong)

60 Victor Reuther op cit. p 137

61 Lichtenstein op cit. p 68

62 Victor Reuther op cit. p 138

63 Victor Reuther op cit. p 138; Lichtenstein op cit. p 69

64 Victor Reuther op cit. p 138; Lichtenstein op cit. p 70

65 Cormier & Eaton op cit. p 72

66 Lichtenstein op cit. p 70

67 Ibid. p 70

68 Victor Reuther op cit. p 139

69 Lichtenstein op cit. p 70

70 Victor Reuther op cit. p 140; Lichtenstein op cit. p 71

71 Lichtenstein op cit. p 71

72 Ibid. p 71

73 Ibid. p 73

74 Ibid. p 72

75 Victor Reuther op cit. p 141

76 Victor Reuther op cit. p 147; Cormier & Eaton op cit. p 76

77 Cormier & Eaton op cit. p 76

78 Cormier & Eaton op cit. p 77, Alinsky op cit. pp 109-110

79 Alinsky op cit. p 107

80 Victor Reuther op cit. p 145; Cormier & Eaton op cit. p 75

81 Fine, *Sit Down* pp 109-112; Victor Reuther op cit. p 144

82 Victor Reuther op cit. p 146

83   Cormier & Eaton op cit. p 78

84   Alinsky op cit. pp 113-114; Fine *Sit Down* p 194

85   Fine *Sit Down* pp 194-195; Cormier & Eaton op cit. p 80, Alinsky op cit. p 116

86   Cormier & Eaton op cit. p 81, Alinsky op cit. p 119

87   Cormier & Eaton op cit. p 81

88   Victor Reuther op cit. p 153; Cormier & Eaton op cit. p 85

89   Fine *Sit Down* p 5; Victor Reuther op cit. p 155

90   Fine *Sit Down* p 5; Victor Reuther op cit. p 157

91   Fine *Sit Down* pp 6-7

92   Genora (Johnson) Dollinger interview with Susan Rosenthal, February 1995 http://www.historyisaweapon.com/defcon1/dollflint. html#preparing (retrieved 2/24/2015)

93   Dubofsky & Van Tine op cit. pp 262-63

94   Fine *Sit Down* pp 252-253; Cormier & Eaton op cit. p 88

95   Cormier & Eaton op cit. p 88, Alinsky op cit. pp 122-123

96   Victor Reuther op cit. p 161

97   Genora (Johnson) Dollinger interview with Susan Rosenthal, op. cit.

98   Ibid.

99   Ibid.

100   Ibid.

101   Ibid.

102   Ibid.

103   Ibid.

104   Fine *Sit Down* p 270

105   Dubofsky & Van Tine op cit. p 266, Alinsky op cit. p 127

106   Fine *Sit Down* p 285; Dubofsky & Van Tine op cit. p 267

107   Fine, Sidney, *Frank Murphy: the Washington Years*, The University of Michigan Press, Ann Arbor, 1984. p 450

108   Ibid. 431

109   Dubofsky & Van Tine op cit. p 267, Alinsky op cit. p 129

110   Dubofsky & Van Tine op cit. p. 270, Alinsky op cit. pp 144-145—Lewis invokes Murphy's ancestors; Fine *Sit Down* p 299—Lewis' account was given at subsequent CIO convention and may be embellished

111   Dubofsky & Van Tine op cit. p. 269

112   Cormier & Eaton p 94, Alinsky op cit. p 139

113   Dubofsky & Van Tine op cit. p. 268; Fine *Sit Down* pp 305-306

114   Dubofsky & Van Tine op cit. p 270, Alinsky op cit. p 146

115   Genora (Johnson) Dollinger interview with Susan Rosenthal, op. cit.

116   Lichtenstein op cit. p 98

117   Ibid. p 99

118   Ibid. p 99

119   Ibid. p 100

120   Ibid. p 101

121   Ibid. p 102

122   Ibid. p 102

123   Dubofsky & Van Tine op cit. p. 273

124   Ibid. p 274

125   Ibid. p 276

126   Ibid. p 278

127   Lichtenstein op cit. p. 116

128   Ibid. p 117

129   Ibid. p 118

130   Ibid. pp 118–119

131   Ibid. p 121

132   Ibid. p 122

133   Victor Reuther op cit. p. 184-85; Lichtenstein op cit. p 114

134   Lichtenstein op cit. p 124

135   Victor Reuther op cit. p 190

136   Cormier & Eaton op cit. p 147

137   Lichtenstein op cit. p.129

[138]   Ibid. p 130

[139]   Ibid. p 130

[140]   Gould & Hickok op cit. p 160; Lichtenstein op cit. p. 133

[141]   Gould & Hickok op cit. p 160; Lichtenstein op cit. p. 133

[142]   Ibid. p 137

[143]   Ibid. p 139

[144]   Ibid. p 140

[145]   Ibid. p 140

[146]   Ibid. p 140

[147]   Ibid. p 142

[148]   Ibid. p 142

[149]   Ibid. p 140

[150]   Cormier & Eaton op cit. p 120

[151]   Ibid. pp 124–125

Chapter V

[1]   Ford, Henry in collaboration with Samuel Crowther, *My Life and Work*, Doubleday, Page & Company, Garden City, New York, 1926 (c 1922). p 50

[2]   ibid. p 51

[3]   Sward, Keith, *The Legend of Henry Ford*, Rinehart & Company, Toronto and New York, 1948. p. 17 -19; Ford op. cit. p 51

[4]   Sward op cit. op cit. p. 17-19; Lacey, Robert, *Ford: the Men and the Machine*, Little Brown and Company, Boston-Toronto, 1986. pp 68–69

[5]   Lacey op. cit. pp 46 – 50, 59–61

[6]   Sward op. cit. p 20

[7]   2aa

[8]   Lacey op cit. pp 78–82

[9]   Lacey op cit. pp 78-82; Sward op cit. p. 22

[10]   Sward op cit. p. 46

11   Lacey op cit. pp 77-78

12   Howe, Irving & Widick, B. J., *The UAW and Walter Reuther*, Random House, New York, 1949 pp 83-84

13   Ibid. p 84

14   Sorensen, Charles with Williamson, Samuel, *My Forty Years With Ford*, W. W. Norton & Company, New York, 1956. pp 125-132

15   Sward op cit. pp 38-40, Sorensen op cit. p 126; Emde's contribution to the success of Ford is ignored by the industrialist in his biographical accounts, but William Knudsen credits him with doing more to revolutionize the automobile industry than any man who ever lived (Sward p 40)

16   Howe & Widdik op cit. p 22; Ford op cit. pp 77-78, 103

17   Howe & Widdik op cit. p 84

18   Howe & Widdik op cit. p 85; Lacey op cit. p 121

19   Ford op cit. p 126; Howe & Widdik op cit. p 5

20   Ford op cit. p 147—; Howe & Widdik op cit. p 5

21   Howe & Widdik op cit. p 90; Ford op cit. p 107

22   Howe & Widdik op cit. p 92; Lacey op. cit. p 367; Maurice Sugar, *The Ford Hunger March*, Meiklejohn Civil Liberties Institute, Berkeley, California, 1980. p 112

23   Dickmeyer, Elisabeth Reuther, Putting the World Together—My Father Walter Reuther: The Liberal Warrior, Living Force Publishing, Lake Orion, Michigan, 2004 p 12; Lacey op. cit. pp 372-373

24   Sward, op cit. p 306, Alinsky, Saul, *John L. Lewis: An Unauthorized Biography*, G. P. Putnam's Sons, New York, 1949 p 101

25   Ford op cit. p 129; Howe & Widdik op cit. p 88

26   Ford op. cit. p 129

27   Baldwin, Neil, *Henry Ford and the Jews: The Mass Production of Hate*, PublicAffairs, New York, 2001. pp 2-3; *McGuffey's 5th Eclectic Reader* pp 198-203 gives an abridged rendition of the court scene where Shylock demands his pound of flesh from the merchant Antonio and refuses to accept six times the sum he was owed instead of the penalty stipulated in the contract. Shylock professes his hatred for Antonio and is not moved by the judge's (not revealed here to be Portia) first four lines of the quality of mercy speech. The scene is removed entirely from the context of the play.

None of the characters are given any development, and the reasons for Shylock's animosity toward Antonio is nowhere mentioned. The student is left to conclude that Shylock's mean thirst for vengeance was simply because it was characteristic of a Jew.

28   Howe & Widdik op cit. p 87

29   Sward op cit. p 160; *The New York Times*, Dec. 20, 1922

30   Lacey op cit. p 219

31   Meier, August & Rudwick, Elliott, *Black Detroit and the Rise of the UAW*, Oxford University Press, New York, 1979.p 6

32   Lacey op cit. pp 307-308;Sward op cit. pp 229-230

33   Meier & Rudwick op cit. pp 59-60

34   Ibid. pp 60–61

35   Lichtenstein, Nelson, The Most Dangerous Man in Detroit—Walter Reuther and the Fate of American Labor, Basic Books, New York, 1995. p 17; Sorensen op cit. p 282 gives a figure of 10,000 cars a day

36   Lewis, David L., *The Public Image of Henry Ford*, Wayne State University Press, Detroit, 1976. p 266—At the time of the NLRB vote on March 21, 1941 the number casting votes at the River Rouge plant were 51,886 for the UAW, 20,364 for the AFL, and 1,958 for no union or a total of 74,208 votes cast that expressed a preference—90,000 workers at height

37   Howe & Widdik op cit. p.29; Cormier, Frank & Eaton, William J., *Reuther*, Prentice-Hall, Edgewood Cliffs, N. J., 1970. p 50

38   Sward op cit. p 223

39   Maurice Sugar, *The Ford Hunger March*, p 25—In Sugar's account of the riot that erupted after the hunger marchers approached the Miller Road access to the Ford plant, Harry Bennett with two others drove out of the Ford plant at a point at which the workers had voted to march back to Detroit and abandon their effort to press their demands at the plant doors. When Bennett's car got close to the marchers, he rolled down the window and began shooting into the crowd. A barrage of stones showered down on Bennett's car and he was struck in the head by one. He kept up the assault until he collapsed from the effects of his injury. In the papers the next day Bennett was variously described as having been shot in the head, courageously charging a mob bare-handed, having created thousands of jobs for needy men, a noted criminologist, and a peacemakerinjured while on the scene only for the purpose of investigation.

Clearly incongruous explanations of his presence at the scene. (see pages 41-43)

40   Cormier & Eaton op cit. p 97

41   Lichtenstein op cit. p 83; Cormier & Eaton op cit. p 101

42   Cormier & Eaton op cit. p 102;Lichtenstein op cit. p 83

43   Cormier & Eaton op cit. pp 102-103

44   Sward op. cit. pp 391–394;Cormier & Eaton op cit. pp 103-107

45   Cormier & Eaton op cit. pp 103-104; Lichtenstein op cit. p 84

46   Sward pp 393-394; Cormier & Eaton op cit. p 106

47   Cormier & Eaton op cit. pp 107-108

48   *Detroit News* retrospective info.detnews.com/history/story/index.cfm?id1728(category=events) (retrieved February 12, 2011) no longer accessible

49   Cormier & Eaton op cit. p 107; Lewis op cit. pp 250-252—Describes Ford's support from smaller newspapers around the country in the wake of the Battle of the Overpass

50   Alinsky op cit. p 156

51   Ibid. p 159

52   Lewis op cit. p 76; Howe & Widdik op cit. p 89;Lewis p 251 & 289-290 lists other public surveys in which Ford ranks high.

53   17a

54   Cormier & Eaton op cit. p 123

55   18

56   Reuther, Victor, The Brothers Reuther and the Story of the UAW: A Memoir, Houghton Mifflin Company, Boston, 1976. p 205; Lichtenstein op cit. p 87

57   Sward op cit. p 397

58   Ibid. pp 397–398

59   Ibid. pp 393–394, 414–415

60   Ibid. p 399; Lacey op cit. p 370

61   Gould, Jean & Hickok, Lorena, *Walter Reuther, Labor's Rugged Individualist*, Dodd, Mead & Company, New York, NY, 1972. pp 154-155

62   Cormier & Eaton op cit. p 147

63   Sward, op cit. p 401

64   Victor Reuther op cit. p 211

65   Sward op cit. p 207

66   Ibid. p 403

67   Ibid. 404

68   Lewis op cit. p 264; Sward op cit. p 406

69   Sward op cit. p 407

70   Howe & Widdik op cit. pp 103-194; Sward op cit. p 408

71   Sward op cit. pp 408-409

72   Ibid. 409

73   Ibid. p 410

74   Ibid. p 411

75   Ibid. p 411

76   *Detroit Free Press*, April 5, 1941

77   Sward p 412

78   Meier & Rudwick op cit. pp 88-89; Lewis op cit. pp 262-265 Ford uses his branch managers to approach newspaper editors and secure favorable coverage for his confrontation with the union. Most papers are inclined to support management and espouse anti-union sentiment to begin with, and readily accede to the Ford requests. The papers helped promote the view that the CIO was synonymous with lawlessness by only showing pictures of CIO pickets beating up Blacks defending the company.

79   Meier & Rudwick op cit. p 89

80   Ibid. pp 99–102

81   White, Walter, *A Man Called White*, The Viking Press, New York, 1948. p 216

82   Sward op cit. p 416

83   Lewis op cit. p 265; Sward op cit. pp 416–417

84   Sorensen op cit. p 268

85   Sward op cit. pp 418-419;Lacey op cit. p 374

86   Sorensen op cit. p 259

87   Sorensen op cit. p 268; Cormier & Eaton op cit. p 162

88   Sorensen op cit. p 271; Cormier & Eaton op cit. p 163

89   Lacey op cit. pp 377-378

90   Sward op cit. p 421

91   Sward op cit. pp 421-422; Gould & Hickok op cit. p 182

92   Sward op cit. pp 422-423

93   Ibid. p 424–429

94   Sward op cit. p 464, Sorensen op cit. pp 324-333 Sorensen provides a
      detailed account of the reorganization of the management at Ford after
      the death of Edsel in 1943. Henry Ford's decision to resume the role of
      president caused a rift in the family and between Ford and Sorensen. In a
      hastily convened board meeting immediately after Edsel's death, Ford was
      named president, Sorensen was made executive vice president, and Craig
      Wibel was appointed vice president and treasurer. Ford told Sorensen that
      they would work together just as in the old days. Sorensen disabused him
      of this notion and told him he should get his grandson Henry back from
      the navy and put him in charge immediately. The elder Ford was not eager
      to see his grandson back at his company, and resisted calls to name him
      to a leadership position. During this period many of the key people were
      leaving the company and Roosevelt was concerned about Ford's ability to
      fulfill its wartime contracts. The government was prepared to nationalize
      the company before Ford relented and named his grandson executive vice
      president.

95   Lacey op cit. p 419

96   Lacey op cit. p 426, pp 420–431; Sward op cit. pp 468-469

97   Sward op cit. p 478; Lacey p 430

98   Lacey op cit. p 433

99   Lacey op cit. pp 437-438;Lewis op cit. pp 431-432—UAW reaction to
      Ford's speech was that "Ford stole a page right out of Walter Reuther's
      book." Reuther first used the term 'human engineering' in an Oct. 19,
      1945 speech.

100   Lacey op cit. p 438

101   Lacey pp 247-249; Henry Ford created what might be called the first
      historical theme park in the United States. Ford began collecting historical
      objects in 1919 shortly after his testimony in a libel suit against the *Chicago*

Tribune revealed an embarrassing lack of knowledge about important events and dates in American history. Ford was castigated in the press for his comment, history is bunk," which he insisted was meant to state that the history taught in school books was bunk. Ford went to great expense to reverse the image of himself that his ill chosen words had created by assembling artifacts that he considered important pieces of American history. He bought the old Wayside Inn that swerved as a setting for many of Longfellow's poems and reassembled it in Greenfield Village. He added the birthplaces and residences of several of his heroes – William Holmes McGuffey, Noah Webster, Luther Burbank, and Stephen Foster. He built replicas of Independence Hall, Constitution Hall, and the Old City Hall in Philadelphia, and restored the Menlo Park laboratory of Edison, the bicycle shop where the Wright brothers experimented with flight, the courthouse where Lincoln first practiced law, and the little schoolhouse where Mary of little lamb fame once attended. In Greenfield Village Ford provided visitors a peek back into the nineteenth century where he felt most comfortable while at the same time doing as much as anyone to hasten its end.

Chapter VI

[1] Burns, James MacGregor, *Roosevelt: The Lion and the Fox,* Harcourt, Brace & World, Inc., New York, 1956. p 425; Black, Conrad, *Franklin Delano Roosevelt: Champion of Freedom*, Public Affairs, New York, 2003 p 568

[2] Black op cit. p 568

[3] Burns op cit. p 427; Black op cit. p 569

[4] Burns op cit. pp 427-428; Black p op cit. 569

[5] Black op cit. p 570; Burns op cit. p 432

[6] Black op cit. p 589; Alinsky, Saul, *John L. Lewis: An Unauthorized Biography*, G. P. Putnam's Sons, New York, 1949 pp 188–190

[7] Lichtenstein, Nelson, The Most Dangerous Man in Detroit—Walter Reuther and the Fate of American Labor, Basic Books, New York, 1995. p 157; Reuther, Victor, The Brothers Reuther and the Story of the UAW: A *Memoir*, Houghton Mifflin Company, Boston, 1976. p 223

[8] Hersh, Seymour, *The Dark Side of Camelot*, Back Bay Books, 1998 p 63

[9] Black op cit. pp 590-91

10   Ibid. p 591

11   Ibid. p 591

12   Ibid. p 577

13   Lichtenstein op cit. p 158; footnote—Studs Terkel, *The Good War* p 316

14   Lichtenstein op cit. p 158

15   Ibid. p 157

16   Ibid. p 157

17   Ibid. p 157

18   Swanberg, *Norman Thomas* p 246, Seidler, Murray, *Norman Thomas, Respectable Rebel,* pp 249-250, 283

19   Walter P. Reuther radio address on the Red Network of the National Broadcasting Company, Dec. 28, 1940

20   FDR Pres. Library

21   Ibid.

22   Ibid.

23   Lichtenstein op cit. p 164

24   Cormier, Frank & Eaton, William J., *Reuther*, Prentice-Hall, Edgewood Cliffs, N. J., 1970. p 186

25   Reuther, Victor, The Brothers Reuther and the Story of the UAW: A Memoir, Houghton Mifflin Company, Boston, 1976. p 226

26   Cormier & Eaton op cit. p 191, Lictenstein op cit. p 165; Catton, Bruce, *The War Lords of Washington*, Harcourt, Brace and Company, New York, 1948. pp 91–106—To retain government control of the war production system and to thwart an industry effort to superimpose an industry oversight committee that would in effect exercise control of the effort, John Lord O'Brian, the general counsel of the OMB decreed that the anti-trust laws would remain in effect during the crisis and that government would exercise control of the process. If government wanted concerted action from an industry, it could first get approval from the Justice Department then send its proposal to an industry committee in writing. Industry (and labor) could not initiate a plan of their own. This policy rendered the Reuther plan illegal. In the end industry rapidly converted the machine tools they claimed could not be used for other purposes when faced with

a prohibition on producing consumer vehicles one month after Pearl Harbor and presented with large defense contracts.

27   Lichtenstein op cit. p 165

28   Ibid. p 165

29   Victor Reuther op cit. p 229

30   Lichtenstein op cit. p 166

31   Cormier & Eaton op cit. pp 188-189

32   Ibid. p 192

33   Lichtenstein op cit. p 167

34   Dickmeyer, Elisabeth Reuther, Putting the World Together—My Father Walter Reuther: The Liberal Warrior, Living Force Publishing, Lake Orion, Michigan, 2004—pp 67-68

35   Lichtenstein op cit. p 169

36   Cormier & Eaton op cit. p 194

37   Lichtenstein op cit. p 170

38   Ibid. p 169

39   Ibid p 170

40   *Milwaukee Journal*, April 1, 1942 page 5

41   Ibid.

42   Cormier & Eaton op cit. p 195

43   Ibid. p 196

44   Ibid. p 196

45   Howe, Irving & Widick, B. J., *The UAW and Walter Reuther*, Random House, New York, 1949 p 200; Lichtenstein op cit. p 185

46   Cormier & Eaton op cit. p 198

47   Ibid. p 199

48   Victor Reuther op cit. p 240

49   Sward, Keith, *The Legend of Henry Ford*, Rinehart & Company, Toronto and New York, 1948. p 430

50   Ibid. pp 433–435

51   Cormier & Eaton op cit. p 211

52 Catton, Bruce, *The War Lords of Washington*, Harcourt, Brace and Company, New York, 1948. p 91; Cormier & Eaton op cit. p 194

53 Cormier & Eaton op cit. p 204

54 Lichtenstein op cit. p 174

55 Ibid. p 174

56 Ibid. p 179

57 Ibid. p 180

58 Ibid. p 180

59 Ibid. p 183

60 Ibid. p 183

61 Ibid. p 183

62 Ibid. p 184

63 Ibid. p 191

64 Ibid. p 191

65 Ibid. p 191

66 Ibid. p 191

67 Ibid. p 192

68 Ibid. p 192

69 Ibid. p 196

70 Cormier & Eaton op cit. p 199

71 Ibid. p 199

72 Ibid. p 199

73 Lichtenstein op cit. p 196

74 Ibid. p 197

75 Cormier & Eaton op cit. p 200

76 Ibid. p 200

77 Lichtenstein op cit. p 199

78 Cormier & Eaton p 200

79 Ibid. p 200

80 79

81   Lichtenstein op cit. p 200

82   Ibid. p 200

83   Cormier & Eaton op cit. p 202

84   Ibid. p 203

85   Lichtenstein op cit. p 198

86   Ibid. p 198

87   Cormier & Eaton op cit. p 205

88   Lichtenstein op cit. p 203

89   Ibid. p 204

90   Ibid. p 205

91   Ibid. p 204

92   Ibid. p 205

93   Ibid. p 205

94   Victor Reuther op cit. p 236

95   Cormier & Eaton op cit. p 209; Lichtenstein op cit. p 206

96   Ibid.

97   Cormier & Eaton op. cit. p 210

98   C. N. Trueman, "The Battle of Kursk," *The History Learning Site,* http://www.historylearningsite.co.uk/world-war-two/famous-battles-of-world-war-two/the-battle-of-kursk/—retrieved July 15, 2015

99   Ibid.

100   Ibid.

101   Alinsky op cit. 164-169

102   Ibid.p 161

103   Ibid. p 164

104   Alinsky op cit. pp 316-317—The cartoon was drawn by a soldier and showed Lewis depicted as a miner shoveling coal on a soldier's grave. It was sent to the Army newspaper *Stars and Stripes* but never printed. In an editorial, the paper described the cartoon and said it did not print the drawing because of its policy of not getting involved in anything deemed political. It went on to state that the cartoon it described expressed the attitude of the majority of men in this and any other theater The editorial

ended, "Speaking for the American soldier, John L. Lewis, damn your coal black soul.'

105 Catton op cit. pp 215-217

106 Ibid. pp 152–153

107 Ibid. p 254

108 Ibid. p 247

109 Ibid. pp 219, 269–273

110 Cormier & Eaton op cit. p 212

111 Ibid. p 212

112 Ibid. pp 212–213

113 Ibid. p 214

114 Ibid. pp 213–214

115 Lichtenstein op. cit. p 176

116 Cormier & Eaton op cit. p 216

117 Schneiderman, Matt, "William Levitt: The king of suburbia," *The Real Deal.* April 30, 2008 http://therealdeal.com/issues_articles/william-levitt-the-king-of-suburbia/

118 Malvina Reynolds (1962) Schroder Music Company—Little boxes lyrics

119 Kushner, David, Two Families, One Tycoon, and the Fight for Civil Rights in America's Legendary Suburb, Walker & Company, New York, 2009 p 44

120 Reuther, Walter P., Swords Into Plowshares: A Proposal to Promote Orderly Conversion From Defense to *Civilian Production*, Statement and Testimony of Walter P. Reuther, President of the UAW, To the Senate Committee On Labor and Public Welfare, December 1, 1969. page 4

121 Cormier & Eaton op cit. p 216

122 Ibid. p 216

123 Ibid. p 216

Chapter VII

1   Sorensen, Charles with Williamson, Samuel, *My Forty Years With Ford*, W. W. Norton & Company, 1956 p 283

2   Gould & Hickok, *Walter Reuther: Labor's Rugged Individualist*, Dodd, Mead& Company, (New York, 1972) p 225, Howe & Widick, *The UAW and Walter Reuther*, Random House, 1949 pp 129-130

3   Gould & Hickok op. cit. p 226,; Howe & Widick op. cit. p 131 states Wilson's counter offer was a 45 hour week

4   Victor Reuther, *The Brothers Reuther and the Story of the UAW*, Houghton Mifflin Company, 1976. p 250

5   Victor Reuther op. cit. p 250; Howe & Widick op. cit. p 132

6   Victor Reuther op. cit. p 250

7   Gould & Hickok op. cit. pp 227-228

8   Cormier & Eaton, *Reuther*, Prentice Hall, 1970 p 222;Howe & Widick op. cit pp 132-136

9   Cormier & Eaton op. cit. p 223

10   Ibid. p 223

11   Ibid. p 222

12   ibid. p 222; Victor Reuther op. cit. p 251

13   Cormier & Eaton op. cit. p 223

14   White, Walter, *A Man Called White*, The Viking Press, New York, 1948. p 217; Howe & Widick op. cit p 138

15   White op. cit. p 217;Cormier & Eaton op. cit. p 224

16   White op. cit. p 218;Cormier & Eaton op. cit. p 224

17   Cormier & Eaton op. cit. p 224

18   Gould & Hickok op. cit. P 231; Howe & Widick op. cit p 139; Halperin, Martin, *UAW Politics in the Cold War Era*, SUNY Press, Albany, 1988. p 77

19   "Reuther, F. O. B. Detroit." *Fortune* (Dec, 1945) p 149-150

20   Lichtenstein, Nelson, The Most Dangerous Man in Detroit—Walter Reuther and the Fate of American Labor, Basic Books, New York, 1995. pp 238-239; Halperin op. cit. p 72, Gould & Hickok op. cit. p 230

21   Gould & Hickok op. cit. p 230

22   Lichtenstein op. cit. p 239

23   Ibid. p 239

24   Lichtenstein op. cit. p239; Halperin op. cit. p 68

25   Halperin op. cit. pp 71-72; Lichtenstein op. cit. p 249

26   Lichtenstein op. cit. p 241

27   Victor Reuther op. cit. p 241

28   Lichtenstein op. cit. p 242

29   Ibid. p 242

30   Halperin op. cit. p 79

31   Ibid. p 79

32   Lichtenstein op. cit. p 240

33   Victor Reuther op. cit. p 256; Halperin op. cit. p 95

34   Victor Reuther op. cit. p 257

35   Halperin op. cit. pp 107-108

36   "Reuther, F. O. B. Detroit." *Fortune* (Dec, 1945) p 149-150

37   Cormier & Eaton op. cit. p 235

38   ibid p 235; Halperin op. cit. pp 96-97

39   Ibid. p 235

40   Cormier & Eaton op. cit. p 238

41   Ibid. p 237

42   Halpern op. cit. p 142

43   Lichtenstein op. cit. p 251

44   "Richard Frankensteen, 'The UAW's 'other guy'," Patricia Zacharias, *Detroit News*—October 22, 1997—A 1975 interview with Frankensteen—info. detnews/history/story/index.cfm?id=1198{category=people   (retrieved June 16, 2011) (no longer accessible on Nov 15, 2014)

45   Ibid.

46   Halperin op. cit. pp 101-102

47   Lichtenstein op. cit. p 251

48   Victor Reuther op. cit. p 260

49   Cormier & Eaton op. cit. p 242

50   Lichtenstein op. cit. p 251; Victor Reuther op. cit. p 259

51   Victor Reuther op. cit. p 260

52   White op. cit. p 335

53   Ibid. p 334

54   Halperin op. cit. p 176; Lichtenstein op. cit. p 258

55   Lichtenstein op. cit. p 258

56   Halperin op. cit. p 179; Lichtenstein op. cit. p 259

57   Halperin op. cit. p 181; Lichtenstein op. cit. p 259

58   Lichtenstein op. cit. p 259

59   Ibid. p 259

60   Cormier & Eaton op. cit. p 247

61   Cormier & Eaton op. cit. p 247; Victor Reuther op. cit. p 261

62   Cormier & Eaton op. cit. p 248; Victor Reuther op. cit. p 262

63   Lichtenstein op. cit. p 268; Cormier & Eaton op. cit. p 249

64   Cormier & Eaton op. cit. p 250

65   Ibid. p 251

66   Ibid. p 251

67   Victor Reuther op. cit. pp 276-277

68   Ibid. p 277

69   Ibid. pp 277-278

70   Ibid. p 284

71   ibid. pp 284

72   Ibid. p 284-286

73   ibid. p 286

74   Gould & Hickok op. cit. p 264; Victor Reuther op. cit. p 279

75   Gould & Hickok op. cit. p 270; Cormier & Eaton op. cit. p 260

76   Dickmeyer, Elisabeth Reuther, Putting the World Together—My Father Walter Reuther: The Liberal Warrior, Living Force Publishing, Lake Orion, Michigan, 2004;Cormier & Eaton op. cit. p 260

77   Lichtenstein op. cit. p 275

78   E. R. Dickmeyer op. cit. p 262

79   Ibid. p 265

80   Ibid. p 265

81   Victor Reuther op. cit. p 281; Lichtenstein op. cit. p 274

82   Victor Reuther op. cit. p 289

83   Gould & Hickok op. cit. pp 270-271; Cormier & Eaton op. cit. p 260

84   Gould & Hickok op. cit. pp 270-271; Cormier & Eaton op. cit. pp 260-261

85   Victor Reuther op. cit. p 290

86   Ibid. pp 292-297

87   Cormier & Eaton op. cit. p 264; Victor Reuther op. cit. p 274

88   Cormier & Eaton op. cit. p 265; Victor Reuther op. cit. p 274

89   Victor Reuther op. cit. p 271; Cormier & Eaton op. cit. pp 262-263

90   Victor Reuther op. cit. pp 276, 297; Cormier & Eaton op. cit. p 267

91   Victor Reuther op. cit. pp 276-277

92   Ibid. pp 274-275

93   Cormier & Eaton op. cit. pp 265-266

94   Ibid. p 266

95   A grand jury witness testified that his wife had been beaten by hoodlums after he was interviewed by Detective DeLamielleure (Cormier & Eaton op. cit. p 263); Victor Reuther reports that a neighbor who had information about his assailants received threatening phone calls shortly after he came forward to the police and was given a box of photos to examine by DeLamielleure. The man suffered a heart attack and subsequently moved to Florida. (Victor Reuther op. cit. pp 288-289)

96   Cormier & Eaton op. cit. p 266

97   Victor Reuther op. cit. p 275

98   Gould & Hickok op. cit. p 273

99   Victor Reuther op. cit. p 297

100   Ibid. p 298

101   Ibid. p 299

102   Ibid. p 299

[103] Ibid. p 299

[104] Ibid. pp 300-301

[105] Gould & Hickok op. cit. pp 276-277

[106] Ibid p 277.

[107] Ibid. p 277

[108] Victor Reuther op. cit. pp 288-289

[109] Ibid. pp 288-289

[110] Cormier & Eaton op. cit. pp 291-292

[111] Victor Reuther op. cit. pp 305-306; Cormier & Eaton op. cit. p 292

[112] Victor Reuther op. cit. p 306

[113] Lichtenstein op. cit. p 278

[114] Ibid. p 278

[115] Cormier & Eaton op. cit. p 291

[116] Lichtenstein op. cit. p 280

[117] Ibid. p 279

[118] Ibid. p 279

[119] Ibid. p 279

[120] Ibid. p 282

[121] Alinsky, Saul, *John L. Lewis: An Unauthorized Biography*, G. P. Putnam's Sons, New York, 1949 pp 330, 343-345 (coal companies paid a royalty of 5 cents per ton of coal mined into a fund administered by three trustees – one from the union, one from the government, and one mutually acceptable to both parties. The royalty payment was raised to 20 cents a ton in 1947. Cormier & Eaton op. cit. p 296 (royalties paid out on a pay-as-workers retire basis)

[122] Cormier & Eaton op. cit. p 296 (royalties paid out on a pay-as-workers retire basis)

[123] Lichtenstein op. cit. p 283; Cormier & Eaton op. cit. p 296

[124] Lichtenstein op. cit. p 284

[125] Ibid. p 274-275

[126] Cormier & Eaton op. cit. pp 298-299

[127] Lichtenstein op. cit. p 280

128 "Reuther's Stock Goes Up: What's Next? Detroit Asks." *New York Times,* May 28, 1950

129 Lichtenstein op. cit. p 280

130 Daniel Bell, "The Treaty of Detroit," *Fortune,* July 1950

131 Lichtenstein op. cit. p 288

132 Ibid. pp 142-143, 289

133 Victor Reuther op. cit. p 312; Gould & Hickok op. cit. p 281

134 Boyle, Kevin, The UAW and the Heyday of American Liberalism, 1945–1968, Cornell University Press, 1998 p 79; Lichtenstein op. cit. p 281

135 Lichtenstein op. cit. p 281

136 Boyle op. cit. pp 79-80

137 Cormier & Eaton op. cit. p 299; Gould & Hickok op. cit. p 282

138 Cormier & Eaton op. cit. p 300

139 Ibid. p 300

140 Ibid. p 300

141 Ibid. p 327

142 Victor Reuther op. cit. pp 312-313

143 ibid. p 313

144 Victor Reuther op. cit. Victor Reuther op. cit. p 314; Cormier & Eaton op. cit. p 329

145 Gould & Hickok op. cit. pp 285-286; Cormier & Eaton op. cit. pp 329-330

146 Cormier & Eaton op. cit. p 330

147 Ibid. p 330

148 Cormier & Eaton op. cit. p 331; Victor Reuther op. cit. p 315 put the strike fund at $125 million which seems to be too high for the 1955 value of the dollar

149 Gould & Hickok op. cit. p 286

150 Cormier & Eaton op. cit. pp 330-331; Gould & Hickok op. cit. p 286

151 Cormier & Eaton op. cit. p 331

152 Gould & Hickok op. cit. p 287

153 Victor Reuther op. cit. p 315; Cormier & Eaton op. cit. p 332

154 Gould & Hickok op. cit. p 287; Lichtenstein op. cit. 285

155 Victor Reuther op. cit. p 316; Cormier & Eaton op. cit. p 333

156 Gould & Hickok op. cit. p 288

157 Victor Reuther op. cit. p 316; Gould & Hickok op. cit. p 288

158 Victor Reuther op. cit. pp 316-317; Gould & Hickok op. cit. pp 288-289

159 Gould & Hickok op. cit. p 289; Cormier & Eaton op. cit. p 335

160 Victor Reuther op. cit. p 317; Cormier & Eaton op. cit. p 335

161 Cormier & Eaton op. cit. p 335 payments to workers during recession of 1958; Victor Reuther op. cit. p 317 During the recession of 1974-1975 GM paid out over $400 million in SUB payments to 88,000 laid off workers

162 Victor Reuther op. cit. p 317; Cormier & Eaton op. cit. p 335

163 Lichtenstein op. cit. p 241

164 Cormier & Eaton op. cit. pp 318-319

165 Ibid. p 313

166 Ibid. p 317

167 Ibid. p 322-323

168 Ibid. p 323

169 Ibid. p 323

170 Ibid. p 317

171 Victor Reuther op. cit. p 364

172 Ibid. p 362

173 Cormier & Eaton op. cit. pp 323-324; Victor Reuther op. cit. p 363

174 Boyle op. cit. p 104

175 Victor Reuther op. cit. p 364

176 Ibid. p 365

177 Ibid. p 367

178 Ibid. p 368

179 Ibid. p 369

180 Ibid. pp 369-370

181 E. R. Dickmeyer op. cit. p 286

182 Ibid. p 286

183 Victor Reuther op. cit. p 370

184 Ibid. pp 372-373

185 Cormier & Eaton op. cit. p 406

186 Treckel, Karl F., The Rise and Fall of the Alliance for Labor Action (1968-1972),Center for Business and Economic Research, Graduate School of Business Administration, Kent State University, Kent, Ohio, 1975. p 5-6, 8-9—The ALA was to be an umbrella organization in which autonomous unions could participate to promote organizingefforts, community organizing, and a social agenda that included national health, free education, and a guaranteed income.

187 Lichtenstein op. cit. p 431; Victor Reuther op. cit. p 380—The combined membership of the two unions was over 3.5 million which represented about 1/4 of the size of the AFL-CIO

188 Gould & Hickok op. cit. p 336; Victor Reuther op. cit. p 380

189 Gould & Hickok op. cit. p 336; Cormier & Eaton op. cit. p 419

190 Lichtenstein op. cit. pp 443-444

Chapter VIII

1 General Motors at nywf64.com, http://nywf64.com/gm01.shtml (retrieved 5/14/2014)

2 International Business Machines at nywf64.com http://nywf64.com/ibm01.shtml (retrieved 5/14/2014)

3 The Walt Disney Corporation under the direction of its founder produced a number of the larger exhibits at the fair

4 Personal recollection during a 1964 training session. I occupied a cubicle adjacent to Mike Supa during part of my time at IBM and remember him once receiving a phone call from T. J. Watson Jr.

5 Analyze This, Village Road Show Pictures TriBeCa Productions, 1999

6 Crowther, Samuel, John H. Patterson Pioneer in Industrial Welfare, Doubleday, Page & Company, Garden City, Long Island and New York, 1923. pp 41-47

7   Crowther op. cit. pp 57-59

8   Ibid. p 63

9   Ibid. pp 58-59

10   Ibid. pp 80-81

11   Ibid. p 90-91

12   Ibid. pp 87-90, 104-106, 154-164

13   Ibid. 190-192, 196

14   Bernstein, Mark, "John H. Patterson—John Patterson rang up success with the incorruptible cashier," *Dayton Innovation Legacy,* http://www.daytoninnovationlegacy.org/patterson.html (retrieved 3/24/2014) p 2

15   Crowther op. cit. pp 201-206, 251-263

16   Crowther op. cit. p 206; Bernstein op. cit. p 2

17   Bernstein op cit. p 2

18   Bernstein op cit. p 2; Belden, Thomas Graham & Belden, Marva Robins, *The Lengthening Shadow: The Life of Thomas J. Watson,* Little, Brown and Company, Boston-Toronto, 1962. p 36

19   Bernstein, Mark, Grand Eccentrics: Turning the Century: Dayton and the Inventing of America, Orange Frazier Press, Wilmington, Ohio, 1996. p 109

20   Bernstein, *Turning the Century* p 109

21   Ibid. p 111

22   Ibid. p 203

23   Crowther op. cit. pp 73-74

24   Ibid. pp 11-12

25   Bernstein, "John H. Patterson" p 2

26   Ibid. p 2

27   Ibid. p 3

28   Tedlow, Richard S., *The Watson Dynasty,* HarperCollins, New York, 2003. pp 51

29   Crowther op. cit. pp 302-304; Tedlow op. cit. p 59

30   Tedlow op cit. p 60

31 Belden, Thomas Graham & Belden, Marva Robins, The Lengthening Shadow: The Life of Thomas J. Watson, Little, Brown and Company, Boston-Toronto, 1962. p 81

32 Belden op. cit. p 77; Bernstein "John H. Patterson" p 3

33 Tedlow op. cit. p 19

34 Ibid. p 20

35 Maney, Kevin, The Maverick and His Machihne: Thomas Watson, Sr. and the Making of IBM, John Wiley & Sons, Hoboken, New Jersey, 2003. p 17

36 Belden op. cit. pp 16-17

37 Maney op. cit. pp 17-18; Tedlow op. cit. pp 25-28; Belden op. cit. pp 17-23

38 Tedlow op. cit. p 28

39 Maney, op. cit. p 16; Tedlow op. cit. p 34

40 Tedlow op. cit. pp 35-36

41 Belden op. cit. pp 33-34

42 Tedlow op. cit. p 42

43 Belden op. cit. p 79

44 Belden op. cit. p 87; Maney op. cit. p 35; Tedlow op. cit. p 66

45 Belden op. cit. p 90

46 Ibid. pp 92-93

47 Maney op. cit. p 63; Belden op. cit. pp 101-102

48 Tedlow op. cit. p 101; Maney op. cit. p 83

49 Maney op. cit. p 49; Black, Edwin, IBM and the Holocaust, Random House, New York, 2001., p 52

50 Maney op. cit. pp 48-49; Black op. cit. pp 45-49, 67; Belden op. cit. pp 112-114

51 Maney op. cit. p 99; Tedlow op. cit. p 103 in 1925 address to salesmen Watson extols the future prospects of IBM

52 Maney op. cit. pp 100-101; Tedlow op. cit. p 124

53 Maney op. cit. pp 101-102

54 Ibid. p 104

55   Ibid. p 104

56   Ibid. p 105

57   Ibid. p 105

58   Zahavi, Gerald, *Workers, Managers, and Welfare Capitalists*, University of Illinois Press, Urbana and Chicago,1988. p 40

59   Maney op. cit. p 102

60   Ibid. pp 106-109

61   Ibid. p 88

62   Ibid. p 139

63   Maney op. cit. p 141—Belden & Belden op. cit. p 162

64   Zahavi op. cit. pp 127-129

65   Ibid. p 137

66   Ibid. p 138

67   Ibid. p 138

68   Ibid. pp 138-139

69   Maney op. cit. p 173

70   ibid. p 172; Address at National Recovery Act pledge card meeting, IBM, NY, Sept.7, 1933

71   FDR Presidential Library, FDR Personal File Box 2480 – 2499, Corr. With T. J. Watson Sr. (1935-36)

72   Ibid.

73   Ibid.

74   Ibid.

75   Maney op. cit. p 156

76   Belden op. cit. p 196; Black op. cit. pp 232-233

77   Black op. cit. p 231

78   Ibid. pp 233-234

79   Belden op. cit. p 195; Black op. cit. p 231

80   Black op. cit. p 233

81   Ibid. p 275

82   Ibid. p 309

83   Ibid. p 310

84   Ibid. p 310

85   Ibid. p 312

86   The New York Times, June 6, 1940

87   Tedlow op. cit. p 128

88   Black op. cit. p 50; Maney op. cit. pp 204-205

89   Black op. cit. pp 74-75

90   Ibid. p 76

91   Ibid. p 103

92   Black op. cit. p 132-133, Maney p 212

93   Black op. cit. pp 104-105

94   Ibid. pp 86-87

95   Ibid. pp 87 & 148

96   Ibid. p 170

97   Ibid. pp 469-470

98   "IBM Statement on Nazi-Era Book and Lawsuit," Armonk, NY, 14 February 2001

99   "Addendum to IBM statement on Nazi-Era Book and Lawsuit, Armonk, NY, 29 March 2002

100   Richard Bernstein, "'IBM and the Holocaust': Assessing the Culpability," *New York Times Review of Books*, March 7, 2001.

101   Ibid; Chomsky, Noam, Rethinking Camelot: JFK, the Vietnam War, and US Political Culture, South End Press, Boston, 1993. p 20—US investment in Germany accelerated rapidly after Hitler came to power.—increasing by some 48.5 percent between 1929 and 1940, while declining sharply everywhere else in continental Europe and barely holding steady in Britain. (cites Christopher Simpson)

102   Black op. cit. p 254

103   Belden op. cit. pp 196-197; Black op. cit. p 121

104   Maney op. cit. p 159; Tedlow op. cit. p 101

105   Maney op. cit. p 175

106   Tedlow op. cit. p 5; Maney op. cit. p 236

[107] Tedlow op. cit. p 5; Maney op. cit. p 236

[108] Maney op. cit. pp 236-237; Watson, Thomas J. Jr. and Petre, Peter, *Father, Son & Co.: My Life at IBM and* Beyond, Bantam Books, 1990. pp 83-84

[109] ibid.

[110] Belden op. cit. p 210; Maney op. cit. p 299

[111] Maney op. cit. p 301

[112] Ibid. pp 301-303

[113] Ibid. pp 305-306

[114] Ibid. pp 305-306

[115] Ibid. p 311

[116] Ibid. p 306

[117] Ibid. pp 303-304

[118] Tedlow op. cit. p 86; Maney op. cit. p 270

[119] Maney op. cit. p 271

[120] Tedlow op. cit. p 136; Maney op. cit. p 274

[121] Watson op. cit. pp 106, 109

[122] Ibid. pp 126-127

[123] Ibid. p 127

[124] Ibid. p 134

[125] Ibid. p 139

[126] Ibid. p 143

[127] Maney op. cit. p 264, 278; Watson op. cit. p 177

[128] Tedlow op. cit. p 168; Maney op. cit. p 280

[129] Maney op. cit. p 166

[130] Ibid. p 143

[131] Ibid. p 143

[132] Ibid. p 144

[133] Ibid.p 128

[134] Ibid. pp 197, 200

[135] Maney op. cit. p 334

[136] Ibid. p 334

[137] Watson op. cit. p 135

[138] Belden op. cit. p 259; Maney op. cit. p 336

[139] Maney op. cit. p 338

[140] Watson op. cit. pp 135-136

[141] Maney op. cit. p 346

[142] Maney op. cit. p 347; Belden op. cit. p 261

[143] Watson op. cit. p 137

[144] Ibid. pp 126-137

[145] Ibid. p 195

[146] Belden op. cit. p 276; Watson op. cit. p 163

[147] Watson op. cit. p 164; Maney op. cit. p 395; Belden op. cit. pp 274, 278-279

[148] Maney op. cit. pp 402-404

[149] Watson op. cit. p 204

[150] Maney op. cit. p 358

[151] Watson op. cit. pp 203-205

[152] Ibid. p 229

[153] Ibid. p 206

[154] Ibid. pp 63-64

[155] Ibid. pp 230-233

[156] Ibid. pp 239-241

[157] Tedlow op. cit. p 170; Maney op. cit. pp 282-283; Watson op. cit. p 176

[158] Watson op. cit. p 176; Tedlow op. cit. p 173

[159] Watson op. cit. p 176

[160] Maney op. cit. pp 424-428

[161] Watson op. cit. p 379

[162] Maney op. cit. p 441

[163] Watson op. cit. p 297

[164] Ibid. p 349

165   Ibid. p 348

166   Ibid. p 347

167   Ibid. 358

168   Ibid. p 350

169   Ibid. p 356

170   Brooks, Frederick P., *The Mythical Man Month (Anniversary Edition)*, Addison Wesley, 1995 p ?

171   Watson op. cit. p 353

172   Ibid. p 344

173   Ibid. pp 345-346, 358—359

174   Ibid. p 317

175   Ibid. p 334

176   Ibid. p 335

177   Ibid. p 338

178   Ibid. p 338

179   Ibid. p 338

180   Ibid. p 339

181   Ibid. pp 371-373

182   Ibid. p 367

183   Ibid. p 373

184   Ibid. p 375

185   Ibid. p 338

186   Reuther, Victor, The Brothers Reuther and the Story of the UAW: A Memoir, Houghton Mifflin Company, Boston, 1976. pp 310-312

187   Watson op. cit. p 267

188   Victor Reuther op. cit. pp 316-317

189   Ibid. p 317

190   Watson op. cit. pp 310-311

191   Ibid. p 312

192   Ibid. pp 311-312

193   Ibid. p 312

194   Ibid. p 383

195   Ibid. p 383

196   Ibid. p 384

197   Ibid. p 384

198   Ibid. p 385

199   Ibid. p 385

200   Ibid. p 387

201   Ibid. pp 387-388

202   Ibid. p 387

203   Maney op. cit. p 441

204   Ibid. p 441

205   Ibid. p 441

206   Carroll, Paul, *Big Blues: The Unmaking of IBM*, Crown Publishers Inc., New York, NY, 1993. p 22

207   Carroll op. cit. p 1

208   Ibid. p 2

209   Brooks, Frederick P., *The Mythical Man Month (Anniversary Edition)*, Addison Wesley, 1995. p 17

210   Carroll op. cit. p 9

211   Ibid. p 18

212   Ibid. p 18

213   Ibid. p 18

214   Ibid. p 24

215   Ibid. p 32

216   Ibid. p 59

217   Tedlow op. cit. p 265

218   Carroll op. cit. pp 181-183

219   Ibid. pp 159-161

220   Ibid. p 181

221 Ibid. p 182

222 Ibid. p 287

223 Ibid. p 263

224 Ibid. p 263

225 Ibid. p 338

226 Gerstner, Louis V., *Who Says Elephants Can't Dance?*, Harper Business, Harper Collins Publishers, New York, 2002. p 37

227 Ibid. p 106

228 Carroll op. cit. p 5

229 Ibid. p 5

230 Ibid. p 5

231 Gerstner op. cit. pp 57-62

232 Ibid. pp 57-62, 130

233 Ibid. pp 57U-62

234 Ibid. p 141-142

235 213

236 Kasparov vs Deep Blue, *Chess Corner*, http://www.chesscorner.com/games/deepblue/deepblu.htm retrieved (1/21/2015)

237 Baker, Stephen, Final Jeopardy:Man vs. Machine and the Quest to Know Everything, Houghton Mifflin Harcourt, Boston, New York, 2011

238 Ibid. pp 68, 79

239 217

240 Jennings, Ken (2011-02-16), "My Puny Human Brain," *Slate*, Newsweek Interactive Co. LLC, retrieved 2011-02-17

241 Bruce Upbin, "IBM's Watson Gets Its First Piece of Business in Healthcare," *Forbes*, Feb. 8, 2013

242 220

243 221

244 Gerstner op. cit. pp 94, 117-116

245 Ibid. p 96

246 Ibid. p 96

247 Ibid. pp 100-101

248 McDonald, Duff, The Firm, The Story of McKinsey and its Secret Influence on American Business, Simon & Schuster, New York, 2013 p 84

249 Ibid. p 244

250 Rebecca Leung, CBS Sixty Minutes, Dec. 9, 2003, "Did IBM Know of a Cancer Link?"

251 229

252 Gerstner op. cit. pp 108-109

253 Ibid. pp 108-109

254 Joni Mitchel, "Both Sides Now"

255 Amazon was substantially ahead of other IaaS cloud services providers in both the Gartner Magic Quadrant ratings of 2013 and 2014. The Magic Quadrant classifies cloud services providers into four categories:Leaders (Amazon and Microsoft), Challengers, Visionaries, and Niche Players. IBM moved from being a Niche player in 2013 to become a Visionary in 2014 with the acquisition of SoftLayer.

256 Thompson, Gabriel, "Holliday Crush," The Nation, 12/16/2013 pp 12-17

Chapter IX

1 Geschwender, James A., Class, Race, and Worker Insurgency: The League of Revolutionary Black Workers, Cambridge University Press, 1977. p 64

2 Geschwender p 64, Howe, Irving & Widick, B. J., The UAW and Walter Reuther, Random House, New York, 1949 p 8

3 Geschwender op. cit. p 18

4 Ibid. p 19

5 Howe & Widick op. cit. p 18

6 Ibid. p 19

7 Ibid. p 11

8 Geschwender op. cit. p 64

[9] White, Walter, *A Man Called White*, The Viking Press, New York, 1948. p 74; Geschwender op. cit. p 65

[10] Geschwender op. cit. p 65

[11] Walter White op. cit. p 74

[12] Walter White op. cit. p 74; Geschwender op. cit. p 65

[13] Walter White op. cit. pp 77-79 The first trial ended with a hung jury. One juror who seemed in the courtroom favorably disposed to the defense proclaimed in the jury room, "I don't give a God damn what the facts are…I'll be burned in hell before I will ever vote to acquit a nigger who has killed a white man." In the second trial the defendants were tried separately and a jury needed only three hours and twenty minutes to bring in a not guilty verdict on Henry Sweet, the defendant for whom the prosecution felt it had its strongest case. In light of the verdict the charges were dropped againstthe other defendants.

[14] Howe & Widick op. cit. p 33; Geschwender op. cit. p 66

[15] Howe & Widick op. cit. p 35; Geschwender op. cit. p 66

[16] Meier, August & Rudwick, Elliott, *Black Detroit and the Rise of the UAW*, Oxford University Press, New York, 1979.p. 10

[17] Meier & Rudwick op. cit. p 12; Ford's Page, *Dearborn Independent*, June 17, 1922

[18] Ibid. p 14

[19] Meier & Rudwick op. cit. p 18

[20] Ibid. p 24

[21] Horace White, "Who Owns the Negro Churches?" *Christian Century* 55 Feb. 9, 1938, pp 176-177

[22] Meier & Rudwick op. cit. p 33

[23] Ibid. pp 40-41

[24] *CIO News*, June 26, 1939

[25] Meier & Rudwick op. cit. pp 42-44

[26] Ibid. pp 28-29

[27] Cormier, Frank & Eaton, William J., *Reuther*, Prentice-Hall, Edgewood Cliffs, N. J., 1970. p 120

28 Reuther, Victor, The Brothers Reuther and the Story of the UAW: A Memoir, Houghton Mifflin Company, Boston, 1976. p 184; Cormier & Eaton op. cit. p 121

29 Meier & Rudwick op. cit. p 46-47, 65

30 Ibid. p 68

31 Ibid. p 68

32 Meier & Rudwick op. cit. p 69

33 Meier & Rudwick op. cit. p 69; Geschwender op. cit. p 28

34 Meier & Rudwick op. cit. p 69-70

35 Ibid. p 70

36 Ibid. pp 70-72

37 Ibid. p 80

38 Ibid. p 80

39 Ibid. pp 82-83

40 Bates, Beth T. "'Double V for Victory' Mobilizes Detroit 1941-1946," *Freedom North* p 20

41 Ibid. p 21

42 Foner, Philip S. & Lewis, Ronald L., editors, Black Workers: A Documentary History From Colonial Times to the *Present*, Temple University Press, Philadelphia, 1989. pp 527-530—A. Philip Randolph provides a justification for the MOWM and a list of demands that the movement wants addressed in an article in *Survey Graphic*, 31 Nov. 1942. His demands include: enforcement of protections stipulated in the Constitution, representation on the war-time agencies, end of segregation in the armed services, and end of discrimination in hiring and training.

43 ibid. pp 527-530; Bates op. cit. pp 21–22

44 Kheel Center for Labor-Management Documentation and Archives, Cornell University Library, rmc.library.cornell.edu/EAP/htmldocs/KCL05298.html

45 Meier & Rudwick op. cit. p 112

46 Ibid. p 121

47 Ibid. p 121

48 Ibid. p 134

49   Ibid. p 133

50   Meier & Rudwick op. cit. p 142

51   Ibid. p 165

52   Ibid. p 168

53   Ibid.pp 168-169

54   Ibid. p 170

55   Ibid. pp 170-171

56   Bates op. cit. p 29; Meier & Rudwick op. cit. p 172 fn

57   Meier & Rudwick op. cit. p 196

58   Ibid. p 219

59   Howe & Widick op. cit. p 36

60   Ibid. p 36; Walter White op. cit. p 226

61   Howe & Widick op. cit. p 37

62   ibid. p 38; Walter White op. cit. p 227; Doody, Colleen, *Detroit's Cold War: The Origins of Postwar Conservatism*, The University of Illinois Press, Urbana, Illinois, 2013. pp 53—toll of arrests and deaths in riot. Walter White reports the toll as 34 dead, 25 of whom were Negroes and 600 injured

63   Meier & Rudwick op. cit. p 195

64   Bates op. cit. p 30; Meier & Rudwick op. cit. pp 212-213

65   Meier & Rudwick op. cit. pp 209-211

66   Howe & Widick op. cit. p 224

67   Meier & Rudwick op. cit. p 211

68   Bates op. cit. p 31

69   Halperin, Martin, *UAW Politics in the Cold War Era*, SUNY Press, Albany, 1988. pp 208-209

70   Stromquist, Shelton, editor, *Labor's Cold War – Local Politics in a Global Context,* University of Illinois Press, Urbana and Chicago, 2008.—David Lewis-Colman, "From Fellow Traveler to Friendly Witness," p 128; *Michigan Chronicle* Editorial "The UAW Convention", Nov 22, 1947; Horace White, "The Facts in our News," *Michigan* Chronicle, Nov 22, 1947.

71 Dickmeyer, Elisabeth Reuther, Putting the World Together—My Father Walter Reuther: The Liberal Warrior, Living Force Publishing, Lake Orion, Michigan, 2004 p. 17

72 E. R. Dickmeyer op. cit. p. 24

73 Lichtenstein, Nelson, The Most Dangerous Man in Detroit—Walter Reuther and the Fate of American Labor, Basic Books, New York, 1995. p 210

74 Stromquist—David Lewis-Colman, "From Fellow Traveler to Friendly Witness," p 121

75 Ibid. p 121

76 Ibid. pp 121-122

77 Ibid. p 130

78 Lichtenstein op. cit. p 373

79 Ibid p 373; Boyle, Kevin, The UAW and the Heyday of American Liberalism, 1945–1968, Cornell University Press, 1998 p 126

80 Lichtenstein op. cit. p 373

81 E R. Dickmeyer op. cit. p 188

82 48

83 49

84 Lichtenstein op. cit. p 373

85 E. R. Dickmeyer op. cit. pp 187-188

86 Geschwender op. cit. pp 40-44

87 Ball, Howard, *Hugo L. Black: Cold Steel Warrior*, Oxford University Press, New York, Oford, 1996. pp 100-106 – Black developed a friendship with NAACP Chairman William White during his Senate years that survived therevelation of his membership in the klan during the confirmation hearings for his nomination to the Supreme Court. Black eased the apprehension of African Americans with his majority opinion in *Chambers v Florida* (1940) in which the Court reversed a murder conviction based on a confession extracted only after five days of continuous interrogation.

88 Williams, Juan, *Eyes on the Prize: America's Civil rights Years, 1954-1965*, Viking Penguin Inc., 1987. pp 100-102, 105,106, 113-118; Woodward, C. Vann, *The Strange Career of Jim Crow*, Second Revised Edition, Oxford University Press, New York, 1966 pp 166-168

[89] Williams op. cit. p 63—In 1955, Claudette Colvin, a 15-year old school girl, and another elderly black woman refused to give up their seats on a Montgomery bus to allow a white passenger to sit down. The elderly lady got off when the driver went to get the police, but Colvin stayed and was dragged off and arrested by the police when they arrived. E. D. Nixon of the local NAACP came to the girl's defense, but decided not to appeal her case to a higher court when it was learned that Colvin was pregnant and did not fit the image of the person that the NAACP wanted to be the face of their campaign against the bus company.

[90] Williams op. cit. pp 188-189

[91] Lichtenstein op. cit. p 381

[92] "Trials: Hung Jury," *Time,* Feb. 14, 1964—retrieved from digital archives

[93] Lichtenstein op. cit. p 384

[94] Boyle op. cit. p 177

[95] Ibid. p 177

[96] Ibid. p 177

[97] Victor Reuther op. cit. p 372

[98] Ibid. p 372

[99] Boyle op. cit. p 177

[100] Boyle op. cit. p 179; Lichtenstein op. cit. pp 385-386

[101] Boyle op. cit. p 179; Lichtenstein op. cit. pp 385-386

[102] Boyle op. cit. pp 179-180

[103] Lichtenstein op. cit. p 386; Boyle op. cit. p 179

[104] www.infoplease.com/spot/marchonwashington.html (retrieved 11/14/13)

[105] L ichtenstein op. cit. pp 386-387

[106] Boyle op. cit. p 175—The bill signed into law by President Johnson was not the tepid legislation first proposed by Kennedy, but one with provisions to eliminate segregation in all public places, broaden the power of the Attorney General to bring suit on behalf of victims of segregation, and to establish a fair employment practices committee. Joe Rauh, Jack Conway, and Andrew Biemilller of the AFL-CIO convinced Congressman Emanuel Celler to add provisions supported by the Leadership Conference on Civil Rights to the administration bill that his Judiciary subcommittee was considering. The New York City Congressman was easily persuaded

and helped steer the strengthened bill through the legislative process in the House.

107 Williams op. cit. p 265

108 Title of song by U2 referred to a Palm Sunday massacre in Derry, NI, not the 1965 march in Selma

109 Williams op. cit. p 273—Judge Frank Johnson presided over the trial for Rosa Parks when she refused to give up her seat to a white bus customer, and he was later the judge at the Federal trial for the three men, who along with FBI informant Gary Rowe, were charged with the murder of Viola Liuzzo. The three were acquitted of the murder charge in a state trial, and were subsequently charged with vilolating Mrs. Liuzzo's civil rights by the Federal government. Judge Johnson insured that the jury selected to hear this case would not contain members of the klan and the White Citizens Councils or people affiliated with the civil rights movement. When the jury appeared to be deadlocked he insisted that they return and try to reach a verdict. After additional deliberation, they found the three defendants guilty, and each was given the maximum sentence of ten years

110 E. R. Dickimeyer op. cit. pp 263-264

111 Williams op. cit. p 282

112 Ibid. p 283

113 Stanton, Mary, From Selma to Sorrow: The Life and Death of Viola Liuzzo, The University of Georgia Press, Athens, Georgia, 1998. p 170— Viola Liuzo sang freedom songs on the drive along highway 80 on the trip into Selma, more to express her defiance than to calm her fears. During the fatal trip back to Montgomery she was hitting speeds of up to 90 miles per hour on the narrow, two-lane road while being chased by the klansmen. When they pulled alongside, FBI informant Gary Rowe later testified that she turned her head and looked straight at them and her mouth flew open. He thought she might have screamed something like Oh God before she was shot. Stanton pp 50-51

114 Lewis, Catherine M., "Charles Weltner (1927-1992)." New Georgia Encyclopedia, 05 September, 2014. Web 21 July 2015

115 "Congress: A Crop of Bright Young Men," *Newsweek*, 11/8/1965 p 31

116 Resignation Speech of Charles Weltner on October 1, 1966, John F Kennedy Library and Museum Profile In Courage Award, http://www.

jfklibrary.org/Events-and-Awards/Profile-in-Courage-Award/Award-Recipients/Charles-Weltner-1991.aspx

[117] Jacobs, Hal, "Lester! The strange but true tale of Georgia's unlikeliest governor," *Creative Loafing,* March 20, 1999

[118] From Robert Lowell's "For the Union Dead"

[119] Walter White op. cit. p 249—Bedell Smith insisted the plan be submitted to Army Chief of Stasff George Marshall. It was originally rejected in Washington before the brass realized there were no other reinforcements available. The original plan to introduce Negro soldiers into existing all-white units was changed to allow all-Black platoons to fight alongside all-white platoons. The inclusion of Negro platoons fighting alongside white platoons persisted until V-E Day at which time the army was re-segregated. Polls of officers and enlisted men taken before and after integration showed only thirty-three and thirty-seven percent respectively of the two groups initially favoring integration and seventy-seven percent of both groups favoring it after the experience. White relates the testimony of several Southern White soldiers about how the experience changedtheir attitude about race (Walter White op. cit. pp 250-251

[120] Harry S. Truman Library and Museum, Official File, Truman Papers—A. Philip Randolph letter to President Truman about army integration dated June 29, 1948 http://www.trumanlibrary.org/whistlestop/study_collections/desegregation/large/documents/index.php?pagenumber=5&documentid=1-5&documentdate=1948-07-07&groupid=retrieved 1/5/2015

[121] Walter White op. cit. p 251

[122] Boeck, Scott, *USA* Today, http://usatoday30.usatoday.com/sports/basketball/2008-02-12-globetrotters_N.htm (updated 2/13/2008) retrieved 1/5/2015

[123] Briley, John David, Career in Crisis: Paul "Bear" Bryant and the Season of Change, Mercer University Press, Macon, Georgia, 2009. p 139

[124] Lichtenstein op. cit. p 375

[125] Ibid. p 375

[126] Ibid. p 376

[127] Ibid. p 376

[128] Ibid. p 377

[129]   Ibid. p 377

[130]   Ibid. pp 375-376

[131]   Ibid. p 378-379

[132]   Ibid. p 379

[133]   ibid. p 380

[134]   Ibid. pp 379-380

[135]   Geschwender op. cit. pp 92-93; Foner op. cit. pp 635-636

[136]   Geschwender op. cit. pp 96-97

[137]   *Battleline* 1 (July 1968); Geschwender op. cit. p 104

[138]   Geschwender op. cit. pp 110-113

[139]   Geschwender op. cit. p 107; Boyle op. cit. p 254

[140]   E. R. Dickmeyer op. cit. p 243

Chapter X

[1]   McCullough, David, *Truman,* Simon & Schuster, New York, 1992. p 489

[2]   Halperin, Martin, *UAW Politics in the Cold War Era,* SUNY Press, Albany, 1988. p 101

[3]   Ibid. pp 101-102

[4]   Ibid. pp 101-102

[5]   Ibid. p 102

[6]   Gaddis, John Lewis, *George F. Kennan: An American Life*, The Penguin Press, New York, 2011 p 216 Kennan reveals it was not the earlier Treasury request that prompted the long telegram but a speech by Stalin that indicated a hardening Soviet attitude toward post-war cooperation with its former allies

[7]   McCullough, *Truman* pp 490-491

[8]   Ibid. pp 490-491

[9]   Gaddis op. cit. pp 218, 231—Forrestal circulates the long telegram to administration officials including Truman, General Gruenther secures the appointment to the Naval War College

10 X (George Kennan), "The Sources of Soviet Power," *Foreign Affairs*, July, 1947, pp 579–580

11 McCullough, *Truman* pp 547-549, 553-554

12 Ibid. p 563

13 Ibid. pp 563, 565

14 Reuther, Victor, The Brothers Reuther and the Story of the UAW: A Memoir, Houghton Mifflin Company, Boston, 1976. p 329

15 Ibid. 330

16 Ibid. p 330

17 Ibid. pp 242-243

18 Ibid. pp 281-282

19 Ibid. p 283

20 Ibid. pp 336-337

21 Ibid. p 337

22 Ibid. 337

23 Ibid. p 337

24 Ibid. p 338

25 Ibid. p 338

26 Ibid. p 339

27 Ibid. p 339

28 "Economics:Cornerstone of Steel," *Time Magazine*, Monday, Jan 21, 1946

29 Hoover, Herbert, "The President's Economic Mission to Germany and Austria," Report 3, p 2

30 "Conferences: Pas de Pagaille," *Time Magazine*, Monday, July 28, 1947

31 Victor Reuther op. cit. pp 341–342

32 Ibid. p 344

33 Ibid. 344

34 Rebecca Page, "Co-determination in Germany—A Beginner's Guide," Hans Böckler Stiftung, www.boeckler.de

35 http://www.country-data.com/cgi-bin/query/r-4980.html—In   1995
    28% of the German workforce (9.8 of 35 million) belonged to the DGB,
    an umbrella organization covering most all unionized workers http://
    www.country-data.com/cgi-bin/query/r-4980.html; http://www.bls.gov/
    news.release/union2.nr0.htm—U. S. union membership—20.1% in
    1983, 11.1% (6.6% in private sector) in 2014

36 37

37 J. Robert Oppenheimer recounts in a 1965 tekevision documentary "The
    Decision to Drop the Bomb, *Atomic Archive,* http://www.atomicarchive.
    com/Movies/Movie8.shtml (retrieved 9/17/2011)

38 Poundstone, William, *Prisoner's Dilemma,* Doubleday, New York, 1992. p
    78

39 Record, Jeffrey, "Nuclear Deterrence, Preventive War, and Counter
    proliferation," *Cato Institute, Policy Analysis* No. 519, July 8, 2004. p 14;
    Poundstone op. cit. p 70

40 Poundstone op. cit. pp 78-79

41 Ibid. p 71

42 Feynman, Richard P. & Leighton, Ralph, "Surely You're Joking, Mr.
    Feynman!"(Adventures of a Curious *Character),* W. W. Norton &
    Company, New York, 1985. pp 135–136

43 Record op. cit. p 14; Poundstone op. cit. pp 142-143

44 Poundstone op. cit. p 68

45 Poundstone footnote on bottom of page 190

46 Poundstone p 166; *Los Angeles Times* July 24, 1989

47 Poundstone op. cit. pp 146-147; Record op. cit. p 14

48 Poundstone op. cit. pp 146-147; Record op. cit. p 14

49 Poundstone p 149

50 Ibid. p 147

51 Ibid. p 149

52 Ibid. pp 150-151

53 Poundstone pp 158-159; *Life* Dec. 11, 1950; *Time* Sept 18, 1950; *Collier's*
    Nov. 11, 1950

54 From Robert Lowell Inauguration Day 1953 at Grant's Tomb

55   Schlesinger, Stephen and Kinzer, Stephen, Bitter Fruit: The Story of the American Coup in Guatemala, Harvard University Press, Cambridge, Mass., 2005 p 75

56   Schlesinger op. cit. p 80; Chapman, Peter, Bananas: How the United Fruit Company Shaped the World, Canongate, New York, NY, 2007. p 116

57   Schlesinger op. cit. pp 80-81

58   Ibid. p 87

59   Ibid. pp 88-89

60   Ibid. p 106—John Foster Dulles, as general counsel to Schroder Banking Corporation handled negotiations arranging a deal with United Fruit to acquire control of the International Railroad of Central America on favorable terms. The deal reinforced United Fruit's monopoly of the banana business and much of the Central American economy. It provided a tidy profit for Schroder Banking and for Dulles and his law firm. Brother Allen Dulles also did legal work in the 1930's for Sullivan and Cromwell and assisted his brother on Schroder bank business. Allen was later named a director of Schroder Banking and the bank became a depository for secret CIA funds for covert operations.

61   Cullather, Nicholas, Secret History: The CIA's Classified Account of Its Operations in Guatemala, 1952-1954, Stanford University Press, Palo Alto, California, 2006. pp 137-142

62   Ibid. p 96—The original CIA trained 480 mercenaries was to be the core of a larger force that would spontaneously arise and join the rebellion. Additional recruits did materialize, but mainly in areas where there was no fighting. In areas where fighting occurred no new troops were forthcoming and the original core shrank dramatically. At the height of the operation the CIA estimated the rebel strength at 1200. It was the CIA bombing runs and the assumed threat of a US invasion that tipped the balance against Arbenz and discouraged the Guatemalan army from fighting, not the rag-tag army of Castillo Armas.

63   Chapman op. cit. pp 145-146—PBHISTORY—no Soviet connection; Cullather op. cit. p 148—CIA internal pre-coup document downplays Arbenz' ties to Communists and states his role model is FDR and his reforms more influenced by the New Deal than from Soviet Russia Cullather pp 165-166 (CIA Document 15, June 19, 1956) The outlawed Communist Party has retreated underground and reconstituted its

organization, setting up new cells and recruiting new members. Whatever its actual strength, the CP would no cause us concern but for the weakness of the Castillo Armas government.

64 Chapman op. cit. pp 135-136, 156

65 Schlesinger op. cit. pp 227-255

66 The flood of refugees from Guatemala and other Central American countries can be traced back to Cold War policy and the sequence of dictators that precipitated the breakdown of civil society

67 Heikal, Mohamed, *Iran: The Untold Story*, Pantheon, New York, NY, 1982. p 30

68 Ibid. p 30

69 Ibid. pp 30-31

70 Ibid. p 31

71 Heikal p 33; Risen, James, "Secrets of History: The CIA in Iran," *The New York Times on the Web, 2000,* Pt I The Roots

72 Heikal op. cit. p 41

73 Ibid. p 39

74 Heikal op. cit. pp 40; Risen, NYT pt. II The Pressure

75 Heikal op. cit. pp 14-15

76 Ibid. pp 14-15

77 Ibid. p 42

78 Ibid. pp 48-51

79 ibid. p 51

80 Abrahamian, Ervand, *A History of Modern Iran*, Cambridge University Press, New York, 2009. pp 114–116

81 Ibid. pp 109-113

82 Heikal op. cit. p 56

83 Ibid. p 62

84 Azimi, Fakhreddin, Mohammed Mosaddeq and the 1953 Coup in Iran, p 34; Behrooz, Maziar, *Mohammed Mosaddeq and the 1953 Coup in Iran*, p 102; Heikal op. cit. p 63

85 Risen, NYT pt I

86 ibjd.

87 Ibid.

88 Risen, NYT Introduction & pt I

89 Risen, NYT pt I

90 Wilber, Donald, CIA Clandestine Service History, "Overthrow of Premier Mossadeq of Iran, November 1952-August 1953," March 1954 pp 23-24; Risen, NYT pt. II The Pressure

91 Wilber op. cit. p 24; Risen, NYT pt. II The Pressure

92 Wilber op. cit. p 30; Risen, NYT pt. II The Pressure

93 Wilber op. cit. p 34

94 Ibid. pp 20, 32

95 Wilber op. cit. p 32; Risen, NYT pt. II The Pressure

96 Risen NYT pt. II The Pressure

97 Wilber op. cit. p 39; Risen, NYT pt. III The Coup

98 Wilber op. cit. p 45; Risen, NYT pt. III The Coup

99 Wilber op. cit. p 56; Risen, NYT pt. III The Coup

100 Wilber op. cit. p 37

101 Azimi, Fakhreddin, Mohammed Mosaddeq and the 1953 Coup in Iran, p 92

102 Wilber op. cit. pp 66 -68; Risen, NYT pt. IV The Success

103 Wilber op. cit. p72; Risen, NYT pt. IV The Success

104 Heikal op. cit. p 23

105 Ibid. p 66

106 Ibid. p 66

107 Ibid. p 66

108 Ibid. p 68

109 Abrahamian op. cit. p 122

110 Heikal op. cit. p 13

111 Cormier, Frank & Eaton, William J., *Reuther*, Prentice-Hall, Edgewood Cliffs, N. J., 1970 p 358

112 Victor Reuther op. cit. p 387

113 Harrison, Selig S., "Reuther in India," *The New Republic,* May 21, 1956

114 Victor Reuther op. cit. p 387

115 Harrison, Selig S. *Reuther in India*

116 Boyle, Kevin, The UAW and the Heyday of American Liberalism, 1945–1968, Cornell University Press, 1998 p 105

117 Lichtenstein, Nelson, The Most Dangerous Man in Detroit—Walter Reuther and the Fate of American Labor, Basic Books, New York, 1995. p 341

118 Harrison, Selig S.; *Reuther in India;* Boyle op. cit. p 105

119 Harrison, Selig S. *Reuther in India*

120 Ibid.

121 Ibid.

122 Cormier & Eaton op. cit. p 361

123 Boyle op. cit. p 105

124 Ibid. p 106

125 Oshinsky, David M., *A Conspiracy So Immense: The World of Joe McCarthy,* The Free Press, A Division of Macmillan, Inc., New York, 1983. p 44

126 Reeves, Thomas C., *The Life and Times of Joe McCarthy: A Biography,* Stein and Day, New York, 1992 p 53

127 Beichman, Arnold, "The Politics of Personal Self-Destruction," *Policy Review* February-March 2006 p 72

128 Boyle op. cit. p 70; McCullough, *Truman* p 765

129 Zinn, Howard, A People's History of the United States—1492–Present, Harper Perennial Modern Classics edition, New York, 2005. p 430

130 Oshinsky op. cit. pp 114-129

131 Ibid. pp 168-172

132 Ibid. pp 174-176

133 McCullough, *Truman* p 814

134 Ibid. pp 910-912

135 Ibid. p 860

136 Crosby S. J., Donald, God, Church, and Flag: Senator Joseph R. McCarthy and the Catholic Church 1950-1957, The University of North Carolina

Press, 1979.—McCarthy emerged during a time when the Catholic clergy, most prominently represented by Cardinal Spellman and Bishop Fulton Sheen, were preaching against Communism from the pulpit, on television, and in the pages of Catholic organs such as *Catholic World*. Catholics as a whole were as divided on McCarthy as their Protestant counterparts and were supportive of the New Deal and the Democratic Pary. pp 12-25

137   Ibid. pp 106, 208-209

138   Eisenhower, Dwight D. The White House Years: Mandate for Change 1953-1956, Doubleday & Company, Garden City, New York, 1963. p 323

139   Eisenhower op. cit. p 323; Oshinsky op. cit. pp 385-386

140   Oshinsky op. cit. p 387

141   Eisenhower op. cit. pp 324, 326-327

142   Oshinsky op. cit. pp 462–463

143   Ibid. pp 398-399

144   Ibid. pp 495-496

145   Caute, David, The Great Fear: The Anti-Communist Purge Under Truman and Eisenhower, Simon and Schuster, New York, 1978 p 166

146   Albert Fried, ed., *McCarthyism: the Great American Red Scare*, Oxford University Press, New York, 1997 p 52

147   ibid. p 31

148   Murphy, Brenda, Congressional Theatre: Dramatizing McCarthyis, on Stage, Film, and Television Cambridge University Press, New York, 1999 pp 16-17

149   Fried op. cit. p 20

150   Cohen, Karl, Forbidden Animation: Censored Cartoons and Blacklisted Animators in America, McFarland & Company, Jefferson, NorthCarolina, 1997 pp 169-170

151   "John Elliott Rankin," *Spartacus Educational*, www.spartacus-educational. com/USARankinJ.html retrieved 4//14/2015

152   Murphy op. cit. p 24

153   Bosworth, Patricia, *Anything Your Little Heart Desires*, Simon & Schuster, NewYork, 1997—Bartley Crum's daughter's account of the events in

his life that led to periods of despndency, barbituate dependency, and death—especially pp 304-306, 321-326, 360-364, 378

154   Gillon, Steven M., Politics and Vision: The ADA And American Liberalism, 1947-1985, Oxford University Press, New York & Oxford, 1987. p 16

155   Ibid. pp 6-7

156   Ibid. pp 7-8, 34

157   Ibid. p 10

158   Ibid. p 9

159   Ibid. pp 11-13

160   Ibid. pp 17, 19-22

161   Ibid. p 19

162   Ibid. p 20

163   Ibid. p 23

164   Ibid. p 20

165   Ibid p 20

166   Ibid. p 22

167   Ibid. p 22

168   Ibid. p 23

169   Halperin, Martin, "I'm fighting for Freedom: Coleman Young, HUAC, and the Detroit African American Community," *Journal of American Ethnic History,* vol. 17, No. 1, Fall 1997. pp 20-21

170   Ibid. pp 23-24

171   Ibid. p 29

172   HUAC Detroit Hearings Part 1 p 2879

173   HUAC Detroit Hearings Part 1 p 2884

174   Halperin (1997 article) p 29; HUAC Detroit Hearings Part 1 p 2889

175   Ibid. p 30

176   Ibid. p 30

177   175

178   176

[179] 177

[180] HUAC Detroit Hearings Part 2 pp 3082-3083

[181] Ibid. p 3083

[182] Widdick, B. J., *Detroit: City of Race and Class Violence*, Revised Edition, Wayne State University Press, Detroit, 1989. pp 130-131

[183] ibid. pp 128-130

[184] Schlesinger, Jr., Arthur M., *Robert Kennedy and His Times*, Houghton Mifflin Company, Boston, 1978 p 148

[185] Kennedy, Robert F., *The Enemy Within*, Harper & Brothers, New York, 1960. p 280

[186] Ibid. p 280

[187] Schlesinger op. cit. p 176; RFK op. cit. p 281

[188] RFK op. cit. p 278

[189] Ibid. p 278

[190] RFK op. cit. p 278; Cormier & Eaton op. cit. p 345

[191] Cormier & Eaton op. cit. pp 345-346

[192] RFK op. cit. pp 266-267

[193] Ibid. p 267

[194] Ibid. p 267

[195] Ibid. pp 267-268

[196] Ibid. p 268

[197] Ibid. pp 268-269

[198] Ibid. p 269

[199] Ibid. p 270

[200] Schlesinger op. cit. pp 174-175; RFK op. cit. p 271

[201] Schlesinger op. cit. pp 174-175; RFK op. cit. p 271

[202] RFK op. cit.p 272

[203] Ibid. p 271

[204] Schlesinger op. cit. p 178; RFK op. cit.p 283

[205] RFK op. cit.p 272

[206] Ibid. pp 281-282

207   Ibid. p 285

208   Ibid. p 286

209   Ibid. p 286

210   Ibid. p 286

211   Ibid. p 287

212   Ibid. p 288

213   Cormier & Eaton op. cit. p 347

214   Schlesinger op. cit. p 176; RFK op. cit. p 275

215   Schlesinger op. cit. p 176; RFK op. cit. p 275

216   Schlesinger op. cit. p 176; RFK op. cit. p 277

217   Dickmeyer, Elisabeth Reuther, Putting the World Together—My Father Walter Reuther: The Liberal Warrior, Living Force Publishing, Lake Orion, Michigan, 2004 p 287

218   Victor Reuther op. cit. p 219; Lichtenstein op. cit. p 348

219   RFK op. cit. p 290

220   Schlesinger op. cit. p 180; RFK op. cit. p 294

221   Cormier & Eaton op. cit. pp 347-348

222   Ibid. p 348

223   Ibid. p 348

224   RFK op. cit. p 285

225   Cormier & Eaton op. cit. pp 349-350

226   Ibid. p 351

227   Ibid. pp 351-352

228   Lichtenstein op. cit. p 348

229   Ibid. pp 348-349

230   Ibid. p 349

231   Ibid. p 349

232   Cormier & Eaton op. cit. p 353

233   RFK op. cit. p 297

234   Ibid. pp 298-299

235 Cormier & Eaton op. cit. p 355

236 Ibid. p 355

237 Victor Reuther op. cit. P 393

238 Cormier & Eaton op. cit. pp 362-363

239 Ibid. p 363

240 Victor Reuther op. cit. p 394

241 Cormier & Eaton op. cit. p 363

242 Victor Reuther op. cit. p 396

243 Reuther, Walter P., *Selected Papers,* Macmillan, New York, 1961. p 299

244 *The New York Times*, Sept. 19, 1959 p 8

245 Walter Reuther, *Selected Papers* p 302

246 Ibid. p 302

247 Ibid. p 303

248 Ibid. p 304

249 Ibid. p 305

250 Victor Reuther op. cit. p 397

251 Walter Reuther, *Selected Papers* pp 310-311

252 Ibid. pp 310-311

253 Ibid. pp 311-312

254 Cormier & Eaton op. cit. p 366

255 Ibid. p 366

256 Lichtenstein op. cit. p 345

257 Khrushchev, Sergei, *Nikita Khrushchev and the Creation of a Superpower*, The Pennsylvania State University, University Park, Pennsylvania, 2000. p 329

258 Kordon, Kyle A., "Khrushchev Comes to America: The Advent of Mutual Understanding," *Voces Novae*, Chapman University Historical Review, Vol. 1, No. 1, 2009.

259 S. Khrushchev, *Superpower* p 305

260 Kordon op. cit.

261 Lichtenstein op. cit. p 344

262   Ibid. p 346

263   Ibid. p 346

264   ibid. p 346; Lichtenstein op. cit. p 344

265   Victor Reuther op. cit. p 346

266   Ibid. p 347

267   Ibid. p 347

268   Ibid. p 347

269   FDR Library

270   Ibid.

271   Ibid.

272   Walter Reuther, *Selected Papers* p 188

273   Victor Reuther op. cit. p 392

274   Lichtenstein op. cit. p 358

275   Ibid. p 358

276   Victor Reuther op. cit. p 392

277   Ibid p 392

278   ibid. p 352 p 352; Lichtenstein op. cit. p 359

279   Victor Reuther op. cit. p 352; Lichtenstein op. cit. p 359

280   Victor Reuther op. cit. p 354

Chapter XI

1   McNamara, Robert S. and James Blight, Robert Brigham, Thomas Biersteker, Col. Herbert Schandler, *Argument* Without End: In Search of Answers to the Vietnam Tragedy, Public Affairs, New York, 1990. p 69

2   Karnow, Stanley, *Vietnam: A Huistory*, Penguin Books, New York, c. 1983. p 133; Schulzinger, Robert D., *A Time* for War: The United States and Vietnam, 1941–1975, Oxford University Press, New York, 1997. p. 8

3   Schulzinger op. cit. p. 11

4   Schultzinger op. cit. p 11; McNamara op. cit. p xxii

5   Schulzinger op. cit. p. 13, Hammer, Ellen J., *The Struggle for Indochina, 1940-1955*, Stanford University Press, Stanford, California, 1955. pp 42-43;—Roosevelt detests DeGaulle,—Schultzinger op. cit. p 19; Tonnesson, Stein, The Vietnameses Revolution of 1945: Roosevelt, Ho Chi Minh, and DeGaulle in a World at War, Sage Publications, Newbury Park, California, 1991. p. 378—Vietminh agreeable to U.S Trusteeship

6   Schulzinger op. cit. p. 37

7   Karnow op. cit. p 208

8   Schulzinger op. cit. p. 57; Hammer op. cit. p 314; Fall, Bernard, *Hell in a Very Small Place: The Siege of Dien Bien Phu*, J. B. Lippincott Company, Philadelphia, New York, *1967.* pp 30, 42-45

9   Schulzinger op. cit. p. 60

10   Fall op. cit. p 133; Schulzinger op. cit. p 60

11   Fall op. cit. p 133; Schulzinger op. cit. p 60

12   Fall op. cit. pp 134-141, 147-154

13   Schulzinger op. cit. p. 62; Karnow op. cit. pp 212-213

14   Schulzinger op. cit. p. 66; Karnow op. cit. p 213

15   FRUS: 1952-1954:13, pp 1411-15 (FRUS = Foreign Relations of the United States)

16   Karnow op. cit. p 208

17   Schulzinger op. cit. p. 75

18   Karnow op. cit. pp 218-220—The basic agreement was worked out in secret meetings between Zhou EnLai and Pierre Mendes-France away from the conference site. Zhou then met secretly with Ho and insisted that the Viet Minh drop their demands for Pathet Lao and Free Khmer occupation of Laos and Cambodia. The final details were worked out in the Geneva villa of Russian Foreign Secretary Vyashlav Molotov.on the July 20th deadline that Mendes-France had set for himself. Molotov gathered Anthony Eden, Mendes-France, Zhou EnLai, and Pham Van Dong together, purposely excluding Bedell Smith and Bao Dai's representative, and acted as an arbiter in resolving the remaining differences. When the French and Vietnamese differed on whether the demarcation line between the north and south of the country would be set at the 18th or 16th parallel, Molotov volunteered, "Let's agree on the 17th." Similarly he resolved the question as to when an election to reunite the country would be held by

asking, "Shall we say two years?" McNamara pp 66-67, 71-72, 79, 83–91, 96—In a series of meetings between American and Vietnamese officials who had positions of responsibility during the American-Vietnamese War, including McNamara and Gen Vo Nguyen Giap on several occasions, revealed the sense of betrayal felt by the Vietnamese toward the Russians and Chinese at Geneva. These discussions also highlighted how the attitude of Dulles and the American delegation in refusing to talk with the Vietnamese at Geneva prevented the U. S. policymakers from developing a real understanding of the situation in Vietnam and the relationship between the various Communist governmentssee also Kiernan (ref. below) p 151; Hammer op. cit. pp 334–337

[19] Schulzinger op. cit. p. 78; Shaplen, Robert, *The Lost Revolution*, Harper & Row, New York, 1965. p 104

[20] Collins to Sec. Of State 7 April 1955, *FRUS 1955-1957:1* p 219; Kolko, Gabriel, *Anatomy of a War: Vietnam, the* United States, and the Modern Historical Experience, Pantheon Books, New York, 1985. p 86 details Diem's reliance on his family

[21] Schulzinger op. cit. p. 85

[22] Collins to Sec. Of State, 5 May 1955, *FRUS 19-1957:1* p 368

[23] Cullather, The Political Economy of United States-Philippines Relations, 1942-1960 pp 102-104 Cullather distills the man from the legend created by Lansdale and an American press that was overly receptive to the message that the government was promoting. Magsaysay the man was genuinely popular and a man with laudable personal qualities, but was much more a traditional politician and much less a social reformer than the legend suggests. Promoting Magsaysay's legend proved very useful to Lansdale in establishing his own. pp 96–122

[24] 16

[25] Schulzinger op. cit. p. 81

[26] Ibid. p 88

[27] Karnow op. cit. p 281

[28] Kolko op. cit. p 89—a conservative estimate 12,000 killed between 1955-1957 and 40,000 jailed by end of 1958, 150,000 political prisoners by end of 1961; Kolko op. cit. p 95 describes Ngo Dinh Can's brutal suppression in the northern provinces during the "Denounce the Communists" campaign

29   Karnow op. cit. p 294

30   McNamara op. cit. 110-111

31   Moyar, Mark, *Triumph Forsaken: the Vietnam War 1954-1965,* Cambridge University Press, Cambridge and New York, 2006. p 286—Moyar believes in the validity of the domino theory and the necessity of preventing a Communist takeover of South Vietnam. He defends Diem and his tactics as being appropriate in the context of Vietnamese culture and the qualities the people expect in a strong, respected leader. He contrasts Diem's Asian view of the requirements for successful leadership with the American preoccupation with imposing its values on a foreign culture. Chomsky (Chomsky, Noam, *Rethinking Camelot: JFK, the Vietnam War, and US Political Culture,* South End Press, Boston, 1993.) pp 72-73 cites American fears that Diem, and in particular Nhu, were sending feelers to the North amid a French inspired push for a neutral solution to the Vietnam problem. Diem was critical of the growing U. S. role in his country and over his course of action and wanted to reduce the size of the American presence. Both Chomsky and Moyar point to the critical role that Ambassador Lodge played in abetting the coup. Lodge was sent to Vietnam as a political ploy to remove him from the scene as a possible Republican candidate in the 1964 election. Lodge was aware of the logic behind his appointment and saw it as an opportunity to blast Kennedy and propel his own political chances if things went badly in Vietnam and he was constrained to follow the administration's script. As a result, Lodge was given extraordinary leeway for an ambassador, and, despite dissatisfaction with his performance, was not replaceable until after the election.

32   Ibid. p 286

33   Schulzinger op. cit. p 155

34   Karnow op. cit. pp 385-386; Schulzinger op. cit. p 151; McNamara op. cit. p 23—In a discussion with General Giap thirty years later, Giap declares that no attack took place on August 4 and that the August 2 attack was not ordered by the Defense Ministry in Hanoi, but by a local commander.

35   Karnow op. cit. p 601; Schulzinger op. cit. p 271

36   Kiernan, Ben, How Pol Pot Came to Power: Colonialism, Nationalism, and Communism in Cambodia, 1930-1975, Yale University Press, New

Haven and London, 2nd Edition, 2004. pp 234-235; Shawcross op. cit. p. 244

37 Kiernan op. cit. pp 250-256; Shawcross, William, Sideshow: Kissinger, Nixon, and the Destruction of Cambodia, Simon & Schuster, 1979. p. 245

38 Shawcross op. cit. p 245

39 Deac, Wilfred, *Road to the Killing Fields: The Cambodia War of 1970-1975*, Texas A&M University Press, College Station, Texas, 1997. p 50— The first targets on March 17, 1969 were designated breakfast, lunch, snack, dinner, dessert, and supper and the campaign became known as Menu. The secret plan was exposed by *New York Times* reporter William Beecher on May 9, 1969, but the article received little attention at the time. Beecher's revelation did jolt the Nixon Administration and set in motion the clandestine wiretapping operation that resulted in Watergate. Shawcross op. cit. p. 26-28

40 Shawcross op. cit. pp 116-117

41 Karnow op. cit. pp 620, 622; Shawcross op. cit. p. 139

42 Shawcross op. cit. pp 144-145 – Kissinger staffers William Watts, Roger Morris, and Tony Lake resigned in protest over the plan to invade Cambodia and their alienation from the Nixon Administration.

43 Karnow op. cit. 621-623; Shawcross op. cit. pp 134-148

44 Gitlin, Todd, *the Sixties: Years of Hope Days of Rage, Bantam Books*, New York, 1987. p 410

45 Karnow op. cit. p 623; Shawcross op. cit. p 149

46 Kiernan op. cit. pp 300-301 Navy intelligence specialist Samuel R. Thorton reported to Seymour Hersh that as early as 1968 the U. S. government was discussing coup plans with Lon Nol. Lon Nol wanted assurance of U. S. aid after the coup, but the Americans made a deeper commitment to infiltrate units of the American-trained Khmer Serei into the Cambodian Army and to insert a specially trained assassination team disguised as Viet Cong guerrilas into Cambodia to kill the Prince. The plan, code-named *Sunshine Park,* according to Thorton was approved at 'the highest levels' in February or March of 1969, but rejected as 'criminal insanity' by Lon Nol. Discussion between Lon Nol and American agents continued and the 'defection' of 640 Khmer Serei fighters prior to the coup signaled U. S. support for the project. See also Deac op. cit. p 67

47 Shawcross op. cit. p 115; Kolko op. cit. p 352 asserts that the coup was not primarily Washington's doing but came with Washington's foreknowledge and was followed immediately by aid to the Lon Nol regime. Deac op. cit. pp 66-67 suggests that American military officers below the top-level commanders encouraged Cambodian officers with whom they had trained and worked closely to go ahead with plans for a coup and assured them of subsequent U. S. support.

48 Shawcross op. cit. p 115

49 Ibid. p 119

50 Shawcross op. cit. p. 119; Kiernan op. cit. pp 300-391

51 Kiernan op. cit. p 301; Shawcross op. cit. p. 119

52 Shawcross op. cit. p 120; Deac op. cit. p 66; Kiernan op. cit. p 301 In February 1970 Green Beret Captain Forrest Lindley was told by superiors that there was going to be a coup

53 Shawcross op. cit. p 117

54 Ibid. p 117

55 Ayres, David M., Anatomy of a Crisis: Education, Development, and the State in Cambodia: 1953-1998, University of Hawaii Press, 2000. p 82; Shawcross op. cit. p 73

56 Shawcross op. cit. p 127; Karnow op. cit. p 621 describes acts of murder and cannibalism but does not mention Lon Nil as one of such victims. Brinkley, Joel, *Cambodia's Curse: The Modern History of a Troubled Land*, Public Affairs, a member of Perseus Books Group (paperback), 2012. pp 20-21—confirms the killing of Lon Nil and two other officials and the cannibalizin of their gall bladders and puts it into the context of ancient Angkor belief that by consuming the organs of a person one is absorbing the power living within the victim.

57 Shawcross p 132

58 Shawcross op. cit. p 132; Deac op. cit. p 75; *The New York Times* April 15, 1970

59 Shawcross op. cit. p 132–133

60 Ibid. p 127

61 Brinkley op. cit. pp 34-35

62 Brinkley op. cit. pp 35-36

63   Kiernan op. cit. pp 120, 122; Shawcross op. cit. p 239; Ayres op. cit. p 43

64   Shawcross op. cit. p 240

65   Shawcross op. cit. pp 240-243

66   Shawcross op. cit. p 257; Kiernan op. cit. pp 298–300—Zhou wanted a neutral Cambodia friendly to China and was prepared to hedge his bets and maintain ties with the Prince, the Khmer Rouge, and Lon Nol for two months after the coup until the U. S. led invasion.

67   Shawcross op. cit. p 258

68   Ibid. p 281

69   Swank, Emory, "The Land in Between: Cambodia Ten Years Later," *Indochina Issues,* Vol. 36, April, 1983,pp 1-7. p 1; Shawcross op. cit. p 281

70   Kiernan op. cit. pp 349-357—In 1852 American 52s dropped 53,500 tons of bombs concentrated mostly in the eastern border regions of Cambodia. From February, 1953 until August of the same year when the menu bumbing was stopped by Congress, the U. S. dropped 257,500 tons on populated rural areas throughout the country. The bombing created many civilian casualties, caused massive relocation inside the country, and swelled the ranks of the Khmer Rouge with angry villagers fleeing the destruction of their ancestral homes.

71   Turse, Nick, Kill Anything That Moves: The Real American War in Vietnam, Metropolitan Books, Henry Holt and Company, New York, 2013. p 11

72   Turse op. cit. pp 12-13—Depaartment of Defense postwar figures estimate 1.2 million civilian casualties in South Vietnam including 195,000 killed. 1975 Senate subcommittee on refugees and war victims came up with 1.4 million with 415,000 killed. More recent analysis in 2008 by researchers from Harvard Medical School and the Institute for Health Metrics and Evaluation at the Univ. of Washington suggest an estimate of 3.8 million violent deaths of combatants and civilians. Official Vietnamese government estimate—3 million deaths total—2 million civilian. ARVN forces 254,000 killed and more than 783,000 wounded NVA and Viet Cong 1 million killed 300,000 missing—McNamara op. cit. p 254— estimates from figures Hanoi was supplying after the war and American estimates that about a million Vietnamese (North and South) were killed each year between the end of 1965 and Johnson' s speech in March of 1968

73 Price, Jennifer, "Findings from the National Veterans' Readjustment Study," National Center for PTSD, U.S. Department of Veteran Affairs, last updated 8/17/2015 www.ptsd.va.gov/professional/research-bio/research/vietnam-vets-study.asp

74 Turse op. cit. pp 94-95

75 Daggett, Stephen, "Cost of Major U.S. Wars," *Congressional Research Service,* June 29, 2010

76 61

77 Papers of John F. Kennedy. Pre-Presidential Papers. Senate Files. Speeches and the Press. Speech Files, 1953-1960. "America's Stake in Vietnam," *American Friends of Vietnam,* Washington, D. C. June 1, 1956, JFKSEN-0895-014 John F. Kennedy Presidential Library and Museum

78 Quote from Kennedy inaugural address

79 From interview with Stanley Karnow in 1979 as part of a WGBH series titled "LBJ Goes to War (1964-1965)" found on WGBH Open Vault at openvault.wgbh.org/catalog/openvault55567 Interview with Maxwell D. Taylor, 1979, Part 4 of 4

Chapter XII

1 Digest of Education Statistics, National Center for Educational Statistics, 2013 Table 303.10

2 Boyle, Kevin, The UAW and the Heyday of American Liberalism, 1945–1968, Cornell University Press, 1998 pp 173-174

3 Ibid. 162, 173

4 Ibid. p 159

5 Ibid. p 159

6 Lichtenstein, Nelson, The Most Dangerous Man in Detroit—Walter Reuther and the Fate of American Labor, Basic Books, p 391; Boyle op. cit. p 159

7 http://www.sds-1960s.org/PortHuronStatement-draft.htm

8 Boyle op. cit. p 159

9 http://www.sds-1960s.org/PortHuronStatement-draft.htm

10 Boyle op. cit. p 182

11   Congressional Record -House February 10, 1964 p 2804 (yeas 290, nays 130, not voting 11) Congressional Record-Senate June 19, 1964 p 14511 (yeas 73, nays 27)

12   Boyle op. cit. p 200

13   www.presidency.uscb.edu/ws/?pid=27931

14   Bentley Historical Library, University of Michigan http://bentley.umich.edu/exhibits/lbj1964/

15   Boyle op. cit. p 189

16   Ibid. pp 189-190

17   Ibid. p 192

18   Boyle op. cit. p 192 -Cormier, Frank & Eaton, William J., *Reuther*, Prentice-Hall, Edgewood Cliffs, N. J., 1970., How tough is WR?", *Look*, 8/10/65

19   Boyle op. cit. p 202

20   Ibid. p 204

21   Ibid. p 204

22   Ibid. p 204

23   Ibid. p 214

24   *Fortune*, June 1965

25   Boyle op. cit. pp 213-215

26   Ibid. p 206

27   Boyle op. cit. p 231; Albert Cleague, "The Black Messiah," *Detroit News* 8/16/68

28   Boyle op. cit. p 194; Lichtenstein op. cit. p 392

29   Boyle op. cit. p 195; Lichtenstein op. cit. p 393

30   Lichtenstein op. cit. p 394; Boyle op. cit. p 195

31   Lichtenstein op. cit. pp 394-395; Victor Reuther minimizes the lasting effects of the rift between his brother and Joseph Rauh and states that Johnson was still considering a vice presidential choice from a list that did not include Humphrey when Walter reported the results of his negotiations in Atlantic City to him the next day. Victor implies that it was only Walter calling in a favor for the service he rendered that got Humphrey on the ticket. (Victor Reuther op. cit. p 450)

[32] Boyle op. cit. pp 207-208

[33] Boyle op. cit. p 219

[34] Levy, Peter B., *The New Left and Labor in the 1960's*, University of Illinois Press, 1994 p 48

[35] Cohen, Adam & Taylor, Elizabeth, American Pharaoh: Mayor Richard J. Daley—His Battle for Chicago and the *Nation*, Little Brown, 2000. p. 446

[36] Boyle op. cit. pp 231-232

[37] Ibid. p 227

[38] Dickmeyer, Elisabeth Reuther, Putting the World Together—My Father Walter Reuther: The Liberal Warrior, Living Force Publishing, Lake Orion, Michigan, 2004 p 316

[39] Boyle op. cit. p 228

[40] Hayward, Stephen F., The Age of Reagan: The Fall of the Old Liberal Order 1964–1980, Three Rivers Press, New York 2001 p 136

[41] ibid. p 136

[42] Ibid. p 137

[43] Boyle op. cit. pp 200-201

[44] Da Cruz, Frank, "ColumbiaUniversity – 1968," *Columbia Librarian*, www.columbia.edu/acis/history/1968 accessed 4/23/2012

[45] Hayward op. cit. p 219

[46] E. R. Dickmeyer op. cit. p 320

[47] 22a

[48] E. R. Dickmeyer op. cit. p 344

[49] Ibid. p 360

[50] Turse, Nick, Kill Anything That Moves: The Real American War in Vietnam, Metropolitan Books, Henry Holt and Company, New York, 2013. pp 228-230, 242-243

[51] Gould, Jean & Hickok, Lorena, *Walter Reuther, Labor's Rugged Individualist*, Dodd, Mead & Company, New York, NY, 1972 p 386

[52] http://academic.regis.edu/jriley/413%20democratic_party_convention_rule.htm

53   Eisenstein, James, "Presidential Primaries of 1976: Where? What? When? Why" Grass Roots Guides on Democracy and Practical Politics," http://eric.ed.gov/?id=ED121647

54   Personal recollection during time in Syracuse

55   Marmor, Theodore R.with Jan S. Marmor, *The Politics of Medicare,* Aldine Publishing Company, Chicago, 1973 pp 68, 72, 74; The Official Social Security Website http://www.ssa.gov/history/tally65.html—The final vote was 307-116 in the House (70 Republicans yea, 68 nay, 2 not voting) and 70-24 in the Senate (13 Republicans yea, 17 nay, 2 not voting)

56   "War on Poverty Revisited," Thomas Sowell, *Capitalism Magazine*; August 17, 2004

57   "What Was Really Great About the Great Society: The Truth About the Conservative Myths," Joseph Califano, The Washington Monthly; October 1999

58   26a

59   Cohen & Taylor op. cit. p 320

60   Ibid. o 490

61   Boyle op. cit. pp 186-187

62   Bob Dylan, "The Times They Are a changin'"

Chapter XIII

1   Hans H. Helbling & James E. Turley, "Oil Price Controls: A Counterproductive Effort," *Federal Reserve Bank of* St. Louis, November, 1975

2   *Newsweek,* October 13, 1980

3   Stockman, David, The Triumph of Politics: Why the Reagan Revolution Failed, Harper & Row, 1986 p 49

4   Ibid. p 10

5   Krugman, Paul, Peddling Prosperity; Economic Sense and Nonsense in the Age of Diminished Expectations, Norton & Co., 1994 p 85

6   Wilentz, Sean, *The Age of Reagan: a History 1974–2008*, Harper Perennial, New York, 2008. pp 140-141

7   Stockman op. cit. p 68

8   Ibid. pp 143-146

9   Edward Cowan, "Tax Cuts Due: But Will Kemp-Roth Be the Plan?" *The New York Times, 1/11/1981*

10   Wilentz op. cit. p 146

11   "Ronald Reagan Signs the Economic Recovery Tax Act of 1981," *The World History Project, 8/13/1981* https://worldhistoryproject.org/1981/8/13/ronald-reagan-signs-the-economic-recovery-tax-act-of-1981

12   Wilentz op. cit. p 146

13   Krugman op. cit. pp 121-122

14   Wilentz op. cit. p 147

15   Ibid. pp 139-140

16   Ibid. p 140

17   Ibid. pp 196-197

18   GDP Yearly Growth from 1973-2009, U. S. Department of Commerce, Bureau of Economic Analysis, www.bea.gov/index.html (retrieved 06/26/2012} Computation taking average of yearly figures over the period in office of each president

19   Krugman op. cit. p 117

20   Ibid. p 127

21   Ibid. p 126

22   **ibid. p 126**

23   Ibid. p 127

24   Phillips, Kevin, Wealth and Democracy: A Political History of the American Rich, Broadway Books, New York, 2002 p*p* 151-154

25   5

26   Denver Post 6/20/2010

27   Krugman op. cit. p 132

28   Ibid. p 134

29   Ibid. p 4

30   Ibid. pp 57-58

31   Time Magazine 8/20/79

32   Lichtenstein, Nelson, The Most Dangerous Man in Detroit—Walter Reuther and the Fate of American Labor, Basic Books p 444

33   Cowie, Jefferson, Stayin' Alive: The 1970's and the Last Days of the Working Class, The New Press, New York, 2010. pp 230-231

34   Smith, Hedrick, *The Power Game: How Washington Works,* Ballantine, 1988. p 31

35   Ibid. p 32

36   Ibid. pp 32-33

37   Data from Center for Responsive Politics, Washington, DC, 1993

38   Smith op. cit. p 135

39   Ibid. p 39

40   Allentown named *Look* Magazine All American City in 1962

41   National Science Board, "Science and Engineering Indicators 2004" http://www.nsf.gov/statistics/seind04/c2/c2s2.htm (retrieved 11/16/2014)—Data compiled by the National Science Foundation indicates that college enrollments increased from 6.962 million in 1967 to 15.593 million in 2000. A substantial contribution to that growth came from 2-year colleges whose enrollment jumped from 1.426 to 6.171 million over the same period. These figures indicate a fairly steady increase of about 250,000 students per year in American colleges and universities over the thirty four years surveyed. The numbers for engineering students do not show the same trajectory. In selected years between 1979 and 2002, enrollments in engineering programs fluctuated between 366,299 in 1979, to a peak of 441,205 in 1983, down to a low of 356,177 in 1996, and rebounding back to 421,178 in 2002. The growth in engineering majors has been relatively flat over a similar period during which the college population has been growing by about 250,000 per year. The percentage of students enrolled in engineering programs dropped from 3.13% in 1979 to 2.48% in 2000.

42   Wilentz op. cit. p 277

43   14

44   Ravitch, Diane, Reign of Error: The Hoax of the Privatization Movement and the Danger to America's Public *Schools,* Alfred A. Knopf, New York, 2013 pp 20-36

45   *The Honneymooners,* "TV-Or Not TV," first aired Oct 1, 1955

46   Krugman op. cit. pp 121-122

47   remarks at the 1977 World Future Society convention by Ken Olsen

48   15a

49   Wilentz op. cit. p 275; Krugman op. cit. p 117—Growth in potential output from '79—'90 averaged 2.3%/year, from '73 -'79 it averaged 2.4%/year, and over the decade from '69—'79 it averaged 2.8%/year. Growth in the 1980s was slower than in the 1970s as a whole, about the same as the growth in the period after 1973.

50   Wilentz op. cit. p 275—The average rate was 19.4% in 1981 and 19.3% in 1989. State and local taxes in mnay areas increased during this period to cover shortfalls in reduced federal assistance.

51   Wilentz pp 199, 307—The federal S&L bailout totaled $370 billion dollar of which $341 was ponied up by the taxpayers

52   calculated from data from U. S. Bureau of Economic Analysis –www. tradingeconomic.com/united-states/gdp-growth-annual   (retrieved 9/23/2010) average of yearly growth during each administration

53   Smith op. cit. p 465

54   Loth, Wilfried, "Moscow, Prague and Warsaw: Overcoming the Brezhnev Doctrine," *Cold War History*, 1, no. 2, 2001: 103-118. p 104

55   Stockman op. cit. p 90

56   Ibid. p 9

57   Wilentz op. cit. pp 274–276—During the decade of the '80's, the share of the nation's wealth held by the top 1% rose from 22% to 39%.— Krugman op. cit. p 126—Private saving rate in the US crashed in the 1980s from 9.1% of disposable income in 1980 to 5.1% in 1987. The overall rate of national saving—public and private had averaged 7.7% in the '70s but was only 3% from '88–'90 Krugman p 127—In the '50s capital spending by govs. at all levels was at 3%/year. since then it, has fallen to 1%/year. The Reagan-Bush policies reinforced this trend. Private investment in the years 1980–1992 was only 17.4% of GDP compared to 18.6% in the 1970s.

58   19a

59   Willard Fazar et al, "Federal Statistical Activities," *The American Statistician* 13(2), 0-12 April 1959. Pp 9-12

60 Tanenbaum, Andrew, *Computer Networks*, 4th ed., Prentice-Hall, Englewood Cliffs, NJ, 2002. p 50-54

61 Ibid. pp 55-56

Chapter XIV

1   Dickmeyer, Elisabeth Reuther, Putting the World Together—My Father Walter Reuther: The Liberal Warrior, Living Force Publishing, Lake Orion, Michigan, 2004 p 388

2   Ibid. pp 331-332

3   Ibid. p 387

4   Ibid. pp 385-386

5   Ibid. p 391

6   *The New York Times*, January 4, 1971. Nixon actually said, "I am now a Keynsian in economics." after taking the dollar off the gold standard. The quote later attributed to him was first stated by the Conservative economist Milton Friedman in a *Time* magazine article in the December 31, 1965 issue

7   Ted Kennedy interview re: Walter Reuther and Introduction to National Health Care Bill, https://www.youtube.com/watch?v=XyZhcjvjFAY (retrieved November, 2013)

8   Ibid.

9   E. R. Dickmeyer op. cit. p 330

10 Ibid. p 330

11 Ibid. p 330

12 Ibid. p 330

13 CBS Evening News with Walter Cronkite, February 18, 1971; see also https://www.youtube.com/watch?v=iGKkPEvD2OM; Gordon, Colin, Dead on Arrival: The Politics of Health Care in Twentieth-Century America, Princeton University Press, Princeton and Oxford, 2003. p 33

14 ibid; also Gordon op. cit. p 33

15 Evening News with John Chancellor, April, 24, 1974 (same youtube clip) see also Gordon op. cit. pp 34-35

16 Ibid.

17 Ibid.

18 Ibid.

19 Ibid.

20 E. R. Dickmeyer op. cit. p 387

21 Ibid. p 387

22 Gordon op. cit. pp 36-37, 119

23 Health Care Legislation Message to Congress, April 25, 1977 by Jimmy Carter found on The American Presidency Project websitewww. presidency.ucsb.edu/ws/index.php?pip=7401#axzz2irDFMNfi retrieved 1/2/2015

24 Hoffman, Beatrix, "Health Care Reform and Social Movements in the United States," *American Journal of Public Health*, January 2003, 93(1) pp. 75-85. p 76

25 Hoffman op. cit. p 76; Gordon op. cit. p 13—opponents characterize proponents of the AALL plan as "Paid Professional Philanthropists, busybody Social Workers, Misguided Clergymen, and Hysterical Women"

26 Hoffman op. cit. p 76

27 Gordon op. cit. p 275; Hoffman op. cit. p 76; Taft, *The A. F. of L. in the Time of Gompers,* pp 364-365; Gompers felt, as many current Conservatives, that a government role in providing health insurance was an infringement on individual liberty. There was strong disagreement with this stand by some of his close associates. William Green, his eventual successor, favored employer provided insurance that is now common.

28 Hoffman op. cit. p 78

29 Gordon op. cit. pp 41-44, 258, 284; Hoffman op. cit. p 78-79

30 Hoffman op. cit. p 78

31 Ibid. p 76

32 E. R. Dickmeyer op. cit. pp 389-390

33 Patricia Spain Ward, "The Medical Antitrust Case of 1938-1943," *American Studies Journal*, University of Kansas, pp 123-153 *https://journals.ku.edu/index.php/amerstud/article/download/2475/2434*

34 Marmor, Theodore R.with Jan S. Marmor, *The Politics of Medicare,* Aldine Publishing Company, Chicago, 1973 pp 8-9; Hoffman pp 76-77

35   Derickson, Alan, "Health Security for All? Social Unionism and Universal Health Insurance 1935-1958," Journal of American History 80 (1994): 1333-1356 see pages 1342-1343; Gordon p 413, Hoffman p 77

36   Hoffman op. cit. p 77

37   Gordon op. cit. pp 21, 144-145, Hoffman op. cit. p 77

38   Marmor op. cit. pp 13-14

39   Ibid. p 15

40   Ibid. pp 18-19

41   Ibid. pp 41-44

42   R. J. Eskow, "'Operation Coffee Cup':Reagan, the AMA, and the First 'Viral Marketing' Campaign Against Medicare," The Huffington Post updated 5/25/2011, retrieved 12/31/2014 www.huffingtonpost.com/rj-eskow/operation-coffeecup-reaga_b_45444.html;Hoffman op. cit. p 78

43   Marmor op. cit. pp 63-64

44   Ibid. pp 61-62

45   Ibid. pp 64-68

46   Derickson op. cit. pp 1349-1351

47   E. R. Dickmeyer op. cit. p 385

48   Cauchon, Dennis, "Medical miscalculation creates doctor shortage," USA Today, posted 3/2/2005—figure up to 15.4% of GDP in 2005 (17.9 % by 2013)

49   See http://solstice.ischool.utexas.edu/tmwi/index.php/Walter_Reuther

50   "Health Insurance Premiums Rise 6.1% in 2007, Less rapidly than in previous years, but still fasteer than wages and inflation," Kaiser Family Foundation (press release – Sept 11, 2007); Eisenberg, Richard, "The End of Employer-Provided Health Insurance," Forbes, 3/11/2015

51   Gordon p 300 gives a figure of 44 million at some time during 2006

52   Stuart M. Butler, "Assuring Affordable Health Care for All Americans," October 2, 1989 lecture delivered at Meharry Medical College in Nashville, Tenn. As part of their conference on "Health Care for the Poor and Underservered." Butler was Director of Domestic Policy Studies at the Heritage Foundation at the time

53 posted on billmoyers.com/2013/10/29/why-republicans-have-no-business-being-upset-about-obamacare/ originally appearing on Robert Reich's blog

54 Avik Roy, "The Torturous History of Conservatives and the Individual Mandate," -*Forbes Magazine,* February 7, 2012

55 Ryan Lizza, "Romney's Dilemma," *The New Yorker,* June 6, 2011

56 Ibid.

57 Ibid.

58 Ibid.

59 Robert Pear, "Senate Passes Health Care Overhaul on Party-Line Vote," *The New York Times*, December 24, 2009

60 Carl Hulse and Adam Nagourney, "Senate GOP Leader Finds Weapon in Unity," *The New York Times*, March 16, 2010; Jonathon Chait, "The Republican Health Care Blunder," *The New Republic,* December 19, 2009

61 In 2010 the Pew Research Center reported that 85% of Americans were familiar with the claim that The Affordable Care Act contained a provision for creating "Death Panels" that would determine if elderly patients should be provided with care and 30% of respondents believed the claim was true

62 Jonathon Cohn, "How They Did It," *The New Republic*, May 21, 2010

63 Ibid.

64 Ibid.

65 Ibid.

66 Ibid.

67 Cole, David, "Obamacare Upheld: How and Why Did Justice Roberts Do It?" *The Nation,* http://www.thenation.com/blog/168655/obamacare-upheld-how-and-why-did-justice-roberts-do-it#, posted June 28, 2012, retrieved 1/2/2105

68 Cohn op. cit

69 See HealthCare.govhttps://www.healthcare.gov/blog/10-health-care-benefits-covered-in-the-health-insurance-marketplace/

70 See HealthCare.gov https://www.healthcare.gov/glossary/health-plan-categories/

71 Ezra Klein and Sarah Kliff, "Obama's last campaign: Inside the White House Plan to sell Obamacare," *The* Washington Post, July 17, 2013

72 Robert Pear, "State's Policies on Health Care Exclude Some of the Poorest," *The New York Times*, May 24, 2013

73 Ibid.

74 Jonathon Cohn, "We Don't Know Everything About Obamacare. But We Know Who's Trying to Sabotage It." *The New Republic*, July 18, 2013; Ezra Klein and Sarah Kliff, "Obama's last campaign: Inside the White House Plan to sell Obamacare," *The Washington Post*, July 17, 2013

75 William Hsiao, Steven Kappel, Jonathon Gruber, "The Vermont Option, Achieving Affordable Universal Health Care," *Vermont Health System Reform*, June 21, 2010; Jay Fitzgerald, "Costs derail Vermont's dream of a Single-payer health plan," *Boston Globe*, January 25, 2015

76 Taylor Lincoln, "Severing the Tie that Binds: Why A Publicly Funded, Universal Health Care System Would be a Boon to U. S. Businesses," *Public Citizen*, April 9, 2014 www.citizen.org

77 In the World Health Organization Report 2000 the U. S. healthcare system is ranked highest for responsiveness. People with generous employer-based plans are unaffected by the cost and inequalities of the system

78 World Health Organization Report 2000 can be found at www.who.int/whr; it can also be retrieved-at www.photius.com/rankings/healthranks.html (retrieved 2/7/2010)

79 WHO Report accessed at above link

80 Ibid.

81 Ibid.

82 Ellen Nolte and C. Martin McKee, "Measuring the Health of Nations: Updating an Earlier Analysis," Health Affairs, 27, No.1 (2008) 58-71 in the report www.photius.com/rankings/healthranks.html

83 Ibid.

84 Ibid.

85 House of Commons 21 June 2000, www.parliament.uk

86 Notte and McKee op. cit.

87   Klein, Ezra, "Our Corrupt Politics: It's Not All Money," *New York Review of Books*, March 22, 2012—In the period from 1998-2011 the AMA spent $264 million on lobbyists, second only to the U. S. Chamber of Commerce. The Health Care Industry taken together spent $4.87 billion during the same period—more than Finance and Energy interests; Gordon op. cit. pp 210, 216, 221-225

88   Cauchon, Dennis, "Medical miscalculation creates doctor shortage," *USA Today*, posted 3/2/2005 The article also points to the problem that doctors cluster in the areas where they want to live, not necessarily where the need is greatest, and specialize in areas that serve the more affluent and better insured. http://usatoday30.usatoday.com/news/health/2005-03-02-doctor-shortage_x.htm retrieved 1/16/2015

89   Ravitch, Diane, Reign of Error: The Hoax of the Privatization Movement and the Danger to America's Public *Schools*, Alfred A. Knopf, New York, 2013—The first 19 chapters present a critical assessment of the privatization movement being pushed by politicians and corporate executives

90   Rodwin, Victor G., "The Health Care System Under French National Health Insurance: Lessons forHealth Reform in the United States," *American Journal of Public Health*, January 2003, Vol. 93, No. 1 pp 31-37, 33

91   Ibid. p 35

92   Ibid. p 35

93   Ibid. p 35

94   Ibid. p 35

95   ibid. p 35

96   Dutton, Paul, "Health Care in France and the United States: Learning from Each Other," *The Brookings* Institution, p 5

97   personal experience in the Spring of 2012

98   Hendricks, Rickey, A Model for National Health Care: the History of Kaiser Permanente, Rutgers University Press, New Brunswick, New Jersey, 1993. pp 12, 26-27

99   Ibid. pp 30-37

100   Ibid. pp 45-49

101   Gould, Jean & Hickok, Lorena, *Walter Reuther, Labor's Rugged Individualist*, Dodd, Mead & Company, New York, NY, 1972 p 293

102   Ibid. p 293

103   Ibid. p 294

104   Ibid. pp 294-295

105   Ibid. p 294

106   Hendricks op. cit. pp 97-100

107   87

108   Hendricks op. cit. pp 80, 86

109   89

110   *The Origins of Managed Health Care*, Jones & Bartlett Publishers, p 4

111   Murata, Stephen, "How Doctors Can Regain Control of Healthcare," *Medical Economics*, 73.9 May 13, 1996 p 178

112   A transcript of the conversation can be found at http://en.wikisource.org/wiki/Transcript_of_taped_conversation_between_President_Richard_Nixon_and_John_D._Ehrlichman_%281971%29_that_led_to_the_HMO_act_of_1973

113   Gordon op. cit. pp 169-171

114   Eming, Shelley, "Q & A With Dr. Paul Ellwood, Jr., MD 'Father of Managed Competition Concept'," *Neurology Today*, November/December 2001, Volume 1, Issue 4, p 36

115   William Greider, "Reviving the Fight for Single-Payer," *The Nation,* Dec. 23/30, 2013

116   Ibid.

117   Ibid.

118   Ibid.

119   Gordon op. cit. p 246

120   Ibid. pp 234-242

121   Hendricks op. cit. pp 215-216

Chapter XV

1   Title of Tom Friedman's book Hot, Flat, and Crowded, Farrar, Straus & Giroux, 2008.

2   Stockholm International Peace Research Institute "The 15 countries with the highest military expenditure in 2011," Table 4.2

3   Reuther, Walter, "The Future of Education" – Address to the National Council for Social Studies of the NEA, Cl Cleveland, Nov 23, 1956

4   n a July 1854 essay. Lincoln went on to elaborate the things he considered belonged to the purview of government—roads, bridges, and the like; providing for the helpless young and afflicted; common schools; the criminal and civil departments.

5   Cowie, Jefferson, Stayin' Alive: The 1970's and the Last Days of the Working Class, The New Press, New York, 2010. pp 1-3

6   Treckel, Karl F., The Rise and Fall of the Alliance for Labor Action (1968-1972),Center for Business and Economic Research, Graduate School of Business Administration, Kent State University, Kent, Ohio, 1975.—The UAW began the two month long strike with a fund of $120 million which it exhausted and was required to borrow $25 million from its ALA partner, the Teamsters, using its resources of Solidarity House and Black Lake as collateral. The UAW reduced its contribution to the ALA and the scope of its social vision to pay off its debt. p 23

7   Schulzinger, Robert D., A Time for War: The United States and Vietnam, 1941–1975, Oxford University Press, New York, 1997 pp 287–288

8   Dickmeyer, Elizabeth Reuther, Putting the World Together—My Father Walter Reuther: The Liberal Warrior, Living Force Publishing, Lake Orion, Michigan, 2004 p 344

9   Cowie op. cit. p 127

10   ibid. p 158

11   Gould, Jean & Hickok, Lorena, Walter Reuther, Labor's Rugged Individualist, Dodd, Mead & Company, New York, NY, 1972. p 378

12   Cowie op. cit. p 45

13   Gould & Hickok op. cit. p 386

14   Ibid. pp 368–369

15   E. R. Dickmeyer op. cit. p 234

16   Cormier, Frank & Eaton, William J., *Reuther*, Prentice-Hall, Edgewood Cliffs, N. J., 1970 p 385

17   Ibid. p 385

18   Cowie op. cit. p 45

19   Ibid. p 46

20   Ibid. p 47

21   Ibid. p 47

22   Ibid. pp 48–49

23   E. R. Dickmeyer op. cit. 2004 p 236

24   Ibid. p 233

25   Ibid. pp 230–231

26   Ibid. p 231; Lichtenstein, Nelson, The Most Dangerous Man in Detroit— Walter Reuther and the Fate of American *Labor*, Basic Books, New York, 1995. p 339; Gould & Hickok op. cit. p 357

27   E. R. Dickmeyer op. cit. p 234

28   Weinberg, Alvin, The First Nuclear Era: The Life and Times of a Technology Fixer, AIP Press, American Institute of Physics, New York, 1994. p 129—A report authored by Lee Haworth projected a nuclear capacity of about 700 gigawatts by 2000. This would require1000 nuclear fueled plants with an average of about 3 times the power output of the Clinch River breeder. By 1993 nuclear power only generated about 100 gigawatts of the nation's electrical power.

29   Reuther, Walter P., Education and the Public Good—The Challenge to Education in a Changing World, Harvard University Press, Cambridge, Massachusetts, 1964 pp 104–128

30   Weinberg op. cit. pp 13–20 presents a concise tutorial on the physics of a nuclear reactor

31   Weinberg op. cit. p 110

32   Fuller, John G., *We Almost Lost Detroit*, Reader's Digest Press, New York, 1975. pp 33-35 describes a meltdown of the Experimental Breeder Reactor 1 at Idaho Falls. This reactor was a prototype for the much larger Fermi 1 being planned by Detroit Edison

33   Ibid. pp 50-51

34   Ibid. pp 54-55

35 WASH-740 released Mar,1957—3,400 dead within 15 miles from plant, another 43,000 upto 44 miles away, Another 182,000 people up to 200 miles away would be exposed to a dose that would double their chance of cancer. Property damage about $7 billion (about 10% of government receipts at the time) (Fuller op. cit. pp 58-59)

36 The Supreme Court voted 7-2 for the project to continue, In dissent Justices Douglas and Black wrote—"Plainly these are not findings that the safety standards have been met. They presuppose…that safety findings can be made after the construction is finished. But when that point is reached, when millions have been invested, the momentum is on the side of the applicant not on the side of the public. The momentum is not only generated by the desire to salvage an investment, no agency wants to be the architect of a white elephant…" (Fuller op. cit. pp 118-119)

37 Fuller op. cit. p 220

38 Ibid. p 234

39 E.R. Dickmeyer op. cit. p 152

40 Boudreau, Jay, "The American Breeder Reactor Gets a Second Chance," *Los Alamos Science*, vol. 2, no. 2, summer/fall 1981 pp 118-119

41 ibid pp 118-119

42 Carter, Jimmy, "Message to the Senate Returning S. 1811 Without Approval," November 5, 1977 *The American Presidency Project*, http://www.presidency.ucsb.edu/ws/print.php?pid=6892 retrieved July 21, 2015

43 Boudreau op. cit. p 118

44 Ibid. p 118

45 Fuller op. cit. pp 13-18, 74-87, 104-115

46 *Pandora's Promise* a 2013 documentary about the nuclear power debate directed by Robert Stone and released by Impact Partners, in association with Vulcan Productions and CNN Films.The documentary presented the positive environmental aspects of nuclear power.

47 Eisenhower, Dwight D. The White House Years: Mandate for Change 1953-1956, Doubleday & Company, Garden City, New York, 1963. pp 251-255; Eisenhower gives the rationale behind the plan, and some of the details in the proposal. Weinberg op. cit. p 129 (1962 forecast of 700 GW)

rice-Anderson Act passed Sept 7, 1957—Private insurers $65 million, US—up to $560 million (F64)

Internationjal Panel on Fissile Materials, "Plutonium separation in Nuclear Power Programs," 1 Sept. 2015, p 13

50   Moir & Teller, "Thorium-Fueled Undergrown Power Plant Based on Molten Salt Technology," *Nuclear Technology*, vol. 151, September 2005 pp 334-340

51   Weinberg op. cit. pp 126-127

52   MacPherson, H. G., "The Molten Salt Reactor Adventure," *Nuclear Science and Engineering*, vol. 90, 1985, pp 374-380

53   Weinberg op. cit. p 199

54   "A Future Energy Giant? India's Thorium-Based Nuclear Plans," *Physics* Oct. 1, 2010—Currently 40% of India's vast population is not connected to the electricity grid. The country plans to incorporate thorium into its pressurized heavy water reactors to breed fissile fuel. Their 3-stage plan does not include molten salt reactors

55   Mark Halper, "The U.S. is helping China build a novel, superior nuclear reactor," *Fortune*, Feb. 2, 2015

56   Mathew L. Wald, "TR-10: Travelling Wave Reactor," MIT Technology Review, Mar/Apr 2009 http://www2.technologyreview.com/article/412188/tr10-traveling-wave-reactor/3/

57   Daniel Trotta, Reuters US News Service, June 29, 2011; http://www.reuters.com/article/2011/06/29/us-usa-war-idUSTRE75S25320110629

58   information from Stockholm International Peace Research Institute—2012 defense spending

59   Ibid.

60   Ibid.

61   Ibid.

62   From NBC Evening News 10/3/2015 and www.Antiwar.com/casualties {retrieved 10/8/2015)—gun deaths (including suicides) 93/day, 33,680/year, 153,000 since 9/11/2001; U. S. military war deaths (as of 10/8/15) Iraq 4493, Afghanistan 2358, civilian contractors 1487

63   Reuther, Walter P., Swords Into Plowshares: A Proposal to Promote Orderly Conversion From Defense to Civilian Production, Statement

and Testimony of Walter P. Reuther, President of the UAW, To the Senate Committee On Labor and Public Welfare, December 1, 1969. p 9

64   Ibid. pp 15-16

65   Ibid. pp 18-26

66   Ibid. p 50

67   Melman, Seymour, "In the Grip of a Permanent War Economy", *Counterpunch*, March 15, 2003.

68   Nick Turse relates the accounts of other My Lai events in his book *Kill Anything That Moves*—The emphasis on body count as a measure of success in the battle and for career advancement for officers and for getting perks like R&R created an atmosphere where killing of civilians was prevalent. Regarding Vietnamese as gooks and dinks facilitated this climate. (p 41-51) Strategy of search and destroy and free fire zones lead to high civilian casualties (pp 51-63)—Kolko pp 345-346 claims the destruction of villages and innocent people had been characteristic of the war from its inception…but were dismissed by mainstream media outlets like the *New York Times* until their support for the war evaporated.

69   Gould & Hickok op. cit. p 376

70   Cowie op. cit. p 290

71   Ibid. p 293

72   Ibid. pp 294, 231

73   Ibid. pp 296-297

74   E.R.Dickmeyer op. cit. forward by David Bonior